NOW you're knitting

super how-to handbook and design treasury

Growing fast in popularity, knitting brings us into a world of luscious yarns in eye-catching colors and sensational textures. And not only are we producing beautiful creations for ourselves and our loved ones, but we are also reaping the benefits of the calming effect that this meditative needlecraft offers.

Even if you weren't knitting yesterday, now you can start today with our easy 10-20-30-minute Learn to Knit method. If you already know the basics, now you have 165 great-looking projects at your fingertips, ranging from stylish sweaters to kids' fun stuff, precious baby outfits, and cozy afghans and pillows for your home. And to please even the most advanced knitters, now you have an easy-to-use collection of 99 knit stitches, to help you jazz up a plain design or create your own. So with this super how-to handbook and design treasury at your side,

NOW you'll be knitting! Enjoy!

LEISURE ARTS, INC.
Little Rock, Arkansas

EDITORIAL STAFF
VICE PRESIDENT AND EDITOR-IN-CHIEF
  Sandra Graham Case
EXECUTIVE DIRECTOR OF PUBLICATIONS
  Cheryl Nodine Gunnells
SENIOR PUBLICATIONS DIRECTOR
  Susan White Sullivan
DIRECTOR OF DESIGNER RELATIONS
  Debra Nettles
DIRECTOR OF RETAIL MARKETING
  Stephen Wilson
SPECIAL PROJECTS DIRECTOR
  Susan Frantz Wiles
KNIT TECHNICAL EDITOR
  Linda Luder
SENIOR ART OPERATIONS DIRECTOR
  Jeff Curtis
ART PUBLICATIONS DIRECTOR
  Rhonda Shelby
ART CATEGORY MANAGER
  Rebecca J. Hester
GRAPHIC ARTISTS
  Karen Allbright, Autumn Hall,
  Stephanie Hamling, Andrea Hazlewood,
  and Dana Vaughn
ART IMAGING DIRECTOR
  Mark Hawkins
IMAGING TECHNICIANS
  Stephanie Johnson and Mark Potter
PUBLISHING SYSTEMS ADMINISTRATOR
  Becky Riddle
PUBLISHING SYSTEMS ASSISTANTS
  Clint Hanson, Josh Hyatt, and John Rose

BUSINESS STAFF
CHIEF OPERATING OFFICER
  Tom Siebenmorgen
VICE PRESIDENT, SALES AND MARKETING
  Pam Stebbins
DIRECTOR OF SALES AND SERVICES
  Margaret Reinold
VICE PRESIDENT, OPERATIONS
  Jim Dittrich
COMPTROLLER, OPERATIONS
  Rob Thieme
RETAIL CUSTOMER SERVICE MANAGER
  Stan Raynor
PRINT PRODUCTION MANAGER
  Fred F. Pruss

Printed in China.

International Standard Book Number
1-57486-547-1

10 9 8 7 6 5 4 3 2 1

2   Contents

40   67   78

Contents

103   118   134   203   242

265   272   294   330   370

Contents

466   472   482   486   498

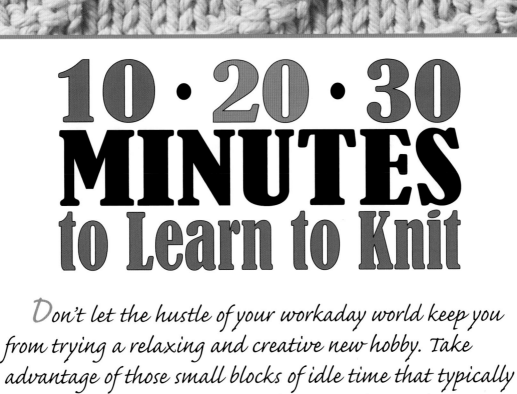

10 · 20 · 30 MINUTES
to Learn to Knit

Don't let the hustle of your workaday world keep you from trying a relaxing and creative new hobby. Take advantage of those small blocks of idle time that typically occur throughout your day and learn to knit. This traditional handicraft is so very simple — everything you do is based on two easy stitches, knit and purl.

Time spent in front of the television or waiting to pick up your child after school can be used to create beautiful items for your home, yourself, and others. Our clear instructions guide you through two methods of knitting, so you can experiment and decide which one works best for you. All it takes is 10, 20, or 30 minutes a day and you can learn to knit — we'll show you how!

Basic Materials

It really only takes two things – a pair of knitting needles and yarn. There are many sizes of needles – try using a pair of 10" straight knitting needles, size 8 (5.00 mm) for learning. Yarn is available in a multitude of sizes and colors, but for learning we recommend a ball or skein of worsted weight yarn in a color you like – but not too dark – a light or bright color will make it easier to see your stitches.

Let's Start Knitting!

MAKING A SLIP KNOT

IN ONLY 10 MINUTES!

Fig. 1a

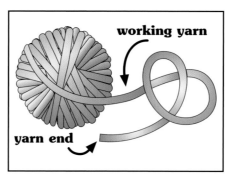

working yarn

yarn end

Pull a 10" length of yarn from the ball. Make a circle and place the working yarn (the yarn coming from the ball) under the circle (Fig. 1a).

Knitting begins with a slip knot. This easy knot will anchor your stitches to the needle and will also count as your first stitch.

Fig. 1b

Insert the needle under the bar just made (Fig. 1b) and pull on both ends of the yarn to complete the slip knot (Fig. 1c).

Practice making a slip knot until you feel confident with this simple beginning stitch.

Fig. 1c

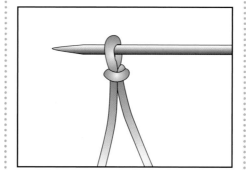

The slip knot counts as your first cast on stitch.

SLINGSHOT CAST ON

In order to begin knitting, it is necessary to cast on a Foundation Row of stitches onto one needle.

Step 1: Pull a 24" length of yarn from the ball. Make a slip knot (Figs. 1a-c, page 8) at the measured distance, pulling gently on both yarn ends to tighten the stitch on the needle (counts as first cast on stitch).

Step 2: Hold the needle with the stitch in your right hand with your index finger resting on the stitch.

Step 3: Place the short end of the yarn over your left thumb, and bring the working yarn up and over your left index finger. Hold both yarn ends in your left palm with your 3 remaining fingers (Fig. 2a).

Step 4: Insert the tip of the needle **under** the first strand of yarn on your left thumb (Fig. 2b).

Step 5: Bring the needle **over** and around the first strand on your index finger (Fig. 2c).

Step 6: Pull the yarn and needle down through the loop on your thumb (Fig. 2d).

Step 7: Slip your thumb out of the loop and bring it toward you, catching the yarn end to form a new loop on your thumb (Fig. 2e) and gently pulling to tighten the new stitch on the needle. Rest your index finger on the new stitch.

Repeat Steps 4-7 for each additional stitch.

Fig. 2a

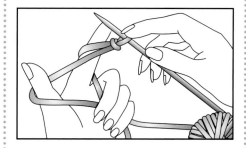

Fig. 2b

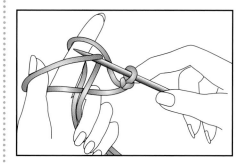

Fig. 2c

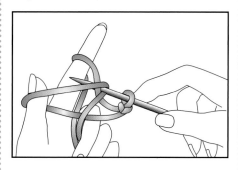

Fig. 2d

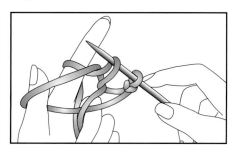

Fig. 2e

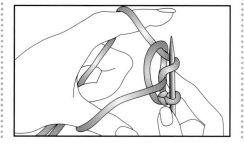

"Cast on" is a term used to describe placing a foundation row of stitches on the needle.

Continue to cast on stitches until you feel comfortable casting on. With practice, your stitches will become neat and even.

helpful hints

To figure how much yarn is needed for casting on, allow approximately 1" of yarn for each stitch to be cast on. Finer yarns require slightly less than 1" per stitch, and heavier yarns require slightly more.

Each cast on stitch needs to be snug, but not tight. This will allow you to easily insert the tip of the needle into the stitch when working the first row. The foundation row needs to be as elastic as the knitting.

After all of your stitches have been cast on, the yarn end may be cut shorter, but leave the end long enough to be woven in later. If the yarn end will be needed to sew a seam, it can be rolled in a ball and pinned to the bottom of the piece after a few rows have been worked.

KNIT STITCH
English Method

Here is the first of the only two stitches used in knitting.

We've included two methods of knitting, the **English Method** and the **Continental Method**. We encourage you to try both methods, whether you're right or left handed, to determine which feels more comfortable. Either method will produce knitting and there is no difference in the resulting piece of work.

Fig. 3a

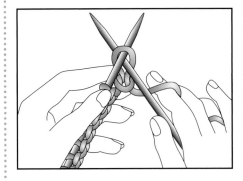

Fig. 3b

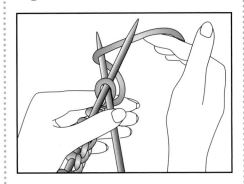

Fig. 3c

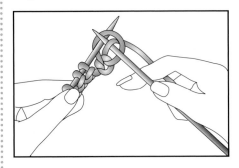

Fig. 3d

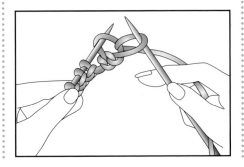

Let's make a practice swatch.
You will knit and purl a total of 16 rows to make the swatch. When you finish, you will have experienced both the knit stitch and the purl stitch using English and Continental Methods.

Cast on 20 stitches.

ROW 1
Step 1: Hold the needle with the cast on stitches in your left hand and the empty needle in your right hand.

Step 2: With the working yarn in **back** of the needles, insert the right needle into the stitch closest to the tip of the left needle as shown in Fig. 3a.

Step 3: Hold the right needle with your left thumb and index finger while you bring the yarn beneath the right needle and between the needles from **back** to **front** (Fig. 3b).

Step 4: With your right hand, bring the right needle (with the loop of yarn) toward you and through the stitch (Figs. 3c & d), slipping the old stitch off the left needle and gently pulling to tighten the new stitch on the shaft of the right needle.

Repeat Steps 2-4 across the row. You should now have one row of 20 stitches.

ROWS 2-4
To begin the next row, switch needles, so the empty needle is in your right hand and the needle with the stitches is in your left hand. Repeat Steps 2-4 across the row.

IN ONLY **20** MINUTES!

Continue your practice swatch knitting Rows 5-8 using the Continental Method.

ROW 5

Step 1: Hold the needle with the stitches in your left hand and the empty needle in your right hand. Loop the working yarn over the index finger of your left hand and hold it loosely across the palm of your hand with your little finger.

Step 2: With the yarn in **back** of the needles, insert the right needle into the stitch closest to the tip of the left needle as shown in Fig. 4a.

Step 3: With your left index finger, bring the yarn between the needles from **left** to **right** (Fig. 4b).

Step 4: With your right hand, bring the right needle (with the loop of yarn) toward you and through the stitch (Figs. 4c & d), slipping the old stitch off the left needle and gently pulling to tighten the new stitch on the shaft of the right needle.

Repeat Steps 2-4 across the row.

ROWS 6-8

To begin the next row, switch needles, so the empty needle is in your right hand and the needle with the stitches is in your left hand. Repeat Steps 2-4 across the row.

Now that you've learned the first stitch, you've completed half of your practice swatch. Turn to page 12 to learn the last stitch.

Fig. 4a

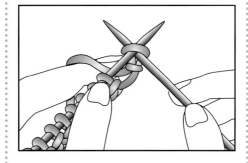

Fig. 4b

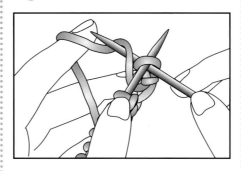

Fig. 4c

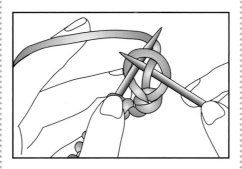

Fig. 4d

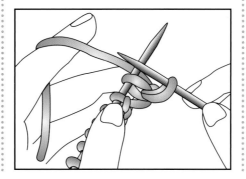

Whether you favor the English or the Continental Method, you'll find that knitting will become easier and your work will be more even with a little bit of practice.

helpful hints

When knitting or purling a stitch, wrap the working yarn around the shaft of the needle. Wrapping the yarn around the tip of the needle will make your stitches too tight.

IN ONLY **20** MINUTES!

Now you're ready to learn purl, the "other stitch." Knitting becomes easy to understand when you realize that knit stitches and purl stitches are the reverse of each other. In each case, you pull a new stitch through an existing stitch. When knitting, you drop the old stitch off to the back of your work. When purling, the old stitch falls to the front of your work.

PURL STITCH
English Method

Fig. 5a

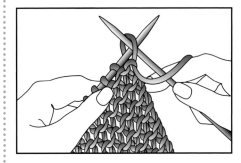

Fig. 5b

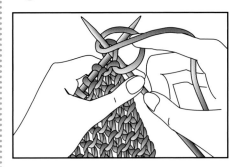

Fig. 5c

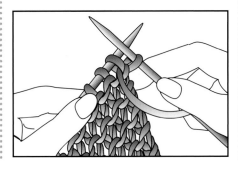

ROW 9

Step 1: Hold the needle with the stitches in your left hand and the empty needle in your right hand.

Step 2: With the yarn in **front** of the needles, insert the right needle into the front of the stitch as shown in Fig. 5a.

Step 3: Hold the right needle with your left thumb and index finger while you bring the yarn **between** the needles from **right** to **left** and around the right needle (Fig. 5b).

Step 4: Move the right needle (with the loop of yarn) through the stitch and away from you (Fig. 5c), slipping the old stitch off the left needle and gently pulling to tighten the new stitch on the shaft of the right needle.

Repeat Steps 2-4 across the row. (Remember to count your stitches - there should still be 20 stitches on the needle.)

ROWS 10-12

Turn your work, switching your needles; repeat Steps 2-4 across the row.

Continental Method

ROW 13

Step 1: Hold the needle with the stitches in your left hand and the empty needle in your right hand. Loop the working yarn over the index finger of your left hand.

Step 2: With the yarn in **front** of the needles, insert the right needle into the front of the stitch as shown in Fig. 6a.

Step 3: With your index finger, bring the yarn **between** the needles from **right** to **left** and around the right needle (Fig. 6b).

Step 4: Move your left index finger forward while moving the right needle (with the loop of yarn) through the stitch and away from you (Fig. 6c), slipping the old stitch off the left needle and gently pulling to tighten the new stitch on the shaft of the right needle.

Repeat Steps 2-4 across the row.

ROWS 14-16

Turn your work, switching your needles; repeat Steps 2-4 across the row.

Now you're ready to finish your swatch. Turn to page 14 to learn how to bind off your stitches.

Fig. 6a

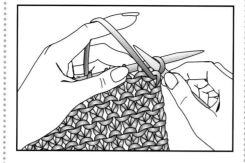

Fig. 6b

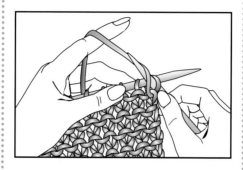

Fig. 6c

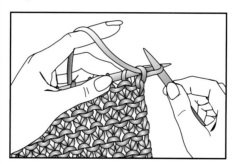

Decide which method, English or Continental, is best for you. When you're ready to complete your swatch, continue using that method as you follow the steps on the next page to bind off all stitches.

Remember, this is only a practice swatch. It doesn't have to be perfect. However, if at any time you're not happy with your work, or if you've made a mistake and would like to correct it, you can. Turn to page 21 to find out how to pick up dropped stitches and how to rip back.

IN ONLY
10
MINUTES!

*All knitting ends
with binding off,
locking each stitch
as you remove it from the
needle. Binding
off is also used for shaping
and to work buttonholes
and pockets.*

helpful hint

Count stitches as you bind off. It takes two stitches to bind off one stitch. Count each stitch as you bind it off, **not** as you knit it.

Bind off loosely versus tightly: Bind off loosely for an edge with elasticity, and bind off tightly for a firm edge. When binding off a crew neck or turtleneck ribbing, always bind off loosely. The bound off stitches should stretch as much as the ribbing does. To make this easier, replace the needle in your right hand with a larger size needle. To guarantee that the shoulders of a garment will always stay firmly in place and will not sag or droop, bind off tightly. Always bind off tightly when using cotton yarn because of its tendency to stretch.

BINDING OFF

Fig. 7a

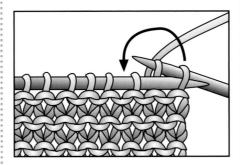

Fig. 7b

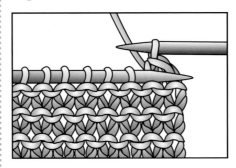

Fig. 7c

Let's practice binding off on the swatch you just made.

Step 1: Knit 2 stitches.

Step 2: With the left needle, bring the first stitch over the second stitch and off the needle (Fig. 7a). One stitch has been bound off and one stitch remains on your right needle (Fig. 7b).

Step 3: Knit the next stitch.

Repeat Steps 2 and 3 until only one stitch remains.

Step 4: To lock the last stitch, cut the yarn (leaving a long end) and bring it up through the last stitch (Fig. 7c), pulling to tighten.

Now that you've finished your swatch, you're ready to learn about basic fabrics. We've included instructions for three more swatches so you can practice making fabrics.

Basic Fabrics
Garter Stitch

IN ONLY **30** MINUTES!

Knitting *every* stitch in *every* row, as you did in the first 8 rows of your swatch, is called Garter Stitch (Photo A). Look closely at your swatch and you will see that each stitch looks like the **gray** stitch in Fig. 8.

Two rows of knitting make one horizontal ridge in your fabric. Garter Stitch is a thick, reversible fabric that does not curl at the edges. You can also achieve Garter Stitch by **purling** *every* stitch in *every* row, as you did on Rows 9-16 of your swatch.

Photo A

Fig. 8

Using the two basic stitches you've just learned — knit and purl — you can easily make fabrics that occur frequently in knitting.

Stockinette Stitch

Stockinette Stitch is the most common knit fabric and is the result of alternating knit and purl rows.

Let's make another swatch while you learn how to knit Stockinette Stitch.

Cast on 20 stitches.

Row 1: Knit each stitch across the row (pages 10 and 11).

Row 2: Purl each stitch across the row (pages 12 and 13).

Rows 3-8: Repeat Rows 1 and 2, 3 times.

Bind off your stitches.

Look at the **knit** side of your fabric (Photo B). This is considered to be the right side of your work. Notice that your fabric is smooth and flat, and that the side edges curl under. Each stitch should resemble a "V" like the **gray** stitch in Fig. 9.

Photo B

Fig. 9

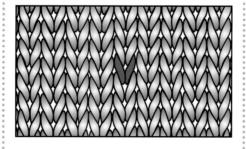

Reverse Stockinette Stitch

Photo C

Fig. 10

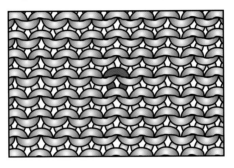

Fig. 11a

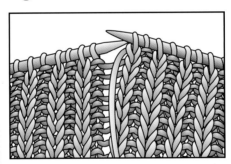

Fig. 11b

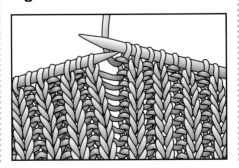

After you've been knitting for a while, you'll easily be able to identify a knit stitch versus a purl stitch.

Reverse Stockinette Stitch is worked the same as Stockinette Stitch with the exception that the **purl** side of your fabric is considered to be the right side.

Now flip your Stockinette Stitch swatch over and look at the **purl** side of your fabric (Photo C). The fabric is bumpy, and the side edges curl slightly toward you.

Each stitch should resemble a bump like the **gray** stitch in Fig. 10.

helpful hints

Alternating knit and purl stitches: Some fabrics are a combination of knit and purl stitches, like Seed (or Moss) Stitch, other textured pattern stitches (Dishcloths, page 28), and also Ribbing.

When working a **purl stitch after a knit stitch**, bring the yarn **between** the needles to the front (in position to purl, Fig. 11a). When working a **knit stitch after a purl stitch**, take the yarn **between** the needles to the back (in position to knit, Fig. 11b).

Seed (or Moss) Stitch

Seed Stitch, also known as Moss Stitch, is a reversible fabric that does not curl at the edges (Photo D). Alternate the knit and purl stitches on the first row. On the following rows, knit the purl stitches and purl the knit stitches as they face you (Fig. 12).

Let's work a swatch as you learn to knit Seed (or Moss) Stitch.

Note: These instructions are for an even number of stitches.

Cast on 20 stitches (abbreviated sts).

Row 1: ★ K1, P1; repeat from ★ across.

Translation: Knit the first stitch (abbreviated K1), purl the next stitch (abbreviated P1), ★ K1, P1; repeat from ★ (all the instructions between the ★ and the semicolon) across the row.

Note: See Understanding Instructions (page 19).

Row 2: ★ P1, K1; repeat from ★ across.

Row 3: ★ K1, P1; repeat from ★ across.

Rows 4-9: Repeat Rows 2 and 3, 3 times for Seed (or Moss) Stitch.

Bind off all sts in pattern.

Photo D

Fig. 12

If you would like to take a break from learning new things, knit the useful kitchen dishcloth on page 28.

helpful hint

Bind off in pattern. Unless otherwise stated, when you're instructed to bind off your stitches, you should always bind off in pattern. In reality, you're working another row.

If you would knit the next row, knit the stitches as you're binding them off. If you would purl the next row, purl the stitches as you're binding them off. If you're doing both, knit and purl the stitches as you're binding them off, as you would if it was a normal row. Binding off ribbing in pattern maintains the elasticity of the ribbing.

Whether you're binding off at the shoulders, the back of the neck, or around the neck or armhole ribbing, your work will be more professional in appearance if that row is worked in pattern.

Ribbing

Ribbing is a wonderful elastic stitch that's often worked at the bottom of sweaters, on cuffs, and around necklines. It can be worked in several combinations of knit and purl stitches.

The most common ribbing is the "knit one, purl one" ribbing, which offers more stretch than other ribbing variations.

Fig. 13a knit purl

Fig. 13b knit purl

Photo E

Alternate the knit and purl stitches on the first row. On the following rows, knit the knit stitches and purl the purl stitches as they face you.

The most common ribbing is knit 1, purl 1 ribbing (abbreviated K1, P1 ribbing) (Fig. 13a).

Knit 2, purl 2 ribbing (abbreviated K2, P2 ribbing) is not quite as elastic as K1, P1 ribbing and is worked in the same manner over a multiple of 4 stitches (Fig. 13b).

Let's make another swatch while you learn to knit Ribbing.

Note: These instructions are for an even number of stitches.
Cast on 20 sts **loosely**.

Row 1: ★ K1, P1; repeat from ★ across.

Rows 2-8: Repeat Row 1, 7 times for K1, P1 ribbing.

Bind off all sts in pattern.

Compare your ribbing to Photo E. Notice that the vertical lines of "V's" (the knit stitches) almost hide the bumps (the purl stitches). When working ribbing, the "V's" must always be knit and the bumps must always be purled (Figs. 13a & b).

Understanding Instructions

Knit instructions are written using abbreviations, symbols, terms, and punctuation marks. This method of writing saves time and space, and is actually easy to read once you understand the knit shorthand

Abbreviations

A list of abbreviations will be included with each leaflet or book, and you should review this list carefully before beginning a project. The list given below are those used for the projects in this section.

K	knit
M1	make one
mm	millimeters
P	purl
PSSO	pass slipped stitch over
SSK	slip, slip, knit
SSP	slip, slip, purl
st(s)	stitch(es)
tbl	through back loop(s)
tog	together
YO	yarn over

Symbols and Terms

★ — work all instructions following a ★ (star) as many **more** times as indicated in addition to the first time.

change to larger size needles — replace the right needle with one larger size needle and work the stitches from the left needle as instructed; at the end of the row, replace the left needle with the other larger size needle.

loosely — (binding off, adding new, or casting on stitches) the work should be as elastic as the knitting.

right vs. left — the side of the garment as if you were wearing it.

right side vs. wrong side — the right side of your work is the side that will show when the piece is finished.

work even — work without increasing or decreasing in the established pattern.

Punctuation

When reading knitting instructions, read from punctuation mark to punctuation mark. Just as in reading, commas (,) mean pause and semicolons (;) mean stop.

colon (:) — the number(s) given after a colon at the end of a row or round denote(s) the number of stitches you should have on that row or round. When repeating rows, the number given is for the last row.

braces { } — contain information or instructions pertaining to multiple sizes.

parentheses ( ) or brackets [ ] — indicate repetition, so you should work the enclosed instructions **as many** times as specified by the number immediately following. Parentheses or brackets may also contain explanatory remarks.

Gauge

Gauge is the number of stitches and rows per inch and is used to determine the finished size of a project. Most knitting patterns specify the gauge that you must match to ensure proper size or fit and to ensure you have enough yarn to complete the project. Before beginning any knitted item, it is absolutely necessary for you to knit a sample swatch in the pattern stitch with the weight of yarn and needle size suggested. It must be large enough for you to measure your gauge, usually a 4" square. After completing the swatch, measure it. If your swatch is larger or smaller than specified, make another, changing needle size to get the correct gauge. Remember, DO NOT HESITATE TO CHANGE NEEDLE SIZE IN ORDER TO MAINTAIN CORRECT GAUGE. Once you have obtained the correct gauge, you should continue to measure the total width of your work every three to four inches to be sure your gauge does not change.

Terminology

U.S. and International terminologies differ slightly. Equivalents are:

KNIT TERMINOLOGY	
UNITED STATES	**INTERNATIONAL**
gauge =	tension
bind off =	cast off
yarn over (YO) =	yarn forward (yfwd) **or**
	yarn around needle (yrn)

KNITTING NEEDLES																
U.S.	0	1	2	3	4	5	6	7	8	9	10	10½	11	13	15	17
U.K.	13	12	11	10	9	8	7	6	5	4	3	2	1	00	000	---
Metric - mm	2	2.25	2.75	3.25	3.5	3.75	4	4.5	5	5.5	6	6.5	8	9	10	12.75

Additional Techniques
Front and Back Loops

Here are a variety of techniques you'll encounter as you knit. You can take the time to learn about all of them now or refer to each as needed.

Sometimes twisted stitches are used for a special effect, such as in the Double-Cozy Boots and the Lattice Afghan.

A slipped stitch is a stitch transferred from the left needle to the right needle, without knitting or purling it.

Fig. 14

back loop   front loop

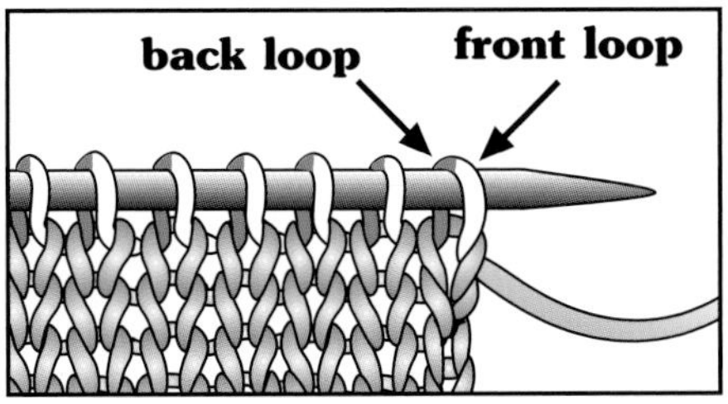

Always work into the front of a stitch unless instructed to work through back loop (abbreviated tbl) (Fig. 14).

Twisted Stitches

Fig. 15

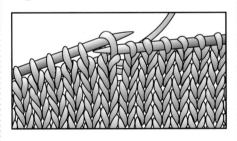

When instructed to knit or purl through **back** loop of a stitch (Fig. 14), the result will be twisted stitches (Fig. 15).

Slipping Stitches

Fig. 16a

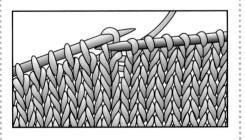

When slipping stitches, in order to prevent twisted stitches, the general rule is, when you're not going to use the slipped stitch again until the next row, slip it as if to purl (Fig. 16a), keeping the front loop to the front. When you're going to use the slipped stitch again on the same row, as in a decrease, slip it as if to knit (Fig. 16b). This will only temporarily twist the stitch.

Fig. 16b

Join New Yarn

Always join new yarn at the beginning of a row, so the ends can be woven in a seam and not be visible on the finished project. Cut the existing yarn leaving a 6" end. Begin the next row with the new ball of yarn, leaving a 6" end to weave in later (see Weaving in Yarn Ends, page 27).

Dropped Stitches

To pick up a dropped stitch, hold the work with the **knit** side facing, insert a crochet hook through the loop of the dropped stitch, hook the strand of yarn immediately above it (Fig. 17a), and pull it through the loop on your hook. Continue in this manner until you have used all of the strands of yarn.

If you were knitting across the row, slip the stitch onto the left needle with the right side of the stitch to the front (Fig. 17b).

If you were purling across the row, slip the stitch onto the right needle with the right side of the stitch to the front. Turn your work again to finish the row.

If a mistake is on the row you just worked, turn the work around so that you are holding the needle with the mistake in your left hand, ★ insert the **right** needle from the **back** into the stitch **below** the next stitch on the left needle (Fig. 17c), slip the stitch off the **left** needle and gently pull the working yarn to unravel the old stitch; repeat from ★ across until the mistake has been eliminated. Turn your work again to finish the row.

If you discover a mistake in a previous row or if you have not maintained correct gauge, it will be necessary to rip out more than one row. Place a safety pin or paper clip through the first and the last stitch in the row with the mistake. Slide all the stitches off the needles and rip back to the first safety pin or paper clip. Hold your knitting in your left hand with the working yarn at the right. ★ Insert a needle from the **back** into the stitch **below** the first stitch and gently pull the working yarn to unravel the old stitch; repeat from ★ until all the stitches are back on a needle.

Fig. 17a

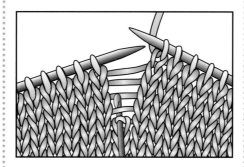

Fig. 17b

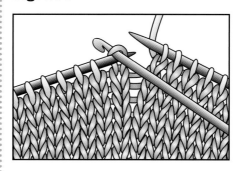

Fig. 17c

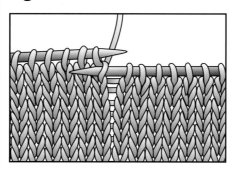

A dropped stitch is a stitch that accidentally slips off your needle and may easily unravel more than one row. It can happen to anyone, but there's an easy solution that will save the day.

helpful hint

There will be much less chance of dropping or splitting stitches if the stitches are picked up with a needle 2 or 3 sizes smaller than the one used to knit them.

Markers

As a convenience to you, we've used markers to help distinguish the beginning of a pattern or the beginning of a round. You may use purchased markers that fit on your needle or you may tie a length of contrasting color yarn around the needle.

The knit increase is the most common increase used.

When increasing across the row, the important point is to reach the total number of stitches needed with the increases spaced as evenly as possible.

The make one increase forms a new stitch by working into the strand between two stitches. The strand is intentionally twisted in order to prevent a hole.

Fig. 18

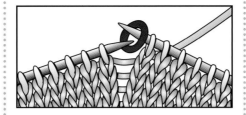

Place markers as instructed. When you reach a marker on a row, slip it from the left needle to the right needle (Fig. 18); remove it when no longer needed.

Increases
Knit Increases

Fig. 19a

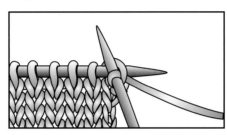

Fig. 19b

To make a knit increase, knit the next stitch but do **not** slip the old stitch off the left needle (Fig. 19a). Insert the right needle into the **back** loop of the **same** stitch (Fig. 19b) and knit it, then slip the old stitch off the left needle.

To increase evenly across a row, add one to the number of increases required and divide that number into the number of stitches on the needle. Subtract one from the result and the new number is the appropriate number of stitches to be worked between each increase. Adjust the number as needed. Sometimes it's necessary to work more or less stitches between increases to arrive at the correct total number of stitches.

Make One Increase

Fig. 20a

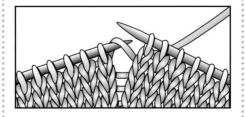

Fig. 20b

To Make One (abbreviated M1), insert the **left** needle under the horizontal strand between the stitches from the **front** (Fig. 20a). Then knit into the **back** of the strand (Fig. 20b), slipping it off the left needle.

After a knit stitch, before a knit stitch: Bring the yarn forward **between** the needles, then back **over** the top of the right needle, so that it is now in position to knit the next stitch (Fig. 21a).

Fig. 21a

After a purl stitch, before a purl stitch: Take the yarn **over** the right needle to the back, then forward **under** it, so that it is now in position to purl the next stitch (Fig. 21b).

Fig. 21b

After a knit stitch, before a purl stitch: Take the yarn forward **between** the needles, then back **over** the top of the right needle and forward **between** the needles again, so that it is now in position to purl the next stitch (Fig. 21c).

Fig. 21c

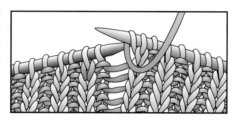

After a purl stitch, before a knit stitch: Take the yarn **over** the right needle to the back, so that it is now in position to knit the next stitch (Fig. 21d).

Fig. 21d

A yarn over (abbreviated YO), another type of increase, is simply placing the yarn over the right needle, creating an extra stitch.

Since the yarn over does produce a hole in the fabric, it's used for a lacy effect or a buttonhole. On the row following a yarn over, you must be careful to keep it on the needle and treat it as a stitch by knitting or purling it as instructed.

Adding New Stitches

Fig. 22a

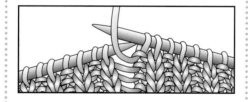

Knit the next stitch, but do **not** slip the old stitch off the left needle (Fig. 22a), insert the left needle into the loop just worked from **front** to **back** and slip it onto the left needle (Fig. 22b). Repeat for required number of stitches.

Fig. 22b

Adding new stitches is a technique used when you need to add on more than one stitch at the beginning or in the middle of a row, such as for the thumb of the mittens or the armhole band on the striped vest.

Decreases
Knit 2 Together

A decrease is made when two or more stitches are worked together to form one stitch.

Decreases can be worked on either the right or wrong side of your fabric. They are used to form decorative patterns and also for armhole and neck shaping.

A decrease will slant either to the right or to the left. Decreases worked at the edge of a piece for shaping usually lean in the same direction as the knitting is shaped. We have indicated which direction each decrease will slant.

Fig. 23

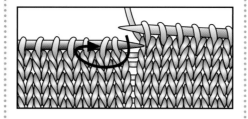

To Knit 2 Together (abbreviated K2 tog), insert the right needle into the **front** of the first two stitches on the left needle as if to **knit** (Fig. 23), then **knit** them together as if they were one stitch. (This decrease slants to the **right**.)

Knit 3 Together

Fig. 24

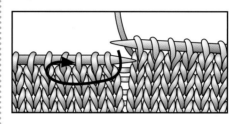

To Knit 3 Together (abbreviated K3 tog), insert the right needle into the **front** of the first three stitches on the left needle as if to **knit** (Fig. 24), then **knit** them together as if they were one stitch. (This decrease slants to the **right**.)

Slip, Slip, Knit

Fig. 25a

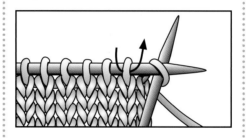

Fig. 25b

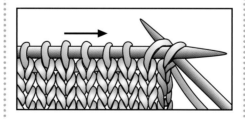

Fig. 25c

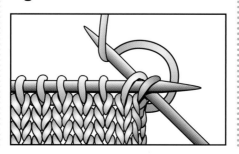

To Slip, Slip, Knit (abbreviated SSK), with the yarn in back of the work, separately slip two stitches as if to **knit** (Fig. 25a). Insert the **left** needle into the **front** of both slipped sts (Fig. 25b) and **knit** them together as if they were one stitch (Fig. 25c). (This decrease slants to the **left**.)

To Slip 1, Knit 1, Pass Slipped Stitch Over (abbreviated slip 1, K1, PSSO), slip one stitch as if to **knit** (Fig. 16b, page 20), then knit the next stitch. With the left needle, bring the slipped stitch over the knit stitch (Fig. 26) and off the needle. (This decrease slants to the **left**.)

To Slip 1, Knit 2 Together, Pass Slipped Stitch Over (abbreviated slip 1, K2 tog, PSSO), slip one stitch as if to **knit** (Fig. 16b, page 20), then knit the next two stitches together (Fig. 23, page 24). With the left needle, bring the slipped stitch over the stitch just made (Fig. 27) and off the needle. (This decrease slants to the **left**.)

To Purl 2 Together (abbreviated P2 tog), insert the right needle into the **front** of the first two stitches on the left needle as if to **purl** (Fig. 28), then **purl** them together as if they were one stitch. (This decrease slants to the **right** on the knit side.)

To Purl 2 Together Through Back Loop (abbreviated P2 tog tbl), insert the right needle into the **back** loop of the next two stitches from **back** to **front** (Fig. 29), then **purl** them together as if they were one stitch. (This decrease slants to the **left** on the knit side.)

To Slip, Slip, Purl (abbreviated SSP), with yarn held in front of work, separately slip two stitches as if to **knit** (Fig. 25a, page 24). Place these two stitches back onto the left needle. Insert the right needle into the **back** loop of both stitches from **back** to **front** (Fig. 30) and purl them together as if they were one stitch. (This decrease slants to the **left** on the knit side.)

Slip 1, Knit 1, Pass Slipped Stitch Over

Fig. 26

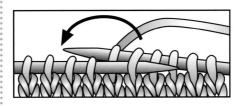

Slip 1, Knit 2 Together, Pass Slipped Stitch Over

Fig. 27

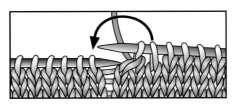

Purl 2 Together

Fig. 28

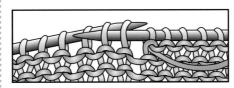

Purl 2 Together Through Back Loop

Fig. 29

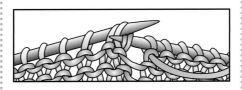

Slip, Slip, Purl

Fig. 30

The knit two together decrease is the most common knit decrease.

The slip one, knit one, PSSO decrease and the slip, slip, knit decrease are interchangeable.

The slip one, knit two together, PSSO decrease uses three stitches and decreases two stitches. It's frequently used in lace patterns like the Baby Blanket.

The purl two together decrease is the most common purl decrease.

The slip, slip, purl decrease resembles the slip, slip, knit decrease.

Finishing

Picking Up Stitches

Several of our projects require you to pick up stitches. Picking up stitches along the edge of a piece allows you to add a neck ribbing on the pullover, a cuff on the slippers, or a band on the dog coat. Stitches can also be picked up in the middle of a row as in the mittens.

A tapestry or yarn needle is best to use for sewing (or weaving) seams because the blunt tip will not split the yarn. Use the same yarn your project was made with to sew the seams. However, if the yarn is textured or bulky, it may be easier to sew the seam with a small, smooth yarn of the same color, such as tapestry yarn or an acrylic needlepoint yarn. Seam weaving is practically invisible and does not add bulk.

Fig. 31a

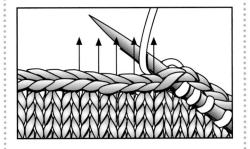

Fig. 31b

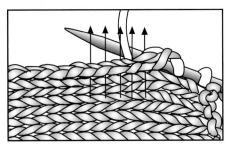

When instructed to pick up stitches, insert the needle from the **front** to the **back** under two strands at the edge of the worked piece (Figs. 31a & b). Wrap the yarn around the needle as if to **knit**, then bring the needle with the yarn back through the stitch to the right side, resulting in a stitch on the needle.
Repeat this along the edge, picking up the required number of stitches. A crochet hook may be helpful to pull yarn through.

Weaving Seams

Fig. 32

With the **right** side of both pieces facing you and the edges even, sew through both sides once to secure the seam. Insert the needle under the bar **between** the first and second stitches on the row and pull the yarn through (Fig. 32). Insert the needle under the next bar on the second side. Repeat from side to side, being careful to match rows. If the edges are different lengths, it may be necessary to insert the needle under two bars at one edge.

If a different yarn is used for the seams, be sure the care instructions for both yarns are the same. If the yarn used to knit your project is machine washable, the seam yarn must also be machine washable.

POM-POM

Cut a piece of cardboard 3" square. Wind the yarn around the cardboard lengthwise until it is approximately ¹/₂" thick in the middle (Fig. 33a). Carefully slip the yarn off the cardboard and firmly tie an 18" length of yarn around the middle (Fig. 33b). Leave yarn ends long enough to attach the pom-pom. Cut the loops on both ends, shake the pom-pom to fluff the strands, and trim the pom-pom into a smooth ball (Fig. 33c).

Twisted Cord

Cut 2 pieces of yarn, each 3 times as long as the desired finished length **or** to the length specified in the instructions. Holding both pieces of yarn together, fasten one end to a stationary object or have another person hold it; twist until **tight**. Fold in half and let it twist itself; knot both ends and cut the loops on the folded end.

Weaving in Yarn Ends

Thread a yarn needle with the yarn end. With **wrong** side facing, weave the needle through a seam or through a few inches of stitches following the contour of the stitches, then reverse the direction and weave it back through several more inches. When the end is secure, clip the yarn off close to your work.

Fig. 33a

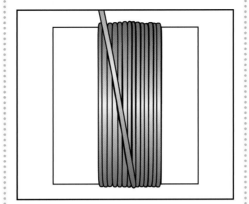

Fig. 33b

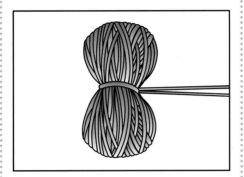

Fig. 33c

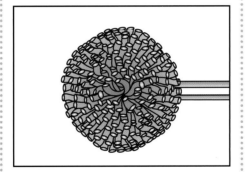

Pom-poms are great to add to the top of a hat, like the one included in the Baby Gift Set, and to lots of other projects.

The twisted cord is easy to make and can be used as a tie for booties and hats.

The assembly and finishing of a design should be done with great care. The techniques given will add value and beauty to your finished projects.

helpful hint

Never tie knots in your yarn. Knots may poke through to the right side and will sometimes come untied and unravel. Weaving in the ends gives a much better result.

Always take time to check your work to be sure the yarn ends do not show on the right side.

PROJECTS

Take a look at the twenty great projects we've selected especially for the beginning knitter. We've listed the projects in order of degree of difficulty, with the simplest first. When you're comfortable making the knit and purl stitches, and the basic knit fabrics, you're ready to begin a project! The extra skills needed to complete each project are specified in the instructions and can be learned as you go. Choose your favorite projects and get ready to have fun!

The Variegated Dishcloth is made in the same manner as the seed stitch swatch you made on page 17, except that you use an odd number of stitches. The Blue Dishcloth also uses knit and purl stitches to create an attractive textured design. Soon you'll be able to finish a couple of rows in 10 minutes! These are perfect beginner projects and can be taken with you wherever you go, since they require only a small amount of cotton yarn to make each one. Let's knit!

BLUE DISHCLOTH

Finished Size: Approximately 10" square

MATERIALS
100% Cotton Worsted Weight Yarn: **MEDIUM 4**
    95 yards
Straight knitting needles, size 8 (5.00 mm)
Yarn needle

Note: See Punctuation (page 19).

Cast on 46 sts.

Rows 1-4: Knit across.

Row 5 (Right side)**:** K9, P2, (K6, P2) 4 times, K3.

Row 6: K3, P1, K2, (P6, K2) 4 times, P5, K3.

Row 7: K7, P2, (K6, P2) 4 times, K5.

Row 8: K3, P3, K2, (P6, K2) 4 times, P3, K3.

Row 9: K5, P2, (K6, P2) 4 times, K7.

Row 10: K3, P5, K2, (P6, K2) 4 times, P1, K3.

Row 11: K3, purl across to last 3 sts, K3.

Rows 12-16: Repeat Rows 6-10.

Row 17: K3, P2, (K6, P2) 4 times, K9.

Row 18: Knit across.

Rows 19-73: Repeat Rows 5-18, 3 times; then repeat Rows 5-17 once **more**.

Rows 74-77: Knit across.

Bind off all sts in knit (page 14).

Weave in yarn ends (page 27).

Design by Linda Luder.

VARIEGATED DISHCLOTH

Finished Size: Approximately 10" square

MATERIALS
100% Cotton Worsted Weight Yarn: **MEDIUM 4**
    125 yards
Straight knitting needles, size 7 (4.50 mm)
Yarn needle

Cast on 51 sts.

Row 1: K1, ★ P1, K1; repeat from ★ across.

Repeat Row 1 for Seed Stitch until Dishcloth measures approximately 10" from cast on edge.

Bind off all sts in pattern (page 14).

Weave in yarn ends (page 27).

Design by Eunice Svinicki.

This warm set is made in ribbing like the swatch you made on page 18, except that you use an odd number of stitches for the Ribbed Scarf. A smaller size needle is used on the first row of each stripe to maintain gauge. The fashionable Ribbed Hat design also incorporates decreases for shaping. In only 30 minutes, you can see the stripes beginning to form.

RIBBED SCARF

Size:	Small	Medium	Large
Finished			
Measurement:	5" x 36"	7" x 44"	9" x 54"

MATERIALS
Worsted Weight Yarn: **MEDIUM 4**
 Grey - $2^1/_2$ {$4^1/_2$-$7^1/_2$} ounces,
  [70{130-210} grams, 140{255-425} yards]
 Burgundy - $1/_2$ ounce, (15 grams, 30 yards)
 Lt Grey - small amount
Straight knitting needles, sizes 5 (3.75 mm)
 and 6 (4.00 mm) **or** sizes needed
 for gauge
Yarn needle

Note: See Gauge (page 19).

GAUGE: With larger size needles, in ribbing,
  24 sts and 18 rows = 4"

Note: If you come to an abbreviation, symbol, term, or punctuation that you haven't learned yet, refer to Understanding Instructions, page 19.

FIRST END
With Grey and larger size needles, cast on 29{41-53} sts **loosely**.

Row 1: P1, (K1, P1) across.

Row 2 (Right side)**:** K1, (P1, K1) across.

Repeat Rows 1 and 2 for ribbing until Scarf measures approximately 2" from cast on edge, ending by working Row 1.

FIRST STRIPE
Row 1: With Burgundy and smaller size needle, knit across.

Row 2: With larger size needle, P1, (K1, P1) across.

Row 3: With larger size needle, K1, (P1, K1) across.

Row 4: With larger size needle, P1, (K1, P1) across; drop Burgundy.

Row 5: With Lt Grey and smaller size needle, knit across.

Row 6: With larger size needle, P1, (K1, P1) across; cut Lt Grey.

Rows 7-10: Repeat Rows 1-4.

Cut Burgundy.

BODY
Row 1: With Grey and smaller size needle, knit across.

Row 2: With larger size needle, P1, (K1, P1) across.

Row 3: With larger size needle, K1, (P1, K1) across.

Repeat Rows 2 and 3 until Scarf measures approximately 32{40-50}" from cast on edge, ending by working Row 2.

SECOND STRIPE
Work same as First Stripe.

SECOND END
Work same as Body for 2".

Bind off all sts **loosely** in ribbing (page 14).

Weave in yarn ends (page 27).

RIBBED HAT

Size:	Small	Medium	Large
Finished			
Measurement:	16"	17"	$18^1/_2$"

MATERIALS
Worsted Weight Yarn: **MEDIUM 4**
 Grey - $2^1/_2$ {3-$3^1/_2$} ounces,
  [70{90-100} grams, 140{170-200} yards]
 Burgundy - $1/_4$ ounce, (10 grams, 15 yards)
 Lt Grey - small amount
Straight knitting needles, sizes 5 (3.75 mm)
 and 6 (4.00 mm) **or** sizes needed
 for gauge
Yarn needle

Note: See Gauge (page 19).

GAUGE: With larger size needles, in ribbing,
  24 sts and 18 rows = 4"

Instructions begin on page 57.

Now you can knit fancy footwear for the whole family! The Ruffle-Top Slippers are knit in Garter Stitch, and you'll use decreases for the toe shaping and increases to complete the attractive ruffle around the ankle. The Double-Cozy Boots are knit in Garter Stitch and Stockinette Stitch, holding two strands of yarn together as one strand for a fun effect and extra warmth. "Yarn overs" form eyelets for the twisted cord ties. Before you know it, you'll be completing 2" in 30 minutes or less. Choose the yarn colors you like and let's get started!

RUFFLE-TOP SLIPPERS

Child Sizes:	Small	Medium	Large
Sole Length:	7¹/₂"	8"	8¹/₂"

Adult Sizes:	Small	Medium	Large
Sole Length:	9"	9¹/₂"	10"

Size Note: Instructions are written for Child sizes in the first set of braces { }, with Adult sizes in the second set of braces. Instructions will be easier to read if you circle all the numbers pertaining to your size. If only one number is given, it applies to all sizes.

MATERIALS

Worsted Weight Yarn:
{2¹/₂-3-3¹/₂}{3¹/₂-4-4} ounces,
[{70-90-100}{100-110-110} grams,
{140-170-200}{200-225-225} yards]
Straight knitting needles, size 9 (5.50 mm) **or**
size needed for gauge
Yarn needle

Note: See Gauge (page 19).

GAUGE: In Garter Stitch (knit every row),
16 sts and 32 rows = 4"

Note: If you come to an abbreviation, symbol, term, or punctuation that you haven't learned yet, refer to Understanding Instructions, page 19.

Extra skills needed: K2 tog (Knit 2 together, Fig. 23, page 24), picking up stitches (Fig. 31b, page 26), and knit increases (Figs. 19a & b, page 22).

BODY

Beginning at heel, cast on {26-26-30}{32-36-38} sts.

Work in Garter Stitch until piece measures {5¹/₄-5³/₄-6¹/₄}{6³/₄-7¹/₄-7³/₄}" from cast on edge.

TOE

Row 1 (Decrease row)**:** K2 tog, knit across to last 2 sts, K2 tog: {24-24-28}{30-34-36} sts.

Row 2: Knit across.

Rows 3-10: Repeat Rows 1 and 2, 4 times: {16-16-20}{22-26-28} sts.

Cut yarn leaving a long end. Thread a yarn needle with the end and separately slip each stitch from the knitting needle onto the yarn, gathering the stitches tightly to close toe, then secure end.
Sew center front seam to within {3¹/₄-3¹/₂-3³/₄}{4-4¹/₄-4¹/₂}" of cast on edge or to desired opening.

CUFF

With **right** side facing, pick up one stitch in edge of each row along opening.

Row 1: Increase in each st across.

Rows 2-6: Knit across.

Bind off all sts in knit.

Sew back seam.
Weave in yarn ends.

Design by Ruth Shepherd.

DOUBLE-COZY BOOTS

Child Sizes:	Small	Medium	Large
Sole Length:	7¹/₂"	8"	8¹/₂"

Adult Sizes:	Small	Medium	Large
Sole Length:	9"	9¹/₂"	10"

Size Note: Instructions are written for Child sizes in the first set of braces { }, with Adult sizes in the second set of braces. Instructions will be easier to read if you circle all the numbers pertaining to your size. If only one number is given, it applies to all sizes.

MATERIALS

Worsted Weight Yarn:
Red - {3¹/₂-4-4¹/₂}{4¹/₂-5-5} ounces,
[{100-110-130}{130-140-140} grams,
{200-225-255}{255-285-285} yards]
Variegated - {1¹/₂-1¹/₂-1¹/₂}{2-2-2} ounces,
[{40-40-40}{60-60-60} grams,
{85-85-85}{115-115-115} yards]
Straight knitting needles, size 7 (4.50 mm) **or**
size needed for gauge
Yarn needle

Entire Boot is worked holding **two** strands of Red together **or** one strand of Red and one strand of Variegated together.

Note: See Gauge (page 19).

GAUGE: With **two** strands of yarn held together, in Garter Stitch (knit every row) **or** in Stockinette Stitch (knit one row, purl one row), 16 sts = 4"

Note: If you come to an abbreviation, symbol, term, or punctuation that you haven't learned yet, refer to Understanding Instructions, page 19.

Extra skills needed: YO (Yarn overs, Fig. 21a, page 23), and the following decreases: K2 tog (Knit 2 together, Fig. 23, page 24), P2 tog (Purl 2 together, Fig. 28, page 25), P2 tog tbl (Purl 2 together through back loop, Fig. 29, page 25), and slip 1, K1, PSSO (Slip 1, knit 1, pass slipped stitch over, Fig. 26, page 25).

SOLE

With **two** strands of Red held together, cast on {60-64-68}{72-76-80} sts.

Work in Garter Stitch until there are {7-7-8}{8-9-9} ridges [{14-14-16}{16-18-18} rows].

Instructions continued on page 57.

This cute gift set is made using a combination of Stockinette Stitch and Garter Stitch for a ridged effect. The Cap, Booties, and Ball are made with worsted weight yarn, while the Baby Toy uses sport weight yarn for a softer touch. Knit one project or all four to make the whole set! Half of the Bootie can be made in just 30 minutes. Your friends will be so impressed by your new skills at the next baby shower!

BABY GIFT SET

MATERIALS (For Cap, Booties, and Ball) **MEDIUM 4**
Worsted Weight Yarn:
Variegated – 1$\frac{1}{2}$ ounces,
(40 grams, 100 yards)
Green – 1$\frac{1}{2}$ ounces,
(40 grams, 100 yards)
Straight knitting needles, size 7 (4.50 mm) **or**
size needed for gauge
Yarn needle
Polyester fiberfill
Small pill bottle with child proof cap
Dried beans, rice, or unpopped popcorn
(See page 37 for Baby Toy)

Note: See Gauge (page 19).

GAUGE: With worsted weight yarn, in Stockinette Stitch (knit one row, purl one row), 20 sts and 28 rows = 4"

Note: If you come to an abbreviation, symbol, term, or punctuation that you haven't learned yet, refer to Understanding Instructions, page 19.

CAP

Finished Size: 6 months

Extra skills needed: K2 tog (Knit 2 together, Fig. 23, page 24), and P2 tog (Purl 2 together, Fig. 28, page 25).

With Green, cast on 80 sts.

Rows 1-7: Knit across.

Cut Green; with Variegated and beginning with a **knit** row, work in Stockinette Stitch until piece measures approximately 3$\frac{1}{2}$" from cast on edge, ending by working a **purl** row.

SHAPING
Row 1: (K3, K2 tog) across: 64 sts.

Row 2 AND ALL WRONG SIDE ROWS: Purl across.

Row 3: (K2, K2 tog) across: 48 sts.

Row 5: (K1, K2 tog) across: 32 sts.

Row 7: K2 tog across: 16 sts.

Row 9: K2 tog across: 8 sts.

Cut yarn leaving a long end. Thread a yarn needle with the end and separately slip each stitch from the knitting needle onto the yarn; gather the stitches tightly to close, then secure end. Weave seam (Fig. 32, page 26).

EAR FLAP (Make 2)
With Green, cast on 26 sts.

Rows 1 and 2 (Border)**:** Knit across.

Note: A **short row** is a row that's not worked all the way from one end to the other. The body of the Ear Flap is worked in Stockinette Stitch, beginning in the center of the Garter Stitch border. Each row works across the center 9 stitches of the body, then a decrease is made using the last stitch on the body and the next stitch on the border. Leaving the remaining stitches unworked, you will stop, **turn** the work, and continue in the opposite direction. Begin working in short rows as follows:

Row 3: Cut Green, slip 8 sts as if to **purl** onto right needle; with Variegated P9, P2 tog, leave remaining sts unworked.

Row 4 (Right side)**:** **Turn**; K9, K2 tog, leave remaining sts unworked.

Row 5: Turn; P9, P2 tog, leave remaining sts unworked.

Rows 6-16: Repeat Rows 4 and 5, 5 times; then repeat Row 4 once **more**.

Slip remaining st on left needle onto right needle.

Bind off all 12 sts **loosely** in purl.

FINISHING
Sew top edge of each Ear Flap to inside edge of Cap Row 7 (top of Garter Stitch), beginning 2" from seam.

Weave in yarn ends.

With Green, make two 12" Twisted Cords (page 27); sew one to bottom of each Ear Flap for tie.

Make a Green pom-pom (Figs. 33a-c, page 27); sew to top of Cap.

Instructions continued on page 36.

BOOTIES

Finished Size: 6 months

Extra skills needed: K2 tog (Knit 2 together, Fig. 23, page 24), and YO (Yarn overs, Fig. 21a, page 23).

SIDES AND BOTTOM

With Green, cast on 44 sts.

Row 1: K 17, P1, K8, P1, K 17.

Row 2 (Right side)**:** Knit across.

Rows 3-23: Repeat Rows 1 and 2, 10 times; then repeat Row 1 once **more**.

Row 24 (Eyelet row)**:** ★ K1, K2 tog, YO; repeat from ★ 2 times **more**, K 26, (YO, K2 tog, K1) 3 times.

Row 25: K 17, P1, K8, P1, K 17.

Row 26: Bind off 10 sts, K 23, bind off remaining 10 sts; cut Green: 24 sts.

TOE

With Variegated and beginning with a **purl** row, work in Stockinette Stitch until Toe measures approximately 1¼", ending by working a **purl** row.

SHAPING

Row 1: K2 tog across: 12 sts.

Row 2: Purl across.

Row 3: K2 tog across; cut yarn leaving a long end for sewing: 6 sts.

FINISHING

Thread a yarn needle with the end and separately slip each stitch from the knitting needle onto the yarn; gather the stitches tightly to close, then secure end. Weave Toe seam (Fig. 32, page 26).

Weave back seam from the top to the Stockinette Stitch lines; secure; do **not** cut yarn. Weave the same yarn through each of the remaining 8 sts; gather tightly and secure.

Weave in yarn ends.

With Variegated, make a 20" Twisted Cord (page 27). Lace Cord through Eyelet row and tie in a bow.

BALL

Extra skills needed: Knit increase (Figs. 19a & b, page 22) and K2 tog (Knit 2 together, Fig. 23, page 24).

With Variegated, cast on 12 sts **loosely**.

Row 1 (Right side)**:** Increase in each st across: 24 sts.

Row 2: Purl across.

Row 3: Increase in each st across: 48 sts.

Rows 4-10: Beginning with a **purl** row, work in Stockinette Stitch for 7 rows.

Note: Carry the yarn not being used **loosely** along the edge, twisting it on every other wrong side row with the yarn being used in order to prevent holes.

Rows 11-14: With Green, knit 4 rows.

Rows 15-18: With Variegated, work in Stockinette Stitch for 4 rows.

Rows 19-24: With Green, knit 6 rows.

Rows 25-28: With Variegated, work in Stockinette Stitch for 4 rows.

Rows 29-32: With Green, knit 4 rows.

Rows 33-40: With Variegated, work in Stockinette Stitch for 8 rows.

Row 41: K2 tog across: 24 sts.

Row 42: Purl across.

Row 43: K2 tog across; cut yarn leaving a long end for sewing: 12 sts.

FINISHING

Thread a yarn needle with the end and separately slip each stitch from the knitting needle onto the yarn; gather the stitches tightly to close, then secure end. Weave one half of the seam (Fig. 32, page 26).

Place beans, rice, or unpopped popcorn in pill bottle for rattle; wrap in a small layer of polyester fiberfill and place in Ball. Stuff polyester fiberfill evenly around bottle, forming Ball into a smooth, round shape. Finish weaving seam; weave yarn through the remaining 12 sts; gather tightly and secure.

Weave in yarn ends.

BABY TOY

Finished Size: 7" tall

MATERIALS
Sport Weight Yarn:
  Green - 55 yards
  Pink - 15 yards
  White - small amount
Straight knitting needles, size 5 (3.75 mm) **or**
  size needed for gauge
Yarn needle
Embroidery needle
Polyester fiberfill
Blue embroidery floss - small amount
White embroidery floss - small amount
1" Gathered eyelet lace - 7"
Sewing needle and thread to match lace

Note: See Gauge (page 19).

GAUGE: In Stockinette Stitch (knit one row,
  purl one row) 24 sts and 32 rows = 4"

Note: If you come to an abbreviation, symbol, term, or punctuation that you haven't learned yet, refer to Understanding Instructions, page 19.

Extra skills needed: Knit increase (Figs. 19a & b, page 22), P2 tog (Purl 2 together, Fig. 28, page 25), M1 (Make one, Figs. 20a & b, page 22), and K2 tog (Knit 2 together, Fig. 23, page 24).

BODY
With Green, cast on 12 sts **loosely**.

Row 1 (Right side)**:** Increase in each st across: 24 sts.

Row 2: Purl across.

Row 3: Increase in each st across: 48 sts.

Beginning with a **purl** row, work in Stockinette Stitch until piece measures approximately 5" from cast on edge, ending by working a **knit** row.

HEAD
Row 1: P2 tog across: 24 sts.

Row 2 (Eyelet row)**:** (K1, M1) twice, K2, ★ M1, K1, M1, K2; repeat from ★ across to last 2 sts, (M1, K1) twice: 40 sts.

Row 3: Purl across; cut Green leaving a long end for sewing.

With Pink, work in Stockinette Stitch for approximately 2", ending by working a **purl** row.

SHAPING
Row 1: K2 tog across: 20 sts.

Row 2: Purl across.

Row 3: K2 tog across; cut yarn leaving a long end for sewing: 10 sts.

FINISHING
Thread a yarn needle with the end and separately slip each stitch from the knitting needle onto the yarn; gather the stitches tightly to close, then secure end. Weave Head seam (Fig. 32, page 26) and stuff Head with polyester fiberfill.

Sew bottom seam; weave back seam, stuffing Body with polyester fiberfill before closing.

Weave in yarn ends.

With White and using photo as a guide, add French knot buttons to front of Body as follows: Bring needle up at 1. Wrap yarn desired number of times around needle and insert needle at 2, holding end of yarn with non-stitching fingers (Fig. 34). Tighten knot; then pull needle through, holding yarn until it must be released.

Fig. 34

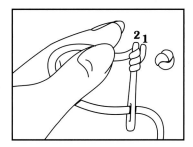

With floss, add facial features as desired.

With White, make a 12" Twisted Cord (page 27). Lace Cord through Eyelet row and tie in a bow in front.

Sew lace around face.

With Green and yarn needle, stitch through stuffed piece to shape arms (see overlay).

Design by Beth MacDonald.

While making these mittens, you'll learn new techniques as you add on stitches for the thumb and work with stitch holders. It's a small project, so you'll learn a lot in a short time. Complete the ribbing for a small size in 30 minutes or less. Striped and multicolor variations are included to help you fashion unique mittens for yourself and everyone you know.

FAMILY MITTENS

Selecting Correct Size Mitten: Size indicates number of inches around palm, measured just above thumb.

Size Note: Instructions are written for sizes 5, 5¹/₂, and 6 in first set of braces { }, with sizes 6¹/₂, 7, and 7¹/₂ in second set of braces, and sizes 8, 8¹/₂, and 9 in third set of braces. Instructions will be easier to read if you circle all the numbers pertaining to your size. If only one number is given, it applies to all sizes.

MATERIALS
Note: Yarn amounts are given for the total amount needed for a pair of mittens. When making any of the variations, divide this amount between the colors used accordingly.
Worsted Weight Yarn:
{1-1-1¹/₄}{1¹/₂-1³/₄-2}{2¹/₄-2¹/₂-2³/₄} ounce(s),
[{30-30-35}{40-50-60}{65-70-80} grams,
{65-65-80}{100-115-135}{145-165-180} yards]
Straight knitting needles, sizes 5 (3.75 mm)
  and 7 (4.50 mm) **or** sizes needed for gauge
Stitch holders - 2
Markers - 2
Yarn needle

Note: See Gauge (page 19).

GAUGE: With larger size needles,
  in Stockinette Stitch (knit one row,
  purl one row), 20 sts and 28 rows = 4"

Note: If you come to an abbreviation, symbol, term, or punctuation that you haven't learned yet, refer to Understanding Instructions, page 19.

Extra skills needed: Increases (page 22), using markers (Fig. 18, page 22), adding new stitches (Figs. 22a & b, page 23), K2 tog (Knit 2 together, Fig. 23, page 24), picking up stitches (Fig. 31a, page 26), and slip 1, K1, PSSO (Slip 1, knit 1, pass slipped stitch over, Fig. 26, page 25).

RIBBING
With smaller size needles, cast on
{23-25-27}{29-31-33}{35-37-39} sts **loosely**.

Row 1: P1, (K1, P1) across.

Row 2 (Right side)**:** K1, (P1, K1) across.

Repeat Rows 1 and 2 until Ribbing measures approximately {2-2¹/₂-2¹/₂}{2³/₄-3-3}{3¹/₄-3¹/₄-3¹/₂}" from cast on edge, ending by working Row 1.

BODY
Change to larger size needles.

Row 1: Knit across increasing {5-5-5}{5-7-7}{7-9-9} sts evenly spaced: {28-30-32}{34-38-40}{42-46-48} sts.

Row 2: Purl across.

For Sizes 8, 8¹/₂, and 9 Only - Rows 3 and 4: Work across in Stockinette Stitch.

SHAPING (All Sizes)
Row 1: Knit {13-14-15}{16-18-19}{20-22-23} sts, place marker, increase twice, place marker, knit across: {30-32-34}{36-40-42}{44-48-50} sts.

Row 2: Purl across.

Row 3 (Increase row)**:** Knit across to next marker, increase, knit to within one st of next marker, increase, knit across: {32-34-36}{38-42-44}{46-50-52} sts.

Repeat Rows 2 and 3, {1-2-2}{3-3-4}{4-5-5} time(s): {34-38-40}{44-48-52}{54-60-62} sts.

Work even in Stockinette Stitch until Mitten measures approximately {3¹/₄-4-4}{4³/₄-5-5¹/₄}{5³/₄-6-6¹/₄}" from cast on edge, ending by working a **purl** row.

THUMB
Row 1: Knit across to next marker and slip these {13-14-15}{16-18-19}{20-22-23} sts just worked onto st holder, remove marker, add on one st; knit added on st, knit across to next marker, remove marker, **turn**; add on one st, slip remaining sts onto second st holder: {10-12-12}{14-14-16}{16-18-18} sts.

Work even until Thumb measures approximately {1¹/₄-1¹/₂-1³/₄}{2-2¹/₄-2¹/₂}{2¹/₂-2³/₄-2³/₄}", ending by working a **purl** row.

Next Row: K2 tog across: {5-6-6}{7-7-8}{8-9-9} sts.

Cut yarn leaving a long end. Thread a yarn needle with the end and separately slip each stitch from the knitting needle onto the yarn; gather the stitches tightly to close, then secure end. Weave seam (Fig. 32, page 26).

HAND
With **right** side facing, slip sts from first st holder onto needle; with same needle, pick up a st in each of 2 added on sts at base of Thumb; slip sts from second st holder onto empty needle and knit across: {28-30-32}{34-38-40}{42-46-48} sts.

Work even until piece measures approximately {4³/₄-6-6}{7-7¹/₂-7³/₄}{8¹/₂-8³/₄-9¹/₄}" from cast on edge, ending by working a **knit** row.

Next Row: Purl {14-15-16}{17-19-20} {21-23-24} sts, place marker, purl across.

SHAPING
Row 1: K2, slip 1 as if to **knit**, K1, PSSO, knit across to within 3 sts of next marker, K2 tog, K1, slip marker, K1, slip 1 as if to **knit**, K1, PSSO, knit across to last 4 sts, K2 tog, K2: {24-26-28}{30-34-36}{38-42-44} sts.

Row 2: Purl across.

Repeat Rows 1 and 2, {1-2-3}{3-4-5}{5-5-5} time(s): {20-18-16}{18-18-16}{18-22-24} sts.

Next Row: K2 tog across: {10-9-8}{9-9-8}{9-11-12} sts.

Cut yarn leaving a long end. Thread a yarn needle with the end and separately slip each stitch from the knitting needle onto the yarn; gather the stitches tightly to close, then secure end. Weave seam.

Weave in yarn ends.

VARIATIONS
3-COLOR STRIPES
Work Ribbing in Main Color (Pink).

Complete Mitten working in the following color sequence: 1 Row **each** of Color A (Green), Color B (Yellow), and Main Color (Pink), carrying the yarns **loosely** along the edge.

Note: The Thumb can be worked with Main Color if the extra yarn ends make the seam too bulky.

MULTI-COLORS
Work Ribbing in Color A (Green), Body in Color B (Rose), Thumb in Color C (Yellow), and Hand in Color D (Blue). Work second Mitten, same as the first, switching the positions of the colors, or with completely different colors.

Designs by Mary Lamb Becker.

These Bunny Mittens use the same basic techniques as the Mittens on page 38, but the thumb and hand are replaced by a mouth. Knit the Ears in just 10 minutes. See how pleased a youngster will be to wear these cute mittens for warmth or just for fun — let's get started!

BUNNY MITTENS

Size:	Small	Medium	Large
Fits Ages:	2-3	4-5	6-7

Size Note: Instructions are written for size Small, with sizes Medium and Large in braces { }. Instructions will be easier to read if you circle all the numbers pertaining to your size. If only one number is given, it applies to all sizes.

MATERIALS

MEDIUM
4

Worsted Weight Yarn:
  White - 2 ounces, (60 grams, 135 yards)
  Pink - small amount
Straight knitting needles, sizes 3 (3.25 mm)
  and 7 (4.50 mm) **or** sizes needed for gauge
Stitch holders - 2
Yarn needle
Craft glue
1/2" Pink pom-poms - 2
3/4" White pom-poms - 2
Round wiggle eyes - 4
Red cloth-backed vinyl - small amount
Ribbon roses - 2 (optional)
Pink blush (optional)

Note: See Gauge (page 19).

GAUGE: With larger size needles,
        in Stockinette Stitch (knit one row,
        purl one row) 20 sts and 28 rows = 4"

Note: If you come to an abbreviation, symbol, term, or punctuation that you haven't learned yet, refer to Understanding Instructions, page 19.

Extra skills needed: K2 tog (Knit 2 together, Fig. 23, page 24), adding new stitches (Figs. 22a & b, page 23), picking up stitches (Fig. 31a, page 26), and knit increases (Figs. 19a & b, page 22).

RIBBING

With White and smaller size needles, cast on 33 sts **loosely**.

Row 1: P1, (K1, P1) across.

Row 2 (Right side)**:** K1, (P1, K1) across.

Repeat Rows 1 and 2 until Ribbing measures approximately 1^3/$_4${2-2}" from cast on edge, ending by working Row 1.

BODY

Change to larger size needles.

Row 1: Knit across working K2 tog decrease 5{3-1} time(s) evenly spaced: 28{30-32} sts.

Beginning with a **purl** row, work even in Stockinette Stitch until Mitten measures approximately 3{3^3/$_4$-4}" from cast on edge, ending by working a **purl** row; cut yarn, leaving a 6" end.

UPPER MOUTH

Row 1: Slip 7{7-8} sts onto st holder; cast on 7{7-8} sts **loosely** onto empty needle, K 14{15-16}, slip remaining 7{8-8} sts onto second st holder, **turn**; add on 7{8-8} sts: 28{30-32} sts.

Work even until Upper Mouth measures approximately 2{2^1/$_4$-2^3/$_4$}", ending by working a **purl** row.

SHAPING
For Sizes Small and Large Only

Row 1: K1, K2 tog, (K2, K2 tog) across to last st, K1: 21{24} sts.

Row 2: Purl across.

Row 3: (K1, K2 tog) across: 14{16} sts.

For Size Medium Only

Row 1: K2, (K2 tog, K2) across: 23 sts.

Row 2: Purl across.

Row 3: K2, (K2 tog, K1) across: 16 sts.

All Sizes

Row 4: Purl across.

Row 5: K2 tog across: 7{8-8} sts.

Cut yarn leaving a long end. Thread a yarn needle with the end and separately slip each stitch from the knitting needle onto the yarn; gather the stitches tightly to close, then secure end. Weave seam (Fig. 32, page 26).

LOWER MOUTH

With **right** side facing, slip 7{7-8} sts from right st holder onto needle and knit across, pick up 14{15-16} sts across cast on edge of Upper Mouth, slip 7{8-8} sts from left st holder onto empty needle and knit across: 28{30-32} sts.

Work even until Lower Mouth measures approximately 1^1/$_2${1^3/$_4$-2^1/$_4$}", ending by working a **purl** row.

SHAPING
Work same as Upper Mouth through Row 5.

Cut yarn leaving a long end. Thread a yarn needle with the end and separately slip each stitch from the knitting needle onto the yarn; gather the stitches tightly to close, then secure end. Weave approximately 1" of seam. (The remaining seam will be woven after Finishing details are complete.)

EARS
FIRST EAR
Note: Instructions are written for Ears to be picked up directly from Mitten and worked without sewing. If desired, they may be worked separately and sewn in place using photo as a guide for placement.

Hold Mitten with tip facing and Upper Mouth up. With White and smaller size needles, pick up 4 sts beginning $2^1/_4\{2^1/_2\text{-}2^3/_4\}$" up from tip and in third st from right edge OR cast on 4 sts **loosely**.

Row 1: Purl across.

Row 2: Increase, K2, increase: 6 sts.

Rows 3-11: Beginning with a **purl** row, work even in Stockinette Stitch for 9 rows.

Row 12: K2 tog, K2, K2 tog: 4 sts.

Row 13: Purl across.

Row 14: K2 tog twice: 2 sts.

Row 15: Purl across.

Bind off all sts in knit.

SECOND EAR
Work same as First Ear, leaving 2{3-4} sts between.

FINISHING
Using photo as a guide for placement:
Attach pom-poms and wiggle eyes.

With a double strand of Pink and yarn needle, embroider a straight stitch from tip of Mitten to nose.

Trace Pattern and cut Tongue from red vinyl.
Attach Tongue to Lower Mouth at joining of Upper and Lower Mouth.

Finish weaving seam.

Weave in yarn ends.

Optional: With Pink blush, lightly color center of Ears. Attach a ribbon rose below one Ear.

Design by Beth MacDonald.

TONGUE PATTERN

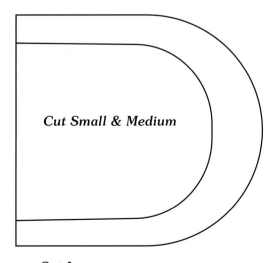

Cut Small & Medium

Cut Large

This classic cable pillow is made with a lacy "yarn over" design. As impressive as cables are, you'll soon see that they aren't hard to make. Practice making a few cables by working the Gauge Swatch. Soon you'll be able to complete several rows of the pillow in 10 minutes! What a lovely way to decorate a room and show off your new skill at the same time!

LACY CABLES PILLOW

MATERIALS

Worsted Weight Yarn: **MEDIUM 4**
 7 ounces, (200 grams, 395 yards)
Straight knitting needles, size 8 (5.00 mm) **or**
 size needed for gauge
Cable needle (see note below)
Yarn needle
Pillow form - 14" square

Note: Cable needles have a point on each end and are available in several shapes and sizes. The size of the cable needle does not have to be the same size as the needles with which you are knitting, but it should not be bigger or it will stretch the stitches out of shape.

Note: See Gauge (page 19).

GAUGE: In pattern, 3 repeats (24 sts) = 4¹/₂";
 24 rows = 4"

Gauge Swatch: 4³/₄"w x 4"h
Cast on 26 sts **loosely**.
Work same as Pillow Cover for 24 rows.
Bind off **loosely** in pattern.

STITCH GUIDE

CABLE (uses next 6 sts)
Slip next 3 sts onto cable needle as if to **purl** and hold them in **back** of work, K3 from left needle (Fig. 35a), K3 from cable needle being sure that the first st you knit is the first one you slipped onto the cable needle (Fig. 35b).

Fig. 35a

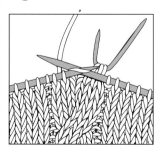

Fig. 35b

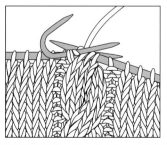

Note: If you come to an abbreviation, symbol, term, or punctuation that you haven't learned yet, refer to Understanding Instructions, page 19.

Extra skills needed: YO (Yarn overs, Fig. 21a, page 23), K2 tog (Knit 2 together, Fig. 23, page 24), and slip 1, knit 1, PSSO, (Slip 1, knit 1, pass slipped stitch over, Fig. 26, page 25).

PILLOW COVER (Make 2)
Cast on 74 sts **loosely**.

Row 1 AND ALL WRONG SIDE ROWS: K2, (P6, K2) across.

Row 2 (Right side)**:** P2, (K6, P2) across.

Row 4: P2, (work Cable, P2) across.

Row 6: P2, (K6, P2) across.

Row 8: P2, ★ K1, YO, K2 tog, K3, P2; repeat from ★ across.

Row 10: P2, ★ slip 1 as if to **knit**, K1, PSSO, YO, K4, P2; repeat from ★ across.

Row 12: P2, ★ K1, YO, K2 tog, K3, P2; repeat from ★ across.

Row 14: P2, (K6, P2) across.

Row 16: P2, (work Cable, P2) across.

Row 18: P2, (K6, P2) across.

Row 20: P2, ★ K3, slip 1 as if to **knit**, K1, PSSO, YO, K1, P2; repeat from ★ across.

Row 22: P2, ★ K4, YO, K2 tog, P2; repeat from ★ across.

Row 24: P2, ★ K3, slip 1 as if to **knit**, K1, PSSO, YO, K1, P2; repeat from ★ across.

Repeat Rows 1-24 for pattern until Pillow measures approximately 13" from cast on edge, ending by working a **wrong** side row.

Bind off all sts **loosely** maintaining knit and purl pattern (do **not** work cables, decreases, or yarn overs).

Cover pillow form with fabric, if desired.

With **wrong** sides together, matching stitches and rows, sew around three sides, insert pillow form and sew last side.

Weave in yarn ends.

This precious Eyelet Baby Blanket is knit with soft yarn on a circular needle in the same way you've been knitting on straight needles, allowing you to work with more stitches at a time. Before long you'll find yourself able to knit a few rows in just 20 minutes. You'll enjoy seeing a precious baby wrapped in this sweet eyelet pattern that shows off your new hobby.

EYELET BABY BLANKET

Finished Size: 34" x 46"

MATERIALS

Worsted Weight Yarn: **4** MEDIUM
  21 ounces, (600 grams, 1,225 yards)
  29" Circular needle, size 8 (5.00 mm)
  or size needed for gauge
  Yarn needle

Note: See Gauge (page 19).

GAUGE: In pattern, 16 sts and 26 rows = 4"

Note: If you come to an abbreviation, symbol, term, or punctuation that you haven't learned yet, refer to Understanding Instructions, page 19.

Extra skills needed: YO (Yarn overs, Fig. 21a, page 23), slip 1, K2 tog, PSSO (Slip 1 as if to knit, knit 2 together, pass slipped stitch over, Fig. 27, page 25), and SSK (Slip, slip, knit, Figs. 25a-c, page 24).

Cast on 137 sts.

Rows 1-8: Knit across.

Row 9: K5, purl across to last 5 sts, K5.

Row 10: Knit across.

Row 11: K5, purl across to last 5 sts, K5.

Row 12: K7, YO, slip 1 as if to **knit**, K2 tog, PSSO, ★ YO, K5, YO, slip 1 as if to **knit**, K2 tog, PSSO; repeat from ★ across to last 7 sts, YO, K7.

Row 13: K5, purl across to last 5 sts, K5.

Row 14: K8, YO, SSK, (K6, YO, SSK) across to last 7 sts, K7.

Row 15: K5, purl across to last 5 sts, K5.

Row 16: Knit across.

Row 17: K5, purl across to last 5 sts, K5.

Row 18: K 11, YO, slip 1 as if to **knit**, K2 tog, PSSO, ★ YO, K5, YO, slip 1 as if to **knit**, K2 tog, PSSO; repeat from ★ across to last 11 sts, YO, K 11.

Row 19: K5, purl across to last 5 sts, K5.

Row 20: K 12, YO, SSK, (K6, YO, SSK) across to last 11 sts, K 11.

Repeat Rows 9-20 for pattern until Blanket measures approximately 45" from cast on edge, ending by working Row 17.

Last 8 Rows: Knit across.

Bind off all sts in knit.

Weave in yarn ends.

The Dog Coat is made using a double seed stitch pattern, increases, and decreases. The pattern is not complicated, but the neck shaping is new, so take your time and read each instruction carefully. In just 10 minutes, you'll be able to knit several rows! On your next walk, you can really show off your new talent as your favorite pooch wears the colorful coat in style!

DOG COAT

Size:	Sm	Med	Lg	X-Lg
Finished Measurement:	12"	14"	16"	18"

(from neck to base of tail)

Size Note: Instructions are written for size Small, with sizes Medium, Large, and X-Large in braces { }. Instructions will be easier to read if you circle all the numbers pertaining to your dog's size. If only one number is given, it applies to all sizes.

MATERIALS

MEDIUM 4

Worsted Weight Yarn:
3{4-5-6} ounces,
[90{110-140-170} grams,
170{225-285-340} yards]
Straight knitting needles, size 7 (4.50 mm) **or**
size needed for gauge
Stitch holder
Markers - 2
³/₄" Buttons - 2
Yarn needle

Note: When making a garment, correct gauge is critical to ensure fit. See Gauge (page 19).

GAUGE: In pattern, 20 sts and 26 rows = 4"

Note: If you come to an abbreviation, symbol, term, or punctuation that you haven't learned yet, refer to Understanding Instructions, page 19.

Extra skills needed: Knit Increases (Figs. 19a & b, page 22), using markers (Fig. 18, page 22), K2 tog (Knit 2 together, Fig. 23, page 24), slip 1, K1, PSSO (Slip 1, knit 1, pass slipped stitch over, Fig. 26, page 25), picking up stitches (Fig. 31b, page 26), and YO (Yarn overs, Fig. 21a, page 23).

BODY

Cast on 40{44-52-56} sts.

Row 1: Knit across.

Rows 2-7: K1, increase, knit across to last 2 sts, increase, K1: 52{56-64-68} sts.

Row 8 (Right side): K6, place marker, knit across to last 6 sts, place marker, K6.

Note: Loop a short piece of yarn around any stitch to mark Row 8 as **right** side.

Rows 9 and 10: Knit across to first marker, (P2, K2) across to next marker, knit across.

Rows 11 and 12: Knit across to first marker, (K2, P2) across to next marker, knit across.

Repeat Rows 9-12 for pattern until Body measures approximately 11{13-15-17}" from cast on edge, ending by working a **wrong** side row.

NECK SHAPING

Note: Both sides of the Neck are worked at the same time, using separate yarn for each side. This guarantees that both sides will be the same length. **Maintain established pattern throughout**.

Note: To maintain established pattern, simply look at a stitch as it faces you and determine whether it is a knit or purl stitch, then proceed with the proper stitch to continue the pattern. (See Basic Fabrics, page 15.)

Row 1: Work across 18{18-20-22} sts, slip next 16{20-24-24} sts onto st holder; with second yarn, work across: 18{18-20-22} sts **each** side.

Row 2 (Decrease row): Work across to within 2 sts of Neck edge, K2 tog; with second yarn, slip 1 as if to **knit**, K1, PSSO, work across: 17{17-19-21} sts **each** side.

Rows 3 and 4: Repeat Row 2: 15{15-17-19} sts **each** side.

Continue to decrease one stitch at **each** Neck edge, every other row, 3{3-4-5} times: 12{12-13-14} sts **each** side.

Work even until Coat measures approximately 14{16¹/₂-18¹/₂-21}" from cast on edge, ending by working a **wrong** side row.

Bind off all sts.

FINISHING
Neckband

With **right** side facing, pick up 18{22-22-24} sts along right Neck edge, slip 16{20-24-24} sts from st holder onto empty needle and knit across, pick up 18{22-22-24} sts along left Neck edge: 52{64-68-72} sts.

Knit 8 rows.

Bind off all sts in knit.

Band
With **right** side facing and beginning
5^1/$_2$(6^1/$_2$-7^1/$_2$-8^1/$_2$)" down from left bound off edge, pick up 10 sts evenly spaced across 2".

Knit every row until Coat fits snugly around Dog's chest.

Next Row (Buttonhole row)**:** K2, YO (buttonhole), K2 tog, K2, K2 tog, YO (buttonhole), K2.

Knit 3 rows.

Bind off all sts in knit.

Sew end of Right Neck to end of Left Neck.

Weave in yarn ends.

Sew Buttons to Body, opposite Band.

Design by Evie Rosen.

The Lattice Afghan is a great example of texture made with your newly learned skills. Some of the stitches are worked through the back loop for a different effect. Its four-row repeat will allow you to quickly see the pattern unfold, but be careful to count your stitches. With a little practice, you'll be able to complete a repeat in about 30 minutes! Finish your afghan with fringe. Imagine your satisfaction when you curl up under this attractive afghan that you knit all by yourself!

LATTICE AFGHAN

Finished Size: 42" x 64"

MATERIALS

Worsted Weight Yarn:
  32 ounces, (910 grams, 2,105 yards)
29" Circular needle, size 8 (5.00 mm)
  or size needed for gauge
Crochet hook (for attaching fringe)
Yarn needle

Note: See Gauge (page 19).

GAUGE: In pattern, one repeat (20 sts) = 5"

Note: If you come to an abbreviation, symbol, term, or punctuation that you haven't learned yet, refer to Understanding Instructions, page 19.

Extra skills needed: tbl (Through back loop, Fig. 14, page 20), YO (Yarn overs, Fig. 21a, page 23), and K2 tog (Knit 2 together, Fig. 23, page 24).

AFGHAN

Cast on 170 sts **loosely**.

Row 1 (Right side)**:** P1, P2 tbl, (K1, P2 tbl) twice, P1, ★ K1, (YO, K2 tog) 4 times, K1, P1, P2 tbl, (K1, P2 tbl) twice, P1; repeat from ★ across.

Row 2: K1, K2 tbl, (P1, K2 tbl) twice, K1, ★ P 10, K1, K2 tbl, (P1, K2 tbl) twice, K1; repeat from ★ across.

Row 3: P1, K8, P1, ★ K1, (K2 tog, YO) 4 times, K1, P1, K8, P1; repeat from ★ across.

Row 4: K1, P8, K1, ★ P 10, K1, P8, K1; repeat from ★ across.

Repeat Rows 1-4 for pattern until Afghan measures approximately 64" from cast on edge, ending by working Row 3.

Bind off all sts **loosely** in pattern.

Weave in yarn ends.

FRINGE

Cut a piece of cardboard 3" x 6". Wind the yarn **loosely** and **evenly** around the length of the cardboard until the card is filled, then cut across one end; repeat as needed. Hold together 4 strands of yarn; fold in half.

With **wrong** side facing and using a crochet hook, draw the folded end up through a stitch and pull the loose ends through the folded end (Fig. 36a); draw the knot up tightly (Fig. 36b).

Repeat in every fourth stitch across short edges of Afghan. Lay flat on a hard surface and trim the ends.

Fig. 36a   **Fig. 36b**

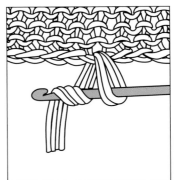   

Design by Jean Lampe.

A vest is a great way to learn how to knit a garment. Get creative, combining 7 colors, including a variegated yarn, in any order that you desire. Stitches for the armhole and Front Bands are added on and worked as you knit the Body, eliminating extra finishing steps. You can have the Ribbing knit in as little as 20 minutes and be on your way to completing your first garment. You'll enjoy getting compliments on your new skills when you wear this appealing vest.

STRIPED VEST

Size:	Small	Medium	Large
Chest			
Measurement:	32-34"	36-38"	40-42"
Finished Chest			
Measurement:	36"	40"	44"

Size Note: Instructions are written for size Small, with sizes Medium and Large in braces { }. Instructions will be easier to read if you circle all the numbers pertaining to your size. If only one number is given, it applies to all sizes.

MATERIALS

Worsted Weight Yarn:
8{9-10¹/₂} ounces,
[230{260-300} grams, 485{550-640} yards]
total of the following colors: Black, Dark Green, Brown, Green, Variegated, Red, and Tan.
Straight knitting needles, size 9 (5.50 mm) **or** size needed for gauge
Stitch holders - 2
Yarn needle

Note: When making a garment, correct gauge is critical to ensure fit. See Gauge (page 19).

GAUGE: In Stockinette Stitch,
16 sts and 22 rows = 4"

Note: If you come to an abbreviation, symbol, term, or punctuation that you haven't learned yet, refer to Understanding Instructions, page 19.

Extra skills needed: Knit Increases (Figs. 19a & b, page 22), adding on stitches (Figs. 22a & b, page 23), SSK (Slip, slip, knit, Figs. 25a-c, page 24), K2 tog (Knit 2 together, Fig. 23, page 24), P2 tog (Purl 2 together, Fig. 28, page 25), and SSP (Slip, slip, purl, Fig. 30, page 25).

Work in desired color sequence throughout.

BACK
RIBBING
Cast on 74{82-90} sts **loosely**.
Work in K1, P1 ribbing for 3 rows increasing one stitch at end of last row: 75{83-91} sts.

BODY
Work in Stockinette Stitch until Back measures approximately 11¹/₂{12-12¹/₂}" from cast on edge, ending by working a **purl** row.

ARMHOLE SHAPING
Row 1: Add on 3 sts (Armhole band), K3 (same sts added on), SSK, knit across to last 2 sts, K2 tog, **turn**; add on 3 sts (Armhole band): 79{87-95} sts.

Row 2 (Decrease row): K3, P2 tog, purl across to last 5 sts, SSP, K3: 77{85-93} sts.

Row 3 (Decrease row): K3, SSK, knit across to last 5 sts, K2 tog, K3: 75{83-91} sts.

Rows 4 thru 7{9-11}: Repeat Rows 2 and 3, 2{3-4} times: 67{71-75} sts.

Instructions continued on page 52.

Row 8{10-12}: K3, purl across to last 3 sts, K3.

Row 9{11-13} (Decrease row)**:** K3, SSK, knit across to last 5 sts, K2 tog, K3: 65{69-73} sts.

Rows 10{12-14} and 11{13-15}: Repeat Rows 8{10-12} and 9{11-13}: 63{67-71} sts.

Row 12{14-16}: K3, purl across to last 3 sts, K3.

Row 13{15-17}: Knit across.

Row 14{16-18}: K3, purl across to last 3 sts, K3.

Row 15{17-19} (Decrease row)**:** K3, SSK, knit across to last 5 sts, K2 tog, K3: 61{65-69} sts.

Rows 16{18-20} thru 19{21-23}: Repeat Rows 12{14-16} thru 15{17-19}: 59{63-67} sts.

Repeat Rows 12{14-16} and 13{15-17} until Armholes measure approximately 7¹/₂{8-8¹/₂}", ending by working a **wrong** side row.

SHOULDER SHAPING

Note: To shape the shoulders, bind off stitches in pattern at the beginning of each row as indicated.

Row 1: Bind off 5{6-6} sts at the beginning of the row, knit across: 54{57-61} sts.

Row 2: Bind off 5{6-6} sts at the beginning of the row, purl across: 49{51-55} sts.

Rows 3 and 4: Bind off 6 sts at the beginning of the row, work across: 37{39-43} sts.

Rows 5 and 6: Bind off 6{6-7} sts at the beginning of the row, work across: 25{27-29} sts.

Slip remaining sts onto st holder; cut yarn.

FRONT

Work same as Back through Row 8{10-12} of Armhole Shaping: 67{71-75} sts.

NECK & ARMHOLE SHAPING

Note: Both sides of the Neck are worked at the same time, using separate yarn for each side. This guarantees that both sides will be the same length. The semicolon (;) separates the instructions for each side and is the signal for you to drop your first yarn and begin working with the second yarn.

Row 1 (Decrease row)**:** K3, SSK, K 25{27-29}, K2 tog, **turn**, add on 3 sts **loosely** (Front Band), **turn**; with second yarn, K3 (Front Band), SSK, knit across to last 5 sts, K2 tog, K3: 33{35-37} sts **each** side.

Row 2: K3, purl across to within 3 sts of Neck edge, K3; with second yarn, K3, purl across to last 3 sts, K3.

Row 3 (Decrease row)**:** K3, SSK, knit across to within 5 sts of Neck edge, K2 tog, K3; with second yarn, K3, SSK, knit across to last 5 sts, K2 tog, K3: 31{33-35} sts **each** side.

Row 4: K3, purl across to within 3 sts of Neck edge, K3; with second yarn, K3, purl across to last 3 sts, K3.

Row 5 (Decrease row)**:** Knit across to within 5 sts of Neck edge, K2 tog, K3; with second yarn, K3, SSK, knit across: 30{32-34} sts **each** side.

Rows 6-11: Repeat Rows 2-5 once, then repeat Rows 2 and 3 once **more**: 25{27-29} sts **each** side.

FOR SIZES MEDIUM & LARGE ONLY
Rows 12 thru {15-19}: Repeat Rows 4 and 5, {2-4} times: 25 sts **each** side.

FOR ALL SIZES

Row 12{16-20}: K3, purl across to within 3 sts of Neck edge, K3; with second yarn, K3, purl across to last 3 sts, K3.

Row 13{17-21}: Knit across; with second yarn, knit across.

Row 14{18-22}: K3, purl across to within 3 sts of Neck edge, K3; with second yarn, K3, purl across to last 3 sts, K3.

Row 15{19-23} (Decrease row)**:** Knit across to within 5 sts of Neck edge, K2 tog, K3; with second yarn, K3, SSK, knit across: 24 sts **each** side.

Rows 16{20-24} thru 31: Repeat Rows 12{16-20} thru 15{19-23}, 4{3-2} times: 20{21-22} sts **each** side.

Repeat Rows 12{16-20} and 13{17-21} until Armholes measure same as Back to Shoulder Shaping, ending by working a **wrong** side row.

SHOULDER SHAPING

Row 1: Bind off 5{6-6} sts at Armhole edge, knit across; with second yarn, knit across.

Row 2: Bind off 5{6-6} sts at Armhole edge, purl across to within 3 sts of Neck edge, K3; with second yarn, K3, purl across: 15{15-16} sts **each** side.

Row 3: Bind off 6 sts at Armhole edge, knit across; with second yarn, knit across.

Row 4: Bind off 6 sts at Armhole edge, purl across to within 3 sts of Neck edge, K3; with second yarn, K3, purl across: 9{9-10} sts **each** side.

Row 5: Bind off 9{9-10} sts; with second yarn, knit across.

Row 6: Bind off 6{6-7} sts, K2: 3 sts.

Slip remaining sts onto st holder; cut yarn.

FINISHING

Sew shoulder seams, leaving 3 sts at each Neck edge free (Front Band).

BACK NECK BAND

Note: Rather than making the Back Neck Band separately and then sewing it to the Back, you will work in short rows, which are rows that are not worked all the way from one end to the other. Each right side row works across 2 stitches from the Front Band, then a decrease is made using the last stitch on the Front Band and the next stitch on the Back neck. Leaving the remaining stitches unworked, you will stop, **turn** the work, and work the next row in the opposite direction.

Begin working in short rows as follows: Slip 25{27-29} sts from Back st holder onto needle; slip 3 sts from Right Front st holder onto same needle.

Row 1: K2, K2 tog, leave remaining sts unworked.

Row 2: Knit across.

Repeat Rows 1 and 2 until only 3 sts remain, ending by working Row 2.

Bind off remaining 3 sts.

Sew Back Neck Band and Left Front Band together.

Sew bottom of Left Front Band to **wrong** side behind Right Front Band.

Weave side seams (Fig. 32, page 26).

This Cable Accent Pullover is knit using a soft, thick yarn and larger size needles, which helps the project go even quicker — you'll need only about 30 minutes to complete the cable repeat! The eight-stitch cable adds style and is fun to complete. How pleased you'll be to wear this pullover and say, "I made it myself!"

CABLE ACCENT PULLOVER

Size:	Small	Medium	Large
Chest			
Measurement:	32-34"	36-38"	40-42"
Finished Chest			
Measurement:	37"	41"	45"

Size Note: Instructions are written for size Small, with sizes Medium and Large in braces { }. Instructions will be easier to read if you circle all the numbers pertaining to your size. If only one number is given, it applies to all sizes.

MATERIALS

Bulky Weight Brushed Acrylic Yarn:
  17{19-21} ounces,
    [480{540-600} grams, 765{855-945} yards]
Straight knitting needles, size 11 (8.00 mm) **or**
  size needed for gauge
16" Circular needle, size 10 (6.00 mm)
Markers - 2
Cable needle (see note below)
Stitch holders - 2
Yarn needle

Note: Cable needles have a point on each end and are available in several shapes and sizes. The size of the cable needle does not have to be the same size as the needles with which you are knitting, but it should not be bigger or it will stretch the stitches out of shape.

Note: When making a garment, correct gauge is critical to ensure fit. See Gauge (page 19).

GAUGE: With larger size needles,
    in Stockinette Stitch,
    12 sts and 16 rows = 4"

STITCH GUIDE

CABLE (uses next 8 sts)
Slip next 4 sts onto cable needle as if to **purl** and hold them in **back** of work, K4 from left needle, K4 from cable needle being sure that the first st you knit is the first one you slipped onto the cable needle.

Note: If you come to an abbreviation, symbol, term, or punctuation that you haven't learned yet, refer to Understanding Instructions, page 19.

Extra skills needed: Using markers (Fig. 18, page 22), K2 tog (Knit 2 together, Fig. 23, page 24), slip 1, K1, PSSO (Slip 1, knit 1, pass slipped stitch over, Fig. 26, page 25), knit increases (Figs. 19a & b, page 22), and picking up sts (Fig. 31b, page 26).

BACK
RIBBING

With larger size needles, cast on 58{64-70} sts **loosely**. Work in K1, P1 ribbing for 2".

BODY

Beginning with a **knit** row, work in Stockinette Stitch until Back measures approximately 27½{28-28½}" from cast on edge, ending by working a **knit** row.

SHOULDER SHAPING

Note: To shape the shoulders, bind off stitches in pattern at the beginning of each row as indicated.

Rows 1 and 2: Bind off 6{7-7} sts at the beginning of the row, work across: 46{50-56} sts.

Rows 3 and 4: Bind off 6{7-8} sts at the beginning of the row, work across: 34{36-40} sts.

Rows 5 and 6: Bind off 7{7-8} sts at the beginning of the row, work across: 20{22-24} sts.

Slip remaining sts onto st holder; cut yarn.

Instructions continued on page 56.

FRONT
RIBBING
With larger size needles, cast on 60{66-72} sts **loosely**.

Work in K1, P1 ribbing for 2".

BODY
Row 1 (Right side)**:** K 25{28-31}, place marker, P1, K8, P1, place marker, knit across.

Row 2: Purl across to marker, K1, P8, K1, purl across.

Row 3: Knit across to marker, P1, K8, P1, knit across.

Row 4: Purl across to marker, K1, P8, K1, purl across.

Row 5: Knit across to marker, P1, work Cable, P1, knit across.

Rows 6-11: Repeat Rows 2 and 3, 3 times.

Repeat Rows 4-11 for pattern until Front measures approximately $24^1/_2${25-25$^1/_2$}" from cast on edge, ending by working a **right** side row.

NECK SHAPING
Note: Both sides of the Neck are worked at the same time, using separate yarn for each side. This guarantees that both sides will be the same length. The semicolon (;) separates the instructions for each side and is the signal for you to drop your first yarn and begin working with the second yarn.

Row 1: Purl across to within 3{4-5} sts of first marker, slip next 16{18-20} sts onto st holder; with second yarn, purl across: 22{24-26} sts **each** side.

Row 2 (Decrease row)**:** Knit across to within 2 sts of Neck edge, K2 tog; with second yarn, slip 1 as if to **knit**, K1, PSSO, knit across: 21{23-25} sts **each** side.

Row 3: Purl across; with second yarn, purl across.

Rows 4-7: Repeat Rows 2 and 3 twice: 19{21-23} sts **each** side.

Work even until Front measures same as Back to Shoulder Shaping, ending by working a **knit** row.

SHOULDER SHAPING
Rows 1 and 2: Bind off 6{7-7} sts at Armhole edge, work across; with second yarn, work across: 13{14-16} sts **each** side.

Rows 3 and 4: Bind off 6{7-8} sts at Armhole edge, work across; with second yarn, work across: 7{7-8} sts **each** side.

Row 5: Bind off 7{7-8} sts; with second yarn, purl across.

Bind off remaining sts.

SLEEVE (Make 2)
RIBBING
With larger size needles, cast on 28{30-32} sts **loosely**.

Work in K1, P1 ribbing for 4".

BODY
Row 1 (Right side)**:** Knit across.

Row 2: Purl across.

Row 3 (Increase row)**:** Increase, knit across to last st, increase: 30{32-34} sts.

Rows 4-17: Repeat Rows 2 and 3, 7 times: 44{46-48} sts.

Continue to increase one stitch at **each** edge in same manner, every fourth row, 7 times: 58{60-62} sts.

Work even until Sleeve measures approximately 17{17$^1/_2$-18}" from cast on edge, ending by working a **purl** row.

SLEEVE CAP
Rows 1-12: Bind off 4 sts at the beginning of the row, work across: 10{12-14} sts.

Bind off remaining sts.

FINISHING
Sew shoulder seams.

Sew Sleeves to Sweater, matching center of last row on Sleeve Cap to shoulder seam and beginning 9$^1/_2${10-10$^1/_2$}" down from seam.

Weave underarm and side in one continuous seam (Fig. 32, page 26).

NECK RIBBING
With **right** side facing and using circular needle, knit 20{22-24} sts from Back st holder, pick up 14 sts along left Front Neck edge, knit 16{18-20} sts from Front st holder, pick up 14 sts along right Front Neck edge, place marker for beginning of round: 64{68-72} sts.

Work in K1, P1 ribbing around for 5".

Bind off all sts **loosely** in ribbing.

Design by Evie Rosen.

RIBBED HAT

Continued from page 30.

Note: If you come to an abbreviation, symbol, term, or punctuation that you haven't learned yet, refer to Understanding Instructions, page 19.

Extra skills needed: K2 tog (Knit 2 together, Fig. 23, page 24), K3 tog (Knit 3 together, Fig. 24, page 24), and P2 tog (Purl 2 together, Fig. 28, page 25).

BODY

With Grey and larger size needles, cast on 96{104-112} sts **loosely**.

Rows 1-5: (K1, P1) across.

Row 6 (Right side)**:** With Burgundy and smaller size needle, knit across.

Row 7: With larger size needle, (K1, P1) across; drop Burgundy.

Row 8: With Lt Grey and smaller size needle, knit across.

Row 9: With larger size needle, (K1, P1) across; cut Lt Grey.

Row 10: With Burgundy and smaller size needle, knit across.

Row 11: With larger size needle, (K1, P1) across; cut Burgundy.

Row 12: With Grey and smaller size needle, knit across.

Row 13: With larger size needle, (K1, P1) across.

Repeat Row 13 until Hat measures approximately 8{9-10}" from cast on edge, ending by working a **right** side row.

SHAPING

Row 1 (Decrease row)**:** K1, P1, (K3 tog, P1) across to last 2 sts, K1, P1: 50{54-58} sts.

Rows 2-6: (K1, P1) across.

Row 7 (Decrease row)**:** K1, K2 tog across to last st, P1: 26{28-30} sts.

Row 8 (Decrease row)**:** P2 tog across: 13{14-15} sts.

Cut yarn leaving a long end. Thread a yarn needle with the end and separately slip each stitch from the knitting needle onto the yarn; gather the stitches tightly to close, then secure end. Weave seam (Fig. 32, page 26), remembering that **right** side of brim is **wrong** side of Hat.

Weave in yarn ends (page 27).

Fold bottom edge to form brim.

DOUBLE-COZY BOOTS

Continued from page 33.

SIDES

Cut **one** strand of Red and add **one** strand of Variegated.

Row 1 (Eyelet row)**:** K2, YO, K2 tog, knit across to last 4 sts, K2 tog, YO, K2.

Row 2 (Decrease row)**:** K4, P2 tog, purl across to last 6 sts, P2 tog tbl, K4: {58-62-66}{70-74-78} sts.

Row 3 (Decrease row)**:** K4, slip 1 as if to **knit**, K1, PSSO, knit across to last 6 sts, K2 tog, K4: {56-60-64}{68-72-76} sts.

Row 4 (Decrease row)**:** K4, P2 tog, purl across to last 6 sts, P2 tog tbl, K4: {54-58-62}{66-70-74} sts.

Row 5 (Decrease **and** Eyelet row)**:** K2, YO, K2 tog, slip 1 as if to **knit**, K1, PSSO, knit across to last 6 sts, K2 tog twice, YO, K2: {52-56-60}{64-68-72} sts.

Repeat Rows 2-5, {1-2-3}{1-2-3} time(s): {44-40-36}{56-52-48} sts.

Repeat Rows 2-4 once: {38-34-30}{50-46-42} sts.

Note: To consolidate the length of an involved pattern, Zeros are sometimes used so that all sizes can be combined. For example, in the instructions below, the Child's size large will not repeat Rows 1-4 at all.

Repeat Rows 1-4, {2-1-0}{3-2-1} time(s): {26-28-30}{32-34-36} sts.

CUFF

Cut Variegated and add second strand of Red.

Row 1 (Eyelet row)**:** K2, YO, K2 tog, knit across to last 4 sts, K2 tog, YO, K2.

Rows 2-4: Knit across.

Rows 5-8: Repeat Rows 1-4.

Bind off all sts.

FINISHING

Fold piece in half; sew bottom and toe seam.

Weave in yarn ends.

With Red, make a {37-37-37}{37-40-40}" Twisted Cord (page 27). Lace Cord through Eyelet rows as for a shoe and tie in a bow at the ankle.

Design by Bev Dillon.

DEEP V-NECK VEST

■■■□ INTERMEDIATE

Size	Finished Chest Measurement
Medium	40¹/₂" (103 cm)
Large	45" (114.5 cm)

Size Note: Instructions are written for size Medium with size Large in braces { }. Instructions will be easier to read if you circle all the numbers pertaining to your size. If only one number is given, it applies to all sizes.

MATERIALS

Medium/Worsted Weight Yarn: 🔵 **④**
14{15} ounces, 905{970} yards **[400{430} grams, 828{887} meters]**
Straight knitting needles, size 9 (5.5 mm) **or** size needed for gauge
24" (61 cm) **and** 31" (78.5 cm) Circular knitting needles, size 9 (5.5 mm) **or** size needed for gauge
Markers
Yarn needle

GAUGE: In pattern,
16 sts and 27 rows = 4" (10 cm)

BACK

With straight needles, cast on 83{92} sts.

Row 1: (K1, P1) across to last 1{0} sts **(see Zeros, page 577)**, K1{0}.

Row 2 (Increase row - right side)**:** K1, ★ [K1, YO twice **(Fig. 16a, page 582)**] 9 times, P9; repeat from ★ across to last 10{1} st(s), (K1, YO twice) 9{0} time(s), K1: 173{182} sts.

Row 3 (Decrease row)**:** Work sts as they face you, knit the knit sts and purl the purl sts, drop YO's of previous row so that sts become 3 times as long: 83{92} sts.

Row 4: K1, (K9, P9) across to last 10{1} st(s), K 10{1}.

Rows 5-10: Work sts as they face you.

Row 11: Work sts as they face you; however, work purl sts (except for edge sts) as follows: Insert right needle into st 8 rows **below** next st, slip loop onto left needle and purl together with next st. Work all 9 purl sts this way forming a puff on right side.

Rows 12 and 13: Repeat Rows 2 and 3.

Row 14 (Increase row)**:** K1, ★ P9, (K1, YO twice) 9 times; repeat from ★ across to last 10{1} st(s), P9{0}, K1: 155{182} sts.

Row 15 (Decrease row)**:** Work sts as they face you, knit the knit sts and purl the purl sts, drop YO's of previous row so that sts become 3 times as long: 83{92} sts.

Row 16: K1, (P9, K9) across to last 10{1} st(s), P9{0}, K1.

Rows 17-22: Work sts as they face you.

Row 23: Work sts as they face you; however, work purl sts (except for edge sts) as follows: Insert right needle into st 8 rows **below** next st, slip loop onto left needle and purl together with next st. Work all 9 purl sts this way forming a puff on right side.

Rows 24 and 25: Repeat Rows 14 and 15.

Repeat Rows 2-25 for pattern until Back measures approximately 12³/₄" (32.5 cm) from cast on edge **or to desired length**.

Instructions continued on page 60.

ARMHOLE SHAPING

Maintain established pattern and maintain an edge st worked in Stockinette Stitch at **each** Armhole edge.

Rows 1 thru 4{8}: Bind off one st, work across in pattern: 79{84} sts.

Next 2 Rows: Bind off 3{4} sts, work across in pattern: 73{76} sts.

Work even until Armholes measure approximately $11^3/_4$" (30 cm).

Bind off all sts.

FRONT

Work same as Back until Front measures 14 rows **less** than Back to Armhole Shaping.

NECK AND ARMHOLE SHAPING

Both sides of Neck are worked at the same time, using separate yarn for **each** side. Maintain established pattern and maintain an edge st worked in Stockinette Stitch at **each** Neck and Armhole edge.

Row 1: Work across 40{46} sts in pattern, increase in next 1{0} st **(see Knit & Purl Increases, page 581)**; with second yarn, work across remaining sts: 42{46} sts **each** side.

Row 2 (Decrease row)**:** Work across in pattern decreasing one st **(see Decreases, page 583)**, one st in, at each neck edge: 41{45} sts **each** side.

Rows 3-5: Work across in pattern.

Rows 6-14: Repeat Rows 2-5 twice, then repeat Row 2 once **more**: 38{42} sts **each** side.

Rows 15-17: Bind off one st, work across in pattern.

Row 18: Bind off one st, work across in pattern decreasing one st at **each** Neck edge: 35{39} sts **each** side.

Large Size ONLY
Row 19: Bind off one st, work across in pattern.

Row 20: Bind off one st, work across in pattern decreasing one st at **each** Neck edge: 37 sts **each** side.

Rows 21 and 22: Bind off one st, work across in pattern: 36 sts **each** side.

Both Sizes
Row 19{23}: Bind off 3{4} sts, work across in pattern.

Row 20{24}: Bind off 3{4} sts, work across in pattern, decreasing one st at **each** Neck edge: 31 sts **each** side.

Next 3 Rows: Work across in pattern.

Large Size ONLY: Decrease one st at **each** Neck edge, every 4th row, 3 times; then decrease every other row once: 27 sts **each** side.

Both Sizes: ★ Decrease one st at **each** Neck edge, every 4th row, 4 times; then decrease every other row once; repeat from ★ 3{2} times **more**: 11{12} sts **each** side.

Bind off remaining sts.

FINISHING

Sew shoulder seams. Sew side seams.

ARMHOLE BAND

With 24" (61 cm) circular needle, cast on 96 sts.

Work in Stockinette Stitch for 10 rounds.

Slip sts onto spare strand of yarn.

Backstitch Band evenly to Armhole edge through live sts; fold Band in half to **wrong** side and sew cast on edge in place.

Repeat around second Armhole.

NECK BAND

With 31" (78.5 cm) circular needle, cast on 164 sts.

Rnd 1: K 82, place marker, K 82.

Rnds 2-4: Knit across to within 2 sts of marker, decrease twice, knit remaining sts: 158 sts.

Rnd 5: Knit around.

Rnds 6-8: Knit across to within one st of marker, increase in each of next 2 sts *(Figs. 10a & b, page 581)*, knit remaining sts: 164 sts.

Rnds 9 and 10: Knit around.

Slip sts onto spare strand of yarn.

Backstitch Band evenly to Neck edge through live sts, beginning at marker and center V; fold Band in half to **wrong** side and sew cast on edge in place.

CABLE CARDIGAN

◼◼◼◻ INTERMEDIATE

Size	Finished Chest Measurement
Small	34" (86.5 cm)
Medium	38" (96.5 cm)
Large	42" (106.5 cm)

Size Note: Instructions are written for size Small with sizes Medium and Large in braces { }. Instructions will be easier to read if you circle all the numbers pertaining to your size. If only one number is given, it applies to all sizes. Garment is designed to fit snugly.

MATERIALS

Medium/Worsted Weight Yarn: 🧶 **4** MEDIUM

Ounces	24{28-30}
Yards	1,400{1,680-1,800}
Grams	680{800-850}
Meters	1,370{1,536-1,646}

24" (61 cm) Circular knitting needles, sizes 10 (6 mm) **and** 11 (8 mm) **or** sizes needed for gauge
Straight knitting needles, size 11 (8 mm)
Cable needle
Markers
Yarn needle
Crochet hook, size J (6 mm)
1¼" (32 mm) Buttons - 4
Sewing needle and thread

Cardigan is worked holding two strands of yarn together, unless otherwise indicated.

GAUGE: With larger size needles, in Stockinette Stitch, 12 sts and 16 rows = 4" (10 cm)

Cardigan is worked in one piece to underarm.

RIBBING

With smaller size circular needle, cast on 117{129-147} sts.

Row 1: K1, (P1, K1) across.

Row 2 (Right side)**:** K2, P1, (K1, P1) across to last 2 sts, K2.

Repeat Rows 1 and 2 until Ribbing measures approximately 2" (5 cm), ending by working Row 2.

Decrease Row: K1, (P1, K1) across to last 2 sts, K2 tog *(Fig. 17, page 583)*: 116{128-146} sts.

Instructions continued on page 64.

BODY

Change to larger size circular needle.

Row 1 (Right side)**:** K1, P1, K4, (P2, K4) across to last 2 sts, P1, K1.

Row 2: K2, (P4, K2) across.

Rows 3 and 4: Repeat Rows 1 and 2.

Row 5: K1, P1, slip next 2 sts onto cable needle and hold in **back** of work, K2 from left needle, K2 from cable needle, ★ P2, slip next 2 sts onto cable needle and hold in **back** of work, K2 from left needle, K2 from cable needle; repeat from ★ across to last 2 sts, P1, K1.

Row 6: K2, (P4, K2) across.

Rows 7-10: Repeat Rows 1 and 2 twice.

Repeat Rows 1-10 for pattern until Body measures approximately 10" (25.5 cm) from cast on edge **or to desired length**, ending by working a **wrong** side row.

Dividing Row: Maintaining established pattern, work across next 26{29-33} sts (Right Front), bind off next 4{4-8} sts, work across next 55{61-63} sts (Back), bind off next 4{4-8} sts, work across remaining 25{28-32} sts (Left Front).

LEFT FRONT

Work only Left Front, leaving remaining sts on circular needle. Maintain established pattern throughout.

Row 1: Work across: 26{29-33} sts.

Row 2 (Decrease row)**:** Decrease *(see Decreases, page 583)*, work across: 25{28-32} sts.

Row 3: Work across.

Rows 4 thru 6{6-8}: Repeat Rows 2 and 3, 1{1-2} time(s); then repeat Row 2 once **more**: 23{26-29} sts.

Work even until Left Front measures 5$\frac{3}{4}${6$\frac{1}{4}$-6$\frac{3}{4}$}"/14.5{16-17} cm above Dividing Row, ending by working a **right** side row.

NECK AND SHOULDER SHAPING

Row 1: Bind off 4{5-8} sts (Neck edge), work across: 19{21-21} sts.

Decrease one stitch at Neck edge, every other row 4 times **AND AT THE SAME TIME** when Left Front measures 7$\frac{3}{4}${8$\frac{1}{4}$-8$\frac{3}{4}$}"/ 19.5{21-22} cm above Dividing Row, bind off 5 sts once at armhole edge (right side row), then 5{6-6} sts once at armhole edge, then remaining 5{6-6} sts.

RIGHT FRONT

Slip Right Front sts onto empty straight needle.

Row 1: With **wrong** side facing, work across: 26{29-33} sts.

Row 2 (Decrease row)**:** Work across to last 2 sts, K2 tog: 25{28-32} sts.

Row 3: Work across.

Rows 4 thru 6{6-8}: Repeat Rows 2 and 3, 1{1-2} time(s); then repeat Row 2 once **more**: 23{26-29} sts.

Work even until Right Front measures 5$\frac{3}{4}${6$\frac{1}{4}$-6$\frac{3}{4}$}"/14.5{16-17} cm above Dividing Row, ending by working a **wrong** side row.

NECK AND SHOULDER SHAPING

Row 1: Bind off 4{5-8} sts (Neck edge), work across: 19{21-21} sts.

Decrease one stitch at Neck edge, every other row 4 times **AND AT THE SAME TIME** when Right Front measures 7$\frac{3}{4}${8$\frac{1}{4}$-8$\frac{3}{4}$}"/ 19.5{21-22} cm above Dividing Row, bind off 5 sts once at armhole edge (wrong side row), then 5{6-6} sts once at armhole edge, then remaining 5{6-6} sts.

BACK

Row 1: With **wrong** side facing and using circular needle, work across: 56{62-64} sts.

Row 2 (Decrease row)**:** [Slip 1, K1, PSSO *(Figs. 19a & b, page 583)*], work across to last 2 sts, K2 tog: 54{60-62} sts.

Row 3: Work across.

Rows 4 thru 6{6-8}: Repeat Rows 2 and 3, 1{1-2} time(s); then repeat Row 2 once **more**: 50{56-56} sts.

Work even until Back measures 7¹/₂{8-8¹/₂}"/ 19{20.5-21.5} cm above Dividing Row, ending by working a **wrong** side row.

NECK AND SHOULDER SHAPING

Both sides of Neck are worked at the same time, using separate yarn for **each** side.

Row 1: Work across first 17{19-19} sts, bind off next 16{18-18} sts, work across: 17{19-19} sts **each** side.

Row 2: Work across to within 2 sts of Neck edge, decrease; with second yarn, decrease, work across: 16{18-18} sts **each** side.

Row 3: Bind off 5 sts, work across to within 2 sts of Neck edge, K2 tog; with second yarn, slip 1, K1, PSSO, work across.

Row 4: Bind off 5 sts, work across; with second yarn, work across: 10{12-12} sts **each** side.

Bind off 5{6-6} sts once at each armhole edge, then bind off remaining 5{6-6} sts.

SLEEVE (Make 2)
RIBBING

With smaller size circular needle, cast on 25{31-35} sts.

Row 1: K1, (P1, K1) across.

Row 2 (Right side)**:** K2, P1, (K1, P1) across to last 2 sts, K2.

Repeat Rows 1 and 2 until Ribbing measures approximately 3" (7.5 cm), ending by working Row 2.

Increase Row: Work across increasing 7{7-9} sts evenly spaced across row *(see Increasing Evenly Across A Row, page 581)*: 32{38-44} sts.

BODY

Change to larger size straight needle.

Row 1 (Right side)**:** K1, P1, K4, (P2, K4) across to last 2 sts, P1, K1.

Row 2: K2, (P4, K2) across.

Row 3: K1, P1, K4, (P2, K4) across to last 2 sts, P1, K1.

Continue in established pattern increasing one stitch at **each** edge, every 6th{4th-6th} row, 7{10-7} times working new stitches in pattern: 46{58-58} sts.

Work even until Sleeve measures approximately 17" (43 cm) from cast on edge **or to desired length**, ending by working a **wrong** side row.

Instructions continued on page 66.

SLEEVE CAP

Rows 1 and 2: Bind off 2{2-4} sts, work across: 42{54-50} sts.

Continuing in pattern, decrease one stitch at **each** edge, every row, 0{6-4} times *(see Zeros, page 577)*; then decrease every other row, 13 times **more**: 16 sts.

Next 4 Rows: Bind off 2 sts, work across: 8 sts.

Bind off remaining sts.

FINISHING

In order to obtain finished measurement, you will have to carefully steam and gently stretch the garment. If you have used wool, after completely finishing, you may wish to wash the cardigan and lay it flat to block, stretching to desired measurement.

Sew shoulder seams.
Sew underarm seam on each Sleeve.

NECKBAND

With **right** side facing, using smaller size needle, and beginning at Right neck edge, pick up 63{67-71} sts evenly spaced across neck edge *(Figs. 34a & b, page 586)*.

Row 1: P1, (K1, P1) across.

Row 2 (Right side): K1, (P1, K1) across.

Repeat Rows 1 and 2 until Neckband measures 1¼" (3 mm), ending by working Row 1.

Bind off all sts in pattern; do **not** finish off last st of bind off.

LEFT FRONT BAND

Slip last st of bind off onto crochet hook.

Row 1: With **right** side facing, sc evenly across Left Front edge *(see Crochet Stitches, pages 588 & 589)*.

Rows 2-7: Ch 1, turn; sc in each sc across.

Finish off.

Trim: With **right** side facing, join yarn with slip st in end of Row 1 of Left Front Band *(see Joining With Slip St, page 589)*; slip st in end of next 6 rows; slip st in each sc across; slip st in end of next 7 rows; finish off.

RIGHT FRONT BAND

Row 1: With **right** side facing, join yarn with sc in end of Row 1 of bottom Ribbing on Right Front *(see Joining With Sc, page 589)*; sc evenly across Right Front edge.

Rows 2 and 3: Ch 1, turn; sc in each sc across.

Place a marker 1" (2.5 cm) from bottom of band for bottom button placement and 1" (2.5 cm) from top of band for top button placement. Evenly space 2 more markers between top and bottom marker for placement of remaining 2 buttons.

Row 4 (Buttonhole row): Ch 1, turn; ★ sc in each sc across to within one st of next marker, ch 3, skip next 2 sc; repeat from ★ 3 times **more**, sc in each sc across (4 buttonholes made).

Row 5: Ch 1, turn; ★ sc in each sc across to next ch-3 sp, 2 sc in ch-3 sp; repeat from ★ 3 times **more**, sc in each sc across.

Rows 6 and 7: Ch 1, turn; sc in each sc across.

Finish off.

Trim: With **right** side facing, join yarn with slip st in end of Row 1 of Right Front Band; slip st in end of next 6 rows; slip st in each sc across; slip st in end of next 7 rows; finish off.

Sew in Sleeves matching center of Sleeve Cap to shoulder seam.
Sew buttons to Left Front Band opposite buttonholes.

Design by Nancy Dent.

CHANEL JACKET

◼◼◼◻ INTERMEDIATE

Shown on page 69.

Size	Finished Chest Measurement
Small	34" (86.5 cm)
Medium	38" (96.5 cm)
Large	42" (106.5 cm)

Size Note: Instructions are written for size Small with sizes Medium and Large in braces { }. Instructions will be easier to read if you circle all the numbers pertaining to your size. If only one number is given, it applies to all sizes.

MATERIALS

Bulky Weight Yarn: **5** BULKY

Ounces   13{14$\frac{1}{2}$-16$\frac{1}{2}$}
Yards   525{590-670}
Grams   370{410-470}
Meters   480{539-613}

Straight knitting needles, sizes 8 (5 cm) **and** 9 (5.5 mm) **or** sizes needed for gauge
Stitch holders - 2
Yarn needle

GAUGE: With larger size needles, in Stockinette Stitch, 14 sts and 17 rows = 4" (10 cm)

BACK
BODY

With smaller size needles, cast on 61{68-75} sts.

Rows 1-3: Knit across.

Change to larger size needles.

Beginning with a **knit** row, work in Stockinette Stitch (knit one row, purl one row) until Back measures approximately 12" (30.5 cm) from cast on edge **or to desired length**, ending by working a **purl** row.

ARMHOLE SHAPING

Rows 1 and 2: Bind off 4{5-6} sts at the beginning of the next 2 rows, work across: 53{58-63} sts.

Row 3 (Decrease row)**:** [Slip 1, K1, PSSO **(Figs. 19a & b, page 583)**], knit across to last 2 sts, K2 tog **(Fig. 17, page 583)**: 51{56-61} sts.

Row 4: Purl across.

Repeat Rows 3 and 4, 2{2-3} times: 47{52-55} sts.

Work even until Armholes measure approximately 8$\frac{1}{2}${9-9$\frac{1}{2}$}"/21.5{23-24} cm, ending by working a **purl** row.

SHOULDER SHAPING

Rows 1 and 2: Bind off 4{5-5} sts at the beginning of the next 2 rows, work across: 39{42-45} sts.

Rows 3 and 4: Bind off 5 sts at the beginning of the next 2 rows, work across: 29{32-35} sts.

Rows 5 and 6: Bind off 5{5-6} sts at the beginning of the next 2 rows, work across: 19{22-23} sts.

Bind off remaining sts.

Instructions continued on page 68.

LEFT FRONT

With smaller size needles, cast on 31{34-38} sts.

Work same as Back to Armhole Shaping.

ARMHOLE SHAPING

Row 1: Bind off 4{5-6} sts, knit across: 27{29-32} sts.

Row 2: Purl across.

Row 3 (Decrease row): Slip 1, K1, PSSO, knit across: 26{28-31} sts.

Repeat Rows 2 and 3, 2{2-3} times: 24{26-28} sts.

Work even until Armhole measures approximately $5^1/2${$6-6^1/2$}"/14{15-16.5} cm, ending by working a **purl** row.

NECK SHAPING

Row 1: Knit across to last 7{8-8} sts, K2 tog, slip remaining 5{6-6} sts onto st holder: 18{19-21} sts.

Row 2: P2 tog *(Fig. 18, page 583)*, purl across: 17{18-20} sts.

Row 3 (Decrease row): Knit across to last 2 sts, K2 tog: 16{17-19} sts.

Row 4: Purl across.

Repeat Rows 3 and 4, 2{2-3} times: 14{15-16} sts.

Work even until Armhole measures approximately $8^1/2${$9-9^1/2$}"/21.5{23-24} cm, ending by working a **purl** row.

SHOULDER SHAPING

Row 1: Bind off 4{5-5} sts, knit across: 10{10-11} sts.

Row 2: Purl across.

Row 3: Bind off 5 sts, knit across: 5{5-6} sts.

Row 4: Purl across.

Bind off remaining sts.

RIGHT FRONT

With smaller size needles, cast on 31{34-38} sts.

Work same as Back to Armhole Shaping, ending by working a **knit** row.

ARMHOLE SHAPING

Row 1: Bind off 4{5-6} sts, purl across: 27{29-32} sts.

Row 2 (Decrease row): Knit across to last 2 sts, K2 tog: 26{28-31} sts.

Row 3: Purl across.

Repeat Rows 2 and 3, 2{2-3} times: 24{26-28} sts.

Work even until Armhole measures approximately $5^1/2${$6-6^1/2$}"/14{15-16.5} cm, ending by working a **knit** row.

NECK SHAPING

Row 1: Purl across to last 7{8-8} sts, P2 tog, slip remaining 5{6-6} sts onto st holder: 18{19-21} sts.

Row 2: Slip 1, K1, PSSO, knit across: 17{18-20} sts.

Row 3 (Decrease row): Purl across to last 2 sts, P2 tog: 16{17-19} sts.

Row 4: Knit across.

Repeat Rows 3 and 4, 2{2-3} times: 14{15-16} sts.

Work even until Armhole measures same as Left Front to Shoulder Shaping, ending by working a **knit** row.

Instructions continued on page 70.

SHOULDER SHAPING

Row 1: Bind off 4{5-5} sts, purl across: 10{10-11} sts.

Row 2: Knit across.

Row 3: Bind off 5 sts, purl across: 5{5-6} sts.

Row 4: Knit across.

Bind off remaining sts.

SLEEVE (Make 2)
BODY

With smaller size needles, cast on 30{34-36} sts.

Rows 1-3: Knit across.

Change to larger size needles.

Beginning with a **knit** row, work 6 rows in Stockinette Stitch.

Increase Row: Increase in first st *(Figs. 10a & b, page 581)*, knit across to last st, increase in last st: 32{36-38} sts.

Continue to increase one stitch at **each** edge, every 6th row, 7{2-4} times **more**; then increase every 8th row, 2{6-5} times: 50{52-56} sts.

Work even until Sleeve measures approximately 17$\frac{1}{4}${17$\frac{3}{4}$-18$\frac{1}{2}$}"/44{45-47} cm from cast on edge **or to desired length**, ending by working a **purl** row.

SLEEVE CAP

Rows 1 and 2: Bind off 4{5-6} sts at the beginning of the next 2 rows, work across: 42{42-44} sts.

Row 3 (Decrease row): Slip 1, K1, PSSO, knit across to last 2 sts, K2 tog: 40{40-42} sts.

Row 4: Purl across.

Repeat Rows 3 and 4, 8{8-9} times: 24 sts.

Bind off 2 sts at the beginning of the next 2 rows, work across: 20 sts.

Bind off 3 sts at the beginning of the next 4 rows, work across: 8 sts.

Bind off remaining sts.

FINISHING

Sew shoulder seams. Set in Sleeves matching center to shoulder seam. Sew underarm and side in one continuous seam.

NECK BAND

With **right** side facing and using smaller size needles, knit 5{6-6} sts from Right Front st holder, pick up 14 sts along Right Neck edge *(Figs. 34a & b, page 586)*, pick up 19{22-23} sts along Back Neck edge, pick up 14 sts along Left Neck edge, slip 5{6-6} sts from Left Front st holder onto empty needle, knit across: 57{62-63} sts.

Rows 1-3: Knit across.

Bind off all sts **loosely**.

Design by Evie Rosen.

FUZZY HOODED JACKET

◼◼◼◻ INTERMEDIATE

Shown on page 73.

Size	Finished Chest Measurement
Small	36" (91.5 cm)
Medium	40" (101.5 cm)
Large	44" (112 cm)

Size Note: Instructions are written for size Small with sizes Medium and Large in braces { }. Instructions will be easier to read if you circle all the numbers pertaining to your size. If only one number is given, it applies to all sizes.

MATERIALS

Bulky Weight Yarn: 🔳 **5** BULKY

Ounces	18$\frac{1}{2}${21-23$\frac{1}{2}$}
Yards	570{650-725}
Grams	530{600-670}
Meters	521{594-663}

Bulky Weight Novelty Eyelash Yarn: 🔳 **5** BULKY

Ounces	16$\frac{1}{2}${19-21$\frac{1}{4}$}
Yards	565{650-730}
Grams	470{540-605}
Meters	517{594-668}

Straight knitting needles, size 11 (8 cm) **or** size needed for gauge
Markers
Stitch holder
1$\frac{1}{2}$" (38 mm) Buttons - 4
Yarn needle
Sewing needle and matching thread

Jacket is worked holding one strand of Bulky Weight yarn and one strand of Bulky Weight Novelty Eyelash yarn held together, unless otherwise indicated.

GAUGE: In Stockinette Stitch,
10 sts and 14 rows = 4" (10 cm)

BACK
BODY
Cast on 47{52-57} sts.

Rows 1-4: Knit across.

Beginning with a **purl** row, work in Stockinette Stitch until Back measures approximately 15$\frac{1}{2}${16$\frac{1}{2}$-17$\frac{1}{2}$}"/39.5{42-44.5} cm from cast on edge **or to desired length**, ending by working a **purl** row.

ARMHOLE SHAPING
Rows 1 and 2: Bind off 2{3-4} sts at the beginning of the next 2 rows, work across: 43{46-49} sts.

Row 3 (Decrease row)**:** [Slip 1, K1, PSSO **(Figs. 19a & b, page 583)**], knit across to last 2 sts, K2 tog **(Fig. 17, page 583)**: 41{44-47} sts.

Row 4: Purl across.

Repeat Rows 3 and 4, 1{2-3} time(s); then repeat Row 3 once **more**: 37{38-39} sts.

Work even until Armholes measure approximately 8$\frac{1}{2}${9-9$\frac{1}{2}$}"/21.5{23-24} cm, ending by working a **knit** row.

SHOULDER SHAPING
Rows 1-6: Bind off 4 sts at the beginning of the next 6 rows, work across: 13{14-15} sts.

Slip remaining sts onto st holder.

Instructions continued on page 72.

LEFT FRONT
BODY
Cast on 23{26-29} sts.

Work same as Back to Armhole Shaping.

ARMHOLE SHAPING
Row 1: Bind off 2{3-4} sts, knit across: 21{23-25} sts.

Row 2: Purl across.

Row 3 (Decrease row): Slip 1, K1, PSSO, knit across: 20{22-24} sts.

Row 4: Purl across.

Repeat Rows 3 and 4, 1{2-3} time(s); then repeat Row 3 once **more**: 18{19-20} sts.

Work even until Armholes measure approximately $6^1/2\{7-7^1/2\}$"/16.5{18-19} cm, ending by working a **knit** row.

NECK SHAPING
Row 1: Bind off 3{4-5} sts, purl across: 15 sts.

Row 2 (Decrease row): Knit across to last 2 sts, K2 tog: 14 sts.

Row 3: Purl across.

Rows 4-7: Repeat Rows 2 and 3 twice: 12 sts.

SHOULDER SHAPING
Row 1: Bind off 4 sts, knit across: 8 sts.

Row 2: Purl across.

Rows 3 and 4: Repeat Rows 1 and 2: 4 sts.

Bind off remaining sts.

RIGHT FRONT
BODY
Cast on 23{26-29} sts.

Work same as Back to Armhole Shaping, ending by working a **knit** row.

ARMHOLE SHAPING
Row 1: Bind off 2{3-4} sts, purl across: 21{23-25} sts.

Row 2: Knit across.

Row 3 (Decrease row): P2 tog **(Fig. 18, page 583)**, purl across: 20{22-24} sts.

Row 4: Knit across.

Repeat Rows 3 and 4, 1{2-3} time(s); then repeat Row 3 once **more**: 18{19-20} sts.

Work even until Armholes measure approximately $6^1/2\{7-7^1/2\}$"/16.5{18-19} cm, ending by working a **purl** row.

NECK SHAPING
Row 1: Bind off 3{4-5} sts, knit across: 15 sts.

Row 2 (Decrease row): Purl across to last 2 sts, P2 tog: 14 sts.

Row 3: Knit across.

Rows 4-7: Repeat Rows 2 and 3 twice: 12 sts.

SHOULDER SHAPING
Row 1: Bind off 4 sts, purl across: 8 sts.

Row 2: Knit across.

Rows 3 and 4: Repeat Rows 1 and 2: 4 sts.

Bind off remaining sts.

Instructions continued on page 74.

SLEEVE (Make 2)
BODY
Cast on 23{26-26} sts.

Rows 1-4: Knit across.

Row 5: Purl across.

Beginning with a **knit** row, work in Stockinette Stitch increasing one stitch at **each** edge *(Figs. 10a & b, page 581)*, every 6th row, 1{0-4} time(s) *(see Zeros, page 577)*; then increase every 8th row, 6{7-4} times: 37{40-42} sts.

Work even until Sleeve measures approximately 17¹/₂{18-18}"/44.5{45.5-45.5} cm from cast edge **or to desired length**, ending by working a **purl** row.

SLEEVE CAP
Rows 1 and 2: Bind off 2{3-4} sts at the beginning of the next 2 rows, work across: 33{34-34} sts.

Row 3 (Decrease row)**:** Slip 1, K1, PSSO, knit across to last 2 sts, K2 tog: 31{32-32} sts.

Row 4: Purl across.

Rows 5 thru 16{16-18}: Repeat Rows 3 and 4, 6{6-7} times: 19{20-18} sts.

Bind off 2{2-1} st(s) at the beginning of the next 2 rows, work across: 15{16-16} sts.

Bind off 2 sts at the beginning of the next 4 rows, work across: 7{8-8} sts.

Bind off remaining sts.

FINISHING
Sew shoulder seams.

HOOD
With **right** side facing, pick up 12 sts evenly spaced along Right Front neck edge *(Figs. 34a & b, page 586)*, knit 13{14-15} sts from Back st holder, pick up 12 sts evenly spaced along Left Front neck edge: 37{38-39} sts.

Row 1 (Wrong side)**:** Purl across.

Row 2: K 13, increase in next st, place marker on right needle, K 9{10-11}, place marker on right needle, increase in next st, knit across: 39{40-41} sts.

Row 3: Purl across.

Row 4: Knit across.

Rows 5-7: Repeat Rows 3 and 4 once, then repeat Row 3 once **more**.

Row 8 (Increase row)**:** Knit across to within one st of next marker, increase in next st, slip marker, knit across to next marker, slip marker, increase in next st, knit across: 41{42-43} sts.

Rows 9-38: Repeat Rows 3-8, 5 times: 51{52-53} sts.

Row 39: P 16, attach second ball of yarn and bind off next 5 sts, P8{9-10}, slip 9{10-11} sts just worked onto st holder, bind off next 5 sts, purl across: 16 sts **each** side.

Row 40: Knit across; with second yarn, knit across.

Row 41: Purl across; with second yarn, purl across.

Rows 42-46: Repeat Rows 40 and 41 twice, then repeat Row 40 once **more**.

Bind off remaining sts on **each** side.

With **right** side facing, slip 9{10-11} sts from st holder onto empty needle and knit across.

Work in Stockinette Stitch on center 9{10-11} sts until piece measures 6¹/₂" (16.5 cm) from bound off sts, ending by working a **knit** row.

Bind off remaining sts.

Referring to Diagram, sew hood seams, sewing A to B and sewing C to D.

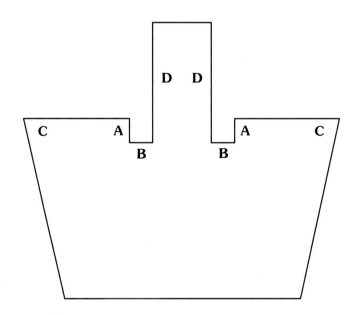

LEFT FRONT BAND
With **right** side facing, pick up 50{54-58} sts along Left Front edge.

Rows 1-6: Knit across.

Bind off all sts.

RIGHT FRONT BAND
With **right** side facing, pick up 50{54-58} sts along Right Front edge.

Rows 1 and 2: Knit across.

Row 3 (Buttonhole row)**:** K3, YO *(Fig. 16a, page 582)*, K2 tog, ★ K7{8-9}, YO, K2 tog; repeat from ★ 3 times **more**, K9.

Rows 4-6: Knit across.

Bind off all sts.

Sew Sleeves into armholes matching bound off sts at underarm and placing center of Cap at shoulder seam.

Sew Sleeve and side seams.

Sew buttons to Left Front Band opposite buttonholes.

Design by Evie Rosen.

BIRDSEYE SHAWL

◼◼◼◻ INTERMEDIATE

Finished Size: 64$\frac{1}{2}$"w (164 cm) at top edge

MATERIALS

Bulky Weight Yarn: **(5) BULKY**
 17$\frac{1}{2}$ ounces, 770 yards
 (500 grams, 704 meters)
 24" (61 cm) Circular knitting needle,
  size 11 (8 mm) **or** size needed for gauge

GAUGE: In Garter Stitch,
  12 sts and 16 rows = 4" (10 cm)

SHAWL

Cast on 4 sts.

Row 1: Knit across.

Row 2 (Increase row)**:** Increase in first st **(Figs. 10a & b, page 581)**, knit across to last st, increase in last st: 6 sts.

Rows 3-11: Repeat Rows 1 and 2, 4 times; then repeat Row 1 once **more**: 14 sts.

Row 12: Increase in first st, K4, K2 tog **(Fig. 17, page 583)**, YO twice **(Fig. 16a, page 582)**, K2 tog, K4, increase in last st: 16 sts.

Row 13: K7, K1 in first YO, P1 in next YO, K7.

Row 14 (Increase row)**:** Increase in first st, knit across to last st, increase in last st: 18 sts.

Row 15: Knit across.

Row 16 (Increase row)**:** Increase in first st, K4, K2 tog, YO twice, K2 tog twice, YO twice, K2 tog, K4, increase in last st: 20 sts.

Row 17: K7, K1 in first YO, P1 in next YO, K2, K1 in first YO, P1 in next YO, K7.

Row 18 (Increase row)**:** Increase in first st, knit across to last st, increase in last st: 22 sts.

Row 19: Knit across.

Row 20 (Increase row)**:** Increase in first st, K4, K2 tog, YO twice, (K2 tog twice, YO twice) across to last 7 sts, K2 tog, K4, increase in last st: 24 sts.

Row 21: K7, K1 in first YO, P1 in next YO, (K2, K1 in first YO, P1 in next YO) across to last 7 sts, K7.

Rows 22-190: Repeat Rows 18-21, 42 times; then repeat Row 18 once **more**: 194 sts.

Rows 191-198: Knit across.

Bind off all sts.

Design by Mary Thomas.

FUZZY LACE PONCHO

◼◼◼◻ INTERMEDIATE

Size	Misses Size (approximate)
X-Small/Small	4-8
Medium/Large	10-16
X-Large	18-20

	Side Length - Short Version (approximate)
X-Small/Small	11" (28 cm)
Medium/Large	14" (35.5 cm)
X-Large	16½" (42 cm)

	Side Length - Long Version (approximate)
X-Small/Small	15½" (39.5 cm)
Medium/Large	17½" (44.5 cm)
X-Large	21" (53.5 cm)

Size Note: Instructions are written for size X-Small /Small with sizes Medium/Large and X-Large in braces { }. Instructions will be easier to read if you circle all the numbers pertaining to your size. If only one number is given, it applies to all sizes.

MATERIALS

Bulky Weight Yarn:

Short Version
Ounces	10{16-21}
Yards	405{645-845}
Grams	280{450-600}
Meters	370{590-773}

Long Version
Ounces	17{22-28}
Yards	685{890-1,130}
Grams	480{620-800}
Meters	626{814-1,033}

Double pointed needles, size 11 (8 mm)
   or size needed for gauge
29" (73.5 cm) Circular knitting needle,
   size 11 (8 mm) **or** size needed for gauge
Markers
Crochet hook (for fringe)

GAUGE: In pattern,
   11 sts and 14 rows = 4" (10 cm)

BODY

Cast on 62{74-82} sts, place marker to mark beginning of rnd *(see Markers and Knitting in the Round, pages 578 & 579)*.

Rnd 1: K 31{37-41}, place marker, knit across.

Rnd 2: K1, YO *(Fig. 16a, page 582)*, knit across to marker, YO, slip marker, K1, YO, knit across to marker, YO: 66{78-86} sts.

Rnd 3: ★ (K2 tog, YO) across to within 3 sts of marker *(Fig. 17, page 583)*, K3; repeat from ★ once **more**.

Rnd 4: K1, YO, knit across to marker, YO, slip marker, K1, YO, knit across to marker, YO: 70{82-90} sts.

Rnd 5: ★ K3, (YO, K2 tog) across to within 2 sts of marker, K2; repeat from ★ once **more**.

Rnd 6: K1, YO, knit across to marker, YO, slip marker, K1, YO, knit across to marker, YO: 74{86-94} sts.

Repeat Rnds 3-6 for pattern until piece measures approximately 11{14-16½}"/28{35.5-42} cm **or** 15½{17½-21}"/39.5{44.5-53.5} cm from cast on edge (at straight edge), ending by working Rnd 4.

Next Rnd: ★ K1, YO, (K2 tog, YO) across to marker; repeat from ★ once **more**.

Last Rnd: Knit around.

Bind off all sts in knit.

Using 3 strands, add 9" (23 cm) fringe to each YO along edge *(Figs. 37a & b, page 588)*.

Design by Kay Meadors.

COTTON CABLE PONCHO
■■■□ INTERMEDIATE

Size	Misses Size
	(approximate)
X-Small/Small	4-8
Medium/Large	10-16
X-Large	18-20

Size Note: Instructions are written for size X-Small /Small with sizes Medium/Large and X-Large in braces { }. Instructions will be easier to read if you circle all the numbers pertaining to your size. If only one number is given, it applies to all sizes.

MATERIALS
Medium/Worsted **④** MEDIUM
Weight Cotton Yarn:
  Ounces   16{24-31}
  Yards   850{1,275-1,645}
  Grams   450{680-880}
  Meters   777{1,166-1,504}
Straight knitting needles, size 10 (6 mm)
    or size needed for gauge
Cable needle
Yarn needle
Crochet hook (for fringe)

GAUGE: In Garter Stitch,
      16 sts and 30 rows = 4" (10 cm)

STITCH GUIDE

CABLE 3 FRONT *(abbreviated C3F)*
Slip next 3 sts onto cable needle and hold in **front** of work, K3 from left needle, K3 from cable needle.
CABLE 3 BACK *(abbreviated C3B)*
Slip next 3 sts onto cable needle and hold in **back** of work, K3 from left needle, K3 from cable needle.

BODY (Make 2)
Cast on 60{72-84} sts.

Row 1: K 11{14-17}, P1, K7, P1, K 20{26-32}, P1, K7, P1, knit across.

When instructed to slip a stitch, always slip as if to **purl**.

Row 2 (Right side)**:** K 11{14-17}, slip 1, K2, increase in each of next 3 sts *(Figs. 10a & b, page 581)*, K2, slip 1, K 20{26-32}, slip 1, K2, increase in each of next 3 sts, K2, slip 1, knit across: 66{78-90} sts.

Note: Loop a short piece of yarn around any stitch to mark Row 2 as **right** side.

Row 3: K 11{14-17}, P1, K 10, P1, K 20{26-32}, P1, K 10, P1, knit across.

Row 4: K 11{14-17}, slip 1, K 10, slip 1, K 20{26-32}, slip 1, K 10, slip 1, knit across.

Row 5: K 11{14-17}, P1, K2, P6, K2, P1, K 20{26-32}, P1, K2, P6, K2, P1, knit across.

Row 6: K 11{14-17}, slip 1, K2, C3F, K2, slip 1, K 20{26-32}, slip 1, K2, C3B, K2, slip 1, knit across.

Row 7: K 11{14-17}, P1, K2, P6, K2, P1, K 20{26-32}, P1, K2, P6, K2, P1, knit across.

Row 8: K 11{14-17}, slip 1, K 10, slip 1, K 20{26-32}, slip 1, K 10, slip 1, knit across.

Rows 9-15: Repeat Rows 7 and 8, 3 times; then repeat Row 7 once **more**.

Repeat Rows 6-15 for pattern until piece measures approximately 23^1/2{29-34}"/ 59.5{73.5-86.5} cm from cast on edge, ending by working Row 6.

Decrease Row: K 11{14-17}, P1, K2, K2 tog 3 times *(Fig. 17, page 583)*, K2, P1, K 20{26-32}, P1, K2, K2 tog 3 times, K2, P1, knit across: 60{72-84} sts.

Next Row:
K 11{14-17}, slip 1, K7, slip 1, K 20{26-32}, slip 1, K7, slip 1, knit across.

Last Row:
K 11{14-17}, P1, K7, P1, K 20{26-32}, P1, K7, P1, knit across.

Bind off all sts in knit.

FINISHING
Using diagram as a guide for placement, sew cast on edge of first piece to side of second piece. Sew bound off edge of second piece to side edge of first piece.

DIAGRAM

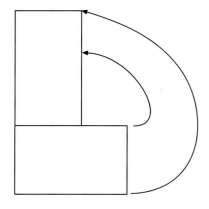

Using 2 strands, add 6" (15 cm) fringe to every other stitch across cast on and bound off edges and to every ridge at end of rows *(Figs. 37a & b, page 588)*.

Design by Kay Meadors.

STRIPED PONCHO
◖◖◼◻ INTERMEDIATE

Size	Misses Size
	(approximate)
X-Small/Small	4-8
Medium/Large	10-16
X-Large	18-20

Size	Side Length - Short Version
X-Small/Small	11" (28 cm)
Medium/Large	14" (35.5 cm)
X-Large	16$^1/_2$" (42 cm)

Size	Side Length - Long Version
X-Small/Small	15" (38 cm)
Medium/Large	18" (45.5 cm)
X-Large	21" (53.5 cm)

Size Note: Instructions are written for size X-Small /Small with sizes Medium/Large and X-Large in braces { }. Instructions will be easier to read if you circle all the numbers pertaining to your size. If only one number is given, it applies to all sizes.

MATERIALS

Bulky Weight Yarn:
Short Version
Brown

Ounces	6{9-12}
Yards	185{275-370}
Grams	170{260-340}
Meters	169{251-338}

Variegated

Ounces	5$^1/_2${8-11}
Yards	240{345-475}
Grams	160{230-310}
Meters	219{315-434}

Long Version
Brown

Ounces	9{13-17}
Yards	275{400-520}
Grams	260{370-480}
Meters	251{366-475}

Variegated

Ounces	8{11$^1/_2$-15$^1/_2$}
Yards	345{495-670}
Grams	230{330-440}
Meters	315{453-613}

Double pointed needles, size 11 (8 mm)
or size needed for gauge
29" (73.5 cm) Circular knitting needle, size 11 (8 mm)
Markers
Crochet hook (for fringe)

GAUGE: In Stockinette Stitch,
11 sts and 16 rows = 4" (10 cm)

BODY

With Brown, cast on 62{74-82} sts, place marker to mark beginning of rnd *(see Markers and Knitting in the Round, pages 578 & 579)*.

Rnd 1: K 31{37-41}, place marker, knit across.

Rnd 2: K1, YO *(Fig. 16a, page 582)*, knit across to marker, YO, slip marker, K1, YO, knit across to marker, YO: 66{78-86} sts.

Rnd 3: With Variegated, knit around.

Rnd 4: K1, YO, knit across to marker, YO, slip marker, K1, YO, knit across to marker, YO: 70{82-90} sts.

Rnd 5: Knit around.

Rnd 6: With Brown, K1, YO, knit across to marker, YO, slip marker, K1, YO, knit across to marker, YO: 74{86-94} sts.

Rnd 7: Knit around.

Rnd 8: K1, YO, knit across to marker, YO, slip marker, K1, YO, knit across to marker, YO: 78{90-98} sts.

Repeat Rnds 3-8 for pattern until piece measures approximately 11{14-16^1/$_2$}"/ 28{35.5-42} cm **or** 15{18-21}"/ 38{45.5-53.5} cm from cast on edge (at straight edge), ending by working Rnd 7.

Last Rnd: ★ K1, YO, (K2 tog, YO) across to marker *(Fig. 17, page 583)*; repeat from ★ once **more**.

Bind off all sts in knit.

Using 3 strands of Variegated, add 6" (15 cm) fringe to each YO on last rnd *(Figs. 37a & b, page 588)*.

Design by Kay Meadors.

FURRY PONCHO

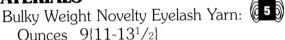 EASY

Size	Misses Size (approximate)
X-Small/Small	4-8
Medium/Large	10-16
X-Large	18-20

Size Note: Instructions are written for size X-Small /Small with sizes Medium/Large and X-Large in braces { }. Instructions will be easier to read if you circle all the numbers pertaining to your size. If only one number is given, it applies to all sizes.

MATERIALS

Bulky Weight Novelty Eyelash Yarn: **BULKY 5**
Ounces 9{11-13$^1/_2$}
Yards   365{445-550}
Grams   260{310-380}
Meters 334{407-503}
Straight knitting needles, size 11 (8 mm)
   or size needed for gauge
Yarn needle

GAUGE: In pattern, 12 sts = 3$^1/_2$" (9 cm);
            14 rows = 4" (10 cm)

BODY (Make 2)
Cast on 52{57-62} sts.

Row 1: Knit across.

Row 2 (Right side)**:** K1, (K2 tog, YO, K1, YO, SSK) across to last st *(Fig. 17, page 583, Fig. 16a, page 582, and Figs. 21a-c, page 584)*, K1.

Row 3: Purl across.

Repeat Rows 2 and 3 for pattern until piece measures approximately 25{28-31}"/ 63.5{71-78.5} cm from cast on edge, ending by working Row 2.

Last Row: Knit across.

Bind off all sts in knit leaving a long end for sewing.

FINISHING

Using diagram as a guide for placement, sew cast on edge of first piece to side of second piece. Sew bound off edge of second piece to side edge of first piece.

DIAGRAM

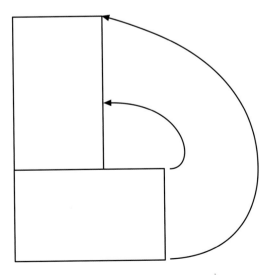

Design by Kay Meadors.

ASYMMETRICAL HALTER

■■■□ INTERMEDIATE

MATERIALS

MC - Medium/Worsted Weight Yarn: **MEDIUM 4**

Ounces	4{5-6-7}
Yards	265{330-395-460}
Grams	110{140-170-200}
Meters	242.5{302-361-420.5}

CC - Medium Weight Novelty Eyelash Yarn: **BULKY 5**

Ounces	$2^1/_2${$2^3/_4$-3-$3^1/_4$}
Yards	85{95-105-110}
Grams	70{80-90-95}
Meters	77.5{87-96-100.5}

29" (73.5 cm) Circular needle,
   size 8 (5 mm) **or** size needed for gauge
Crochet hook, size I (5.5 mm)
Marker
Stitch holder

GAUGE: In Stockinette Stitch,
         18 sts and 24 rows = 4" (10 cm)

SIZE	Finished Body Measurement
X-Small	26" (66 cm)
Small	30" (76 cm)
Medium	34" (86.5 cm)
Large	38" (96.5 cm)

Size Note: Instructions are written for size X-Small with sizes Small, Medium, and Large in braces { }. Instructions will be easier to read if you circle all the numbers pertaining to your size. If only one number is given, it applies to all sizes.

BODY

With CC, cast on 118{136-154-172} sts, place marker to mark beginning of rnd *(see Markers and Knitting in the Round, pages 578 & 579).*

Knit around for 2" (5 cm).

Drop CC, with MC knit around until Body measures approximately $10^1/_2${11-$11^1/_2$-12}"/ 26.5{28-29-30.5} cm from cast on edge **or desired length to armhole.**

Dividing Rnd (Right side)**:** K1, [slip 1, K1, PSSO *(Figs. 19a & b, page 583)*], K 53{62-71-80}, K2 tog *(Fig. 17, page 583)*, K1, slip 57{66-75-84} sts just worked onto st holder (Back), K1, slip 1, K1, PSSO, knit across to last 3 sts, K2 tog, K1: 57{66-75-84} sts.

FRONT
Row 1 (Decrease row)**:** P1, P2 tog *(Fig. 18, page 583)*, purl across: 56{65-74-83} sts.

Row 2 (Decrease row)**:** K1, slip 1, K1, PSSO, knit across to last 3 sts, K2 tog, K1: 54{63-72-81} sts.

Rows 3 thru 26{32-38-44}: Repeat Rows 1 and 2, 12{15-18-21} times: 18 sts.

Row 27{33-39-45} (Decrease row)**:** P1, P2 tog, purl across: 17 sts.

Row 28{34-40-46} (Decrease row)**:** Knit across to last 3 sts, K2 tog, K1: 16 sts.

Rows 29{35-41-47} thru 40{46-52-58}: Repeat last 2 rows, 6 times: 4 sts.

Row 41{47-53-59}: P1, P2 tog, P1: 3 sts.

Row 42{48-54-60}: P3 tog *(Fig. 24, page 584)*; finish off.

BACK
With **wrong** side facing, slip sts from st holder onto circular needle.

Work same as Front.

FINISHING
See Crochet Stitches, pages 588 & 589.

BOTTOM TRIM
Rnd 1: With **wrong** side of Body facing, using a crochet hook, and working around cast on edge, join CC with sc in any st; sc in each st around; join with slip st to first sc.

Rnd 2: Ch 1, sc in Front Loop Only of each sc around; join with slip st to **both** loops of first sc, finish off.

TOP TRIM
Rnd 1: With **wrong** side facing and using a crochet hook, join CC with sc in first st of Dividing Rnd; sc in each st around working 3 sc in st on last row of Front and Back; join with slip st to first sc.

Rnd 2: Ch 1, sc in Front Loop Only of each sc around working 3 sc in center sc of each 3-sc group; join with slip st to **both** loops of first sc, finish off.

FIRST STRAP
With **right** side of Front facing, using a crochet hook, and holding 2 strands of CC together, join yarn with slip st in center sc of 3-sc group on Top Trim; work a chain approximately 8{9-10-11}"/20.5{23-25.5-28} cm long; lay top flat and join with slip st to sc on Back edge directly opposite joining slip st, finish off.

SECOND STRAP
With **right** side of Back facing, using a crochet hook, and holding 2 strands of CC together, join yarn with slip st in center sc of 3-sc group on Top Trim; work a chain approximately 8{9-10-11}"/20.5{23-25.5-28} cm long; lay top flat and join with slip st to sc on Front edge directly opposite joining slip st, finish off.

Design by Joyce M. Wu.

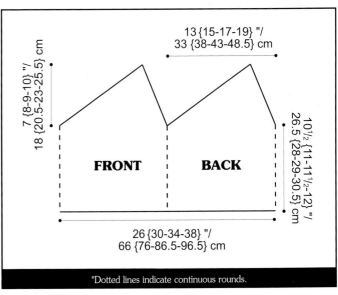

13 {15-17-19} "/
33 {38-43-48.5} cm

7 {8-9-10} "/
18 {20.5-23-25.5} cm

10½ {11-11½-12} "/
26.5 {28-29-30.5} cm

FRONT   **BACK**

26 {30-34-38} "/
66 {76-86.5-96.5} cm

Dotted lines indicate continuous rounds.

V-NECK TANK

SIZE	Finished Body Measurement
X-Small	26" (66 cm)
Small	29$\frac{1}{2}$" (75 cm)
Medium	34" (86.5 cm)
Large	37$\frac{1}{2}$" (95.5 cm)

Size Note: Instructions are written for size X-Small with sizes Small, Medium, and Large in braces { }. Instructions will be easier to read if you circle all the numbers pertaining to your size. If only one number is given, it applies to all sizes.

MATERIALS

Bulky Weight Yarn:

Ounces	8{9-11-12$\frac{1}{2}$}
Yards	245{280-340-385}
Grams	230{260-310-360}
Meters	224{256-311-352}

29" (73.5 cm) Circular needle, size 10 (6 mm) **or** size needed for gauge
Crochet hook, size J (6 mm)
Stitch holders - 3
Marker
Yarn needle

GAUGE: In Stockinette Stitch, 14 sts and 20 rows = 4" (10 cm)

BODY

Cast on 92{104-120-132} sts, place marker to mark beginning of rnd *(see Markers and Knitting in the Round, pages 578 & 579)*.

Knit around until Body measures approximately 12$\frac{1}{2}${13-13$\frac{1}{2}$-14}"/ 32{33-34.5-35.5} cm from cast on edge **or desired length to armhole**.

Dividing Rnd: K1, [slip 1, K1, PSSO *(Figs. 19a & b, page 583)*], K 17{20-24-27}, K2 tog *(Fig. 17, page 583)*, K1, ★ slip 21{24-28-31} sts just worked onto st holder, K1, slip 1, K1, PSSO, K 17{20-24-27}, K2 tog, K1; repeat from ★ 2 times **more**: 21{24-28-31} sts.

RIGHT FRONT

Row 1 (Decrease row)**:** P1, P2 tog *(Fig. 18, page 583)*, purl across: 20{23-27-30} sts.

Row 2 (Decrease row)**:** Knit across to last 3 sts, K2 tog, K1: 19{22-26-29} sts.

Row 3 (Decrease row)**:** P1, P2 tog, purl across: 18{21-25-28} sts.

Working in Stockinette Stitch, continue to decrease one stitch at armhole edge, *every row, 1{3-11-9} time(s)* **more**; then decrease *every other row, 12{14-10-14} times*: 5{4-4-5} sts.

Work even until Armhole measures approximately 7{8-8-9}"/18{20.5-20.5-23} cm, ending by working a **purl** row.

Bind off all sts in **knit**.

LEFT FRONT

With **wrong** side facing, slip sts from next st holder (to the left of the Right Front) onto empty needle: 21{24-28-31} sts.

Row 1 (Decrease row)**:** Purl across to last 3 sts, P2 tog tbl *(Fig. 20, page 583)*, P1: 20{23-27-30} sts.

Row 2 (Decrease row)**:** K1, slip 1, K1, PSSO, knit across: 19{22-26-29} sts.

Row 3 (Decrease row)**:** Purl across to last 3 sts, P2 tog tbl, P1: 18{21-25-28} sts.

Continue to decrease one stitch at armhole edge, *every row, 1{3-11-9} time(s)* **more**; then decrease *every other row, 12{14-10-14} times*: 5{4-4-5} sts.

Work even until Armhole measures approximately 7{8-8-9}"/18{20.5-20.5-23} cm, ending by working a **purl** row.

Bind off all sts in **knit**.

LEFT BACK

With **wrong** side facing, slip sts from next st holder (to the left of the Left Front) onto empty needle: 21{24-28-31} sts.

Work same as Right Front.

RIGHT BACK

With **wrong** side facing, slip sts from st holder onto empty needle: 21{24-28-31} sts.

Work same as Left Front.

FINISHING

Sew shoulder seams.

BOTTOM HEM

Turn cast on edge ¹/₂" (12 mm) to wrong side and sew in place.

TRIMS

See Crochet Stitches, pages 588 & 589.

NECK TRIM

With **right** side facing, using a crochet hook, and working in end of rows, join yarn with sc in either shoulder seam; sc evenly around; join with slip st to first sc, finish off.

ARMHOLE TRIM

With **right** side facing, using a crochet hook, and working in end of rows, join yarn with sc in either shoulder seam; sc evenly around; join with slip st to first sc, finish off.

Repeat for remaining Armhole.

Design by Joyce M. Wu.

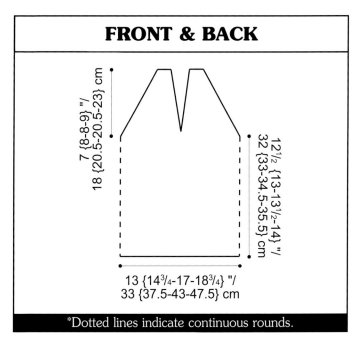

FRONT & BACK

7 {8-8-9} "/
18 {20.5-20.5-23} cm

12½ {13-13½-14} "/
32 {33-34.5-35.5} cm

13 {14³/₄-17-18³/₄} "/
33 {37.5-43-47.5} cm

*Dotted lines indicate continuous rounds.

ONE-SHOULDER TOP

Finished Bust Size:

Small	Medium	Large	Ex-Large
29^1/$_2$"	34"	39"	44"
[75 cm]	[86.5 cm]	[99 cm]	[112 cm]

Size Note: Instructions are written for size Small with sizes Medium, Large, and Ex-Large in braces { }. Instructions will be easier to read, if you circle all the numbers pertaining to your size.

MATERIALS

FINE 2

Sport Weight Yarn:
  Black - 2{2^1/$_2$-3-3^1/$_2$} Ounces
  335{420-505-590} Yards
  57{71-85-100} Grams
  306{384-462-539} Meters
Bulky Weight Novelty
Eyelash Yarn: **BULKY 5**
  Pink - 25{30} Yards
  23{27.5} Meters
Straight knitting needles, sizes 6 [4.25 mm]
  and 8 [5.00 mm] **or** sizes needed for gauge
Crochet hook, size F [4.00 mm]

GAUGE: With larger size needles,
  in Stockinette Stitch,
  20 sts and 26 rows = 4" [10 cm]

BACK
RIBBING

With smaller size needles and Black, cast on 66{78-90-102} sts **loosely**.

Work in K1, P1 ribbing for 2" [5 cm] increasing 10 sts evenly spaced across last row: 76{88-100-112} sts.

BODY

Change to larger size needles.

Work in Stockinette Stitch [knit one row, purl one row] until Back measures approximately 9" [23 cm], ending by working a **purl** row.

SHAPING

Row 1: Bind off 9{9-9-10} sts, knit across: 67{79-91-102} sts.

Row 2 [Decrease row]**:** Purl across to last 2 sts, P2 tog *(Fig. 18, page 583)*: 66{78-90-101} sts.

Row 3 [Decrease row]**:** [Slip 1 as if to **knit**, K1, PSSO *(Figs. 19a & b, page 583)*], knit across: 65{77-89-100} sts.

Rows 4-9: Repeat Rows 2 and 3, 3 times: 59{71-83-94} sts.

Row 10: Bind off 10{10-10-11} sts, purl across to last 2 sts, P2 tog: 48{60-72-82} sts.

Instructions continued on page 92.

Row 11 [Decrease row]**:** Slip 1 as if to **knit**, K1, PSSO [Neck edge], knit across to last 2 sts, K2 tog **(Fig. 17, page 583)** [Armhole edge]: 46{58-70-80} sts.

Row 12 [Decrease row]**:** Purl across to last 2 sts, P2 tog: 45{57-69-79} sts.

Repeat Rows 11 and 12, 2{3-4-4} times: 39{48-57-67} sts.

Next Row: Slip 1 as if to **knit**, K1, PSSO, knit across: 38{47-56-66} sts.

Next Row: Purl across to last 2 sts, P2 tog: 37{46-55-65} sts.

Continue to decrease one stitch at Neck edge ONLY, every row, 8{22-33-42} times **more**; then decrease every other row, 14{7-3-0} times **(see Zeros, page 577)**: 15{17-19-23} sts.

Bind off all sts.

FRONT
RIBBING
Work same as Back: 76{88-100-112} sts.

BODY
Change to larger size needles.

Work in Stockinette Stitch until Front measures approximately 9" [23 cm], ending by working a **knit** row.

SHAPING
Row 1: Bind off 9{9-9-10} sts, purl across: 67{79-91-102} sts.

Row 2 [Decrease row]**:** Knit across to last 2 sts, K2 tog: 66{78-90-101} sts.

Row 3 [Decrease row]**:** P2 tog, purl across: 65{77-89-100} sts.

Rows 4-9: Repeat Rows 2 and 3, 3 times: 59{71-83-94} sts.

Row 10: Bind off 10{10-10-11} sts, knit across to last 2 sts, K2 tog: 48{60-72-82} sts.

Row 11 [Decrease row]**:** P2 tog, purl across: 47{59-71-81} sts.

Row 12 [Decrease row]**:** Slip 1 as if to **knit**, K1, PSSO [Armhole edge], knit across to last 2 sts, K2 tog [Neck edge]: 45{57-69-79} sts.

Repeat Rows 11 and 12, 2{3-4-4} times: 39{48-57-67} sts.

Next Row: P2 tog, purl across: 38{47-56-66} sts.

Next Row: Knit across to last 2 sts, K2 tog: 37{46-55-65} sts.

Continue to decrease one stitch at neck edge ONLY, every row, 8{22-33-42} times **more**; then decrease every other row, 14{7-3-0} times: 15{17-19-23} sts.

Bind off all sts.

FINISHING

Sew shoulder seam.
Sew side seams.

ARMHOLE EDGING

With **right** side facing and using crochet hook, join Black with slip st at side seam *(see Crochet Stitches, pages 588 & 589)*; ch 1, sc evenly around Armhole edge; join with slip st to first sc, finish off.

EDGING

With **right** side facing, using larger size needles and Pink, pick up 124{128-136-144} sts evenly spaced around bound off sts and along Neck edge *(Figs. 34a & b, page 586)*: 124{128-136-144} sts.

Work in Garter Stitch for 9 rows.

Bind off all sts **loosely**.

Design by Darla Sims.

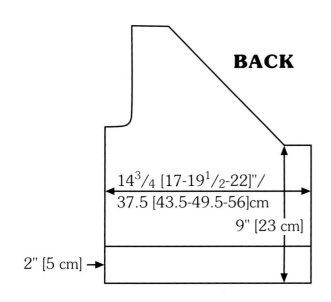

BACK

$14^3/_4$ [17-19$^1/_2$-22]"/
37.5 [43.5-49.5-56]cm

9" [23 cm]

2" [5 cm] →

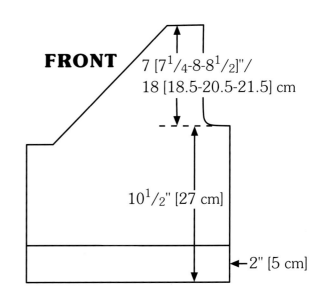

FRONT

7 [7$^1/_4$-8-8$^1/_2$]"/
18 [18.5-20.5-21.5] cm

10$^1/_2$" [27 cm]

← 2" [5 cm]

SUMMER CARDIGAN

Finished Bust Size:

Medium	Large
42"	46"
[106.5 cm]	[117 cm]

Size Note: Instructions are written for size Medium with size Large in braces { }. Instructions will be easier to read, if you circle all the numbers pertaining to your size.

MATERIALS

Sport Weight Yarn:
   7{8} Ounces
   955{1090} Yards
   199{227} Grams
   873{997} Meters
Straight knitting needles, sizes 2 [2.75 mm]
   and 5 [3.75 mm] **or** sizes needed for gauge
Markers
3 Buttons

GAUGE: With larger size needles,
   in Pattern Stitch,
   22 sts and 28 rows = 4" [10 cm]

PATTERN STITCH [multiple of 6 sts + 3]
Row 1 [Right side]: ★ K3, YO (*Fig. 16a, page 582*), slip 1 as if to **purl**, K2 tog (*Fig. 17, page 583*), PSSO, YO; repeat from ★ across to last 3 sts, K3.
Row 2: Purl across.
Row 3: K2, ★ K2 tog, YO, K1, YO, [slip 1 as if to **knit**, K1, PSSO (*Figs. 19a & b, page 583*)], K1; repeat from ★ across to last st, K1.
Rows 4-7: Repeat Rows 2 and 3, twice.
Row 8: Purl across.
Row 9: K1, K2 tog, YO, ★ K3, YO, slip 1 as if to **purl**, K2 tog, PSSO, YO; repeat from ★ across to last 6 sts, K3, YO, slip 1 as if to **knit**, K1, PSSO, K1.

Row 10: Purl across.
Row 11: K2, ★ YO, slip 1 as if to **knit**, K1, PSSO, K1, K2 tog, YO, K1; repeat from ★ across to last st, K1.
Rows 12-15: Repeat Rows 10 and 11, twice.
Row 16: Purl across.
Repeat Rows 1-16 for pattern.

BACK
RIBBING

With smaller size needles, cast on 104 {116} sts **loosely**.

Work in K1, P1 ribbing for 2¹/₂" [6.5 cm], increasing 13 sts evenly spaced across last row **(see Increasing Evenly Across A Row, page 581)**: 117 {129} sts.

BODY

Change to larger size needles.

Work in Pattern Stitch until Back measures approximately 10¹/₄ {10¹/₂}"/26 {26.5 cm} from cast on edge, ending by working a **right** side row.

SLEEVE SHAPING

Add on 24 sts **loosely (Figs. 5a & b, page 580)**: 141 {153} sts.

Row 1: K6, place marker, purl across, add on 24 sts **loosely**: 165 {177} sts.

Note: Maintain established pattern throughout.

Row 2: K6, place marker, work across to marker, K6.

Row 3: K6, work across to marker, K6.

Repeat Row 3 until Sleeves measure approximately 8 {8¹/₂}"/20.5 {21.5 cm}, ending by working a **wrong** side row.

Instructions continued on page 96.

NECK SHAPING
Row 1: Work across 68 {74} sts, bind off 29 sts, work across: 68 {74} sts **each** side.

Note: Both sides of Neck are worked at the same time, using separate yarn for **each** side.

Rows 2 and 3: Work across; with second ball, bind off 5 sts, work across: 63 {69} sts **each** side.

Rows 4 and 5: Work across; with second ball, bind off 3 sts, work across: 60 {66} sts **each** side.

Row 6: Bind off 60 {66} sts; with second ball, work across.

Bind off remaining sts.

RIGHT FRONT
RIBBING
With smaller size needles, cast on 52 {58} sts **loosely**.

Work in K1, P1 ribbing for $2^1/_2$" [6.5 cm], increasing 5 sts evenly spaced across last row: 57 {63} sts.

BODY
Change to larger size needles.

Work in Pattern Stitch until Front measures approximately 5" [12.5 cm] from cast on edge, ending by working a **wrong** side row.

NECK SHAPING
Note: Maintain established pattern throughout.

Row 1: Bind off 3 sts, work across: 54 {60} sts.

Row 2: Work across.

Row 3: Bind off 2 sts, work across: 52 {58} sts.

Rows 4 & 5: Repeat Rows 2 and 3: 50 {56} sts.

Row 6: Work across.

Row 7 [Decrease row]**:** Decrease, work across: 49 {55} sts.

Rows 8-17: Repeat Rows 6 and 7, 5 times: 44 {50} sts.

Rows 18-20: Work across.

Row 21 [Decrease row]**:** Decrease, work across: 43 {49} sts.

Rows 22-33: Repeat Rows 18-21, 3 times: 40 {46} sts.

Rows 34-37: Work across.

SLEEVE SHAPING
Cast on 24 sts **loosely**: 64 {70} sts.

Row 1: K6, place marker, work across.

Row 2 [Decrease row]**:** Decrease, work across to marker, K6: 63 {69} sts.

Row 3: K6, work across.

Row 4: Work across to marker, K6.

Rows 5-7: Repeat Rows 3 and 4, once; then repeat Row 3, once **more**.

Rows 8-25: Repeat Rows 2-7, 3 times: 60 {66} sts.

Work even, knitting 6 sts at Sleeve edge on every row, until Sleeve measures same as Back.

Bind off all sts.

LEFT FRONT
Work same as Right Front to Neck Shaping, ending by working a **right** side row.

Work Neck and Sleeve Shaping same as Right Front.

FINISHING

Sew shoulder seams.

Sew underarm and weave side in one continuous seam *(Fig. 36, page 587)*.

RIGHT FRONT BAND

With larger size needles, cast on 8 sts **loosely**.

Rows 1-6: Knit across.

Row 7 [Buttonhole row - first half]**:** K3, bind off 2 sts, K3.

Row 8 [Buttonhole row - second half]**:** K3, add on 2 sts, K3.

Rows 9-26: Knit across.

Rows 27-48: Repeat Rows 7-26, once; then repeat Rows 7 and 8 once **more**.

Rows 49-54: Knit across.

Bind off all sts.

Sew to Right Front.

LEFT FRONT BAND

With larger size needles, cast on 8 sts **loosely**. Knit 54 rows.

Bind off all sts.

Sew to Left Front.

Add buttons.

COLLAR

With smaller size needles, cast on 270 sts **loosely**.

Rows 1 and 2: Work in K1, P1 ribbing.

Note: Maintaining ribbing, begin working in short rows as follows:

Rows 3 and 4: Work across to last 2 sts, wrap next st as follows: with yarn in **front**, slip 1 as if to **purl**, bring yarn in back, and slip the same st back to the left needle; **turn**.

Rows 5-19: Work across to within 2 sts of wrapped st, wrap next st; **turn**.

Row 20: Work across all sts on left needle, knitting or purling the wrap and the st it wraps together.

Row 21: Work across all sts, knitting or purling the wrap and the st it wraps together.

Bind off all sts **loosely** in ribbing.

With **right** sides facing you, sew bound off edge to Neck edge so that seam is hidden when Collar is folded back.

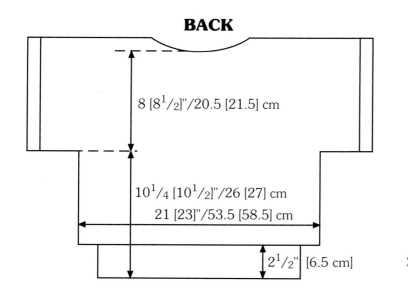

BACK

8 [8$^1/_2$]"/20.5 [21.5] cm

10$^1/_4$ [10$^1/_2$]"/26 [27] cm

21 [23]"/53.5 [58.5] cm

2$^1/_2$" [6.5 cm]

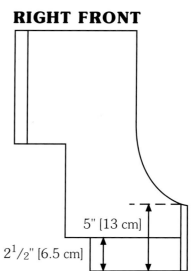

RIGHT FRONT

5" [13 cm]

2$^1/_2$" [6.5 cm]

TUBE TOP
Shown on page 95.

Finished Bust Size:

Medium	Large
34-36"	38-40"
[86.5-91.5 cm]	[96.5-101.5 cm]

Size Note: Instructions are written for size Medium with size Large, in braces { }. Instructions will be easier to read, if you circle all the numbers pertaining to your size.

MATERIALS

Sport Weight Yarn:
  3{3¹/₂} Ounces
  410{475} Yards
  85{100} Grams
  375{434} Meters
Straight knitting needles, sizes 2 [2.75 mm]
  or sizes needed for gauge

GAUGE: In Body pattern,
  27 sts and 32 rows = 4" [10 cm]

STITCH GUIDE

> **TWISTED RIB**
> **Row 1:** ★ K1 through back loop *(Fig. 4a, page 580)*, P1; repeat from ★ across.
> Repeat Row 1 for Twisted Rib.

BACK
BOTTOM BAND
Cast on 102 {114} sts **loosely**.

Work in Twisted Rib for 1¹/₂" [4 cm], increasing 14 sts evenly spaced across last row *(see Increases, page 581)*: 116 {128} sts.

BODY
Row 1 [Right side]**:** K1, P2, ★ K2, P4; repeat from ★ across to last 5 sts, K2, P2, K1.

Row 2: P1, K2, P2, ★ K4, P2; repeat from ★ across to last 3 sts, K2, P1.

Repeat Rows 1 and 2 for pattern until piece measures approximately 8" [20.5 cm] from cast on edge.

TOP BAND
Row 1: Work in Twisted Rib, decreasing 6 sts evenly spaced across *(see Decreases, page 583)*: 110 {122} sts.

Continue in Twisted Rib for 1" [2.5 cm].

Bind off all sts **loosely** in Rib.

FRONT
BOTTOM BAND
Cast on 102 {114} sts **loosely**.

Work in Twisted Rib for 1¹/₂" [4 cm], increasing 20 sts evenly spaced across last row: 122 {134} sts.

BODY
Work same as Back until piece measures approximately 8" [20.5 cm] from cast on edge.

SHAPING
Note: Maintaining pattern, begin working in short rows as follows:

Rows 1 and 2: Work across to last 10 sts, wrap next st as follows: with yarn in **front**, slip 1 as if to **purl**, bring yarn in back, and slip the same st back to the left needle; **turn**.

Rows 3-6: Work across to within 10 sts of wrapped st, wrap next st; **turn**.

Row 7: Work across all sts on left needle, knitting or purling the wrap and the st it wraps together.

TOP BAND
Row 1: Work in Twisted Rib, knitting or purling the wrap and the st it wraps together and decreasing 6 sts evenly spaced across: 116 {128} sts.

Continue in Twisted Rib for 1" [2.5 cm].

Bind off all sts **loosely** in Rib.

FINISHING
Weave side seams *(Fig. 36, page 587)*.

BACK

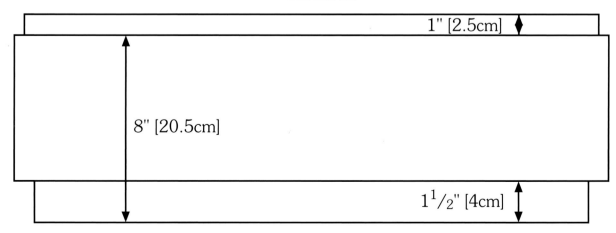

1" [2.5cm]

8" [20.5cm]

1¹/₂" [4cm]

SLEEVELESS V-NECK TOP

Finished Bust Size:
Small	Medium	Large
34"	38"	42"
[86.5 cm]	[96.5 cm]	[106.5 cm]

Size Note: Instructions are written for size Small with sizes Medium and Large in braces { }. Instructions will be easier to read, if you circle all the numbers pertaining to your size.

MATERIALS
Medium/Worsted Weight Yarn: **4**
$3^1/_2${4-4$^1/_2$} Ounces
580{665-750} Yards
100{114-130} Grams
530{608-686} Meters
Straight knitting needles, sizes 4 [3.5 mm] **and** 7 [4.5 mm] **or** sizes needed for gauge
Crochet hook, size E [3.5 mm]

GAUGE: With larger size needles, in Stockinette Stitch, 20 sts and 26 rows = 4" [10 cm]

BACK
RIBBING
With smaller size needles, cast on 70 {80-90} sts.

Work in K1, P1 ribbing for 3" [7.5 cm] increasing 16 sts evenly spaced across last row *(see Increasing Evenly Across A Row, page 581)*: 86 {96-106} sts.

BODY
Change to larger size needles.

Work in Stockinette Stitch [knit one row, purl one row] until piece measures approximately 9" [23 cm] from cast on edge **or desired length to underarm**, ending by working a **purl** row.

ARMHOLE SHAPING
Rows 1 and 2: Bind off 4 {5-6} sts at the beginning of the next 2 rows, work across: 78 {86-94} sts.

Row 3 [Decrease row]**:** K2 tog *(Fig. 17, page 583)*, knit across to last 2 sts, K2 tog: 76 {84-92} sts.

Row 4: Purl across.

Repeat Rows 3 and 4, 4 {5-6} times: 68 {74-80} sts.

Work even until Armholes measure approximately 8 {8$^1/_2$-9}"/20.5 {21.5-23 cm}, ending by working a **purl** row.

SHOULDER SHAPING
Rows 1 and 2: Bind off 4 {5-6} sts at the beginning of the next 2 rows, work across: 60 {64-68} sts.

Rows 3 and 4: Bind off 5 {5-6} sts at the beginning of the next 2 rows, work across: 50 {54-56} sts.

Rows 5 and 6: Bind off 5 {6-6} sts at the beginning of the next 2 rows, work across: 40 {42-44} sts.

Bind off remaining sts.

FRONT
Work same as Back until Armholes measure approximately 3" [7.5 cm], ending by working a **purl** row: 68 {74-80} sts.

Instructions continued on page 102.

NECK SHAPING

Note: Both sides of Neck are worked at the same time, using a separate ball for **each** side.

Row 1 [Decrease row]**:** K 32 {35-38}, K2 tog; with second ball, K2 tog, knit across: 33 {36-39} sts **each** side.

Row 2 [Decrease row]**:** Purl across to last 2 sts, P2 tog *(Fig. 18, page 583)*; with second ball, P2 tog, purl across: 32 {35-38} sts **each** side.

Continue to decrease one stitch at each Neck edge, every row, 12 {10-9} times **more**; then decrease every other row, 6 {9-11} times: 14 {16-18} sts **each** side.

Work even until Armholes measure same as Back to Shoulder Shaping, ending by working a **purl** row.

SHOULDER SHAPING

Rows 1 and 2: Bind off 4 {5-6} sts at Armhole edge, work across: 10 {11-12} sts **each** side.

Rows 3 and 4: Bind off 5 {5-6} sts at Armhole edge, work across: 5 {6-6} sts **each** side.

Row 5: Bind off 5 {6-6} sts; work across.

Bind off remaining sts.

FINISHING

Sew shoulder seams.

Sew side seams.

NECK EDGING

Rnd 1: With **right** side facing and using crochet hook, join yarn with slip st at shoulder seam *(see Crochet Stitches, pages 588 & 589)*; ch 1, sc evenly around Neck edge; join with slip st to first sc.

Rnd 2: Ch 1, do **not** turn, working from **left** to **right**, ★ insert hook in sc to right of hook *(Fig. 44a, page 589)*, YO and draw through, under and to left of loop on hook [2 loops on hook] *(Fig. 44b, page 589)*, YO and draw through both loops on hook *(Fig. 44c, page 589)* **(Reverse Single Crochet made,** *Fig. 44d, page 589)*; repeat from ★ around; join with slip st to first st, finish off.

ARMHOLE EDGING

Rnd 1: With **right** side facing and using crochet hook, join yarn with slip st at underarm seam; ch 1, sc evenly around Armhole edge; join with slip st to first sc.

Rnd 2: Ch 1, do **not** turn; work Reverse Single Crochet in each sc around; join with slip st to first st, finish off.

Repeat for second Armhole.

Design by Barbara B. Rondeau.

PEEKABOO CROP TOP
Shown on page 105.

◼◼◼◻ INTERMEDIATE

Finished Bust Size:

Small	Medium	Large
36"	40"	44"
[91.5 cm]	[101.5 cm]	[112 cm]

Size Note: Instructions are written for size Small with sizes Medium and Large in braces { }. Instructions will be easier to read, if you circle all the numbers pertaining to your size.

MATERIALS

Medium/Worsted Weight Yarn: **MEDIUM 4**
3{3-3^1/$_2$} Ounces
600{600-700} Yards
85{85-100} Grams
549{549-640} Meters
31" Circular knitting needle, sizes 3 [3.25 mm] **and** 5 [3.75 mm] **or** sizes needed for gauge
3 Stitch holders
Yarn needle
^{3}/$_4$" Buttons - 6

GAUGE: With larger size needle,
In Garter Stitch,
20 sts and 32 rows = 4" [10 cm]

BODY
BOTTOM BAND

With smaller size needle, cast on 185 {205-225} sts **loosely**.

Work in Garter Stitch [knit every row] for 3 rows.

Buttonhole Row 1 [Right side]**:** K2, bind off 2 sts, knit across.

Note: Loop a short piece of yarn around any stitch to mark last row as **right** side.

Buttonhole Row 2: Knit across to bound off sts, add on 2 sts *(Figs. 5a & b, page 580)*, K2.

Work in Garter Stitch until piece measures 1" [2.5 cm].

Change to larger size needle.

Continue in Garter Stitch until Bottom Band measures approximately 1^1/$_2$" [4 cm] from cast on edge, ending by working a **wrong** side row.

Work Buttonhole Rows 1 and 2.

Work in Garter Stitch for 2 rows.

FIRST PANEL
Row 1 [Right side]**:** Bind off 15 sts, knit across: 170 {190-210} sts.

Row 2: Bind off 15 sts, K4, purl across to last 5 sts, K5: 155 {175-195} sts.

Row 3: Knit across.

Row 4: K5, purl across to last 5 sts, K5.

Repeat Rows 3 and 4 until Body measures approximately 4" [10 cm] from cast on edge, ending by working a **wrong** side row.

CENTER BAND
Rows 1 and 2: Add on 15 sts, knit across: 185 {205-225} sts.

Rows 3 and 4: Knit across.

Rows 5 and 6: Work Buttonhole Rows 1 and 2.

Continue in Garter Stitch until Center Band measures approximately 1^1/$_2$" [4 cm], ending by working a **wrong** side row.

Work Buttonhole Rows 1 and 2.

Work in Garter Stitch for 2 rows.

SECOND PANEL
Work same as First Panel until Body measures approximately 8" [20.5 cm] from cast on edge, ending by working a **wrong** side row: 155 {175-195} sts.

Instructions continued on page 104.

TOP BAND

Rows 1 and 2: Add on 15 sts, knit across: 185 {205-225} sts.

Rows 3 and 4: Knit across.

Rows 5 and 6: Work Buttonhole Rows 1 and 2.

Rows 7 and 8: Knit across.

ARMHOLE SHAPING

Row 1 [Right side]**:** K 40 {45-49}, slip 40 {45-49} sts just worked onto st holder [Left Back], bind off 15 {16-17} sts [Armhole], knit across: 130 {144-159} sts.

Row 2: K 40 {45-49}, slip 40 {45-49} sts just worked onto st holder [Right Back], bind off 15 {16-17} sts [Armhole], knit across: 75 {83-93} sts.

FRONT

Continue in Garter Stitch until Armholes measure approximately 1" [2.5 cm], ending by working a **wrong** side row.

NECK SHAPING

Row 1: K 20 {23-26}, slip 20 {23-26} sts just worked onto st holder [Left Strap], bind off 35 {37-41} sts [Neck], knit across: 20 {23-26} sts.

RIGHT STRAP

Row 1: K5, P 10 {13-16}, K5.

Row 2: Knit across.

Repeat Rows 1 and 2 until Armhole measures approximately 6^1/$_2$ {6^3/$_4$-7}"/16.5 {17-18 cm}, ending by working a **wrong** side row.

Bind off all sts.

LEFT STRAP

With **wrong** side facing, slip 20 {23-26} sts from Front st holder onto empty needle.

Beginning with Row 1, work same as Right Strap.

LEFT BACK

With **wrong** side facing, slip 40 {45-49} sts from Left Back st holder onto empty needle.

Work in Garter Stitch until Armhole measures approximately 1^1/$_2$" [4 cm], ending by working a **wrong** side row.

Work Buttonhole Rows 1 and 2.

Work in Garter Stitch for 2 rows.

Next Row: Bind off 20 {22-23} sts, knit across: 20 {23-26} sts.

STRAP

Beginning with Row 1, work same as Front Right Strap.

RIGHT BACK

With **right** side facing, slip 40 {45-49} sts from Right Back st holder onto empty needle.

Work in Garter Stitch until Armhole measures approximately 2" [5 cm], ending by working a **right** side row.

Next Row: Bind off 20 {22-23} sts, knit across: 20 {23-26} sts.

STRAP

Beginning with Row 2, work same as Front Right Strap.

FINISHING

Sew shoulder seams.
Add buttons.

Design by Helené Rush.

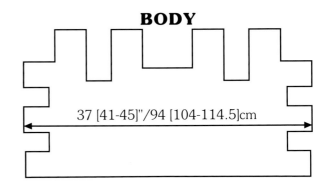

BODY

37 [41-45]"/94 [104-114.5]cm

FURRY HALTER

Finished Bust Size:

Small	Medium	Large
32"	36"	40"
[81.5 cm]	[91.5 cm]	[101.5 cm]

Size Note: Instructions are written for size Small with sizes Medium and Large in braces { }. Instructions will be easier to read, if you circle all the numbers pertaining to your size.

MATERIALS

Bulky Weight Novelty Eyelash Yarn:
Red - 3¹/₂{4-5} Ounces
130{150-185} Yards
100{115-145} Grams
119{137-169} Meters
Variegated - 3¹/₂{4-5} Ounces
145{165-205} Yards
100{115-145} Grams
133{151-187} Meters

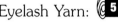

Medium/Weight Novelty Ribbon Yarn:
50 yards, 45.5 meters
Straight knitting needles, size 11 [8 mm]
or size needed for gauge
Crochet hook size J [6 cm]

Halter is worked holding 2 strands of **each** Novelty Eyelash Yarn together throughout.

GAUGE: In Stockinette Stitch,
10 sts and 11 rows = 4" [10 cm]

Instructions begin on page 108.

HALTER

Cast on 44 {48-54} sts.

SMALL AND MEDIUM ONLY

Rows 1 and 2: Knit across.

Row 3: SSK *(Figs. 21a-c, page 581)*, K1, YO *(Fig. 16a, page 582)*, K2 tog *(Fig. 17, page 583)*, knit across to last 5 sts, K2 tog, YO, K1, K2 tog: 42 {46} sts.

Row 4: Purl across.

Row 5: SSK, knit across to last 2 sts, K2 tog: 40 {44} sts.

Row 6: Purl across.

Repeat Rows 5 and 6 until 22 {24} sts remain.

Work even until Halter measures 9 {10}"/23 {25.5} cm ending with a **purl** row.

Bind off all sts in knit.

LARGE ONLY

Rows 1 and 2: Knit across.

Row 3: K2, YO *(Fig. 16a, page 582)*, K2 tog *(Fig. 17, page 583)*, knit across to last 4 sts, K2 tog, YO, K2.

Row 4: Purl across.

Row 5: SSK, knit across to last 2 sts, K2 tog: 52 sts.

Row 6: Purl across.

Repeat Rows 5 and 6 until 28 sts remain.

Work even until Halter measures 11" [28 cm] ending with a **purl** row.

Bind off all sts in **knit**.

STRAPS
FIRST SIDE

Join one strand of each yarn with slip st in first st of bound off edge *(see Crochet Stitches, pages 588 & 589)*; make a ch 45" [114.5 cm] long, knot end, cut yarn.

SECOND SIDE

Join one strand of each yarn with slip st in last st of bound off edge; make a ch 45" [114.5 cm] long, knot end, cut yarn.

FINISHING

Cross Straps in back, thread through yarn overs of Row 3 and tie.

Using one strand of Novelty Ribbon yarn, add fringe to each st of cast on edge; knot ends.

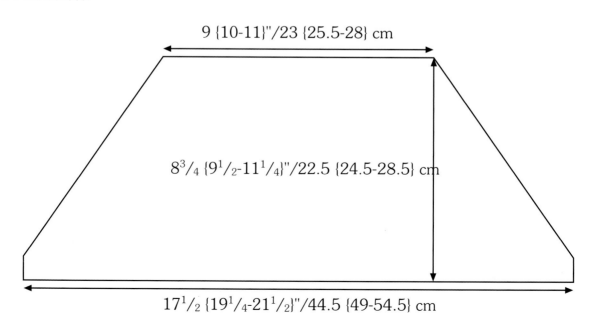

9 {10-11}"/23 {25.5-28} cm

$8^3/_4$ {$9^1/_2$-$11^1/_4$}"/22.5 {24.5-28.5} cm

$17^1/_2$ {$19^1/_4$-$21^1/_2$}"/44.5 {49-54.5} cm

FUZZY OFF-SHOULDER TOP

Shown on page 111.

◼◼◼◻ INTERMEDIATE

Finished Bust Size:

Small	Medium	Large
32"	35$\frac{1}{2}$"	39$\frac{1}{2}$"
[81.5 cm]	[91 cm]	[100 cm]

Size Note: Instructions are written for size Small with sizes Medium and Large in braces { }. Instructions will be easier to read, if you circle all the numbers pertaining to your size.

MATERIALS

Bulky Weight Novelty Eyelash Yarn:
 Pink - 6{7-8} Ounces
  265{310-355} Yards
  107.5{199-227.5} Grams
  242.5{283.5-324.5} Meters
Bulky Weight Yarn:
 Variegated - 2$\frac{1}{2}${3-3$\frac{1}{2}$} Ounces
  130{155-180} Yards
  71{85.5-100} Grams
  119{141.5-164.5} Meters
Sport Weight Yarn:
 Ecru - 1$\frac{1}{2}$ ounces, 100 yards
  [42.5 grams, 91.5 meters]
31" [78.5 cm] Circular needle, size 11 [8 mm]
 and size 13 [9 mm] **or** sizes needed for gauge
Markers
Stitch holders

GAUGE: With one strand of Bulky Weight Yarn,
 in Stockinette Stitch,
  13 sts and 17 rows = 4" [10 cm]

BODY

With Variegated, cast on 104 {116-128} sts, place marker to mark beginning of rnd *[see Markers and Knitting in the Round, pages 578 & 579].*

Knit each round until Body measures approximately 2$\frac{1}{2}$" [6.5 cm] from cast on edge.

SHAPE WAIST

Decrease Rnds: Decrease 2 sts evenly *[see Decreasing Evenly in a Rnd, page 583]* every other rnd 6 {4-3} times: 92 {108-122} sts.

Work even knitting every rnd until Body measures approximately 6" [15.5 cm] from cast on edge.

Note: Increases are made by knitting into the front **and** into the back of a stitch.

Increase Rnds: Increase 2 sts evenly *(see Increasing Evenly Across a Row/Rnd, page 581)* every other rnd 6 {4-3} times: 104 {116-128} sts.

Work even knitting every rnd until Body measures approximately 9 {10-11}"/23 {25.5-28} cm from cast on edge.

Dividing Rnd: Bind off 6 sts, K 46 {52-58}, slip 46 {52-58} sts just worked onto st holder [Front], bind off 6 sts, K 46 {52-58} [Back].

ARMHOLE SHAPING
BACK

Row 1: Bind off 2 sts, purl across: 44 {50-56} sts.

Row 2 [Right side]: Bind off 2 sts, knit across: 42 {48-54} sts.

Rows 3-5: Repeat Rows 1 and 2 once, then repeat Row 1 once **more**: 36 {42-48} sts.

Row 6: Knit across.

Slip remaining sts onto st holder.

Instructions continued on page 110.

FRONT

With **wrong** side facing, slip 46 {52-58} sts from Front st holder onto needle.

Work same as Back.

YOKE

Holding one strand of Ecru Sport Weight yarn and 2 strands of Bulky Weight Novelty Eyelash yarn together, add on 18 sts **(Figs. 5a & b, page 580)**, place marker, with **right** side facing, knit 36 {42-48} sts from Back st holder, place marker, add on 18 sts, place marker, knit 36 {42-48} sts from Front st holder, place marker: 108 {120-132} sts.

Rnds 1-4: Knit around.

Rnd 5 [Decrease Rnd]: ★ Knit across to marker, slip marker, K2 tog **(Fig. 17, page 583)**, knit across to 2 sts before next marker, K2 tog, slip marker; repeat from ★ once **more**.

Rnds 6-11: Repeat Rnds 4 and 5, 3 times: 96 {108-120} sts.

Rnd 12: Knit around.

Rnds 13-15: Holding 3 strands of Bulky Weight Novelty Eyelash yarn together, knit around.

Rnds 16-20: With larger size needle, knit around.

Bind off all sts **loosely** in **knit**.

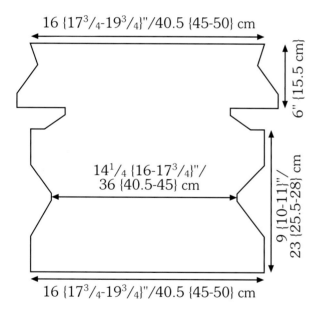

16 {17³/₄-19³/₄}"/40.5 {45-50} cm

6" {15.5 cm}

14¹/₄ {16-17³/₄}"/ 36 {40.5-45} cm

9 {10-11}"/ 23 {25.5-28} cm

16 {17³/₄-19³/₄}"/40.5 {45-50} cm

RIBBON SCARF

◖◼☐◗ EASY

Finished Size: 6" x 72" (15 cm x 183 cm)

MATERIALS

MEDIUM ❨4❩

Novelty Ribbon Yarn
[1³/₄ ounces, 110 yards
(50 grams, 100 meters) per ball]:
3 balls
Straight knitting needles, size 9 (5.5 mm) **or**
size needed for gauge

GAUGE: In Stockinette Stitch,
18 sts and 24 rows = 4" (10 cm)

SCARF

Cast on 27 sts.

Rows 1-12: Knit across.

Row 13: K1, [YO 3 times *(Fig. 16a, page 582)*, K1] across: 105 sts.

Row 14: K1, (drop 3 YO's of previous row, K1) across: 27 sts.

Rows 15 and 16: Knit across.

Repeat Rows 13-16 until Scarf measures approximately 70" (178 cm) from cast on edge, ending by Working Row 14.

Last 11 Rows: Knit across.

Bind off **loosely** in **knit**.

FELTED PURSE

■■□□ EASY

Finished Size: 10"w x 9"h (25.5 cm x 23 cm)

Finished size is only an approximate, as size will vary with the yarn choice as well as the amount of felting. The Purse will be oversized and will shrink down during the felting process.

MATERIALS

Super Bulky Weight Yarn **SUPER BULKY 6**
  [1³/₄ ounces, 55 yards
    (50 grams, 50 meters) per ball]:
  Variegated - 4 balls
Bulky Weight Novelty Eyelash Yarn **BULKY 5**
  [1³/₄ ounces, 60 yards
    (50 grams, 54 meters) per ball]:
  Blue - 1 ball
Double pointed knitting needles, size 13
  (9 mm) **or** size needed for gauge
Marker
Yarn needle

GAUGE: With Variegated, in Stockinette Stitch,
    10 sts and 14 rows = 4" (10 cm)

BODY

With Variegated, cast on 66 sts, divide sts evenly onto three double pointed needles **(see Knitting in the Round, page 579)**, place marker to mark beginning of rnd **(Fig. 1, page 578)**.

Holding one strand of Variegated, knit around until Body measures approximately 4" (10 cm) from cast on edge.

Holding one strand **each** of Blue with Variegated, purl around until Body measures approximately 6" (15 cm) from cast on edge, cut Blue.

With Variegated, knit around until Body measures approximately 10" (25.5 cm) from cast on edge.

Holding one strand **each** of Blue with Variegated, purl around until Body measures approximately 12" (30.5 cm) from cast on edge, cut Blue.

With Variegated, knit around until Body measures approximately 13" (33 cm) from cast on edge.

Bind off all sts in **knit.**

Sew bottom seam.

I-CORD HANDLE (Make 2)

Using double pointed needles, cast on 3 sts, ★ K3, do not **turn**, slide sts to opposite end of needle; repeat from ★ until cord measures 36" (91.5 cm) or desired length before felting.

Bind off all sts.

Using photo as a guide for placement, sew Handle to inside of Body.

Felt Purse (see Felting, below).

FELTING

The yarn used to make The Purse is Lion Brand Landscapes. Landscapes is a yarn made with an acrylic core (50%) that is wrapped with a wool wrap (50%). It does not felt exactly as 100% Wool felts and may need additional washing to fully felt.

Purse should be felted as follows:
Wash by machine on a long setting with hot water/cold water rinse with detergent with several pieces of clothing to agitate. Wash items several times if necessary with hot water depending on how quickly the project felts. To felt additionally, dry by machine on a regular setting until almost dry. Remove from dryer and lie flat to shape. Trim excess "fuzzies" with small scissors or sweater shaver.

Felting is not an exact science, the rate of felting varies depending on how it is washed, water temperature, detergent and amount of agitation.

BOBBLED SCARF & TAM

■■■□ INTERMEDIATE

MATERIALS

Medium/Worsted Weight
Brushed Acrylic Yarn: [MEDIUM 4]
  5 ounces, 385 yards (140 grams, 352 meters)
Straight knitting needles, sizes 6 (4.25 mm)
  and 9 (5.5 mm) **or** sizes needed for gauge
Yarn needle

GAUGE: With larger size needles in pattern,
    18 sts and 24 rows = 4" (10 cm)

STITCH GUIDE

> **BOBBLE**
> (K1, P1) twice **all** in next stitch, (**turn**, P4,
> **turn**, K4) twice, slip second, third, and fourth
> stitch on right needle over first stitch.

SCARF

With larger size needles, cast on 26 sts.

Row 1: K2, P2 tog **(Fig. 18, page 583)**, YO
(Fig. 16b, page 582), P2, (K5, P2 tog, YO, P2)
twice, K2.

Row 2 (Right side)**:** P2, K2 tog **(Fig. 17,
page 583)**, YO **(Fig. 16a, page 582)**, K2, (P5,
K2 tog, YO, K2) twice, P2.

Rows 3-7: Repeat Rows 1 and 2 twice, then
repeat Row 1 once **more**.

Row 8: P2, K2 tog, YO, K2, (P2, work Bobble,
P2, K2 tog, YO, K2) twice, P2.

Repeat Rows 1-8 until Scarf measures
approximately 41" (104 cm) from cast on edge,
ending by working Row 7.

Bind off all stitches in pattern.

TAM
RIBBING

With smaller size needles, cast on 90 sts **loosely**.

Work K1, P1 ribbing for 1" (2.5 cm) increasing
45 sts evenly spaced across last row: 135 sts.

CROWN

Change to larger size needles.

Row 1: P1, K 15, P2 tog **(Fig. 18, page 583)**,
YO **(Fig. 16b, page 582)**, (P2, K 15, P2 tog,
YO) across to last 3 sts, P3.

Row 2 (Right side)**:** K1, K2 tog **(Fig. 17,
page 583)**, YO **(Fig. 16a, page 582)**, K2,
P 15; repeat from ★ across to last st, K1.

Rows 3-7: Repeat Rows 1 and 2 twice, then
repeat Row 1 once **more.**

Row 8: K1, (K2 tog, YO, K2, P7, work Bobble,
P7) across to last st, K1.

Rows 9-18: Repeat Rows 1-8 once, then
repeat Rows 1 and 2 once **more.**

Row 19: P1, place marker **(Fig. 1, page 578)**,
K 15, place marker, P2 tog, YO, (P2, place
marker, K 15, place marker, P2 tog, YO) across
to last 3 sts, P3.

SHAPING
Row 1: K1, (K2 tog, YO, K2, P2 tog, purl to
within 2 sts of marker, P2 tog) across to last st,
K1: 121 sts.

Row 2: P1, knit to marker, P2 tog, YO, (P2,
knit to marker, P2 tog, YO) across to last 3 sts,
P3.

Row 3: K1, (K2 tog, YO, K2, purl to marker)
across to last st, K1.

Row 4: P1, knit to marker, P2 tog, YO, (P2,
knit to marker, P2 tog, YO) across to last 3 sts,
P3.

Row 5: K1, (K2 tog, YO, K2, P2 tog, P4, work Bobble, P4, P2 tog) across to last st, K1: 107 sts.

Rows 6-8: Repeat Rows 2-4.

Rows 9-12: Repeat Rows 1-4: 93 sts.

Row 13: K1, (K2 tog, YO, K2, P2 tog, P2, work Bobble, P2, P2 tog) across to last st, K1: 79 sts.

Rows 14-16: Repeat Rows 2-4.

Rows 17-20: Repeat Rows 1-4: 65 sts.

Row 21: K1, (K2 tog, YO, K2, P2 tog, work Bobble, P2 tog) across to last st, K1: 51 sts.

Rows 22-24: Repeat Rows 2-4.

Row 25: K1, ★ K2 tog, YO, K2, P3 tog *(Fig. 24, page 584)*; repeat from ★ across to last st, K1: 37 sts.

Row 26: Knit across.

Row 27: P2 tog across to last st, P1: 19 sts.

Row 28: Knit across.

Row 29: P2 tog across to last st, P1; cut yarn leaving an 18" (45.5 cm) end: 10 sts.

Thread yarn needle with end and weave through sts of last row, gathering **tightly** to close. With same end, weave seam *(Fig. 36, page 587)* and secure.

Designs by Brooke Shellflower.

LONG & LUSH SCARF

Finished Size: 4" x 73" (10 cm x 185.5 cm)

■■□□ **EASY**

MATERIALS

Bernat® Bling Bling **BULKY 5**
[1³/₄ ounces, 90 yards
(50 grams, 82 meters) per ball]:
#65040 Night Club - 4 balls
29" (73.5 cm) Circular knitting needle,
size 10¹/₂ (6.5 mm) **or** size needed for
gauge
Crochet hook for fringe

Scarf is worked lengthwise holding two strands
of yarn together throughout.

GAUGE: In Stockinette Stitch,
12 sts and 16 rows = 4" (10 cm)

SCARF

Cast on 220 sts.

Beginning with a **purl** row, work in Stockinette
Stitch for 16 rows (purl one row, knit one row).

Bind off all sts in **purl**.

Holding two strands of yarn together, each 18"
(45.5 cm) long, add fringe in end of each row
across short edges of Scarf *(Figs. 37a & b,
page 588)*.

SHOULDER PURSE

Finished Size: 8" tall (20.5 cm)

◧■□□ EASY

MATERIALS

Bernat® Bling Bling [BULKY 5]
[1³/₄ ounces, 90 yards
(50 grams, 82 meters) per ball]:
  #65530 Moulin Rouge - 2 balls
  #65415 Twinkle Toes - 2 balls
Double pointed needles, size 11 (5 mm) **or**
  size needed for gauge
Yarn needle
Optional lining: 12" x 24" (30.5 cm x 61 cm)
  fabric, sewing needle, and thread

Purse is worked holding two strands of yarn
together throughout.

GAUGE: In Stockinette Stitch,
        11 sts = 4" (10 cm)

PURSE

With Moulin Rouge, cast on 40 sts, place marker
to mark beginning of rnd *(see Markers and
Knitting in the Round, pages 578 & 579)*.

Knit each round until Purse measures
approximately 4" (10 cm) from cast on edge.

With Twinkle Toes, knit each round until Purse
measures approximately 6" (15 cm) from cast
on edge.

Decrease Rnd: Knit around decreasing 2 sts
evenly spaced *(see Decreasing Evenly in a
Round and Fig. 17, page 583)*: 38 sts.

Next Rnd: Knit around.

Next 6 Rnds: Repeat last 2 rounds, 3 times:
32 sts.

Bind off remaining sts in **knit**.

FINISHING

With **right** side together, sew cast on edge
closed.

I-CORD STRAP

With Twinkle Toes and leaving a long end for
sewing, cast on 3 sts.

★ K3, do **not** turn; slide sts to opposite end of
needle; repeat from ★ until Strap measures
approximately 24" (61 cm) **or** to desired length.

Bind off all sts.

Cut yarn, leaving a long end for sewing.

Thread yarn needle with one long end and sew
Strap to inside of Purse at one side.

Repeat for other end.

Optional Lining: Using Purse for pattern, cut
2 pieces of fabric, adding ¹/₂" (13 mm) along the
top edge and ⁵/₈" (16 mm) seam allowance
along remaining edges. With right sides together,
sew side and bottom seams. Fold top edge ¹/₄"
(7 mm) to wrong side twice and sew in place.
With wrong sides together, sew Lining inside
Purse along top edge.

CAPELET

Finished Size: One Size Fits Most

■■□□ EASY

MATERIALS
Bernat® Bling Bling
BULKY 5
[1³/₄ ounces, 90 yards
(50 grams, 82 meters) per ball]:
   #65208 Sassy Sparkle - 6 balls
Straight knitting needles, size 15 (10 mm) **or**
size needed for gauge
Yarn needle

Capelet is worked holding two strands of yarn
together throughout.

GAUGE: In pattern, 12 sts = 5 (12.75 cm)

CAPELET
Cast on 34 sts.

Rows 1-5: Knit across.

Row 6: K1, ★ YO *(Fig. 16c, page 582)*,
P2 tog *(Fig. 18, page 583)*; repeat from ★
across to last st, K1.

Repeat Row 6 until Capelet measures
approximately 34" (86.5 cm) from cast on edge
or to desired length.

Last 5 Rows: Knit across.

Bind off all sts in **knit.**

Cut yarn, leaving a long end for sewing.

Thread yarn needle with long end. Matching sts,
sew cast on edge to bound off edge (Front).

BAND
Cast on 12 sts.

Work in Garter Stitch (knit each row) until Band
measures approximately 6" (15 cm) from cast on
edge.

Bind off all sts in **knit.**

Cut yarn, leaving a long end for sewing.

FINISHING
With Front of Capelet facing, wrap Band around
seam. Matching sts, sew cast on edge to bound
off edge and tack in place on Capelet.

SHAWL

Finished Size: One Size Fits Most

■■□□ EASY

MATERIALS

Bernat® Bling Bling
[1³/₄ ounces, 90 yards
(50 grams, 82 meters) per ball]:
    #65244 Spotlight Sage - 6 balls
29" (73.5 cm) Circular knitting needle,
size 17 (12.75 mm) **or** size needed
for gauge

GAUGE: In pattern,
    13 sts = 4" (10 cm)
    12 rows = 5" (12.5 cm)

SHAWL
Cast on 3 sts.

Row 1 (Right side)**:** P1, [YO *(Fig. 16b, page 582)*, P1] twice: 5 sts.

Row 2: K1, YO *(Fig. 16a, page 582)*, knit across to last st, YO, K1: 7 sts.

Row 3: P1, YO, purl across to last st, YO, P1: 9 sts.

Rows 4-95: Repeat Rows 2 and 3, 46 times: 193 sts.

Bind off all sts **loosely** in **knit**.

Note: Finished shape is a 90-degree triangle.

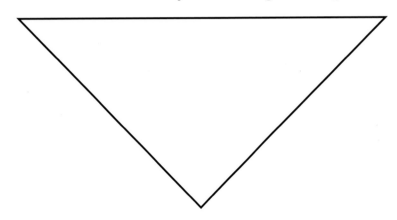

GARTER RIDGE TUNIC

◼︎◼︎◼︎◻︎ INTERMEDIATE

Size	Finished Chest Measurement
X-Small	37$^1/_4$" (94.5 cm)
Small	41" (104 cm)
Medium	45$^1/_4$" (115 cm)
Large	49$^3/_4$" (126.5 cm)
X-Large	53$^1/_4$" (135.5 cm)

MATERIALS

Medium/Worsted Weight Yarn: [MEDIUM 4]

Ounces	{22-23$^1/_2$}{26-27$^1/_2$-29}
Yards	{1,025-1,095}{1,210-1,280-1,350}
Grams	{620-670}{740-780-820}
Meters	{937-1,001}{1,106-1,170-1,234}

Straight knitting needles, sizes 6 (4 mm) **and**
 8 (5 mm) **or** sizes needed for gauge
24" (61 cm) Circular needle, size 6 (4 mm)
Markers
Yarn needle

GAUGE: With larger size needles,
 in Stockinette Stitch,
 18 sts and 24 rows = 4" (10 cm)

Size Note: Instructions are written with sizes X-Small and Small in the first set of braces { } and sizes Medium, Large, and X-Large in the second set of braces. Instructions will be easier to read if you circle all the numbers pertaining to your size. If only one number is given, it applies to all sizes.

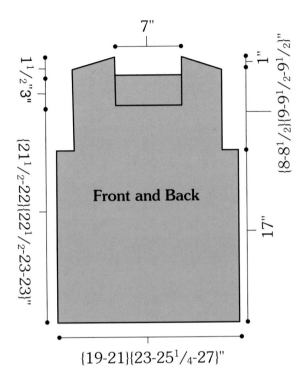

7"

1$^1/_2$"
3"
1"

{8-8$^1/_2$}{9-9$^1/_2$-9$^1/_2$}"

{21$^1/_2$-22}{22$^1/_2$-23-23}"

17"

Front and Back

{19-21}{23-25$^1/_4$-27}"

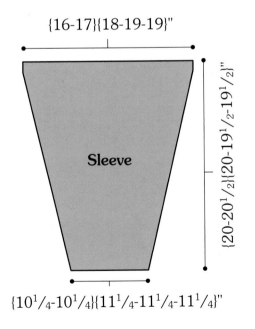

{16-17}{18-19-19}"

{20-20$^1/_2$}{20-19$^1/_2$-19$^1/_2$}"

Sleeve

{10$^1/_4$-10$^1/_4$}{11$^1/_4$-11$^1/_4$-11$^1/_4$}"

Note: Sweater includes two edge stitches.

Instructions begin on page 128.

BACK

With smaller size straight needles, cast on {78-85}{94-103-110} sts.

Rows 1-9: Knit across.

Row 10: Knit across increasing {8-9}{10-11-12} sts evenly spaced using M1 *(see Increasing Evenly Across A Row, page 581 and Figs. 14a & b, page 582)*: {86-94}{104-114-122} sts.

Change to larger size needles.

Row 11 (Right side)**:** Knit across.

Row 12: K6, purl across to last 6 sts, K6.

Repeat Rows 11 and 12 until piece measures approximately 4$^1/_2$" (11.5 cm) from cast on edge, ending by working Row 12.

Beginning with a **knit** row, work in Stockinette Stitch until piece measures approximately {12-12$^1/_2$}{13-13$^1/_2$-13$^1/_2$}"/ {30.5-32}{33-34.5-34.5} cm from cast on edge, ending by working a **purl** row.

GARTER RIDGE

Row 1 (Right side)**:** Purl across.

Row 2: Purl across.

Row 3: Knit across.

Row 4: Purl across.

Repeat Rows 1-4 for pattern until piece measures approximately 17" (43 cm) from cast on edge, ending by working Row 2.

ARMHOLE SHAPING

Row 1: Bind off {7-10}{12-14-16} sts, knit across: {79-84}{92-100-106} sts.

Row 2: Bind off {7-10}{12-14-16} sts, purl across: {72-74}{80-86-90} sts.

Repeat Rows 1-4 of Garter Ridge pattern until piece measures approximately {19-19$^1/_2$}{20-20$^1/_2$-20$^1/_2$}"/ {48.5-49.5}{51-52-52} cm from cast on edge, ending by working a **wrong** side row.

Beginning with a **knit** row, work in Stockinette Stitch until piece measures approximately {24$^1/_2$-25}{25$^1/_2$-26-26}"/ {62-63.5}{65-66-66} cm from cast on edge, ending by working a **knit** row.

NECK SHAPING

Note: Both sides of Neck are worked at the same time, using separate yarn for **each** side.

Row 1: Purl {20-21}{24-27-29} sts; with second yarn, bind off next 32 sts, purl across: {20-21}{24-27-29} sts **each** side.

Work even until piece measures approximately {25-25$^1/_2$}{26-26$^1/_2$-26 $^1/_2$}"/ {63.5-65}{66-67.5-67.5} cm from cast on edge, ending by working a **purl** row.

SHOULDER SHAPING

Rows 1-4: Bind off {7-7}{8-9-10} sts, work across; with second yarn, work across: {6-7}{8-9-9} sts **each** side.

Row 5: Bind off remaining sts on first side; with second yarn, knit across.

Bind off remaining sts in **purl**.

FRONT

Work same as Back until piece measures approximately {21¹/₂-22}{22¹/₂-23-23}"/ {54.5-56}{57-58.5-58.5} cm from cast on edge, ending by working a **purl** row: {72-74}{80-86-90} sts.

NECK SHAPING

Note: Both sides of Neck are worked at the same time, using separate yarn for **each** side.

Row 1: Knit {20-21}{24-27-29} sts; with second yarn, bind off next 32 sts, knit across: {20-21}{24-27-29} sts **each** side.

Complete same as Back.

SLEEVE (Make 2)

With smaller size straight needles, cast on {42-42}{46-46-46} sts.

Rows 1-9: Knit across.

Row 10: Knit across increasing {4-4}{5-5-5} sts evenly spaced across using M1: {46-46}{51-51-51} sts.

Change to larger size needles.

Beginning with a **purl** row, work in Stockinette Stitch increasing one stitch at **each** edge **(Figs. 10a & b, page 581)**, every fourth row, {0-0}{0-8-8} times **(see Zeros, page 577)**; then increase every sixth row, {3-12}{14-9-9} times; then increase every eighth row, {10-3}{1-0-0} time(s): {72-76}{81-85-85} sts.

Work even until Sleeve measures approximately {20-20¹/₂}{20-19¹/₂-19¹/₂}"/ {51-52}{51-49.5-49.5} cm from cast on edge, ending by working a **purl** row.

Bind off all sts in **knit**.

FINISHING

Sew shoulder seams.

NECKBAND

With **right** side facing and using circular needle, pick up one st in left shoulder seam **(Figs. 34a & b, page 586)**, pick up 18 sts evenly spaced along left Front Neck edge, place marker **(see Markers, page 578)**, pick up 32 sts across Front Neck edge, place marker, pick up 18 sts evenly spaced along right Front Neck edge, pick up one st in shoulder seam, pick up 6 sts evenly spaced along right Back Neck edge, place marker, pick up 32 sts across Back Neck edge, place marker, pick up 6 sts evenly spaced along left Back Neck edge, place marker to mark beginning of rnd: 114 sts.

Rnd 1: ★ Purl across to next marker, K1, purl across to within one st of next marker, K1; repeat from ★ once **more**, purl across.

Rnd 2 (Decrease row): ★ Knit across to within 2 sts of next marker, SSK **(Figs. 21a-c, page 584)**, K1, K2 tog **(Fig. 17, page 583)**, knit across to within 3 sts of next marker, SSK, K1, K2 tog; repeat from ★ once **more**, knit across: 106 sts.

Rnds 3-9: Repeat Rnds 1 and 2, 3 times; then repeat Rnd 1 once **more**: 82 sts.

Bind off all sts **loosely** in **knit**.

Sew Sleeves to Tunic, matching center of last row on Sleeve to shoulder seam, and sewing top of Sleeve along Armhole edge and sides of Sleeve to bound off edges **(see Sewing in Sleeves, page 587)**.

Weave underarm and side in one continuous seam **(Fig. 36, page 587)**, leaving lower 3¹/₂" (9 cm) of Tunic unsewn for side slits.

Design by Melissa Leapman.

REFINED-RIBBING PULLOVER

■■■□ INTERMEDIATE

Size	Finished Chest Measurement
X-Small	37$\frac{1}{4}$" (94.5 cm)
Small	41$\frac{1}{4}$" (105 cm)
Medium	45$\frac{1}{4}$" (115 cm)
Large	49$\frac{1}{4}$" (125 cm)
X-Large	53$\frac{1}{4}$" (135.5 cm)

Size Note: Instructions are written with sizes X-Small and Small in the first set of braces { } and sizes Medium, Large, and X-Large in the second set of braces. Instructions will be easier to read if you circle all the numbers pertaining to your size. If only one number is given, it applies to all sizes.

MATERIALS

Medium/Worsted Weight Yarn: MEDIUM ④

Ounces {24-25$\frac{1}{2}$}{27-29-31}
Yards {1,120-1,190}{1,255-1,350-1,445}
Grams {680-720}{770-820-880}
Meters {1,024-1,088}{1,148-1,234-1,321}

Straight knitting needles, size 8 (5 mm) **or** size needed for gauge

16" (40.5 cm) Circular needle, size 8 (5 mm)

Marker

Yarn needle

GAUGE: In pattern, 18 sts and 24 rows = 4" (10 cm)

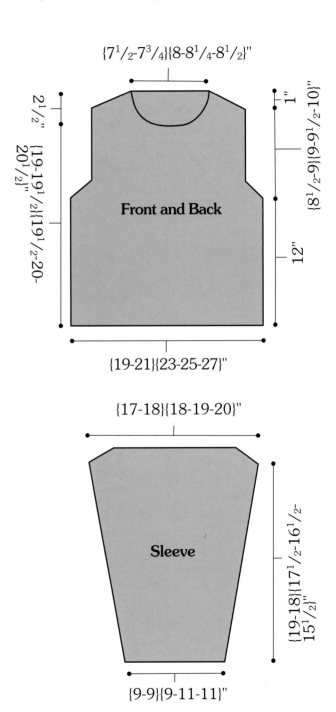

{7$\frac{1}{2}$-7$\frac{3}{4}$}{8-8$\frac{1}{4}$-8$\frac{1}{2}$}"

2$\frac{1}{2}$"

1"

{8$\frac{1}{2}$-9}{9-9$\frac{1}{2}$-10}"

{19-19$\frac{1}{2}$}{19$\frac{1}{2}$-20-20$\frac{1}{2}$}"

Front and Back

12"

{19-21}{23-25-27}"

{17-18}{18-19-20}"

Sleeve

{19-18}{17$\frac{1}{2}$-16$\frac{1}{2}$-15$\frac{1}{2}$}"

{9-9}{9-11-11}"

Note: Sweater includes two edge stitches.

Instructions begin on page 132.

BACK

Cast on {86-95}{104-113-122} sts.

Row 1: (P1, K1) twice, (P6, K1, P1, K1) across to last st, P1.

Row 2 (Right side)**:** P1, (K1, P1) twice, ★ K4, P1, (K1, P1) twice; repeat from ★ across.

Repeat Rows 1 and 2 for pattern until piece measures approximately 12" (30.5 cm) from cast on edge, ending by working a **wrong** side row.

ARMHOLE SHAPING

Note: Maintain established pattern throughout.

Rows 1-9: Decrease *(see Decreases, pages 583 & 584)*, work across to last 2 sts, decrease: {68-77}{86-95-104} sts.

Work even until piece measures approximately {20¹/₂-21}{21-21¹/₂-22}"/ {52-53.5}{53.5-54.5-56} cm from cast on edge, ending by working a **wrong** side row.

SHOULDER SHAPING

Rows 1-4: Bind off {6-7}{8-10-11} sts, work across: {44-49}{54-55-60} sts.

Rows 5 and 6: Bind off {5-7}{9-9-11} sts, work across: {34-35}{36-37-38} sts.

Bind off remaining sts in pattern.

FRONT

Work same as Back until Front measures approximately {19-19¹/₂}{19¹/₂-20-20¹/₂}"/ {48.5-49.5}{49.5-51-52} cm from cast on edge, ending by working a **wrong** side row: {68-77}{86-95-104} sts.

NECK SHAPING

Note: Both sides of Neck are worked at the same time, using separate yarn for **each** side.

Row 1: Work across {27-31}{35-39-43} sts; with second yarn, bind off next {14-15}{16-17-18} sts, work across: {27-31}{35-39-43} sts **each** side.

Rows 2 and 3: Work across; with second yarn, bind off 3 sts, work across: {24-28}{32-36-40} sts **each** side.

Rows 4-7: Work across; with second yarn, bind off 2 sts, work across: {20-24}{28-32-36} sts **each** side.

Rows 8-10: Work across to within 2 sts of Neck edge, decrease; with second yarn, decrease, work across: {17-21}{25-29-33} sts **each** side.

Work even until Front measures same as Back to Shoulder Shaping, ending by working a **wrong** side row.

SHOULDER SHAPING

Rows 1-4: Bind off {6-7}{8-10-11} sts, work across; with second yarn, work across: {5-7}{9-9-11} sts **each** side.

Row 5: Bind off remaining sts on first side; with second yarn, work across.

Bind off remaining sts in pattern.

SLEEVE (Make 2)
BODY

Cast on {41-41}{41-50-50} sts.

Row 1: (P1, K1) twice, (P6, K1, P1, K1) across to last st, P1.

Row 2 (Right side)**:** P1, (K1, P1) twice, ★ K4, P1, (K1, P1) twice; repeat from ★ across.

Repeating Rows 1 and 2 for pattern and working new stitches in pattern, increase one stitch at **each** edge **(see Knit and Purl Increases, page 581)**, every fourth row, {0-9}{10-7-16} times **(see Zeros, page 577)**; then increase every sixth row, {18-11}{10-11-4} times: {77-81}{81-86-90} sts.

Work even until Sleeve measures approximately {19-18}{17^1/$_2$-16^1/$_2$-15^1/$_2$}"/ {48.5-45.5}{44.5-42-39.5} cm from cast on edge, ending by working a **wrong** side row.

SLEEVE SHAPING

Row 1 (Decrease row)**:** Decrease, work across to last 2 sts, decrease: {75-79}{79-84-88} sts.

Row 2: Work across.

Rows 3-10: Repeat Rows 1 and 2, 4 times: {67-71}{71-76-80} sts.

Rows 11 and 12: Decrease, work across to last 2 sts, decrease: {63-67}{67-72-76} sts.

Bind off remaining sts in pattern.

FINISHING

Sew shoulder seams.

NECKBAND

With **right** side facing and using circular needle, pick up 16 sts evenly spaced along left Front Neck edge **(Figs. 34a & b, page 586)**, pick up {14-15}{16-17-18} sts across Front Neck edge, pick up 16 sts evenly spaced along right Front Neck edge, pick up {34-35}{36-37-38} sts across Back neck edge, place marker to mark beginning of rnd **(see Markers, page 578)**: {80-82}{84-86-88} sts.

Rnds 1-9: Knit around.

Bind off all sts **loosely** in **knit**.

Sew Sleeves to Pullover, matching center of last row on Sleeve Shaping to shoulder seam.

Weave underarm and side in one continuous seam **(Fig. 36, page 587)**.

Design by Melissa Leapman.

RUFFLED-HEM CARDIGAN

◼◼◼◻ **INTERMEDIATE**

Size	Finished Chest Measurement
X-Small	37$\frac{1}{2}$" (95.5 cm)
Small	42" (106.5 cm)
Medium	46$\frac{1}{2}$" (118 cm)
Large	51" (129.5 cm)
X-Large	55$\frac{1}{2}$" (141 cm)

Size Note: Instructions are written with sizes X-Small and Small in the first set of braces { } and sizes Medium, Large, and X-Large in the second set of braces. Instructions will be easier to read if you circle all the numbers pertaining to your size. If only one number is given, it applies to all sizes.

MATERIALS

Medium/Worsted Weight Yarn: **4**
  Ounces {23$\frac{3}{4}$-25$\frac{3}{4}$}{28-30-31$\frac{1}{2}$}
  Yards   {1,105-1,200}{1,305-1,395-1,465}
  Grams   {670-730}{800-850-890}
  Meters {1,010-1,097}{1,193-1,276-1,340}
Straight knitting needles, size 8 (5 mm) **or** size needed for gauge
24" (61 cm) Circular needle, size 7 (4.5 mm)
Markers
Yarn needle
Sewing needle and thread
$\frac{3}{4}$" (19 mm) Buttons - {6-6}{7-7-7}

GAUGE: With larger size needles,
    in Stockinette Stitch,
    18 sts and 24 rows = 4" (10 cm)

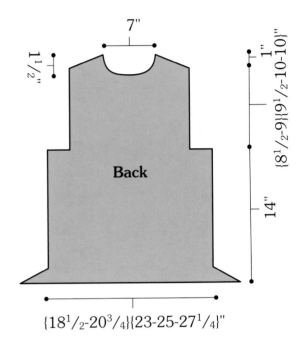

Back

7"
1$\frac{1}{2}$"
1"
{8$\frac{1}{2}$-9}{9$\frac{1}{2}$-10-10}"
14"

{18$\frac{1}{2}$-20$\frac{3}{4}$}{23-25-27$\frac{1}{4}$}"

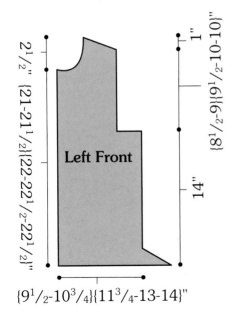

Left Front

2$\frac{1}{2}$"
{21-21$\frac{1}{2}$}{22-22$\frac{1}{2}$-22$\frac{1}{2}$}"
1"
{8$\frac{1}{2}$-9}{9$\frac{1}{2}$-10-10}"
14"

{9$\frac{1}{2}$-10$\frac{3}{4}$}{11$\frac{3}{4}$-13-14}"

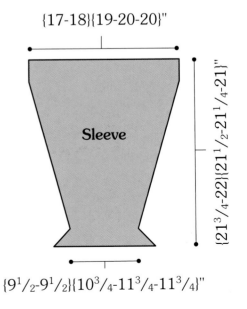

Sleeve

{17-18}{19-20-20}"
{21$\frac{3}{4}$-22}{21$\frac{1}{2}$-21$\frac{1}{4}$-21}"

{9$\frac{1}{2}$-9$\frac{1}{2}$}{10$\frac{3}{4}$-11$\frac{3}{4}$-11$\frac{3}{4}$}"

Note: Sweater includes two edge stitches.

Instructions begin on page 136.

BACK
RUFFLE

With straight needles,
cast on {211-237}{263-289-315} sts.

Row 1 (Right side)**:** P3, (K 10, P3) across.

Row 2: K3, (P 10, K3) across.

Row 3: P3, ★ SSK *(Figs. 21a-c, page 584)*, K6, K2 tog *(Fig. 17, page 583)*, P3; repeat from ★ across: {179-201}{223-245-267} sts.

Row 4: K3, (P8, K3) across.

Row 5: P3, (SSK, K4, K2 tog, P3) across: {147-165}{183-201-219} sts.

Row 6: K3, (P6, K3) across.

Row 7: P3, (SSK, K2, K2 tog, P3) across: {115-129}{143-157-171} sts.

Row 8: K3, (P4, K3) across.

Row 9: P3, (SSK, K2 tog, P3) across: {83-93}{103-113-123} sts.

Rows 10 and 11: Knit across.

BODY

Beginning with a **purl** row, work in Stockinette Stitch until piece measures approximately 14" (35.5 cm) from cast on edge, ending by working a **purl** row.

ARMHOLE SHAPING

Note: Maintain established pattern throughout.

Rows 1 and 2: Bind off {9-13}{15-17-21} sts, work across: {65-67}{73-79-81} sts.

Work even until piece measures approximately {22-22^1/$_2$}{23-23^1/$_2$-23^1/$_2$}"/ {56-57}{58.5-59.5-59.5} cm from cast on edge, ending by working a **knit** row.

NECK SHAPING

Note: Both sides of Neck are worked at the same time, using separate yarn for **each** side.

Row 1: Purl {18-19}{22-25-26} sts; with second yarn, bind off next 29 sts, purl across: {18-19}{22-25-26} sts **each** side.

Row 2: Knit across to within 2 sts of Neck edge, K2 tog; with second yarn, SSK, knit across: {17-18}{21-24-25} sts **each** side.

Work even until piece measures approximately {22^1/$_2$-23}{23^1/$_2$-24-24}"/ {57-58.5}{59.5-61-61} cm from cast on edge, ending by working a **purl** row.

SHOULDER SHAPING

Rows 1-4: Bind off {6-6}{7-8-8} sts, work across; with second yarn, work across: {5-6}{7-8-9} sts **each** side.

Row 5: Bind off remaining sts on first side; with second yarn, knit across.

Bind off remaining sts in **purl**.

LEFT FRONT

With straight needles,
cast on {107-120}{133-146-159} sts.

Work same as Back until piece measures approximately 14" (35.5 cm) from cast on edge, ending by working a **purl** row: {43-48}{53-58-63} sts.

ARMHOLE SHAPING

Row 1: Bind off {9-13}{15-17-21} sts, knit across: {34-35}{38-41-42} sts.

Work even until Left Front measures approximately {21-21$\frac{1}{2}$}{22-22$\frac{1}{2}$-22$\frac{1}{2}$}"/ {53.5-54.5}{56-57-57} cm from cast on edge, ending by working a **knit** row.

NECK SHAPING

Row 1: Bind off 7 sts, purl across: {27-28}{31-34-35} sts.

Row 2: Knit across.

Row 3: Bind off 4 sts, purl across: {23-24}{27-30-31} sts.

Row 4: Knit across.

Row 5: Bind off 3 sts, purl across: {20-21}{24-27-28} sts.

Row 6: Knit across.

Row 7: Bind off 2 sts, purl across: {18-19}{22-25-26} sts.

Row 8: Knit across to last 2 sts, K2 tog: {17-18}{21-24-25} sts.

Work even until Left Front measures same as Back to Shoulder Shaping, ending by working a **purl** row.

SHOULDER SHAPING

Row 1: Bind off {6-6}{7-8-8} sts, knit across: {11-12}{14-16-17} sts.

Row 2: Purl across.

Row 3: Bind off {6-6}{7-8-8} sts, knit across: {5-6}{7-8-9} sts.

Row 4: Purl across.

Bind off remaining sts in **knit**.

RIGHT FRONT

With straight needles,
cast on {107-120}{133-146-159} sts.

Work same as Back until piece measures approximately 14" (35.5 cm) from cast on edge, ending by working a **knit** row: {43-48}{53-58-63} sts.

ARMHOLE SHAPING

Row 1: Bind off {9-13}{15-17-21} sts, purl across: {34-35}{38-41-42} sts.

Work even until Right Front measures approximately {21-21$\frac{1}{2}$}{22-22$\frac{1}{2}$-22$\frac{1}{2}$}"/ {53.5-54.5}{56-57-57} cm from cast on edge, ending by working a **purl** row.

Instructions continued on page 138.

NECK SHAPING

Row 1: Bind off 7 sts, knit across: {27-28}{31-34-35} sts.

Row 2: Purl across.

Row 3: Bind off 4 sts, knit across: {23-24}{27-30-31} sts.

Row 4: Purl across.

Row 5: Bind off 3 sts, knit across: {20-21}{24-27-28} sts.

Row 6: Purl across.

Row 7: Bind off 2 sts, knit across: {18-19}{22-25-26} sts.

Row 8: Purl across to last 2 sts, P2 tog *(Fig. 18, page 583)*: {17-18}{21-24-25} sts.

Work even until Right Front measures same as Back to Shoulder Shaping, ending by working a **knit** row.

SHOULDER SHAPING

Row 1: Bind off {6-6}{7-8-8} sts, purl across: {11-12}{14-16-17} sts.

Row 2: Knit across.

Row 3: Bind off {6-6}{7-8-8} sts, purl across: {5-6}{7-8-9} sts.

Row 4: Knit across.

Bind off remaining sts in **purl**.

SLEEVE (Make 2)

With straight needles, cast on {107-107}{120-133-133} sts.

Rows 1-11: Work same as Back: {43-43}{48-53-53} sts.

Row 12: Purl across.

Row 13: Knit across.

Row 14: Purl across.

Row 15 (Increase row)**:** Increase *(Figs. 10a & b, page 581)*, knit across to last st, increase: {45-45}{50-55-55} sts.

Continue to increase one stitch at **each** edge, every fourth row, {0-8}{11-13-16} times **more** *(see Zeros, page 577)*; then increase every sixth row, {16-10}{7-5-2} times: {77-81}{86-91-91} sts.

Work even until Sleeve measures approximately {21³/₄-22}{21¹/₂-21¹/₄-21}"/ {55-56}{54.5-54-53.5} cm from cast on edge, ending by working a **purl** row.

Bind off all sts in **knit**.

FINISHING

Sew shoulder seams.

NECKBAND

With **right** side facing and using circular needle, pick up 24 sts evenly spaced along Right Front Neck edge *(Figs. 34a & b, page 586)*, pick up one st in shoulder seam, pick 44 sts evenly spaced along Back Neck edge, pick up one st in shoulder seam, pick up 24 sts evenly spaced along Left Front Neck edge: 94 sts.

Knit each row until Neckband measures approximately 1" (2.5 cm).

Bind off all sts in **knit**.

BUTTON BAND

With **right** side facing and using circular needle, pick up {107-110}{113-116-116} sts evenly spaced across Neckband and Left Front edge, ending at Row 11 of Ruffle.

Knit each row until Button Band measures approximately 1" (2.5 cm).

Bind off all sts in **knit**.

BUTTONHOLE BAND

With **right** side facing and using circular needle, pick up {107-110}{113-116-116} sts evenly spaced across Right Front edge and Neckband, beginning at Row 11 of Ruffle.

Knit each row until Buttonhole Band measures approximately $^1/_2$" (12 mm).

Mark placement of buttonholes on Right Front, placing the first marker $^1/_2$" (12 mm) from bottom edge of Buttonhole Band and placing the last marker $^1/_2$" (12 mm) from top edge; then evenly space {4-4}{5-5-5} more markers for remaining buttonholes.

Buttonhole Row: ★ Knit across to next marker, bind off next 2 sts (buttonhole); repeat from ★ {5-5}{6-6-6} times **more**, knit across.

Next Row: ★ Knit across to bound off sts, **turn**; add on 2 sts *(Figs. 5a & b, page 580)*, **turn**; repeat from ★ {5-5}{6-6-6} times **more**, knit across.

Work even until Buttonhole Band measures approximately 1" (2.5 cm).

Bind off all sts in **knit**.

Sew Sleeves to Cardigan, matching center of last row on Sleeve to shoulder seam, and sewing top of Sleeve along Armhole edge and sides of Sleeve to bound off edges *(see Sewing in Sleeves, page 587)*.

Weave underarm and side in one continuous seam *(Fig. 36, page 587)*.

Sew buttons to Button Band opposite buttonholes.

Design by Melissa Leapman.

DRESSY JACKET

■■■□ INTERMEDIATE

Also shown on page 143.

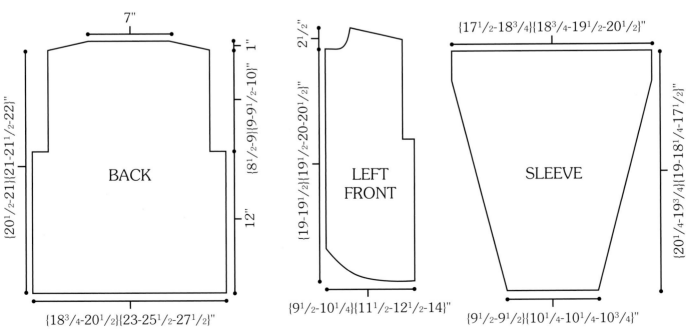

BACK

7"

1"

{8¹/₂-9}{9-9¹/₂-10}"

12"

{20¹/₂-21}{21-21¹/₂-22}"

{18³/₄-20¹/₂}{23-25¹/₂-27¹/₂}"

LEFT FRONT

2¹/₂"

{19-19¹/₂}{19¹/₂-20-20¹/₂}"

{9¹/₂-10¹/₄}{11¹/₂-12¹/₂-14}"

SLEEVE

{17¹/₂-18³/₄}{18³/₄-19¹/₂-20¹/₂}"

{20¹/₄-19³/₄}{19-18¹/₄-17¹/₂}"

{9¹/₂-9¹/₂}{10¹/₄-10¹/₄-10³/₄}"

Note: Sweater includes two edge stitches.

Size	Finished Chest Measurement
Small	36^1/$_2$" (92.5 cm)
Medium	39^1/$_2$" (100.5 cm)
Large	44^1/$_2$" (113 cm)
X-Large	49^1/$_2$" (125.5 cm)
XX-Large	54" (137 cm)

Size Note: Instructions are written with sizes Small and Medium in the first set of braces, and with sizes Large, X-Large, and XX-Large in the second set of braces { }. Instructions will be easier to read if you circle all the numbers pertaining to your size. If only one number is given, it applies to all sizes.

MATERIALS
Bulky Weight Yarn: **5** BULKY
    Ounces {26-28}{30-32-35}
    Yards {800-865}{925-985-1,080}
    Grams {740-800}{850-910-990}
    Meters {731.5-791}{846-900.5-987.5}
Straight knitting needles, size 10 (6 mm) **or** size needed for gauge
Crochet hook, size K (6.5 mm)
Yarn needle
Sewing needle and thread
1" (25 mm) Button - 1

GAUGE: In Seed Stitch,
    13 sts and 26 rows = 4" (10 cm)
    In Stockinette Stitch,
    14 sts and 20 rows = 4" (10 cm)

BACK
Cast on {61-67}{75-83-89} sts.

Row 1 (Right side)**:** K1, (P1, K1) across.

Repeat Row 1 (Seed Stitch) until Back measures approximately 12" (30.5 cm) from cast on edge, ending by working a **wrong** side row.

ARMHOLE SHAPING
Maintain established pattern throughout.

Rows 1 and 2: Bind off {4-4}{5-5-6} sts, work across in Seed Stitch: {53-59}{65-73-77} sts.

Work even until Back measures approximately {20^1/$_2$-21}{21-21^1/$_2$-22}"/{52-53.5}{53.5-54.5-56} cm from cast on edge, ending by working a **wrong** side row.

SHOULDER SHAPING
Rows 1-4: Bind off {5-6}{7-8-9} sts, work across in Seed Stitch: {33-35}{37-41-41} sts.

Rows 5 and 6: Bind off {5-6}{7-9-9} sts, work across in Seed Stitch: 23 sts.

Bind off remaining sts.

LEFT FRONT
Cast on {17-19}{23-27-31} sts.

Row 1 (Right side)**:** P1, (K1, P1) across.

Row 2 (Increase row)**:** Add on 3 sts **(Figs. 5a & b, page 580)**, work across in Seed Stitch: {20-22}{26-30-34} sts.

Row 3: Work across in Seed Stitch.

Rows 4 and 5: Repeat Rows 2 and 3: {23-25}{29-33-37} sts.

Row 6 (Increase row)**:** Add on 2 sts, work across in Seed Stitch: {25-27}{31-35-39} sts.

Row 7: Work across in Seed Stitch.

Rows 8-10: Repeat Rows 6 and 7 once, then repeat Row 6 once **more**: {29-31}{35-39-43} sts.

Rows 11-13: Work across in Seed Stitch.

Row 14 (Increase row)**:** Add on one st, work across in Seed Stitch: {30-32}{36-40-44} sts.

Instructions continued on page 142.

Rows 15-18: Repeat Rows 11-14: {31-33}{37-41-45} sts.

Work even until Left Front measures same as Back to Armhole Shaping, ending by working a **wrong** side row.

ARMHOLE SHAPING

Maintain established pattern throughout.

Row 1: Bind off {4-4}{5-5-6} sts, work across in Seed Stitch: {27-29}{32-36-39} sts.

Work even until Left Front measures approximately {19-19½}{19½-20-20½}"/ {48.5-49.5}{49.5-51-52} cm from cast on edge, ending by working a **right** side row.

NECK SHAPING

Row 1: Bind off 4 sts, work across in Seed Stitch: {23-25}{28-32-35} sts.

Row 2: Work across in Seed Stitch.

Row 3: Bind off 3 sts, work across in Seed Stitch: {20-22}{25-29-32} sts.

Row 4: Work across in Seed Stitch.

Row 5: Bind off {3-2}{2-2-3} sts, work across in Seed Stitch: {17-20}{23-27-29} sts.

Row 6: Work across in Seed Stitch to last 2 sts, decrease *(Fig. 17 or Fig. 18, page 583)*: {16-19}{22-26-28} sts.

Row 7: Decrease, work across in Seed Stitch: {15-18}{21-25-27} sts.

Work even until Left Front measures same as Back to Shoulder Shaping, ending by working a **wrong** side row.

SHOULDER SHAPING

Row 1: Bind off {5-6}{7-8-9} sts, work across in Seed Stitch: {10-12}{14-17-18} sts.

Row 2: Work across in Seed Stitch.

Rows 3 and 4: Repeat Rows 1 and 2: {5-6}{7-9-9} sts.

Bind off remaining sts.

RIGHT FRONT

Cast on {17-19}{23-27-31} sts.

Row 1 (Right side)**:** P1, (K1, P1) across.

Row 2: P1, (K1, P1) across.

Row 3 (Increase row)**:** Add on 3 sts, work across in Seed Stitch: {20-22}{26-30-34} sts.

Row 4: Work across in Seed Stitch.

Rows 5 and 6: Repeat Rows 3 and 4: {23-25}{29-33-37} sts.

Row 7 (Increase row)**:** Add on 2 sts, work across in Seed Stitch: {25-27}{31-35-39} sts.

Row 8: Work across in Seed Stitch.

Rows 9-11: Repeat Rows 7 and 8 once, then repeat Row 7 once **more**: {29-31}{35-39-43} sts.

Rows 12-14: Work across in Seed Stitch.

Row 15 (Increase row)**:** Add on one st, work across in Seed Stitch: {30-32}{36-40-44} sts.

Rows 16-19: Repeat Rows 12-15: {31-33}{37-41-45} sts.

Work even until Right Front measures same as Back to Armhole Shaping, ending by working a **right** side row.

Instructions continued on page 144.

ARMHOLE SHAPING
Maintain established pattern throughout.

Row 1: Bind off {4-4}{5-5-6} sts, work across in Seed Stitch: {27-29}{32-36-39} sts.

Work even until Right Front measures approximately {19-19$\frac{1}{2}$}{19$\frac{1}{2}$-20-20$\frac{1}{2}$}"/ {48.5-49.5}{49.5-51-52} cm from cast on edge, ending by working a **wrong** side row.

NECK SHAPING
Row 1: Bind off 4 sts, place marker around first bound off st to mark button loop placement, work across in Seed Stitch: {23-25}{28-32-35} sts.

Row 2: Work across in Seed Stitch.

Row 3: Bind off 3 sts, work across in Seed Stitch: {20-22}{25-29-32} sts.

Row 4: Work across in Seed Stitch.

Row 5: Bind off {3-2}{2-2-3} sts, work across in Seed Stitch: {17-20}{23-27-29} sts.

Row 6: Work across in Seed Stitch to last 2 sts, decrease: {16-19}{22-26-28} sts.

Row 7: Decrease, work across in Seed Stitch: {15-18}{21-25-27} sts.

Work even until Right Front measures same as Back to Shoulder Shaping, ending by working a **right** side row.

SHOULDER SHAPING
Row 1: Bind off {5-6}{7-8-9} sts, work across in Seed Stitch: {10-12}{14-17-18} sts.

Row 2: Work across in Seed Stitch.

Rows 3 and 4: Repeat Rows 1 and 2: {5-6}{7-9-9} sts.

Bind off remaining sts.

SLEEVE (Make 2)
Cast on {31-31}{33-33-35} sts **loosely**.

Row 1 (Right side)**:** K1, (P1, K1) across.

Work in Seed Stitch increasing one stitch at **each** edge **(see Increases, page 581)**, every sixth row, {0-1}{1-7-14} times **(see Zeros, page 577)**; then increase every eighth row, {6-14}{13-8-2} times; then increase every tenth row, {7-0}{0-0-0} times: {57-61}{61-63-67} sts.

Work even until Sleeve measures approximately {20$\frac{1}{4}$-19$\frac{3}{4}$}{19-18$\frac{1}{4}$-17$\frac{1}{2}$}"/ {51.5-50}{48.5-46.5-44.5} cm from cast on edge, ending by working a **wrong** side row.

Bind off all sts in Seed Stitch.

FINISHING
Sew shoulder seams.

Sew Sleeves to Jacket, matching center of last row on Sleeve to shoulder seam, and sewing top of Sleeve along Armhole edge and sides of Sleeve to bound off edges **(see Sewing in Sleeves, page 587)**.

Weave underarm and side in one continuous seam **(Fig. 36, page 587)**.

EDGING
With **right** side facing and using crochet hook, join yarn with sc in right side seam **(see Joining With Sc, page 589)**; sc evenly across Right Front edge to marker **(Fig. 42, page 589)**, sc in marked st, remove marker, ch 7 (button loop made), slip st in last sc made **(Fig. 41, page 589)**, sc evenly around entire edge; join with slip st to first sc, finish off.

SLEEVE EDGING
With **right** side facing and using crochet hook, join yarn with sc in seam; sc evenly around edge; join with slip st to first sc, finish off.

Repeat for second Sleeve.

Sew button opposite button loop.

Design by Melissa Leapman.

HOODED SWEATER COAT

◖◼◼◻ INTERMEDIATE

Long Version shown on page 149.

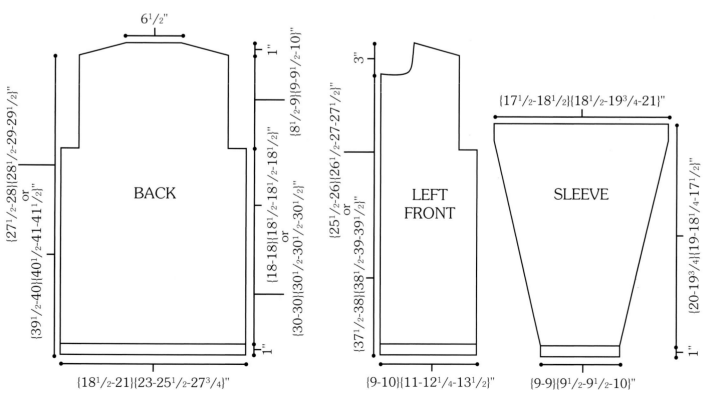

BACK

6¹/₂"

1"

{8¹/₂-9}{9-9¹/₂-10}"

{27¹/₂-28}{28¹/₂-29-29¹/₂}"
or
{39¹/₂-40}{40¹/₂-41-41¹/₂}"

{18-18}{18¹/₂-18-18¹/₂}"
or
{30-30}{30¹/₂-30¹/₂-30¹/₂}"

1"

{18¹/₂-21}{23-25¹/₂-27³/₄}"

LEFT FRONT

3"

{25¹/₂-26}{26¹/₂-27-27¹/₂}"
or
{37¹/₂-38}{38¹/₂-39-39¹/₂}"

{9-10}{11-12¹/₄-13¹/₂}"

SLEEVE

{17¹/₂-18¹/₂}{18¹/₂-19³/₄-21}"

{20-19³/₄}{19-18¹/₄-17¹/₂}"

1"

{9-9}{9¹/₂-9¹/₂-10}"

Instructions begin on page 146.

Note: Sweater includes two edge stitches.

Size	Finished Chest Measurement	
Small	36"	(91.5 cm)
Medium	40$\frac{1}{2}$"	(103 cm)
Large	45"	(114.5 cm)
X-Large	50"	(127 cm)
XX-Large	54$\frac{1}{2}$"	(138.5 cm)

Size Note: Instructions are written with sizes Small and Medium in the first set of braces, and with sizes Large, X-Large, and XX-Large in the second set of braces { }. Instructions will be easier to read if you circle all the numbers pertaining to your size. If only one number is given, it applies to all sizes.

MATERIALS

Bulky Weight Yarn:
Short Version
Ounces {33$\frac{1}{2}$-36}{38$\frac{1}{2}$-41-44}
Yards {1,035-1,110}{1,185-1,265-1,355}
Grams {950-1,020}{1,090-1,160-1,250}
Meters {946.5-1,015}{1,083.5-1,156.5-1,239}
Long Version
Ounces {41$\frac{1}{2}$-45}{48$\frac{1}{2}$-52$\frac{1}{2}$-56$\frac{1}{2}$}
Yards {1,280-1,390}{1,495-1,620-1,740}
Grams {1,180-1,280}{1,380-1,490-1,600}
Meters {1,170.5-1,271}{1,367-1,481.5-1,591}

Straight knitting needles, sizes 9 (5.5 mm) **and** 10 (6 mm) **or** sizes needed for gauge
31" (78.5 cm) Circular needles, sizes 9 (5.5 mm) **and** 10 (6 mm)
Marker
Yarn needle
Sewing needle and thread
1" (25 mm) Buttons - 8

GAUGE: With larger size needles, in Reverse Stockinette Stitch, 14 sts and 20 rows = 4" (10 cm)

BACK
RIBBING
With larger size straight needles, cast on {65-73}{81-89-97} sts.

Row 1: K1, (P1, K1) across.

Row 2 (Right side)**:** P1, (K1, P1) across.

Repeat Rows 1 and 2 until Ribbing measures approximately 1" (2.5 cm) from cast on edge, ending by working a **wrong** side row.

BODY
Beginning with a **purl** row, work in Reverse Stockinette Stitch until Back measures approximately {19-19}{19$\frac{1}{2}$-19$\frac{1}{2}$-19$\frac{1}{2}$}"/ {48.5-48.5}{49.5-49.5-49.5} cm from cast on edge for Short Version or approximately {31-31}{31$\frac{1}{2}$-31$\frac{1}{2}$-31$\frac{1}{2}$}"/{78.5-78.5}{80-80-80} cm from cast on edge for Long Version, ending by working a **knit** row.

ARMHOLE SHAPING
Rows 1 and 2: Bind off {7-8}{9-10-11} sts, work across: {51-57}{63-69-75} sts.

Work even until Back measures approximately {27$\frac{1}{2}$-28}{28$\frac{1}{2}$-29-29$\frac{1}{2}$}"/{70-71}{72.5-73.5-75} cm from cast on edge for Short Version or approximately {39$\frac{1}{2}$-40}{40$\frac{1}{2}$-41-41$\frac{1}{2}$}"/ {100.5-101.5}{103-104-105.5} cm from cast on edge for Long Version, ending by working a **knit** row.

SHOULDER SHAPING
Rows 1-4: Bind off {5-6}{7-8-9} sts, work across: {31-33}{35-37-39} sts.

Rows 5 and 6: Bind off {4-5}{6-7-8} sts, work across: 23 sts.

Bind off remaining sts.

LEFT FRONT
RIBBING
With larger size straight needles, cast on {31-35}{39-43-47} sts.

Row 1: K1, (P1, K1) across.

Row 2 (Right side)**:** P1, (K1, P1) across.

Repeat Rows 1 and 2 until Ribbing measures approximately 1" (2.5 cm) from cast on edge, ending by working a **wrong** side row.

BODY
Beginning with a **purl** row, work in Reverse Stockinette Stitch until Left Front measures approximately {2$\frac{1}{2}$-3}{3$\frac{1}{2}$-4-4$\frac{1}{2}$}"/ {6.5-7.5}{9-10-11.5} cm from cast on edge for Short Version or approximately {14$\frac{1}{2}$-15}{15$\frac{1}{2}$-16-16$\frac{1}{2}$}"/{37-38}{39.5-40.5-42} cm from cast on edge for Long Version, ending by working a **knit** row.

POCKET OPENING
Both sides of Pocket Opening are worked at the same time, using separate yarn for **each** side.

Row 1: Purl {7-10}{11-13-14} sts; with second yarn, purl across.

Row 2: Knit {24-25}{28-30-33} sts; with second yarn, knit across.

Repeat Rows 1 and 2 until piece measures approximately {8$\frac{1}{2}$-9}{9$\frac{1}{2}$-10-10$\frac{1}{2}$}"/ {21.5-23}{24-25.5-26.5} cm from cast on edge for Short Version or approximately {20$\frac{1}{2}$-21}{21$\frac{1}{2}$-22-22$\frac{1}{2}$}"/{52-53.5}{54.5-56-57} cm from cast on edge for Long Version, ending by working Row 1.

Next Row: Knit {24-25}{28-30-33} sts, cut yarn; with second yarn, knit across.

Working across all stitches, continue in Reverse Stockinette Stitch until Left Front measures same as Back to Armhole Shaping, ending by working a **knit** row.

ARMHOLE SHAPING
Row 1: Bind off {7-8}{9-10-11} sts, purl across: {24-27}{30-33-36} sts.

Work even until Left Front measures approximately {25$\frac{1}{2}$-26}{26$\frac{1}{2}$-27-27$\frac{1}{2}$}"/{65-66}{67.5-68.5-70} cm from cast on edge for Short Version or approximately {37$\frac{1}{2}$-38}{38$\frac{1}{2}$-39-39$\frac{1}{2}$}"/ {95.5-96.5}{98-99-100.5} cm from cast on edge for Long Version, ending by working a **purl** row.

NECK SHAPING
Row 1: Bind off 3 sts, knit across: {21-24}{27-30-33} sts.

Row 2: Purl across.

Row 3: Bind off 2 sts, knit across: {19-22}{25-28-31} sts.

Rows 4 and 5: Repeat Rows 2 and 3: {17-20}{23-26-29} sts.

Row 6: Purl across to last 2 sts, P2 tog *(Fig. 18, page 583)*: {16-19}{22-25-28} sts.

Row 7: SSK *(Figs. 21a-c, page 584)*, knit across: {15-18}{21-24-27} sts.

Row 8: Purl across.

Row 9: SSK, knit across: {14-17}{20-23-26} sts.

Work even until Left Front measures same as Back to Shoulder Shaping, ending by working a **knit** row.

SHOULDER SHAPING
Row 1: Bind off {5-6}{7-8-9} sts, purl across: {9-11}{13-15-17} sts.

Row 2: Knit across.

Rows 3 and 4: Repeat Rows 1 and 2: {4-5}{6-7-8} sts.

Bind off remaining sts.

RIGHT FRONT
RIBBING
With larger size straight needles, cast on {31-35}{39-43-47} sts.

Instructions continued on page 148.

Row 1: K1, (P1, K1) across.

Row 2 (Right side): P1, (K1, P1) across.

Repeat Rows 1 and 2 until Ribbing measures approximately 1" (2.5 cm) from cast on edge, ending by working a **wrong** side row.

BODY

Beginning with a **purl** row, work in Reverse Stockinette Stitch until Right Front measures approximately {2^1/$_2$-3}{3^1/$_2$-4-4^1/$_2$}"/ {6.5-7.5}{9-10-11.5} cm from cast on edge for Short Version or approximately {14^1/$_2$-15}{15^1/$_2$-16-16^1/$_2$}"/{37-38}{39.5-40.5-42} cm from cast on edge for Long Version, ending by working a **knit** row.

POCKET OPENING

Both sides of Pocket Opening are worked at the same time, using separate yarn for **each** side.

Row 1: Purl {24-25}{28-30-33} sts; with second yarn, purl across.

Row 2: Knit {7-10}{11-13-14} sts; with second yarn, knit across.

Repeat Rows 1 and 2 until piece measures approximately {8^1/$_2$-9}{9^1/$_2$-10-10^1/$_2$}"/ {21.5-23}{24-25.5-26.5} cm from cast on edge for Short Version or approximately {20^1/$_2$-21}{21^1/$_2$-22-22^1/$_2$}"/{52-53.5}{54.5-56-57} cm from cast on edge for Long Version, ending by working Row 1.

Next Row: Knit {7-10}{11-13-14} sts, cut yarn; with second yarn, knit across.

Working across all stitches, continue in Reverse Stockinette Stitch until Right Front measures same as Back to Armhole Shaping, ending by working a **purl** row.

ARMHOLE SHAPING

Row 1: Bind off {7-8}{9-10-11} sts, knit across: {24-27}{30-33-36} sts.

Work even until Right Front measures same as Left Front to Neck Shaping, ending by working a **knit** row.

NECK SHAPING

Row 1: Bind off 3 sts, purl across: {21-24}{27-30-33} sts.

Row 2: Knit across.

Row 3: Bind off 2 sts, purl across: {19-22}{25-28-31} sts.

Rows 4 and 5: Repeat Rows 2 and 3: {17-20}{23-26-29} sts.

Row 6: Knit across to last 2 sts, K2 tog **(Fig. 17, page 583)**: {16-19}{22-25-28} sts.

Row 7: SSP **(Fig. 22, page 584)**, purl across: {15-18}{21-24-27} sts.

Row 8: Knit across.

Row 9: SSP, purl across: {14-17}{20-23-26} sts.

Work even until Right Front measures same as Back to Shoulder Shaping, ending by working a **purl** row.

SHOULDER SHAPING

Row 1: Bind off {5-6}{7-8-9} sts, knit across: {9-11}{13-15-17} sts.

Row 2: Purl across.

Rows 3 and 4: Repeat Rows 1 and 2: {4-5}{6-7-8} sts.

Bind off remaining sts.

POCKET
RIBBING

With **right** side facing and using smaller size straight needles, pick up 21 sts evenly spaced across end of rows along center Front edge of Pocket Opening **(Fig. 34a, page 586)**.

Row 1: K1, (P1, K1) across.

Row 2 (Right side): P1, (K1, P1) across.

Repeat Rows 1 and 2 until Ribbing measures approximately 1" (2.5 cm).

Bind off all sts in pattern.

LINING

With **right** side facing and using larger size straight needles, pick up 21 sts evenly spaced across end of rows along remaining vertical edge of Pocket Opening.

Beginning with a **knit** row, work in Reverse Stockinette Stitch until Lining measures approximately 6" (15 cm).

Bind off all sts.

Insert Lining through Pocket Opening and sew Lining in place to **wrong** side of Front.

Sew side edges of Pocket Ribbing to **right** side of Front.

Repeat for second Pocket Opening.

SLEEVE (Make 2)
RIBBING

With larger size straight needles, cast on {31-31}{33-33-35} sts **loosely**.

Row 1: K1, (P1, K1) across.

Row 2 (Right side)**:** P1, (K1, P1) across.

Repeat Rows 1 and 2 until Ribbing measures approximately 1" (2.5 cm) from cast on edge, ending by working a **wrong** side row.

BODY

Beginning with a purl row, work in Reverse Stockinette Stitch increasing one stitch at **each** edge **(see Increases, page 581)**, every other row, {0-0}{0-0-5} times **(see Zeros, page 577)**; then increase every fourth row, {3-10}{10-18-14} times; then increase every sixth row, {12-7}{6-0-0} times: {61-65}{65-69-73} sts.

Work even until Sleeve measures approximately {21-20^3/$_4$}{20-19^1/$_4$-18^1/$_2$}"/{53.5-52.5}{51-49-47}cm from cast on edge, ending by working a **knit** row.

Bind off all sts in **purl**.

Instructions continued on page 150.

FINISHING

Sew shoulder seams.

HOOD

With **right** side facing and using larger size circular needle, pick up 20 sts evenly spaced along Right Front Neck edge *(Figs. 34a & b, page 586)*, pick up 24 sts across Back Neck bound off edge, pick up 20 sts evenly spaced along Left Front Neck edge: 64 sts.

Beginning with a **knit** row, work in Reverse Stockinette Stitch until Hood measures approximately $9^1/_2$" (24 cm), ending by working a **knit** row.

SHAPING

Row 1 (Decrease row): P 30, P2 tog, place marker *(Fig. 1, page 578)*, P2 tog tbl *(Fig. 20, page 583)*, purl across: 62 sts.

Row 2: Knit across.

Row 3 (Decrease row): Purl across to within 2 sts of marker, P2 tog, slip marker, P2 tog tbl, purl across: 60 sts.

Rows 4-14: Repeat Rows 2 and 3, 5 times; then repeat Row 2 once **more**: 50 sts.

Bind off remaining sts in **purl**.

Sew top Hood seam.

FRONT BAND

With **right** side facing and using smaller size circular needle, pick up
{102-104}{106-108-110} sts evenly spaced across Right Front edge for Short Version or {150-152}{154-156-158} sts evenly spaced across Right Front edge for Long Version, pick up 95 sts evenly spaced around edge of Hood, pick up {102-104}{106-108-110} sts evenly spaced across Left Front edge for Short Version or {150-152}{154-156-158} sts evenly spaced across Left Front edge for Long Version: {299-303}{307-311-315} sts for Short Version or {395-399}{403-407-411} sts for Long Version.

Row 1: P1, (K1, P1) across.

Row 2 (Right side): K1, (P1, K1) across.

Mark placement of buttons on Right Front, placing first marker $^1/_2$" (1.25 cm) from top of neck edge for either length and placing last marker 2" (5 cm) from lower edge for Short Version or 14" (35.5 cm) from lower edge for Long Version; then evenly space six more markers for remaining buttons.

Row 3: ★ Work in established ribbing across to next marker, bind off 3 sts in pattern; repeat from ★ 7 times **more**, work across in established ribbing.

Row 4: ★ Work in established ribbing across to bound off sts, **turn**; add on 3 sts *(Figs. 5a & b, page 580)*; **turn**; repeat from ★ 7 times **more**, work across in established ribbing.

Row 5: P1, (K1, P1) across.

Row 6: K1, (P1, K1) across.

Bind off all sts in ribbing.

Sew Sleeves to Coat, matching center of last row on Sleeve to shoulder seam, and sewing top of Sleeve along Armhole edge and sides of Sleeve to bound off edges *(see Sewing in Sleeves, page 587)*.

Weave underarm and side in one continuous seam *(Fig. 36, page 587)*.

Sew buttons to Button Band opposite buttonholes.

Design by Melissa Leapman.

COLOR-BLOCK PULLOVER

■■□□ **EASY**

Also shown on page 183.

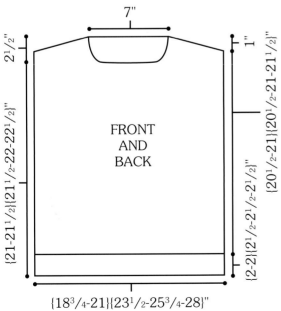

7"

2¹/₂"

1"

FRONT
AND
BACK

{21-21¹/₂}{21¹/₂-22-22¹/₂}"

{20¹/₂-21}{20¹/₂-21-21¹/₂}"

{2-2}{2¹/₂-2¹/₂-2¹/₂}"

{18³/₄-21}{23¹/₂-25³/₄-28}"

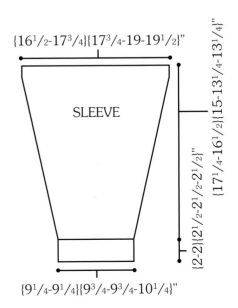

{16¹/₂-17³/₄}{17³/₄-19-19¹/₂}"

SLEEVE

{17¹/₄-16¹/₂}{15-13¹/₄-13¹/₄}"

{2-2}{2¹/₂-2¹/₂-2¹/₂}"

{9¹/₄-9¹/₄}{9³/₄-9³/₄-10¹/₄}"

Instructions begin on page 152.

Note: Sweater includes two edge stitches.

Size	Finished Chest Measurement
Small	36^1/$_2$" (92.5 cm)
Medium	41" (104 cm)
Large	45^3/$_4$" (116 cm)
X-Large	50^1/$_4$" (127.5 cm)
XX-Large	55" (139.5 cm)

Size Note: Instructions are written with sizes Small and Medium in the first set of braces, and with sizes Large, X-Large, and XX-Large in the second set of braces { }. Instructions will be easier to read if you circle all the numbers pertaining to your size. If only one number is given, it applies to all sizes.

MATERIALS

Bulky Weight Yarn:
Lt Purple -
Ounces {11^1/$_2$-13}{13^1/$_2$-14^1/$_2$-16}
Yards {355-400}{415-445-495}
Grams {330-370}{380-410-450}
Meters {324.5-366}{379.5-407-452.5}
Purple -
Ounces {11^1/$_2$-13}{13^1/$_2$-14^1/$_2$-16}
Yards {355-400}{415-445-495}
Grams {330-370}{380-410-450}
Meters {324.5-366}{379.5-407-452.5}
Ecru -
Ounces {2^1/$_2$-2^3/$_4$}{3^1/$_2$-3^3/$_4$-4}
Yards {75-85}{110-115-125}
Grams {70-80}{100-105-110}
Meters {68.5-77.5}{100.5-105-114.5}
Straight knitting needles, size 10 (6 mm) **or**
size needed for gauge
16" (40.5 cm) Circular needle, size 9 (5.5 mm)
Marker
Yarn needle

GAUGE: With larger size needles,
in Stockinette Stitch,
14 sts and 20 rows = 4" (10 cm)

BACK
RIBBING
With larger size needles and Ecru,
cast on {66-74}{82-90-98} sts **loosely**.

Work in K1, P1 ribbing for
{2-2}{2^1/$_2$-2^1/$_2$-2^1/$_2$}"/{5-5}{6.5-6.5-6.5} cm.

Cut Ecru.

BODY
Row 1 (Right side)**:** With Purple, knit
{33-37}{41-45-49} sts; with Lt Purple **(Fig. 30, page 585)**, knit across.

Row 2: Purl {33-37}{41-45-49} sts; with Purple, purl across.

Work in Stockinette Stitch using established colors, until Back measures approximately {11^1/$_2$-11^1/$_2$}{12-12^1/$_2$-12^1/$_2$}"/{29-29}{30.5-32-32} cm from cast on edge, ending by working a **purl** row; cut both colors.

Next Row: With Lt Purple, knit {33-37}{41-45-49} sts; with Purple, knit across.

Next Row: Purl {33-37}{41-45-49} sts; with Lt Purple, purl across.

Continue in Stockinette Stitch using newly established colors, until Back measures approximately {22^1/$_2$-23}{23-23^1/$_2$-24}"/{57-58.5}{58.5-59.5-61} cm from cast on edge, ending by working a **purl** row.

SHOULDER SHAPING
Maintain established colors throughout.

Rows 1-4: Bind off {7-8}{10-11-12} sts, work across: {38-42}{42-46-50} sts.

Rows 5 and 6: Bind off {7-9}{9-11-13} sts, work across: 24 sts.

Bind off remaining sts.

FRONT
Work same as Back until Front measures approximately {21-21^1/$_2$}{21^1/$_2$-22-22^1/$_2$}"/{53.5-54.5}{54.5-56-57} cm from cast on edge, ending by working a **purl** row.

NECK SHAPING

Both sides of Neck are worked at the same time, using separate yarn for **each** side. Maintain established colors throughout.

Row 1 (Right side)**:** Knit {27-31}{35-39-43} sts; with second yarn, bind off 12 sts, knit across: {27-31}{35-39-43} sts **each** side.

Rows 2 and 3: Work across; with second yarn, bind off 3 sts, work across: {24-28}{32-36-40} sts **each** side.

Rows 4 and 5: Work across; with second yarn, bind off 2 sts, work across: {22-26}{30-34-38} sts **each** side.

Row 6: Purl across to within 2 sts of Neck edge, SSP *(Fig. 22, page 584)*; with second yarn, P2 tog *(Fig. 18, page 583)*, purl across: {21-25}{29-33-37} sts **each** side.

Work even until Front measures same as Back to Shoulder Shaping, ending by working a **purl** row.

SHOULDER SHAPING

Rows 1-4: Bind off {7-8}{10-11-12} sts, work across; with second yarn, work across: {7-9}{9-11-13} sts.

Row 5: Bind off remaining sts on first side; with second yarn, knit across.
Bind off remaining sts.

SLEEVE (Make 2)
RIBBING

With larger size needles and Ecru, cast on {32-32}{34-34-36} sts **loosely**.

Work in K1, P1 ribbing for {2-2}{2^1/$_2$-2^1/$_2$-2^1/$_2$}"/{5-5}{6.5-6.5-6.5} cm.

Cut Ecru.

BODY

Row 1 (Right side)**:** With Lt Purple, knit {16-16}{17-17-18} sts; with Purple, knit across.

Row 2: Purl {16-16}{17-17-18} sts; with Lt Purple, purl across.

Repeat Rows 1 and 2, {0-0}{0-1-1} time(s) *(see Zeros, page 577)*.

Increase Row: Increase *(Figs. 10a & b, page 581)*, knit in established colors across to last st, increase: {34-34}{36-36-38} sts.

Continue in Stockinette Stitch using established colors, increasing one stitch at **each** edge, every other row, {0-0}{0-2-2} times; then increase, every fourth row, {0-7}{7-13-13} times; then increase every sixth row, {12-7}{6-0-0} times: {58-62}{62-66-68} sts.

Work even until Sleeve measures approximately {19^1/$_4$-18^1/$_2$}{17^1/$_2$-15^3/$_4$-15^3/$_4$}"/ {49-47}{44.5-40-40} cm from cast on edge, ending by working a **purl** row.

Bind off all sts in **knit**.

FINISHING
Sew shoulder seams.

NECK RIBBING
With **right** side facing, using circular needle and Ecru, pick up 13 sts evenly spaced along left Front Neck edge *(Figs. 34a & b, page 586)*, pick up 12 sts across Front bound off edge, pick up 13 sts evenly spaced along right Front Neck edge, pick up 24 sts across Back Neck bound off edge, place marker to mark beginning of rnd *(Fig. 1, page 578)*: 62 sts.

Work in K1, P1 ribbing around for 1" (2.5 cm).

Bind off all sts **loosely** in ribbing.

Sew Sleeves to Pullover, matching center of last row on Sleeve to shoulder seam and beginning {8^1/$_4$-9}{9-9^1/$_2$-9^3/$_4$}"/{21-23}{23-24-25} cm down from seam.

Weave underarm and side in one continuous seam *(Fig. 36, page 587)*.

Design by Melissa Leapman.

CASUAL PULLOVER

■■□□ EASY

Also shown on page 157.

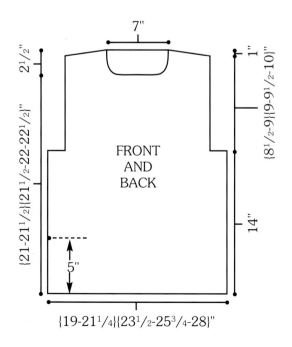

7"

2¹/₂"

1"

{8¹/₂-9}{9-9¹/₂-10}"

{21-21¹/₂}{21¹/₂-22-22¹/₂}"

FRONT
AND
BACK

14"

5"

{19-21¹/₄}{23¹/₂-25³/₄-28}"

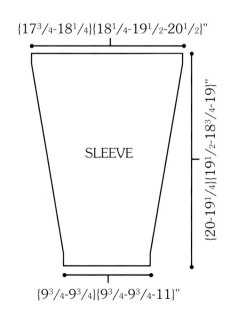

{17³/₄-18¹/₄}{18¹/₄-19¹/₂-20¹/₂}"

SLEEVE

{20-19¹/₄}{19¹/₂-18³/₄-19}"

{9³/₄-9³/₄}{9³/₄-9³/₄-11}"

Note: Sweater includes two edge stitches.

Size	Finished Chest Measurement
Small	$36^1/_2$" (92.5 cm)
Medium	$41^1/_4$" (105 cm)
Large	$45^3/_4$" (116 cm)
X-Large	$50^1/_4$" (127.5 cm)
XX-Large	55" (139.5 cm)

Size Note: Instructions are written with sizes Small and Medium in the first set of braces, and with sizes Large, X-Large, and XX-Large in the second set of braces { }. Instructions will be easier to read if you circle all the numbers pertaining to your size. If only one number is given, it applies to all sizes.

MATERIALS

Bulky Weight Yarn: **BULKY 5**
Ounces {27-$29^1/_2$}{32-$34^1/_2$-$37^1/_2$}
Yards {835-910}{985-1,065-1,155}
Grams {770-840}{910-980-1,070}
Meters {763.5-832}{900.5-974-1,056}
Straight knitting needles, size 10 (6 mm) **or** size needed for gauge
16" (40.5 cm) Circular needle, size 9 (5.5 mm)
Marker
Yarn needle

GAUGE: With larger size needles, in Alternating Rib pattern, 14 sts and 20 rows = 4" (10 cm)

PATTERN STITCH

ALTERNATING RIB
Row 1 (Right side)**:** K2, (P2, K2) across.
Row 2: P2, (K2, P2) across.
Row 3: K2, (P2, K2) across.
Row 4: P2, (K2, P2) across.
Row 5: K2, (P2, K2) across.
Rows 6 and 7: P2, (K2, P2) across.

Row 8: K2, (P2, K2) across.
Row 9: P2, (K2, P2) across.
Row 10: K2, (P2, K2) across.
Row 11: P2, (K2, P2) across.
Rows 12 and 13: K2, (P2, K2) across.
Repeat Rows 2-13 for pattern.

BACK

With larger size needles, cast on {66-74}{82-90-98} sts.

Work in Alternating Rib pattern until Back measures approximately 14" (35.5 cm) from cast on edge, ending by working a **wrong** side row.

ARMHOLE SHAPING

Maintain established pattern throughout.

Rows 1 and 2: Bind off {4-4}{8-8-12} sts, work across: {58-66}{66-74-74} sts.

Work even until Back measures approximately {$22^1/_2$-23}{23-$23^1/_2$-24}"/{57-58.5}{58.5-59.5-61} cm from cast on edge, ending by working a **wrong** side row.

SHOULDER SHAPING

Rows 1-4: Bind off {6-7}{7-8-8} sts, work across: {34-38}{38-42-42} sts.

Rows 5 and 6: Bind off {5-7}{7-9-9} sts, work across: 24 sts.

Bind off remaining sts.

FRONT

Work same as Back until Front measures approximately {21-$21^1/_2$}{$21^1/_2$-22-$22^1/_2$}"/{53.5-54.5}{54.5-56-57} cm from cast on edge, ending by working a **wrong** side row: {58-66}{66-74-74} sts.

Instructions continued on page 156.

NECK SHAPING
Both sides of Neck are worked at the same time, using separate yarn for **each** side.

Row 1 (Right side)**:** Work across {23-27}{27-31-31} sts; with second yarn, bind off 12 sts, work across: {23-27}{27-31-31} sts **each** side.

Rows 2 and 3: Work across; with second yarn, bind off 3 sts, work across: {20-24}{24-28-28} sts **each** side.

Rows 4 and 5: Work across; with second yarn, bind off 2 sts, work across: {18-22}{22-26-26} sts **each** side.

Row 6: Work across to within 2 sts of Neck edge, SSP **(Fig. 22, page 584)**; with second yarn, P2 tog **(Fig. 18, page 583)**, work across: {17-21}{21-25-25} sts **each** side.

Work even until Front measures same as Back to Shoulder Shaping, ending by working a **wrong** side row.

SHOULDER SHAPING
Rows 1-4: Bind off {6-7}{7-8-8} sts, work across; with second yarn, work across: {5-7}{7-9-9} sts **each** side.

Row 5: Bind off remaining sts on first side; with second yarn, work across.

Bind off remaining sts.

SLEEVE (Make 2)
With larger size needles, cast on {34-34}{34-34-38} sts.

Rows 1-4: Work in Alternating Rib pattern.

Row 5 (Increase row)**:** Increase **(Figs. 10a & b or Fig. 11, page 581)**, work in Alternating Rib pattern across to last st, increase: {36-36}{36-36-40} sts.

Continue increasing one stitch at **each** edge and adding new stitches in pattern, every fourth row, {0-4}{6-14-16} times **(see Zeros, page 577)**; then increase every sixth row, {13-10}{8-2-0} times: {62-64}{64-68-72} sts.

Work even until Sleeve measures approximately {20-19^1/$_4$}{19^1/$_2$-18^3/$_4$-19}"/{51-49}{49.5-48-48.5} cm from cast on edge, ending by working a **wrong** side row.

Bind off all sts in pattern.

FINISHING
Sew shoulder seams.

NECK RIBBING
With **right** side facing and using circular needle, pick up 16 sts evenly spaced along left Front Neck edge **(Figs. 34a & b, page 586)**, pick up 12 sts across Front bound off edge, pick up 16 sts evenly spaced along right Front Neck edge, pick up 24 sts across Back Neck bound off edge, place marker to mark beginning of rnd **(Fig. 1, page 578)**: 68 sts.

Work in K2, P2 ribbing around for 1" (2.5 cm).

Bind off all sts **loosely** in ribbing.

Sew Sleeves to Pullover, matching center of last row on Sleeve to shoulder seam, and sewing top of Sleeve along Armhole edge and sides of Sleeve to bound off edges **(see Sewing in Sleeves, page 587)**.

Weave underarm and side in one continuous seam **(Fig. 36, page 587)**, leaving lower 5" (12.5 cm) on Front and Back open for side slits.

Design by Melissa Leapman.

STRIPED TURTLENECK

■■□□ **EASY**

Also shown on page 161.

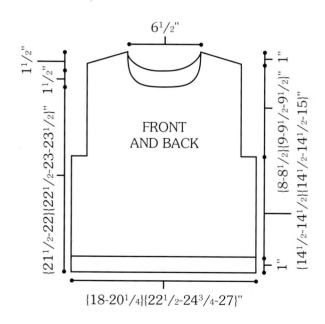

FRONT
AND BACK

6¹/₂"

1¹/₂"

1¹/₂"

{21¹/₂-22}{22¹/₂-23-23¹/₂}"

{18-20¹/₄}{22¹/₂-24³/₄-27}"

1"

{14¹/₂-14¹/₂}{14¹/₂-14¹/₂-15}"

{8-8¹/₂}{9-9¹/₂-9¹/₂}"

1"

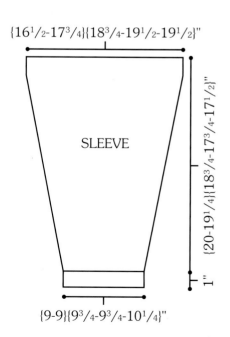

SLEEVE

{16¹/₂-17³/₄}{18³/₄-19¹/₂-19¹/₂}"

{20-19¹/₄}{18³/₄-17³/₄-17¹/₂}"

1"

{9-9}{9³/₄-9³/₄-10¹/₄}"

Note: Sweater includes two edge stitches.

Size	Finished Chest Measurement	
Small	35"	(89 cm)
Medium	39^1/$_2$"	(100.5 cm)
Large	44"	(112 cm)
X-Large	48^1/$_2$"	(123 cm)
XX-Large	53"	(134.5 cm)

Size Note: Instructions are written with sizes Small and Medium in the first set of braces, and with sizes Large, X-Large, and XX-Large in the second set of braces { }. Instructions will be easier to read if you circle all the numbers pertaining to your size. If only one number is given, it applies to all sizes.

MATERIALS

Bulky Weight Yarn:
Blue -
 Ounces {23-25}{27-29-31^1/$_2$}
 Yards {710-770}{835-895-970}
 Grams {650-710}{770-820-890}
 Meters {649-704}{763.5-818.5-887}
Lt Blue -
 Ounces {4-4}{4^1/$_2$-5-5^1/$_2$}
 Yards {125-125}{140-155-170}
 Grams {110-110}{130-140-160}
 Meter {114.5-114.5}{128-141.5-155.5}
Straight knitting needles, sizes 9 (5.5 mm) **and** 10 (6 mm) **or** sizes needed for gauge
16" (40.5 cm) Circular needle, size 9 (5.5 mm)
Stitch holders - 2
Marker
Yarn needle

GAUGE: With larger size needles,
 in Stockinette Stitch,
 14 sts and 20 rows = 4" (10 cm)

BACK
RIBBING
With smaller size straight needles and Blue, cast on {62-70}{78-86-94} sts **loosely.**

Work in K1, P1 ribbing for 1" (2.5 cm) increasing one stitch at end of last row: {63-71}{79-87-95} sts.

BODY
Change to larger size needles.

Rows 1-4: With Lt Blue and beginning with a **knit** row, work in Stockinette Stitch.

Rows 5-8: With Blue, work in Stockinette Stitch.

Rows 9-12: With Lt Blue, work in Stockinette Stitch.

Rows 13-36: Repeat Rows 5-12, 3 times.

With Blue, work in Stockinette Stitch until Back measures approximately {15^1/$_2$-15^1/$_2$}{15^1/$_2$-15^1/$_2$-16}"/{39.5-39.5}{39.5-39.5-40.5} cm from cast on edge, ending by working a **purl** row.

ARMHOLE SHAPING
Rows 1 and 2: Bind off {6-6}{7-7-9} sts, work across: {51-59}{65-73-77} sts.

Work even until Back measures approximately {23-23^1/$_2$}{24-24^1/$_2$-25}"/{58.5-59.5}{61-62-63.5} cm from cast on edge, ending by working a **knit** row.

NECK SHAPING
Both sides of Neck are worked at the same time, using separate yarn for **each** side.

Row 1: Purl {16-20}{23-27-29} sts, slip next 19 sts onto st holder; with second yarn, purl across: {16-20}{23-27-29} sts **each** side.

Instructions continued on page 160.

Row 2: Knit across to within 2 sts of Neck edge, K2 tog *(Fig. 17, page 583)*; with second yarn, SSK *(Figs. 21a-c, page 584)*, knit across: {15-19}{22-26-28} sts **each** side.

Row 3: Purl across to within 2 sts of Neck edge, SSP *(Fig. 22, page 584)*; with second yarn, P2 tog *(Fig. 18, page 583)*, purl across: {14-18}{21-25-27} sts **each** side.

SHOULDER SHAPING
Rows 1-4: Bind off {5-6}{7-8-9} sts, work across; with second yarn, work across: {4-6}{7-9-9} sts **each** side.

Row 5: Bind off remaining sts on first side; with second yarn, knit across.

Bind off remaining sts.

FRONT
Work same as Back until Front measures approximately {21^1/$_2$-22}{22^1/$_2$-23-23^1/$_2$}"/ {54.5-56}{57-58.5-59.5}cm from cast on edge, ending by working a **purl** row: {51-59}{65-73-77} sts.

NECK SHAPING
Both sides of Neck are worked at the same time, using separate yarn for **each** side.

Row 1: Knit {20-24}{27-31-33} sts, slip next 11 sts onto st holder; with second yarn, knit across: {20-24}{27-31-33} sts **each** side.

Rows 2-5: Work across; with second yarn, bind off 2 sts, work across: {16-20}{23-27-29} sts **each** side.

Row 6: Purl across to within 2 sts of Neck edge, SSP; with second yarn, P2 tog, purl across: {15-19}{22-26-28} sts **each** side.

Row 7: Knit across to within 2 sts of Neck edge, K2 tog; with second yarn SSK, knit across: {14-18}{21-25-27} sts **each** side.

Row 8: Purl across; with second yarn, purl across.

Row 9: Knit across; with second yarn, knit across.

Row 10: Purl across; with second yarn, purl across.

SHOULDER SHAPING
Rows 1-4: Bind off {5-6}{7-8-9} sts, work across; with second yarn, work across: {4-6}{7-9-9} sts **each** side.

Row 5: Bind off remaining sts on first side; with second yarn, knit across.

Bind off remaining sts.

SLEEVE (Make 2)
RIBBING
With smaller size straight needles and Blue, cast on {32-32}{34-34-36} sts **loosely**.

Work in K1, P1 ribbing for 1" (2.5 cm).

BODY
Change to larger size needles.

Sleeve is worked as follows, alternating 4 rows Lt Blue and 4 rows Blue until 3 stripes of Lt Blue have been worked; then complete Sleeve with Blue.

Beginning with a **knit** row, work in Stockinette Stitch increasing one stitch at **each** edge *(see Increases, page 581)*, every fourth row, {0-6}{11-17-16} times *(see Zeros, page 577)*; then increase every sixth row, {13-9}{5-0-0} times: {58-62}{66-68-68} sts.

Work even until Sleeve measures approximately {21-20^1/$_4$}{19^3/$_4$-18^3/$_4$-18^1/$_2$}"/ {53.5-51.5}{50-47.5-47} cm from cast on edge, ending by working a **purl** row.

Bind off all sts in **knit**.

FINISHING

Sew shoulder seams.

NECK RIBBING

With **right** side facing, using circular needle and Blue, pick up 20 sts evenly spaced along left Front Neck edge *(Figs. 34a & b, page 586)*, slip 11 sts from Front st holder onto second end of circular needle and knit across, pick up 28 sts evenly spaced along right Neck edge, knit across 19 sts from Back st holder, pick up 8 sts evenly space along left Back Neck edge, place marker to mark beginning of rnd *(Fig. 1, page 578)*: 86 sts.

Work in K1, P1 ribbing for 7" (18 cm).

Bind off all sts **loosely** in ribbing.

Sew Sleeves to Pullover, matching center of last row on Sleeve to shoulder seam, and sewing top of Sleeve along Armhole edge and sides of Sleeve to bound off edges *(see Sewing in Sleeves, page 587)*.

Weave underarm and side in one continuous seam *(Fig. 36, page 587)*.

Design by Melissa Leapman.

ZIPPERED NECK PULLOVER

▰▰▰▱ INTERMEDIATE

Also shown on page 165.

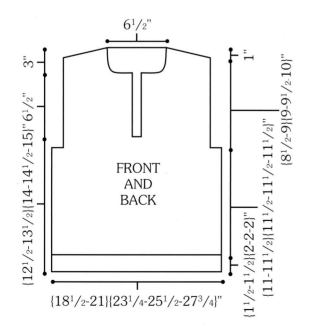

6½"

3"

1"

{12½-13½}{14-14½-15}" 6½"

{8½-9}{9-9½-10}"

{11-11½}{11½-11½-11½}"

{1½-1½}{2-2-2}"

FRONT
AND
BACK

{18½-21}{23¼-25½-27¾}"

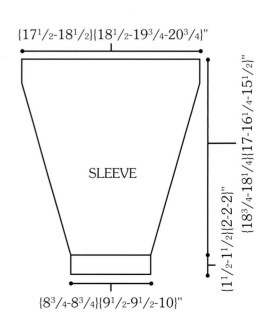

{17½-18½}{18½-19¾-20¾}"

{18¾-18¼}{17-16¼-15½}"

SLEEVE

{1½-1½}{2-2-2}"

{8¾-8¾}{9½-9½-10}"

Note: Sweater includes two edge stitches.

Size	Finished Chest Measurement
Small	36" (91.5 cm)
Medium	40^1/$_2$" (103 cm)
Large	45^1/$_4$" (115 cm)
X-Large	49^3/$_4$" (126.5 cm)
XX-Large	54^1/$_4$" (138 cm)

Size Note: Instructions are written with sizes Small and Medium in the first set of braces, and with sizes Large, X-Large, and XX-Large in the second set of braces { }. Instructions will be easier to read if you circle all the numbers pertaining to your size. If only one number is given, it applies to all sizes.

MATERIALS
Bulky Weight Yarn:
  Variegated -
    Ounces {24^1/$_2$-27^1/$_2$}{29^1/$_2$-32-34^1/$_2$}
    Yards   {755-850}{910-985-1,065}
    Grams   {700-780}{840-910-980}
    Meters {690.5-777}{832-900.5-974}
  Dk Grey - ^{1}/$_2$ ounce, 15 yards
            (20 grams, 13.5 meters)
Straight knitting needles, size 10 (6 mm) **or**
    size needed for gauge
Stitch holder
Yarn needle
Sewing needle and thread
9" (23 cm) Sport zipper

GAUGE: In Reverse Stockinette Stitch,
      14 sts and 20 rows = 4" (10 cm)

BACK
RIBBING
With Dk Grey,
cast on {64-72}{80-88-96} sts **loosely**.

Row 1: (K1, P1) across; cut Dk Grey.

With Variegated, work in K1, P1 ribbing for {1^1/$_2$-1^1/$_2$}{2-2-2}"/{4-4}{5-5-5} cm increasing one stitch at end of last row (*see Increases, page 581*): {65-73}{81-89-97} sts.

BODY
Beginning with a **purl** row, work in Reverse Stockinette Stitch until Back measures approximately {12^1/$_2$-13}{13^1/$_2$-13^1/$_2$-13^1/$_2$}"/ {32-33}{34.5-34.5-34.5} cm from cast on edge, ending by working a **knit** row.

ARMHOLE SHAPING
Rows 1 and 2: Bind off {4-4}{5-5-6} sts, work across: {57-65}{71-79-85} sts.

Work even until Back measures approximately {21-22}{22^1/$_2$-23-23^1/$_2$}"/{53.5-56}{57-58.5-59.5} cm from cast on edge, ending by working a **knit** row.

SHOULDER SHAPING
Rows 1-4: Bind off {6-7}{8-9-10} sts, work across: {33-37}{39-43-45} sts.

Rows 5 and 6: Bind off {5-7}{8-10-11} sts, work across: 23 sts.

Bind off remaining sts.

FRONT
Work same as Back until Front measures approximately {12^1/$_2$-13^1/$_2$}{14-14^1/$_2$-15}"/ {32-34.5}{35.5-37-38} cm from cast on edge, ending by working a **knit** row: {65-65}{71-79-85} sts.

NECK OPENING
Both sides of Neck are worked at the same time, using separate yarn for **each** side.

SIZE SMALL ONLY
Row 1: Bind off 4 sts, P 26, slip next 3 sts onto st holder; with second yarn, purl across.

Row 2: Bind off 4 sts, knit across; with second yarn, knit across: 27 sts **each** side.

Instructions continued on page 164.

SIZES MEDIUM THRU XX-LARGE ONLY
Row 1: Purl {31}{34-38-41} sts, slip next 3 sts onto st holder; with second yarn, purl across: {31}{34-38-41} sts **each** side.

ALL SIZES
Work even until Front measures approximately {19-20}{20½-21-21½}"/{48.5-51}{52-53.5-54.5} cm from cast on edge, ending by working a **knit** row.

NECK SHAPING
Rows 1 and 2: Work across; with second yarn, bind off 4 sts, work across: {23-27}{30-34-37} sts **each** side.

Rows 3 and 4: Work across; with second yarn, bind off 3 sts, work across: {20-24}{27-31-34} sts **each** side.

Row 5: Purl across to within 2 sts of Neck edge, P2 tog *(Fig. 18, page 583)*; with second yarn, SSP *(Fig. 22, page 584)*, purl across: {19-23}{26-30-33} sts **each** side.

Row 6: Knit across to within 2 sts of Neck edge, SSK *(Figs. 21a-c, page 584)*; with second yarn, K2 tog *(Fig. 17, page 583)*, knit across: {18-22}{25-29-32} sts **each** side.

Row 7: Purl across to within 2 sts of Neck edge, P2 tog; with second yarn, SSP, purl across: {17-21}{24-28-31} sts **each** side.

Work even until Front measures same as Back to Shoulder Shaping, ending by working a **knit** row.

SHOULDER SHAPING
Rows 1-4: Bind off {6-7}{8-9-10} sts, work across; with second yarn, work across: {5-7}{8-10-11} sts **each** side.

Row 5: Bind off remaining sts on first side; with second yarn, purl across.

Bind off remaining sts.

SLEEVE (Make 2)
RIBBING
With Dk Grey, cast on {30-30}{32-32-34} sts **loosely**.

Row 1: (K1, P1) across; cut Dk Grey.

With Variegated, work in K1, P1 ribbing for {1½-1½}{2-2-2}"/{4-4}{5-5-5} cm increasing one stitch at end of last row: {31-31}{33-33-35} sts.

BODY
Beginning with a **purl** row, work in Reverse Stockinette Stitch increasing one stitch at **each** edge, every other row, {0-0}{0-4-9} times *(see Zeros, page 577)*; then increase every fourth row, {6-13}{14-14-10} times; then increase every sixth row, {9-4}{2-0-0} times: {61-65}{65-69-73} sts.

Work even until Sleeve measures approximately {20¼-19¾}{19-18¼-17½}"/{51.5-50}{48.5-46.5-44.5} cm from cast on edge, ending by working a **knit** row.

Bind off all sts in **purl**.

FINISHING
Sew shoulder seams.

NECK RIBBING
With **right** side facing and Variegated, pick up 20 sts evenly spaced across right Front Neck edge *(Figs. 34a & b, page 586)*, pick up 23 sts across Back Neck bound off edge, pick up 20 sts evenly spaced across left Front Neck edge: 63 sts.

Row 1: P1, (K1, P1) across.

Row 2 (Right side): K1, (P1, K1) across.

Repeat Rows 1 and 2 until Ribbing measures approximately 2½" (6.5 cm), ending by working Row 2; cut Variegated.

Last Row: With Dk Grey, P1, (K1, P1) across.

Bind off all sts **loosely** in ribbing.

ZIPPER FACING

With **right** side facing and Dk Grey, pick up 32 sts evenly spaced along left edge of center Front Neck Opening, slip 3 sts from st holder onto empty needle and knit across, pick up 32 sts evenly spaced along right edge of center Front Neck Opening: 67 sts.

Bind off all sts in **knit**.

Sew in zipper.

Sew Sleeves to Pullover, matching center of last row on Sleeve to shoulder seam, and sewing top of Sleeve along Armhole edge and sides of Sleeve to bound off edges **(see Sewing in Sleeves, page 587)**.

Weave underarm and side in one continuous seam **(Fig. 36, page 587)**.

Design by Melissa Leapman.

CROPPED COWL NECK PULLOVER

■□□□ **EASY**

Also shown on page 169.

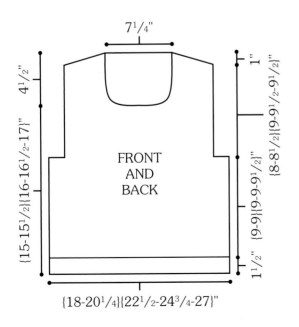

7¹/₄"

4¹/₂"

1"

{15-15¹/₂}{16-16¹/₂-17}"

{8-8¹/₂}{9-9¹/₂-9¹/₂}"

{9-9}{9-9¹/₂-9¹/₂}"

1¹/₂"

FRONT
AND
BACK

{18-20¹/₄}{22¹/₂-24³/₄-27}"

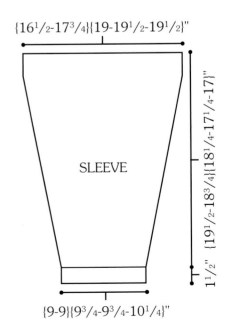

{16¹/₂-17³/₄}{19-19¹/₂-19¹/₂}"

{19¹/₂-18³/₄}{18¹/₄-17¹/₄-17}"

1¹/₂"

SLEEVE

{9-9}{9³/₄-9³/₄-10¹/₄}"

Note: Sweater includes two edge stitches.

Size	Finished Chest Measurement	
Small	35"	(89 cm)
Medium	39^1/$_2$"	(100.5 cm)
Large	44"	(112 cm)
X-Large	48^1/$_2$"	(123 cm)
XX-Large	53"	(134.5 cm)

Size Note: Instructions are written with sizes Small and Medium in the first set of braces, and with sizes Large, X-Large, and XX-Large in the second set of braces { }. Instructions will be easier to read if you circle all the numbers pertaining to your size. If only one number is given, it applies to all sizes.

MATERIALS

Bulky Weight Yarn:
- Ounces {22^1/$_2$-24^1/$_2$}{27^1/$_2$-29-31^1/$_2$}
- Yards {695-755}{850-895-970}
- Grams {640-700}{780-820-890}
- Meters {635.5-690.5}{777-818.5-887}

Straight knitting needles, sizes 9 (5.5 mm) **and** 10 (6 mm) **or** sizes needed for gauge
16" (40.5 cm) Circular needles, sizes 9 (5.5 mm), 10 (6 mm), **and** 11 (8 mm)
Stitch holders - 2
Marker
Yarn needle

GAUGE: With larger size straight needles, in Stockinette Stitch, 14 sts and 20 rows = 4" (10 cm)

BACK
RIBBING

With smaller size straight needles, cast on {62-70}{78-86-94} sts **loosely**.

Work in K1, P1 ribbing for 1^1/$_2$" (4 cm) increasing one stitch at end of last row *(see Increases, page 581)*: {63-71}{79-87-95} sts.

BODY

Change to larger size straight needles.

Beginning with a **knit** row, work in Stockinette Stitch until Back measures approximately {10^1/$_2$-10^1/$_2$}{10^1/$_2$-10^1/$_2$-11}"/ {26.5-26.5}{26.5-26.5-28} cm from cast on edge, ending by working a **purl** row.

ARMHOLE SHAPING

Rows 1 and 2: Bind off {6-6}{7-7-9} sts, work across: {51-59}{65-73-77} sts.

Work even until Back measures approximately {18^1/$_2$-19}{19^1/$_2$-20-20^1/$_2$}"/ {47-48.5}{49.5-51-52} cm from cast on edge, ending by working a **purl** row.

SHOULDER SHAPING

Rows 1-4: Bind off {4-6}{7-8-9} sts, work across: {35-35}{37-41-41} sts.

Rows 5 and 6: Bind off {5-5}{6-8-8} sts, work across: 25 sts.

Slip remaining sts onto st holder.

FRONT

Work same as Back until Front measures approximately {15-15^1/$_2$}{16-16^1/$_2$-17}"/ {38-39.5}{40.5-42-43} cm from cast on edge, ending by working a **purl** row: {51-59}{65-73-77} sts.

Instructions continued on page 168.

NECK SHAPING

Both sides of Neck are worked at the same time, using separate yarn for **each** side.

Row 1: Knit {18-22}{25-29-31} sts, slip next 15 sts onto st holder; with second yarn, knit across: {18-22}{25-29-31} sts **each** side.

Rows 2-5: Work across; with second yarn, bind off 2 sts, work across: {14-18}{21-25-27} sts **each** side.

Row 6: Purl across to within 2 sts of Neck edge, SSP *(Fig. 22, page 584)*; with second yarn, P2 tog *(Fig. 18, page 583)*, purl across: {13-17}{20-24-26} sts **each** side.

Work even until Front measures same as Back to Shoulder Shaping, ending by working a **purl** row.

SHOULDER SHAPING

Rows 1-4: Bind off {4-6}{7-8-9} sts, work across; with second yarn, work across: {5-5}{6-8-8} sts **each** side.

Row 5: Bind off remaining sts on first side; with second yarn, knit across.

Bind off remaining sts.

SLEEVE (Make 2)
RIBBING

With smaller size straight needles, cast on {32-32}{34-34-36} sts **loosely**.

Work in K1, P1 ribbing for $1^1/_2$" (4 cm).

BODY

Change to larger size straight needles.

Beginning with a **knit** row, work in Stockinette Stitch increasing one stitch at **each** edge, every fourth row, {0-2}{6-12-9} times *(see Zeros, page 577)*; then increase every sixth row, {7-13}{10-5-7} times; then increase every eighth row, {6-0}{0-0-0} times: {58-62}{66-68-68} sts.

Work even until Sleeve measures approximately {21-20$^1/_4$}{19$^3/_4$-18$^3/_4$-18$^1/_2$}"/ {53.5-51.5}{50-47.5-47} cm from cast on edge, ending by working a **purl** row.

Bind off all sts in **knit**.

FINISHING

Sew shoulder seams.

COWL NECK

With **right** side facing and using smallest size circular needle, pick up 22 sts evenly spaced along left Front Neck edge *(Figs. 34a & b, page 586)*, slip 15 sts from Front st holder onto second end of circular needle and knit across, pick up 22 sts evenly spaced along right Front Neck edge, slip 25 sts from Back st holder onto second end of circular needle and knit across, place marker to mark beginning of rnd *(Fig. 1, page 578)*: 84 sts.

Purl every rnd until Cowl Neck measures approximately $2^1/_2$" (6.5 cm).

Change to medium size circular needle.

Purl every rnd until Cowl Neck measures approximately 5" (12.5 cm).

Change to largest size circular needle.

Purl every rnd until Cowl Neck measures approximately 8" (20.5 cm).

Work in (K1, P1) ribbing for 4 rnds.

Bind off all sts **loosely** in ribbing.

Turn Cowl Neck to **right** side.

Sew Sleeves to Pullover, matching center of last row on Sleeve to shoulder seam, and sewing top of Sleeve along Armhole edge and sides of Sleeve to bound off edges.

Weave underarm and side in one continuous seam *(Fig. 36, page 587)*.

Design by Melissa Leapman.

TRENDY SLEEVELESS PULLOVER

■■□□ **EASY**

Also shown on page 173.

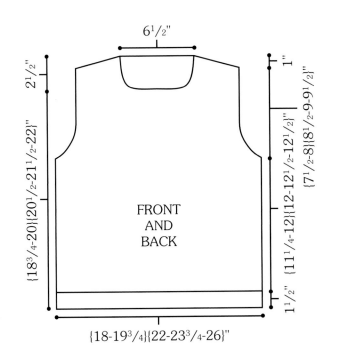

6¹/₂"

2¹/₂"

1"

{18³/₄-20}{20¹/₂-21¹/₂-22}"

{7¹/₂-8}{8¹/₂-9-9¹/₂}"

{11¹/₄-12}{12-12¹/₂-12¹/₂}"

FRONT
AND
BACK

1¹/₂"

{18-19³/₄}{22-23³/₄-26}"

Note: Sweater includes two edge stitches.

Size	Finished Chest Measurement
Small	35" (89 cm)
Medium	38$^{1}/_{4}$" (97 cm)
Large	43" (109 cm)
X-Large	46$^{1}/_{4}$" (117.5 cm)
XX-Large	51" (129.5 cm)

Size Note: Instructions are written with sizes Small and Medium in the first set of braces, and with sizes Large, X-Large, and XX-Large in the second set of braces { }. Instructions will be easier to read if you circle all the numbers pertaining to your size. If only one number is given, it applies to all sizes.

MATERIALS

Bulky Weight Yarn:

Ounces {13$^{1}/_{2}$-15$^{1}/_{2}$}{18-20-22$^{1}/_{2}$}
Yards {415-480}{555-615-695}
Grams {380-440}{510-570-640}
Meters {379.5-439}{507.5-562.5-635.5}
Straight knitting needles, sizes 9 (5.5 mm) **and** 10 (6 mm) **or** sizes needed for gauge
16" (40.5 cm) Circular needle, size 9 (5.5 mm)
Stitch holders - 2
Marker
Yarn needle

GAUGE: With larger size needles, in Stockinette Stitch, 14 sts and 20 rows = 4" (10 cm)

BACK
RIBBING

With smaller size straight needles, cast on {63-69}{77-83-91} sts **loosely**.

Row 1: K1, (P1, K1) across.

Row 2 (Right side)**:** P1, (K1, P1) across.

Repeat Rows 1 and 2 until Ribbing measures approximately 1$^{1}/_{2}$" (4 cm) from cast on edge, ending by working a **wrong** side row.

BODY

Change to larger size needles.

Beginning with a **knit** row, work Stockinette Stitch until Back measures approximately {12$^{3}/_{4}$-13$^{1}/_{2}$}{13$^{1}/_{2}$-14-14}"/ {32.5-34.5}{34.5-35.5-35.5} cm from cast on edge, ending by working a **purl** row.

ARMHOLE SHAPING

Row 1 (Decrease row)**:** K1, (P1, K1) twice, P3 tog tbl *(Fig. 28, page 585)*, knit across to last 8 sts, P3 tog *(Fig. 24, page 584)*, K1, (P1, K1) twice: {59-65}{73-79-87} sts.

Row 2: (P1, K1) 3 times, purl across to last 6 sts, (K1, P1) 3 times.

Repeat Rows 1 and 2, {1-2}{4-5-7} time(s): {55-57}{57-59-59} sts.

Next Row (Decrease row)**:** K1, (P1, K1) twice, P2 tog tbl *(Fig. 20, page 583)*, knit across to last 7 sts, P2 tog *(Fig. 18, page 583)*, K1, (P1, K1) twice: {53-55}{55-57-57} sts.

Next Row: (P1, K1) 3 times, purl across to last 6 sts, (K1, P1) 3 times.

Repeat last 2 rows, {4-3}{2-2-1} time(s): {45-49}{51-53-55} sts.

Work even until Back measures approximately {20$^{1}/_{4}$-21$^{1}/_{2}$}{22-23-23$^{1}/_{2}$}"/ {51.5-54.5}{56-58.5-59.5} cm from cast on edge, ending by working a **wrong** side row.

SHOULDER SHAPING

Rows 1-4: Bind off {4-4}{5-5-5} sts, work across: {29-33}{31-33-35} sts.

Rows 5 and 6: Bind off {3-5}{4-5-6} sts, work across: 23 sts.

Slip remaining sts onto st holder.

Instructions continued on page 172.

FRONT

Work same as Back until Front measures approximately {18³/₄-20}{20¹/₂-21¹/₂-22}"/ {47.5-51}{52-54.5-56} cm from cast on edge, ending by working a **wrong** side row: {45-49}{51-53-55} sts.

NECK SHAPING

Both sides of Neck are worked at the same time, using separate yarn for **each** side. Maintain established pattern throughout.

Row 1: Work across {17-19}{20-21-22} sts, slip next 11 sts onto st holder; with second yarn, work across: {17-19}{20-21-22} sts **each** side.

Rows 2 and 3: Work across; with second yarn, bind off 3 sts, work across: {14-16}{17-18-19} sts **each** side.

Rows 4 and 5: Work across; with second yarn, bind off 2 sts, work across: {12-14}{15-16-17} sts **each** side.

Row 6: Work across to last 2 sts, P2 tog tbl; with second yarn, P2 tog, work across: {11-13}{14-15-16} sts **each** side.

Work even until Front measures same as Back to Shoulder Shaping, ending by working a **wrong** side row.

SHOULDER SHAPING

Rows 1-4: Bind off {4-4}{5-5-5} sts, work across; with second yarn, work across: {3-5}{4-5-6} sts **each** side.

Row 5: Bind off remaining sts on first side; with second yarn, work across.

Bind off remaining sts.

FINISHING

Sew shoulder seams.

NECK RIBBING

With **right** side facing, slip 23 sts from Back st holder onto circular needle and knit across, pick up 14 sts evenly spaced along left Front Neck edge **(Figs. 34a & b, page 586)**, slip 11 sts from Front st holder onto second end of circular needle and knit across, pick up 14 sts evenly spaced along right Front Neck edge, place marker to mark beginning of rnd **(Fig. 1, page 578)**: 62 sts.

Work in K1, P1 ribbing around for 2¹/₂" (6.5 cm).

Knit 7 rnds.

Bind off all sts **loosely** in **knit**.

Weave side seams **(Fig. 36, page 587)**.

Design by Melissa Leapman.

V-NECK SWEATER COAT

■■■□ INTERMEDIATE

Long Version shown on page 177.

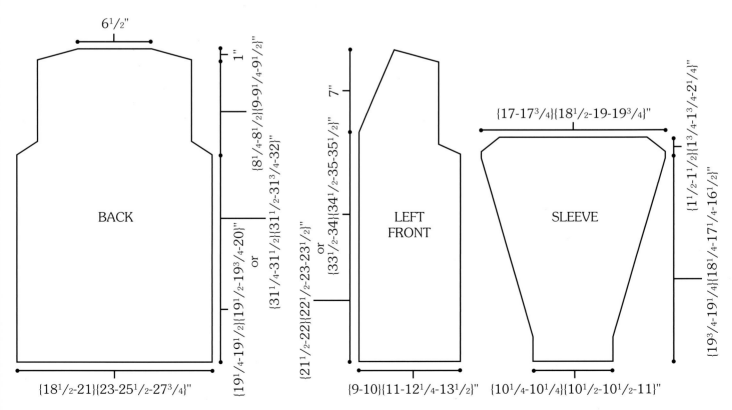

BACK

6¹/₂"

1"

{8¹/₄-8¹/₂}{9-9¹/₄-9¹/₂}"

{31¹/₄-31¹/₂}{31¹/₂-31³/₄-32}"
or
{21¹/₂-22}{22¹/₂-23-23¹/₂}"

{19¹/₄-19¹/₂}{19¹/₂-19³/₄-20}"
or

{18¹/₂-21}{23-25¹/₂-27³/₄}"

LEFT FRONT

7"

{33¹/₂-34}{34¹/₂-35-35¹/₂}"

{9-10}{11-12¹/₄-13¹/₂}"

SLEEVE

{17-17³/₄}{18¹/₂-19-19³/₄}"

{1¹/₂-1¹/₂}{1³/₄-1³/₄-2¹/₄}"

{19³/₄-19¹/₄}{18¹/₄-17¹/₄-16¹/₂}"

{10¹/₄-10¹/₄}{10¹/₂-10¹/₂-11}"

Note: Sweater includes two edge stitches.

Size	Finished Chest Measurement
Small	36$^1/_2$" (92.5 cm)
Medium	41$^1/_4$" (105 cm)
Large	45$^3/_4$" (116 cm)
X-Large	50$^1/_4$" (127.5 cm)
XX-Large	55" (139.5 cm)

Size Note: Instructions are written with sizes Small and Medium in the first set of braces, and with sizes Large, X-Large, and XX-Large in the second set of braces { }. Instructions will be easier to read if you circle all the numbers pertaining to your size. If only one number is given, it applies to all sizes.

MATERIALS

Bulky Weight Yarn:
   Short Version
      Ounces {33$^1/_2$-36$^1/_2$}{39$^1/_2$-42$^1/_2$-46}
      Yards {1,035-1,125}{1,220-1,310-1,420}
      Grams {950-1,040}{1,120-1,210-1,310}
      Meters {946.5-1,028.5}{1,115.5-1,198-1,298.5}
   Long Version
      Ounces {39-42$^1/_2$}{46-50-54$^1/_2$}
      Yards {1,205-1,310}{1,420-1,540-1,680}
      Grams {1,110-1,210}{1,310-1,420-1,550}
      Meters {1,102-1,198}{1,298.5-1,408-1,536}
Straight knitting needles, sizes 9 (5.5 mm) **and** 10 (6 mm) **or** sizes needed for gauge
16" (40.5 cm) Circular needle, size 9 (5.5 mm)
Stitch holders - 3
Yarn needle
Sewing needle and thread
1$^1/_2$" (38 mm) Buttons - 8

GAUGE: With larger size needles,
     in Stockinette Stitch,
      14 sts and 20 rows = 4" (10 cm)

BACK
BAND

With smaller size straight needles, cast on {55-62}{69-76-82} sts.

Rows 1-8: Knit across.

BODY

Change to larger size needles.

Knit across increasing {10-11}{12-13-15} sts evenly spaced *(see Increases, page 581)*: {65-73}{81-89-97} sts.

Beginning with a **purl** row, work in Stockinette Stitch until Back measures approximately {19$^1/_4$-19$^1/_2$}{19$^1/_2$-19$^3/_4$-20}"/{49-49.5}{49.5-50-51} cm from cast on edge for Short Version or approximately {31$^1/_4$-31$^1/_2$}{31$^1/_2$-31$^3/_4$-32}"/ {79.5-80}{80-80.5-81.5} cm from cast on edge for Long Version, ending by working a **purl** row.

ARMHOLE SHAPING

Row 1 (Decrease row): SSK *(Figs. 21a-c, page 584)*, knit across to last 2 sts, K2 tog *(Fig. 17, page 583)*: {63-71}{79-87-95} sts.

Row 2 (Decrease row): P2 tog *(Fig. 18, page 583)*, purl across to last 2 sts, SSP *(Fig. 22, page 584)*: {61-69}{77-85-93} sts.

Repeat Rows 1 and 2, {2-2}{3-3-4} times; then repeat Row 1 once **more**: {51-59}{63-71-75} sts.

Work even until Back measures approximately {27$^1/_2$-28}{28$^1/_2$-29-29$^1/_2$}"/{70-71}{72.5-73.5-75} cm from cast on edge for Short Version or approximately {39$^1/_2$-40}{40$^1/_2$-41-41$^1/_2$}"/ {100.5-101.5}{103-104-105.5} cm from cast on edge for Long Version, ending by working a **purl** row.

Instructions continued on page 176.

SHOULDER SHAPING

Rows 1-4: Bind off {5-6}{7-8-9} sts, work across: {31-35}{35-39-39} sts.

Rows 5 and 6: Bind off {4-6}{6-8-8} sts, work across: 23 sts.

Bind off remaining sts.

POCKET LINING (Make 2)

With larger size needles, cast on 21 sts.

Work in Stockinette Stitch until Pocket Lining measures approximately 6" {15 cm} from cast on edge, ending by working a **purl** row.

Slip sts onto st holder.

LEFT FRONT
BAND

With smaller size straight needles, cast on {26-30}{33-37-40} sts.

Rows 1-8: Knit across.

BODY

Change to larger size needles.

Knit across increasing {5-5}{6-6-7} sts evenly spaced: {31-35}{39-43-47} sts.

Beginning with a **purl** row, work in Stockinette Stitch until Left Front measures approximately 8½" (21.5 cm) from cast on edge for Short Version or approximately 20½" (52 cm) from cast on edge for Long Version, ending by working a **purl** row.

Pocket Placement Row: Knit {5-7}{9-11-13} sts, slip next 21 sts onto st holder (Pocket Band), slip 21 sts from Pocket Lining st holder onto left needle and knit across.

Work even until Left Front measures same as Back to Armhole Shaping, ending by working a **purl** row.

ARMHOLE SHAPING

Row 1 (Decrease row)**:** SSK, knit across: {30-34}{38-42-46} sts.

Row 2 (Decrease row)**:** Purl across to last 2 sts, SSP: {29-33}{37-41-45} sts.

Repeat Rows 1 and 2, {2-2}{3-3-4} times; then repeat Row 1 once **more**: {24-28}{30-34-36} sts.

Work even until Left Front measures approximately {21½-22}{22½-23-23½}"/ {54.5-56}{57-58.5-59.5} cm from cast on edge for Short Version or approximately {33½-34}{34½-35-35½}"/ {85-86.5}{87.5-89-90} cm from cast on edge for Long Version, ending by working a **purl** row.

NECK SHAPING

Row 1 (Decrease row)**:** Knit across to last 3 sts, K2 tog, K1: {23-27}{29-33-35} sts.

Row 2: Purl across.

Rows 3-11: Repeat Rows 1 and 2, 4 times; then repeat Row 1 once **more**: {18-22}{24-28-30} sts.

Row 12: Purl across.

Row 13: Knit across.

Row 14: Purl across.

Row 15 (Decrease row)**:** Knit across to last 3 sts, K2 tog, K1: {17-21}{23-27-29} sts.

Rows 16-27: Repeat Rows 12-15, 3 times: {14-18}{20-24-26} sts.

Work even until Left Front measures same as Back to Shoulder Shaping, ending by working a **purl** row.

SHOULDER SHAPING

Row 1: Bind off {5-6}{7-8-9} sts, knit across: {9-12}{13-16-17} sts.

Row 2: Purl across.

Rows 3 and 4: Repeat Rows 1 and 2: {4-6}{6-8-8} sts.

Bind off remaining sts.

RIGHT FRONT

Work same as Left Front to Armhole Shaping, ending by working a **knit** row: {31-35}{39-43-47} sts.

ARMHOLE SHAPING

Row 1 (Decrease row)**:** P2 tog, purl across: {30-34}{38-42-46} sts.

Row 2 (Decrease row)**:** Knit across to last 2 sts, K2 tog: {29-33}{37-41-45} sts.

Repeat Rows 1 and 2, {2-2}{3-3-4} times; then repeat Row 1 once **more**: {24-28}{30-34-36} sts.

Work even until Right Front measures same as Left Front to Neck Shaping, ending by working a **purl** row.

NECK SHAPING

Row 1 (Decrease row)**:** K1, SSK, knit across: {23-27}{29-33-35} sts.

Row 2: Purl across.

Rows 3-11: Repeat Rows 1 and 2, 4 times; then repeat Row 1 once **more**: {18-22}{24-28-30} sts.

Row 12: Purl across.

Row 13: Knit across.

Row 14: Purl across.

Instructions continued on page 178.

Row 15 (Decrease row)**:** K1, SSK, knit across: {17-21}{23-27-29} sts.

Rows 16-27: Repeat Rows 12-15, 3 times: {14-18}{20-24-26} sts.

Work even until Right Front measures same as Back to Shoulder Shaping, ending by working a **knit** row.

SHOULDER SHAPING
Row 1: Bind off {5-6}{7-8-9} sts, purl across: {9-12}{13-16-17} sts.

Row 2: Knit across.

Rows 3 and 4: Repeat Rows 1 and 2: {4-6}{6-8-8} sts.

Bind off remaining sts.

SLEEVE (Make 2)
BAND
With smaller size straight needles, cast on {30-30}{31-31-32} sts.

Rows 1-8: Knit across.

BODY
Change to larger size needles.

Knit across increasing {6-6}{6-6-7} sts evenly spaced: {36-36}{37-37-39} sts.

Beginning with a **purl** row, work in Stockinette Stitch increasing one stitch at **each** edge, every fourth row, {0-0}{3-8-10} times (*see Zeros, page 577*); then increase every sixth row, {5-10}{11-7-5} times; then increase every eighth row, {7-3}{0-0-0} times: {60-62}{65-67-69} sts.

Work even until Sleeve measures approximately {19³/₄-19¹/₄}{18¹/₄-17¹/₄-16¹/₂}"/ {50-49}{46.5-44-42} cm from cast on edge, ending by working a **purl** row.

SLEEVE CAP
Row 1 (Decrease row)**:** SSK, knit across to last 2 sts, K2 tog: {58-60}{63-65-67} sts.

Row 2 (Decrease row)**:** P2 tog, purl across to last 2 sts, SSP: {56-58}{61-63-65} sts.

Repeat Rows 1 and 2, {2-2}{3-3-4} times; then repeat Row 1 once **more**: {46-48}{47-49-47} sts.

Bind off remaining sts in **purl**.

FINISHING
POCKET BAND
With **right** side facing, slip 21 sts from Pocket Band st holder onto smaller size straight needle.

Row 1: Knit across decreasing 4 sts evenly spaced: 17 sts.

Rows 2-8: Knit across.

Bind off all sts in **knit**.

Repeat for remaining Pocket Band.

Sew Pocket Linings to **wrong** side of Fronts.

Sew Pocket Band edges to **right** side of Fronts.

BUTTON BAND
With **right** side facing, using circular needle, and beginning at Neck Shaping, pick up {70-72}{74-76-78} sts evenly spaced along Left Front edge for Short Version or {108-110}{112-114-116} sts evenly spaced along Left Front edge for Long Version (*Figs. 34a & b, page 586*).

Knit every row until Button Band measures approximately 1¹/₂" (4 cm).

Bind off all sts in **knit**.

BUTTONHOLE BAND

With **right** side facing and using circular needle, pick up {70-72}{74-76-78} sts evenly spaced along Right Front edge to Neck Shaping for Short Version or pick up {108-110}{112-114-116} sts evenly spaced along Right Front edge to Neck Shaping for Long Version.

Rows 1-4: Knit across.

Mark placement of buttons on Right Front, placing first marker ³/₄" (2 cm) from beginning of Neck Shaping for either length and placing last marker 2" (5 cm) from lower edge for Short Version or 14" (35.5 cm) from lower edge for Long Version; then evenly space six more markers for remaining buttons.

Row 5 (Buttonhole row): ★ Knit across to next marker, bind off 4 sts; repeat from ★ 7 times **more**, knit across.

Row 6: ★ Knit across to bound off sts, **turn**; add on 4 sts **(Figs. 5a & b, page 580)**; **turn**; repeat from ★ 7 times **more**, knit across.

Knit every row until Buttonhole Band measures approximately 1¹/₂" (4 cm).

Bind off all sts in **knit**.

BELT (Optional)

With smaller size straight needles, cast on 7 sts.

Work in Garter Stitch until Belt measures approximately 64" (1.75 meters) from cast on edge.

Bind off all sts in **knit**.

COLLAR

With larger size straight needles, cast on 6 sts.

Work in Garter Stitch increasing one stitch at **each** edge, every fourth row, 6 times; then increase every sixth row, 4 times: 26 sts.

Work even until piece measures 7" (18 cm) from last increase row.

Next Row (Decrease row): SSK, knit across to last 2 sts, K2 tog: 24 sts.

Continue in Garter Stitch decreasing one stitch at **each** edge, every sixth row, 3 times; then decrease every fourth row, 6 times: 6 sts.

Last 3 Rows: Knit across.

Bind off all sts in **knit**.

Sew shoulder seams.

Sew cast on edge of Collar to top of Buttonhole Band and bound off edge of Collar to Button Band; then sew Collar to neck edge.

Sew Sleeves to Coat, matching center of last row on Sleeves to shoulder seam, and sewing top of Sleeve and Sleeve Cap along Armhole Shaping and Armhole edge.

Weave underarm and side in one continuous seam **(Fig. 36, page 587)**.

Sew buttons to Button Band opposite buttonholes.

Design by Melissa Leapman.

CABLED HIGH-NECK PULLOER

◖■◻◻ **EASY**

Also shown on page 183.

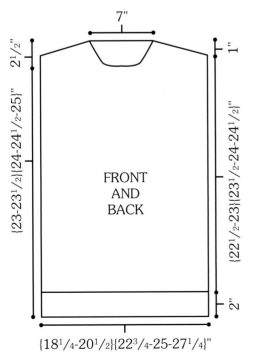

7"

2¹/₂"

1"

{23-23¹/₂}{24-24¹/₂-25}"

{22¹/₂-23}{23¹/₂-24-24¹/₂}"

FRONT
AND
BACK

2"

{18¹/₄-20¹/₂}{22³/₄-25-27¹/₄}"

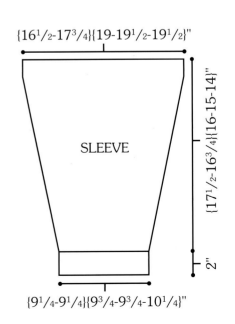

{16¹/₂-17³/₄}{19-19¹/₂-19¹/₂}"

{17¹/₂-16³/₄}{16-15-14}"

SLEEVE

2"

{9¹/₄-9¹/₄}{9³/₄-9³/₄-10¹/₄}"

Note: *Sweater includes two edge stitches.*

Size	Finished Chest Measurement
Small	35$\frac{1}{4}$" (89.5 cm)
Medium	40" (101.5 cm)
Large	44$\frac{1}{2}$" (113 cm)
X-Large	49" (124.5 cm)
XX-Large	53$\frac{1}{2}$" (136 cm)

Size Note: Instructions are written with sizes Small and Medium in the first set of braces, and with sizes Large, X-Large, and XX-Large in the second set of braces { }. Instructions will be easier to read if you circle all the numbers pertaining to your size. If only one number is given, it applies to all sizes.

MATERIALS

Bulky Weight Yarn:

Ounces {27$\frac{1}{2}$-30}{33$\frac{1}{2}$-36-38$\frac{1}{2}$}
Yards {850-925}{1,035-1,110-1,185}
Grams {780-850}{950-1,020-1,090}
Meters {777-846}{946.5-1,015-1,083.5}
Straight knitting needles, sizes 9 (5.5 mm) **and**
10 (6 mm) **or** sizes needed for gauge
16" (40.5 cm) Circular needle, size 9 (5.5 mm)
Cable needle
Stitch holders - 2
Markers
Yarn needle

GAUGE: With larger size needles,
in Reverse Stockinette Stitch,
14 sts and 20 rows = 4" (10 cm)

BACK
RIBBING

With smaller size straight needles,
cast on {68-76}{84-92-100} sts **loosely**.

Work in K1, P1 ribbing for 2" (5 cm).

PATTERN STITCH

CABLE PANEL (uses 12 sts)
Row 1 (Right side): Knit across.
Row 2: Purl across.
Row 3: Knit across.
Row 4: Purl across.
Row 5: Slip next 3 sts onto cable needle and hold in **back** of work, K3 from left needle, K3 from cable needle, slip next 3 sts onto cable needle and hold in **front** of work, K3 from left needle, K3 from cable needle.
Row 6: Purl across.
Repeat Rows 1-6 for pattern.

BODY

Change to larger size needles.

Row 1 (Right side): Purl {28-32}{36-40-44} sts, place marker *(Fig. 1, page 578)*, work Row 1 of Cable Panel, place marker, purl across.

Row 2: Knit across to next marker, work next row of Cable Panel, knit across.

Row 3: Purl across to next marker, work next row of Cable Panel, purl across.

Repeat Rows 2 and 3 for pattern until Back measures approximately {24$\frac{1}{2}$-25}{25$\frac{1}{2}$-26-26$\frac{1}{2}$}"/ {62-63.5}{65-66-67.5} cm from cast on edge, ending by working a **wrong** side row.

SHOULDER SHAPING

Maintain established pattern throughout.

Rows 1-4: Bind off {7-9}{10-11-13} sts, work across: {40-40}{44-48-48} sts.

Rows 5 and 6: Bind off {8-8}{10-12-12} sts, work across: 24 sts.

Make a note of which Cable Panel row you ended with, so you can continue working the Cable Panel later in the Neck Ribbing.

Slip remaining 24 sts onto st holder.

Instructions continued on page 182.

FRONT

Work same as Back until Front measures approximately {23-23 1/2}{24-24 1/2-25}"/ {58.5-59.5}{61-62-63.5} cm from cast on edge, ending by working a **wrong** side row.

Make a note of which Cable Panel row you ended with, so you can continue working the Cable Panel later in the Neck Ribbing.

NECK SHAPING

Both sides of Neck are worked at the same time, using separate yarn for **each** side.

Row 1 (Right side)**:** Purl across to next marker, remove marker and slip next 12 sts of Cable Panel onto st holder, remove next marker; with second yarn, purl across: {28-32}{36-40-44} sts **each** side.

Rows 2 and 3: Work across; with second yarn, bind off 3 sts, work across: {25-29}{33-37-41} sts **each** side.

Rows 4 and 5: Work across; with second yarn, bind off 2 sts, work across: {23-27}{31-35-39} sts **each** side.

Row 6: Knit across to within 2 sts of Neck edge, K2 tog **(Fig. 17, page 583)**; with second yarn, SSK **(Figs. 21a-c, page 584)**, knit across: {22-26}{30-34-38} sts **each** side.

Work even until Front measures same as Back to Shoulder Shaping, ending by working a **knit** row.

SHOULDER SHAPING

Rows 1-4: Bind off {7-9}{10-11-13} sts, work across; with second yarn, work across: {8-8}{10-12-12} sts **each** side.

Row 5: Bind off remaining sts on first side; with second yarn, purl across.

Bind off remaining sts.

SLEEVE (Make 2)
RIBBING

With smaller size straight needles, cast on {32-32}{34-34-36} sts **loosely**.

Work in K1, P1 ribbing for 2" (5 cm).

BODY

Change to larger size needles.

Beginning with a **purl** row, work in Reverse Stockinette Stitch increasing one stitch at **each** edge **(Figs. 10a & b, page 581)**, every fourth row, {0-9}{12-17-16} times **(see Zeros, page 577)**; then increase every sixth row, {13-6}{4-0-0} times: {58-62}{66-68-68} sts.

Work even until Sleeve measures approximately {19 1/2-18 3/4}{18-17-16}"/ {49.5-47.5}{45.5-43-40.5} cm from cast on edge, ending by working a **knit** row.

Bind off all sts in **purl**.

FINISHING

Sew shoulder seams.

NECK RIBBING

With **right** side facing, slip 24 sts from Back st holder onto circular needle and K6, work next row of Cable Panel across next 12 sts, K6, pick up 13 sts evenly spaced along left Front Neck edge **(Figs. 34a & b, page 586)**, slip 12 sts from Front st holder onto second end of circular needle and work next row of Cable Panel, pick up 13 sts evenly spaced along right Front Neck edge, place marker to mark beginning of rnd: 62 sts.

Rnd 1: (K1, P1) 3 times, work next row of Cable Panel, P1, (K1, P1) 9 times, work next row of Cable Panel, P1, (K1, P1) 6 times.

Repeat Rnd 1 until Ribbing measures approximately 2" (5 cm).

Bind off all sts **loosely** in pattern.

Sew Sleeves to Pullover, matching center of last row on Sleeve to shoulder seam, and beginning {8^1/$_4$-9}{9^1/$_2$-9^3/$_4$-9^3/$_4$}"/ {21-23}{24-25-25} cm down from seam.

Weave underarm and side in one continuous seam **(Fig. 36, page 587)**.

Design by Melissa Leapman.

TEXTURED CABLE PULLOVER

◖◼◼◼▭ INTERMEDIATE

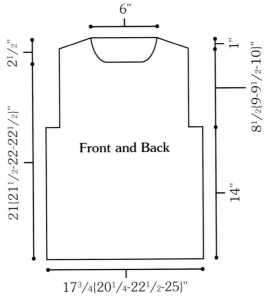

6"

2¹/₂"

1"

8¹/₂{9-9¹/₂-10}"

21{21¹/₂-22-22¹/₂}"

Front and Back

14"

17³/₄{20¹/₄-22¹/₂-25}"

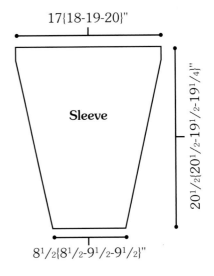

17{18-19-20}"

20¹/₂{20¹/₂-19¹/₂-19¹/₄}"

Sleeve

8¹/₂{8¹/₂-9¹/₂-9¹/₂}"

Size	Finished Chest Measurement	
Small	35"	(89 cm)
Medium	40"	(101.5 cm)
Large	44¹/₂"	(113 cm)
X-Large	49¹/₂"	(125.5 cm)

Size Note: Instructions are written for size Small with sizes Medium, Large, and X-Large in braces { }. Instructions will be easier to read if you circle all the numbers pertaining to your size. If only one number is given, it applies to all sizes.

Note: Sweater includes two edge stitches.

MATERIALS

Worsted Weight Yarn: **(4)** MEDIUM

Ounces	21$\frac{1}{2}${24-26$\frac{1}{2}$-29}
Yards	1,410{1,575-1,740-1,905}
Grams	610{680-750-820}
Meters	1,289{1,440-1,591-1,742}

Straight knitting needles, size 8 (5 mm) **or** size needed for gauge
16" (40.75 cm) Circular needle, size 7 (4.5 mm)
Cable needle
Stitch holder
Markers
Yarn needle

GAUGE: With straight needles, in pattern, 20 sts and 28 rows = 4" (10 cm)

BACK

With straight needles, cast on 94{106-118-130} sts.

Row 1 (Right side): K1, (P1, K1) 18{21-24-27} times, P2, place marker **(see Markers, page 578)**, K4, slip next 2 sts onto cable needle and hold in **back** of work, K2, K2 from cable needle, slip next 2 sts onto cable needle and hold in **front** of work, K2, K2 from cable needle, K4, place marker, P1, (K1, P1) 19{22-25-28} times.

Row 2: K1, (P1, K1) across to marker, P 16, K2, P1, (K1, P1) across.

Row 3: P1, (K1, P1) across to marker, K2, slip next 2 sts onto cable needle and hold in **back** of work, K2, K2 from cable needle, K4, slip next 2 sts onto cable needle and hold in **front** of work, K2, K2 from cable needle, K2, P2, K1, (P1, K1) across.

Row 4: P1, (K1, P1) across to within 2 sts of marker, K2, P 16, K1, (P1, K1) across.

Row 5: K1, (P1, K1) across to within 2 sts of marker, P2, slip next 2 sts onto cable needle and hold in **back** of work, K2, K2 from cable needle, K8, slip next 2 sts onto cable needle and hold in **front** of work, K2, K2 from cable needle, P1, (K1, P1) across.

Row 6: K1, (P1, K1) across to marker, P 16, K2, P1, (K1, P1) across.

Row 7: P1, (K1, P1) across to marker, K4, slip next 2 sts onto cable needle and hold in **back** of work, K2, K2 from cable needle, slip next 2 sts onto cable needle and hold in **front** of work, K2, K2 from cable needle, K4, P2, K1, (P1, K1) across.

Row 8: P1, (K1, P1) across to within 2 sts of marker, K2, P 16, K1, (P1, K1) across.

Row 9: K1, (P1, K1) across to within 2 sts of marker, P2, K2, slip next 2 sts onto cable needle and hold in **back** of work, K2, K2 from cable needle, K4, slip next 2 sts onto cable needle and hold in **front** of work, K2, K2 from cable needle, K2, P1, (K1, P1) across.

Row 10: K1, (P1, K1) across to marker, P 16, K2, P1, (K1, P1) across.

Row 11: P1, (K1, P1) across to marker, slip next 2 sts onto cable needle and hold in **back** of work, K2, K2 from cable needle, K8, slip next 2 sts onto cable needle and hold in **front** of work, K2, K2 from cable needle, P2, K1, (P1, K1) across.

Row 12: P1, (K1, P1) across to within 2 sts of marker, K2, P 16, K1, (P1, K1) across.

Row 13: K1, (P1, K1) across to within 2 sts of marker, P2, K4, slip next 2 sts onto cable needle and hold in **back** of work, K2, K2 from cable needle, slip next 2 sts onto cable needle and hold in **front** of work, K2, K2 from cable needle, K4, P1, (K1, P1) across.

Repeat Rows 2-13 for pattern until Back measures approximately 14" (35.5 cm) from cast on edge, ending by working a **wrong** side row.

ARMHOLE SHAPING

Note: Maintain established patterns throughout.

Rows 1 and 2: Bind off 7{9-9-11} sts, work across: 80{88-100-108} sts.

Work even until Back measures approximately 22$\frac{1}{2}${23-23$\frac{1}{2}$-24}"/57{58.5-59.5-61} cm from cast on edge, ending by working a **wrong** side row.

Instructions continued on page 186.

SHOULDER SHAPING

Rows 1-6: Bind off 6{7-8-9} sts, work across: 44{46-52-54} sts.

Rows 7 and 8: Bind off 5{6-9-10} sts, work across: 34 sts.

Slip remaining sts onto st holder.

FRONT

Work same as Back until Front measures approximately 21{21$\frac{1}{2}$-22-22$\frac{1}{2}$}"/ 53.5{54.5-56-57} cm from cast on edge, ending by working a **wrong** side row: 80{88-100-108} sts.

NECK SHAPING

Row 1: Work across 32{36-42-46} sts, bind off next 16 sts, work across: 32{36-42-46} sts **each** side.

Note: Both sides of Neck are worked at the same time, using separate yarn for **each** side.

Rows 2 and 3: Work across; with second yarn, bind off 3 sts, work across: 29{33-39-43} sts **each** side.

Rows 4-7: Work across; with second yarn, bind off 2 sts, work across: 25{29-35-39} sts **each** side.

Rows 8 and 9: Work across to within 2 sts of neck edge, decrease *(see Decreases, pages 583 & 584)*; with second yarn, decrease, work across: 23{27-33-37} sts **each** side.

Work even until Front measures same as Back to Shoulder Shaping, ending by working a **wrong** side row.

SHOULDER SHAPING

Rows 1-6: Bind off 6{7-8-9} sts, work across; with second yarn, work across: 5{6-9-10} sts **each** side.

Row 7: Bind off remaining sts on first side; with second yarn, work across.

Bind off remaining sts.

SLEEVE (Make 2)
SIZE SMALL ONLY

With straight needles, cast on 43 sts **loosely**.

Row 1 (Right side)**:** K1, (P1, K1) across.

Rows 2 and 3: P1, (K1, P1) across.

Rows 4 and 5: K1, (P1, K1) across.

Increase as instructed, working a knit increase before and after a purl stitch and a purl increase before and after a knit stitch *(see Knit and Purl Increases, page 581)*.

Row 6: Increase, K1, (P1, K1) across to last st, increase: 45 sts.

Adding new stitches in pattern, continue to increase one stitch at **each** edge, every sixth row, 20 times **more**: 85 sts.

Work even until Sleeve measures approximately 20$\frac{1}{2}$" (52 cm) from cast on edge.

Bind off all sts.

SIZES MEDIUM, LARGE, AND X-LARGE ONLY

With straight needles, cast on {43-47-47} sts **loosely**.

Row 1 (Right side)**:** K1, (P1, K1) across.

Rows 2 and 3: P1, (K1, P1) across.

Increase as instructed, working a knit increase before and after a purl stitch and a purl increase before and after a knit stitch *(see Knit and Purl Increases, page 581)*.

Row 4: Increase, P1, (K1, P1) across to last st, increase: {45-49-49} sts.

Adding new stitches in pattern, continue to increase one stitch at **each** edge, every fourth row, {10-14-24} times **more**; then increase every sixth row, {13-9-2} times: {91-95-101} sts.

Work even until Sleeve measures approximately {20$\frac{1}{2}$-19$\frac{1}{2}$-19$\frac{1}{4}$}"/{52-49.5-49} cm from cast on edge.

Bind off all sts.

FINISHING

Sew shoulder seams.

NECK RIBBING

With **right** side facing, slip 34 sts from Back st holder onto circular needle and knit across, pick up 19 sts evenly spaced along left Front Neck edge **(Figs. 34a & b, page 586)**, pick up 16 sts across bound off sts on Front, pick up 19 sts evenly spaced along right Front Neck edge, place marker to mark beginning of rnd: 88 sts.

Work in K1, P1 ribbing around for 1" (2.5 cm).

Bind off all sts **loosely** in ribbing.

Sew Sleeves to Pullover, matching center of last row on Sleeve to shoulder seam and sewing top of Sleeve along Armhole edge and sides of Sleeve to bound off edges.

Weave underarm and side in one continuous seam **(Fig. 36, page 587)**, leaving lower 3{3-3^1/$_2$-3^1/$_2$}"/7.5{7.5-9-9} cm on Body open for side slits.

Design by Melissa Leapman.

UPDATED BARN JACKET

Long Version shown on page 189. Short Version shown on page 191.

■■■□ INTERMEDIATE

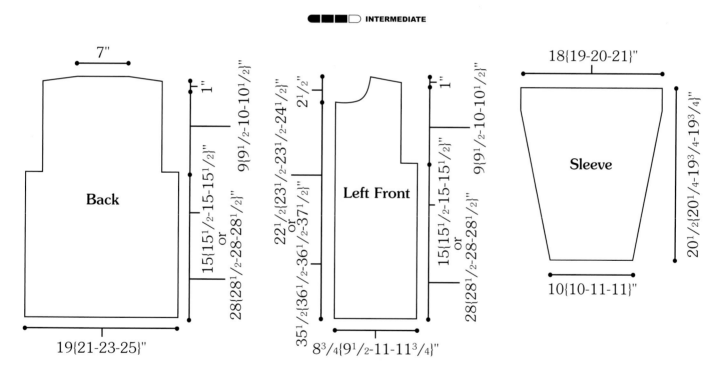

Size	Finished Chest Measurement	
Small	37"	(94 cm)
Medium	41"	(104 cm)
Large	45^1/$_2$"	(115.5 cm)
X-Large	49^1/$_2$"	(125.5 cm)

Size Note: Instructions are written for size Small with sizes Medium, Large, and X-Large in braces { }. Instructions will be easier to read if you circle all the numbers pertaining to your size. If only one number is given, it applies to all sizes.

Note: Sweater includes two edge stitches.

Instructions begin on page 188.

MATERIALS

Worsted Weight Yarn: 🧶 **MEDIUM 4**

Short Version

Ounces	19{21-23-25}
Yards	1,245{1,380-1,510-1,640}
Grams	540{600-650-710}
Meters	1,138.5{1,262-1,380.5-1,499.5}

Long Version

Ounces	29{32-34$^1/_2$-37$^1/_2$}
Yards	1,680{1,855-2,000-2,175}
Grams	820{910-980-1,070}
Meters	1,536{1,696-1,829-1,989}

Straight knitting needles, sizes 7 (4.5 mm)
and 8 (5 mm) **or** sizes needed for gauge
36" (91.5 cm) Circular needle, size 7 (4.5 mm)
Stitch holders - 3
Markers
Yarn needle
Sewing needle and thread
$^7/_8$" (2.25 cm) Buttons - 7

GAUGE: With larger size needles,
in Stockinette Stitch,
18 sts and 26 rows = 4" (10 cm)

BACK

With smaller size straight needles, cast on
85{95-103-113} sts *(Figs. 2a-e, page 9)*.

Rows 1-6: Knit across.

Row 7 (Right side)**:** ★ K2 tog *(Fig. 17, page 583)*, YO *(Fig. 16a, page 582)*; repeat
from ★ across to last st, K1.

Row 8: ★ P2 tog *(Fig. 18, page 583)*, YO
(Fig. 16b, page 582); repeat from ★ across to last
st, P1.

Rows 9 and 10: Repeat Rows 7 and 8.

Rows 11-17: Knit across.

Change to larger size needles.

Beginning with a **purl** row, work in Stockinette
Stitch until Back measures approximately
15{15$^1/_2$-15-15$^1/_2$}"/38{39.5-38-39.5} cm from
cast on edge for Short Version or approximately
28{28$^1/_2$-28-28$^1/_2$}"/71{72.5-71-72.5} cm from
cast on edge for Long Version, ending by working
a **purl** row.

ARMHOLE SHAPING

Rows 1 and 2: Bind off 7{9-9-11} sts, work
across: 71{77-85-91} sts.

Work even until Back measures approximately
24{25-25-26}"/61{63.5-63.5-66} cm from cast
on edge for Short Version or approximately
37{38-38-39}"/94{96.5-96.5-99} cm from cast
on edge for Long Version, ending by working a
purl row.

SHOULDER SHAPING

Rows 1-4: Bind off 7{8-9-10} sts, work across:
43{45-49-51} sts.

Rows 5 and 6: Bind off 6{7-9-10} sts, work
across: 31 sts.

Bind off remaining sts in **knit**, placing marker
around center st for Collar placement.

POCKET LINING (Make 2)

With larger size needles, cast on 23 sts.

Work in Stockinette Stitch until Pocket Lining
measures approximately 5" (12.5 cm) from cast
on edge, ending by working a **purl** row.

Slip sts onto st holder.

LEFT FRONT

With smaller size straight needles, cast on
39{43-49-53} sts.

Work same as Back until Left Front measures
approximately 6" (15 cm) from cast on edge for
Short Version or approximately 19" (48.5 cm)
from cast on edge for Long Version, ending by
working a **purl** row.

Pocket Placement Row:

Knit 8{10-13-15} sts, slip next 23 sts onto st holder (Pocket Band), slip 23 sts from Pocket Lining st holder onto left needle and knit across.

Work even until Left Front measures same as Back to Armhole Shaping, ending by working a **purl** row.

ARMHOLE SHAPING

Row 1: Bind off 7{9-9-11} sts, knit across: 32{34-40-42} sts.

Work even until Left Front measures approximately 22^1/$_2${23^1/$_2$-23^1/$_2$-24^1/$_2$}"/57{59.5-59.5-62} cm from cast on edge for Short Version or approximately 35^1/$_2${36^1/$_2$-36^1/$_2$-37^1/$_2$}"/90{92.5-92.5-95.5} cm from cast on edge for Long Version, ending by working a **knit** row.

NECK SHAPING

Row 1: Bind off 5{4-6-5} sts, purl across: 27{30-34-37} sts.

Row 2: Knit across.

Row 3: Bind off 3 sts, purl across: 24{27-31-34} sts.

Row 4: Knit across.

Row 5: Bind off 2 sts, purl across: 22{25-29-32} sts.

Row 6: Knit across to within 2 sts of Neck edge, K2 tog: 21{24-28-31} sts.

Row 7: Bind off one st, purl across: 20{23-27-30} sts.

Work even until Left Front measures same as Back to Shoulder Shaping, ending by working a **purl** row.

Instructions continued on page 190.

SHOULDER SHAPING

Row 1: Bind off 7{8-9-10} sts, knit across: 13{15-18-20} sts.

Row 2: Purl across.

Rows 3 and 4: Repeat Rows 1 and 2: 6{7-9-10} sts.

Bind off remaining sts in **knit**.

RIGHT FRONT

Work same as Left Front to Armhole Shaping, ending by working a **knit** row: 39{43-49-53} sts.

ARMHOLE SHAPING

Row 1: Bind off 7{9-9-11} sts, purl across: 32{34-40-42} sts.

Work even until Right Front measures same as Left Front to Neck Shaping, ending by working a **purl** row.

NECK SHAPING

Row 1: Bind off 5{4-6-5} sts, knit across: 27{30-34-37} sts.

Row 2: Purl across.

Row 3: Bind off 3 sts, knit across: 24{27-31-34} sts.

Row 4: Purl across.

Row 5: Bind off 2 sts, knit across: 22{25-29-32} sts.

Row 6: Purl across to within 2 sts of Neck edge, P2 tog: 21{24-28-31} sts.

Row 7: Bind off one st, knit across: 20{23-27-30} sts.

Work even until Right Front measures same as Back to Shoulder Shaping, ending by working a **knit** row.

SHOULDER SHAPING

Row 1: Bind off 7{8-9-10} sts, purl across: 13{15-18-20} sts.

Row 2: Knit across.

Rows 3 and 4: Repeat Rows 1 and 2: 6{7-9-10} sts.

Bind off remaining sts in **purl**.

SLEEVE (Make 2)

With smaller size straight needles, cast on 45{45-49-49} sts.

Rows 1-6: Knit across.

Row 7 (Right side)**:** (K2 tog, YO) across to last st, K1.

Row 8: (P2 tog, YO) across to last st, P1.

Rows 9 and 10: Repeat Rows 7 and 8.

Rows 11-17: Knit across.

Change to larger size needles.

Beginning with a **purl** row, work in Stockinette Stitch increasing one stitch at **each** edge *(Figs. 10a & b, page 581)*, every fourth row, 0{4-9-16} times *(see Zeros, page 577)*; then increase every sixth row, 14{16-12-7} times; then increase every eighth row, 4{0-0-0} times: 81{85-91-95} sts.

Work even until Sleeve measures approximately $20\frac{1}{2}${$20\frac{1}{4}$-$19\frac{3}{4}$-$19\frac{3}{4}$}"/52{51.5-50-50} cm from cast on edge, ending by working a **purl** row.

Bind off all sts in **knit**.

FINISHING

Sew shoulder seams.

POCKET BAND

With **right** side facing, slip 23 sts from Pocket Band st holder onto smaller size straight needle and knit across.

Knit each row for 1" (2.5 cm).

Bind off all sts in **knit**.

Repeat for remaining Pocket Band.

Sew Pocket Linings to wrong side of Fronts.

Sew Pocket Band edges to right side of Fronts.

BUTTON BAND

With **right** side facing and using circular needle, pick up 126{130-130-134} sts evenly spaced across Left Front edge for Short Version or 194{200-200-204} sts evenly spaced across Left Front edge for Long Version **(Figs. 34a & b, page 586)**.

Work in K1, P1 ribbing for $1^1/2$" (3.75 cm).

Bind off all sts in ribbing.

BUTTONHOLE BAND

With **right** side facing and using circular needle, pick up 126{130-130-134} sts evenly spaced across Right Front edge for Short Version or 194{200-200-204} sts evenly spaced across Right Front edge for Long Version.

Work in K1, P1 ribbing for $^3/4$" (2 cm).

Mark placement of buttons on Right Front, placing first marker $^1/2$" (1.25 cm) from top edge for either length and placing last marker $^1/2$" (1.25 cm) from lower edge for Short Version or $13^1/2$" (34.5 cm) from lower edge for Long Version; then evenly space five more markers for remaining buttons.

Next Row: ★ Work in established ribbing across to next marker, bind off 2 sts in pattern; repeat from ★ 6 times **more**, work across in established ribbing.

Instructions continued on page 192.

Next Row: ★ Work in established ribbing across to bound off sts, **turn**; add on 2 sts *(Figs. 5a & b, page 580)*, **turn**; repeat from ★ 6 times **more**, work across in established ribbing.

Work even until Buttonhole Band measures 1¹/₂" (3.75 cm).

Bind off all sts in ribbing.

COLLAR

With **right** side facing, using circular needle and beginning at center top edge of Buttonhole Band, pick up 3 sts along edge of Buttonhole Band, pick up 14 sts evenly spaced along Right Front Neck edge, pick up one st in shoulder seam, place marker *(see Markers, page 578)*, pick up 12 sts evenly spaced across Back to marked st, place marker, pick up 12 sts evenly spaced across to shoulder seam, place marker, pick up one st in shoulder seam, pick up 14 sts evenly spaced along Left Front neck edge, pick up 3 sts along Button Band edge ending at center of Band: 60 sts.

Row 1: Knit across.

Row 2 (Right side)**:** ★ Knit across to next marker, slip marker, M1 *(Figs. 14a & b, page 582)*; repeat from ★ once **more**, knit across to next marker, M1, slip marker, knit across: 63 sts.

Row 3: Knit across.

Row 4: Knit across to next marker, slip marker, M1, ★ knit across to next marker, M1, slip marker; repeat from ★ once **more**, knit across: 66 sts.

Rows 5-17: Repeat Rows 1-4, 3 times, then repeat Row 1 once **more**: 84 sts.

Row 18: ★ Knit across to next marker, remove marker, M1; repeat from ★ 2 times **more**, knit across: 87 sts.

Row 19: (K2 tog, YO) across to last st, K1.

Row 20: (P2 tog, YO) across to last st, P1.

Rows 21 and 22: Repeat Rows 19 and 20.

Rows 23-28: Knit across.

Bind off all sts **loosely** in **knit**.

Sew Sleeves to Jacket, matching center of last row on Sleeve to shoulder seam, and sewing top of Sleeve along Armhole edge and sides of Sleeve to bound off edges.

Weave underarm and side in one continuous seam *(Fig. 36, page 587)*.

Sew buttons to Button Band opposite buttonholes.

Design by Melissa Leapman.

ROLLED HIGH-NECK PULLOVER

Also shown on page 195.

■■■□ INTERMEDIATE

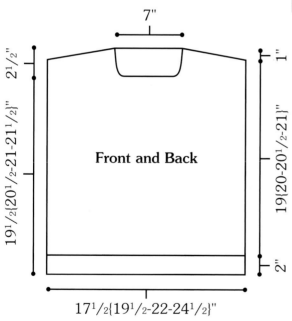

7"

2¹/₂"

1"

19¹/₂{20¹/₂-21-21¹/₂}"

19{20-20¹/₂-21}"

Front and Back

2"

17¹/₂{19¹/₂-22-24¹/₂}"

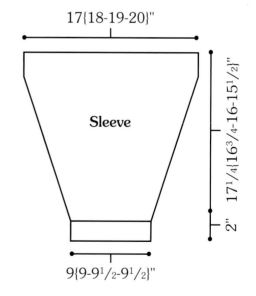

17{18-19-20}"

17¹/₄{16³/₄-16-15¹/₂}"

Sleeve

2"

9{9-9¹/₂-9¹/₂}"

Size	Finished Chest Measurement	
Small	34"	(86.5 cm)
Medium	38"	(96.5 cm)
Large	43"	(109 cm)
X-Large	48¹/₂"	(123 cm)

Size Note: Instructions are written for size Small with sizes Medium, Large, and X-Large in braces { }. Instructions will be easier to read if you circle all the numbers pertaining to your size. If only one number is given, it applies to all sizes.

Note: Sweater includes two edge stitches.

Instructions begin on page 194.

MATERIALS

Worsted Weight Yarn: **MEDIUM 4**

MC (Tan or Lt Purple) -
Ounces 16{17-18^1/$_2$-20^1/$_2$}
Yards   1,052{1,115-1,215-1,345}
Grams   450{480-530-580}
Meters 962{1,019.5-1,111-1230}
Color A (Black or Dk Purple) -
Ounce   1
Yards   65
Grams   30
Meters 59.5
Color B (Ecru or White) -
Ounce   1
Yards   65
Grams   30
Meters 59.5
Straight knitting needles, sizes 7 (4.5 mm)
and 8 (5 mm) **or** sizes needed for gauge
16" (40.75 cm) Circular needle, size 7 (4.5 mm)
Stitch holders - 2
Marker
Yarn needle

GAUGE: With larger size needles,
in Stockinette Stitch,
18 sts and 26 rows = 4" (10 cm)

BACK
RIBBING

With MC and smaller size straight needles,
cast on 79{87-99-111} sts **loosely (Figs. 2a-e,
page 9)**.

Row 1: K1, (P1, K1) across.

Row 2 (Right side): P1, (K1, P1) across.

Repeat Rows 1 and 2 until Ribbing measures
2" (5 cm), ending by working Row 1.

BODY

Change to larger size needles.

Beginning with a **knit** row, work in Stockinette
Stitch until Back measures approximately
12^1/$_2${13^1/$_2$-14-14^1/$_2$}"/32{34.5-35.5-37} cm
from cast on edge, ending by working a **purl**
row; cut MC.

With Color A, work in Stockinette Stitch for
7 rows; cut Color A.

With Color B, work in Stockinette Stitch for
7 rows; cut Color B.

With MC, work in Stockinette Stitch until Back
measures approximately 21{22-22^1/$_2$-23}"/
53.5{56-57-58.5} cm from cast on edge, ending
by working a **purl** row.

SHOULDER SHAPING

Rows 1-4: Bind off 8{9-11-13} sts, work
across: 47{51-55-59} sts.

Rows 5 and 6: Bind off 8{10-12-14} sts, work
across: 31 sts.

Slip remaining sts onto st holder.

FRONT

Work same as Back until Front measures
approximately 19^1/$_2${20^1/$_2$-21-21^1/$_2$}"/
49.5{52-53.5-54.5} cm from cast on edge,
ending by working a **purl** row.

NECK SHAPING

Note: Both sides of Neck are worked at the
same time, using separate yarn for **each** side.

Row 1: Knit 32{36-42-48} sts, slip next 15 sts
onto st holder; with second yarn, knit across:
32{36-42-48} sts **each** side.

Rows 2 and 3: Work across; with second yarn,
bind off 3 sts, work across: 29{33-39-45} sts
each side.

Rows 4-7: Work across; with second yarn, bind off
2 sts, work across: 25{29-35-41} sts **each** side.

Rows 8 and 9: Work across; with second yarn,
bind off one st, work across: 24{28-34-40} sts
each side.

Work even until Front measures same as Back to
Shoulder Shaping, ending by working a **purl** row.

SHOULDER SHAPING

Rows 1-4: Bind off 8{9-11-13} sts, work across; with second yarn, work across: 8{10-12-14} sts **each** side.

Row 5: Bind off remaining sts on first side; with second yarn, knit across.

Bind off remaining sts.

SLEEVE (Make 2)
RIBBING

With MC and smaller size straight needles, cast on 41{41-43-43} sts **loosely**.

Row 1: K1, (P1, K1) across.

Row 2 (Right side)**:** P1, (K1, P1) across.

Repeat Rows 1 and 2 until Ribbing measures 2" (5 cm), ending by working Row 2.

BODY

Change to larger size needles.

Beginning with a **purl** row, work in Stockinette Stitch increasing one stitch at **each** edge **(Figs. 10a & b, page 581)**, every other row, 0{0-0-2} times **(see Zeros, page 577)**; then increase every fourth row, 2{9-15-22} times; then increase every sixth row, 16{11-6-0} times: 77{81-85-91} sts.

Work even until Sleeve measures approximately 19^1/$_4${18^3/$_4$-18-17^1/$_2$}"/49{47.5-45.5-44.5} cm from cast on edge, ending by working a **purl** row.

Bind off all sts in **knit**.

FINISHING

Sew shoulder seams.

NECK RIBBING

With **right** side facing and MC, slip 31 sts from Back st holder onto circular needle and knit across, pick up 16 sts evenly spaced along left Front Neck edge **(Figs. 34a & b, page 586)**, slip 15 sts from Front st holder onto second end of circular needle and knit across, pick up 16 sts evenly spaced along right Front Neck edge, place marker to mark beginning of rnd **(see Markers, page 578)**: 78 sts.

Work in K1, P1 ribbing around for 3" (7.5 cm).

Knit 7 rounds.

Bind off all sts **loosely** in **knit**, allowing edge to roll.

Sew Sleeves to Pullover, matching center of last row on Sleeve to shoulder seam and beginning 8^1/$_2${9-9^1/$_2$-10}"/21.5{23-24-25.5} cm down from seam.

Weave underarm and side in one continuous seam **(Fig. 36, page 587)**.

Design by Melissa Leapman.

CABLED CARDIGAN VEST

◖■■■▢ **INTERMEDIATE**

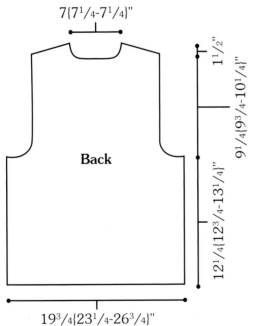

$7\{7^1/_4$-$7^1/_4\}$"

$1^1/_2$"

$9^1/_4\{9^3/_4$-$10^1/_4\}$"

Back

$12^1/_4\{12^3/_4$-$13^1/_4\}$"

$19^3/_4\{23^1/_4$-$26^3/_4\}$"

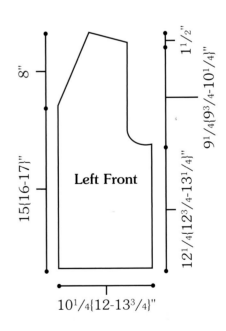

$1^1/_2$"

8"

$9^1/_4\{9^3/_4$-$10^1/_4\}$"

$15\{16$-$17\}$"

Left Front

$12^1/_4\{12^3/_4$-$13^1/_4\}$"

$10^1/_4\{12$-$13^3/_4\}$"

Size	Finished Chest Measurement	
Small	40"	(101.5 cm)
Medium	47"	(119.5 cm)
Large	54"	(137 cm)

Size Note: Instructions are written for size Small with sizes Medium and Large in braces { }. Instructions will be easier to read if you circle all the numbers pertaining to your size. If only one number is given, it applies to all sizes.

Note: Sweater includes two edge stitches.

MATERIALS

Worsted Weight Yarn: **MEDIUM 4**

Ounces	14{17-21}
Yards	920{1,115-1,380}
Grams	400{480-600}
Meters	841{1,019.5-1,262}

Straight knitting needles, sizes 7 (4.5 mm)
  and 8 (5 mm) **or** sizes needed for gauge
Cable needle
Stitch holders - 2
Yarn needle
Sewing needle and thread
$7/8$" (2.25 cm) Button

GAUGE: With larger size needles, in pattern,
  Each repeat (11 sts) = $1^3/4$" (4.5 cm);
  24 rows = 4" (10 cm)

BACK

With larger size needles, cast on 126{148-170} sts
(Figs. 2a-e, page 9).

Row 1 (Right side)**:** K5, ★ P1, slip next st onto cable needle and hold in **back** of work, K1, P1 from cable needle, slip next st onto cable needle and hold in **front** of work, P1, K1 from cable needle, P1, K5; repeat from ★ across.

Row 2: P5, ★ K1, P1, K2, P1, K1, P5; repeat from ★ across.

Row 3: K5, ★ P1, slip next st onto cable needle and hold in **front** of work, P1, K1 from cable needle, slip next st onto cable needle and hold in **back** of work, K1, P1 from cable needle, P1, K5; repeat from ★ across.

Row 4: P5, ★ K2, P2, K2, P5; repeat from ★ across.

Row 5: K5, ★ P2, slip next st onto cable needle and hold in **back** of work, K1, K1 from cable needle, P2, K5; repeat from ★ across.

Row 6: P5, ★ K2, P2, K2, P5; repeat from ★ across.

Repeat Rows 1-6 for pattern until Back measures approximately $12^1/4$ {$12^3/4$-$13^1/4$}"/ 31{32.5-33.5} cm from cast on edge, ending by working a **wrong** side row.

ARMHOLE SHAPING

Note: Maintain established pattern throughout.

Rows 1 and 2: Bind off 7{9-11} sts, work across: 112{130-148} sts.

Rows 3 and 4: Bind off 5{6-8} sts, work across: 102{118-132} sts.

Rows 5 and 6: Bind off 3{4-6} sts, work across: 96{110-120} sts.

Row 7 (Decrease row)**:** SSK *(Figs. 21a-c, page 584)*, work across to last 2 sts, K2 tog *(Fig. 17, page 583)*: 94{108-118} sts.

Row 8 (Decrease row)**:** P2 tog *(Fig. 18, page 583)*, work across to last 2 sts, SSP *(Fig. 22, page 584)*: 92{106-116} sts.

Continue to decrease one stitch at **each** edge, every row, 1{2-3} time(s) **more**; then decrease every other row, 3{4-5} times: 84{94-100} sts.

Work even until Back measures approximately $21^1/2$ {$22^1/2$-$23^1/2$}"/54.5{57-59.5} cm from cast on edge, ending by working a **wrong** side row.

NECK SHAPING

Note: Both sides of Neck are worked at the same time, using separate yarn for **each** side.

Row 1: Work across 20{24-27} sts; with second yarn, bind off next 44{46-46} sts, work across: 20{24-27} sts **each** side.

Row 2: Work across to within 2 sts of Neck edge, decrease; with second yarn, decrease, work across: 19{23-26} sts **each** side.

SHOULDER SHAPING

Rows 1-6: Bind off 5{6-7} sts, work across; with second yarn, work across: 4{5-5} sts **each** side.

Row 7: Bind off remaining sts on first side; with second yarn, work across.

Bind off remaining sts.

Instructions continued on page 198.

LEFT FRONT

With larger size needles, cast on 67{78-89} sts.

Row 1 (Right side): K5, ★ P1, slip next st onto cable needle and hold in **back** of work, K1, P1 from cable needle, slip next st onto cable needle and hold in **front** of work, P1, K1 from cable needle, P1, K5; repeat from ★ across to last 7 sts, P1, (K1, P1) across (Front band).

Row 2: K1, (P1, K1) 3 times, P5, ★ K1, P1, K2, P1, K1, P5; repeat from ★ across.

Row 3: K5, ★ P1, slip next st onto cable needle and hold in **front** of work, P1, K1 from cable needle, slip next st onto cable needle and hold in **back** of work, K1, P1 from cable needle, P1, K5; repeat from ★ across to last 7 sts, P1, (K1, P1) across.

Row 4: K1, (P1, K1) 3 times, P5, ★ K2, P2, K2, P5; repeat from ★ across.

Row 5: K5, ★ P2, slip next st onto cable needle and hold in **back** of work, K1, K1 from cable needle, P2, K5; repeat from ★ across to last 7 sts, P1, (K1, P1) across.

Row 6: K1, (P1, K1) 3 times, P5, ★ K2, P2, K2, P5; repeat from ★ across.

Repeat Rows 1-6 for pattern until Left Front measures same as Back to Armhole Shaping, ending by working a **wrong** side row.

ARMHOLE SHAPING

Note: Maintain established pattern throughout.

Row 1: Bind off 7{9-11} sts, work across to last 7 sts, P1, (K1, P1) across: 60{69-78} sts.

Row 2: K1, (P1, K1) 3 times, work across.

Row 3: Bind off 5{6-8} sts, work across to last 7 sts, P1, (K1, P1) across: 55{63-70} sts.

Row 4: K1, (P1, K1) 3 times, work across.

Row 5: Bind off 3{4-6} sts, work across to last 7 sts, P1, (K1, P1) across: 52{59-64} sts.

Row 6 (Decrease row): K1, (P1, K1) 3 times, work across to last 2 sts, K2 tog: 51{58-63} sts.

Row 7 (Decrease row): SSK, work across to last 7 sts, P1, (K1, P1) across: 50{57-62} sts.

Continue to decrease one stitch at Armhole edge, every row, 1{2-3} time(s) **more**; then decrease every other row, 3{4-5} times: 46{51-54} sts.

Work even until Left Front measures approximately 15{16-17}"/38{40.5-43} cm from cast on edge, ending by working a **wrong** side row.

NECK SHAPING

Row 1 (Decrease row): Work across to last 8 sts, P2 tog, work across: 45{50-53} sts.

Row 2: Work across.

Rows 3 thru 31{35-35}: Repeat Rows 1 and 2, 14{16-16} times; then repeat Row 1 once **more**: 30{33-36} sts.

Next 3 Rows: Work across.

Next Row: Work across to last 8 sts, K2 tog, work across: 29{32-35} sts.

Repeat last 4 rows, 3{2-2} times: 26{30-33} sts.

Work even until Left Front measures same as Back to Shoulder Shaping, ending by working a **wrong** side row.

SHOULDER SHAPING

Row 1: Bind off 5{6-7} sts, work across: 21{24-26} sts.

Row 2: Work across.

Rows 3-6: Repeat Rows 1 and 2 twice: 11{12-12} sts.

Row 7: Bind off 4{5-5} sts, work across: 7 sts.

Slip remaining sts onto st holder (Front Band); cut yarn.

RIGHT FRONT

With larger size needles, cast on 67{78-89} sts.

Row 1 (Right side)**:** P1, (K1, P1) 3 times (Front band), K5, ★ P1, slip next st onto cable needle and hold in **back** of work, K1, P1 from cable needle, slip next st onto cable needle and hold in **front** of work, P1, K1 from cable needle, P1, K5; repeat from ★ across.

Row 2: P5, ★ K1, P1, K2, P1, K1, P5; repeat from ★ across to last 7 sts, K1, (P1, K1) across.

Row 3: P1, (K1, P1) 3 times, K5, ★ P1, slip next st onto cable needle and hold in **front** of work, P1, K1 from cable needle, slip next st onto cable needle and hold in **back** of work, K1, P1 from cable needle, P1, K5; repeat from ★ across.

Row 4: P5, ★ K2, P2, K2, P5; repeat from ★ across to last 7 sts, K1, (P1, K1) across.

Row 5: P1, (K1, P1) 3 times, K5, ★ P2, slip next st onto cable needle and hold in **back** of work, K1, K1 from cable needle, P2, K5; repeat from ★ across.

Row 6: P5, ★ K2, P2, K2, P5; repeat from ★ across to last 7 sts, K1, (P1, K1) across.

Repeat Rows 1-6 for pattern until Right Front measures same as Back to Armhole Shaping, ending by working a **right** side row.

ARMHOLE SHAPING

Note: Maintain established pattern throughout.

Row 1: Bind off 7{9-11} sts, work across to last 7 sts, K1, (P1, K1) across: 60{69-78} sts.

Row 2: P1, (K1, P1) 3 times, work across.

Row 3: Bind off 5{6-8} sts, work across to last 7 sts, K1, (P1, K1) across: 55{63-70} sts.

Row 4: P1, (K1, P1) 3 times, work across.

Row 5: Bind off 3{4-6} sts, work across to last 7 sts, K1, (P1, K1) across: 52{59-64} sts.

Row 6 (Decrease row)**:** P1, (K1, P1) 3 times, work across to last 2 sts, K2 tog: 51{58-63} sts.

Row 7 (Decrease row)**:** SSK, work across to last 7 sts, K1, (P1, K1) across: 50{57-62} sts.

Continue to decrease one stitch at Armhole edge, every row, 1{2-3} time(s) **more**; then decrease every other row, 3{4-5} times: 46{51-54} sts.

Work even until Right Front measures approximately 15{16-17}"/38{40.5-43} cm from cast on edge, ending by working a **right** side row.

NECK SHAPING

Row 1 (Decrease row)**:** Work across to last 8 sts, K2 tog, work across: 45{50-53} sts.

Row 2: Work across.

Rows 3-5: Repeat Rows 1 and 2 once, then repeat Row 1 once **more**: 43{48-51} sts.

Row 6: P1, K1, bind off next 2 sts **(buttonhole)**, work across.

Row 7: Work across to last 6 sts, K2 tog, P1, K1; **turn**; add on 2 sts *(Figs. 5a & b, page 580)*, **turn**; P1, K1: 42{47-50} sts.

Row 8: Work across.

Rows 9 thru 31{35-35}: Repeat Rows 1 and 2, 11{13-13} times; then repeat Row 1 once **more**: 30{33-36} sts.

Next 3 Rows: Work across.

Next Row: Work across to last 8 sts, K2 tog, work across: 29{32-35} sts.

Repeat last 4 rows, 3{2-2} times: 26{30-33} sts.

Work even until Right Front measures same as Back to Shoulder Shaping, ending by working a **right** side row.

Instructions continued on page 205.

CABLED SLEEVE PULLOVER

Also shown on page 195.

■■■□ INTERMEDIATE

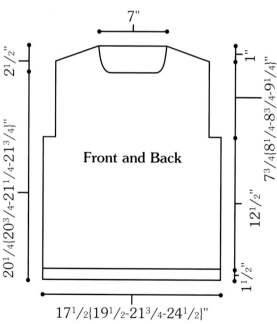

7"

2¹/₂"

1"

7³/₄{8¹/₄-8³/₄-9¹/₄}"

Front and Back

12¹/₂"

20¹/₄{20³/₄-21¹/₄-21³/₄}"

1¹/₂"

17¹/₂{19¹/₂-21³/₄-24¹/₂}"

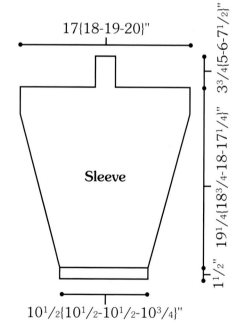

17{18-19-20}"

3³/₄{5-6-7¹/₂}"

Sleeve

19¹/₄{18³/₄-18-17¹/₄}"

1¹/₂"

10¹/₂{10¹/₂-10¹/₂-10³/₄}"

Size	Finished Chest Measurement	
Small	33¹/₂"	(85 cm)
Medium	38"	(96.5 cm)
Large	42¹/₂"	(108 cm)
X-Large	48"	(122 cm)

Size Note: Instructions are written for size Small with sizes Medium, Large, and X-Large in braces { }. Instructions will be easier to read if you circle all the numbers pertaining to your size. If only one number is given, it applies to all sizes.

Note: Sweater includes two edge stitches.

MATERIALS

Worsted Weight Yarn: 🧶 MEDIUM 4

Ounces	20{21½-23-25½}
Yards	1,310{1,410-1,510-1,675}
Grams	570{610-650-720}
Meters	1,198{1,289.5-1,380.5-1,531.5}

Straight knitting needles, sizes 7 (4.5 mm)
  and 8 (5 mm) **or** sizes needed for gauge
16" (40.75 cm) Circular needle, size 7 (4.5 mm)
Cable needle
Stitch holders - 2
Marker
Yarn needle

GAUGE: With larger size needles,
    in pattern,
    18 sts and 28 rows = 4" (10 cm)

BACK
RIBBING

With smaller size straight needles,
cast on 78{88-98-110} sts **loosely (Figs. 2a-e, page 9)**.

Work in K1, P1 ribbing for 1½" (3.75 cm).

BODY

Change to larger size needles.

Row 1 (Right side)**:** (K1, P1) across.

Row 2: (P1, K1) across.

Repeat Rows 1 and 2 for pattern until Back
measures approximately 14" (35.5 cm) from cast
on edge, ending by working a **wrong** side row.

ARMHOLE SHAPING

Note: Maintain established pattern throughout.

Rows 1 and 2: Bind off 6 sts, work across:
66{76-86-98} sts.

Work even until Back measures approximately
21¾{22¼-22¾-23¼}"/55{56.5-58-59} cm
from cast on edge, ending by working a **wrong**
side row.

SHOULDER SHAPING

Rows 1-4: Bind off 6{7-9-11} sts, work across:
42{48-50-54} sts.

Rows 5 and 6: Bind off 5{8-9-11} sts, work
across: 32 sts.

Slip remaining sts onto st holder.

FRONT

Work same as Back until Front measures
approximately 20¼{20¾-21¼-21¾}"/
51.5{52.5-54-55} cm from cast on edge, ending by
working a **wrong** side row: 66{76-86-98} sts.

NECK SHAPING

Note: Both sides of Neck are worked at the same
time, using separate yarn for **each** side.

Row 1: Work across 26{31-36-42} sts, slip next
14 sts onto st holder; with second yarn, work
across: 26{31-36-42} sts **each** side.

Rows 2 and 3: Work across; with second yarn,
bind off 3 sts, work across: 23{28-33-39} sts
each side.

Rows 4 and 5: Work across; with second yarn,
bind off 2 sts, work across: 21{26-31-37} sts
each side.

Rows 6-9: Work across to within 2 sts of Neck
edge, decrease **(see Decreases, pages 583 &
584)**; with second yarn, decrease, work across:
17{22-27-33} sts **each** side.

Work even until Front measures same as Back to
Shoulder Shaping.

SHOULDER SHAPING

Rows 1-4: Bind off 6{7-9-11} sts, work across; with
second yarn, work across: 5{8-9-11} sts **each** side.

Row 5: Bind off remaining sts on first side; with
second yarn, work across.

Bind off remaining sts.

Instructions continued on page 202.

SLEEVE (Make 2)
RIBBING
With smaller size straight needles, cast on 52{52-52-56} sts **loosely**.

Work in K1, P1 ribbing for $1^1/_2$" (4 cm).

BODY
Change to larger size needles.

Row 1 (Right side)**:** (K1, P1) 10{10-10-11} times, place marker *(see Markers, page 578)*, K 12, place marker, (P1, K1) across.

Row 2: (K1, P1) across to within 2 sts of marker, K2, P 12, K2, (P1, K1) across.

Row 3: (K1, P1) across to marker, slip next 4 sts onto cable needle and hold in **back** of work, K4, K4 from cable needle, K4, (P1, K1) across.

Row 4: (K1, P1) across to within 2 sts of marker, K2, P 12, K2, (P1, K1) across.

Row 5: Increase 0{0-1-1} time(s) *(see Figs. 10a & b, page 581 and Zeros, page 577)*, work across in established pattern to marker, K 12, work across in established pattern to last 0{0-1-1} st(s), increase 0{0-1-1} time(s): 52{52-54-58} sts.

Row 6: Work across in established pattern to within 2 sts of marker, K2, P 12, K2, work across in established pattern.

Row 7: Increase 0{1-0-0} time(s), work across in established pattern to marker, K4, slip next 4 sts onto cable needle and hold in **front** of work, K4, K4 from cable needle, work across in established pattern to last 0{1-0-0} st(s), increase 0{1-0-0} time(s): 52{54-54-58} sts.

Row 8: Work across in established pattern to within 2 sts of marker, K2, P 12, K2, work across in established pattern.

Maintaining established patterns and working each new stitch in pattern, increase one stitch at **each** edge, every fourth row, 0{0-8-11} times; then increase every sixth row, 8{17-12-9} times; then increase every eighth row, 8{1-0-0} time(s): 84{90-94-98} sts.

Work even until Sleeve measures approximately $20^3/_4${$20^1/_2$-$19^1/_2$-$18^3/_4$}"/52.5{51.5-49.5-47.5} cm from cast on edge.

SADDLE
Rows 1 and 2: Bind off 35{38-40-42} sts at beginning of the row, work across, removing all markers on Row 2: 14 sts.

Work even for $3^3/_4${5-6-$7^1/_2$}"/ 9.5{12.5-15-19} cm.

Bind off remaining sts in pattern.

FINISHING
Sew long edges of each Saddle to bound off edges of Back and Front.

Sew Sleeves to Pullover, sewing top of Sleeve along Armhole edge and sides of Sleeve to bound off edges.

NECKBAND
With **right** side facing, slip 32 sts from Back st holder onto circular needle and knit across, pick up 18 sts evenly spaced along left edge *(Figs. 34a & b, page 586)*, slip 14 sts from Front st holder onto second end of circular needle and knit across, pick up 18 sts evenly spaced along right edge, place marker to mark beginning of rnd: 82 sts.

Work in K1, P1 ribbing around for 4" (10 cm).

Bind off all sts **loosely** in ribbing.

Weave underarm and side in one continuous seam *(Fig. 36, page 587)*.

Design by Melissa Leapman.

SWEATER JACKET

Shown on page 205.

◖◼◼◻ INTERMEDIATE

BACK

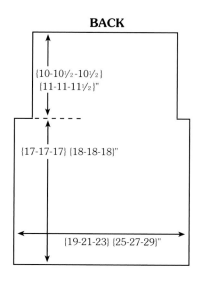

FRONT

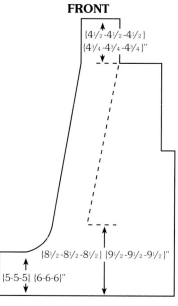

SLEEVE

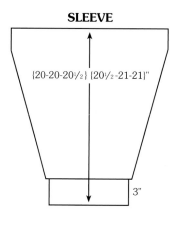

Size:	XS	S	M	L	XL	XXL
Finished						
Chest						
Measurement:	38"	42"	46"	50"	54"	58"

Size Note: Instructions are written for sizes X-Small, Small, and Medium in first braces { } with sizes Large, X-Large, and XX-Large in second braces. Instructions will be easier to read if you circle all the numbers pertaining to your size. If only one number is given, it applies to all sizes.

MATERIALS

Lion Brand Homespun® Yarn **or** any Bulky Weight Yarn:

BULKY ⑤

{32-34-36}{40-43-47} ounces,
[{910-970-1,020}{1,140-1,220-1,330} grams,
{985-1,050-1,110}{1,235-1,325-1,450} yards**]**

Straight knitting needles, sizes 8 (5.00 mm) **and** 10 (6.00 mm) **or** sizes needed for gauge
Crochet hook, size K (6.50 mm)
Markers
Yarn needle

GAUGE: With larger size needles, in pattern,
12 sts and 22 rows = 4"

BACK

With larger size needles,
cast on {59-65-71}{77-83-89} sts.

Row 1: K1, (P1, K1) across.

Repeat Row 1 until Back measures approximately {17-17-17}{18-18-18}" from cast on edge.

ARMHOLE SHAPING

Note: Maintain established pattern throughout.

Rows 1 and 2: Bind off {5-5-5}{7-7-7} sts, work across: {49-55-61}{63-69-75} sts.

Work even until Armholes measure approximately {10-10½-10½}{11-11-11½}".

Bind off all sts in pattern.

FRONT (Make 2)

With larger size needles,
cast on {59-65-71}{77-83-89} sts.

Row 1: K1, (P1, K1) across.

Repeat Row 1 until piece measures approximately {5-5-5}{6-6-6}" from cast on edge.

Instructions continued on page 204.

POCKET SHAPING

Note: Maintain established pattern throughout.

Row 1: Bind off {12-12-12}{15-15-15} sts, work across: {47-53-59}{62-68-74} sts.

Row 2 (Decrease row)**:** Work across to last 2 sts, decrease *(see Decreases, page 583)*: {46-52-58}{61-67-73} sts.

Row 3 (Decrease row)**:** Decrease, work across: {45-51-57}{60-66-72} sts.

Repeat Rows 2 and 3, {2-3-5}{5-6-8} times; then repeat Row 2 {0-1-0}{0-1-0} time **more** *(see Zeros, page 577)*: {41-44-47}{50-53-56} sts.

Work even until Front measures approximately {8½-8½-8½}{9½-9½-9½}" from cast on edge, ending last row at Pocket Shaping edge.

NECK AND ARMHOLE SHAPING

Note: Maintain established pattern throughout.

Row 1: Work across 12 sts for Collar, place marker *(see Markers, page 578)*, decrease, work across: {40-43-46}{49-52-55} sts.

Continue to decrease in same manner, every sixth row, {1-0-0}{2-2-1} time(s); then decrease every eighth row, {11-12-12}{11-11-12} times **AND AT THE SAME TIME**, when Front measures approximately {17-17-17}{18-18-18}" from cast on edge, bind off {5-5-5}{7-7-7} sts at armhole edge: {23-26-29}{29-32-35} sts.

Work even until Armhole measures approximately {10-10½-10½}{11-11-11½}", ending last row at Armhole edge.

Next Row: Bind off {11-14-17}{17-20-23} sts at Armhole edge, work across remaining sts: 12 sts.

Work even on remaining Collar sts for {4½-4½-4½}{4¾-4¾-4¾}".

Bind off all sts in pattern.

SLEEVE (Make 2)
RIBBING

With smaller size needles, cast on {35-35-35}{38-38-38} sts **loosely**.

Row 1: K2, (P1, K2) across.

Row 2 (Right side)**:** K1, P1, (K2, P1) across.

Repeat Rows 1 and 2 until Ribbing measures approximately 3", ending by working Row 1 and increasing {0-0-0}{1-1-1} st at end of last row *(see Increases, page 581)*: {35-35-35}{39-39-39} sts.

BODY

Change to larger size needles.

Rows 1 thru {6-4-4}{4-6-4}: K1, (P1, K1) across.

Row {7-5-5}{5-7-5} (Increase row)**:** Increase, P1, (K1, P1) across to last st, increase: {37-37-37}{41-41-41} sts.

Maintaining pattern, continue to increase one stitch at **each** edge, every fourth row, {0-2-0}{1-0-4} time(s); then increase every sixth row, {12-12-14}{12-13-11} times: {61-65-65}{67-67-71} sts.

Work even until Sleeve measures approximately {20-20-20½}{20½-21-21}" from cast on edge.

Bind off all sts **loosely** in pattern.

FINISHING

Sew shoulder seams.

Fold lower edge of each Front in half, bringing Pocket Shaping to right side of Front and matching side edges. Sew bottom edge of Pocket seams. Sew center back seam of Collar. Sew Collar to Back neck edge.

With **right** side facing, single crochet along edge of Pockets and Collar.

Matching center of Sleeve to shoulder seam, sew top of Sleeve along Armhole edge and sides of Sleeve to bound off edges.

Working through all thicknesses, weave underarm and side in one continuous seam *(Fig. 36, page 587)*.

CABLED CARDIGAN VEST *Continued from page 199.*

SHOULDER SHAPING

Row 1: Bind off 5{6-7} sts, work across: 21{24-26} sts.

Row 2: Work across.

Rows 3-6: Repeat Rows 1 and 2 twice: 11{12-12} sts.

Row 7: Bind off 4{5-5} sts, work across: 7 sts.

Slip remaining sts onto st holder (Front Band); do **not** cut yarn.

FINISHING

Sew shoulder and side seams.

FRONT BAND

Slip sts from Right Front Band st holder onto larger size needle and work even in established ribbing until Band, when slightly stretched, fits along Back neck edge to center back.

Bind off all sts in ribbing.

Repeat for Left Front Band.

Sew ends of Front Bands together at Back neck edge.

Sew Front Bands to Back neck edge.

ARMHOLE BAND (Make 2)

With smaller size needles, cast on 7 sts.

Work in K1, P1 ribbing until Band measures approximately 20{21-22}"/51{53.5-56} cm from cast on edge.

Bind off all sts in ribbing.

Sew cast on and bound off edges together.

Pin Bands in place along each Armhole; then sew in place.

Sew button to Left Front Band opposite buttonhole.

Design by Melissa Leapman.

CHENILLE JACKET

◼◼◼◻ INTERMEDIATE

BACK	FRONT	SLEEVE
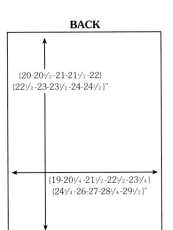	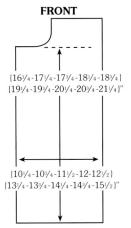	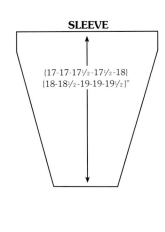

BACK:
{20-20½-21-21½-22}
{22½-23-23½-24-24½}"
{19-20¼-21½-22½-23¾}
{24¾-26-27-28¼-29½}"

FRONT:
{16¾-17¼-17¾-18¼-18¾}
{19¼-19¾-20¼-20¾-21¼}"
{10¼-10¾-11½-12-12½}
{13¼-13¾-14½-14¾-15½}"

SLEEVE:
{17-17-17½-17½-18}
{18-18½-19-19-19½}"

Size: ____
Chest Measurement: ____"
Finished Chest
Measurement: ____"

MATERIALS

Lion Brand Wool-Ease® Yarn **or**
  any Worsted Weight Yarn:
    ____ ounces,
      (____ grams,
       ____ yards)
Lion Brand Chenille Thick & Quick®
  Yarn **or** any Chunky Chenille Yarn:
    ____ yards
Straight knitting needles, sizes 7 (4.50 mm) **and**
  8 (5.00 mm) **or** sizes needed for gauge
16" Circular needle, size 7 (4.50 mm)
Yarn needle

GAUGE: With larger size needles, in pattern,
    14 sts and 24 rows = 4"

When instructed to slip a stitch, always slip as if to **purl**.

BACK

With smaller size straight needles and worsted weight
yarn, cast on ____ sts **loosely**.

Note: Carry unused yarn **loosely** along edge.
Change to larger size needles.

Row 1 (Right side): With Chenille, knit across.
Row 2: K1, purl across to last st, K1.

32	34	36	38	40	42	44	46	48	50
32	34	36	38	40	42	44	46	48	50
39½	41¾	44½	46½	48¾	51¼	53½	55½	57¾	60½
7½	8	8½	9	9½	10	10½	11	12	12½
210	230	240	260	270	280	300	310	340	350
495	525	560	590	625	655	690	720	790	820
285	300	330	345	370	385	415	440	465	495
69	73	77	81	85	89	93	97	101	105

Instructions continued on page 208.

Row 3: With worsted weight yarn, K1, purl ____ st(s), WYB slip 1, (P5, WYB slip 1) across to last ____ st(s), purl ____ st(s), K1.

Row 4: Knit ____ st(s), WYF slip 1, (K5, WYF slip 1) across to last ____ st(s), knit ____ st(s).

Rows 5 and 6: Repeat Rows 3 and 4.

Row 7: With Chenille, knit across.

Row 8: K1, purl across to last st, K1.

Row 9: With worsted weight yarn, K1, purl ____ sts, WYB slip 1, (P5, WYB slip 1) across to last ____ sts, purl ____ sts, K1.

Row 10: Knit ____ sts, WYF slip 1, (K5, WYF slip 1) across to last ____ sts, knit ____ sts.

Rows 11 and 12: Repeat Rows 9 and 10.

Repeat Rows 1-12 for pattern until Back measures approximately ____" from cast on edge, ending by working Row 2 or Row 8.

With worsted weight yarn, bind off all sts **loosely** in **knit**.

LEFT FRONT

With smaller size straight needles and worsted weight yarn, cast on ____ sts **loosely**.

Note: Carry unused yarn **loosely** along edge. Change to larger size needles.

Row 1 (Right side)**:** With Chenille, knit across.

Row 2: K1, purl across to last st, K1.

Row 3: With worsted weight yarn, K1, purl ____ sts, WYB slip 1, (P5, WYB slip 1) across to last ____ st(s), purl ____ sts, K1.

Row 4: Knit ____ st(s), WYF slip 1, (K5, WYF slip 1) across to last ____ st(s), knit ____ st(s).

Rows 5 and 6: Repeat Rows 3 and 4.

Row 7: With Chenille, knit across.

Row 8: K1, purl across to last st, K1.

Row 9: With worsted weight yarn, K1, purl ____ st(s), WYB slip 1, (P5, WYB slip 1) across to last ____ sts, purl ____ st(s), K1.

Row 10: Knit ____ sts, WYF slip 1, (K5, WYF slip 1) across to last ____ sts, knit ____ sts.

Rows 11 and 12: Repeat Rows 9 and 10.

32	34	36	38	40	42	44	46	48	50
0	5	1	0	5	1	0	5	1	0
1	6	2	1	6	2	1	6	2	1
0	5	1	0	5	1	0	5	1	0
1	6	2	1	6	2	1	6	2	1
1	6	2	1	6	2	1	6	2	1
1	6	2	1	6	2	1	6	2	1
3	2	4	3	2	4	3	2	4	3
4	3	5	4	3	5	4	3	5	4
3	2	4	3	2	4	3	2	4	3
4	3	5	4	3	5	4	3	5	4
4	3	5	4	3	5	4	3	5	4
4	3	5	4	3	5	4	3	5	4
20	20½	21	21½	22	22½	23	23½	24	24½
37	39	41	43	45	47	49	51	53	55
5	0	4	5	0	4	5	0	4	5
6	1	5	6	1	5	6	1	5	6
5	0	4	5	0	4	5	0	4	5
6	1	5	6	1	5	6	1	5	6
6	1	5	6	1	5	6	1	5	6
6	1	5	6	1	5	6	1	5	6
2	3	1	2	3	1	2	3	1	2
3	4	2	3	4	2	3	4	2	3
2	3	1	2	3	1	2	3	1	2
3	4	2	3	4	2	3	4	2	3
3	4	2	3	4	2	3	4	2	3
3	4	2	3	4	2	3	4	2	3

32	34	36	38	40	42	44	46	48	50
16¾	17¼	17¾	18¼	18¾	19¼	19¾	20¼	20¾	21¼

Repeat Rows 1-12 for pattern until Left Front measures approximately ____" from cast on edge, ending by working Row 1 or Row 7.

NECK SHAPING

Note: Maintain established pattern throughout.

Row 1: Bind off 10 sts, work across: ____ sts.
Row 2: Work across.
Row 3: Bind off 3 sts, work across: ____ sts.
Row 4: Work across.
Row 5: Decrease *(see Decreases, page 583)*, work across: ____ sts.

Repeat Rows 4 and 5, ____ time(s): ____ sts.

32	34	36	38	40	42	44	46	48	50
27	29	31	33	35	37	39	41	43	45
24	26	28	30	32	34	36	38	40	42
23	25	27	29	31	33	35	37	39	41
1	1	2	2	3	3	4	4	5	5
22	24	25	27	28	30	31	33	34	36

Work even until Front measures same as Back, ending by working pattern Row 2 or Row 8.

With worsted weight yarn, bind off all sts **loosely** in **knit**.

RIGHT FRONT

Work same as Left Front to Neck Shaping, ending by working Row 2 or Row 8.

NECK SHAPING

Work same as Left Front.

SLEEVE (Make 2)

With smaller size straight needles and worsted weight yarn, cast on ____ sts **loosely**.

32	34	36	38	40	42	44	46	48	50
31	31	33	33	35	35	37	39	41	43

Note: Carry unused yarn **loosely** along edge.
Change to larger size needles.

Row 1 (Right side)**:** With Chenille, knit across.
Row 2: K1, purl across to last st, K1.
Row 3: With worsted weight yarn, K1, purl ____ st(s), WYB slip 1, (P5, WYB slip 1) across to last ____ st(s), purl ____ st(s), K1.
Row 4: Knit ____ st(s), WYF slip 1, (K5, WYF slip 1) across to last ____ st(s), knit ____ st(s).
Rows 5 and 6: Repeat Rows 3 and 4.
Row 7 (Increase row)**:** With Chenille, increase *(Figs. 10a & b, page 581)*, knit across to last st, increase: ____ sts.
Row 8: K1, purl across to last st, K1.

32	34	36	38	40	42	44	46	48	50
2	2	0	0	1	1	2	0	1	2
3	3	1	1	2	2	3	1	2	3
2	2	0	0	1	1	2	0	1	2
3	3	1	1	2	2	3	1	2	3
3	3	1	1	2	2	3	1	2	3
3	3	1	1	2	2	3	1	2	3
33	33	35	35	37	37	39	41	43	45

Instructions continued on page 210.

32	34	36	38	40	42	44	46	48	50
6	6	4	4	5	5	6	4	5	6
7	7	5	5	6	6	7	5	6	7
6	6	4	4	5	5	6	4	5	6
7	7	5	5	6	6	7	5	6	7
7	7	5	5	6	6	7	5	6	7
7	7	5	5	6	6	7	5	6	7
35	35	37	37	39	39	41	43	45	47
14	14	14	14	14	14	15	16	16	16
63	63	65	65	67	67	71	75	77	79
17	17	17½	17½	18	18	18½	19	19	19½
25	25	27	27	29	29	31	31	33	33
85	85	87	87	89	89	91	91	93	93
9	9	9¼	9¼	9½	9½	10	11	11	11¼

Row 9: With worsted weight yarn, K1, purl ____ sts, WYB slip 1, (P5, WYB slip 1) across to last ____ sts, purl ____ sts, K1.

Row 10: Knit ____ sts, WYF slip 1, (K5, WYF slip 1) across to last ____ sts, knit ____ sts.

Rows 11 and 12: Repeat Rows 9 and 10.

Row 13 (Increase row)**:** With Chenille, increase, knit across to last st, increase: ____ sts.

Maintaining pattern and working new sts in pattern, continue to increase one stitch at **each** edge, every sixth row, ____ times **more**: ____ sts.

Work even until Sleeve measures approximately ____" from cast on edge, ending by working a **wrong** side row.

With worsted weight yarn, bind off all sts **loosely** in **knit**.

FINISHING
Sew shoulder seams.

NECK BAND
With **right** side facing, using circular needle and worsted weight yarn, pick up 30 sts along Right Front neck edge **(Figs. 34a & b, page 586)**, pick up ____ sts across Back neck edge, pick up 30 sts along Left Front neck edge: ____ sts.

Beginning with a **knit** row, work in Reverse Stockinette Stitch for 6 rows.

Bind off all sts **loosely** in **knit**.

Turn bound off edge to inside and sew to edge along picked up sts.

Sew Sleeves to Sweater, matching center of last row on Sleeve to shoulder seam and beginning ____" down from seam.

Sew underarm and side in one continuous seam.

WIDE-RIBBED PULLOVER

Shown on page 213.

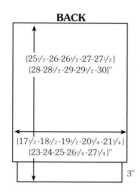

BACK

{25½-26-26½-27-27½}
{28-28½-29-29½-30}"

{17½-18½-19½-20¼-21¼}
{23-24-25-26¼-27¼}"

3"

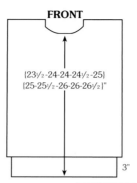

FRONT

{23½-24-24-24½-25}
{25-25½-26-26-26½}"

3"

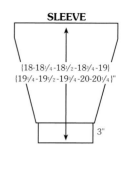

SLEEVE

{18-18¼-18½-18¾-19}
{19¼-19½-19¾-20-20¼}"

3"

Size: ____

Chest Measurement: ____"

Finished Chest Measurement: ____"

MATERIALS

Lion Brand Wool-Ease® Yarn **or** any Worsted Weight Yarn:

____ ounces,

(____ grams,

____ yards)

Straight knitting needles, sizes 6 (4.00 mm) **and** 8 (5.00 mm) **or** sizes needed for gauge

16" Circular needle, size 6 (4.00 mm)

Stitch holders - 2

Markers

Yarn needle

GAUGE: With larger size needles, in Stockinette Stitch, 18 sts and 24 rows = 4"

BACK

With smaller size needles, cast on ____ sts **loosely**. Beginning with a **knit** row, work in Stockinette Stitch for 6 rows to form rolled edge.

RIBBING

Row 1 (Right side)**:** Knit ____ st(s), purl ____ st(s), (K2, P2) across to last ____ st(s), knit ____ st(s), purl ____ st.

Row 2: Purl ____ st(s), knit ____ st(s), (P2, K2) across to last ____ st(s), purl ____ st(s), knit ____ st.

32	34	36	38	40	42	44	46	48	50
32	34	36	38	40	42	44	46	48	50
35	37	39	41½	43½	46	48	50	52½	54½
18	19	20	21	23	24	26	27	29	30
510	540	570	600	650	680	740	770	820	850
1,180	1,250	1,315	1,380	1,510	1,575	1,705	1,775	1,905	1,970
98	104	110	116	122	128	134	140	146	152
0	0	2	1	0	0	2	1	0	0
2	1	2	2	2	1	2	2	2	1
0	3	2	1	0	3	2	1	0	3
0	2	2	1	0	2	2	1	0	2
0	1	0	0	0	1	0	0	0	1
0	0	2	1	0	0	2	1	0	0
2	1	2	2	2	1	2	2	2	1
0	3	2	1	0	3	2	1	0	3
0	2	2	1	0	2	2	1	0	2
0	1	0	0	0	1	0	0	0	1

Instructions continued on page 212.

Repeat Rows 1 and 2 until Ribbing measures approximately 3", ending by working Row 2.

BODY

Change to larger size needles.

Row 1 (Right side): Knit ____ sts, P2, (K 10, P2) across to last ____ sts, knit ____ sts.
Row 2: Purl ____ sts, K2, (P 10, K2) across to last ____ sts, purl ____ sts.

Repeat Rows 1 and 2 for pattern until Back measures approximately ____" from cast on edge, ending by working a **wrong** side row.

Last Row: Bind off ____ sts, work in pattern across next ____ sts, slip ____ sts just worked onto st holder, bind off remaining ____ sts.

FRONT

Work same as Back until Front measures approximately ____" from cast on edge, ending by working a **wrong** side row.

NECK SHAPING

Note: Maintain established pattern throughout.
Row 1: Work across ____ sts, slip last ____ sts worked onto st holder, work across: ____ sts **each** side.
Note: Both sides of Neck are worked at the same time, using separate yarn for **each** side.
Rows 2 and 3: Work across; with second yarn, bind off 3 sts at neck edge, work across: ____ sts **each** side.
Rows 4-9: Work across; with second yarn, bind off 2 sts at neck edge, work across: ____ sts **each** side.
Row 10: Work across; with second yarn, work across.
Row 11 (Decrease row): Work across to within 2 sts of Neck edge, decrease *(see Decreases, page 583)*; with second yarn, decrease, work across: ____ sts **each** side.
Rows 12 and 13: Repeat Rows 10 and 11: ____ sts **each** side.

Work even until Front measures same as Back, ending by working a **wrong** side row. Bind off remaining sts.

SLEEVE (Make 2)

With smaller size needles, cast on ____ sts **loosely**.

32	34	36	38	40	42	44	46	48	50
0	3	6	9	0	3	6	9	0	3
0	3	6	9	0	3	6	9	0	3
0	3	6	9	0	3	6	9	0	3
0	3	6	9	0	3	6	9	0	3
0	3	6	9	0	3	6	9	0	3
0	3	6	9	0	3	6	9	0	3
25½	26	26½	27	27½	28	28½	29	29½	30
32	35	37	40	43	46	48	51	54	57
33	33	35	35	35	35	37	37	37	37
34	34	36	36	36	36	38	38	38	38
32	35	37	40	43	46	48	51	54	57
23½	24	24	24½	25	25	25½	26	26	26½
55	58	62	65	68	71	75	78	81	84
12	12	14	14	14	14	16	16	16	16
43	46	48	51	54	57	59	62	65	68
40	43	45	48	51	54	56	59	62	65
34	37	39	42	45	48	50	53	56	59
33	36	38	41	44	47	49	52	55	58
32	35	37	40	43	46	48	51	54	57
38	38	42	42	42	46	46	46	50	50

Beginning with a **knit** row, work in Stockinette Stitch for 6 rows to form rolled edge.

RIBBING
Row 1 (Right side)**:** K2, (P2, K2) across.
Row 2: P2, (K2, P2) across.

Repeat Rows 1 and 2 until Ribbing measures approximately 3", ending by working a **wrong** side row.

BODY
Change to larger size needles.
Row 1 (Right side)**:** Knit across increasing ____ sts evenly spaced (*see Increases, page 581*): ____ sts.
Row 2: Purl ____ st(s), K2, (P 10, K2) across to last ____ st(s), purl ____ st(s).
Row 3 (Increase row)**:** Increase, knit ____ st(s), P2, (K 10, P2) across to last ____ st(s), knit ____ st(s), increase: ____ sts.

32	34	36	38	40	42	44	46	48	50
14	14	12	12	14	12	12	14	12	12
52	52	54	54	56	58	58	60	62	62
1	1	2	2	3	4	4	5	6	6
1	1	2	2	3	4	4	5	6	6
1	1	2	2	3	4	4	5	6	6
0	0	1	1	2	3	3	4	5	5
0	0	1	1	2	3	3	4	5	5
0	0	1	1	2	3	3	4	5	5
54	54	56	56	58	60	60	62	64	64

Instructions continued on page 214.

32	34	36	38	40	42	44	46	48	50
2	2	3	3	4	5	5	6	7	7
2	2	3	3	4	5	5	6	7	7
2	2	3	3	4	5	5	6	7	7
1	1	2	2	3	4	4	5	6	6
1	1	2	2	3	4	4	5	6	6
1	1	2	2	3	4	4	5	6	6
56	56	58	58	60	62	62	64	66	66
6	11	12	18	21	22	27	31	34	37
14	12	12	9	8	8	6	4	3	2
96	102	106	112	118	122	128	134	140	144
18	18¼	18½	18¾	19	19¼	19½	19¾	20	20¼
0	0	1	1	1	1	2	2	2	2
0	0	1	1	1	1	2	2	2	2
0	0	1	1	1	1	2	2	2	2
17	17	19	19	19	19	21	21	21	25
1	1	2	2	2	2	0	0	0	0
2	2	2	2	2	2	1	1	1	1
1	1	2	2	2	2	3	3	3	3
1	1	2	2	2	2	2	2	2	2
0	0	0	0	0	0	1	1	1	1
17	17	19	19	19	19	21	21	21	25
80	80	88	88	88	88	96	96	96	104
0	0	1	1	1	1	2	2	2	2
2	2	1	1	1	1	0	0	0	0
2	2	1	1	1	1	0	0	0	0
8½	9	9½	10	10½	11	11½	12	12½	13

Row 4: Purl _____ sts, K2, (P 10, K2) across
to last _____ sts,
purl _____ sts.

Row 5 (Increase row)**:** Increase, knit _____ st(s),
P2, (K 10, P2) across to last _____ st(s),
knit _____ st(s), increase:
_____ sts.

Working in established pattern, continue to
increase one stitch at **each** edge in same manner,
every other row, _____ times **more**;
then increase every fourth row, _____ times:
_____ sts.

Work even until Sleeve measures approximately _____"
from cast on edge, ending by working a **wrong** side row.
Bind off all sts **loosely** in pattern.

FINISHING
Sew shoulder seams.

NECK RIBBING
With **right** side facing, using circular needle and working
across Back st holder, purl _____ st(s),
K2, (P2, K2) across to last _____ st(s),
purl _____ st(s), pick up
_____ sts along left Front Neck edge **(Fig. 34a,
page 586)**, working across Front st holder, knit _____ st(s),
purl _____ st(s), (K2, P2) across
to last _____ st(s),
knit _____ st(s),
purl _____ st, pick up
_____ sts along right Front Neck edge, place marker for
beginning of rnd **(see Markers, page 578)**: _____ sts.

Rnd 1: Purl _____ st(s), K2, (P2, K2) around
to last _____ st(s),
purl _____ st(s).

Repeat Rnd 1 until Ribbing measures approximately 3".

Next 6 Rnds: Knit around.
Bind off all sts **loosely** in **knit**.

Sew Sleeves to Sweater, matching center of last row on
Sleeve to shoulder seam and beginning _____" down
from seam.
Weave underarm and side in one continuous seam
(Fig. 36, page 587).

PATCHWORK PULLOVER

Shown on pages 213 and 219.

■■■□ INTERMEDIATE

BACK
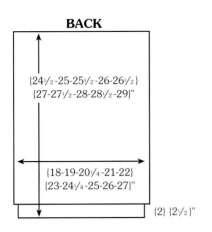
{24½-25-25½-26-26½}
{27-27½-28-28½-29}"

{18-19-20¼-21-22}
{23-24¼-25-26-27}"

{2} {2½}"

FRONT
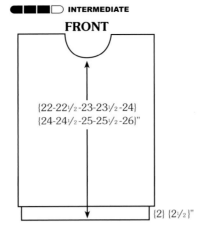
{22-22½-23-23½-24}
{24-24½-25-25½-26}"

{2} {2½}"

SLEEVE
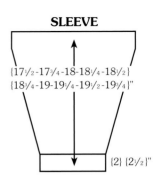
{17½-17¾-18-18¼-18½}
{18¾-19-19¼-19½-19¾}"

{2} {2½}"

Size: ____
Chest Measurement: ____"
Finished Chest
  Measurement: ____"

MATERIALS
Lion Brand Wool-Ease® yarn **or** any
  Worsted Weight Yarn:

MEDIUM 4

  Color A (Red or Green) - ____ ounces,
    (____ grams,
     ____ yards)
  Color B (Blue or Grey) - ____ ounces,
    (____ grams,
     ____ yards)
  Color C (Ecru) - ____ ounces,
    (____ grams,
     ____ yards)
  Color D (Navy or Dk Grey) - ____ ounces,
    (____ grams,
     ____ yards)
Straight knitting needles, sizes 6 (4.00 mm) **and**
  8 (5.00 mm) **or** sizes needed for gauge
16" Circular needles, sizes 6 (4.00 mm) **and**
  7 (4.50 mm)
Stitch holders - 2
Yarn needle

32	34	36	38	40	42	44	46	48	50
32	34	36	38	40	42	44	46	48	50
36	38	40½	42	44	46	48½	50	52	54
6½	7	7½	8	8½	9	9½	10	10½	11
180	200	210	230	240	260	270	280	300	310
425	460	495	525	560	590	625	655	690	720
3	3½	3½	4	4	4½	4½	5	5	5½
90	100	100	110	110	130	130	140	140	160
195	230	230	260	260	295	295	330	330	360
2½	3	3	3	3½	3½	3½	4	4	4½
70	90	90	90	100	100	100	110	110	130
165	195	195	195	230	230	230	260	260	295
2½	3	3	3	3½	3½	3½	4	4	4½
70	90	90	90	100	100	100	110	110	130
165	195	195	195	230	230	230	260	260	295

GAUGE: With larger size needles, in Stockinette Stitch,
  18 sts and 24 rows = 4"

CHANGING COLORS
Use a separate skein of yarn for each color area, always
keeping the skeins on the **wrong** side of the garment. When
changing colors, always pick up the new color yarn from
beneath the dropped yarn and keep the color which has just
been worked to the left **(Fig. A)**. This will prevent holes in the
finished piece. Take extra care to keep your tension even.

Fig. A

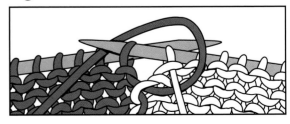

Instructions begin on page 216.

BACK
RIBBING

With smaller size straight needles and Color D,
cast on ____ sts;
with Color B, cast on ____ sts;
with Color C, cast on ____ sts:
____ sts.

Row 1: K1, (P1, K1) across using established colors.
Row 2 (Right side)**:** P1, (K1, P1) across using established colors.

Repeat Rows 1 and 2 for ____", ending by working a **right** side row.

BODY

Change to larger size straight needles.

Continuing with established colors and beginning with a **purl** row, work in Stockinette Stitch for ____ rows.

Next Row: With Color D, purl ____ sts,
with Color B, purl ____ sts,
with Color D, purl ____ sts.
Continuing with newly established colors and beginning with a **knit** row, work in Stockinette Stitch for ____ rows.

Next Row: With Color C, knit ____ sts,
with Color B, knit ____ sts,
with Color D, knit ____ sts.
Continuing with newly established colors and beginning with a **purl** row, work in Stockinette Stitch for ____ rows.

Next Row: With Color C, knit ____ sts,
with Color A, knit ____ sts,
with Color D, knit ____ sts.
Continuing with newly established colors and beginning with a **purl** row, work in Stockinette Stitch for ____ rows.

Next Row: With Color C, knit ____ sts,
with Color A, knit ____ sts,
with Color B, knit ____ sts.
Continuing with newly established colors and beginning with a **purl** row, work in Stockinette Stitch for ____ rows.

32	34	36	38	40	42	44	46	48	50
16	16	17	17	18	19	20	21	22	23
34	37	39	42	43	45	48	49	50	51
33	34	37	38	40	41	43	45	47	49
83	87	93	97	101	105	111	115	119	123
2	2	2	2	2	2½	2½	2½	2½	2½
34	36	36	38	38	38	40	40	40	42
23	25	27	28	29	30	32	33	34	35
44	46	49	52	54	56	59	61	63	65
16	16	17	17	18	19	20	21	22	23
28	30	30	30	32	32	32	32	34	34
23	25	27	28	29	30	32	33	34	35
37	37	39	41	43	45	47	49	51	53
23	25	27	28	29	30	32	33	34	35
23	23	25	25	25	25	25	27	27	27
23	25	27	28	29	30	32	33	34	35
37	37	39	41	43	45	47	49	51	53
23	25	27	28	29	30	32	33	34	35
27	27	27	27	29	29	29	29	31	31
23	25	27	28	29	30	32	33	34	35
37	37	39	41	43	45	47	49	51	53
23	25	27	28	29	30	32	33	34	35
19	19	19	19	19	19	21	21	21	21

With established colors, bind off ____ sts,
knit next ____ sts,
slip ____ sts just worked onto st holder,
bind off remaining ____ sts.

FRONT
RIBBING

With smaller size straight needles and Color C,
cast on ____ sts;
with Color B, cast on ____ sts;
with Color D, cast on ____ sts:
____ sts.

Row 1: P1, (K1, P1) across using established colors.
Row 2 (Right side)**:** K1, (P1, K1) across using established colors.

Repeat Rows 1 and 2 for ____", ending by working a **right** side row.

BODY

Change to larger size straight needles.
Continuing with established colors and beginning with a **purl** row, work in Stockinette Stitch for ____ rows.

Next Row: With Color D, purl ____ sts,
with Color B, purl ____ sts,
with Color D, purl ____ sts.
Continuing with newly established colors and beginning with a **knit** row, work in Stockinette Stitch for ____ rows.

Next Row: With Color D, knit ____ sts,
with Color B, knit ____ sts,
with Color C, knit ____ sts.
Continuing with newly established colors and beginning with a **purl** row, work in Stockinette Stitch for ____ rows.

Next Row: With Color D, knit ____ sts,
with Color A, knit ____ sts,
with Color C, knit ____ sts.
Continuing with newly established colors and beginning with a **purl** row, work in Stockinette Stitch for ____ rows.

Next Row: With Color B, knit ____ sts,
with Color A, knit ____ sts,
with Color C, knit ____ sts.

32	34	36	38	40	42	44	46	48	50
24	26	28	30	31	32	35	36	37	39
34	34	36	36	38	40	40	42	44	44
35	35	37	37	39	41	41	43	45	45
24	26	28	30	31	32	35	36	37	39
33	34	37	38	40	41	43	45	47	49
34	37	39	42	43	45	48	49	50	51
16	16	17	17	18	19	20	21	22	23
83	87	93	97	101	105	111	115	119	123
2	2	2	2	2	2½	2½	2½	2½	2½
34	36	36	38	38	38	40	40	40	42
16	16	17	17	18	19	20	21	22	23
44	46	49	52	54	56	59	61	63	65
23	25	27	28	29	30	32	33	34	35
28	30	30	30	32	32	32	32	34	34
23	25	27	28	29	30	32	33	34	35
37	37	39	41	43	45	47	49	51	53
23	25	27	28	29	30	32	33	34	35
23	23	25	25	25	25	25	27	27	27
23	25	27	28	29	30	32	33	34	35
37	37	39	41	43	45	47	49	51	53
23	25	27	28	29	30	32	33	34	35
27	27	27	27	29	29	29	29	31	31
23	25	27	28	29	30	32	33	34	35
37	37	39	41	43	45	47	49	51	53
23	25	27	28	29	30	32	33	34	35

Instructions continued on page 218.

Continuing with newly established colors and beginning with a **purl** row, work in Stockinette Stitch for ____ rows.

NECK SHAPING

Note: Both sides of Neck are worked in established colors and pattern at the same time, using separate yarns for **each** side.

Row 1: Purl across ____ sts,
slip next ____ sts onto st holder; with next yarn, purl across: ____ sts **each** side.
Rows 2 and 3: Work across; with next yarn, bind off 4 sts at neck edge, work across: ____ sts **each** side.
Rows 4-7: Work across; with next yarn, bind off 3 sts at neck edge, work across: ____ sts **each** side.
Rows 8-11: Work across; with next yarn, bind off 2 sts at neck edge, work across: ____ sts **each** side.
Row 12: Knit across to last 2 sts at Neck edge, K2 tog *(Fig. 17, page 583)*; with next yarn, **[**slip 1, K1, PSSO *(Figs. 19a & b, page 583)***]**, knit across: ____ sts **each** side.

Continuing with established colors and beginning with a **purl** row, work in Stockinette Stitch for ____ rows.

Bind off remaining sts.

SLEEVE (Make 2)
RIBBING

With smaller size straight needles and Color A, cast on ____ sts **loosely**.

Work in K1, P1 ribbing for ____" increasing 7 sts evenly spaced across last row *(see Increases, page 581)*: ____ sts.

BODY

Change to larger size straight needles.

Beginning with a **knit** row, work in Stockinette Stitch increasing one st at **each** edge, every other row, ____ times;
then increase every fourth row, ____ times;
then increase every sixth row, ____ times:
____ sts.

Work even until Sleeve measures approximately ____" from cast on edge, ending by working a **purl** row.

Bind off all sts **loosely**.

32	34	36	38	40	42	44	46	48	50
4	4	4	4	4	2	2	2	2	2
39	41	43	45	46	47	50	51	52	54
5	5	7	7	9	11	11	13	15	15
39	41	43	45	46	47	50	51	52	54
35	37	39	41	42	43	46	47	48	50
29	31	33	35	36	37	40	41	42	44
25	27	29	31	32	33	36	37	38	40
24	26	28	30	31	32	35	36	37	39
3	3	3	3	3	5	7	7	7	7
40	40	44	44	48	48	48	52	52	52
2	2	2	2	2	2½	2½	2½	2½	2½
47	47	51	51	55	55	55	59	59	59
0	0	0	0	0	1	4	4	9	12
7	12	11	17	19	22	21	21	19	18
9	6	7	3	2	0	0	0	0	0
79	83	87	91	97	101	105	109	115	119
17½	17¾	18	18¼	18½	18¾	19	19¼	19½	19¾

FINISHING

Using photo as a guide for placement and Color D, work an overcast stitch over 2 sts and 4 rows apart over block color changes on Front and Back. Sew shoulder seams.

NECK RIBBING

With **right** side facing and using smaller size circular needle, knit _____ sts from Back st holder, pick up 24 sts evenly spaced along left Neck edge *(Figs. 34a & b, page 586)*, knit _____ sts from Front st holder, pick up 24 sts evenly spaced along right Neck edge, place marker *(see Markers, page 578)*: _____ sts.

Rnds 1-12: (K1, P1) around.
Change to larger size circular needle.

Rnds 13-16: (K1, P1) around.
Bind off all sts **very loosely** in ribbing.

Fold Neck Ribbing in half to **wrong** side and sew in place.

Sew Sleeves to sweater, matching center of last row on Sleeve to shoulder seam and beginning _____" down from seam.

Weave underarm and side in one continuous seam *(Fig. 36, page 587)*.

32	34	36	38	40	42	44	46	48	50
35	35	37	37	39	41	41	43	45	45
5	5	7	7	9	11	11	13	15	15
88	88	92	92	96	100	100	104	108	108
8½	9	9½	10	10½	11	11½	12	12½	13

CABLES GALORE PULLOVER

◼◼◼◻ INTERMEDIATE

BACK
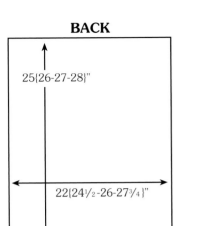

25{26-27-28}"

22{24½-26-27¾}"

2½"

FRONT
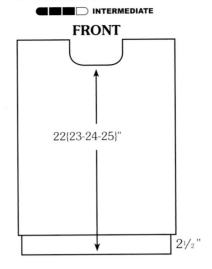

22{23-24-25}"

2½"

SLEEVE
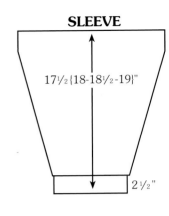

17½{18-18½-19}"

2½"

Size:	Small	Medium	Large	X-Large
Finished Chest Measurement:	44"	49"	52"	55½"

Size Note: Instructions are written for size Small with sizes Medium, Large, and X-Large in braces { }. Instructions will be easier to read if you circle all the numbers pertaining to your size. If only one number is given, it applies to all sizes.

MATERIALS
Lion Brand Homespun® Yarn **or** any Bulky Weight Yarn:
    30{34-37-40} ounces,
      [850{970-1,050-1,140} grams,
        925{1,050-1,140-1,235} yards]
Straight knitting needles, sizes 9 (5.50 mm) **and** 11 (8.00 mm) **or** sizes needed for gauge
16" Circular needles, sizes 8 (5.00 mm) **and** 9 (5.50 mm)
Cable needle
Stitch holders - 2
Markers
Yarn needle

GAUGE: With larger size needles, in Stockinette Stitch,
    10 sts and 15 rows = 4"
    first cable panel (13 sts) = 3½" wide
    second cable panel (17 sts) = 4¼" wide
    center cable panel (18 sts) = 5¼" wide

STITCH GUIDE

RIGHT TWIST *(abbreviated RT)* (uses 2 sts)
Knit second stitch on left needle *(Fig. A)* making sure **not** to drop off, then knit the first stitch *(Fig. B)* letting both stitches drop off left needle together.

Fig. A
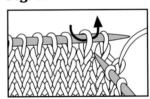

Fig. B
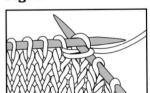

FRONT CABLE *(abbreviated FC)* (uses 6 sts)
Slip 3 sts onto cable needle and hold in **front** of work, K3 from left needle, K3 from cable needle.

BACK CABLE *(abbreviated BC)* (uses 6 sts)
Slip 3 sts onto cable needle and hold in **back** of work, K3 from left needle, K3 from cable needle.

FRONT CROSS (uses next 5 sts)
Slip 3 sts onto cable needle and hold in **front** of work, K2 from left needle, slip last st from cable needle back onto left needle and purl it, K2 from cable needle.

BACK CROSS (uses next 5 sts)
Slip 3 sts onto cable needle and hold in **back** of work, K2 from left needle, slip last st from cable needle back onto left needle and purl it, K2 from cable needle.

Instructions begin on page 222.

BACK
RIBBING

With smaller size straight needles, cast on 86{94-98-102} sts **loosely**.

Row 1: K2, (P2, K2) across.

Row 2: P2, (K2, P2) across.

Repeat Rows 1 and 2 until Ribbing measures approximately 2½", ending by working Row 2.

BODY

Change to larger size straight needles.

Row 1 (Right side)**:** Purl 0{2-4-6} sts *(see Zeros, page 577)*, RT 0{1-1-1} time, P2, K9, P2, RT, P2, K 13, P2, RT, P2, K2, (P1, K2) 4 times, P2, RT, P2, K 13, P2, RT, P2, K9, P2, RT 0{1-1-1} time, purl 0{2-4-6} sts.

Row 2: Knit 0{2-4-6} sts, purl 0{2-2-2} sts, K2, P9, K2, P2, K2, P 13, (K2, P2) twice, (K1, P2) 4 times, K2, P2, K2, P 13, K2, P2, K2, P9, K2, purl 0{2-2-2} sts, knit 0{2-4-6} sts.

Row 3: Purl 0{2-4-6} sts, RT 0{1-1-1} time, P2, BC, K3, P2, RT, P2, BC, K1, FC, P2, RT, P2, K2, (P1, work Front Cross) twice, P2, RT, P2, BC, K1, FC, P2, RT, P2, BC, K3, P2, RT 0{1-1-1} time, purl 0{2-4-6} sts.

Row 4: Repeat Row 2.

Rows 5 and 6: Repeat Rows 1 and 2.

Row 7: Purl 0{2-4-6} sts, RT 0{1-1-1} time, P2, K3, FC, P2, RT, P2, BC, K1, FC, P2, RT, P2, (work Back Cross, P1) twice, K2, P2, RT, P2, BC, K1, FC, P2, RT, P2, K3, FC, P2, RT 0{1-1-1} time, purl 0{2-4-6} sts.

Row 8: Repeat Row 2.

Repeat Rows 1-8 for pattern until Back measures approximately 25{26-27-28}" from cast on edge, ending by working a **wrong** side row.

Last Row: Bind off first 29{32-33-34} sts, work across next 27{29-31-33} sts in pattern, slip 28{30-32-34} sts just worked onto st holder, bind off remaining 29{32-33-34} sts.

FRONT

Work same as Back until Front measures approximately 22{23-24-25}" from cast on edge, ending by working a **wrong** side row.

NECK SHAPING

Note: Maintain established pattern throughout.

Row 1: Work across first 50{55-58-61} sts, slip 14{16-18-20} sts just worked onto st holder, work across: 36{39-40-41} sts **each** side.

Note: Both sides of Neck are worked at the same time, using separate yarn for **each** side.

Rows 2-5: Work across; with second yarn, bind off 2 sts at neck edge, work across: 32{35-36-37} sts **each** side.

Row 6: Work across; with second yarn, work across.

Row 7 (Decrease row)**:** Work across to within 2 sts of Neck edge, decrease *(see Decreases, page 583)*; with second yarn, decrease, work across: 31{34-35-36} sts **each** side.

Rows 8-11: Repeat Rows 6 and 7 twice: 29{32-33-34} sts **each** side.

Work even until Front measures same as Back, ending by working a **wrong** side row.

Bind off remaining sts.

SLEEVE (Make 2)
RIBBING

With smaller size straight needles, cast on 38 sts **loosely**.

Row 1: K2, (P2, K2) across.

Row 2: P2, (K2, P2) across.

Repeat Rows 1 and 2 until Ribbing measures approximately 2½", ending by working Row 2 **and** increasing one stitch at **each** end of last row *(Figs. 10a & b, page 581)*: 40 sts.

BODY

Change to larger size straight needles.

Row 1 (Right side)**:** K7, P2, RT, P2, K2, (P1, K2) 4 times, P2, RT, P2, K7.

Row 2: P7, (K2, P2) twice, (K1, P2) 4 times, K2, P2, K2, P7.

Row 3 (Increase row)**:** Increase, FC, P2, RT, P2, K2, (P1, work Front Cross) twice, P2, RT, P2, BC, increase: 42 sts.

Row 4: P8, (K2, P2) twice, (K1, P2) 4 times, K2, P2, K2, P8.

Row 5 (Increase row)**:** Increase, K7, P2, RT, P2, K2, (P1, K2) 4 times, P2, RT, P2, K7, increase: 44 sts.

Row 6: P9, (K2, P2) twice, (K1, P2) 4 times, K2, P2, K2, P9.

Row 7 (Increase row)**:** Increase, K2, FC, P2, RT, P2, (work Back Cross, P1) twice, K2, P2, RT, P2, BC, K2, increase: 46 sts.

Row 8: P 10, (K2, P2) twice, (K1, P2) 4 times, K2, P2, K2, P 10.

Rows 9-17: Working in same pattern as Rows 1-8 and working new sts in Stockinette Stitch, continue to increase one stitch at **each** edge, every other row, 5 times **more**: 56 sts.

Row 18: K2, P 13, (K2, P2) twice, (K1, P2) 4 times, K2, P2, K2, P 13, K2.

Row 19 (Increase row)**:** Increase, P1, BC, K1, FC, P2, RT, P2, K2, (P1, work Front Cross) twice, P2, RT, P2, BC, K1, FC, P1, increase: 58 sts.

Row 20: P1, K2, P 13, (K2, P2) twice, (K1, P2) 4 times, K2, P2, K2, P 13, K2, P1.

Maintaining pattern and working new sts in Stockinette Stitch, continue to increase one stitch at **each** edge, every other row, 0{1-2-3} time(s) **more**; then increase every fourth row, 7 times: 72{74-76-78} sts.

Work even until Sleeve measures approximately 17$\frac{1}{2}$\{18-18$\frac{1}{2}$-19\}" from cast on edge, ending by working a **wrong** side row.

Bind off all sts **loosely** in pattern.

FINISHING

Sew shoulder seams.

MOCK TURTLENECK

With **right** side facing and using smaller size circular needle, knit 28{30-32-34} sts from Back st holder, pick up 13 sts along left Front Neck edge **(Fig. 34a, page 586)**, knit 14{16-18-20} sts from Front st holder, pick up 13 sts along right Front Neck edge, place marker for beginning of rnd **(see Markers, page 578)**: 68{72-76-80} sts.

Work in K2, P2 ribbing around for 2".

Change to larger size circular needle.

Continue in K2, P2 ribbing around for 2" **more**.

Bind off all sts **loosely** in ribbing.

Sew Sleeves to Sweater, matching center of last row on Sleeve to shoulder seam and beginning 10$\frac{1}{4}$\{10$\frac{3}{4}$-11$\frac{1}{4}$-11$\frac{3}{4}$\}" down from seam.

Weave underarm and side in one continuous seam **(Fig. 36, page 587)**.

STRIPED CARDIGAN

■■■□ INTERMEDIATE

Size	Finished Chest Measurement	
X-Small	32"	(81.5 cm)
Small	36"	(91.5 cm)
Medium	40"	(101.5 cm)
Large	44"	(112 cm)
1X	48"	(122 cm)
2X	52"	(132 cm)

Size Note: Instructions are written with sizes X-Small, Small, and Medium in the first set of braces { } and sizes Large, 1X, and 2X in the second set of braces. Instructions will be easier to read if you circle all the numbers pertaining to your size. If only one number is given, it applies to all sizes.

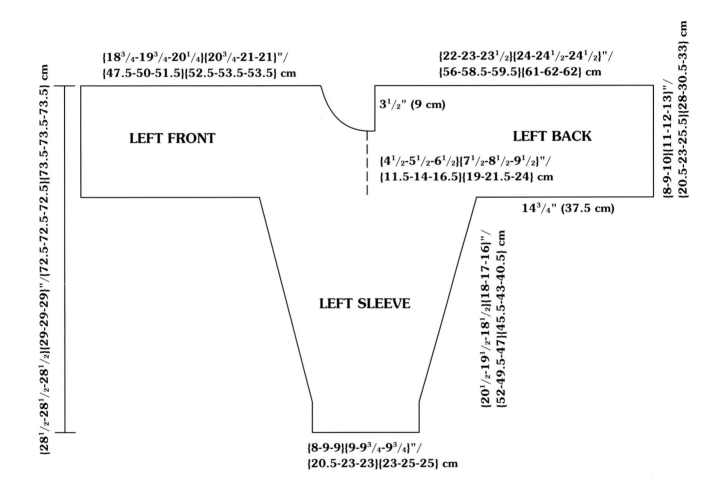

{18³/₄-19³/₄-20¹/₄}{20³/₄-21-21}"/ {47.5-50-51.5}{52.5-53.5-53.5} cm

{22-23-23¹/₂}{24-24¹/₂-24¹/₂}"/ {56-58.5-59.5}{61-62-62} cm

{8-9-10}{11-12-13}"/ {20.5-23-25.5}{28-30.5-33} cm

{28¹/₂-28¹/₂-28¹/₂}{29-29-29}"/{72.5-72.5-72.5}{73.5-73.5-73.5} cm

LEFT FRONT

3¹/₂" (9 cm)

LEFT BACK

{4¹/₂-5¹/₂-6¹/₂}{7¹/₂-8¹/₂-9¹/₂}"/ {11.5-14-16.5}{19-21.5-24} cm

14³/₄" (37.5 cm)

LEFT SLEEVE

{20¹/₂-19¹/₂-18¹/₂}{18-17-16}"/ {52-49.5-47}{45.5-43-40.5} cm

{8-9-9}{9-9³/₄-9³/₄}"/ {20.5-23-23}{23-25-25} cm

Instructions begin on page 226.

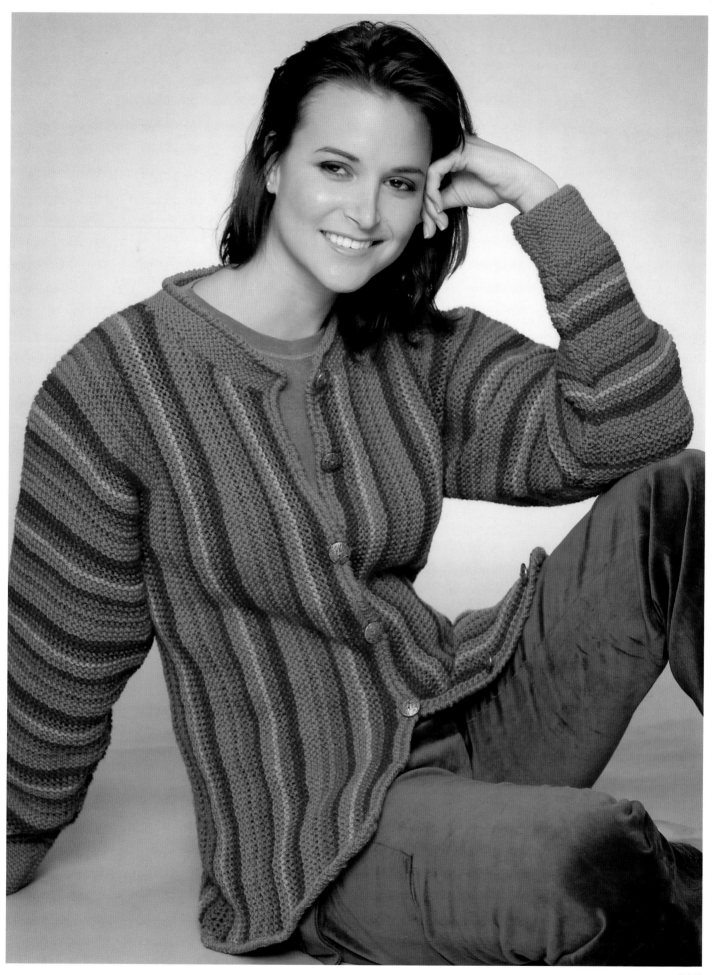

MATERIALS

Medium/Worsted Weight Yarn:

Orange
Ounces {11-12-13}{14-15-15¹/₂}
Yards {660-720-780}{840-900-930}
Grams {310-340-370}{400-430-440}
Meters {604-658-713}{768-823-850}

Green **and** Red
Ounces {5¹/₂-6-6¹/₂}{7-7¹/₂-7³/₄}
Yards {330-360-390}{420-450-465}
Grams {160-170-180}{200-210-220}
Meters {302-329-357}{384-411-425}

Brown
Ounces {3¹/₂-4-4¹/₄}{4¹/₂-5-5}
Yards {210-240-255}{270-300-300}
Grams {100-110-120}{130-140-140}
Meters {192-219-233}{247-274-274}

Lt Brown
Ounces {2-2-2¹/₄}{2¹/₂-2¹/₂-2³/₄}
Yards {120-120-135}{150-150-165}
Grams {60-60-65}{70-70-80}
Meters {110-110-123}{137-137-151}

Two 29" (73.5 cm) Circular knitting needles,
   size 7 (4.5 mm) **or** size needed for gauge
Note: A pair of straight knitting needles can be
substituted for one of the circular knitting needles
which is used to work the 3-needle bind off.
16" (40.5 cm) Circular knitting needle,
   size 6 (4 mm)
Crochet hook (for Edging), size G (4 mm)
Markers (for buttonholes)
Stitch holders - 2
³/₄" (19 mm) Buttons - 7
Yarn needle

GAUGE: With larger size needle(s),
   in Garter Stitch,
   18 sts and 36 rows = 4" (10 cm)
   (see Basic Fabrics, page 578)

Cardigan is worked in two pieces, from Sleeve cuff to center of Front and Back.

STRIPE SEQUENCE

★ 2 Rows Green, 2 rows Orange, 4 rows Brown, 2 rows Red, 4 rows Orange, 2 rows Lt Brown, 4 rows Green, 4 rows Red, 6 rows Orange; repeat from ★ for sequence.

LEFT SIDE
SLEEVE

With smaller size circular needle, using Orange, and leaving a long end for sewing, cast on {36-40-40}{40-44-44} sts; do **not** join.

Knit 23 rows for Garter Stitch (12 ridges).

Change to larger size circular needle.

Follow Stripe Sequence throughout.

Row 24 (Increase row - right side)**:** K1, M1 *(Figs. 14a & b, page 582)*, knit across to last st, M1, K1: {38-42-42}{42-46-46} sts.

Note: Loop a short piece of yarn around any stitch to mark Row 24 as **right** side.

Continue to increase one stitch at **each** edge, every fourth row, {0-0-0}{7-12-16} times *(see Zeros, page 577)*; then increase every sixth row, {0-8-21}{17-12-8} times; then increase every eighth row, {9-12-1}{0-0-0} time(s); then increase every tenth row, {8-0-0}{0-0-0} times: {72-82-86}{90-94-94} sts.

Work even until Sleeve measures approximately {20¹/₂-19¹/₂-18¹/₂}{18-17-16}"/ {52-49.5-47}{45.5-43-40.5} cm from cast on edge, ending by working a **wrong** side row.

LEFT FRONT & BACK

Row 1: Add on 66 sts (Back) *(Figs. 5a & b, page 580)*, knit across, add on 66 sts (Front): {204-214-218}{222-226-226} sts.

Work even until Front and Back measures {4¹/₂-5¹/₂-6¹/₂}{7¹/₂-8¹/₂-9¹/₂}"/ {11.5-14-16.5}{19-21.5-24} cm, ending by working a **wrong** side row.

NECK SHAPING

Back and Front are worked at the same time, using separate yarn for **each** piece.

Row 1: Knit {99-104-106}{108-110-110} sts (Back), slip next 6 sts onto st holder; with second yarn, K2 tog *(Fig. 17, page 583)*, knit across (Front): {99-104-106}{108-110-110} sts on Back and {98-103-105}{107-109-109} sts on Front.

Row 2: Knit across; with second yarn, knit across.

Row 3 (Decrease row)**:** Knit across; with second yarn, K2 tog, knit across: {97-102-104}{106-108-108} sts on Front.

Rows 4-29: Repeat Rows 2 and 3, 13 times: {84-89-91}{93-95-95} sts on Front.

Rows 30 and 31: Knit across; with second yarn, knit across.

Row 32: Bind off all sts on Front; with second yarn, knit across.

Leave all sts on needle for joining center Back seam; cut yarn.

Note: If you are using a straight needle instead of a second circular needle, slip sts onto straight knitting needle, beginning at bottom edge.

RIGHT SIDE

Work same as Left Side to Neck Shaping.

NECK SHAPING

Front and Back are worked at the same time, using separate yarn for **each** piece.

Row 1 (Decrease row)**:** Knit {97-102-104}{106-108-108} sts (Front), K2 tog, slip next 6 sts onto st holder; with second yarn, knit across (Back): {98-103-105}{107-109-109} sts on Front and {99-104-106}{108-110-110} sts on Back.

Row 2: Knit across; with second yarn, knit across.

Row 3 (Decrease row)**:** Knit across to within 2 sts of Neck edge, K2 tog; with second yarn, knit across: {97-102-104}{106-108-108} sts on Front.

Rows 4-29: Repeat Rows 2 and 3, 13 times: {84-89-91}{93-95-95} sts on Front.

Rows 30 and 31: Knit across; with second yarn, knit across.

Row 32: Knit across; with second yarn, bind off all sts on Front.

Leave sts on circular needle, do **not** cut yarn.

Instructions continued on page 228.

FINISHING

Using 3-needle bind off method *(Fig. 33, page 586)*, join Left Back to Right Back.

NECKBAND

With **right** side facing, using Orange and smaller size circular needle, pick up 24 sts evenly spaced along right Neck edge *(Fig. 34a, page 586)*, slip 6 sts from st holder onto second end of circular needle and knit across, pick up 32 sts evenly spaced across Back Neck edge, slip 6 sts from st holder onto second end of circular needle and knit across, pick up 24 sts evenly spaced along left Neck edge: 92 sts.

Knit 9 rows.

Bind off all sts.

With long ends, weave Sleeve seam *(Fig. 36, page 587)* and join Front and Back *(Figs. 35a & b, page 587)* in one continuous seam.

BODY EDGING

Mark placement of buttonholes on Right Front, placing a marker between third and fourth stitches from bottom edge and from top edge; then evenly space 5 more markers between stitches for remaining buttonholes.

Rnd 1 (Buttonhole rnd)**:** With **right** side facing and crochet hook *(see Crochet Stitches, pages 588 & 589)*, join Orange with slip st in either side seam; ch 1, working 2 sts in each corner, sc evenly around to within one st of next marker, [ch 2, skip next 2 sts **(buttonhole made)**], ★ sc in each st across to within one st of next marker, ch 2, skip next 2 sts; repeat from ★ 5 times **more**, sc evenly spaced around; join with slip st to first sc.

Rnd 2: Ch 1, working from **left** to **right**, work reverse sc in each sc around *(Figs. 44a-d, page 589)* working 2 reverse sc in each ch-2 sp; join with slip st to first sc, finish off.

Sew buttons to Left Front opposite buttonholes.

Design by Doreen L. Marquart.

TRI-COLOR PULLOVER

Shown on page 231.

■■■□ INTERMEDIATE

Size	Finished Chest Measurement	
X-Small	32"	(81.5 cm)
Small	36½"	(92.5 cm)
Medium	40"	(101.5 cm)
Large	44½"	(113 cm)
1X	48"	(122 cm)
2X	52½"	(133.5 cm)

Size Note: Instructions are written with sizes X-Small, Small, and Medium in the first set of braces { } and sizes Large, 1X, and 2X in the second set of braces. Instructions will be easier to read if you circle all the numbers pertaining to your size. If only one number is given, it applies to all sizes.

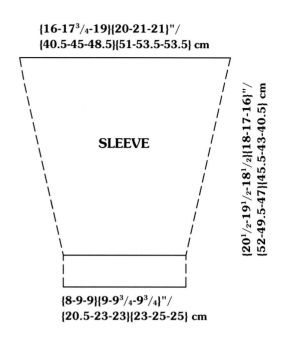

{16-17³/₄-19}{20-21-21}"/
{40.5-45-48.5}{51-53.5-53.5} cm

SLEEVE

{20½-19½-18½}{18-17-16}"/
{52-49.5-47}{45.5-43-40.5} cm

{8-9-9}{9-9³/₄-9³/₄}"/
{20.5-23-23}{23-25-25} cm

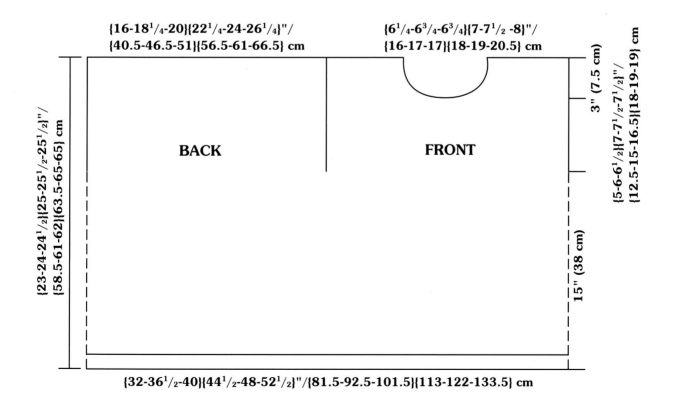

{16-18¼-20}{22¼-24-26¼}"/
{40.5-46.5-51}{56.5-61-66.5} cm

{6¼-6³/₄-6³/₄}{7-7½ -8}"/
{16-17-17}{18-19-20.5} cm

3" (7.5 cm)

{5-6-6½}{7-7½-7½}"/
{12.5-15-16.5}{18-19-19} cm

BACK

FRONT

{23-24-24½}{25-25½-25½}"/
{58.5-61-62}{63.5-65-65} cm

15" (38 cm)

{32-36½-40}{44½-48-52½}"/{81.5-92.5-101.5}{113-122-133.5} cm

Dotted lines indicate continuous rounds.

Instructions begin on page 230.

MATERIALS

Medium/Worsted Weight Yarn:

Gold

Ounces {8-9-9^1/$_2$}{10^1/$_2$-11-11}

Yards {525-590-625}{690-725-725}

Grams {230-260-270}{300-310-310}

Meters {480-539-572}{631-663-663}

Rust

Ounces {6^1/$_2$-7^1/$_2$-8}{9-9^1/$_2$-10^1/$_2$}

Yards {420-480-515}{580-610-675}

Grams {180-210-230}{260-270-300}

Meters {384-439-471}{530-558-617}

Green

Ounces {1^1/$_2$-1^1/$_2$- 1^1/$_2$}{1^1/$_2$-2-2}

Yards {90-90-90}{90-120-120}

Grams {40-40-40}{40-60-60}

Meters {82.5-82.5-82.5}{82.5-110-110}

Two 29" (73.5 cm) Circular knitting needles, size 7 (4.5 mm) **or** size needed for gauge

Note: A pair of straight knitting needles can be substituted for one of the circular knitting needles which is used to work the Front and the 3-needle bind off.

16" (40.5 cm) Circular knitting needle, size 6 (4 mm)

8" (20.5 cm) Double pointed needle sets, sizes 6 (4 mm) **and** 7 (4.5 mm)

Marker

Stitch holders - 3

Yarn needle

GAUGE: With larger size needle(s),
in Stockinette Stitch,
18 sts and 24 rows = 4" (10 cm);
in Garter Stitch,
18 sts and 36 rows = 4" (10 cm)
(see Basic Fabrics, page 578)

Pullover is worked in the round to the underarm.

FRONT & BACK
BORDER

With larger size circular needle and Green, cast on {144-164-180}{200-216-236} sts, place marker to mark beginning of rnd *(see Markers and Knitting in the Round, pages 578 & 579)*.

Rnd 1 (Right side)**:** Knit around.

Rnd 2: Purl around.

Rnds 3-6: Repeat Rnds 1 and 2 twice.

Note: When changing colors, always pick up the new color yarn from beneath the dropped yarn and keep the color which has just been worked to the left *(Fig. 30, page 585)*. This will prevent holes in the finished piece. Carry the yarn not in use loosely across the wrong side and take extra care to keep your tension even.

Rnd 7: (With Rust K2, with Gold K2) around.

Rnd 8: (With Rust K2, with Gold P2) around.

Rnds 9-12: Repeat Rnds 7 and 8 twice; at end of last rnd, cut Gold and drop Rust to **wrong** side.

Rnds 13-16: With Green, repeat Rnds 1 and 2 twice; at end of last rnd, cut Green.

BODY

With Rust, work in Stockinette Stitch (knit every round) until piece measures approximately 15" (38 cm) from cast on edge.

Instructions continued on page 232.

FRONT ARMHOLE SHAPING

Row 1: With second circular needle or straight needle and Gold, knit {72-82-90}{100-108-118} sts, leave remaining {72-82-90} {100-108-118} sts on first circular needle for Back (to be worked later).

Work in Garter Stitch (knit every row) until Armholes measure approximately {5-6-6^1/$_2$}{7-7^1/$_2$-7^1/$_2$}"/ {12.5-15-16.5}{18-19-19} cm, ending by working a **wrong** side row.

NECK SHAPING

Both sides of Neck are worked at the same time, using separate yarn for **each** side.

Row 1: Knit {28-32-36}{40-44-48} sts, slip next {16-18-18}{20-20-22} sts onto st holder; with second yarn, knit across: {28-32-36}{40-44-48} sts **each** side.

Row 2: Knit across; with second yarn, knit across.

Row 3 (Decrease row)**:** Knit across to within 3 sts of neck edge, K2 tog **(Fig. 17, page 583)**, K1; with second yarn, K1, SSK **(Figs. 21a-c, page 584)**, knit across: {27-31-35}{39-43-47} sts **each** side.

Rows 4 thru {13-13-13}{13-15-15}: Repeat Rows 2 and 3, {5-5-5}{5-6-6} times: {22-26-30}{34-37-41} sts **each** side.

Work even until piece measures approximately {23-24-24^1/$_2$}{25-25^1/$_2$-25^1/$_2$}"/ {58.5-61-62}{63.5-65-65} cm from cast on edge, ending by working a **wrong** side row; cut Gold.

Slip remaining sts onto st holders.

BACK ARMHOLE SHAPING

With **right** side facing, larger size circular needle and Gold, work in Garter Stitch until Armholes measure approximately {8-9-9^1/$_2$}{10-10^1/$_2$-10^1/$_2$}"/ {20.5-23-24}{25.5-26.5-26.5} cm, ending by working a **wrong** side row; do **not** cut Gold.

Using 3-needle bind off method **(Fig. 33, page 586)**, join Front to Back at right shoulder.

Slip sts from Front left shoulder st holder onto large size needle; join Front to Back at left shoulder, leaving last {28-30-30}{32-34-36} sts on Back circular needle for Neck Border.

SLEEVE (Make 2)
BORDER

Using smaller size double pointed needles and Green, cast on {36-40-40}{40-44-44} sts, place marker to mark beginning of rnd.

Work same as Front and Back Border.

BODY

Change to larger size double pointed needles.

Rnd 1: With Gold, knit around.

Rnd 2 (Increase rnd)**:** Do **not** slip marker, work knit left invisible increase **(Figs. 13a & b, page 581)**, slip marker, K1 (first st), work knit right invisible increase **(Fig. 12a, page 581)**, knit around: {38-42-42}{42-46-46} sts.

Working in Stockinette Stitch and increasing in same manner, increase every other rnd, {0-0-0}{5-8-11} times *(see Zeros, page 577)*; then increase every fourth rnd, {0-9-21}{19-16-13} times; then increase every sixth rnd, {17-10-1}{0-0-0} time(s): {72-80-86}{90-94-94} sts.

Work even until Sleeve measures approximately {20$\frac{1}{2}$-19$\frac{1}{2}$-18$\frac{1}{2}$}{18-17-16}"/ {52-49.5-47}{45.5-43-40.5} cm from cast on edge, ending by working a purl rnd to form a ridge.

Bind off all sts in knit; leave a long end for sewing.

FINISHING
NECK BORDER
With **right** side facing, using smaller size circular needle and Green, knit {28-30-30}{32-34-36} sts across Back neck, pick up 16 sts evenly spaced along left Neck edge *(Fig. 34a, page 586)*, slip {16-18-18}{20-20-22} sts from Front st holder onto second end of circular needle and knit across, pick up 16 sts evenly spaced along right Neck edge, place marker to mark beginning of rnd: {76-80-80}{84-86-90} sts.

Rnd 1: Purl around.

Rnd 2: Knit around.

Rnd 3: Purl around decreasing {4-4-4}{4-2-2} sts evenly spaced *(Fig. 18, page 583)*: {72-76-76}{80-84-88} sts.

Rnd 4: (With Rust K2, with Gold K2) around.

Rnd 5: (With Rust K2, with Gold P2) around.

Rnds 6 and 7: Repeat Rnds 4 and 5.

Rnd 8: Cut Rust and Gold; with Green, knit around.

Rnd 9: Purl around.

Rnd 10: Knit around.

Bind off **loosely** in **purl**.

With long end, sew Sleeves to armholes matching stitch between increases at lower armhole.

Design by Doreen L. Marquart.

VARIEGATED CARDIGAN

■■■□ INTERMEDIATE

Size	Finished Chest Measurement	
X-Small	32"	(81.5 cm)
Small	36"	(91.5 cm)
Medium	40"	(101.5 cm)
Large	44"	(112 cm)
1X	48"	(122 cm)
2X	52"	(132 cm)

Size Note: Instructions are written with sizes X-Small, Small, and Medium in the first set of braces { } and sizes Large, 1X, and 2X in the second set of braces. Instructions will be easier to read if you circle all the numbers pertaining to your size. If only one number is given, it applies to all sizes.

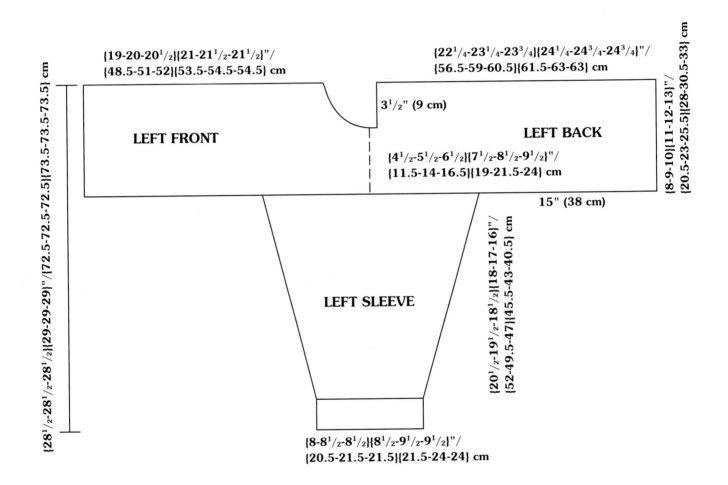

{19-20-20½}{21-21½-21½}"/ {48.5-51-52}{53.5-54.5-54.5} cm

{22¼-23¼-23¾}{24¼-24¾-24¾}"/ {56.5-59-60.5}{61.5-63-63} cm

{8-9-10}{11-12-13}"/ {20.5-23-25.5}{28-30.5-33} cm

3½" (9 cm)

LEFT FRONT

LEFT BACK

{4½-5½-6½}{7½-8½-9½}"/ {11.5-14-16.5}{19-21.5-24} cm

15" (38 cm)

{28½-28½-28½}{29-29-29}"/{72.5-72.5-72.5}{73.5-73.5-73.5} cm

{20½-19½-18½}{18-17-16}"/ {52-49.5-47}{45.5-43-40.5} cm

LEFT SLEEVE

{8-8½-8½}{8½-9½-9½}"/ {20.5-21.5-21.5}{21.5-24-24} cm

Instructions begin on page 236.

MATERIALS

MEDIUM 4

Medium/Worsted Weight Yarn:
- Ounces {19-21-23}{25-27-28}
- Yards {940-1,040-1,140}
  {1,240-1,340-1,390}
- Grams {540-600-650}{710-770-800}
- Meters {860-951-1,042}
  {1,134-1,225-1,271}

Two 29" (73.5 cm) Circular knitting needles,
  size 8 (5 mm) **or** size needed for gauge
Note: A pair of straight knitting needles can be
substituted for one of the circular knitting needles
which is used to work the 3-needle bind off.
16" (40.5 cm) Circular knitting needle,
  size 7 (4.5 mm)
Crochet hook (for Edging), size H (5 mm)
Markers (for buttonholes)
Stitch holders - 2
$3/4$" (19 mm) Buttons - 7
Yarn needle

GAUGE: With larger size needle(s),
in Stockinette Stitch,
16 sts and 24 rows = 4" (10 cm);
in Garter Stitch,
16 sts and 36 rows = 4" (10 cm)
(see Basic Fabrics, page 578)

Cardigan is worked in two pieces, from Sleeve
cuff to center of Front and Back.

LEFT SIDE
SLEEVE

With smaller size circular needle and leaving a long
end for sewing, cast on {32-34-34}{34-38-38} sts;
do **not** join.

Knit 25 rows for Garter Stitch (13 ridges).

Change to larger size circular needle.

Row 26 (Increase row - right side)**:** K1, M1
(Figs. 14a & b, page 582), knit across to last st,
M1, K1: {34-36-36}{36-40-40} sts.

Beginning with a **purl** row, work in Stockinette
Stitch, increasing one stitch at **each** edge, every
other row, {0-0-0}{2-5-8} times ***(see Zeros,
page 577)***; then increase every fourth row,
{0-8-17}{20-17-14} times; then increase every sixth
row, {11-10-3}{0-0-0} times; then increase every
eighth row, {4-0-0}{0-0-0} times:
{64-72-76}{80-84-84} sts.

Work even until Sleeve measures approximately
{20$1/2$-19$1/2$-18$1/2$}{18-17-16}"/
{52-49.5-47}{45.5-43-40.5} cm from cast on edge,
ending by working a **purl** row.

LEFT FRONT & BACK

Row 1: Add on 60 sts (Back) ***(Figs. 5a & b,
page 580)***, knit across, add on 60 sts (Front):
{184-192-196}{200-204-204} sts.

Knit every row (Garter Stitch), until Front and Back
measures {4$1/2$-5$1/2$-6$1/2$}{7$1/2$-8$1/2$-9$1/2$}"/
{11.5-14-16.5}{19-21.5-24} cm, ending by
working a **wrong** side row.

NECK SHAPING

Back and Front are worked at the same time,
using separate yarn for **each** piece.

Row 1: Knit {89-93-95}{97-99-99} sts (Back), slip
next 6 sts onto st holder; with second yarn, K2 tog
(Fig. 17, page 583), knit across (Front):
{89-93-95}{97-99-99} sts on Back and
{88-92-94}{96-98-98} sts on Front.

Row 2: Knit across; with second yarn, knit across.

Row 3 (Decrease row)**:** Knit across; with second
yarn, K2 tog, knit across: {87-91-93}{95-97-97} sts
on Front.

Rows 4-25: Repeat Rows 2 and 3, 11 times:
{76-80-82}{84-86-86} sts on Front.

Work even until Front and Back measure {8-9-10}
{11-12-13}"/{20.5-23-25.5}{28-30.5-33} cm,
ending by working a **right** side row.

Last Row: Bind off all sts on Front; with second yarn, knit across.

Leave all stitches on needle for joining center Back seam; cut yarn.

Note: If you are using a straight needle instead of a second circular knitting needle, slip sts onto straight knitting needle, beginning at bottom edge.

RIGHT SIDE
Work same as Left Side to Neck Shaping.

NECK SHAPING
Front and Back are worked at the same time, using separate yarn for **each** piece.

Row 1 (Decrease row)**:** Knit {87-91-93}{95-97-97} sts (Front), K2 tog, slip next 6 sts onto st holder; with second yarn, knit across (Back): {88-92-94}{96-98-98} sts on Front and {89-93-95}{97-99-99} sts on Back.

Row 2: Knit across; with second yarn, knit across.

Row 3 (Decrease row)**:** Knit across to within 2 sts of Neck edge, K2 tog; with second yarn, knit across: {87-91-93}{95-97-97} sts on Front.

Rows 4-25: Repeat Rows 2 and 3, 11 times: {76-80-82}{84-86-86} sts on Front.

Work even until Front and Back measure same as Left Side, ending by working a **right** side row.

Last Row: Knit across; with second yarn, bind off all sts on Front.

Leave sts on circular needle, do **not** cut yarn.

FINISHING
Using 3-needle bind off method *(Fig. 33, page 586)*, join Left Back to Right Back.

NECKBAND
With **right** side facing and using smaller size circular needle, pick up 20 sts evenly spaced along right Neck edge *(Fig. 34a, page 586)*, slip 6 sts from st holder onto second end of circular needle and knit across, pick up 28 sts evenly spaced across Back Neck edge, slip 6 sts from st holder onto second end of circular needle and knit across, pick up 20 sts evenly spaced along left Neck edge: 80 sts.

Knit 10 rows.

Bind off all sts.

With long ends, weave Sleeve seam *(Fig. 36, page 587)* and join Front and Back *(Figs. 35a & b, page 587)* in one continuous seam.

BODY EDGING
Mark placement of buttonholes on Right Front, placing a marker between third and fourth stitches from bottom edge and from top edge; then evenly space 5 more markers between stitches for remaining buttonholes.

Rnd 1 (Buttonhole rnd)**:** With **right** side facing and crochet hook *(see Crochet Stitches, pages 588 & 589)*, join yarn with slip st in either side seam; ch 1, working 2 sc in each corner, sc evenly around to within one st of next marker, [ch 2, skip next 2 sts **(buttonhole made)**], ★ sc in each st across to within one st of next marker, ch 2, skip next 2 sts; repeat from ★ 5 times **more**, sc evenly spaced around; join with slip st to first sc.

Rnd 2: Ch 1, working from **left** to **right**, work reverse sc in each sc around *(Figs. 44a-d, page 589)* working 2 reverse sc in each ch-2 sp; join with slip st to first sc, finish off.

Sew buttons to Left Front opposite buttonholes.

Design by Doreen L. Marquart.

STRIPED-YOKE PULLOVER

◀▬■■■▭ INTERMEDIATE

Size	Finished Chest Measurement
X-Small	32" (81.5 cm)
Small	36$^1/_2$" (92.5 cm)
Medium	40" (101.5 cm)
Large	44" (112 cm)
1X	48" (122 cm)
2X	52" (132 cm)

Size Note: Instructions are written with sizes X-Small, Small, and Medium in the first set of braces { } and sizes Large, 1X, and 2X in the second set of braces. Instructions will be easier to read if you circle all the numbers pertaining to your size. If only one number is given, it applies to all sizes.

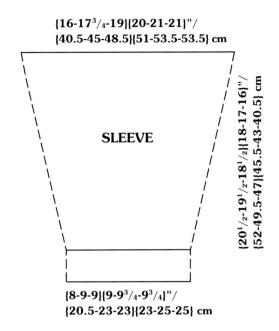

{16-17$^3/_4$-19}{20-21-21}"/ {40.5-45-48.5}{51-53.5-53.5} cm

SLEEVE

{20$^1/_2$-19$^1/_2$-18$^1/_2$}{18-17-16}"/ {52-49.5-47}{45.5-43-40.5} cm

{8-9-9}{9-9$^3/_4$-9$^3/_4$}"/ {20.5-23-23}{23-25-25} cm

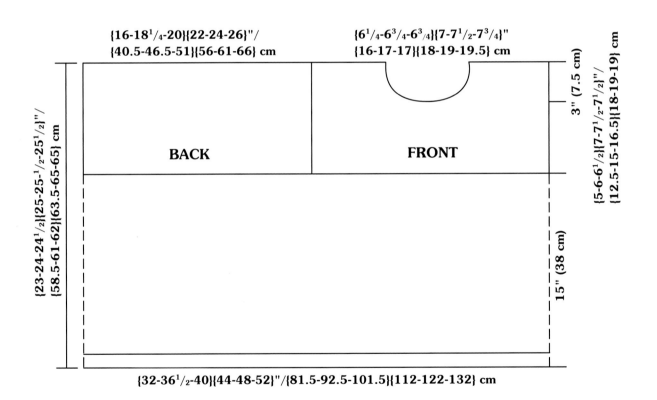

{16-18$^1/_4$-20}{22-24-26}"/ {40.5-46.5-51}{56-61-66} cm

{6$^1/_4$-6$^3/_4$-6$^3/_4$}{7-7$^1/_2$-7$^3/_4$}" {16-17-17}{18-19-19.5} cm

3" (7.5 cm)

{23-24-24$^1/_2$}{25-25-25$^1/_2$}"/ {58.5-61-62}{63.5-65-65} cm

BACK

FRONT

{5-6-6$^1/_2$}{7-7$^1/_2$-7$^1/_2$}"/ {12.5-15-16.5}{18-19-19} cm

15" (38 cm)

{32-36$^1/_2$-40}{44-48-52}"/{81.5-92.5-101.5}{112-122-132} cm

Dotted lines indicate continuous rounds.

Instructions begin on page 240.

MATERIALS

Medium/Worsted Weight Yarn:

Brown

Ounces	{14-15^1/$_2$-16^1/$_2$}{17^1/$_2$-18-18^1/$_2$}
Yards	{780-865-920}{975-1,005-1,030}
Grams	{400-440-470}{500-510-530}
Meters	{713-791-841}{892-919-942}

Lt Blue

Ounces	{1^3/$_4$-2-2^1/$_2$}{3-3^1/$_2$-3^1/$_2$}
Yards	{100-110-140}{170-195-195}
Grams	{50-60-70}{90-100-100}
Meters	{91-101-128}{155-178-178}

Blue **and** Cream

Ounces	{1^1/$_4$-1^1/$_2$-1^1/$_2$}{2-2^1/$_2$-2^1/$_2$}
Yards	{70-85-85}{110-140-140}
Grams	{35-40-40}{60-70-70}
Meters	{64-77.5-77.5}{101-128-128}

Two 29" (73.5 cm) Circular knitting needles, size 7 (4.5 mm) **or** size needed for gauge

Note: A pair of straight knitting needles can be substituted for one of the circular knitting needles which is used to work the Front and the 3-needle bind off.

16" (40.5 cm) Circular knitting needle, size 6 (4 mm)

8" (20.5 cm) Double pointed needle sets, sizes 6 (4 mm) **and** 7 (4.5 mm)

Marker

Stitch holders - 3

Yarn needle

GAUGE: With larger size needle(s), in Stockinette Stitch, 18 sts and 24 rows = 4" (10 cm); in Garter Stitch, 18 sts and 36 rows = 4" (10 cm) *(see Basic Fabrics, page 578)*

Pullover is worked in the round to the underarm.

FRONT & BACK
BORDER

With larger size circular needle and Brown, cast on {144-164-180}{198-216-234} sts, place marker to mark beginning of rnd *(see Markers and Knitting in the Round, pages 578 & 579)*.

Work in Garter Stitch (purl one rnd, knit one rnd) for 10 rnds.

BODY

Work in Stockinette Stitch (knit every rnd) until piece measures approximately 15" (38 cm) from cast on edge.

FRONT ARMHOLE SHAPING
STRIPE SEQUENCE

★ 4 Rows Lt Blue, 2 rows Brown, 2 rows Blue, 2 rows Lt Blue, 4 rows Cream, 2 rows Blue, 4 rows Brown; repeat from ★ for sequence.

Row 1: With second circular needle or straight needle and Lt Blue, knit {72-82-90}{99-108-117} sts, leave remaining {72-82-90}{99-108-117} sts on first circular needle for Back (to be worked later).

Work in Garter Stitch (knit every row) in Stripe Sequence until Armholes measure approximately {5-6-6^1/$_2$}{7-7^1/$_2$-7^1/$_2$}"/ {12.5-15-16.5}{18-19-19} cm, ending by working a **wrong** side row.

NECK SHAPING

Both sides of Neck are worked at the same time, using separate yarn for **each** side.

Row 1: Knit {28-32-36}{40-44-48} sts, slip next {16-18-18}{19-20-21} sts onto st holder; with second yarn, knit across: {28-32-36}{40-44-48} sts **each** side.

Row 2: Knit across; with second yarn, knit across.

Row 3 (Decrease row)**:** Knit across to within 3 sts of neck edge, K2 tog **(Fig. 17, page 583)**, K1; with second yarn, K1, SSK **(Figs. 21a-c, page 584)**, knit across: {27-31-35}{39-43-47} sts **each** side.

Rows 4 thru {13-13-13}{13-15-15}: Repeat Rows 2 and 3, {5-5-5}{5-6-6} times: {22-26-30}{34-37-41} sts **each** side.

Work even until piece measures approximately {23-24-24^1/$_2$}{25-25^1/$_2$-25^1/$_2$}"/ {58.5-61-62}{63.5-65-65} cm from cast on edge, ending by working a **wrong** side row; cut yarns.

Slip remaining sts onto st holders.

BACK ARMHOLE SHAPING
With **right** side facing, larger size circular needle and Lt Blue, work in Garter Stitch in same Stripe Sequence as Front until Armholes measure approximately {8-9-9^1/$_2$}{10-10^1/$_2$-10^1/$_2$}"/ {20.5-23-24}{25.5-26.5-26.5} cm, ending by working a **wrong** side row; do **not** cut yarn.

Using 3-needle bind off method **(Fig. 33, page 586)**, join Front to Back at right shoulder.

Slip sts from Front left shoulder st holder onto large size needle; join Front to Back at left shoulder, leaving last {28-30-30}{31-34-35} sts on Back circular needle for Neck Border.

SLEEVE (Make 2)
BORDER
Using smaller size double pointed needles and Lt Blue, cast on {36-40-40}{40-44-44} sts, place marker to mark beginning of rnd.

Work in Garter Stitch for 24 rounds in the same Stripe Sequence as Front Armhole Shaping, page 9; cut yarn.

BODY
Change to larger size double pointed needles.

Rnd 1: With Brown, knit around.

Rnd 2 (Increase rnd)**:** Do **not** slip marker, work knit left invisible increase **(Figs. 13a & b, page 581)**, slip marker, K1 (first st), work knit right invisible increase **(Fig. 12a, page 581)**, knit around: {38-42-42}{42-46-46} sts.

Working in Stockinette Stitch and increasing in same manner, increase every other rnd, {0-0-2}{8-11-14} times **(see Zeros, page 577)**; then increase every fourth rnd, {0-12-20}{16-13-10} times; then increase every sixth rnd, {17-7-0}{0-0-0} times: {72-80-86}{90-94-94} sts.

Work even until Sleeve measures approximately {20^1/$_2$-19^1/$_2$-18^1/$_2$}{18-17-16}"/ {52-49.5-47}{45.5-43-40.5} cm from cast on edge.

Bind off all sts in knit; leave a long end for sewing.

FINISHING
NECK BORDER
With **right** side facing, using smaller size circular needle and Brown, knit {28-30-30}{31-34-35} sts across Back neck, pick up 16 sts evenly spaced along left Neck edge **(Fig. 34a, page 586)**, slip {16-18-18}{19-20-21} sts from Front st holder onto second end of circular needle and knit across, pick up 16 sts evenly spaced along right Neck edge, place marker to mark beginning of rnd: {76-80-80}{82-86-88} sts.

Work in Garter Stitch (purl one rnd, knit one rnd) for 6 rnds.

Bind off all sts **loosely** in **purl**.

With long end, sew Sleeves to armholes matching stitch between increases at lower armhole.

Design by Doreen L. Marquart.

TEXTURED CARDIGAN

◼◼◼◻ INTERMEDIATE

Size	Finished Chest Measurement
X-Small	32" (81.5 cm)
Small	36$^1/_2$" (92.5 cm)
Medium	40" (101.5 cm)
Large	44$^1/_2$" (113 cm)
1X	48" (122 cm)
2X	52$^1/_2$" (133.5 cm)

Size Note: Instructions are written with sizes X-Small, Small, and Medium in the first set of braces { } and sizes Large, 1X, and 2X in the second set of braces. Instructions will be easier to read if you circle all the numbers pertaining to your size. If only one number is given, it applies to all sizes.

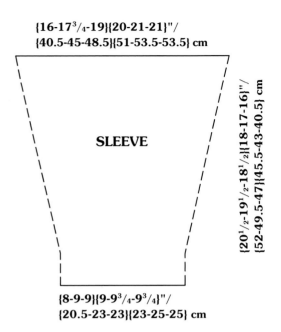

{16-17$^3/_4$-19}{20-21-21}"/
{40.5-45-48.5}{51-53.5-53.5} cm

SLEEVE

{20$^1/_2$-19$^1/_2$-18$^1/_2$}{18-17-16}"/
{52-49.5-47}{45.5-43-40.5} cm

{8-9-9}{9-9$^3/_4$-9$^3/_4$}"/
{20.5-23-23}{23-25-25} cm

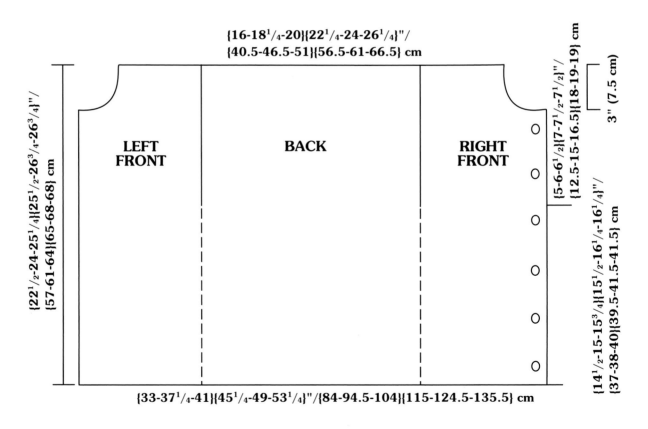

{16-18$^1/_4$-20}{22$^1/_4$-24-26$^1/_4$}"/
{40.5-46.5-51}{56.5-61-66.5} cm

LEFT FRONT

BACK

RIGHT FRONT

{22$^1/_2$-24-25$^1/_4$}{25$^1/_2$-26$^3/_4$-26$^3/_4$}"/
{57-61-64}{65-68-68} cm

3" (7.5 cm)

{5-6-6$^1/_2$}{7-7$^1/_2$-7$^1/_2$}"/
{12.5-15-16.5}{18-19-19} cm

{14$^1/_2$-15-15$^3/_4$}{15$^1/_2$-16$^1/_4$-16$^1/_4$}"/
{37-38-40}{39.5-41.5-41.5} cm

{33-37$^1/_4$-41}{45$^1/_4$-49-53$^1/_4$}"/{84-94.5-104}{115-124.5-135.5} cm

Dotted lines indicate one continuous piece.

Instructions begin on page 243.

MATERIALS

Medium/Worsted Weight Yarn: **4**
  Ounces {19-22-24}{26-28^1/$_2$-29^1/$_2$}
  Yards {1,220-1,415-1,545}
          {1,670-1,830-1,895}
  Grams {540-620-680}{740-810-840}
  Meters {1,116-1,294-1,413}
          {1,527-1,673-1,733}
Two 29" (73.5 cm) Circular knitting needles,
  size 7 (4.5 mm) **or** size needed for gauge
Note: A pair of straight knitting needles can be
substituted for one of the circular knitting needles
which is used to work the Front Armhole
Shapings and the 3-needle bind off.
16" (40.5 cm) Circular knitting needle,
  size 6 (4 mm)
8" (20.5 cm) Double pointed needle set,
  size 7 (4.5 mm)
Marker
Stitch holders - 3
^{7}/$_8$" (22 mm) Buttons - 6
Yarn needle

GAUGE: With larger size needle(s),
           in Double Moss Stitch,
           18 sts and 28 rows = 4" (10 cm)
           (see Basic Fabrics, page 578)

STITCH GUIDE

DOUBLE MOSS STITCH
(multiple of 4 sts)
Rows 1 and 2: (K2, P2) across.
Rows 3 and 4: (P2, K2) across.

Cardigan is worked in one piece to underarm.

FRONT & BACK

With larger size circular needle, cast on
{148-168-184}{204-220-240} sts.

Rows 1-4: Work in Double Moss Stitch.

Maintain established Double Moss Stitch
throughout.

Row 5 (Buttonhole row - right side)**:** Work 3 sts,
bind off next 2 sts, work across.

Row 6: Work across to bound off sts, add on 2 sts
(Figs. 5a & b, page 580), work across last 3 sts.

Work {24-26-28}{28-30-30} rows.

Repeat buttonhole Rows 5 and 6.

Work even and continue to form buttonholes,
spacing them the same distance apart, until
4 buttonholes have been worked.

Work {18-14-14}{12-12-12} rows.

RIGHT FRONT ARMHOLE SHAPING

Row 1: With second circular needle or straight
needles, work across {38-43-47}{52-56-61} sts,
leave remaining {110-125-137}{152-164-179} sts
on circular needle for Back and Left Front (to be
worked later).

Work {5-11-13}{15-17-17} rows.

Repeat buttonhole Rows 5 and 6.

Work {24-26-28}{28-30-30} rows.

Repeat buttonhole Rows 5 and 6.

NECK SHAPING

Row 1: Work across {9-9-9}{10-10-11} sts and slip onto st holder, work across: {29-34-38}{42-46-50} sts.

Row 2 (Decrease row)**:** Work across to last 2 sts, decrease *(see Decreases, page 583)*: {28-33-37}{41-45-49} sts.

Row 3 (Decrease row)**:** Decrease, work across: {27-32-36}{40-44-48} sts.

Row 4 (Decrease row)**:** Work across to last 2 sts, decrease: {26-31-35}{39-43-47} sts.

Row 5: Work across.

Repeat Rows 4 and 5, {4-5-5}{5-6-6} times: {22-26-30}{34-37-41} sts.

Work even until Right Front measures approximately {22^1/$_2$-24-25^1/$_4$} {25^1/$_2$-26^3/$_4$-26^3/$_4$}"/{57-61-64}{65-68-68} cm from cast on edge, ending by working a **wrong** side row.

Slip remaining sts onto st holder; cut yarn.

BACK ARMHOLE SHAPING

Row 1: With **right** side facing, work across {72-82-90}{100-108-118} sts on circular needle, slip remaining {38-43-47}{52-56-61} sts onto st holder for Left Front.

Work even until Back measures same as Right Front, ending by working a **wrong** side row.

Leave all sts on circular needle; cut yarn.

LEFT FRONT ARMHOLE SHAPING

With **right** side facing, slip sts from st holder onto second circular needle or straight needle: {38-43-47}{52-56-61} sts.

Work even until Left Front measures same as Right Front to Neck Shaping, ending by working a **right** side row.

NECK SHAPING

Work same as Right Front, leaving all sts on needle; do **not** cut yarn.

Using 3-needle bind off method *(Fig. 33, page 586)*, join Front to Back at left shoulder.

Join Front to Back at right shoulder, leaving last {28-30-30}{32-34-36} sts on Back circular needle for Neck Border.

Instructions continued on page 246.

SLEEVE (Make 2)

Using double pointed needles *(Fig. 3b, page 579)*, cast on {36-40-40}{40-44-44} sts, place marker to mark beginning of rnd *(Fig. 1, page 578)*.

Rnds 1 and 2: (K2, P2) around.

Rnd 3 (Increase rnd)**:** Do **not** slip marker, work purl left invisible increase *(Fig. 13c, page 581)*, slip marker, P1 (first st), work purl right invisible increase *(Fig. 12b, page 581)*, P1, K2, (P2, K2) around to last st, P1: {38-42-42}{42-46-46} sts.

Rnd 4: P3, K2, (P2, K2) around to last st, P1.

Rnds 5 and 6: K3, P2, (K2, P2) around to last st, K1.

Working in established Double Moss Stitch, increasing in same manner and working a knit or purl invisible increase as needed, increase every fourth rnd, {0-0-6}{14-18-21} times *(see Zeros, page 577)*; then increase every sixth rnd, {1-13-16}{10-6-3} time(s); then increase every eighth rnd, {16-6-0}{0-0-0} times: {72-80-86}{90-94-94} sts.

Work even until Sleeve measures approximately {20^1/$_2$-19^1/$_2$-18^1/$_2$}{18-17-16}"/ {52-49.5-47}{45.5-43-40.5} cm from cast on edge.

Bind off all sts in pattern; leave a long end for sewing.

FINISHING
NECK BORDER

With **right** side facing and using smaller size circular needle, knit {9-9-9}{10-10-11} sts from Right Front st holder, pick up 14 sts along right Front Neck edge *(Fig. 34a, page 586)*, knit {28-30-30}{32-34-36} sts from Back circular needle, pick up 14 sts along left Front Neck edge, slip {9-9-9}{10-10-11} sts from Left Front st holder onto second end of circular needle and knit across: {74-76-76}{80-82-86} sts.

Knit 4 rows.

Bind off all sts **loosely** in **knit**.

With long end, sew Sleeves to armholes matching stitch between increases at lower armhole.
the purl rows; if fewer, use a smaller size needle for the purl rows.

Design by Doreen L. Marquart.

LATTICE PULLOVER

 INTERMEDIATE

Also shown on page 249.

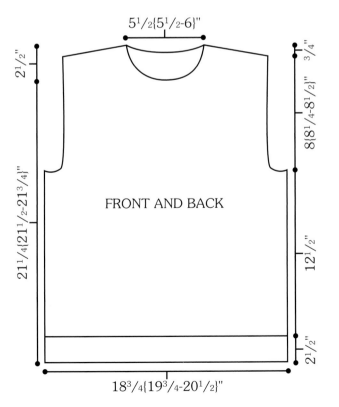

5¹/₂{5¹/₂-6}"

2¹/₂"

³/₄"

8{8¹/₄-8¹/₂}"

21¹/₄{21¹/₂-21³/₄}"

FRONT AND BACK

12¹/₂"

2¹/₂"

18³/₄{19³/₄-20¹/₂}"

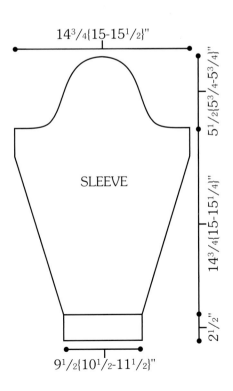

14³/₄{15-15¹/₂}"

5¹/₂{5³/₄-5³/₄}"

14³/₄{15-15¹/₄}"

SLEEVE

2¹/₂"

9¹/₂{10¹/₂-11¹/₂}"

Instructions begin on page 248.

Note: Sweater includes two edge stitches.

Size	Finished Chest Measurement
Small	36¹/₂" (92.5 cm)
Medium	38¹/₂" (98 cm)
Large	40¹/₂" (103 cm)

Size Note: Instructions are written for size Small with sizes Medium and Large in braces { }. Instructions will be easier to read if you circle all the numbers pertaining to your size. If only one number is given, it applies to all sizes.

MATERIALS

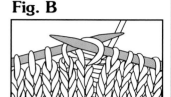

Worsted Weight Yarn:

Ounces	17{18-19}
Yards	925{980-1,030}
Grams	480{510-540}
Meters	846{896-942}

Straight knitting needles, sizes 7 (4.5 mm) **and** 9 (5.5 mm) **or** sizes needed for gauge
16" (40.5 cm) Circular needle, size 7 (4.5 mm)
Stitch holders - 2
Marker
Yarn needle

GAUGE: With larger size needles,
    3 pattern repeats (24 sts) and
    32 rows = 5¹/₂" (14 cm)

Gauge Swatch: 6"w x 5¹/₂"h (15.25 cm x 14 cm)
With larger size needles, cast on 26 sts.
Work same as Back Body for 32 rows following instructions for size Small.
Bind off all sts in **purl**.

STITCH GUIDE

LEFT CROSS (uses next 2 sts)
Skip next stitch on left needle, knit the next stitch through back loop but do **not** slip off needle *(Fig. A)*. With yarn in back, insert the right needle into the skipped stitch as if to **purl** *(Fig. B)*, slip both stitches off the left needle.

Fig. A	Fig. B
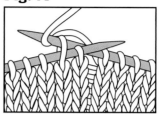	

RIGHT CROSS (uses next 2 sts)
Skip next stitch on left needle, with yarn in back, insert the right needle into the next stitch as if to **purl**, knit the skipped stitch, slipping both stitches off the left needle.

BACK
RIBBING

With smaller size straight needles, cast on 81{85-89} sts **loosely** *(Figs. 2a-e, page 9)*.

Row 1: P1, (K1, P1) across.

Row 2 (Right side)**:** K1, (P1, K1) across.

Repeat Rows 1 and 2 until Ribbing measures 2¹/₂" (6.5 cm), ending by working Row 2 and increasing one stitch at end of row *(Figs. 10a & b, page 581)*: 82{86-90} sts.

BODY

Change to larger size needles.

Row 1 AND ALL WRONG SIDE ROWS:
Purl across.

Row 2: K4{6-4}, work Left Cross, (K6, work Left Cross) across to last 4{6-4} sts, K4{6-4}.

Row 4: K3{5-3}, work Right Cross, work Left Cross, (K4, work Right Cross, work Left Cross) across to last 3{5-3} sts, K3{5-3}.

Row 6: K2{4-2}, work Right Cross, K2, work Left Cross, (K2, work Right Cross, K2, work Left Cross) across to last 2{4-2} sts, K2{4-2}.

Row 8: K1{3-1}, (work Right Cross, K4, work Left Cross) across to last 1{3-1} st(s), K1{3-1}.

Row 10: K8{2-8}, work Right Cross, (K6, work Right Cross) across to last 8{2-8} sts, K8{2-8}.

Row 12: K1{3-1}, (work Left Cross, K4, work Right Cross) across to last 1{3-1} st(s), K1{3-1}.

Row 14: K2{4-2}, work Left Cross, K2, work Right Cross, (K2, work Left Cross, K2, work Right Cross) across to last 2{4-2} sts, K2{4-2}.

Row 16: K3{5-3}, work Left Cross, work Right Cross, (K4, work Left Cross, work Right Cross) across to last 3{5-3} sts, K3{5-3}.

Repeat Rows 1-16 for pattern until Back measures approximately 15" (38 cm) from cast on edge, ending by working a **wrong** side row.

Instructions continued on page 250.

ARMHOLE SHAPING

Maintain established pattern throughout.

Rows 1 and 2: Bind off 5 sts, work across: 72{76-80} sts.

Row 3 (Decrease row)**:** K1, [slip 1, K1, PSSO *(Figs. 19a & b, page 583)*], work across to last 3 sts, K2 tog *(Fig. 17, page 583)*, K1: 70{74-78} sts.

Row 4 (Decrease row)**:** P1, P2 tog *(Fig. 18, page 583)*, purl across to last 3 sts, SSP *(Fig. 22, page 584)*, P1: 68{72-76} sts.

Row 5 (Decrease row)**:** K1, slip 1, K1, PSSO, work across to last 3 sts, K2 tog, K1: 66{70-74} sts.

Row 6: Purl across.

Rows 7 thru 15{17-19}: Repeat Rows 5 and 6, 4{5-6} times; then repeat Row 5 once **more**: 56{58-60} sts.

Work even until Back measures approximately 23{23^1/$_4$-23^1/$_2$}"/58.5{59-59.5} cm from cast on edge, ending by working a **wrong** side row.

NECK & SHOULDER SHAPING

Both sides of Neck are worked at the same time using separate yarn for **each** side.

Row 1: Work across 18{19-19} sts, slip next 20{20-22} sts onto st holder; with second yarn, work across: 18{19-19} sts **each** side.

Row 2: Purl across to within 3 sts of Neck edge, SSP, P1; with second yarn, P1, P2 tog, purl across: 17{18-18} sts **each** side.

Row 3: Bind off 8 sts, work across to within 3 sts of Neck edge, K2 tog, K1; with second yarn, K1, slip 1, K1, PSSO, work across.

Row 4: Bind off 8 sts, purl across; with second yarn, purl across: 8{9-9} sts **each** side.

Row 5: Bind off remaining sts on first side; with second yarn, work across.

Bind off remaining sts.

FRONT

Work same as Back until Front measures approximately 21^1/$_4${21^1/$_2$-21^3/$_4$}"/54{54.5-55} cm from cast on edge, ending by working a **wrong** side row: 56{58-60} sts.

NECK SHAPING

Both sides of Neck are worked at the same time using separate yarn for **each** side.

Row 1: Work across 23{24-24} sts, slip next 10{10-12} sts onto st holder; with second yarn, work across: 23{24-24} sts **each** side.

Row 2 (Decrease row)**:** Purl across to within 3 sts of Neck edge, SSP, P1; with second yarn, P1, P2 tog, purl across: 22{23-23} sts **each** side.

Row 3 (Decrease row)**:** Work across to within 3 sts of Neck edge, K2 tog, K1; with second yarn, K1, slip 1, K1, PSSO, work across: 21{22-22} sts **each** side.

Rows 4 and 5: Repeat Rows 2 and 3: 19{20-20} sts **each** side.

Row 6: Purl across; with second yarn, purl across.

Continue to decrease one stitch at **each** Neck edge, every other row, 3 times: 16{17-17} sts **each** side.

Work even until Front measures same as Back to Shoulder Shaping, ending by working a **wrong** side row.

SHOULDER SHAPING
Rows 1 and 2: Bind off 8 sts, work across; with second yarn, work across: 8{9-9} sts **each** side.

Row 3: Bind off remaining sts on first side; with second yarn, work across.

Bind off remaining sts.

SLEEVE (Make 2)
RIBBING
With smaller size straight needles, cast on 41{45-49} sts **loosely**.
Row 1: P1, (K1, P1) across.

Row 2 (Right side)**:** K1, (P1, K1) across.

Repeat Rows 1 and 2 until Ribbing measures $2^1/2$" (6.5 cm), ending by working Row 2 and increasing one stitch at end of row: 42{46-50} sts.

BODY
Change to larger size needles.

Work in pattern same as Back, increasing one stitch at **each** edge **(see Increases, page 581)**, every sixth row, 10{5-1} time(s), working new stitches in pattern; then increase every eighth row, 1{5-8} time(s): 64{66-68} sts.

Work even until Sleeve measures approximately $17^1/4${$17^1/2$-$17^3/4$}"/44{44.5-45} cm from cast on edge, ending by working a **wrong** side row.

SLEEVE CAP
Maintain established pattern throughout.

Rows 1 and 2: Bind off 5 sts, work across: 54{56-58} sts.

Row 3 (Decrease row)**:** K1, slip 1, K1, PSSO, work across to last 3 sts, K2 tog, K1: 52{54-56} sts.

Row 4 (Decrease row)**:** P1, P2 tog, purl across to last 3 sts, SSP, P1: 50{52-54} sts.

Row 5 (Decrease row)**:** K1, slip 1, K1, PSSO, work across to last 3 sts, K2 tog, K1: 48{50-52} sts.

Continue to decrease one stitch at **each** edge, every other row, 3{3-5} times; then decrease every fourth row, 4{5-4} times: 34 sts.

Work even until Sleeve Cap measures approximately $5^1/2${$5^3/4$-$5^3/4$}"/14{14.5-14.5} cm, ending by working a **wrong** side row.

Next 4 Rows: Bind off 6 sts, work across: 10 sts.

Bind off remaining sts in **knit**.

FINISHING
Weave shoulder seams **(Figs. 35a & b, page 587)**.

NECK RIBBING
With **right** side facing, slip 20{20-22} sts from Back st holder onto circular needle and knit across, pick up 20 sts evenly spaced along left Neck edge **(Fig. 34a, page 586)**, slip 10{10-12} sts from Front st holder onto second end of circular needle and knit across, pick up 20 sts evenly spaced along right Neck edge, place marker to mark beginning of rnd **(Fig. 1, page 578)**: 70{70-74} sts.

Work in K1, P1 ribbing around for 1" (2.5 cm).

Bind off all sts **loosely** in ribbing.

Sew Sleeves to Sweater, placing center of last row on Sleeve Cap at shoulder seam and matching bound off stitches.

Weave underarm and side in one continuous seam **(Fig. 36, page 587)**.

Design by Dale Rieves Potter.

MAN'S CREWNECK PULLOVER ◀■■■▢ INTERMEDIATE

Also shown on page 249.

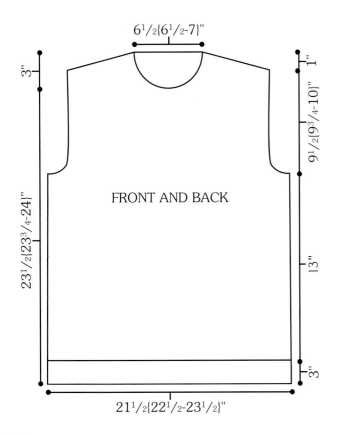

6^1/$_2${6^1/$_2$-7}"

3"

9^1/$_2${9^3/$_4$-10}" 1"

FRONT AND BACK

23^1/$_2${23^3/$_4$-24}"

13"

3"

21^1/$_2${22^1/$_2$-23^1/$_2$}"

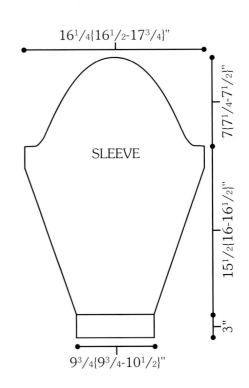

16^1/$_4${16^1/$_2$-17^3/$_4$}"

7{7^1/$_4$-7^1/$_2$}"

SLEEVE

15^1/$_2${16-16^1/$_2$}"

3"

9^3/$_4${9^3/$_4$-10^1/$_2$}"

Note: Sweater includes two edge stitches.

Size	Finished Chest Measurement	
Small	42"	(106.5 cm)
Medium	44¹/₂"	(113 cm)
Large	46"	(117 cm)

Size Note: Instructions are written for size Small with sizes Medium and Large in braces { }. Instructions will be easier to read if you circle all the numbers pertaining to your size. If only one number is given, it applies to all sizes.

MATERIALS
Worsted Weight Yarn: MEDIUM 4

Ounces	24{25-27}
Yards	1,305{1,360-1,465}
Grams	680{710-770}
Meters	1,193.5{1,243.5-1,339.5}

Straight knitting needles, sizes 7 (4.5 mm) **and** 10 (6 mm) **or** sizes needed for gauge
16" (40.5 cm) Circular needle, size 7 (4.5 mm)
Stitch holders - 2
Marker
Yarn needle

GAUGE: With larger size needles, in pattern, 20 sts and 24 rows = 4" (10 cm)

Gauge Swatch: 4" (10 cm) square
With larger size needles, cast on 20 sts.
Row 1 (Right side): K4, P1, K1 tbl *(Fig. 4a, page 580)*, P1, K7, P1, K1 tbl, P1, K3.
Row 2: P3, K1, K1 tbl, K1, P7, K1, K1 tbl, K1, P4.
Rows 3-24: Repeat Rows 1 and 2, 11 times.
Bind off all sts in pattern.

BACK
RIBBING
With smaller size straight needles, cast on 107{113-117} sts **loosely** *(Figs. 2a-e, page 9)*.

Row 1: (P1, K1) 4{3-4} times, K1 tbl *(Fig. 4a, page 580)*, ★ K1, (P1, K1) 4 times, K1 tbl; repeat from ★ across to last 8{6-8} sts, (K1, P1) 4{3-4} times.

Row 2: (K1, P1) 4{3-4} times, K1 tbl, ★ P1, (K1, P1) 4 times, K1 tbl; repeat from ★ across to last 8{6-8} sts, (P1, K1) 4{3-4} times.

Repeat Rows 1 and 2 until Ribbing measures 3" (7.5 cm), ending by working Row 1.

BODY
Change to larger size needles.

Row 1 (Right side)**:** K7{5-7}, P1, K1 tbl, P1, ★ K7, P1, K1 tbl, P1; repeat from ★ across to last 7{5-7} sts, K7{5-7}.

Row 2: P7{5-7}, K1, K1 tbl, K1, ★ P7, K1, K1 tbl, K1; repeat from ★ across to last 7{5-7} sts, P7{5-7}.

Repeat Rows 1 and 2 for pattern until Back measures approximately 16" (40.5 cm) from cast on edge, ending by working Row 2.

ARMHOLE SHAPING
Maintain established pattern throughout.

Rows 1 and 2: Bind off 7 sts, work across: 93{99-103} sts.

Row 3 (Decrease row)**:** K1, [slip 1, K1, PSSO *(Figs. 19a & b, page 583)*], work across to last 3 sts, K2 tog *(Fig. 17, page 583)*, K1: 91{97-101} sts.

Row 4 (Decrease row)**:** P1, P2 tog *(Fig. 18, page 583)*, work across to last 3 sts, SSP *(Fig. 22, page 584)*, P1: 89{95-99} sts.

Row 5 (Decrease row)**:** K1, slip 1, K1, PSSO, work across to last 3 sts, K2 tog, K1: 87{93-97} sts.

Row 6: Work across.

Instructions continued on page 254.

Rows 7 thru 13{15-17}: Repeat Rows 5 and 6, 3{4-5} times; then repeat Row 5 once **more**: 79{83-85} sts.

Work even until Back measures approximately 25$\frac{1}{2}${25$\frac{3}{4}$-26}"/65{65.5-66} cm from cast on edge, ending by working a **wrong** side row.

SHOULDER SHAPING
Rows 1-4: Bind off 8 sts, work across: 47{51-53} sts.

Rows 5 and 6: Bind off 7{9-9} sts, work across: 33{33-35} sts.

Slip remaining sts onto st holder.

FRONT
Work same as Back until Front measures approximately 23$\frac{1}{2}${23$\frac{3}{4}$-24}"/59.5{60.5-61} cm from cast on edge, ending by working a **wrong** side row: 79{83-85} sts.

NECK SHAPING
Both sides of Neck are worked at the same time, using separate yarn for **each** side.

Row 1: Work across 29{31-32} sts, slip next 21 sts onto st holder; with second yarn, work across: 29{31-32} sts **each** side.

Row 2 (Decrease row)**:** Work across to within 3 sts of Neck edge, SSP, P1; with second yarn, P1, P2 tog, work across: 28{30-31} sts **each** side.

Row 3 (Decrease row)**:** Work across to within 3 sts of Neck edge, K2 tog, K1; with second yarn, K1, slip 1, K1, PSSO, work across: 27{29-30} sts **each** side.

Row 4 (Decrease row)**:** Work across to within 3 sts of Neck edge, SSP, P1; with second yarn, P1, P2 tog, work across: 26{28-29} sts **each** side.

Row 5: Work across; with second yarn, work across.

Rows 6 thru 10{10-12}: Repeat Rows 4 and 5, 2{2-3} times; then repeat Row 4 once **more**: 23{25-25} sts.

Work even until Armholes measure same as Back to Shoulder Shaping, ending by working a **wrong** side row.

SHOULDER SHAPING
Rows 1-4: Bind off 8 sts, work across; with second yarn, work across: 7{9-9} sts.

Row 5: Bind off remaining sts on first side; with second yarn, work across.

Bind off remaining sts.

SLEEVE (Make 2)
RIBBING
With smaller size straight needles, cast on 49{49-53} sts **loosely**.

Row 1: (P1, K1) 2{2-3} times, K1 tbl, ★ K1, (P1, K1) 4 times, K1 tbl; repeat from ★ 3 times **more**, (K1, P1) 2{2-3} times.

Row 2: (K1, P1) 2{2-3} times, K1 tbl, ★ P1, (K1, P1) 4 times, K1 tbl; repeat from ★ 3 times **more**, (P1, K1) 2{2-3} times.

Repeat Rows 1 and 2 until Ribbing measures 3" (7.5 cm), ending by working Row 1.

BODY
Change to larger size needles.

Row 1 (Right side)**:** K3{3-5}, P1, K1 tbl, P1, ★ K7, P1, K1 tbl, P1; repeat from ★ 3 times **more**, K3{3-5}.

Row 2: P3{3-5}, K1, K1 tbl, K1, ★ P7, K1, K1 tbl, K1; repeat from ★ 3 times **more**, P3{3-5}.

Repeat Rows 1 and 2 for pattern, increasing one stitch at **each** edge *(see Increases, page 581)*, every fourth row, 11{12-14} times, working new stitches in pattern; then increase every sixth row, 5{5-4} times: 81{83-89} sts.

Work even until Sleeve measures approximately 18$\frac{1}{2}${19-19$\frac{1}{2}$}"/47{48.5-49.5} cm from cast on edge, ending by working a **wrong** side row.

SLEEVE CAP

Maintain established pattern throughout.

Rows 1 and 2: Bind off 7 sts, work across: 67{69-75} sts.

Row 3 (Decrease row)**:** K1, slip 1, K1, PSSO, work across to last 3 sts, K2 tog, K1: 65{67-73} sts.

Row 4 (Decrease row)**:** P1, P2 tog, work across to last 3 sts, SSP, P1: 63{65-71} sts.

Row 5 (Decrease row)**:** K1, slip 1, K1, PSSO, work across to last 3 sts, K2 tog, K1: 61{63-69} sts.

Row 6: Work across.

Rows 7 thru 29{31-41}: Repeat Rows 5 and 6, 11{12-17} times; then repeat Row 5 once **more**: 37{37-33} sts.

Continue to decrease one stitch at **each** edge, every fourth row, 3{3-1} time(s): 31 sts.

Work even until Sleeve Cap measures approximately 7{7$\frac{1}{4}$-7$\frac{1}{2}$}"/18{18.5-19} cm, ending by working a **wrong** side row.

Next 4 Rows: Bind off 5 sts, work across: 11 sts.

Bind off remaining sts in pattern.

FINISHING

Weave shoulder seams *(Figs. 35a & b, page 587)*.

NECK RIBBING

With **right** side facing, slip 33{33-35} sts from Back st holder onto circular needle and knit across, pick up 18 sts evenly spaced along left Front Neck edge *(Fig. 34a, page 586)*, slip 21 sts from Front st holder onto second end of circular needle and knit across, pick up 18 sts evenly spaced along right Front Neck edge, place marker to mark beginning of rnd *(Fig. 1, page 578)*: 90{90-92} sts.

Work in K1, P1 ribbing around for 1" (2.5 cm).

Bind off all sts **loosely** in ribbing.

Sew Sleeves to Sweater, placing center of last row on Sleeve Cap at shoulder seam and matching bound off stitches.

Weave underarm and side in one continuous seam *(Fig. 36, page 587)*.

Design by Dale Rieves Potter.

HERRINGBONE PULLOVER

■■■□ INTERMEDIATE

Also shown on page 259.

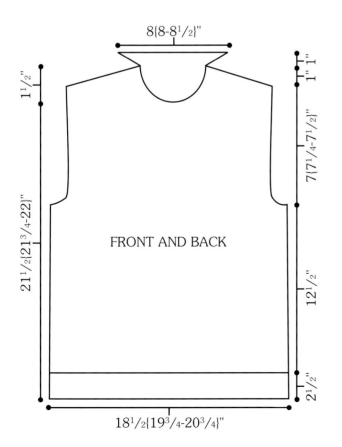

8{8-8¹/₂}"

1¹/₂"

7{7¹/₄-7¹/₂}"

1" 1"

21¹/₂{21³/₄-22}"

FRONT AND BACK

12¹/₂"

2¹/₂"

18¹/₂{19³/₄-20³/₄}"

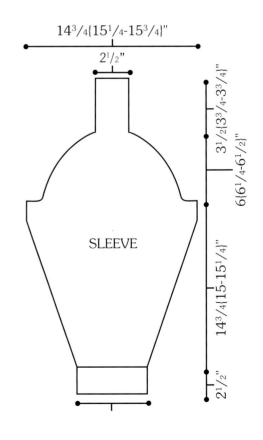

14³/₄{15¹/₄-15³/₄}"

2¹/₂"

3¹/₂{3³/₄-3³/₄}"

6{6¹/₄-6¹/₂}"

SLEEVE

14³/₄{15-15¹/₄}"

2¹/₂"

Note: Sweater includes two edge stitches.

Size	Finished Chest Measurement	
Small	36"	(91.5 cm)
Medium	38"	(96.5 cm)
Large	40^1/$_2$"	(103 cm)

Size Note: Instructions are written for size Small with sizes Medium and Large in braces { }. Instructions will be easier to read if you circle all the numbers pertaining to your size. If only one number is given, it applies to all sizes.

MATERIALS

Worsted Weight Yarn:

Ounces	15{16-17}
Yards	815{870-925}
Grams	430{450-480}
Meters	745{795.5-846}

Straight knitting needles, sizes 7 (4.5 mm) **and** 10 (6 mm) **or** sizes needed for gauge
16" (40.5 cm) Circular needle, size 7 (4.5 mm)
Stitch holders - 4
Marker
Yarn needle

GAUGE: With larger size needles,
3 pattern repeats
(18 sts) = 5" (12.75 cm);
24 rows = 3^1/$_2$" (9 cm)

Gauge Swatch: 5^1/$_2$"w x 3^1/$_2$"h (14 cm x 9 cm)
With larger size needles, cast on 20 sts.

Row 1 AND ALL WRONG SIDE ROWS: Purl across.

When instructed to slip a stitch that is not used in a decrease, with yarn in front, always slip as if to **purl**.

Row 2: K4, slip 3, (K3, slip 3) twice, K1.
Row 4: (K3, slip 3) 3 times, K2.
Row 6: K2, (slip 3, K3) across.
Row 8: K1, slip 3, (K3, slip 3) twice, K4.
Row 10: K1, slip 2, K3, (slip 3, K3) twice, slip 1, K1.
Row 12: K1, slip 1, K3, (slip 3, K3) twice, slip 2, K1.
Rows 13-24: Repeat Rows 1-12.
Bind off all sts **loosely** in **purl**.

BACK
RIBBING

With smaller size straight needles, cast on 67{71-75} sts **loosely (Figs. 2a-e, page 9)**.

Row 1: P1, (K1, P1) across.

Row 2 (Right side)**:** K1, (P1, K1) across.

Repeat Rows 1 and 2 until Ribbing measures 2^1/$_2$" (6.5 cm), ending by working Row 2.

BODY

Change to larger size needles.

Row 1 AND ALL WRONG SIDE ROWS: Purl across.

When instructed to slip a stitch that is not used in a decrease, with yarn in front, always slip as if to **purl**.

Row 2: K3{5-1}, (slip 3, K3) 5{5-6} times, slip 1, (K3, slip 3) 5{5-6} times, K3{5-1}.

Row 4: K2{4-1}, slip 3{3-2}, (K3, slip 3) across to last 2{4-6} sts, K2{4-3}, slip 0{0-2} *(see Zeros, page 577)*, K 0{0-1}.

Row 6: K 0{0-1}, slip 0{0-1}, K1{3-3}, (slip 3, K3) 5 times, slip 2, K1, slip 2, (K3, slip 3) 5 times, K1{3-3}, slip 0{0-1}, K 0{0-1}.

Row 8: K1{2-4}, slip 2{3-3}, (K3, slip 3) 5 times, K1, (slip 3, K3) 5 times, slip 2{3-3}, K1{2-4}.

Row 10: K1{1-0}, slip 1{3-0}, (K3, slip 3) across to last 5{1-3} st(s), K3{1-3}, slip 1{0-0}, K1{0-0}.

Row 12: K4{1-2}, slip 3{2-3}, (K3, slip 3) 4{5-5} times, K5, (slip 3, K3) 4{5-5} times, slip 3{2-3}, K4{1-2}.

Repeat Rows 1-12 for pattern until Back measures approximately 15" (38 cm) from cast on edge, ending by working a **wrong** side row.

Instructions continued on page 258.

ARMHOLE SHAPING

Maintain established pattern throughout.

Rows 1 and 2: Bind off 4 sts, work across: 59{63-67} sts.

Row 3 (Decrease row)**:** K1, [slip 1, K1, PSSO *(Figs. 19a & b, page 583)*], work across to last 3 sts, K2 tog *(Fig. 17, page 583)*, K1: 57{61-65} sts.

Row 4 (Decrease row)**:** P1, P2 tog *(Fig. 18, page 583)*, purl across to last 3 sts, SSP *(Fig. 22, page 584)*, P1: 55{59-63} sts.

Row 5 (Decrease row)**:** K1, slip 1, K1, PSSO, work across to last 3 sts, K2 tog, K1: 53{57-61} sts.

Row 6: Purl across.

Rows 7 thru 13{15-17}: Repeat Rows 5 and 6, 3{4-5} times; then repeat Row 5 once **more**: 45{47-49} sts.

Work even until Back measures approximately 22{22^1/$_4$-22^1/$_2$}"/56{56.5-57} cm from cast on edge, ending by working a **wrong** side row.

SHOULDER SHAPING

Rows 1-4: Bind off 4 sts, work across: 29{31-33} sts.

Rows 5 and 6: Bind off 4{5-5} sts, work across: 21{21-23} sts.

SHAPING

The Back is increased to form a "tab" that will be sewn to a portion of the Sleeve Saddle.

Row 1 (Increase row)**:** K1, Right Invisible Increase *(Fig. 12a, page 581)*, work across to last st, Left Invisible Increase *(Figs. 13a & b, page 581)*, K1: 23{23-25} sts.

Row 2: Purl across.

Rows 3-7: Repeat Rows 1 and 2 twice, then repeat Row 1 once **more**: 29{29-31} sts.

Slip remaining sts onto st holder.

FRONT

Work same as Back until Front measures approximately 21^1/$_2${21^3/$_4$-22}"/ 54.5{55-56} cm from cast on edge, ending by working a **wrong** side row: 45{47-49} sts.

NECK & SHOULDER SHAPING

Both sides of Neck are worked at the same time, using separate yarn for **each** side.

Row 1: Work across 18{19-19} sts, slip next 9{9-11} sts onto st holder; with second yarn, work across: 18{19-19} sts **each** side.

Row 2 (Decrease row)**:** Purl across to within 3 sts of Neck edge, SSP, P1; with second yarn, P1, P2 tog, purl across: 17{18-18} sts **each** side.

Row 3 (Decrease row)**:** Work across to within 3 sts of Neck edge, K2 tog, K1; with second yarn, K1, slip 1, K1, PSSO, work across: 16{17-17} sts **each** side.

Row 4: Repeat Row 2: 15{16-16} sts **each** side.

Row 5: Work across; with second yarn, work across.

Row 6: Repeat Row 2: 14{15-15} sts **each** side.

Row 7: Bind off 4 sts, work across; with second yarn, work across.

Row 8: Bind off 4 sts, purl across to within 3 sts of Neck edge, SSP, P1; with second yarn, P1, P2 tog, purl across: 9{10-10} sts **each** side.

Row 9: Bind off 4 sts, work across; with second yarn, work across.

Row 10: Bind off 4 sts, work across to within 3 sts of Neck edge, P2 tog tbl, P1; with second yarn, P1, P2 tog, purl across: 4{5-5} sts **each** side.

Row 11: Bind off remaining sts on first side; with second yarn, work across.

Bind off remaining sts.

SLEEVE (Make 2)
RIBBING

With smaller size straight needles, cast on 43{45-47} sts **loosely**.

Row 1: P1, (K1, P1) across.

Row 2 (Right side)**:** K1, (P1, K1) across.

Repeat Rows 1 and 2 until Ribbing measures 2¹/₂" (6.5 cm), ending by working Row 2.

BODY

Change to larger size needles.

Row 1 AND ALL WRONG SIDE ROWS:
Purl across.

Row 2: K 0{0-1}, slip 0{0-1}, K3{4-3}, (slip 3, K3) 3 times, slip 1, (K3, slip 3) 3 times, K3{4-3}, slip 0{0-1}, K 0{0-1}.

Row 4: K2{3-4}, slip 3, (K3, slip 3) across to last 2{3-4} sts, K2{3-4}.

Row 6: K1{2-3}, (slip 3, K3) 3 times, slip 2, K1, slip 2, (K3, slip 3) 3 times, K1{2-3}.

Row 8: K1{1-2}, slip 2{3-3}, (K3, slip 3) 3 times, K1, (slip 3, K3) 3 times, slip 2{3-3}, K1{1-2}.

Row 10: K1{1-0}, slip 1{2-0}, K3{3-1}, (slip 3, K3) across to last 2{3-4} sts, slip 1{2-3}, K1.

Row 12: K4{1-1}, slip 3{1-2}, (K3, slip 3) 2{3-3} times, K5, (slip 3, K3) 2{3-3} times, slip 3{1-2}, K4{1-1}.

Rows 13-15: Repeat Rows 1-3.

Row 16 (Increase row)**:** K1, Right Invisible Increase, K1{2-3}, slip 3, (K3, slip 3) across to last 2{3-4} sts, K1{2-3}, Left Invisible Increase, K1: 45{47-49} sts.

Working new stitches in pattern, continue to increase one stitch at **each** edge, every sixteenth row, 4 times **more**: 53{55-57} sts.

Instructions continued on page 260.

Work even until Sleeve measures approximately 17$\frac{1}{4}${17$\frac{1}{2}$-17$\frac{3}{4}$}"/44{44.5-45} cm from cast on edge, ending by working a **wrong** side row.

SLEEVE CAP
Maintain established pattern throughout.

Rows 1 and 2: Bind off 4 sts, work across: 45{47-49} sts.

Row 3 (Decrease row)**:** K1, slip 1, K1, PSSO, work across to last 3 sts, K2 tog, K1: 43{45-47} sts.

Row 4 (Decrease row)**:** P1, P2 tog, purl across to last 3 sts, SSP, P1: 41{43-45} sts.

Row 5 (Decrease row)**:** K1, slip 1, K1, PSSO, work across to last 3 sts, K2 tog, K1: 39{41-43} sts.

Continue to decrease one stitch at **each** edge, every other row, 1{2-3} time(s); then decrease every fourth row, 8 times: 21 sts.

Work even until Sleeve Cap measures approximately 6{6$\frac{1}{4}$-6$\frac{1}{2}$}"/15{16-16.5} cm, ending by working a **wrong** side row.

SADDLE
Rows 1 and 2: Bind off 6 sts, work across: 9 sts.

For Right Sleeve
Work even until Saddle measures approximately 3$\frac{1}{2}${3$\frac{3}{4}$-3$\frac{3}{4}$}"/9{9.5-9.5} cm, ending by working a **right** side row.

Bind off 4 sts, slip remaining 5 sts onto st holder.

For Left Sleeve
Work even until Saddle measures approximately 3$\frac{1}{2}${3$\frac{3}{4}$-3$\frac{3}{4}$}"/9{9.5-9.5} cm, ending by working a **wrong** side row.

Bind off 4 sts, slip remaining 5 sts onto st holder.

FINISHING
Sew long edges of each Saddle to bound off edges of Back and Front at shoulders, sewing 4 bound off stitches on top of Saddle to "tab" on Back. Sew Sleeve Cap to Armhole, matching bound off stitches.

NECK RIBBING
With **right** side facing and using circular needle, knit 29{29-31} sts from Back st holder, slip 5 sts from Sleeve st holder onto second end of circular needle and knit across, pick up 11 sts evenly spaced along left Front Neck edge **(Fig. 34a, page 586)**, slip 9{9-11} sts from Front st holder onto second end of circular needle and knit across, pick up 11 sts evenly spaced along right Front Neck edge, knit 5 sts from Sleeve st holder, place marker to mark beginning of rnd **(Fig. 1, page 578)**: 70{70-74} sts.

Work in K1, P1 ribbing around for 1$\frac{1}{4}$" (3 cm).

Bind off all sts **loosely** in ribbing.

Weave underarm and side in one continuous seam **(Fig. 36, page 587)**.

Design by Dale Rieves Potter.

DIAGONAL STRIPES PULLOVER 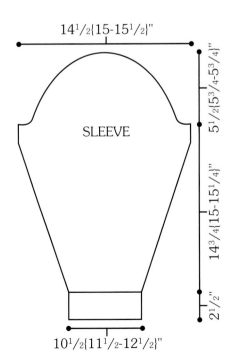 INTERMEDIATE

Also shown on page 263.

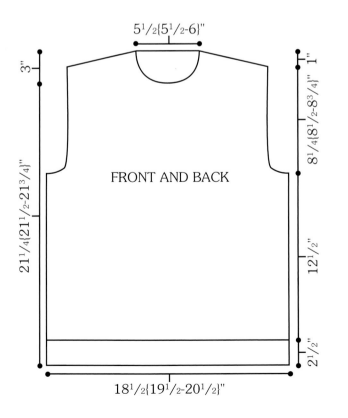

5^1/$_2${5^1/$_2$-6}"

FRONT AND BACK

3"

21^1/$_4${21^1/$_2$-21^3/$_4$}"

8^1/$_4${8^1/$_2$-8^3/$_4$}" 1"

12^1/$_2$"

2^1/$_2$"

18^1/$_2${19^1/$_2$-20^1/$_2$}"

14^1/$_2${15-15^1/$_2$}"

SLEEVE

5^1/$_2${5^3/$_4$-5^3/$_4$}"

14^3/$_4${15-15^1/$_4$}"

2^1/$_2$"

10^1/$_2${11^1/$_2$-12^1/$_2$}"

Instructions begin on page 262.

Note: Sweater includes two edge stitches.

Size	Finished Chest Measurement	
Small	36"	(91.5 cm)
Medium	38"	(96.5 cm)
Large	40"	(101.5 cm)

Size Note: Instructions are written for size Small with sizes Medium and Large in braces { }. Instructions will be easier to read if you circle all the numbers pertaining to your size. If only one number is given, it applies to all sizes.

MATERIALS
Worsted Weight Yarn:
    Ounces   18{19-20}
    Yards   980{1,030-1,085}
    Grams   510{540-570}
    Meters   896{942-992}
Straight knitting needles, sizes 7 (4.5 mm) **and** 10 (6 mm) **or** sizes needed for gauge
16" (40.5 cm) Circular needle, size 7 (4.5 mm)
Stitch holders - 2
Marker
Yarn needle

GAUGE: With larger size needles, in pattern,
        16 sts = 4" (10 cm);
        24 rows = 3¹/₂" (9 cm)

Gauge Swatch: 4¹/₂"w x 3¹/₂"h
                (11.5 cm x 9 cm)
With larger size needles, cast on 18 sts.
Work same as Back Body for 24 rows.
Bind off all sts in pattern.

BACK
RIBBING
With smaller size straight needles, cast on 74{78-82} sts **loosely (Figs. 2a-e, page 9)**.

Row 1: P2, (K2, P2) across.

Row 2: K2, (P2, K2) across.

Repeat Rows 1 and 2 until Ribbing measures 2¹/₂" (6.5 cm), ending by working Row 1.

BODY
Change to larger size needles.

Row 1 (Right side)**:** K1, P2, (K2, P2) across to last 3 sts, K3.

Row 2: P1, K1, P2, (K2, P2) across to last 2 sts, K1, P1.

Row 3: K3, P2, (K2, P2) across to last st, K1.

Row 4: P2, (K2, P2) across.

Repeat Rows 1-4 for pattern until Back measures approximately 15" (38 cm) from cast on edge, ending by working a **wrong** side row.

ARMHOLE SHAPING
Maintain established pattern throughout.

Rows 1 and 2: Bind off 4 sts, work across: 66{70-74} sts.

Row 3 (Decrease row)**:** **[**Slip 1, K1, PSSO **(Figs. 19a & b, page 583)]**, work across to last 2 sts, K2 tog **(Fig. 17, page 583)**: 64{68-72} sts.

Row 4 (Decrease row)**:** P2 tog **(Fig. 18, page 583)**, work across to last 2 sts, SSP **(Fig. 22, page 584)**: 62{66-70} sts.

Rows 5-7: Repeat Rows 3 and 4 once, then Repeat Row 3 once **more**: 56{60-64} sts.

Row 8: Work across.

Row 9 (Decrease row)**:** Slip 1, K1, PSSO, work across to last 2 sts, K2 tog: 54{58-62} sts.

Rows 10 thru 13{15-17}: Repeat Rows 8 and 9, 2{3-4} times: 50{52-54} sts.

Work even until Back measures approximately 23¹/₄{23¹/₂-23³/₄}"/59{59.5-60.5} cm from cast on edge, ending by working a **wrong** side row.

SHOULDER SHAPING

Rows 1 and 2: Bind off 4{5-5} sts, work across: 42{42-44} sts.

Rows 3-6: Bind off 5 sts, work across: 22{22-24} sts.

Slip remaining sts onto st holder.

FRONT

Work same as Back until Front measures approximately $21^1/_4${$21^1/_2$-$21^3/_4$}"/ 54{54.5-55} cm from cast on edge, ending by working a **wrong** side row: 50{52-54} sts.

NECK SHAPING

Both sides of Neck are worked at the same time, using separate yarn for **each** side.

Row 1: Work across 19{20-20} sts, slip next 12{12-14} sts onto st holder; with second yarn, work across: 19{20-20} sts **each** side.

Row 2 (Decrease row)**:** Work across to within 2 sts of Neck edge, SSP; with second yarn, P2 tog, work across: 18{19-19} sts **each** side.

Row 3 (Decrease row)**:** Work across to within 2 sts of Neck edge, K2 tog; with second yarn, slip 1, K1, PSSO, work across: 17{18-18} sts **each** side.

Row 4 (Decrease row)**:** Work across to within 2 sts of Neck edge, SSP; with second yarn, P2 tog, work across: 16{17-17} sts **each** side.

Row 5: Work across; with second yarn, work across.

Rows 6-8: Repeat Rows 4 and 5 once, then repeat Row 4 once **more**: 14{15-15} sts **each** side.

Work even until Front measures same as Back to Shoulder Shaping, ending by working a **wrong** side row.

SHOULDER SHAPING

Rows 1 and 2: Bind off 4{5-5} sts, work across; with second yarn, work across: 10 sts **each** side.

Rows 3 and 4: Bind off 5 sts, work across; with second yarn, work across: 5 sts **each** side.

Row 5: Bind off remaining sts on first side; with second yarn, work across.

Bind off remaining sts.

Instructions continued on page 264.

SLEEVE (Make 2)
RIBBING
With smaller size straight needles, cast on 42{46-50} sts **loosely**.

Row 1: P2, (K2, P2) across.

Row 2: K2, (P2, K2) across.

Repeat Rows 1 and 2 until Ribbing measures 2¹/₂" (6.5 cm), ending by working Row 1.

BODY
Change to larger size needles.

Row 1 (Right side)**:** K1, P2, (K2, P2) across to last 3 sts, K3.

Row 2: P1, K1, P2, (K2, P2) across to last 2 sts, K1, P1.

Row 3: K3, P2, (K2, P2) across to last st, K1.

Row 4: P2, (K2, P2) across.

Repeat Rows 1-4 for pattern, increasing one stitch at **each** edge **(see Increases, page 581)**, every tenth{twelfth-fourteenth} row, 8{7-6} times, working new stitches in pattern: 58{60-62} sts.

Work even until Sleeve measures approximately 17¹/₄{17¹/₂-17³/₄}"/44{44.5-45} cm from cast on edge, ending by working a **wrong** side row.

SLEEVE CAP
Maintain established pattern throughout.

Rows 1 and 2: Bind off 4 sts, work across: 50{52-54} sts.

Row 3 (Decrease row)**:** Slip 1, K1, PSSO, work across to last 2 sts, K2 tog: 48{50-52} sts.

Row 4 (Decrease row)**:** P2 tog, work across to last 2 sts, SSP: 46{48-50} sts.

Row 5 (Decrease row)**:** Slip 1, K1, PSSO, work across to last 2 sts, K2 tog: 44{46-48} sts.

Rows 6-8: Work across.

Rows 9 thru 33{37-41}: Repeat Rows 5-8, 6{7-8} times; then repeat Row 5 once **more**: 30 sts.

Work even until Sleeve Cap measures approximately 5¹/₂{5³/₄-6}"/14{14.5-15} cm, ending by working a **wrong** side row.

Next 4 Rows: Bind off 5 sts, work across: 10 sts.

Bind off remaining sts in pattern.

FINISHING
Weave shoulder seams **(Figs. 35a & b, page 587)**.

NECK RIBBING
With **right** side facing, slip 22{22-24} sts from Back st holder onto circular needle and knit across, pick up 21 sts evenly spaced along left Front Neck edge **(Fig. 34a, page 586)**, slip 12{12-14} sts from Front st holder onto second end of circular needle and knit across, pick up 21 sts evenly spaced along right Front Neck edge, place marker to mark beginning of rnd **(Fig. 1, page 578)**: 76{76-80} sts.

Rnds 1-4: (K2, P2) around.

Rnds 5-12: Knit around.

Bind off all sts **loosely** in **knit**.

Sew Sleeves to Sweater, placing center of last row on Sleeve Cap at shoulder seam and matching bound off stitches.

Weave underarm and side in one continuous seam **(Fig. 36, page 587)**.

Design by Dale Rieves Potter.

MAN'S V-NECK PULLOVER

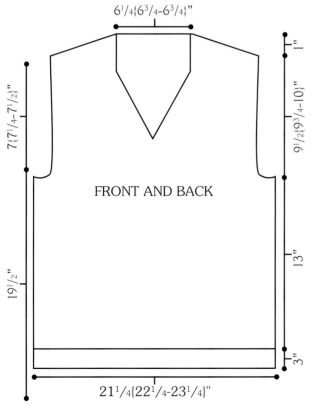

FRONT AND BACK

$6^1/_4\{6^3/_4-6^3/_4\}$"

$7\{7^1/_4-7^1/_2\}$"

1"

$9^1/_2\{9^3/_4-10\}$"

13"

3"

$19^1/_2$"

$21^1/_4\{22^1/_4-23^1/_4\}$"

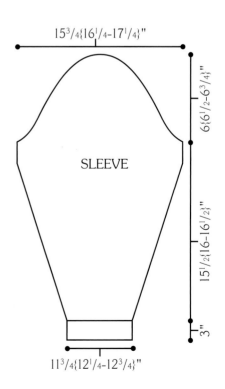

SLEEVE

$15^3/_4\{16^1/_4-17^1/_4\}$"

$6\{6^1/_2-6^3/_4\}$"

$15^1/_2\{16-16^1/_2\}$"

3"

$11^3/_4\{12^1/_4-12^3/_4\}$"

Instructions begin on page 266.

Note: Sweater includes two edge stitches.

Size	Finished Chest Measurement	
Small	42"	(106.5 cm)
Medium	44"	(112 cm)
Large	46"	(117 cm)

Size Note: Instructions are written for size Small with sizes Medium and Large in braces { }. Instructions will be easier to read if you circle all the numbers pertaining to your size. If only one number is given, it applies to all sizes.

MATERIALS

Worsted Weight Yarn: **MEDIUM 4**

    Ounces   19{20-21}
    Yards   1,030{1,085-1,140}
    Grams   540{570-600}
    Meters   942{992-1,042.5}

Straight knitting needles, sizes 7 (4.5 mm) **and**
    10 (6 mm) **or** sizes needed for gauge
16" (40.5 cm) Circular needle, size 7 (4.5 mm)
Stitch holders - 2
Markers
Yarn needle

GAUGE: With larger size needles,
        in Stockinette Stitch,
        16 sts and 20 rows = 4" (10 cm)

Gauge Swatch: 4" (10 cm) square
With larger size needles, cast on 16 sts.
Work in Stockinette Stitch for 20 rows.
Bind off all sts.

BACK
RIBBING

With smaller size straight needles, cast on 87{91-95} sts **loosely (Figs. 2a-e, page 9)**.

Row 1: P1, (K1, P1) across.

Row 2: K1, (P1, K1) across.

Repeat Rows 1 and 2 until Ribbing measures 3" (7.5 cm), ending by working Row 1.

BODY
Change to larger size needles.

Row 1 (Right side)**:** K1, P 11{13-15}, K 21, P 21, K 21, P 11{13-15}, K1.

Row 2: P1, K 11{13-15}, P 21, K 21, P 21, K 11{13-15}, P1.

Repeat Rows 1 and 2 until Back measures approximately 15" (38 cm) from cast on edge, ending by working Row 2.

Next Row: K1, P 12{14-16}, K 20, P 21, K 20, P 12{14-16}, K1.

Next Row: P1, K 13{15-17}, P 19, K 21, P 19, K 13{15-17}, P1.

Next Row: K1, P 14{16-18}, K 18, P 21, K 18, P 14{16-18}, K1.

Next Row: P1, K 15{17-19}, P 17, K 21, P 17, K 15{17-19}, P1.

ARMHOLE SHAPING

Row 1: Bind off 6 sts, P9{11-13}, K 17, P 21, K 17, P 15{17-19}, K1: 81{85-89} sts.

Row 2: Bind off 6 sts, K9{11-13}, P 17, K 21, P 17, K9{11-13}, P1: 75{79-83} sts.

Row 3: K1, P2 tog *(Fig. 18, page 583)*, P8{10-12}, K 16, P 21, K 16, P8{10-12}, SSP *(Fig. 22, page 584)*, K1: 73{77-81} sts.

Row 4: P1, [slip 1, K1, PSSO *(Figs. 19a & b, page 583)*], K7{9-11}, P 16, K 21, P 16, K7{9-11}, K2 tog *(Fig. 17, page 583)*, P1: 71{75-79} sts.

Row 5: K1, P2 tog, P7{9-11}, K 15, P 21, K 15, P7{9-11}, SSP, K1: 69{73-77} sts.

Row 6: P1, K8{10-12}, P 15, K 21, P 15, K8{10-12}, P1.

Row 7: K1, P2 tog, P7{9-11}, K 14, P 21, K 14, P7{9-11}, SSP, K1: 67{71-75} sts.

Row 8: P1, K8{10-12}, P 14, K 21, P 14, K8{10-12}, P1.

Row 9: K1, P2 tog, P7{9-11}, K 13, P 21, K 13, P7{9-11}, SSP, K1: 65{69-73} sts.

Row 10: P1, K8{10-12}, P 13, K 21, P 13, K8{10-12}, P1.

Row 11: K1, P2 tog, P7{9-11}, K 12, P 21, K 12, P7{9-11}, SSP, K1: 63{67-71} sts.

Row 12: P1, K8{10-12}, P 12, K 21, P 12, K8{10-12}, P1.

Row 13: K1, P2 tog, P7{9-11}, K 11, P 21, K 11, P7{9-11}, SSP, K1: 61{65-69} sts.

Row 14: P1, K8{10-12}, P 11, K 21, P 11, K8{10-12}, P1.

FOR SIZE SMALL ONLY

Row 15: K1, P8, K 11, P 21, K 11, P8, K1.

Row 16: P1, K8, P 11, K 21, P 11, K8, P1.

Rows 17 and 18: Repeat Rows 15 and 16.

FOR SIZE MEDIUM ONLY

Row 15: K1, P2 tog, P8, K 11, P 21, K 11, P8, SSP, K1: 63 sts.

Row 16: P1, K9, P 11, K 21, P 11, K9, P1.

Row 17: K1, P9, K 11, P 21, K 11, P9, K1.

Row 18: Repeat Row 16.

FOR SIZE LARGE ONLY

Row 15: K1, P2 tog, P 10, K 11, P 21, K 11, P 10, SSP, K1: 67 sts.

Row 16: P1, K 11, P 11, K 21, P 11, K 11, P1.

Row 17: K1, P2 tog, P9, K 11, P 21, K 11, P9, SSP, K1: 65 sts.

Row 18: P1, K 10, P 11, K 21, P 11, K 10, P1.

FOR ALL SIZES

Row 19: K1, P8{9-10}, K 10, P 23, K 10, P8{9-10}, K1.

Row 20: P1, K8{9-10}, P 10, K 23, P 10, K8{9-10}, P1.

Row 21: K1, P8{9-10}, K9, P 25, K9, P8{9-10}, K1.

Row 22: P1, K8{9-10}, P9, K 25, P9, K8{9-10}, P1.

Row 23: K1, P8{9-10}, K8, P 27, K8, P8{9-10}, K1.

Row 24: P1, K8{9-10}, P8, K 27, P8, K8{9-10}, P1.

Row 25: K1, P8{9-10}, K7, P 29, K7, P8{9-10}, K1.

Row 26: P1, K8{9-10}, P7, K 29, P7, K8{9-10}, P1.

Row 27: K1, P8{9-10}, K6, P 31, K6, P8{9-10}, K1.

Row 28: P1, K8{9-10}, P6, K 31, P6, K8{9-10}, P1.

Row 29: K1, P8{9-10}, K5, P 33, K5, P8{9-10}, K1.

Instructions continued on page 268.

Row 30: P1, K8{9-10}, P5, K 33, P5, K8{9-10}, P1.

Row 31: K1, P8{9-10}, K4, P 35, K4, P8{9-10}, K1.

Row 32: P1, K8{9-10}, P4, K 35, P4, K8{9-10}, P1.

Row 33: K1, P8{9-10}, K3, P 37, K3, P8{9-10}, K1.

Row 34: P1, K8{9-10}, P3, K 37, P3, K8{9-10}, P1.

Row 35: K1, P8{9-10}, K2, P 39, K2, P8{9-10}, K1.

Row 36: P1, K8{9-10}, P2, K 39, P2, K8{9-10}, P1.

Row 37: K1, P8{9-10}, K1, P 41, K1, P8{9-10}, K1.

Row 38: P1, K8{9-10}, P1, K 41, P1, K8{9-10}, P1.

Row 39: K1, purl across to last st, K1.

Row 40: P1, knit across to last st, P1.

Repeat Rows 39 and 40 until Back measures approximately 25$\frac{1}{2}${25$\frac{3}{4}$-26}"/65{65.5-66} cm from cast on edge, ending by working Row 40.

SHOULDER SHAPING
Rows 1-4: Bind off 6 sts, work across: 37{39-41} sts.

Rows 5 and 6: Bind off 6{6-7} sts, work across: 25{27-27} sts.

Slip remaining sts onto st holder.

FRONT
Work same as Back through Row 18 of Armhole Shaping: 61{63-65} sts.

NECK SHAPING
Both sides of Neck are worked at the same time, using separate yarn for **each** side.

Row 19: K1, P8{9-10}, K 10, P 10, K1, slip next st onto st holder; with second yarn, K1, P 10, K 10, P8{9-10}, K1: 30{31-32} sts **each** side.

Row 20: P1, K8{9-10}, P 10, K8, K2 tog, P1; with second yarn, P1, slip 1, K1, PSSO, K8, P 10, K8{9-10}, P1: 29{30-31} sts **each** side.

Row 21: K1, P8{9-10}, K9, P 10, K1; with second yarn, K1, P 10, K9, P8{9-10}, K1.

Row 22: P1, K8{9-10}, P9, K8, K2 tog, P1; with second yarn, P1, slip 1, K1, PSSO, K8, P9, K8{9-10}, P1: 28{29-30} sts **each** side.

Row 23: K1, P8{9-10}, K8, P 10, K1; with second yarn, K1, P 10, K8, P8{9-10}, K1.

Row 24: P1, K8{9-10}, P8, K8, K2 tog, P1; with second yarn, P1, slip 1, K1, PSSO, K8, P8, K8{9-10}, P1: 27{28-29} sts **each** side.

Row 25: K1, P8{9-10}, K7, P 10, K1; with second yarn, K1, P 10, K7, P8{9-10}, K1.

Row 26: P1, K8{9-10}, P7, K8, K2 tog, P1; with second yarn, P1, slip 1, K1, PSSO, K8, P7, K8{9-10}, P1: 26{27-28} sts **each** side.

Row 27: K1, P8{9-10}, K6, P 10, K1; with second yarn, K1, P 10, K6, P8{9-10}, K1.

Row 28: P1, K8{9-10}, P6, K8, K2 tog, P1; with second yarn, P1, slip 1, K1, PSSO, K8, P6, K8{9-10}, P1: 25{26-27} sts **each** side.

Row 29: K1, P8{9-10}, K5, P 10, K1; with second yarn, K1, P 10, K5, P8{9-10}, K1.

Row 30: P1, K8{9-10}, P5, K8, K2 tog, P1; with second yarn, P1, slip 1, K1, PSSO, K8, P5, K8{9-10}, P1: 24{25-26} sts **each** side.

Row 31: K1, P8{9-10}, K4, P 10, K1; with second yarn, K1, P 10, K4, P8{9-10}, K1.

Row 32: P1, K8{9-10}, P4, K8, K2 tog, P1; with second yarn, P1, slip 1, K1, PSSO, K8, P4, K8{9-10}, P1: 23{24-25} sts **each** side.

Row 33: K1, P8{9-10}, K3, P 10, K1; with second yarn, K1, P 10, K3, P8{9-10}, K1.

Row 34: P1, K8{9-10}, P3, K8, K2 tog, P1; with second yarn, P1, slip 1, K1, PSSO, K8, P3, K8{9-10}, P1: 22{23-24} sts **each** side.

Row 35: K1, P8{9-10}, K2, P 10, K1; with second yarn, K1, P 10, K2, P8{9-10}, K1.

Row 36: P1, K8{9-10}, P2, K8, K2 tog, P1; with second yarn, P1, slip 1, K1, PSSO, K8, P2, K8{9-10}, P1: 21{22-23} sts **each** side.

Row 37: K1, P8{9-10}, K1, P 10, K1; with second yarn, K1, P 10, K1, P8{9-10}, K1.

Row 38: P1, K8{9-10}, P1, K8, K2 tog, P1; with second yarn, P1, slip 1, K1, PSSO, K8, P1, K8{9-10}, P1: 20{21-22} sts **each** side.

Row 39: K1, purl across to within one st of Neck edge, K1; with second yarn, K1, purl across to last st, K1.

Row 40: P1, knit across to within 3 sts of Neck edge, K2 tog, P1; with second yarn, P1, slip 1, K1, PSSO, knit across to last st, P1: 19{20-21} sts **each** side.

Rows 41 thru 42{44-44}: Repeat Rows 39 and 40, 1{2-2} time(s): 18{18-19} sts **each** side.

Row 43{45-45}: K1, purl across to within one st of Neck edge, K1; with second yarn, K1, purl across to last st, K1.

Row 44{46-46}: P1, knit across to within one st of Neck edge, P1; with second yarn, P1, knit across to last st, P1.

Repeat Rows 43{45-45} and 44{46-46} until Front measures same as Back to Shoulder Shaping, ending by working Row 44{46-46}.

SHOULDER SHAPING
Maintain established pattern throughout.

Rows 1-4: Bind off 6 sts, work across; with second yarn, work across: 6{6-7} sts.

Row 5: Bind off remaining sts on first side; with second yarn, work across.

Bind off remaining sts.

SLEEVE (Make 2)
RIBBING
With smaller size straight needles, cast on 49{51-53} sts **loosely**.

Row 1: P1, (K1, P1) across.

Row 2: K1, (P1, K1) across.

Repeat Rows 1 and 2 until Ribbing measures 3" (7.5 cm), ending by working Row 1.

BODY
Change to larger size needles.

Row 1 (Right side): K1, P 13{14-15}, place marker **(Fig. 1, page 578)**, K 21, place marker, P 13{14-15}, K1.

Row 2: P1, knit across to next marker, purl across to next marker, knit across to last st, P1.

Row 3: K1, purl across to next marker, knit across to next marker, purl across to last st, K1.

Instructions continued on page 270.

Repeat Rows 2 and 3 for pattern, increasing one stitch at **each** edge *(see Increases, page 581)*, every sixth row, 1{0-3} time(s) *(see Zeros, page 577)*; then increase every eighth row, 7{8-6} times: 65{67-71} sts.

Work even until Sleeve measures approximately $18^1/_2$\{19-$19^1/_2$\}"/47{48.5-49.5} cm from cast on edge, ending by working a **wrong** side row and removing markers.

SLEEVE CAP
Row 1: Bind off 6 sts, P 16{17-19}, K 19, P 22{23-25}, K1: 59{61-65} sts.

Row 2: Bind off 6 sts, K 16{17-19}, P 19, K 16{17-19}, P1: 53{55-59} sts.

Row 3: K1, P2 tog, P 15{16-18}, K 17, P 15{16-18}, SSP, K1: 51{53-57} sts.

Row 4: P1, slip 1, K1, PSSO, K 14{15-17}, P 17, K 14{15-17}, K2 tog, P1: 49{51-55} sts.

Row 5: K1, P2 tog, P 14{15-17}, K 15, P 14{15-17}, SSP, K1: 47{49-53} sts.

Row 6: P1, K 15{16-18}, P 15, K 15{16-18}, P1.

Row 7: K1, P2 tog, P 14{15-17}, K 13, P 14{15-17}, SSP, K1: 45{47-51} sts.

Row 8: P1, K 15{16-18}, P 13, K 15{16-18}, P1.

Row 9: K1, P2 tog, P 14{15-17}, K 11, P 14{15-17}, SSP, K1: 43{45-49} sts.

Row 10: P1, K 15{16-18}, P 11, K 15{16-18}, P1.

Row 11: K1, P2 tog, P 14{15-17}, K9, P 14{15-17}, SSP, K1: 41{43-47} sts.

Row 12: P1, K 15{16-18}, P9, K 15{16-18}, P1.

Row 13: K1, P2 tog, P 14{15-17}, K7, P 14{15-17}, SSP, K1: 39{41-45} sts.

Row 14: P1, K 15{16-18}, P7, K 15{16-18}, P1.

FOR SIZE SMALL ONLY
Row 15: K1, P 16, K5, P 16, K1.

Row 16: P1, K 16, P5, K 16, P1.

Row 17: K1, P2 tog, P 15, K3, P 15, SSP, K1: 37 sts.

Row 18: P1, K 16, P3, K 16, P1.

Row 19: K1, (P 17, K1) twice.

Row 20: P1, (K 17, P1) twice.

Row 21: K1, P2 tog, purl across to last 3 sts, SSP, K1: 35 sts.

Row 22: P1, knit across to last st, P1.

Row 23: K1, purl across to last st, K1.

Row 24: P1, knit across to last st, P1.

Rows 25-29: Repeat Rows 21-24 once, then repeat Row 21 once **more**: 31 sts.

FOR SIZE MEDIUM ONLY
Row 15: K1, P2 tog, P 15, K5, P 15, SSP, K1: 39 sts.

Row 16: P1, K 16, P5, K 16, P1.

Row 17: K1, P2 tog, P 15, K3, P 15, SSP, K1: 37 sts.

Row 18: P1, K 16, P3, K 16, P1.

Row 19: K1, (P 17, K1) twice.

Row 20: P1, (K 17, P1) twice.

Row 21: K1, P2 tog, purl across to last 3 sts, SSP, K1: 35 sts.

Row 22: P1, knit across to last st, P1.

Row 23: K1, purl across to last st, K1.

Row 24: P1, knit across to last st, P1.

Rows 25-29: Repeat Rows 21-24 once, then repeat Row 21 once **more**: 31 sts.

FOR SIZE LARGE ONLY
Row 15: K1, P2 tog, P 17, K5, P 17, SSP, K1: 43 sts.

Row 16: P1, K 18, P5, K 18, P1.

Row 17: K1, P2 tog, P 17, K3, P 17, SSP, K1: 41 sts.

Row 18: P1, K 18, P3, K 18, P1.

Row 19: K1, P2 tog, P 17, K1, P 17, SSP, K1: 39 sts.

Row 20: P1, (K 18, P1) twice.

Row 21: K1, P2 tog, purl across to last 3 sts, SSP, K1: 37 sts.

Row 22: P1, knit across to last st, P1.

Row 23: K1, P2 tog, purl across to last 3 sts, SSP, K1: 35 sts.

Row 24: P1, knit across to last st, P1.

Row 25: K1, purl across to last st, K1.

Row 26: P1, knit across to last st, P1.

Rows 27-31: Repeat Rows 23-26 once, then repeat Row 23 once **more**: 31 sts.

FOR ALL SIZES
Work even until Sleeve Cap measures approximately 6{6^1/$_2$-6^3/$_4$}"/15{16.5-17} cm, ending by working a **wrong** side row.

Next 4 Rows: Bind off 5 sts, work across: 11 sts.

Bind off remaining sts.

FINISHING
Weave shoulder seams *(Figs. 35a & b, page 587)*.

NECK RIBBING
With **right** side facing, slip 25{27-27} sts from Back st holder onto circular needle and knit across, pick up 28{30-32} sts evenly spaced along left Front Neck edge *(Fig. 34a, page 586)*, place marker, slip st from Front st holder onto second end of circular needle and knit it, pick up 29{31-33} sts evenly spaced along right Front Neck edge, place marker to mark beginning of rnd: 83{89-93} sts.

Rnd 1: K1, (P1, K1) across to within 2 sts of marker, K2 tog, slip marker, K1, slip 1, K1, PSSO, P1, (K1, P1) across: 81{87-91} sts.

Rnd 2: Work in established ribbing to within 2 sts of marker, K2 tog, slip marker, K1, slip 1, K1, PSSO, work in established ribbing around: 79{85-89} sts.

Repeat Rnd 2 until ribbing measures approximately 1" (2.5 cm).

Bind off all sts **loosely** in ribbing.

Sew Sleeves to Sweater, placing center of last row on Sleeve Cap at shoulder seam and matching bound off stitches.

Weave underarm and side in one continuous seam *(Fig. 36, page 587)*.

Design by Dale Rieves Potter.

HOODED PULLOVER

Long Sleeve Version shown on page 275.

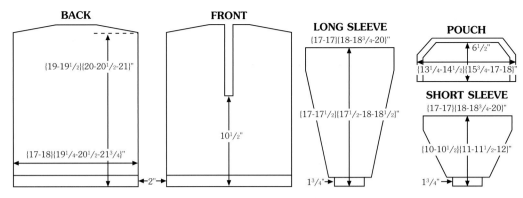

BACK

{19-19^1/$_2$}{20-20^1/$_2$-21}"

{17-18}{19^1/$_4$-20^1/$_2$-21^3/$_4$}"

←2"→

FRONT

10^1/$_2$"

LONG SLEEVE
{17-17}{18-18^3/$_4$-20}"

{17-17^1/$_2$}{17^1/$_2$-18-18^1/$_2$}"

1^3/$_4$"→

POUCH
6^1/$_2$"
{13^1/$_4$-14^1/$_2$}{15^3/$_4$-17-18}"

SHORT SLEEVE
{17-17}{18-18^3/$_4$-20}"

{10-10^1/$_2$}{11-11^1/$_2$-12}"

1^3/$_4$"→

Size:	32	34	36	38	40
Finished Chest Measurement:	34"	36"	38^1/$_2$"	41"	43^1/$_2$"

Size Note: Instructions are written with sizes 32 and 34 in the first set of braces, and with sizes 36, 38, and 40 in the second set of braces { }. Instructions will be easier to read if you circle all the numbers pertaining to your size. If only one number is given, it applies to all sizes.

MATERIALS

Bulky Weight Yarn: **⑤ BULKY**

Short Sleeve Version
{20-22}{24-26-28} ounces,
[{570-620}{680-740-800} grams,
{675-680}{740-800-865} yards**]**

Long Sleeve Version
{22-24}{26-28-30} ounces,
[{620-680}{740-800-850} grams,
{680-740}{800-865-925} yards**]**

Straight knitting needles, size 10^1/$_2$ (6.50 mm) **or** size needed for gauge
29" Circular needle, size 10^1/$_2$ (6.50 mm)
Markers - 3
Yarn needle
Sewing needle and thread
^{7}/$_8$" Buttons - 3

GAUGE: In Stockinette Stitch, 13 sts and 17 rows = 4"

BACK
BAND
Cast on {57-61}{65-69-73} sts **loosely**.

Rows 1-10: K1, (P1, K1) across.

BODY

Beginning with a **knit** row, work in Stockinette Stitch until Back measures approximately {19-19^1/$_2$}{20-20^1/$_2$-21}" from cast on edge, ending by working a **purl** row.

SHOULDER SHAPING

Rows 1-4: Bind off {6-7}{8-9-10} sts at the beginning of the row, work across: 33 sts.

Bind off remaining sts.

FRONT

Work same as Back until Front measures approximately 10^1/$_2$" from cast on edge, ending by working a **purl** row.

PLACKET OPENING

Row 1: Knit {26-28}{30-32-34} sts, bind off next 5 sts; knit across: {26-28}{30-32-34} sts **each** side.

Note: Both sides of Placket Opening are worked at the same time, using separate yarn for **each** side.

Work even until Front measures same as Back to Shoulder Shaping, ending by working a **purl** row.

SHOULDER SHAPING

Rows 1-4: Bind off {6-7}{8-9-10} sts at Armhole edge, work across; with second yarn, work across: 14 sts **each** side.

HOOD

Row 1: Slip 14 sts from left Front onto circular needle; cut yarn on Left Front only; with same circular needle, knit across right Front, holding Back with **right** side facing, pick up 33 sts across Back neck edge **(Figs. 34a & b, page 586)**, knit across left Front: 61 sts.

Instructions continued on page 274.

Rows 2-10: Work in Stockinette Stitch for 9 rows.

Row 11 (Increase row)**:** K 29, increase
(Figs. 10a & b, page 581), K1, increase, knit across: 63 sts.

Rows 12-20: Work in Stockinette Stitch for 9 rows.

Row 21: K 30, increase, K1, increase, knit across: 65 sts.

Rows 22-30: Work in Stockinette Stitch for 9 rows.

Row 31: K 31, increase, K1, increase, knit across: 67 sts.

Rows 32-40: Work in Stockinette Stitch for 9 rows.

Row 41: K 32, increase, K1, increase, knit across: 69 sts.

Work even until Hood measures approximately 11", ending by working a **purl** row.

SHAPING
Row 1: K 29, bind off next 11 sts, knit across: 29 sts **each** side.

Note: Both sides are worked at the same time, using separate yarn for **each** side.

Rows 2-5: Work across; with second yarn, bind off 5 sts, work across: 19 sts **each** side.

Bind off remaining sts.

SHORT SLEEVE VERSION
(Make 2)
BAND
Cast on {39-39}{41-43-43} sts **loosely**.

Rows 1-8: K1, (P1, K1) across.

Row 9 (Right side)**:** Knit across increasing 6 sts evenly spaced *(see Increasing Evenly Across A Row, page 581)*: {45-45}{47-49-49} sts.

BODY
Beginning with a **purl** row, work in Stockinette Stitch increasing one stitch at **each** edge, every fourth row, {2-1}{3-2-7} time(s); then increase every sixth row, {3-4}{3-4-1} time(s): {55-55}{59-61-65} sts.

Work even until Sleeve measures approximately {10-10½}{11-11½-12}" from cast on edge, ending by working a **purl** row.

Bind off all sts **loosely** in **knit**.

LONG SLEEVE VERSION
(Make 2)
BAND
Cast on {21-21}{23-25-25} sts **loosely**.

Rows 1-8: K1, (P1, K1) across.

Row 9 (Right side)**:** Knit across increasing {8-8}{8-8-10} sts evenly spaced *(see Increasing Evenly Across A Row, page 581)*: {29-29}{31-33-35} sts.

BODY
Beginning with a **purl** row, work in Stockinette Stitch increasing one stitch at **each** edge, every fourth row, {13-13}{14-14-15} times: {55-55}{59-61-65} sts.

Work even until Sleeve measures approximately {17-17½}{17½-18-18½}" from cast on edge, ending by working a **purl** row.

Bind off all sts **loosely** in **knit**.

FINISHING
Sew top Hood seam. Sew shoulder seams.

BUTTON PLACKET
With **right** side facing, using circular needle and beginning at right Front Placket Opening, pick up {131-133}{137-139-143} sts evenly spaced around to bound off sts.

Rows 1-3: K1, (P1, K1) across.

Place 3 markers on right front Button Placket for buttonhole placement, placing first marker in stitch corresponding with shoulder seam, second marker one inch from bound off stitches, and third marker evenly spaced between first and second markers.

Row 4 (Buttonhole Row): (Work across to next marker, bind off next st in pattern) 3 times, work across.

Row 5: ★ Work across to bound off st; **turn**, add on one st **(Figs. 5a & b, page 580)**; **turn**; repeat from ★ 2 times **more**, work across.

Rows 6 and 7: K1, (P1, K1) across.

Bind off remaining sts **loosely** in pattern.

Sew Button Placket to bound off stitches on Front.
Sew buttons opposite buttonholes.

POUCH
Cast on {43-47}{51-55-59} sts **loosely**.

Row 1: K1, (P1, K1) twice, purl across to last 5 sts, K1, (P1, K1) twice.

Row 2 (Right side)**:** (K1, P1) twice, knit across to last 4 sts, (P1, K1) twice.

Rows 3-11: Repeat Rows 1 and 2, 4 times; then repeat Row 1 once **more**.

Row 12 (Decrease row)**:** (K1, P1) twice, [slip 1 as if to **knit**, K1, PSSO **(Figs. 19a & b, page 583)**], knit across to last 6 sts, K2 tog **(Fig. 17, page 583)**, (P1, K1) twice: {41-45}{49-53-57} sts.

Rows 13-15: Repeat Rows 1 and 2, then repeat Row 1 once **more**.

Repeat Rows 12-15 until Pouch measures approximately $6^1/2$" from cast on edge, ending by working a **right** side row.

Last 7 Rows: K1, (P1, K1) across.

Bind off remaining sts in pattern.

Sew Pouch to Front, sewing cast on edge of Pouch just above Band and sew bound off edge to Front $1/2$" below Button Placket.

Sew Sleeves to Sweater, matching center of last row on Sleeve to shoulder seam and beginning {$8^1/2$-$8^1/2$}{9-$9^1/2$-10}" down from seam.

Weave underarm and side in one continuous seam **(Fig. 36, page 587)**.

Design by Tammy Kreimeyer.

TEXTURED CARDIGAN VEST

BACK

LEFT FRONT

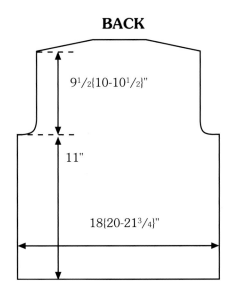

$9^1/_2${10-10$^1/_2$}"

11"

18{20-21$^3/_4$}"

9{10-10$^3/_4$}"

Size:	Small	Medium	Large
Finished Chest			
Measurement:	36"	40"	43$^1/_2$"

Size Note: Instructions are written for size Small with sizes Medium and Large in braces { }. Instructions will be easier to read if you circle all the numbers pertaining to your size. If only one number is given, it pertains to all sizes.

MATERIALS

Bulky Weight Yarn:
   Tan - 11$^3/_4${13-14$^1/_2$} ounces,
     [340{370-410} grams, 360{400-450} yards]
   Blue - 5$^1/_4${6-6$^1/_2$} ounces,
     [150{170-180} grams, 160{185-200} yards]
Straight knitting needles, size 10 (6.00 mm) **or**
   size needed for gauge
29" Circular needle, size 8 (5.00 mm)
Marker
Yarn needle
Sewing needle and thread
$^3/_4$" Buttons - 5

GAUGE: With larger size needles, in pattern,
    13 sts and 28 rows = 4"

SLIP STITCH PATTERN

When instructed to slip a stitch, always slip as if to **purl**.
On **right** side rows, always hold yarn in **back**.
Row 1 (Right side): With Tan, knit across.
Row 2: Knit across.
Carry unused yarn **loosely** along the edge.
Row 3: With Blue K1, (slip 1, K1) across.
Row 4: K1, (WYF slip 1, WYB K1) across.
Row 5: With Tan, knit across.
Row 6: Knit across.
Row 7: With Blue K2, slip 1, (K1, slip 1) across to last 2 sts, K2.
Row 8: K2, WYF slip 1, (WYB K1, WYF slip 1) across to last 2 sts, WYB K2.
Repeat Rows 1-8 for pattern.

BACK

With Tan and larger size needles,
cast on 61{67-73} sts **loosely**.

Row 1: Purl across.

Row 2 (Right side): Knit across.

Row 3: Purl across.

Beginning with Row 1 of Slip Stitch Pattern, work until Back measures approximately 11" from bottom of rolled edge, ending by working pattern Row 4.

ARMHOLE SHAPING

Rows 1 and 2: With Tan, bind off 3 sts at the beginning of the row, knit across: 55{61-67} sts.

Row 3 (Decrease row)**:** With Blue K2 tog *(Fig. 17, page 583)*, K1, (slip 1, K1) across to last 2 sts, K2 tog: 53{59-65} sts.

Row 4: K2, WYF slip 1, (WYB K1, WYF slip 1) across to last 2 sts, K2.

Row 5 (Decrease row)**:** With Tan K2 tog, knit across to last 2 sts, K2 tog: 51{57-63} sts.

Row 6: Knit across.

Row 7 (Decrease row)**:** With Blue K2 tog, slip 1, (K1, slip 1) across to last 2 sts, K2 tog: 49{55-61} sts.

Beginning with Row 4 of Slip Stitch Pattern, work even until Armholes measure approximately 9$\frac{1}{2}${10-10$\frac{1}{2}$}", ending by working pattern Row 4 or Row 8; cut Blue.

SHOULDER SHAPING

Note: Maintain established pattern throughout.

Rows 1 and 2: With Tan, bind off 5{5-7} sts at the beginning of the row, work across: 39{45-47} sts.

Rows 3-6: Bind off 5{6-6} sts at the beginning of the row, work across: 19{21-23} sts.

With Tan, bind off remaining sts.

Instructions continued on page 278.

LEFT FRONT

With Tan and larger size needles, cast on 29{33-35} sts **loosely**.

Work same as Back to Armhole Shaping.

ARMHOLE SHAPING

Row 1: With Tan, bind off 3 sts, knit across: 26{30-32} sts.

Row 2: Knit across.

Row 3 (Decrease row)**:** With Blue K2 tog, (K1, slip 1) across to last 2 sts, K2: 25{29-31} sts.

Row 4: K2, WYF slip 1, (WYB K1, WYF slip 1) across to last 2 sts, K2.

Row 5 (Decrease row)**:** With Tan K2 tog, knit across: 24{28-30} sts.

Row 6: Knit across.

Row 7 (Decrease row)**:** With Blue K2 tog, (slip 1, K1) across: 23{27-29} sts.

Rows 8-16: Beginning with Row 4 of Slip Stitch Pattern, work even for 9 rows.

NECK SHAPING

Row 1 (Decrease row)**:** With Tan, knit across to last 2 sts, K2 tog: 22{26-28} sts.

Row 2: Knit across.

Row 3: With Blue K2, (slip 1, K1) across.

Row 4: K1, WYF slip 1, (WYB K1, WYF slip 1) across to last 2 sts, K2.

Row 5 (Decrease row)**:** With Tan, knit across to last 2 sts, K2 tog: 21{25-27} sts.

Row 6: Knit across.

Row 7: With Blue K1, (slip 1, K1) across.

Row 8: K1, (WYF slip 1, WYB K1) across.

Rows 9 thru 29{37-37}: Repeat Rows 1-8, 2{3-3} times; then repeat Rows 1-5 once **more**: 15{17-19} sts.

Beginning with Row 2 of Slip Stitch Pattern, work even until Armhole measures same as Back to Shoulder Shaping, ending by working pattern Row 4 or Row 8; cut Blue.

SHOULDER SHAPING

Note: Maintain established pattern throughout.

Row 1: With Tan, bind off 5{5-7} sts, knit across: 10{12-12} sts.

Row 2: Knit across.

Row 3: With Blue, bind off 5{6-6} sts, work across: 5{6-6} sts.

Row 4: Work across.

With Tan, bind off remaining sts.

RIGHT FRONT

With Tan and larger size needles, cast on 29{33-35} sts **loosely**.

Work same as Back to Armhole Shaping.

ARMHOLE SHAPING

Row 1: With Tan, knit across.

Row 2: Bind off 3 sts, knit across: 26{30-32} sts.

Row 3 (Decrease row)**:** With Blue K2, (slip 1, K1) across to last 2 sts, K2 tog: 25{29-31} sts.

Row 4: K2, WYF slip 1, (WYB K1, WYF slip 1) across to last 2 sts, K2.

Row 5 (Decrease row)**:** With Tan, knit across to last 2 sts, K2 tog: 24{28-30} sts.

Row 6: Knit across.

Row 7 (Decrease row)**:** With Blue (K1, slip 1) across to last 2 sts, K2 tog: 23{27-29} sts.

Rows 8-16: Beginning with Row 4 of Slip Stitch Pattern, work even for 9 rows.

NECK SHAPING
Row 1 (Decrease row)**:** With Tan K2 tog, knit across: 22{26-28} sts.

Row 2: Knit across.

Row 3: With Blue (K1, slip 1) across to last 2 sts, K2.

Row 4: K2, (WYF slip 1, WYB K1) across.

Row 5 (Decrease row)**:** With Tan K2 tog, knit across: 21{25-27} sts.

Row 6: Knit across.

Row 7: With Blue K1, (slip 1, K1) across.

Row 8: K1, (WYF slip 1, WYB K1) across.

Rows 9 thru 29{37-37}: Repeat Rows 1-8, 2{3-3} times; then repeat Rows 1-5 once **more**: 15{17-19} sts.

Beginning with Row 2 of Slip Stitch Pattern, work even until Armhole measures same as Back to Shoulder Shaping, ending by working pattern Row 4 or Row 8; cut Blue.

SHOULDER SHAPING
Note: Maintain established pattern throughout.

Row 1: With Tan, knit across.

Row 2: Bind off 5{5-7} sts, knit across: 10{12-12} sts.

Row 3: With Blue, work across.

Row 4: Bind off 5{6-6} sts, work across; cut Blue: 5{6-6} sts.

Row 5: With Tan, knit across.

Bind off remaining sts.

FINISHING
Sew shoulder seams.

FRONT AND NECK RIBBING
With **right** side facing, using Tan and circular needle, and allowing bottom edge to stay rolled, pick up 52 sts evenly spaced across Right Front to Neck Shaping *(Figs. 34a & b, page 586)*, place marker *(Fig. 1, page 578)*, pick up 51{55-59} sts evenly spaced across to shoulder seam, pick up 19{21-23} sts across Back neck edge, pick up 51{55-59} sts evenly spaced across Left Front Neck Shaping, pick up 52 sts evenly spaced across to bottom edge: 225{235-245} sts.

Row 1: P1, (K1, P1) across.

Row 2: K1, (P1, K1) across.

Row 3 (Buttonhole row)**:** P1, (K1, P1) across to marker, bind off next st in pattern, ★ (K1, P1) 5 times, bind off next st in pattern; repeat from ★ across to last 2 sts, K1, P1.

Row 4: K1, P1, K1, **turn**; add on one st *(Figs. 5a & b, page 580)*, **turn**; ★ K1, (P1, K1) 5 times, **turn**; add on one st, **turn**; repeat from ★ 3 times **more**, K1, (P1, K1) across.

Row 5: P1, (K1, P1) across.

Bind off all sts **loosely** in ribbing.

ARMHOLE RIBBING
With **right** side facing, using Tan and circular needle, and starting at underarm seam, pick up 70{76-78} sts evenly spaced around armhole edge; place marker to mark beginning of rnd.

Work in K1, P1 ribbing for 1".

Bind off all sts **loosely** in ribbing.

Repeat for second armhole.

Weave side seams *(Fig. 36, page 587)*.

Sew buttons to Left Front opposite buttonholes.

Design by Tammy Kreimeyer.

BULKY RIBBED PULLOVER

BACK

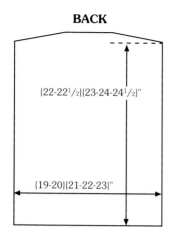

FRONT

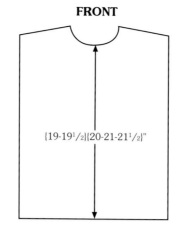

SLEEVE

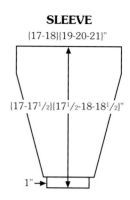

Size:	32	34	36	38	40
Finished Chest					
Measurement:	38"	40"	42"	44"	46"

Size Note: Instructions are written with sizes 32 and 34 in the first set of braces { }, and with sizes 36, 38, and 40 in the second set of braces { }. Instructions will be easier to read if you circle all the numbers pertaining to your size. If only one number is given, it applies to all sizes.

MATERIALS

Bulky Weight Yarn: **BULKY 5**

Brown - {$8^1/_2$-9}{$9^1/_2$-$10^1/_2$-11} ounces,
[{240-260}{270-300-310} grams,
{260-280}{295-325-340} yards]
Variegated - {$8^1/_2$-9}{$9^1/_2$-$10^1/_2$-11} ounces,
[{240-260}{270-300-310} grams,
{260-280}{295-325-340} yards]
Cream - {$8^1/_2$-9}{$9^1/_2$-$10^1/_2$-11} ounces,
[{240-260}{270-300-310} grams,
{260-280}{295-325-340} yards]
Straight knitting needles, size $10^1/_2$ (6.50 mm) **or** size needed for gauge
16" Circular needle, size 9 (5.50 mm)
Stitch holders - 2
Marker
Yarn needle

GAUGE: With larger size needles, in pattern,
16 sts and 16 rows = 4"

BACK

With Brown and larger size needles, cast on {78-82}{86-90-94} sts **loosely**.

Rows 1-4: Beginning with a **purl** row, work in Stockinette Stitch.

Row 5: P2, (K2, P2) across.

Row 6 (Right side)**:** K2, (P2, K2) across.

Repeat Rows 5 and 6 for pattern until Back measures approximately {8-8}{$8^1/_4$-$8^1/_2$-$8^3/_4$}" from bottom of rolled edge.

With Variegated, work even until Back measures approximately {$15^3/_4$-16}{$16^1/_2$-17-$17^1/_2$}" from bottom of rolled edge.

With Cream, work even until Back measures approximately {22-$22^1/_2$}{23-24-$24^1/_2$}" from bottom of rolled edge, ending by working Row 5.

SHOULDER SHAPING

Note: Maintain established pattern throughout.

Rows 1-4: Bind off {9-9}{10-10-11} sts at the beginning of the row, work across: {42-46}{46-50-50} sts.

Rows 5 and 6: Bind off {8-10}{9-11-11} sts at the beginning of the row, work across: {26-26}{28-28-28} sts.

Slip remaining sts onto st holder.

Instructions continued on page 282.

FRONT

Work same as Back until Front measures approximately {19-19$\frac{1}{2}$}{20-21-21$\frac{1}{2}$}" from bottom of rolled edge, ending by working Row 5.

NECK SHAPING

*Note: Both sides of Neck are worked at the same time, using separate yarn for **each** side. Maintain established pattern throughout.*

Row 1: Work across {32-34}{35-37-39} sts, slip next {14-14}{16-16-16} sts onto st holder; with second yarn, work across: {32-34}{35-37-39} sts **each** side.

Row 2 (Decrease row)**:** Work across to within 2 sts of Neck edge, decrease **(see Decreases, pages 583 & 584)**; with second yarn, decrease, work across: {31-33}{34-36-38} sts **each** side.

Row 3 (Decrease row)**:** Work across to within 2 sts of Neck edge, decrease; with second yarn, decrease, work across: {30-32}{33-35-37} sts **each** side.

Row 4: Work across; with second yarn, work across.

Rows 5-12: Repeat Rows 3 and 4, 4 times: {26-28}{29-31-33} sts **each** side.

SHOULDER SHAPING

Rows 1-4: Bind off {9-9}{10-10-11} sts at Armhole edge, work across; with second yarn, work across: {8-10}{9-11-11} sts **each** side.

Row 5: Bind off {8-10}{9-11-11} sts; with second yarn, work across.

Bind off remaining sts.

SLEEVE (Make 2)
COLOR SEQUENCE

Work {5$\frac{1}{2}$-5$\frac{3}{4}$}{5$\frac{3}{4}$-6-6}" with Brown, {5$\frac{3}{4}$-5$\frac{3}{4}$}{5$\frac{3}{4}$-6-6$\frac{1}{4}$}" with Variegated, and complete Sleeve with Cream.

With larger size needles, cast on 30 sts **loosely**.

Rows 1-4: Beginning with a **purl** row, work in Stockinette Stitch.

Row 5: Purl across increasing 6 sts evenly spaced **(Fig. 11, page 581)**: 36 sts.

Rows 6 and 7: (K2, P2) across.

Beginning with the next row and working new stitches in pattern, increase one stitch at **each** edge, every other row, {3-6}{10-13-16} times; then increase every fourth row, {13-12}{10-9-8} times: {68-72}{76-80-84} sts.

Work even until Sleeve measures approximately {17-17$\frac{1}{2}$}{17$\frac{1}{2}$-18-18$\frac{1}{2}$}" from bottom of rolled edge.

Bind off all sts **loosely** in pattern.

FINISHING

Sew shoulder seams.

NECK EDGING

With **right** side facing and Cream, slip {26-26}{28-28-28} sts from Back st holder onto circular needle and knit across, pick up 16 sts evenly spaced along left Front Neck edge **(Fig. 34b, page 586)**, slip {14-14}{16-16-16} sts from Front st holder onto second end of circular needle and knit across, pick up 16 sts evenly spaced along right Front Neck edge, place marker to mark beginning of rnd **(Fig. 1, page 578)**: {72-72}{76-76-76} sts.

Knit 7 rnds.

Bind off all sts **loosely** in **knit**.

Sew Sleeves to Sweater, matching center of last row on Sleeve to shoulder seam and beginning {8$\frac{1}{2}$-9}{9$\frac{1}{2}$-10-10$\frac{1}{2}$}" down from seam.

Weave underarm and side in one continuous seam **(Fig. 36, page 587)**.

Design by Tammy Kreimeyer.

CHILD'S RAGLAN ARAN PULLOVER

Shown on page 285.

▆▆▆▶ **EXPERIENCED**

Size:	2	4	6	8	10	12
Chest Measurement:	22"	24"	25½"	27"	28½"	30"
Finished Measurement:	25"	27"	29"	31"	33"	35"

Size Note: Instructions are written with sizes 2, 4, and 6 in the first set of braces { } and with sizes 8, 10, and 12 in the second set of braces. Instructions will be easier to read if you circle all the numbers pertaining to your size.

MATERIALS

Worsted Weight Yarn: **⬗ 4 ⬖** MEDIUM
{11-13-15}{17-19-21} ounces,
[{310-370-430}{480-540-600} grams,
{690-815-945}{1,070-1,195-1,320} yards]
Straight knitting needles, sizes 5 (3.75 mm) **and**
7 (4.50 mm) **or** sizes needed for gauge
24" Circular needles, size 5 (3.75 mm)
Markers
Cable needle
Stitch holders - 4
Yarn needle

GAUGE: With large size needles, in Seed Stitch,
16 sts and 28 rows = 4"

Gauge Swatch: 4" square
With large size needles, cast on 16 sts **loosely**.
Row 1: (K1, P1) across.
Row 2: (P1, K1) across.
Rows 3-28: Repeat Rows 1 and 2, 13 times.
Bind off all sts **loosely** in established pattern.

Note: Row gauge is very important in raglans. To correct your gauge, see Gauge, page 576.

SEED STITCH (abbreviated Seed St)
Knit the purl sts and purl the knit sts as they face you.

TRIPLE CABLE (uses next 10 sts)
Row 1: K2, P2, with yarn in **front** slip 2 sts as if to **purl**, P2, K2.
Row 2 (Right side)**:** P2, slip next 2 sts onto cable needle and hold in **back** of work, K1 from left needle, K2 from cable needle, slip next st onto cable needle and hold in **front** of work, K2 from left needle, K1 from cable needle, P2.
Rows 3-6: Repeat Rows 1 and 2, twice.
Row 7: K2, P6, K2.
Row 8: P2, K6, P2.
Rows 9-12: Repeat Rows 7 and 8, twice.
Repeat Rows 1-12 for pattern.

DAISY STITCH PANEL (uses next 11 sts)
DAISY STITCH (uses next 3 sts)
P3 tog and leave on left needle, YO *(Fig. 16b, page 582)* and purl the same 3 sts tog again and slip off left needle.

Row 1: Work Daisy Stitch, (K1, work Daisy Stitch) twice.
Row 2 (Right side)**:** Knit across.
Row 3: P1, K1, (work Daisy Stitch, K1) twice, P1.
Row 4: Knit across.
Repeat Rows 1-4 for pattern.

Instructions begin on page 284.

DIAMOND (uses next 19 sts)

POPCORN
[K1, (K1 tbl, K1) twice] **all** in next st: 5 sts.

BACK TWIST *(abbreviated BT)* (uses next 3 sts)
Slip next st onto cable needle and hold in **back** of work, K2 from left needle, P1 from cable needle.

FRONT TWIST *(abbreviated FT)*
(uses next 3 sts)
Slip next 2 sts onto cable needle and hold in **front** of work, P1 from left needle, K2 from cable needle.

Row 1: K3, work Popcorn, K3, P2, K1, P2, K3, work Popcorn, K3: 27 sts.
Row 2 (Right side)**:** P3, K5 tog tbl (Popcorn completed), P3, slip next 3 sts onto cable needle and hold in **front** of work, K2 from left needle, slip last st from cable needle back onto left needle and purl it, K2 from cable needle, P3, K5 tog tbl, P3: 19 sts.
Row 3: K7, P2, K1, P2, K7.
Row 4: P6, BT, P1, FT, P6.
Row 5: K6, P2, K3, P2, K6.
Row 6: P5, BT, P3, FT, P5.
Row 7: K5, P2, K2, work Popcorn, K2, P2, K5: 23 sts.
Row 8: P4, BT, P2, K5 tog tbl, P2, FT, P4: 19 sts.
Row 9: K4, P2, K7, P2, K4.
Row 10: P3, BT, P7, FT, P3.
Row 11: K3, P2, K2, work Popcorn, K3, work Popcorn, K2, P2, K3: 27 sts.
Row 12: P2, BT, P2, K5 tog tbl, P3, K5 tog tbl, P2, FT, P2: 19 sts.
Row 13: K2, P2, K 11, P2, K2.
Row 14: P2, K2, P11, K2, P2.
Row 15: K2, P2, K3, (work Popcorn, K3) twice, P2, K2: 27 sts.
Row 16: P2, FT, P2, K5 tog tbl, P3, K5 tog tbl, P2, BT, P2: 19 sts.
Row 17: K3, P2, K9, P2, K3.
Row 18: P3, FT, P7, BT, P3.
Row 19: K4, P2, K3, work Popcorn, K3, P2, K4: 23 sts.
Row 20: P4, FT, P2, K5 tog tbl, P2, BT, P4: 19 sts.
Row 21: K5, (P2, K5) twice.
Row 22: P5, FT, P3, BT, P5.
Row 23: K6, P2, K3, P2, K6.
Row 24: P6, FT, P1, BT, P6.
Repeat Rows 1-24 for pattern.

BACK
TWISTED RIBBING
With small size needles, cast on {75-79-83}{87-91-95} sts **loosely**.

Row 1: P1, (K1 tbl, P1) across *(Figs. 4a & b, page 580)*.

Row 2 (Right side)**:** K1 tbl, (P1, K1 tbl) across.

Rows 3-10: Repeat Rows 1 and 2, 4 times.

BODY
Change to large size needles.

Row 1: K1, (P1, K1) {3-4-5}{6-7-8} times, place marker *(Fig. 1, page 578)*, work Row 1 of Triple Cable, place marker, work Row 1 of Daisy Stitch Panel, place marker, work Row 1 of Diamond, place marker, work Row 1 of Daisy Stitch Panel, place marker, work Row 1 of Triple Cable, place marker, K1, (P1, K1) across.

Row 2: K1, (P1, K1) across to next marker (Seed St), work next row of Triple Cable, work next row of Daisy Stitch Panel, work next row of Diamond, work next row of Daisy Stitch Panel, work next row of Triple Cable, K1, (P1, K1) across (Seed St).

Repeat Row 2 until Back measures approximately {8-9-10}{11-11½-12}" from cast on edge or desired length to underarm, ending by working a **wrong** side row.

RAGLAN SHAPING
Note #1: Maintain established pattern throughout.
Note #2: The stitch counts given are based on 19 sts for the Diamond. Add 4 sts to the stitch count for each Popcorn being worked.

Rows 1 and 2: Bind off 3 sts at the beginning of next 2 rows, work across: {69-73-77}{81-85-89} sts.

Row 3 (Decrease row)**:** K1, [slip 1 as if to **knit**, K1, PSSO *(Figs. 19a & b, page 583)*], work across to last 3 sts, K2 tog *(Fig. 17, page 583)*, K1: {67-71-75}{79-83-87} sts.

Instructions continued on page 286.

Row 4: P2, work across to last 2 sts, P2.

Repeat Rows 3 and 4, {20-22-24}{24-26-26} times: {27-27-27}{31-31-35} sts.

Slip remaining sts onto st holder; cut yarn.

FRONT

Work same as Back through Row 4 of Raglan Shaping.

Repeat Rows 3 and 4, {13-15-17}{17-19-19} times; then repeat Row 3 once **more**: {39-39-39}{43-43-47} sts.

NECK SHAPING

Note: Both sides of Neck are worked at the same time, using a separate yarn for **each** side.

Row 1: P2, work across 13 sts, slip {9-9-9}{13-13-17} sts onto st holder; with second yarn, work across to last 2 sts, P2: 15 sts **each** side.

Row 2 (Decrease row)**:** K1, slip 1 as if to **knit**, K1, PSSO, work across to within 2 sts of Neck edge, K2 tog; with second yarn, slip 1 as if to **knit**, K1, PSSO, work across to last 3 sts, K2 tog, K1: 13 sts **each** side.

Row 3 (Decrease row)**:** P2, work across to within 2 sts of Neck edge, P2 tog *(Fig. 18, page 583)*; with second yarn, P2 tog, work across to last 2 sts, P2: 12 sts **each** side.

Row 4 (Decrease row)**:** K1, slip 1 as if to **knit**, K1, PSSO, work across to within 2 sts of Neck edge, K2 tog; with second yarn, slip 1 as if to **knit**, K1, PSSO, work across to last 3 sts, K2 tog, K1: 10 sts **each** side.

Row 5: P2, work across; with second yarn, work across to last 2 sts, P2.

Rows 6-9: Repeat Rows 4 and 5, twice: 6 sts **each** side.

Row 10: K1, slip 1 as if to **knit**, K1, PSSO, K1, K2 tog; with second yarn, slip 1 as if to **knit**, K1, PSSO, K1, K2 tog, K1: 4 sts **each** side.

Row 11: Work across; with second yarn, work across.

Row 12: Slip 1 as if to **knit**, K1, PSSO, K2 tog; with second yarn, slip 1 as if to **knit**, K1, PSSO, K2 tog: 2 sts **each** side.

Row 13: P2 tog, cut yarn and pull through st; with second yarn, P2 tog, cut yarn and pull through st.

SLEEVE (Make 2)
TWISTED RIBBING

With small size needles, cast on {27-29-31}{35-37-39} sts **loosely**.

Row 1: P1, (K1 tbl, P1) across.

Row 2 (Right side)**:** K1 tbl, (P1, K1 tbl) across.

Repeat Rows 1 and 2, {4-5-5}{6-6-6} times increasing 8 sts evenly spaced across last row *(Figs. 10a & b, page 583)*: {35-37-39}{43-45-47} sts.

BODY

Change to large size needles.

Row 1: K{0-1-0}{0-1-0} *(see Zeros, page 577)*, (P1, K1) {1-1-2}{3-3-4} times, place marker, work Row 1 of Triple Cable, place marker, work Row 1 of Daisy Stitch Panel, place marker, work Row 1 of Triple Cable, place marker, (K1, P1) across to last {0-1-0}{0-1-0} st, K{0-1-0}{0-1-0}.

Row 2: K{0-1-0}{0-1-0}, (P1, K1) across to next marker (Seed St), work next row of Triple Cable, work next row of Daisy Stitch Panel, work next row of Triple Cable, (K1, P1) across to last {0-1-0}{0-1-0} st, K{0-1-0}{0-1-0} (Seed St).

Note: Work new stitches in Seed St.

Repeat Row 2 for pattern, increasing one stitch at **each** edge, every {6-6-8}{10-12-12} rows, {2-4-1}{6-5-6} times, then increase every {8-8-10}{0-0-0} rows, {4-3-5}{0-0-0} times: {47-51-51}{55-55-59} sts.

Work even until Sleeve measures approximately {9-10½-11¾}{13-14¼-15½}" from cast on edge or desired length to underarm, ending by working a **wrong** side row.

RAGLAN SHAPING

Note: Maintain established pattern throughout.

Rows 1 and 2: Bind off 3 sts at the beginning of next 2 rows, work across: {41-45-45}{49-49-53} sts.

Row 3: K2, work across to last 2 sts, K2.

Row 4: P2, work across to last 2 sts, P2.

Row 5 (Decrease row)**:** K1, slip 1 as if to **knit**, K1, PSSO, work across to last 3 sts, K2 tog, K1: {39-43-43}{47-47-51} sts.

Continue to decrease one stitch at **each** edge in same manner, every fourth row, {3-4-6}{5-7-6} times **more**, then decrease every other row, {13-13-11}{13-11-13} times, ending by working a **wrong** side row: {7-9-9}{11-11-13} sts.

Slip remaining sts onto st holder; cut yarn.

FINISHING

Weave raglan seams *(Fig. 36, page 587)*.
Weave underarm and side seam in one continuous seam.

TWISTED NECK RIBBING

With **right** side facing and using small size circular needles, pick up 13 sts along left Front Neck edge *(Fig. 34a, page 586)*, knit {9-9-9}{13-13-17} sts from Front st holder, pick up 13 sts along right Front Neck edge, slip sts from left Sleeve, Back, and right Sleeve st holders onto empty needle and knit across, place marker for beginning of rnd: {76-80-80}{92-92-104} sts.

Rnd 1: (K1 tbl, P1) around.

Rnd 2: (K1, P1) around.

Repeat Rnds 1 and 2 until Neck Ribbing measures approximately 2".

Bind off all sts **loosely** in established twisted ribbing.

Fold Neck Ribbing to wrong side and sew **loosely** in place.

Design by Tammy Kreimeyer.

FINE RAGLAN TURTLENECK

Shown on page 285.

INTERMEDIATE

Size: ____

Chest Measurement: ____"

Finished Chest Measurement: ____"

MATERIALS
Sport Weight Yarn: FINE **2**

Long Sleeve Version
 ____ ounces,
 (____ grams,
 ____ yards)

Short Sleeve Version
 ____ ounces,
 (____ grams,
 ____ yards)

Note: Add ____ ounce for Turtleneck Version.
Straight knitting needles, sizes 3 (3.25 mm) **and**
5 (3.75 mm) **or** sizes needed for gauge
16" Circular needles, size 3 (3.25 mm)
Marker
Stitch holders - 4
Tapestry needle

GAUGE: With large size needles, in Stockinette Stitch,
 24 sts and 30 rows = 4"

Note: Row gauge is very important in raglans. To
correct your gauge, see Gauge, page 576.

32	34	36	38	40	42	44	46	48	50
32	34	36	38	40	42	44	46	48	50
36	38	40	42	44	46	49	51	53	55
12	13	14	14½	15	16	17	18	19	20
340	370	400	410	430	450	480	510	540	570
1235	1335	1440	1490	1545	1645	1750	1850	1955	2055
9	9½	10	11	12	13	13½	14	15	16
260	270	280	310	340	370	380	400	430	450
925	980	1030	1130	1235	1335	1390	1440	1545	1645
1	1	1	1	1	1	1	1	1	1
110	116	122	128	134	140	150	156	162	168
2	2	2	2	2	2½	2½	2½	2½	2½
15	15	15	16	16	16	16	16	16	16

BACK
RIBBING
With small size needles, cast on ____ sts **loosely**.

Work in K1, P1 ribbing for approximately ____".

BODY
Change to large size needles.

Work in Stockinette Stitch until Back measures
approximately ____" from cast on edge or desired
length to underarm, ending by working a **purl** row.

32	34	36	38	40	42	44	46	48	50
5	5	5	6	8	8	10	12	15	16
100	106	112	116	118	124	130	132	132	136
98	104	110	114	116	122	128	130	130	134
2	1	1	0	0	0	0	0	0	0
29	33	34	37	38	41	42	43	43	44
36	36	40	40	40	40	44	44	44	46
52	52	56	56	56	56	60	62	62	68
15	15	15	16	16	16	16	18	18	20
22	22	26	24	24	24	28	26	26	28
15	15	15	16	16	16	16	18	18	20
13	13	13	14	14	14	14	16	16	18
7	7	7	7	7	7	7	8	8	10
4	4	4	5	5	5	5	6	6	6

RAGLAN SHAPING

Rows 1 and 2: Bind off ____ sts at the beginning of next 2 rows, work across: ____ sts.

Row 3 (Decrease row)**:** K1, SSK *(Figs. 21a-c, page 584)*, knit across to last 3 sts, K2 tog *(Fig. 17, page 583)*, K1: ____ sts.

Continue to decrease one stitch at **each** edge in same manner, every fourth row, ____ times **more (see Zeros, page 577)**; then decrease every other row, ____ times, ending by working a **right** side row.

Slip remaining ____ sts onto st holder; cut yarn.

FRONT

Work same as Back until ____ sts remain, ending by working a **right** side row.

NECK SHAPING

Note: Both sides of Neck are worked at the same time, using a separate yarn for **each** side.

Row 1: Purl ____ sts, slip ____ sts onto st holder; with second yarn, purl across: ____ sts **each** side.

Row 2 (Decrease row)**:** K1, SSK, knit across to within 2 sts of neck edge, K2 tog; with second yarn, SSK, knit across to last 3 sts, K2 tog, K1: ____ sts **each** side.

Row 3: Purl across; with second yarn, purl across.

Continue to decrease one stitch at **each** armhole edge in same manner, every other row, ____ times **more** AND AT THE SAME TIME decrease one stitch at **each** neck edge, every other row, ____ times.

Bind off remaining 2 sts on each side.

LONG SLEEVE (Make 2)

RIBBING

With small size needles, cast on ____ sts **loosely**.

Work in K1, P1 ribbing for approximately ____"
increasing ____ sts evenly spaced across last row
(*Figs. 10a & b, page 581*): ____ sts.

BODY

Change to large size needles.

Work in Stockinette Stitch, increasing one stitch at **each**
edge, every ____ rows,
____ times;
then increase every ____ rows,
____ times:
____ sts.

Work even until Sleeve measures approximately ____"
from cast on edge or desired length to underarm,
ending by working a **purl** row.

RAGLAN SHAPING

Rows 1 and 2: Bind off ____ sts at the beginning of
next 2 rows, work across: ____ sts.

Row 3 (Decrease row)**:** K1, SSK, knit across to last
3 sts, K2 tog, K1: ____ sts.

Row 4: Purl across.

Row 5: K1, slip 1 as if to **purl**, knit across to last
2 sts, slip 1 as if to **purl**, K1.

Row 6: Purl across.

Row 7 (Decrease row)**:** K1, SSK, knit across to last
3 sts, K2 tog, K1: ____ sts.

Repeat Rows 4-7, ____ times; then repeat Rows 6 and
7, ____ times **more**.

Slip remaining ____ sts onto st holder; cut yarn.

32	34	36	38	40	42	44	46	48	50
48	50	52	52	54	56	56	62	64	64
2½	2½	2½	2½	2½	3	3	3	3	3
6	6	6	6	6	8	8	8	8	8
54	56	58	58	60	64	64	70	72	72
6	6	6	4	6	4	4	4	4	4
8	11	10	1	16	1	5	1	2	7
8	8	8	6	0	6	6	6	6	6
5	3	4	15	0	15	12	15	14	11
80	84	86	90	92	96	98	102	104	108
17½	17½	17¾	18	18¼	18½	18¾	19	19¼	19½
5	5	5	6	8	8	10	12	15	16
70	74	76	78	76	80	78	78	74	76
68	72	74	76	74	78	76	76	72	74
66	70	72	74	72	76	74	74	70	72
4	4	5	5	7	8	11	12	14	14
23	25	24	25	22	23	18	17	13	14
12	12	14	14	14	14	16	16	16	16

SHORT SLEEVE (Make 2)

RIBBING

With small size needles, cast on ____ sts **loosely**.

Work in K1, P1 ribbing for approximately 1".

BODY

Change to large size needles.

Work even in Stockinette Stitch until Sleeve measures approximately ____" from cast on edge or desired length to underarm, ending by working a **purl** row.

RAGLAN SHAPING

Work same as Long Sleeve.

FINISHING

Weave raglan seams *(Fig. 36, page 587)*.
Weave side and underarm in one continuous seam.

NECK RIBBING

With **right** side facing and circular needle,
knit ____ sts from left Sleeve st holder,
pick up ____ sts along left Front neck edge
(Fig. 34a, page 586),
knit ____ sts from Front st holder,
pick up ____ sts along right Front neck edge,
knit ____ sts from right Sleeve st holder,
knit ____ sts from Back st holder, place marker for beginning of rnd *(Fig. 1, page 578)*: ____ sts.

Work in K1, P1 ribbing for approximately ____" for Crewneck version **or** ____" for Turtleneck version or to desired length.

Bind off all sts **loosely** in established ribbing.

Design by Marion Graham.

32	34	36	38	40	42	44	46	48	50
80	84	86	90	92	96	98	102	104	108
3	3	3	3	3	3	3	3½	3½	3½
12	12	14	14	14	14	16	16	16	16
16	16	16	16	16	16	16	18	18	22
22	22	26	24	24	24	28	26	26	28
16	16	16	16	16	16	16	18	18	22
12	12	14	14	14	14	16	16	16	16
36	36	40	40	40	40	44	44	44	46
114	114	126	124	124	124	136	138	138	150
1	1	1	1	1	1¼	1¼	1¼	1¼	1¼
5	5	5	5	5	5	5	5	5	5

RIBBON PONCHO

SIZE	GIRLS SIZE
	(approximate)
Small	2-4
Medium	6-8
Large	10-12

Size Note: Instructions are written for size Small with sizes Medium and Large in braces { }. Instructions will be easier to read if you circle all the numbers pertaining to your child's size. If only one number is given, it applies to all sizes.

MATERIALS

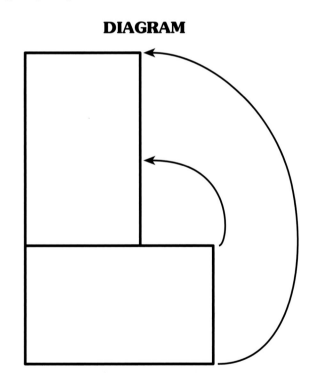

Bulky Weight Ribbon Yarn
   [1³/₄ ounces, 110 yards
   (50 grams, 100 meters) per ball]:
      4{5-5} balls
Knitting needles, size 13 (9 mm) **or** size
   needed for gauge
Yarn needle

GAUGE: In pattern,
         9 sts and 11 rows = 3" (7.5 cm)

BODY (Make 2)

Cast on 30{36-42} sts.

Rows 1-3: Knit across.

Row 4 (Right side)**:** Knit across wrapping yarn around needle twice as you knit each st: 60{72-84} sts.

Row 5: (Knit next st, drop next st off of left needle) across: 30{36-42} sts.

Rows 6 and 7: Knit across.

Repeat Rows 4-7 until piece measures approximately 20{22-24}"/51{56-61} cm from cast on edge, ending by working Row 7.

Bind off all sts in **knit**, leaving a long end for sewing.

FINISHING

Using diagram as a guide for placement, sew cast on edge of first piece to side of second piece. Sew bound off edge of second piece to side edge of first piece.

Design by Kay Meadors.

DIAGRAM

FUR TRIM PONCHO

SIZE	GIRLS SIZE
	(approximate)
Small	2-4
Medium	6-8
Large	10-12

Size Note: Instructions are written for size Small with sizes Medium and Large in braces { }. Instructions will be easier to read if you circle all the numbers pertaining to your child's size. If only one number is given, it applies to all sizes.

MATERIALS
Bulky Weight Yarn **5** BULKY
[2½ ounces, 57 yards
(70 grams, 52 meters) per ball]:
Variegated - 3{3-4} balls
Bulky Weight Novelty Eyelash Yarn **5** BULKY
[1¾ ounces, 64 yards
(50 grams, 58 meters) per ball]:
Orange - 1{1-2} ball(s)
16" (40.5 cm) Circular knitting needle,
size 13 (9 mm) **or** size needed for gauge
2 Markers (use different colors)

GAUGE: In pattern,
9 sts and 13 rnds = 4" (10 cm)

BODY
With Variegated, cast on 52 sts, place marker to mark beginning of rnd *(see Markers and Knitting in the Round, pages 578 & 579)*.

Rnd 1: Knit 26 sts, place marker, knit around.

Rnd 2: ★ (K1, YO) twice *(Fig. 16a, page 582)*, [slip 1, K2 tog, PSSO *(Figs. 26a & b, page 584)*, YO, K1, YO] across to next marker; repeat from ★ once **more**: 56 sts.

Rnd 3 AND ALL ODD-NUMBERED RNDS: Knit around.

Rnd 4: ★ K1, YO, K2, YO, slip 1, K2 tog, PSSO, (YO, K1, YO, slip 1, K2 tog, PSSO) across to within 2 sts of next marker, YO, K2, YO; repeat from ★ once **more**: 60 sts.

Rnd 6: ★ K1, YO, K2 tog, YO, K1, (YO, slip 1, K2 tog, PSSO, YO, K1) across to within 2 sts of next marker, YO, SSK *(Figs. 21a-c, page 584)*, YO; repeat from ★ once **more**: 64 sts.

Rnd 8: ★ K1, YO, K1, K2 tog, YO, K1, (YO, slip 1, K2 tog, PSSO, YO, K1) across to within 3 sts of next marker, YO, SSK, K1, YO; repeat from ★ once **more**: 68 sts.

Repeat Rnds 2-9 for pattern until Body measures approximately 10{12-14}"/25.5{30.5-35.5} cm from cast on edge (from straight edge to straight edge), ending by working an even-numbered rnd; cut yarn.

Last Rnd: Using two strands of Orange, knit around.

Bind off as follows: P2, return 2 sts on right needle back to left needle, purl these 2 sts tog *(Fig. 18, page 583)*, ★ P1, return 2 sts on right needle back to left needle, purl these 2 sts tog; repeat from ★ around.

NECK EDGING
With **right** side facing and using two strands of Orange, pick up 52 sts around cast on edge *(Fig. 34b, page 586)*.

Bind off all sts in same manner as lower edge of Poncho.

Design by Kay Meadors.

FAMILY TOBOGGANS
◼◼◻◻ EASY

SIZE (HEAD MEASUREMENT):
Child
2-4 (16½")   6-8 (18")   10-12 (19½")
Adult
7 (21")   8 (22½")   9 (24")

Size Note: Instructions are written for Children's sizes in first braces { } with Adult sizes in second braces { }. Instructions will be easier to read if you circle all the numbers pertaining to your size.

MATERIALS
MEDIUM 4

Worsted Weight Yarn:
(3½-3½-4)(4-4½-4½) ounces,
[(100-100-110)(110-130-130) grams,
(200-200-225) (225-255-255) yards]
Straight knitting needles, sizes 5 (3.75 mm)
and 7 (4.50 mm) **or** sizes needed for gauge
Markers
Yarn needle

GAUGE: With larger size needles,
in Stockinette Stitch,
20 sts and 28 rows = 4"

For striped Cap, change colors every 2 rows in Body.

RIBBING
With smaller size needles, cast on {78-84-90}{102-108-114} sts **very loosely**.

Work in K1, P1 ribbing for {1-1-1}{1½-1½-1½}".

BODY
Change to larger size needles.

Work in Stockinette Stitch until Cap measures {3½-4-4½}{5-5½-6}" from cast on edge, ending by working a **purl** row.

TOP SHAPING
Row 1 (Decrease row):
K {10-11-12}{14-15-16}, slip 1 as if to **knit**, K2 tog, PSSO *(Fig. 19a & b, page 583)*, ★ place marker *(Fig. 1, page 578)*, K {10-11-12}{14-15-16}, slip one as if to **knit**, K2 tog, PSSO; repeat from ★ across: {66-72-78}{90-96-102} sts.

Row 2: Purl across.

Row 3 (Decrease row): Knit across to within 3 sts of next marker, slip 1 as if to **knit**, K2 tog, PSSO, ★ slip marker, knit across to within 3 sts of next marker, slip 1 as if to **knit**, K2 tog, PSSO; repeat from ★ across: {54-60-66}{78-84-90} sts.

Row 4: Purl across.

Repeat Rows 3 and 4, {4-4-5}{6-6-7} times: {6-12-6}{6-12-6} sts.

Cut yarn, leaving a 20" (51 cm) end. Thread yarn needle with end and weave through remaining sts, pulling firmly to close; sew seam *(Fig. A)*.

Add pom-pom.

Fig. A

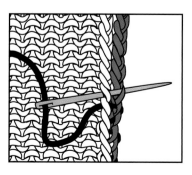

Design by Marion Graham.

FURRY & FUZZY SET

SCARF

Finished Size: 7" x 60" (18 cm x 152.5 cm)

MATERIALS

Bulky Weight Yarn: **5** BULKY
  300 yards (274 meters)
  16" (40.5 cm) Circular needle, size 11 (8 mm)
    or size needed for gauge
Markers

GAUGE: In Stockinette Stitch,
      8 sts and 16 rnds = 4" (10 cm)

SCARF

With Blue, cast on 30 sts, place marker to mark beginning of rnd **(see Markers and Knitting in the Round, pages 578 & 579).**

Rnds 1-6: Knit around.

Rnd 7: Purl around.

Rnd 8: Knit around.

Rnds 9-12: Repeat Rnds 7 and 8, 2 times.

Rnds 13-18: Knit around.

Repeat Rnds 7-18 until Scarf measures 59" (150 cm) from cast on edge, ending by working Rnd 18.

Bind off all sts in **knit**.

Matching sts sew each end closed.

TAM

Finished Brim Circumference:
18" (45.5 cm)

MATERIALS

Bulky Weight Yarn: **5** BULKY
  Blue - 75 yards (68.5 meters)
  White - 40 yards (36.5 meters)
Double pointed needles, size 8 (5 mm)
  (set of 5) **or** size needed for gauge
Markers

GAUGE: In Stockinette Stitch,
      12 sts and 20 rnds = 4" (10 cm)

BRIM

With Blue, cast on 54 sts. Divide sts evenly on 4 double pointed needles **(Fig. 3b, page 579)**, place marker to mark beginning of rnd **(Fig. 1, page 578)**.

Working in K1, P1 ribbing around until Brim measures 1 1/2" (4 cm) from cast on edge.

BODY

Increase Rnd: [K2, M1 **(Figs. 14a & b, page 582)**] around: 81 sts.

Work in Stockinette Stitch until Body measures 4 1/2" (11.5 cm) from Increase Rnd.

Instructions continued on page 300.

CROWN

Rnd 1: Decrease 6 sts evenly around *(see Decreasing Evenly in a Round, page 583)*: 75 sts.

Rnd 2: [K3, K2 tog *(Fig. 17, page 583)*] around: 60 sts.

Rnds 3-7: Knit around.

Rnd 8: (K2, K2 tog) around: 45 sts.

Rnds 9-13: Knit around.

Rnd 14: (K1, K2 tog) around: 30 sts.

Rnds 15-18: Knit around.

Rnd 19: K2 tog around: 15 sts.

Rnds 20-23: Knit around.

Rnd 24: K2 tog around to last 3 sts, K3 tog *(Fig. 23, page 584)*, cut yarn leaving a long end for weaving: 7 sts.

FINISHING

Weave yarn through remaining sts on Rnd 24, pull tightly and secure end.

POM-POM

With White, make Pom-pom *(Figs. 38a-c, page 588)*. Attach Pom-pom to top of Tam.

MUFF

Finished Size: 12" (30.5 cm) wide

MATERIALS
Bulky Weight Yarn:
    $4^1/_2$ ounces, 155 yards
    (130 grams, 141.5 meters)
Sport Weight Yarn:
    2 ounces, 185 yards
    (60 grams, 169 meters)
16" (40.5 cm) Circular needle, size 10 (6 mm)
or size needed for gauge
Markers
Yarn needle

Muff is worked holding one strand of each yarn together throughout.

GAUGE: In Stockinette Stitch,
    12 sts and 16 rnds = 4" (10 cm)

MUFF
Cast on 36 sts, place marker to mark beginning of rnd *(see Markers and Knitting in the Round, pages 578 & 579)*.

Knit each rnd until Muff measures 12" (30.5 cm) from cast on edge.

Next 2 Rnds: Knit around increasing 7 sts evenly around *(see Increasing Evenly Across a Round, page 581)*: 43 sts.

Knit each rnd until Muff measures $23^1/_2$" (59.5 cm).

Next 2 Rnds: Knit around decreasing 7 sts evenly around *(see Decreasing Evenly in a Round, page 583)*: 36 sts.

Bind off all sts in **knit**.

ASSEMBLY
With **wrong** side together, working in cast on edge and bind off edge, sew Muff together.

FUN SOCKS

Shown on page 303.

◀■■■▢ INTERMEDIATE

Size Note: Instructions are written for size Small with sizes Medium and Large in braces { }. Instructions will be easier to read if you circle all the numbers pertaining to your size. If only one number is given, it applies to all sizes.

FINISHED FOOT CIRCUMFERENCE

SMALL	MEDIUM	LARGE
7$\frac{1}{2}$"	8"	8$\frac{1}{2}$"

MATERIALS

SUPER FINE **1**

Fingering Weight Yarn:
  400 yards (366 meters)
Double pointed knitting needles, sizes
  1 (2.25 mm) **and** 2 (2.75 mm) (sets of 5) **or**
  sizes needed for gauge
Markers
Stitch holder
Tapesty needle

GAUGE: With smaller size needles,
    in Stockinette Stitch,
    28 sts and 36 rows = 4" (10 cm)

CUFF

With larger size needles cast on 52{56-60} sts. Divide sts evenly onto 4 double pointed needles *(Fig. 3b, page 579)*, place marker at beginning of round *(Fig. 1, page 578)*, join.

Work in K2, P2 ribbing for 2" (5 cm).

Knit each round until Cuff measures approximately 3$\frac{1}{4}${3$\frac{1}{2}$-3$\frac{3}{4}$}"/8.5{9-9.5} cm from cast on edge.

Changing to smaller size needles, knit each round until Cuff measures approximately 6$\frac{1}{2}${7-7$\frac{1}{2}$}"/16.5{18-19} cm, from cast on edge.

Slip last 26{28-30} sts worked on stitch holder to work Instep later: 26{28-30} sts.

HEEL FLAP

Row 1: (Slip 1 as if to **purl** WYB, K1) across working sts onto one needle.

Row 2: (Slip 1 as if to **purl** WYF, P1) across.

Repeat Rows 1 and 2 until Heel Flap measures approximately 2$\frac{3}{4}${3-3$\frac{1}{4}$}"/7{7.5-8.5} cm, ending by working Row 2.

TURN HEEL

Begin working in short rows as follows:

Row 1: Knit across to last 11 sts, SSK *(Figs. 21a-c, page 584)*, K1, **turn**, leave last 8 sts unworked: 17{19-21} sts.

Row 2 (Right side)**:** Slip 1, P6{8-10}, P2 tog *(Fig. 18, page 583)*, P1, **turn**: 8{10-12} sts.

Row 3: Slip 1, K7{9-11}, SSK, K1, **turn**: 9{11-13} sts.

Row 4: Slip 1, P8{10-12}, P2 tog, P1, **turn**: 10{12-14} sts.

Repeat Rows 3 and 4 adding one st before decrease until all Heel sts have been worked, ending by working **right** side row: 16{18-20} sts.

Instructions continued on page 302.

GUSSET

Knit 9{10-11} sts; place marker (this is now the end of rnd marker); with another needle, knit 9{10-11} sts, pick up 19{21-23} sts along edge of Heel Flap **(Fig. 34a, page 583)**, place marker, (with another needle, knit 14{16-18} sts of instep) twice; place marker, with another needle, pick up 19{21-23} sts along edge of Heel Flap, knit 9{10-11} sts: 79{88-97} sts.

Rnd 1: Knit around.

Rnd 2: Knit around to within 3 sts of first marker, K2 tog **(Fig. 17, page 583)**, K1, slip marker, knit to second marker, slip marker, K1, SSK, knit around.

Repeat Rnds 1 and 2 until 52{56-60} sts remain.

Note: Keep markers in place for Toe shaping.

FOOT

Work even knitting each round until Foot measures approximately 6$\frac{1}{2}${7$\frac{1}{2}$-8}"/16.5{19-20.5} cm from back of heel or 1$\frac{3}{4}${2-2}"/4.5{5-5} cm less than total desired Foot length from back of Heel.

TOE

Rnd 1: Knit around to within 3 sts of first marker, K2 tog, K1, slip marker, K1, SSK, knit around to within 3 sts of second marker, K2 tog, K1, slip marker, K1, SSK, knit around.

Rnd 2: Knit around.

Repeat Rnds 1 and 2 until 20 sts remain.

FINISHING

Knit across first 5 sts of rnd. 10 sts will be for the top of foot and 10 sts will be for the bottom of the foot. Graft remaining stitches together **(Fig. A and B)**.

GRAFTING

Stitches to be woven are held on two knitting needles, with one behind the other and wrong sides together. Threaded yarn needle should be on right side of work. Work in the following sequence, pulling yarn through as if to knit or as if to purl with even tension and keeping yarn under points of needles to avoid tangling and extra loops.

Step 1: Purl first stitch on front needle, leave on **(Fig. A)**.
Step 2: Knit first stitch on back needle, leave on **(Fig. B)**.
Step 3: Knit first stitch on front needle, slip off.
Step 4: Purl next stitch on front needle, leave on.
Step 5: Purl first stitch on back needle, slip off.
Step 6: Knit next stitch on back needle, leave on.

Repeat Steps 3-6 across until all stitches are worked off the needles.

Fig. A

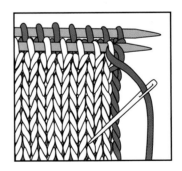

Fig. B

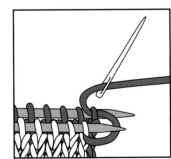

Self-striping yarn creates a unique pattern as you knit.

OPEN PETAL POSY

Make the first of what can become a bouquet of pretty Posies.

MATERIALS

Worsted Weight Acrylic Yarn: 4 MEDIUM
   7 yards (6.5 meters) for **each** Posy
Straight knitting needles, size 8 (5 mm)
Yarn needle

> Have some scrap pieces of yarn or paper clips ready to use as markers. Loop these around the stitches we tell you so that later you'll know which stitches to sew through to form the petals of your Posy.

Cast on 81 stitches.

Step 1: Bind off your first stitch **(Figs. 7a-c, page 14)** and place a marker **(see Fig. A)**.

Step 2: Bind off the next 16 stitches and place another marker. Continue binding off 16 stitches and placing markers until there are 15 stitches remaining on the left needle, then bind off the remaining stitches. Leaving an arm's length of yarn for sewing, cut the working yarn.

Thread a yarn needle with the long end. Fold the strip like a fan so that all the marked stitches are together **(see Fig. B)**. Inserting the needle in the first marked stitch, weave the needle and yarn through each marked stitch and through the last bound off stitch **(see Fig. C)**. Pull the yarn up tightly. Remove the markers. Knot the yarn ends together, and cut the yarn close to the project.

Fig. A

Fig. B

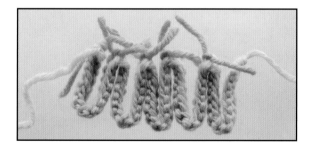

Fig. C

Project Ideas:

Pin, glue, or sew these colorful Posies on hats, bookbags, jackets, purses, shoes, scarves, or photo albums. Stitch or string the Posies together to use as a colorful lampshade trim or glue them to magnets for a special touch on the family fridge. Be sure to make plenty to share with friends!

DOG'S TOY BALL

You can make this toy using one strand of worsted weight yarn and size 8 needles. Follow the same basic ball pattern to make larger toys in more than one color. With the larger projects, you'll learn to knit with multiple strands of yarn held together while using a size 10 needle. Make one of each size and compare them when you're finished.

MATERIALS

MEDIUM 4

Worsted Weight Yarn:
    Small Ball - 24 yards (22 meters)
    Medium Ball - 32 yards
        (29.5 meters) **each** of 2 colors
        (We used 2 strands of the
        same color.)
    Large Ball - 36 yards (33 meters)
        each of 3 colors
Scrap yarn or polyester fiberfill for
    stuffing
Straight knitting needles:
    size 8 (5 mm) for Small Ball
    size 10 (6 mm) for Medium **and**
    Large Balls
Yarn needle

Basic Ball

Follow the instructions using one strand of yarn and the smaller size needles to make the Small Ball. After you're comfortable with the pattern and with working the increases and decreases, you can make the Medium Ball by holding two strands of yarn together and using the larger size needles. Treat the two strands of yarn as if you were knitting with one strand of yarn. The Large Ball is knit by holding three strands of yarn together and using the larger size needles.

Cast on 6 stitches (be sure you cast on **loosely** so you can increase easily in each stitch on Row 1).

ROW 1

Step 1: Knit the first stitch but do **not** slip it off the left needle **(see Fig. A)**.

Fig. A

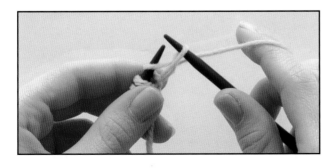

Step 2: Instead, knit into the **back** of the **same** stitch **(see Fig. B)**, then slip it off the left needle. You now have two stitches on the right needle and have made your first knit increase.

Fig. B

Step 3: Repeat Steps 1 and 2 to increase in each remaining stitch across the row: you'll now have 12 stitches.

Instructions continued on page 308.

Row 2: Purl each stitch across the row: you'll still have 12 stitches.

Row 3: Increase in each stitch across the row: you'll now have 24 stitches.

Row 4: Purl each stitch across the row: you'll still have 24 stitches.

Row 5: Increase in each stitch across the row: you'll now have 48 stitches.

Row 6: Purl each stitch across the row: you'll still have 48 stitches and should continue to have 48 stitches through Row 20.

Row 7: Knit each stitch across the row.

Row 8: Purl each stitch across the row.

Rows 9-20: Repeat Rows 7 and 8, 6 times.

Sometimes a set of parentheses will be followed by a direction, such as "across" or "across to the last 4 stitches," instead of a number. In these cases, you'll repeat the instructions inside the parentheses until you've finished the row or reached the number of stitches we say. Then, you'd be told how to work the remaining stitches.

Row 21: (Knit 2 stitches together) across the row **(Fig. 23, page 24)**: you'll now have 24 stitches.

Row 22: Purl each stitch across the row: you'll still have 24 stitches.

Row 23: (Knit 2 stitches together) across the row: you'll now have 12 stitches.

Row 24: Purl each stitch across the row: you'll still have 12 stitches.

Row 25: (Knit 2 stitches together) across the row; cut the working yarn leaving a long end for sewing: you'll now have 6 stitches.

Thread a yarn needle with the long end and weave it through the 6 stitches on the needle, removing the knitting needle and pulling the stitches closed tightly. Make a knot to secure the yarn. Do not remove the yarn needle and do not cut the yarn end.

Make the yarn stuffing: Using leftover yarn, wrap the yarn 18 times around 4 fingers of one hand twice. This is about 6 yards (5.5 meters) of yarn. Cut and set aside. Repeat this as many times as needed.

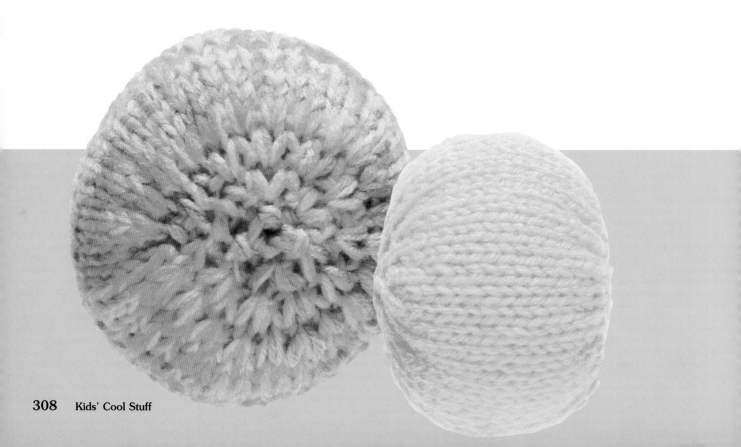

Weave the seam: With the **right** side of the piece facing you and the edges lined up, insert the needle under the bar between the first and second stitches on the row and pull the yarn through **(see Fig. C)**.

Fig. C

Insert the needle under the next bar on the second side. Repeat from side to side across **only** half of the seam, being careful to line up the rows and pulling the seam closed as you work.

Stuff the toy firmly with scrap yarn or polyester fiberfill.

Finish weaving the seam, stuffing the toy as you go. Weave the yarn end through the beginning 6 stitches; pull the yarn tightly to close and make a knot to secure the yarn. Insert the needle inside the ball and push it out the other side. Cut the yarn end close to the ball.

Shape the Ball with your hands like you are making a snowball.

Project Ideas:

Play with color combos and types of yarn to make balls with different patterns. When you are comfortable with this pattern and are creating these toys in no time, you may want to consider donating a few to a local veterinary clinic or animal rescue service.

LEG WARMERS

These Leg Warmers are great for active girls!

Finished Size: 26³/₄" (68 cm) long

MATERIALS

Worsted Weight Yarn: **MEDIUM 4**
  7¹/₂ ounces, 455 yards
    (210 grams, 416 meters)
Straight knitting needles, sizes 6
  (4 mm) **and** 8 (5 mm) **or** sizes
  needed for gauge **(see Gauge,
  page 576)**
Yarn needle

GAUGE: With larger size needles,
  in Stockinette Stitch,
  18 stitches and
  24 rows = 4" (10 cm)

Gauge Swatch: 4" (10 cm) square
With larger size needles, cast on
18 stitches.
Row 1 (Right side)**:** Knit each stitch
across.
Row 2: Purl each stitch across.
Rows 3-24: Repeat Rows 1 and 2, 11
times.
Bind off all stitches in **knit**.

LEG WARMER (Make 2)
UPPER CUFF
With larger size needles, cast on
44 stitches **loosely**.

Row 1: (Knit 1, purl 1) across: you'll have
22 knit stitches and 22 purl stitches.

Repeat Row 1 until Upper Cuff
measures 4" (10 cm).

BODY

Work in Stockinette Stitch (knit one row,
purl one row) until the piece measures
about 21" (53.5 cm) from the cast on
edge, ending by working a **purl** row.

SHAPING
Row 1: Knit 1, knit 2 stitches together
(Fig. 23, page 24), knit each stitch
across to the last 3 stitches, knit
2 stitches together, knit 1: you'll now have
42 stitches and should continue to have
42 stitches through Row 4.

Instructions continued on page 312.

Row 2: Purl each stitch across.

Row 3: Knit each stitch across.

Row 4: Purl each stitch across.

Row 5: Knit 1, knit 2 stitches together, knit each stitch across to the last 3 stitches, knit 2 stitches together, knit 1: you'll now have 40 stitches and should continue to have 40 stitches through Row 8.

Rows 6-8: Repeat Rows 2-4.

Row 9: Knit 1, knit 2 stitches together, knit each stitch across to the last 3 stitches, knit 2 stitches together, knit 1: you'll now have 38 stitches and should continue to have 38 stitches through Row 12.

Rows 10-12: Repeat Rows 2-4.

Row 13: Knit 1, knit 2 stitches together, knit each stitch across to the last 3 stitches, knit 2 stitches together, knit 1: you'll have 36 stitches and should continue to have 36 stitches through Row 16.

Rows 14-16: Repeat Rows 2-4.

LOWER CUFF
Begin using the smaller size needles.

Changing needle sizes is easy! Just work one row using one of the new size needles in your right hand; then you can start the next row using both of the new size needles.

Row 1: (Knit 1, purl 1) across: you'll have 18 knit stitches and 18 purl stitches.

Repeat Row 1 until Lower Cuff measures 3" (7.5 cm).

Bind off all stitches **loosely** in ribbing.

Since ribbing is made by alternating knit stitches with purl stitches, you should bind off in the same way – knit stitches are bound off in knit and purl stitches are bound off in purl.

FINISHING
Fold Leg Warmer lengthwise, with the **right** side facing you and the edges lined up. Weave the back seam **(Fig. C, page 309)**. Weave in the yarn ends.

Project Ideas:

Stripes are cool. Try your hand at combining scrap yarn for a pair of really funky Leg Warmers. Or make extra pairs to match your favorite winter outfits.

COZY HAND MITTS

Fingerless hand mitts are all the rage! They're quick and easy to knit, and they keep hands warm while allowing freer movement than traditional gloves or mittens.

MATERIALS

Worsted Weight Yarn: **MEDIUM 4**
  80 yards (73 meters)
  Straight knitting needles, sizes 8 (5 mm)
    or size needed for gauge
  Yarn needle

GAUGE: In Stockinette Stitch,
  18 stitches and
  24 rows = 4" (10 cm)

Gauge Swatch: 4" (10 cm) square
Cast on 18 stitches.
Row 1 (Right side)**:** Knit each stitch across.
Row 2: Purl each stitch across.
Rows 3-24: Repeat Rows 1 and 2, 11 times.
Bind off all stitches in knit.

MITT (Make 2)
WRIST RIBBING

Leaving a long end for sewing, cast on 32 stitches loosely.

Row 1: (Knit 2, purl 2) across. Repeat Row 1 until the ribbing measures 2" (5 cm).

BODY

Work in Stockinette Stitch (knit one row, purl one row) until the piece measures 4" (10 cm) from the cast on edge, ending by working a **purl** row.

PALM RIBBING

Row 1: (Knit 2, purl 2) across.

Repeat Row 1 until the ribbing measures 2" (5 cm).

Bind off all stitches in ribbing, leaving a long end for sewing.

FINISHING

Thread the yarn needle with the first long end. Fold the Mitt with the **right** side facing you and the edges lined up. Weave the Wrist Ribbing and the side of the Body for the first 2$\frac{1}{2}$" as follows:

Sew through **both** sides once to secure the seam. Insert the needle under the bar between the first and second stitches on the row and pull the yarn through **(Fig. A)**. Insert the needle under the next bar on the second side. Repeat from side to side, being careful to line up the rows and pulling the seam closed as you work. Weave in the yarn end. Thread the yarn needle with the second yarn end. Weave the Palm Ribbing and the side of Body for the last 2$\frac{1}{4}$", leaving a 1$\frac{1}{4}$" opening for your thumb. Weave in the yarn end.

Fig. A

SCARF

Size	Finished Measurement
Small	5½" x 43" (14 cm x 109 cm)
Medium	6½" x 46½" (16.5 cm x 118 cm)
Large	7¼" x 50" (18.5 cm x 127 cm)

Size Note: Instructions are written for size Small with sizes Medium and Large in braces { }. Instructions will be easier to read if you circle all the numbers pertaining to your size. If only one number is given, it applies to all sizes.

MATERIALS

Medium/Worsted Weight Yarn: **MEDIUM 4**
  4½{5½-7} ounces, 210{255-325} yards
  130{160-200} grams, 192{233-297} meters
Knitting needles, size 8 (5 mm) **or** size needed
  for gauge *(see Gauge, page 576)*
Stitch markers - 2
Yarn needle

GAUGE: In pattern, 17 stitches = 4" (10 cm);
  24 rows = 3" (7.5 cm)

Gauge Swatch: 4" wide x 3" high
(10 cm x 7.5 cm)
Cast on 17 stitches.
Work same as Body for 24 rows.
Bind off all stitches in **knit**.

BODY

Cast on 23{27-31} stitches.

Rows 1-8: Knit each stitch across the row.

Row 9: Knit 4 stitches, place a stitch marker on the right needle *(Fig. 1, page 578)*, purl each stitch across to the last 4 stitches, place a stitch marker on the right needle, knit the last 4 stitches.

Instructions continued on page 316.

Row 10 (Right side): Knit each stitch across the row, slipping the markers.

Row 11: Knit each stitch across to the first marker, purl each stitch across to the next marker, knit the last 4 stitches.

Rows 12-20: Knit each stitch across the row, slipping the markers.

Row 21: Knit each stitch across to the first marker, purl each stitch across to the next marker, knit the last 4 stitches.

Repeat Rows 10-21 for pattern until Scarf measures approximately 42{45¹/₂-49}"/106.5{115.5-124.5} cm from cast on edge, ending by working Row 11 and removing both markers on last row worked.

Last 8 Rows: Knit each stitch across the row.

Bind off all stitches in **knit**.

ELF HAT

Size	Finished Head Circumference
Small	16¹/₄" (41.5 cm)
Medium	17" (43 cm)
Large	18" (45.5 cm)

Size Note: Instructions are written for size Small with sizes Medium and Large in braces { }. Instructions will be easier to read if you circle all the numbers pertaining to your size. If only one number is given, it applies to all sizes.

MATERIALS
Medium/Worsted Weight Yarn:
3¹/₂{4-4¹/₂} ounces, 165{185-210} yards
100{110-130} grams, 151{169-192} meters
Knitting needles, size 8 (5 mm) **or** size needed for gauge (**see Gauge, page 576**)
Yarn needle

Note: Gauge is very important in this project (**see Gauge, page 576**).

GAUGE: In pattern, 17 stitches = 4" (10 cm); 24 rows = 3" (7.5 cm)

Gauge Swatch: 4" wide x 3" high (10 cm x 7.5 cm)
Cast on 17 stitches.
Work same as Body, page 318, for 24 rows.
Bind off all stitches in **knit**.

Instructions continued on page 318.

BODY

Cast on 69{73-77} stitches.

Rows 1-8: Knit each stitch across the row.

Row 9: Purl each stitch across the row.

Row 10 (Right side)**:** Knit each stitch across the row.

Row 11: Purl each stitch across the row.

Rows 12-20: Knit each stitch across the row.

Row 21: Purl each stitch across the row.

Row 22: Knit each stitch across the row.

Row 23: Purl each stitch across the row.

Rows 24-47: Repeat Rows 12-23 twice.

Rows 48-55: Knit each stitch across the row.

Row 56: Knit 8 stitches, knit 2 stitches together **(Fig. 23, page 24)**, ★ knit 11{12-13} stitches, knit 2 stitches together; repeat from ★ across to last 7 stitches, knit the last 7 stitches: you will now have 64{68-72} stitches.

Row 57: Purl each stitch across the row.

Row 58: Knit 7 stitches, knit 2 stitches together, ★ knit 10{11-12} stitches, knit 2 stitches together; repeat from ★ across to last 7 stitches, knit the last 7 stitches: you will now have 59{63-67} stitches.

Row 59: Purl each stitch across the row.

Rows 60-67: Knit each stitch across the row.

Row 68: Knit 6 stitches, knit 2 stitches together, ★ knit 9{10-11} stitches, knit 2 stitches together; repeat from ★ across to last 7 stitches, knit the last 7 stitches: you will now have 54{58-62} stitches.

Row 69: Purl each stitch across the row.

Row 70: Knit 6 stitches, knit 2 stitches together, ★ knit 8{9-10} stitches, knit 2 stitches together; repeat from ★ across to last 6 stitches, knit the last 6 stitches: you will now have 49{53-57} stitches.

Row 71: Purl each stitch across the row.

Rows 72-79: Knit each stitch across the row.

Row 80: Knit 5 stitches, knit 2 stitches together, ★ knit 7{8-9} stitches, knit 2 stitches together; repeat from ★ across to last 6 stitches, knit the last 6 stitches: you will now have 44{48-52} stitches.

Row 81: Purl each stitch across the row.

Row 82: Knit 5 stitches, knit 2 stitches together, ★ knit 6{7-8} stitches, knit 2 stitches together; repeat from ★ across to last 5 stitches, knit the last 5 stitches: you will now have 39{43-47} stitches.

Row 83: Purl each stitch across the row.

Rows 84-91: Knit each stitch across the row.

Row 92: Knit 4 stitches, knit 2 stitches together, ★ knit 5{6-7} stitches, knit 2 stitches together; repeat from ★ across to last 5 stitches, knit the last 5 stitches: you will now have 34{38-42} stitches.

Row 93: Purl each stitch across the row.

Row 94: Knit 4 stitches, knit 2 stitches together, ★ knit 4{5-6} stitches, knit 2 stitches together; repeat from ★ across to last 4 stitches, knit the last 4 stitches: you will now have 29{33-37} stitches.

Row 95: Purl each stitch across the row.

Rows 96-103: Knit each stitch across the row.

Row 104: Knit 3 stitches, knit 2 stitches together, ★ knit 3{4-5} stitches, knit 2 stitches together; repeat from ★ across to last 4 stitches, knit the last 4 stitches: you will now have 24{28-32} stitches.

Row 105: Purl each stitch across the row.

Row 106: Knit 3 stitches, knit 2 stitches together, ★ knit 2{3-4} stitches, knit 2 stitches together; repeat from ★ across to last 3 stitches, knit the last 3 stitches: you will now have 19{23-27} stitches.

Row 107: Purl each stitch across the row.

Rows 108-115: Knit each stitch across the row.

Row 116: Knit 2 stitches, knit 2 stitches together, ★ knit 1{2-3} stitch(es), knit 2 stitches together; repeat from ★ across to last 3 stitches, knit the last 3 stitches: you will now have 14{18-22} stitches.

Row 117: Purl each stitch across the row.

Instructions continued on page 320.

SIZE SMALL ONLY

Row 118: Knit 2 stitches together across the row: you will now have 7 stitches.

Row 119: Purl each stitch across the row.

Cut the working yarn, leaving a 36" (91.5 cm) end for sewing. See Finishing, page 321.

SIZE MEDIUM ONLY

Row 118: Knit 2 stitches, knit 2 stitches together, ★ knit 1 stitch, knit 2 stitches together; repeat from ★ across to last 2 stitches, knit the last 2 stitches: you will now have 13 stitches.

Row 119: Purl each stitch across the row.

Rows 120-127: Knit each stitch across the row.

Row 128: Knit 1 stitch, knit 2 stitches together across the row: you will now have 7 stitches.

Row 129: Purl each stitch across the row.

Cut the working yarn, leaving a 36" (91.5 cm) end for sewing. See Finishing, page 321.

SIZE LARGE ONLY

Row 118: Knit 2 stitches, ★ knit 2 stitches together, knit 2 stitches; repeat from ★ across: you will now have 17 stitches.

Row 119: Purl each stitch across the row.

Rows 120-127: Knit each stitch across the row.

Row 128: ★ Knit 1 stitch, knit 2 stitches together; repeat from ★ across to last 2 stitches, knit the last 2 stitches: you will now have 12 stitches.

Row 129: Purl each stitch across the row.

Row 130: Knit 2 stitches together across the row: you will now have 6 stitches.

Row 131: Purl each stitch across the row.

Cut the working yarn, leaving a 36" (91.5 cm) end for sewing. See Finishing, page 321.

FINISHING

Thread a yarn needle with the long end and **insert it through** the remaining stitches on the needle, removing the knitting needle. **Pull the yarn** tightly to close, then **make a knot** to secure the yarn. **Do not remove the yarn** needle and do not cut the yarn. **Weave the seam** *(Fig. 32, page 26)*. Once you get to the first row, make a knot to secure the yarn. **Hide the yarn end** by weaving through several inches in one direction **and then weaving back** in the opposite direction.

TASSEL

Cut a piece of cardboard 3" (7.5 cm) wide and as long as you want your finished tassel to be. Wind a double strand of yarn around the cardboard approximately 12 times. Cut an 18" (45.5 cm) length of yarn and insert it under all of the strands at the top of the cardboard; pull up **tightly** and tie securely. Leave the yarn ends long enough to attach the tassel. Cut the yarn at the opposite end of the cardboard and then remove it *(Fig. A)*. Cut a 6" (15 cm) length of yarn and wrap it **tightly** around the tassel twice, 1" (2.5 cm) below the top *(Fig. B)*; tie securely. Trim the ends.

Fig. A

Fig. B

TWISTED CORD

Cut one piece of yarn, 24" (61 cm) long or 3 times as long as the desired finished length. Insert one end through the top of the Tassel. Let someone hold one end with the Tassel near that end; twist the other end in the direction of the natural twist until it is **tight**. Bring the ends together, placing the Tassel at the folded end; let go of the Tassel and let the yarn twist around itself. Knot the end and attach it to the top of the Hat.

CITRUS VEST

INTERMEDIATE

BACK AND FRONT

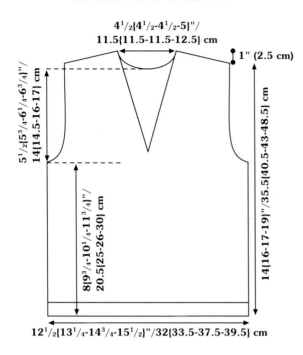

4¹/₂{4¹/₂-4¹/₂-5}"/
11.5{11.5-11.5-12.5} cm

1" (2.5 cm)

5¹/₂{5³/₄-6¹/₄-6³/₄}"/
14{14.5-16-17} cm

8{9³/₄-10¹/₄-11³/₄}"/
20.5{25-26-30} cm

14{16-17-19}"/35.5{40.5-43-48.5} cm

12¹/₂{13¹/₄-14³/₄-15¹/₂}"/32{33.5-37.5-39.5} cm

Note: Sweater width includes two edge stitches.

Size	Finished Chest Measurement	
2	24"	(61 cm)
4	25¾"	(65.5 cm)
6	28½"	(72.5 cm)
8	30¼"	(77 cm)

Size Note: Instructions are written for size 2 with sizes 4, 6, and 8 in braces { }. Instructions will be easier to read if you circle all the numbers pertaining to your child's size. If only one number is given, it applies to all sizes.

MATERIALS

Medium/worsted weight 100% cotton yarn:

Green

Ounces	4½{6-6½-8}	
Yards	220{295-315-390}	
Grams	130{170-180-230}	
Meters	201{270-288-357}	

Coral 1 ounce, 50 yards
(30 grams, 45.5 meters)
Yellow - ¾ ounce, 35 yards
(20 grams, 32 meters)
White - ¾ ounce, 35 yards
(20 grams, 32 meters)
Orange - ¾ ounce, 35 yards
(20 grams, 32 meters)
Straight knitting needles, size 7 (4.5 mm) **or** size needed for gauge
16" (40.5 cm) Circular needle, size 6 (4 mm)
Stitch holder
Markers - 2
Yarn needle

MEDIUM 4

GAUGE: With larger size needles, in Stockinette Stitch, 18 sts and 24 rows = 4" (10 cm)

BACK
RIBBING

With Coral and larger size needles, Slingshot cast on 56{60-66-70} sts **loosely (Figs. 2a-e, page 9)**; cut Coral.

With Green, work in K1, P1 ribbing for 6{6-10-10} rows.

Instructions continued on page 324.

BODY

Beginning with a **purl** row, work in Stockinette Stitch for 3 rows.

The edge stitch will be sewn into the seam and not be seen on the finished garment, so it is unnecessary to change colors for that stitch. Keeping this in mind, follow the Chart, beginning and ending at size indicated, and working the repeat across.

Work in Stockinette Stitch following Chart (see **Using Colors, pages 585 & 586)**, Rows 1-30.

With Green, work even until Back measures approximately 8{9¾-10¼-11¾}"/ 20.5{25-26-30} cm from cast on edge, ending by working a **purl** row.

ARMHOLE SHAPING

Rows 1 and 2: Bind off 3{4-4-5} sts, work across: 50{52-58-60} sts.

Rows 3 and 4: Bind off 2{2-3-3} sts, work across: 46{48-52-54} sts.

Row 5 (Decrease row)**:** K1, SSK **(Figs. 21a-c, page 584)**, knit across to last 3 sts, K2 tog **(Fig. 17, page 583)**, K1: 44{46-50-52} sts.

Row 6 (Decrease row)**:** P1, P2 tog **(Fig. 18, page 583)**, purl across to last 3 sts, P2 tog tbl **(Fig. 20, page 583)**, P1: 42{44-48-50} sts.

Continue to decrease one stitch at **each** edge, every other row, 1{1-2-2} time(s): 40{42-44-46} sts.

Work even until Back measures approximately 13½{15½-16½-18½}"/34.5{39.5-42-47} cm from cast on edge, ending by working a **purl** row.

NECK SHAPING

Both sides of Neck are worked at the same time, using separate yarn for **each** side.

Row 1: Knit 12{13-14-14} sts, slip next 16{16-16-18} sts onto st holder; with second yarn, knit across: 12{13-14-14} sts **each** side.

Row 2: Purl across to within 3 sts of Neck edge, P2 tog tbl, P1; with second yarn, P1, P2 tog, purl across: 11{12-13-13} sts **each** side.

Row 3: Knit across to within 3 sts of Neck edge, K2 tog, K1; with second yarn, K1, SSK, knit across: 10{11-12-12} sts **each** side.

Row 4: Purl across; with second yarn, purl across.

SHOULDER SHAPING

Rows 1-4: Bind off 3{4-4-4} sts at Armhole edge, work across; with second yarn, work across: 4{3-4-4} sts **each** side.

Row 5: Bind off remaining sts on first side; with second yarn, knit across.

Bind off remaining sts.

CHART

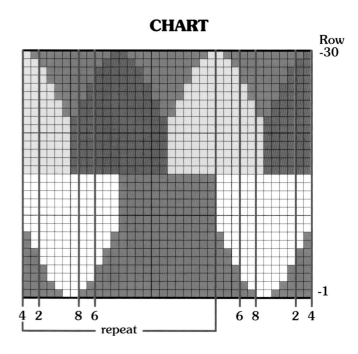

Row -30

4 2   8 6   6 8   2 4
|_____ repeat _____|

-1

KEY

■ Green   □ White
■ Coral   ■ Orange
■ Yellow

FRONT

Work same as Back to Armhole Shaping, ending by working a **purl** row.

ARMHOLE & NECK SHAPING

Rows 1 and 2: Bind off 3{4-4-5} sts, work across: 50{52-58-60} sts.

Both sides of Neck are worked at the same time, using separate yarn for **each** side.

Row 3: Bind off 2{2-3-3} sts, K 22{23-25-26} sts; with second yarn, knit across.

Row 4: Bind off 2{2-3-3} sts, purl across to within 3 sts of Neck edge, P2 tog tbl, P1; with second yarn, P1, P2 tog, purl across: 22{23-25-26} sts **each** side.

Row 5: K1, SSK, knit across; with second yarn, knit across to last 3 sts, K2 tog, K1: 21{22-24-25} sts **each** side.

Row 6 (Decrease row)**:** P1, P2 tog, purl across to within 3 sts of Neck edge, P2 tog tbl, P1; with second yarn, P1, P2 tog, purl across to last 3 sts, P2 tog tbl, P1: 19{20-22-23} sts **each** side.

Row 7: Knit across; with second yarn, knit across.

Rows 8 thru 9{9-11-11}: Repeat Rows 6 and 7, 1{1-2-2} time(s): 17{18-18-19} sts **each** side.

Continue to decrease one stitch at **each** Neck edge, every other row, 3{2-0-0} times **more (see Zeros, page 577)**; then decrease every fourth row, 4{5-6-7} times: 10{11-12-12} sts **each** side.

Work even until Front measures same as Back to Shoulder Shaping, ending by working a **purl** row.

SHOULDER SHAPING

Work same as Back.

FINISHING

Sew shoulder seams **(Figs. 35a & b, page 587)**.

NECK RIBBING

With **right** side facing, using Green and circular needle, pick up 36{38-40-42} sts evenly spaced along left Neck edge **(Fig. 34a, page 586)**, place marker **(Fig. 1, page 578)**, pick up 36{38-40-42} sts evenly spaced along right Neck edge, slip 16{16-16-18} sts from Back st holder onto second end of circular needle and knit across, place marker to mark beginning of rnd: 88{92-96-102} sts.

Rnd 1 (Decrease rnd)**:** (K1, P1) across to within 2 sts of next marker, K2 tog, slip marker, SSK, (P1, K1) around: 86{90-94-100} sts.

Rnds 2-5 (Decrease rnd)**:** Work in established ribbing to within 2 sts of next marker, K2 tog, slip marker, SSK, work in established ribbing around: 78{82-86-92} sts.

Cut Green; with Coral, bind off all sts **loosely** in ribbing.

Weave side seams **(Fig. 36, page 587)**.

ARMHOLE RIBBING

With **right** side facing, using Green and circular needle, and beginning at side seam, pick up 58{64-68-78} sts evenly spaced around entire Armhole edge, place marker to mark beginning of rnd.

Work in K1, P1 ribbing for ¾" (2 cm); cut Green.

With Coral, bind off all sts **loosely** in ribbing.

Repeat around second Armhole.

Design by Melissa Leapman.

TRIANGLES PULLOVER

◀▬▬▬▭ INTERMEDIATE

BACK AND FRONT

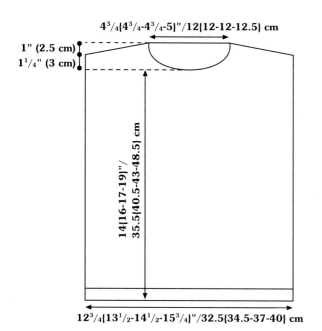

4³/₄{4³/₄-4³/₄-5}"/12{12-12-12.5} cm

1" (2.5 cm)
1¹/₄" (3 cm)

14{16-17-19}"/35.5{40.5-43-48.5} cm

12³/₄{13¹/₂-14¹/₂-15³/₄}"/32.5{34.5-37-40} cm

SLEEVE

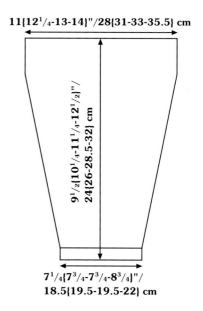

11{12¹/₄-13-14}"/28{31-33-35.5} cm

9¹/₂{10¹/₄-11¹/₄-12¹/₂}"/24{26-28.5-32} cm

7¹/₄{7³/₄-7³/₄-8³/₄}"/18.5{19.5-19.5-22} cm

Note: Sweater width includes two edge stitches.

Size	Finished Chest Measurement	
2	24½"	(62 cm)
4	26¼"	(66.5 cm)
6	28"	(71 cm)
8	30¾"	(78 cm)

Size Note: Instructions are written for size 2 with sizes 4, 6, and 8 in braces { }. Instructions will be easier to read if you circle all the numbers pertaining to your child's size. If only one number is given, it applies to all sizes.

MATERIALS

Medium/worsted weight 100% cotton yarn: **MEDIUM 4**

White

Ounces	9{10¼-11-12}
Yards	440{500-535-585}
Grams	260{290-310-340}
Meters	402{457-489-535}

Green

Ounces	1¾{2-2-2½}
Yards	85{100-100-110}
Grams	50{60-60-65}
Meters	77.5{91-91-101}

Yellow, Red, **and** Purple **each**

Ounces	1½{1¾-1¾-2}
Yards	75{85-85-100}
Grams	40{50-50-60}
Meters	68.5{77.5-77.5-91}

Straight knitting needles, size 7 (4.5 mm) **or** size needed for gauge
16" (40.5 cm) Circular needle, size 6 (4 mm)
Stitch holders - 2
Marker
Yarn needle

GAUGE: With larger size needles, in Stockinette Stitch, 18 sts and 24 rows = 4" (10 cm)

Instructions begin on page 328.

BACK
RIBBING

With Green and larger size needles, Slingshot cast on 57{61-65-71} sts **loosely** *(Figs. 2a-e, page 9)*; cut Green.

Row 1: With White, K1, (P1, K1) across.

Row 2: P1, (K1, P1) across.

Rows 3 thru 6{6-10-10}: Repeat Rows 1 and 2, 2{2-4-4} times.

BODY

Beginning with a **purl** row, work in Stockinette Stitch following Chart *(see Using Colors, pages 585 & 586)* until Back measures approximately 14{16-17-19}"/35.5{40.5-43-48.5} cm from cast on edge, ending by working a **purl** row.

> The edge stitch will be sewn into the seam and not be seen on the finished garment, so it is unnecessary to change colors for that stitch. Keeping this in mind, follow the Chart, beginning and ending at size indicated, and working the repeat across.

SHOULDER SHAPING

> Maintain established Chart pattern throughout.

Rows 1-4: Bind off 6{7-7-8} sts, work across: 33{33-37-39} sts.

Rows 5 and 6: Bind off 6{6-8-8} sts, work across: 21{21-21-23} sts.

Slip remaining sts onto st holder.

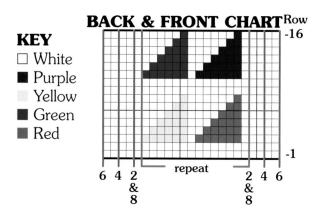

BACK & FRONT CHART

KEY
- □ White
- ■ Purple
- ░ Yellow
- ■ Green
- ■ Red

Row -16

-1

6 4 2
&
8

repeat

2 4 6
&
8

FRONT

Work same as Back until Front measures 8 rows less than Back to Shoulder Shaping, ending by working a **purl** row.

NECK SHAPING

> Both sides of Neck are worked at the same time, using separate yarn for **each** side. Maintain established Chart pattern throughout.

Row 1: Knit 23{25-27-29} sts, slip next 11{11-11-13} sts onto st holder; with second yarn, knit across: 23{25-27-29} sts **each** side.

Row 2 (Decrease row): Purl across to within 3 sts of Neck edge, P2 tog tbl *(Fig. 20, page 583)*, P1; with second yarn, P1, P2 tog *(Fig. 18, page 583)*, purl across: 22{24-26-28} sts **each** side.

Row 3 (Decrease row): Knit across to within 3 sts of Neck edge, K2 tog *(Fig. 17, page 583)*, K1; with second yarn, K1, SSK *(Figs. 21a-c, page 584)*, knit across: 21{23-25-27} sts **each** side.

Rows 4 and 5: Repeat Rows 2 and 3: 19{21-23-25} sts **each** side.

Row 6: Purl across; with second yarn, purl across.

Row 7: Repeat Row 3: 18{20-22-24} sts **each** side.

Row 8: Purl across; with second yarn, purl across.

SHOULDER SHAPING

Rows 1-4: Bind off 6{7-7-8} sts at Armhole edge, work across; with second yarn, work across: 6{6-8-8} sts **each** side.

Row 5: Bind off remaining sts on first side; with second yarn, knit across.

Bind off remaining sts.

SLEEVE (Make 2)
RIBBING

With Green and larger size needles, Slingshot cast on 33{35-35-39} sts **loosely**; cut Green.

Row 1: With White, K1, (P1, K1) across.

Row 2: P1, (K1, P1) across.

Rows 3 thru 6{6-10-10}: Repeat Rows 1 and 2, 2{2-4-4} times.

BODY

Beginning with a **purl** row, work in Stockinette Stitch following Chart and AT THE SAME TIME increase one stitch at **each** edge *(see Increases, page 581)*, working each new stitch in pattern, every fourth row, 2{7-11-6} times; then increase every sixth row, 6{3-1-6} time(s): 49{55-59-63} sts.

Work even until Sleeve measures approximately 9½{10¼-11¼-12½}"/24{26-28.5-32} cm from cast on edge, ending by working a **purl** row.

Bind off all sts in **knit**.

SLEEVE CHART

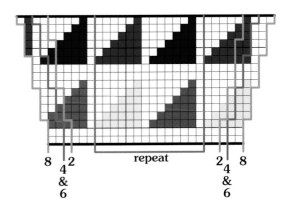

8 2
 4
 &
 6

repeat

2 8
4
&
6

KEY
- □ White
- ■ Green
- ■ Purple
- ■ Red
- ▨ Yellow

FINISHING

Sew shoulder seams *(Figs. 35a & b, page 587)*.

NECK RIBBING

With **right** side facing and White, slip 21{21-21-23} sts from Back st holder onto circular needle and knit across, pick up 13 sts evenly spaced along left Front Neck edge *(Figs. 34a & b, page 586)*, slip 11{11-11-13} sts from Front st holder onto second end of circular needle and knit across, pick up 13 sts evenly spaced along right Front Neck edge, place marker to mark beginning of rnd *(Fig. 1, page 578)*: 58{58-58-62} sts.

Work in K1, P1 ribbing around for ¾" (2 cm); cut White.

With Green, bind off all sts **loosely** in ribbing.

Sew Sleeves to Sweater, matching center of last row on Sleeve to shoulder seam and beginning 5½{6-6½-7}"/14{15-16.5-18} cm down from seam.

Weave underarm and side in one continuous seam *(Fig. 36, page 587)*.

Design by Melissa Leapman.

STRIPES & BLOCKS PULLOVER
◼◼◼◻ INTERMEDIATE

BACK AND FRONT

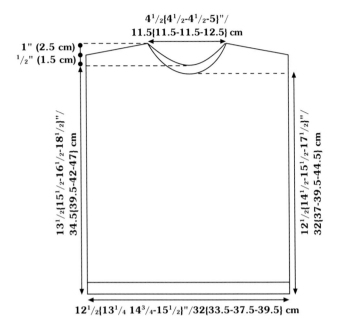

4¹/₂{4¹/₂-4¹/₂-5}"/
11.5{11.5-11.5-12.5} cm

1" (2.5 cm)
¹/₂" (1.5 cm)

13¹/₂{15¹/₂-16¹/₂-18¹/₂}"/
34.5{39.5-42-47} cm

12¹/₂{14¹/₂-15¹/₂-17¹/₂}"/
32{37-39.5-44.5} cm

12¹/₂{13¹/₄ 14³/₄-15¹/₂}"/32{33.5-37.5-39.5} cm

SLEEVE

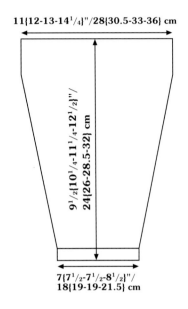

11{12-13-14¹/₄}"/28{30.5-33-36} cm

9¹/₂{10¹/₄-11¹/₄-12¹/₂}"/
24{26-28.5-32} cm

7{7¹/₂-7¹/₂-8¹/₂}"/
18{19-19-21.5} cm

Note: Sweater width includes two edge stitches.

Size	Finished Chest Measurement	
2	24"	(61 cm)
4	25¾"	(65.5 cm)
6	28½"	(72.5 cm)
8	30¼"	(77 cm)

Size Note: Instructions are written for size 2 with sizes 4, 6, and 8 in braces { }. Instructions will be easier to read if you circle all the numbers pertaining to your child's size. If only one number is given, it applies to all sizes.

MATERIALS
Medium/worsted weight 100% cotton yarn:
MEDIUM 4

Coral
- Ounces 2¾{3-3¼-3½}
- Yards 135{145-160-170}
- Grams 80{90-95-100}
- Meters 123{133-146-155}

Yellow
- Ounces 2½{2¾-3-3¼}
- Yards 120{135-145-160}
- Gram 70{80-90-95}
- Meters 110{123-133-146}

Green
- Ounces 2½{2¾-3-3¼}
- Yards 120{135-145-160}
- Grams 70{80-90-95}
- Meters 110{123-133-146}

Orange
- Ounces 2½{2¾-3-3¼}
- Yards 120{135-145-160}
- Grams 70{80-90-95}
- Meters 110{123-133-146}

White
- Ounces 1½{1¾-2½-2¾}
- Yards 75{85-120-135}
- Grams 40{50-70-80}
- Meters 68.5{77.5-110-123}

Straight knitting needles, size 7 (4.5 mm) **or** size needed for gauge
16" (40.5 cm) Circular needle, size 6 (4 mm)
Stitch holders - 2
Marker
Yarn needle

GAUGE: With larger size needles, in Stockinette Stitch, 18 sts and 24 rows = 4" (10 cm)

Instructions begin on page 332.

BACK
RIBBING

With Coral and larger size needles, Slingshot cast on 56{60-66-70} sts **loosely** *(Figs. 2a-e, page 9)*; cut Coral.

With White, work in K1, P1 ribbing for 6{6-10-10} rows; at end of last row, cut White.

BODY

Row 1: With Yellow, purl 28{30-33-35} sts, drop Yellow; with Coral *(Fig. 30, page 585)*, purl across.

Work in Stockinette Stitch in established colors until Back measures approximately 8¼{9¼-10-11}"/ 21{23.5-25.5-28} cm from cast on edge, ending by working a **purl** row; cut Coral and Yellow.

Next Row: With Green, knit 28{30-33-35} sts, drop Green; with Orange, knit across.

Work in Stockinette Stitch in established colors until Back measures approximately 13½{15½-16½-18½}"/34.5{39.5-42-47} cm from cast on edge, ending by working a **purl** row; cut Orange.

NECK SHAPING

Both sides of Neck are worked at the same time, using separate yarn for **each** side. Maintain established color pattern throughout.

Row 1: Knit 20{22-25-26} sts, slip next 16{16-16-18} sts onto st holder; with Orange, knit across: 20{22-25-26} sts **each** side.

Row 2: Purl across to within 3 sts of Neck edge, P2 tog tbl *(Fig. 20, page 583)*, P1; with second yarn, P1, P2 tog *(Fig. 18, page 583)*, purl across: 19{21-24-25} sts **each** side.

Row 3: Knit across to within 3 sts of Neck edge, K2 tog *(Fig. 17, page 583)*, K1; with second yarn, K1, SSK *(Figs. 21a-c, page 584)*, knit across: 18{20-23-24} sts **each** side.

SHOULDER SHAPING

Rows 1-4: Bind off 6{7-8-8} sts at Armhole edge, work across; with second yarn, work across: 6{6-7-8} sts **each** side.

Row 5: Bind off remaining sts on first side; with second yarn, purl across.

Bind off remaining sts.

FRONT

Work same as Back until Front measures 6 rows less than Back to Neck Shaping, ending by working a **purl** row; cut Orange.

NECK SHAPING

Both sides of Neck are worked at the same time, using separate yarn for **each** side. Maintain established color pattern throughout.

Row 1: Knit 23{25-28-29} sts, slip next 10{10-10-12} sts onto st holder; with Orange, knit across: 23{25-28-29} sts **each** side.

Row 2: Purl across to within 3 sts of Neck edge, P2 tog tbl, P1; with second yarn, P1, P2 tog, purl across: 22{24-27-28} sts **each** side.

Row 3: Knit across to within 3 sts of Neck edge, K2 tog, K1; with second yarn, K1, SSK, knit across: 21{23-26-27} sts **each** side.

Row 4 (Decrease row)**:** Purl across to within 3 sts of Neck edge, P2 tog tbl, P1; with second yarn, P1, P2 tog, purl across: 20{22-25-26} sts **each** side.

Row 5: Knit across; with second yarn, knit across.

Rows 6-9: Repeat Rows 4 and 5 twice: 18{20-23-24} sts **each** side.

SHOULDER SHAPING

Work same as Back.

LEFT SLEEVE
RIBBING

With Green and larger size needles, Slingshot cast on 32{34-34-38} sts **loosely**; cut Green.

With White, work in K1, P1 ribbing for 6{6-10-10} rows; at end of last row, cut White.

BODY

With Orange and beginning with a **purl** row, work in Stockinette Stitch, alternating 6 rows of Orange with 6 rows of Yellow and AT THE SAME TIME increase one stitch at **each** edge *(see Increases, page 581)*, every fourth row, 6{7-11-11} times; then increase every sixth row, 3{3-1-2} time(s): 50{54-58-64} sts.

Work even until Sleeve measures approximately 9½{10¼-11¼-12½}"/24{26-28.5-32} cm from cast on edge, ending by working a **purl** row.

Bind off all sts in **knit**.

RIGHT SLEEVE
RIBBING

With Orange and larger size needles, Slingshot cast on 32{34-34-38} sts **loosely**; cut Orange.

With White, work in K1, P1 ribbing for 6{6-10-10} rows; at end of last row, cut White.

BODY

With Green and beginning with a **purl** row, work in Stockinette Stitch, alternating 6 rows of Green with 6 rows of Coral and AT THE SAME TIME increase one stitch at **each** edge, every fourth row, 6{7-11-11} times; then increase every sixth row, 3{3-1-2} time(s): 50{54-58-64} sts.

Work even until Sleeve measures approximately 9½{10¼-11¼-12½}"/24{26-28.5-32} cm from cast on edge, ending by working a **purl** row.

Bind off all sts in **knit**.

FINISHING

Sew shoulder seams *(Figs. 35a & b, page 587)*.

NECK EDGING

With **right** side facing and White, slip 16{16-16-18} sts from Back st holder onto circular needle and knit across, pick up 19 sts evenly spaced along left Neck edge *(Fig. 34a, page 586)*, slip 10{10-10-12} sts from Front st holder onto second end of circular needle and knit across, pick up 19 sts evenly spaced along right Neck edge, place marker to mark beginning of rnd *(Fig. 1, page 578)*: 64{64-64-68} sts.

FOR ROLLED EDGE OPTION

Work in K1, P1 ribbing for 2 rounds; cut White.

With Coral, knit 4 rounds.

Bind off all sts **loosely** in **knit**.

FOR RIBBING OPTION

Work in K1, P1 ribbing around for ¾" (2 cm); cut White.

With Coral, bind off all sts **loosely** in ribbing.

Sew Sleeves to Sweater, matching center of last row on Sleeve to shoulder seam and beginning 5½{6-6½-7}"/14{15-16.5-18} cm down from seam.

Weave underarm and side in one continuous seam *(Fig. 36, page 587)*.

Design by Melissa Leapman.

BRIGHT STRIPES CARDIGAN

■■■□ INTERMEDIATE

BACK

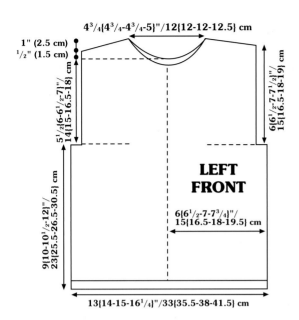

4³/₄{4³/₄-4³/₄-5}"/12{12-12-12.5} cm

1" (2.5 cm)
¹/₂" (1.5 cm)

5¹/₂{6-6¹/₂-7}"/14{15-16.5-18} cm

6{6¹/₂-7-7¹/₂}"/15{16.5-18-19} cm

9{10-10¹/₂-12}"/23{25.5-26.5-30.5} cm

LEFT FRONT

6{6¹/₂-7-7³/₄}"/15{16.5-18-19.5} cm

13{14-15-16¹/₄}"/33{35.5-38-41.5} cm

SLEEVE

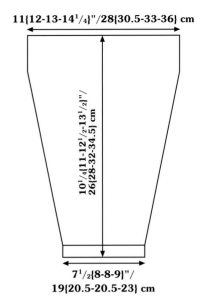

11{12-13-14¹/₄}"/28{30.5-33-36} cm

10¹/₄{11-12-13¹/₂}"/26{28-32-34.5} cm

7¹/₂{8-8-9}"/19{20.5-20.5-23} cm

Note: Sweater width includes two edge stitches.

Size	Finished Chest Measurement	
2	25¹/₄"	(64 cm)
4	27"	(68.5 cm)
6	28³/₄"	(73 cm)
8	32"	(81.5 cm)

Size Note: Instructions are written for size 2 with sizes 4, 6, and 8 in braces { }. Instructions will be easier to read if you circle all the numbers pertaining to your child's size. If only one number is given, it applies to all sizes.

MATERIALS

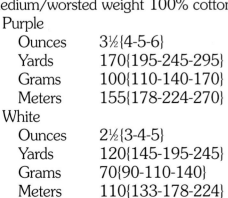

MEDIUM
4

Medium/worsted weight 100% cotton yarn:

Purple
Ounces	3¹/₂{4-5-6}	
Yards	170{195-245-295}	
Grams	100{110-140-170}	
Meters	155{178-224-270}	

White
Ounces	2¹/₂{3-4-5}
Yards	120{145-195-245}
Grams	70{90-110-140}
Meters	110{133-178-224}

Yellow
Ounces	2{2¹/₂-3-3¹/₂}
Yards	100{120-145-170}
Grams	60{70-90-100}
Meters	91{110-133-155}

Red
Ounces	2{2¹/₄-2³/₄-3³/₄}
Yards	100{110-135-160}
Grams	60{65-80-95}
Meters	91{101-123-146}

Green
Ounce(s)	1{1¹/₄-1¹/₄-1¹/₂}
Yards	50{60-60-75}
Grams	30{35-35-40}
Meters	45.5{55-55-68.5}

Straight knitting needles, size 7 (4.5 mm) **or** size needed for gauge
16" (40.5 cm) Circular needle, size 6 (4 mm)
Stitch holder
Markers
³/₄" (19 mm) Buttons - 6
Yarn needle

GAUGE: With larger size needles, in Stockinette Stitch, 18 sts and 24 rows = 4" (10 cm)

Instructions begin on page 336.

STRIPE SEQUENCE

BACK
RIBBING

With Yellow and larger size needles, Slingshot cast on 59{63-67-73} sts **loosely** *(Figs. 2a-e, page 9)*; cut Yellow.

Row 1: With Purple, K1, (P1, K1) across.

Row 2: P1, (K1, P1) across.

Rows 3 thru 6{6-10-10}: Repeat Rows 1 and 2, 2{2-4-4} times; at end of last row, cut Purple.

BODY

With Red and beginning with a **purl** row, work in Stockinette Stitch in Stripe Sequence until Back measures approximately 9{10-10½-12}"/ 23{25.5-26.5-30.5} cm from cast on edge, ending by working a **purl** row.

ARMHOLE SHAPING

Maintain established Stripe Sequence throughout.

Rows 1 and 2: Bind off 5{5-6-6} sts, work across: 49{53-55-61} sts.

Work even until Back measures approximately 14½{16-17-19}"/37{40.5-43-48.5} cm from cast on edge, ending by working a **purl** row.

NECK SHAPING

Both sides of Neck are worked at the same time, using separate yarn for **each** side.

Row 1: Knit 16{18-19-21} sts, slip next 17{17-17-19} sts onto st holder; with second yarn, knit across: 16{18-19-21} sts **each** side.

Row 2: Purl across to within 3 sts of Neck edge, P2 tog tbl *(Fig. 20, page 583)*, P1; with second yarn, P1, P2 tog *(Fig. 18, page 583)*, purl across: 15{17-18-20} sts **each** side.

Row 3: Knit across to within 3 sts of Neck edge, K2 tog *(Fig. 17, page 583)*, K1; with second yarn, K1, SSK *(Figs. 21a-c, page 584)*, knit across: 14{16-17-19} sts **each** side.

SHOULDER SHAPING

Rows 1-4: Bind off 5{5-6-6} sts at Armhole edge, work across; with second yarn, work across: 4{6-5-7} sts **each** side.

Row 5: Bind off remaining sts on first side; with second yarn, purl across.

Bind off remaining sts.

LEFT FRONT
RIBBING

With Yellow and larger size needles, Slingshot cast on 27{29-31-35} sts **loosely**; cut Yellow.

Row 1: With Purple, P1, (K1, P1) across.

Row 2: K1, (P1, K1) across.

Rows 3 thru 6{6-10-10}: Repeat Rows 1 and 2, 2{2-4-4} times; at end of last row, cut Purple.

BODY

With Red and beginning with a **purl** row, work in Stockinette Stitch in Stripe Sequence until Left Front measures same as Back to Armhole Shaping, ending by working a **purl** row.

ARMHOLE SHAPING

Maintain established Stripe Sequence throughout.

Row 1: Bind off 5{5-6-6} sts, knit across: 22{24-25-29} sts.

Work even until Left Front measures 3 rows less than Back to Neck Shaping, ending by working a **knit** row.

NECK SHAPING

Row 1: Bind off 3{3-3-4} sts, purl across: 19{21-22-25} sts.

Row 2: Knit across.

Row 3: Bind off 3{3-3-4} sts, purl across: 16{18-19-21} sts.

Row 4: Knit across to within 3 sts of Neck edge, K2 tog, K1: 15{17-18-20} sts.

Row 5: P1, P2 tog, purl across: 14{16-17-19} sts.

Rows 6 and 7: Work across.

SHOULDER SHAPING

Row 1: Bind off 5{5-6-6} sts, knit across: 9{11-11-13} sts.

Row 2: Purl across.

Row 3: Bind off 5{5-6-6} sts, knit across: 4{6-5-7} sts.

Row 4: Purl across.

Bind off remaining sts.

RIGHT FRONT

Work same as Left Front to Armhole Shaping, ending by working a **knit** row.

ARMHOLE SHAPING

Maintain established Stripe Sequence throughout.

Row 1: Bind off 5{5-6-6} sts, purl across: 22{24-25-29} sts.

Work even until Right Front measures 4 rows less than Back to Neck Shaping, ending by working a **purl** row.

NECK SHAPING

Row 1: Bind off 3{3-3-4} sts, knit across: 19{21-22-25} sts.

Row 2: Purl across.

Row 3: Bind off 3{3-3-4} sts, knit across: 16{18-19-21} sts.

Row 4: Purl across to within 3 sts of Neck edge, P2 tog tbl, P1: 15{17-18-20} sts.

Row 5: K1, SSK, knit across: 14{16-17-19} sts.

Rows 6 and 7: Work across.

Instructions continued on page 338.

SHOULDER SHAPING

Row 1: Bind off 5{5-6-6} sts, purl across: 9{11-11-13} sts.

Row 2: Knit across.

Row 3: Bind off 5{5-6-6} sts, purl across: 4{6-5-7} sts.

Row 4: Knit across.

Bind off remaining sts.

SLEEVE (Make 2)
RIBBING

With Yellow and larger size needles, Slingshot cast on 34{36-36-40} sts **loosely**; cut Yellow.

With Purple, work in K1, P1 ribbing for 6{6-10-10} rows; at end of last row, cut Purple.

BODY

With Red and beginning with a **purl** row, work in Stockinette Stitch, in Stripe Sequence, increasing one stitch at **each** edge *(see Increases, page 581)*, every fourth row, 1{2-5-5} time(s); then increase every sixth row, 7{7-6-7} times: 50{54-58-64} sts.

Work even until Sleeve measures approximately 10¼{11-12½-13½}"/26{28-32-34.5} cm from cast on edge, ending by working a **purl** row.

Bind off all sts in **knit**.

FINISHING

Sew shoulder seams *(Figs. 35a & b, page 587)*.

BUTTON BAND

With **right** side facing, using Purple and circular needle, pick up 72{80-86-94} sts evenly spaced across Left Front edge for Girl's and Right Front edge for Boy's *(Fig. 34a, page 586)*.

Girl's Only - Rows 1-5: (P1, K1) across.

Boy's Only - Rows 1-5: (K1, P1) across.

Cut Purple; with Yellow, bind off all sts in ribbing.

BUTTONHOLE BAND

With **right** side facing, using Purple and circular needle, pick up 72{80-86-94} sts evenly spaced across remaining Front edge.

Girl's Only - Rows 1 and 2: (K1, P1) across.

Boy's Only - Rows 1 and 2: (P1, K1) across.

Mark placement of buttonholes, placing first marker in fifth stitch from bottom edge. Evenly space four more markers for remaining buttons, remembering that last button will go on Neck Band.

Row 3 (Buttonhole row): ★ Work in established ribbing across to next marker, remove marker, bind off next 2 sts in pattern; repeat from ★ 4 times **more**, work in established ribbing across.

Row 4: ★ Work in established ribbing across to bound off sts, **turn**; add on 2 sts *(Figs. 5a & b, page 580)*, **turn**; repeat from ★ 4 times **more**, work across in established ribbing.

Row 5: Work across in established ribbing.

Cut Purple; with Yellow, bind off all sts in ribbing.

NECK RIBBING

With **right** side facing, using Purple and circular needle, pick up 30{30-30-32} sts evenly spaced along Right Neck edge *(Figs. 34a & b, page 386)*, slip 17{17-17-19} sts from Back st holder onto second end of circular needle and knit across, pick up 30{30-30-32} sts evenly spaced along Left Neck edge: 77{77-77-83} sts.

Row 1: P1, (K1, P1) across.

Row 2: K1, (P1, K1) across.

Girl's Only - Row 3 (Buttonhole row): Work in established ribbing across to last 4 sts, bind off next 2 sts in pattern, P1.

Boy's Only - Row 3 (Buttonhole row): P1, K1, bind off next 2 sts in pattern, work in established ribbing across.

Row 4: Work in established ribbing across to bound off sts, **turn**; add on 2 sts, **turn**; work in established ribbing across.

Row 5: P1, (K1, P1) across.

Cut Purple; with Yellow, bind off all sts in ribbing.

Matching center of last row on Sleeve to shoulder seam, sew top of Sleeve along Armhole edge and sides of Sleeve to bound off edges *(see Diagram, page 587)*.

Weave underarm and side in one continuous seam *(Fig. 36, page 587)*.

Sew buttons to Button Band opposite buttonholes.

Design by Melissa Leapman.

SPORTY HOODED PULLOVER  INTERMEDIATE

BACK

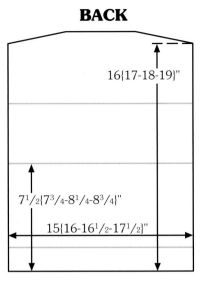

16{17-18-19}"

7¹/₂{7³/₄-8¹/₄-8³/₄}"

15{16-16¹/₂-17¹/₂}"

FRONT

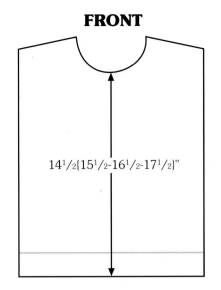

14¹/₂{15¹/₂-16¹/₂-17¹/₂}"

SLEEVE

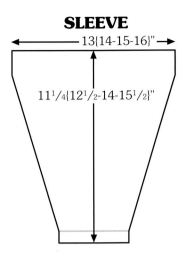

13{14-15-16}"

11¹/₄{12¹/₂-14-15¹/₂}"

Note: Sweater width includes two edge stitches.

Size:	6	8	10	12
Finished Chest				
Measurement:	29"	31"	32"	34"

Size Note: Instructions are written for size 6 with sizes 8, 10, and 12 in braces { }. Instructions will be easier to read if you circle all the numbers pertaining to your child's size. If only one number is given, it applies to all sizes.

MATERIALS

MEDIUM **4**

Worsted Weight Yarn:
  Blue - 7½{8½-10-11} ounces,
    [210{240-280-310} grams,
    425{480-565-620} yards]
  Green - 2¼{2½-2¾-3¼} ounces,
    [65{70-80-95} grams,
    125{140-155-185} yards]
  Gold - ¾{¾-1-1} ounce,
    [20{20-30-30} grams, 40{40-55-55} yards]
Straight knitting needles, sizes 9 (5.50 mm)
  and 10 (6.00 mm) **or** sizes needed for gauge
24" Circular needle, size 10 (6.00 mm)
Stitch holders - 2
Marker
Yarn needle

GAUGE: With larger size needles, in Stockinette
    Stitch, 16 sts and 22 rows = 4"

BACK
RIBBING

With Gold and smaller size straight needles, cast on 60{64-66-70} sts **loosely (Figs. 2a-e, page 9)**; cut Gold.

With Blue, work in K1, P1 ribbing for 10{10-12-12} rows.

BODY

Change to larger size straight needles.

Beginning with a **purl** row, work in Stockinette Stitch until Back measures approximately 7½{7¾-8¼-8¾}" from cast on edge; cut Blue.

With Gold, work in Stockinette Stitch for 3 rows; cut Gold.

With Green, work in Stockinette Stitch for 16 rows; cut Green.

With Gold, work in Stockinette Stitch for 3 rows; cut Gold.

With Blue, work in Stockinette Stitch until Back measures approximately 16{17-18-19}" from cast on edge, ending by working a **purl** row.

Instructions continued on page 342.

SHOULDER SHAPING

Rows 1-4: Bind off 6{6-6-7} sts at the beginning of the row, work across: 36{40-42-42} sts.

Rows 5 and 6: Bind off 5{6-7-6} sts at the beginning of the row, work across: 26{28-28-30} sts.

Slip remaining sts onto st holder.

FRONT

Work same as Back until Front measures approximately 14½{15½-16½-17½}" from cast on edge, ending by working a **purl** row.

NECK SHAPING

Note: Both sides of Neck are worked at the same time, using separate yarn for **each** side.

Row 1: Knit 20{21-22-23} sts, K2 tog *(Fig. 17, page 583)*, slip next 16{18-18-20} sts onto st holder; with second yarn, [slip 1 as if to **knit**, K1, PSSO *(Figs. 19a & b, page 583)*], knit across: 21{22-23-24} sts **each** side.

Row 2 (Decrease row)**:** Purl across to within 2 sts of Neck edge, P2 tog tbl *(Fig. 20, page 583)*; with second yarn, P2 tog *(Fig. 18, page 583)*, purl across: 20{21-22-23} sts **each** side.

Row 3 (Decrease row)**:** Knit across to within 2 sts of Neck edge, K2 tog; with second yarn, slip 1 as if to **knit**, K1, PSSO, knit across: 19{20-21-22} sts **each** side.

Rows 4 and 5: Repeat Rows 2 and 3: 17{18-19-20} sts **each** side.

Rows 6-8: Work across; with second yarn, work across.

SHOULDER SHAPING

Rows 1-4: Bind off 6{6-6-7} sts at Armhole edge, work across; with second yarn, work across: 5{6-7-6} sts **each** side.

Row 5: Bind off remaining sts on first side; with second yarn, knit across.

Bind off remaining sts.

SLEEVE (Make 2)
RIBBING

With Gold and smaller size needles, cast on 32{32-38-38} sts **loosely**; cut Gold.

With Blue, work in K1, P1 ribbing for 10{10-12-12} rows.

BODY

Change to larger size straight needles.

Beginning with a **purl** row, work in Stockinette Stitch increasing one stitch at **each** edge *(see Increases, page 581)*, every fourth row, 10{12-7-9} times; then increase every sixth row, 0{0-4-4} times *(see Zeros, page 577)*: 52{56-60-64} sts.

Work even until Sleeve measures approximately 11¼{12½-14-15½}" from cast on edge, ending by working a **purl** row.

Bind off all sts **loosely** in **knit**.

FINISHING
Sew shoulder seams.

HOOD
With **right** side facing and Blue, slip 8{9-9-10} sts from Front st holder onto circular needle leaving 8{9-9-10} sts on st holder, (K1, P1) twice, K4{5-5-6}, pick up 14 sts evenly spaced along right Front Neck edge *(Fig. 34a, page 586)*, slip 26{28-28-30} sts from Back st holder onto second end of circular needle and knit across, pick up 14 sts evenly spaced along left Front Neck edge, slip remaining 8{9-9-10} sts from Front st holder onto second end of circular needle, K4{5-5-6} sts, (P1, K1) twice: 70{74-74-78} sts.

Row 1: (P1, K1) twice, purl across 62{66-66-70} sts increasing 8 sts evenly spaced, (K1, P1) twice: 78{82-82-86} sts.

Row 2 (Right side)**:** (K1, P1) twice, knit across to last 4 sts, (P1, K1) twice.

Row 3: (P1, K1) twice, purl across to last 4 sts, (K1, P1) twice.

Repeat Rows 2 and 3 until Hood measures approximately 7½{8-8½-9}", ending by working a **wrong** side row.

SHAPING
Note: Maintain established pattern throughout.

Row 1: Work across 37{39-39-41} sts, slip 1 as if to **knit**, K1, PSSO, place marker *(Fig. 1, page 578)*, K2 tog, work across: 76{80-80-84} sts.

Row 2: Work across.

Row 3 (Decrease row)**:** Work across to within 2 sts of marker, slip 1 as if to **knit**, K1, PSSO, slip marker, K2 tog, work across: 74{78-78-82} sts.

Row 4: Work across.

Rows 5-16: Repeat Rows 3 and 4, 6 times: 62{66-66-70} sts.

Bind off all sts **loosely** in pattern.

Sew top seam of Hood.

Sew Sleeves to Sweater, matching center of last row on Sleeve to shoulder seam and beginning 6½{7-7½-8}" down from seam.

Weave underarm and side in one continuous seam *(Fig. 36, page 587)*.

Design by Melissa Leapman.

CLASSIC V-NECK CARDIGAN

BACK

LEFT FRONT

SLEEVE

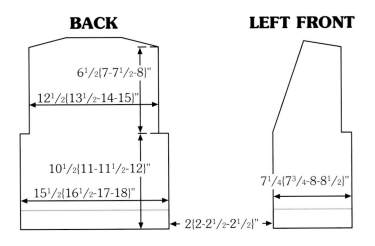

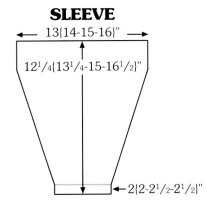

Note: Sweater width includes two edge stitches.

Size:	6	8	10	12
Finished Chest				
Measurement:	30"	32"	33"	35"

Size Note: Instructions are written for size 6 with sizes 8, 10, and 12 in braces { }. Instructions will be easier to read if you circle all the numbers pertaining to your child's size. If only one number is given, it applies to all sizes.

MATERIALS

Worsted Weight Yarn: **(4) MEDIUM**
  Blue - 7½{8½-9½-11} ounces,
  [210{240-270-310} grams,
  425{480-535-620} yards]
  Khaki - 2¼{2½-2¾-3} ounces,
  [65{70-80-90} grams,
  125{140-155-170} yards]
Straight knitting needles, sizes 9 (5.50 mm)
  and 10 (6.00 mm) **or** sizes needed for gauge
29" Circular needle, size 9 (5.50 mm)
Stitch holder
Marker
Sewing needle and thread
Yarn needle
⅝" Buttons - 5{5-6-6}

GAUGE: In Stockinette Stitch,
      16 sts and 22 rows = 4"

BACK
RIBBING
With Khaki and smaller size straight needles, cast on 62{66-68-72} sts **loosely**.

Work in K1, P1 ribbing for 2{2-2½-2½}".

BODY
Change to larger size needles.

Row 1: Purl across; cut Khaki.

With Blue and beginning with a **knit** row, work in Stockinette Stitch until Back measures approximately 10½{11-11½-12}" from cast on edge, ending by working a **purl** row.

ARMHOLE SHAPING
Rows 1 and 2: Bind off 6 sts at the beginning of the row, work across: 50{54-56-60} sts.

Work even until Armholes measure approximately 6½{7-7½-8}", ending by working a **purl** row.

Instructions continued on page 346.

SHOULDER SHAPING
Rows 1-4: Bind off 5{6-6-6} sts at the beginning of the row, work across: 30{30-32-36} sts.

Rows 5 and 6: Bind off 6{5-6-7} sts at the beginning of the row, work across: 18{20-20-22} sts.

Slip remaining sts onto st holder.

LEFT FRONT
RIBBING
With Khaki and smaller size straight needles, cast on 28{30-32-34} sts **loosely**.

Work in K1, P1 ribbing for 2{2-2½-2½}".

BODY
Change to larger size needles.

Row 1: Purl across increasing 1{1-0-0} st(s) *(see Zeros, page 577 and Fig. 11, page 581)*; cut Khaki: 29{31-32-34} sts.

With Blue and beginning with a **knit** row, work in Stockinette Stitch until Left Front measures same as Back to Armhole Shaping, ending by working a **purl** row.

ARMHOLE AND NECK SHAPING
Row 1: Bind off 6 sts, knit across: 23{25-26-28} sts.

Row 2: Purl across.

Row 3 (Decrease row)**:** Knit across to last 3 sts, K2 tog *(Fig. 17, page 583)*, K1: 22{24-25-27} sts.

Continue to decrease one stitch at Neck edge, every fourth row, 6{7-7-8} times **more**: 16{17-18-19} sts.

Work even until Armhole measures same as Back to Shoulder Shaping, ending by working a **purl** row.

SHOULDER SHAPING
Row 1: Bind off 5{6-6-6} sts, knit across: 11{11-12-13} sts.

Row 2: Purl across.

Rows 3 and 4: Repeat Rows 1 and 2: 6{5-6-7} sts.

Bind off remaining sts.

RIGHT FRONT
Work same as Left Front to Armhole and Neck Shaping, ending by working a **knit** row.

ARMHOLE AND NECK SHAPING
Row 1: Bind off 6 sts, purl across: 23{25-26-28} sts.

Row 2: Knit across.

Row 3: Purl across.

Row 4 (Decrease row)**:** K1, **[**slip 1 as if to **knit**, K1, PSSO *(Figs. 19a & b, page 583)***]**, knit across: 22{24-25-27} sts.

Continue to decrease one stitch at Neck edge, every fourth row, 6{7-7-8} times **more**: 16{17-18-19} sts.

Work even until Armhole measures same as Back to Shoulder Shaping, ending by working a **knit** row.

SHOULDER SHAPING
Row 1: Bind off 5{6-6-6} sts, purl across: 11{11-12-13} sts.

Row 2: Knit across.

Rows 3 and 4: Repeat Rows 1 and 2: 6{5-6-7} sts.

Bind off remaining sts.

SLEEVE (Make 2)

RIBBING

With Khaki and smaller size straight needles, cast on 32{32-38-38} sts **loosely**.

Work in K1, P1 ribbing for 2{2-2½-2½}".

BODY

Change to larger size needles.

Row 1: Purl across; cut Khaki.

With Blue and beginning with a **knit** row, work in Stockinette Stitch increasing one stitch at **each edge** *(see Increases, page 581)*, every other row, 1{3-0-0} time(s); then increase every fourth row, 9{9-8-10} times; then increase every sixth row, 0{0-3-3} times: 52{56-60-64} sts.

Work even until Sleeve measures approximately 12¼{13¼-15-16½}" from cast on edge, ending by working a **purl** row.

Bind off all sts **loosely** in **knit**.

FINISHING

Sew shoulder seams.

NECK RIBBING

With **right** side facing, using Khaki and circular needle, pick up 62{62-66-66} sts evenly spaced across Right Front to Neck Shaping *(Fig. 34a, page 586)*, place marker for Girl's only *(Fig. 1, page 578)*, pick up 36{40-42-44} sts evenly spaced across Right Front Neck edge, slip 18{20-20-22} sts from Back st holder onto second end of circular needle and knit across, pick up 35{39-41-43} sts evenly spaced across Left Front Neck Shaping, pick up 62{62-66-66} sts evenly spaced across Left Front: 213{223-235-241} sts.

Row 1: P1, (K1, P1) across.

Row 2 (Right side)**:** K1, (P1, K1) across.

Girl's Cardigan Only - Row 3 (Buttonhole row)**:** P1, (K1, P1) across to marker, remove marker, bind off next 2 sts in pattern, ★ P1, (K1, P1) 5{5-4-4} times, bind off next 2 sts in pattern; repeat from ★ across to last 3 sts, P1, K1, P1.

Boy's Cardigan Only - Row 3 (Buttonhole row)**:** P1, K1, P1, bind off next 2 sts in pattern, ★ P1, (K1, P1) 5{5-4-4} times, bind off next 2 sts in pattern; repeat from ★ 3{3-4-4} times **more**, P1, (K1, P1) across.

Row 4: ★ Work in established ribbing across to bound off sts, **turn**; add on 2 sts *(Figs. 5a & b, page 580)*, **turn**; repeat from ★ 4{4-5-5} times **more**, work across in established ribbing.

Row 5: P1, (K1, P1) across.

Bind off all sts in ribbing.

Matching center of last row on Sleeve to shoulder seam, sew top of Sleeve along Armhole edge and sides of Sleeve to bound off edges.

Weave underarm and side in one continuous seam *(Fig. 36, page 587)*.

Sew buttons to Front opposite buttonholes.

Design by Melissa Leapman.

DAPPLED PULLOVER

 INTERMEDIATE

BACK

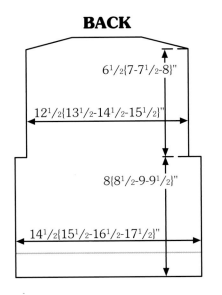

6¹/₂{7-7¹/₂-8}"

12¹/₂{13¹/₂-14¹/₂-15¹/₂}"

8{8¹/₂-9-9¹/₂}"

14¹/₂{15¹/₂-16¹/₂-17¹/₂}"

FRONT

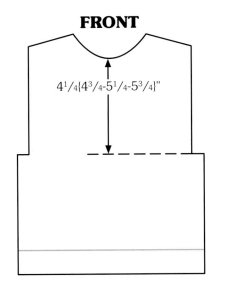

4¹/₄{4³/₄-5¹/₄-5³/₄}"

SLEEVE

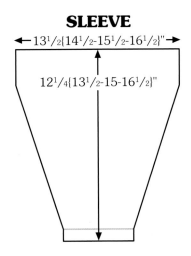

13¹/₂{14¹/₂-15¹/₂-16¹/₂}"

12¹/₄{13¹/₂-15-16¹/₂}"

Note: Sweater width includes two edge stitches.

Size:	6	8	10	12
Finished Chest Measurement:	28"	30"	32"	34"

Size Note: Instructions are written for size 6 with sizes 8, 10, and 12 in braces { }. Instructions will be easier to read if you circle all the numbers pertaining to your child's size. If only one number is given, it applies to all sizes.

MATERIALS

Worsted Weight Yarn: **MEDIUM 4**
Green - 4{5-6-6½} ounces,
[110{140-170-180} grams,
225{285-340-365} yards]
Tan - 2¼{2½-3-3¼} ounces,
[65{70-90-95} grams,
125{140-170-185} yards]
Red - 2¼{2½-3-3¼} ounces,
[65{70-90-95} grams,
125{140-170-185} yards]
Yellow - 2¼{2½-3-3¼} ounces,
[65{70-90-95} grams,
125{140-170-185} yards]
Straight knitting needles, sizes 9 (5.50 mm) **and** 10 (6.00 mm) **or** sizes needed for gauge
16" Circular needle, size 9 (5.50 mm)
Stitch holders - 2
Marker
Yarn needle

Before beginning Pullover, see Fair Isle Knitting, pages 352 through 354.

GAUGE: With larger size needles,
in Stockinette Stitch,
16 sts and 18 rows = 4"

Gauge Swatch: 4½"w x 4"h
With Green and larger size needles, cast on 18 sts **loosely**.
Row 1 (Wrong side)**:** Purl across.
Rows 2-18: Beginning with a **knit** row, work in Stockinette Stitch following Chart.
Bind off all sts **loosely** in **purl**.

CHART

KEY

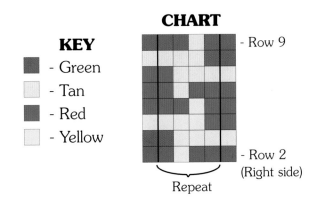

- Green
- Tan
- Red
- Yellow

- Row 9

- Row 2
(Right side)

Repeat

On **right** side rows, work Chart from **right** to **left**.
On **wrong** side rows, work Chart from **left** to **right**.

Instructions begin on page 350.

BACK
RIBBING

With Tan and smaller size straight needles, cast on 58{62-66-70} sts **loosely (Figs. 2a-e, page 9)**; cut Tan.

With Green, work in K1, P1 ribbing for 10{10-12-12} rows.

BODY

Change to larger size needles.

Row 1: Purl across.

Beginning Row 2 with a **knit** row, work in Stockinette Stitch following Chart, page 39, until Back measures approximately 8{8½-9-9½}" from cast on edge, ending by working a **purl** row.

ARMHOLE SHAPING

Note: Maintain established Chart pattern throughout.

Rows 1 and 2: Bind off 4 sts at the beginning of the row, work across: 50{54-58-62} sts.

Work even until Armholes measure approximately 6½{7-7½-8}", ending by working a **purl** row.

SHOULDER SHAPING

Rows 1-4: Bind off 5{6-6-7} sts at the beginning of the row, work across: 30{30-34-34} sts.

Rows 5 and 6: Bind off 6{5-7-6} sts at the beginning of the row, work across: 18{20-20-22} sts.

Slip remaining sts onto st holder.

FRONT

Work same as Back until Armholes measure approximately 4¼{4¾-5¼-5¾}", ending by working a **purl** row: 50{54-58-62} sts.

NECK SHAPING

Note: Both sides of Neck are worked at the same time, using separate yarn for **each** side. Maintain established Chart pattern throughout.

Row 1: Knit 23{24-26-27} sts, slip next 4{6-6-8} sts onto st holder; with second yarn, knit across: 23{24-26-27} sts **each** side.

Rows 2 and 3: Work across; with second yarn, bind off 3 sts at Neck edge, work across: 20{21-23-24} sts **each** side.

Rows 4 and 5: Work across; with second yarn, bind off 2 sts at Neck edge, work across: 18{19-21-22} sts **each** side.

Row 6: Purl across; with second yarn, purl across.

Row 7 (Decrease row)**:** Knit across to within 2 sts of Neck edge, K2 tog **(Fig. 17, page 583)**; with second yarn, [slip 1 as if to **knit**, K1, PSSO **(Figs. 19a & b, page 583)**], work across: 17{18-20-21} sts **each** side.

Rows 8-10: Repeat Rows 6 and 7 once, then repeat Row 6 once **more**: 16{17-19-20} sts **each** side.

SHOULDER SHAPING

Rows 1-4: Bind off 5{6-6-7} sts at Armhole edge, work across; with second yarn, work across: 6{5-7-6} sts **each** side.

Row 5: Bind off remaining sts on first side; with second yarn, knit across.

Bind off remaining sts.

SLEEVE (Make 2)
RIBBING
With Tan and smaller size straight needles, cast on 30{34-38-38} sts **loosely**; cut Tan.

With Green, work in K1, P1 ribbing for 10{10-12-12} rows.

BODY
Change to larger size needles.

Row 1: Purl across.

Beginning Row 2 with a **knit** row, work in Stockinette Stitch following Chart. Working each new stitch in pattern, increase one stitch at **each edge (see Increases, page 581)**, every other row, 8{5-3-3} times; then increase every fourth row, 4{7-9-11} times: 54{58-62-66} sts.

Work even until Sleeve measures approximately 12¼{13½-15-16½}" from cast on edge, ending by working a **purl** row.

Bind off all sts **loosely** in **knit**.

FINISHING
Sew shoulder seams.

NECK RIBBING
With **right** side facing and Green, slip 18{20-20-22} sts from Back st holder onto circular needle and knit across, pick up 20 sts evenly spaced along left Front Neck edge **(Figs. 34a & b, page 586)**, slip 4{6-6-8} sts from Front st holder onto second end of circular needle and knit across, pick up 20 sts evenly spaced along right Front Neck edge, place marker to mark beginning of rnd **(Fig. 1, page 578)**: 62{66-66-70} sts.

Work in K1, P1 ribbing around for 2½".

Knit 7 rnds.

Bind off all sts **loosely** in **knit**.

Matching center of last row on Sleeve to shoulder seam, sew top of Sleeve along Armhole edge and sides of Sleeve to bound off edges.

Weave underarm and side in one continuous seam **(Fig. 36, page 587)**.

Design by Melissa Leapman.

FAIR ISLE KNITTING

Fair Isle Knitting is a Stockinette Stitch technique that uses two colors across a row. Read all instructions and practice any techniques that are new to you before beginning your sweater.

STOCKINETTE STITCH

Stockinette Stitch is the result of alternating knit rows (right side) and purl rows. The knit side is smooth and flat *(Fig. A)*, and the purl side is bumpy *(Fig B)*.

Fig. A

Fig. B

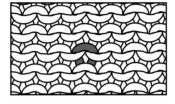

WORKING WITH TWO COLORS

The two methods of knitting, English (holding the yarn with the right hand) and Continental (holding the yarn with the left hand), are easily combined when knitting in Fair Isle *(Figs. C & D)*. It might be awkward at first, but it is faster than only using one method and allows the stitches to be uniform. If you aren't familiar with one of the methods, practice it until you are comfortable using that method *(see pages 10-13)*.

Fig. C

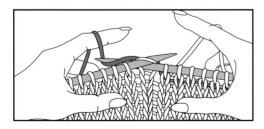

Fig. D

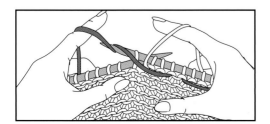

STRANDING

Stranding is the method in which the color not in use is carried across the **wrong** side of the fabric. It gives a nice appearance on the right side and also provides added warmth. Carry the yarn **loosely** across one to 4 sts, about 1" or less, without twisting the strands of yarn *(Fig. E)*. Notice that each color is carried across the wrong side **without** crossing each other.

Fig. E

When you use the English and the Continental method together, the strands automatically lie with the color that is held in your right hand on top. If one color is used more often than the other, always hold that color in the hand you usually knit with and the other color in the hand using the less familiar method. It is important to be consistent.

If you only use one method of knitting, you must concentrate on always bringing one color from underneath and the other from the top. It is important to be consistent.

Spread your stitches on the right hand needle as you knit so that you will have the correct tension on the yarn that is being carried. The stitches should be spread as much as the approximate gauge, so that the yarn carried will lie flat against the fabric. Carrying the strand slightly too loose is better than too tight, but be careful not to provide too much yarn as the stitches at end of the color section will enlarge. It's important to maintain the elasticity of the fabric.

At the end of the row, twist the unused color before the last stitch *(Fig. F)* and then over the second stitch on the next row *(Fig. G)*.

Fig. F

Fig. G

CHECKING YOUR TENSION

The fabric should look smooth and even on the right side *(Fig. H)* without a puckered uneven appearance *(Fig. I)*. The strands on the wrong side should lie flat *(Fig. J)* without pulling the fabric or distorting the shape of the stitches *(Fig. K)*. If the strands are pulled too tight, the gauge will also be too tight making the garment too small.

Fig. H

Fig. I

Fig. J

Fig. K

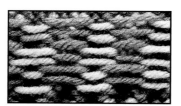

TWISTING STRANDS

If the strands are carried more than an inch, it can be difficult to keep tension. The strands can be easily snagged when putting the garment on or pulling it off. To avoid carrying the yarn across 5 stitches, as in the Zesty Stripes Pullover, page 355, twist the carried color at its midpoint with the yarn in use. Make sure the carried yarn doesn't show on the right side or tighten the tension.

Drop the color you are using, lay the other color to your left on top of it, pick up the color you were using and continue working. The unused color is attached to the fabric *(Fig. L)*.

Fig. L

BOBBINS

Bobbins and yarn holders can be used to keep yarn manageable. Wind small amounts and refill as necessary.

CHANGING COLORS

Always start a new ball or skein at the beginning or end of a row, never in the middle. The yarn can be carried up the side, twisting it every few rows or it can be cut leaving a long end, and the ends can be woven into the edge after the seam has been sewn or in the back of the work.

Instructions continued on page 354.

FOLLOWING A CHART

Designs for Fair Isle knitting are worked from a chart. It is easier to follow a chart than written instructions and you can also see what the pattern looks like. The chart shows each stitch as a square indicating what color each stitch should be. Visualize the chart as your fabric, beginning at the bottom edge.

Only one pattern repeat is given on the chart, and it is indicated by a heavy vertical line and a bracketed indication. This section is to be repeated across the row. There is an extra stitch on each side of the repeat, indicating the first and last stitch of the row. These are edge stitches that will be woven into the seam, allowing the pattern to be continuous between the Back and the Front of the garment.

If the chart is symmetrical, it doesn't matter which direction the chart is followed. If the chart is **not** symmetrical, work as follows: On **right** side rows, follow the chart from **right** to **left**; on **wrong** side rows, follow the chart from **left** to **right**.

For ease in following the chart, place a ruler on the chart above the row being worked to help keep your place.

BINDING OFF

When binding off stitches for the Shoulder Shaping or for the Sleeves, use the dominant color on the last row worked. When sewing the seam, the same color will be used, allowing it to blend in with the bind off row.

SLEEVES

The Sleeves for any of the sweaters can be knit in Fair Isle or with one color. If the instructions are not given for a solid Sleeve, adjust the amount of yarn purchased accordingly. Maintain the stitch gauge given *(see Gauge, page 576)*.

Increases will look smoother and it will be easier to weave the seam if you use the Right and Left Invisible Increases *(Figs. 12a & b and 13a & b, page 581)*.

For Fair Isle Sleeves, stitches are increased at each edge while maintaining the color pattern.

ZESTY STRIPES PULLOVER

Shown on pages 356 and 357.

BACK　**FRONT**

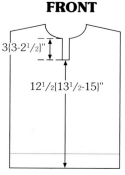

17{18-19}"

3{3-2½}"

12½{13½-15}"

14¾{16¾-18¾}"

SLEEVE

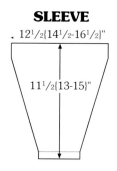

12½{14½-16½}"

11½{13-15}"

Note: Sweater width includes two edge stitches.

Size:	Small	Medium	Large
Finished Chest			
Measurement:	28½"	32½"	36½"

Size Note: Instructions are written for size Small with sizes Medium and Large in braces { }. Instructions will be easier to read if you circle all the numbers pertaining to your child's size. If only one number is given, it applies to all sizes.

MATERIALS

Worsted Weight Yarn:

Solid Sleeve Version

Color A (Blue) - 6½{8-9½} ounces,
 [180{230-270} grams, 365{450-535} yards]
Color B (Yellow) - 2½{3-4} ounces,
 [70{90-110} grams, 140{170-225} yards]
Color C (Teal) - 1¼{1½-1¾} ounces,
 [35{40-50} grams, 70{85-100} yards]
Color D (Maroon) - 1{1¼-1½} ounce(s),
 [30{35-40} grams, 55{70-85} yards]

Fair Isle Sleeve Version

Color A (Lavender) - 4½{5½-6½} ounces,
 [130{160-180} grams, 255{310-365} yards]
Color B (Yellow) - 4{5-6} ounces,
 [110{140-170} grams, 225{285-340} yards]
Color C (Teal) - 1¾{2-2½} ounces,
 [50{60-70} grams, 100{115-140} yards]
Color D (Pink) - 1¾{2-2½} ounces,
 [50{60-70} grams, 100{115-140} yards]
Straight knitting needles, sizes 9 (5.50 mm) **and** 10 (6.00 mm) **or** sizes needed for gauge
24" Circular needle, size 9 (5.50 mm)
Stitch holders - 2
Yarn needle
Sewing needle and thread
5" Zipper

Before beginning Pullover, see Fair Isle Knitting, pages 352 through 354.

GAUGE: With larger size needles,
 in Fair Isle pattern,
 16 sts and 18 rows = 4"
 in solid Stockinette Stitch,
 16 sts and 22 rows = 4"

Gauge Swatch: 4¾"w x 4"h
With Color A and larger size needles, cast on 19 sts **loosely**.
Row 1 (Wrong side)**:** Purl across.
Rows 2-18: Beginning with a **knit** row, work in Stockinette Stitch following Chart.
Bind off all sts **loosely** in **purl**.

CHART

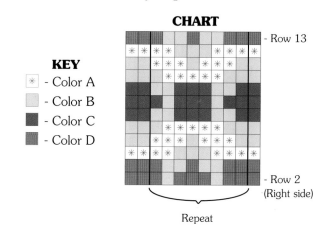

- Row 13

KEY

✳	- Color A
	- Color B
■	- Color C
▨	- Color D

- Row 2
(Right side)

Repeat

On **right** side rows, work Chart from **right** to **left**.
On **wrong** side rows, work Chart from **left** to **right**.

Instructions begin on page 358.

BACK
RIBBING

With Color C and smaller size straight needles, cast on 59{67-75} sts **loosely** (*Figs. 2a-e, page 9*); cut Color C.

With Color A, work in K1, P1 ribbing for 10{10-12} rows.

BODY

Change to larger size needles.

Row 1: Purl across.

Beginning Row 2 with a **knit** row, work in Stockinette Stitch following Chart, page 355, until Back measures approximately 17{18-19}" from cast on edge, ending by working a **purl** row.

SHOULDER SHAPING

Note: Maintain established Chart pattern throughout.

Rows 1-4: Bind off 7{8-9} sts at the beginning of the row, work across: 31{35-39} sts.

Rows 5 and 6: Bind off 6{7-8} sts at the beginning of the row, work across: 19{21-23} sts.

Slip remaining sts onto st holder.

FRONT

Work same as Back until Front measures approximately 12½{13½-15}" from cast on edge, ending by working a **purl** row.

NECK OPENING

Note: Both sides of Neck are worked at the same time, using separate yarn for **each** side. Maintain established Chart pattern throughout.

Row 1: Knit 28{32-36} sts, slip next 3 sts onto st holder; with second yarn, knit across: 28{32-36} sts **each** side.

Work even until Neck Opening measures approximately 3{3-2½}", ending by working a **purl** row.

NECK SHAPING

Rows 1 and 2: Work across; with second yarn, bind off 4{5-6} sts at Neck edge, work across: 24{27-30} sts **each** side.

Rows 3 and 4: Work across; with second yarn, bind off 2 sts at Neck edge, work across: 22{25-28} sts **each** side.

Row 5 (Decrease row)**:** Knit across to within 2 sts of Neck edge, K2 tog (*Fig. 17, page 583*); with second yarn, [slip 1 as if to **knit**, K1, PSSO (*Figs. 19a & b, page 583*)], knit across: 21{24-27} sts **each** side.

Row 6: Purl across; with second yarn, purl across.

Row 7: Repeat Row 5: 20{23-26} sts **each** side.

SHOULDER SHAPING

Rows 1-4: Bind off 7{8-9} sts at Armhole edge, work across; with second yarn, work across: 6{7-8} sts **each** side.

Row 5: Bind off remaining sts on first side; with second yarn, purl across.

Bind off remaining sts.

SOLID SLEEVE VERSION (Make 2)
RIBBING

With Color C and smaller size straight needles, cast on 32{32-38} sts **loosely**; cut Color C.

With Color A, work in K1, P1 ribbing for 10{10-12} rows.

BODY

Change to larger size needles.

Row 1: Purl across increasing 2{2-4} sts evenly spaced (*see Increasing Evenly Across A Row and Fig. 11, page 581*): 34{34-42} sts.

Beginning with a **knit** row, work in Stockinette Stitch increasing one stitch at **each** edge (*see Increases, page 581*), every fourth row, 3{11-6} times; then increase every sixth row, 5{1-6} time(s): 50{58-66} sts.

Work even until Sleeve measures approximately 11½{13-15}" from cast on edge, ending by working a **purl** row.

Bind off all sts **loosely** in **knit**.

FAIR ISLE SLEEVE VERSION (Make 2)
RIBBING

With Color C and smaller size straight needles, cast on 32{32-38} sts **loosely**; cut Color C.

With Color A, work in K1, P1 ribbing for 10{10-12} rows.

BODY

Change to larger size needles.

Row 1: Purl across increasing 2{2-4} sts evenly spaced *(see Increasing Evenly Across A Row and Fig. 11, page 581)*: 34{34-42} sts.

Beginning Row 2 with a **knit** row, work in Stockinette Stitch following Chart. Working each new stitch in pattern, increase one stitch at **each** edge *(see Increases, page 581)*, every other row, 0{4-1} time(s) *(see Zeros, page 577)*; then increase every fourth row, 8{8-11} times: 50{58-66} sts.

Work even until Sleeve measures approximately 11½{13-15}" from cast on edge, ending by working a **purl** row.

Bind off all sts **loosely** in **knit**.

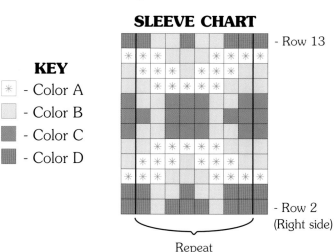

SLEEVE CHART

- Row 13

KEY
- ✳ - Color A
- ☐ - Color B
- ☐ - Color C
- ☐ - Color D

- Row 2
(Right side)

Repeat

On **right** side rows, work Chart from **right** to **left**.
On **wrong** side rows, work Chart from **left** to **right**.

FINISHING

Sew shoulder seams.

NECK RIBBING

With **right** side facing, using Color A and circular needle, pick up 17{18-19} sts evenly spaced along right Front Neck edge *(Figs. 34a & b, page 586)*, slip 19{21-23} sts from Back st holder onto second end of circular needle and knit across, pick up 17{18-19} sts evenly spaced along left Front Neck edge: 53{57-61} sts.

Row 1: K1, (P1, K1) across.

Row 2 (Right side)**:** P1, (K1, P1) across.

Repeat Rows 1 and 2, 4{4-5} times; cut Color A.

With Color C, bind off all sts **loosely** in ribbing.

ZIPPER FACING

To pick up and knit stitches, pick up a stitch and place it on the left needle, then knit the stitch.

With **right** side facing, using Color A and circular needle, pick up and knit 24 sts evenly spaced along left Front neck opening, slip 3 sts from st holder onto second end of circular needle and knit across, pick up and knit 24 sts evenly spaced along right Front neck opening: 51 sts.

Bind off all sts **loosely** in **knit**.

Sew in zipper along Zipper Facing.

Sew Sleeves to Sweater, matching center of last row on Sleeve to shoulder seam and beginning 6¼{7¼-8¼}" down from seam.

Weave underarm and side in one continuous seam *(Fig. 36, page 587)*.

Design by Melissa Leapman.

SOFT RIPPLES LAYETTE

DRESS OR GOWN ◼◼◼◼ EXPERIENCED

Size: Newborn, 3 months and 6 months

Note: Yarn amounts, Gauge and length are given for Newborn, with 3 months and 6 months in braces { }. Proper measurement is obtained by using different needle sizes as recommended under Materials.

MATERIALS

Baby Yarn, approximately:

Dress

$1^3/_4${2-$2^1/_4$} ounces, 305{350-395} yards, [50{60-65} grams, 279{320-361} meters]

Gown

4{$4^1/_2$-5} ounces, 700{790-875} yards, [110{130-140} grams, 640{722-800} meters]

For Newborn size ONLY:

24" (61 cm) Circular needle, size 3 (3.25 mm) **or** size needed for gauge

For 3 months size ONLY:

24" (61 cm) Circular needle, size 4 (3.5 mm) **or** size needed for gauge

For 6 months size ONLY:

24" (61 cm) Circular needle, size 5 (3.75 mm) **or** size needed for gauge

2 Stitch holders - for Gown Only
Crochet hook, size D (3 mm)
Button

GAUGE: One pattern (35 sts) = 3{$3^1/_4$-$3^1/_2$}"/ 7.5{8.25-9} cm; 26 rows = $2^1/_4${$2^1/_2$-$2^3/_4$}"/ 5.75{6.25-7} cm

Work Gauge Swatch as follows:
Cast on 35 sts **loosely.**
Rows 1 and 2: Knit across.
Row 3: Purl across.
Row 4: K2 tog 6 times *(Fig. 17, page 583)*, YO *(Fig. 16a, page 582)*, (K1, YO) 11 times, K2 tog 6 times.
Rows 5-24: Repeat Rows 1-4, 5 times.
Rows 25 and 26: Knit across.
Bind off all sts **loosely.**

YOKE

Cast on 49 sts **loosely.**

Rows 1-4: Knit across.

Row 5: K1, ★ P3, K1; repeat from ★ across.

Row 6 (Right side)**:** P1, ★ K1, [YO *(Fig. 16a, page 582)*, K1] twice, P1; repeat from ★ across: 73 sts.

Row 7: K1, ★ P5, K1; repeat from ★ across.

Row 8: P1, ★ K5, P1; repeat from ★ across.

Row 9: K1, ★ P5, K1; repeat from ★ across.

Row 10: P1, ★ K2, YO, K1, YO, K2, P1; repeat from ★ across: 97 sts.

Row 11: K1, ★ P7, K1; repeat from ★ across.

Row 12: P1, ★ K7, P1; repeat from ★ across.

Row 13: K1, ★ P7, K1; repeat from ★ across.

Row 14: P1, ★ K3, YO, K1, YO, K3, P1; repeat from ★ across: 121 sts.

Row 15: K1, ★ P9, K1; repeat from ★ across.

Row 16: P1, ★ K9, P1; repeat from ★ across.

Row 17: K1, ★ P9, K1; repeat from ★ across.

Row 18: P1, ★ K4, YO, K1, YO, K4, P1; repeat from ★ across: 145 sts.

Row 19: K1, ★ P 11, K1; repeat from ★ across.

Row 20: P1, ★ K 11, P1; repeat from ★ across.

Row 21: K1, P 11, ★ knit into the front **and** into the back of the next st, P 11; repeat from ★ across to last st, K1: 156 sts.

Row 22: K1, YO, [slip 1, K1, PSSO *(Figs. 19a & b, page 583)*], K7, K2 tog *(Fig. 17, page 583)*, YO, ★ K2, YO, slip 1, K1, PSSO, K7, K2 tog, YO; repeat from ★ across to last st, K1.

Row 23: K2, P9, ★ K4, P9; repeat from ★ across to last 2 sts, K2.

Row 24: K2, YO, slip 1, K1, PSSO, K5, K2 tog, YO, ★ K4, YO, slip 1, K1, PSSO, K5, K2 tog, YO; repeat from ★ across to last 2 sts, K2.

Row 25: Purl across.

Instructions continued on page 362.

Row 26: K3, YO, slip 1, K1, PSSO, K3, K2 tog, YO, ★ K6, YO, slip 1, K1, PSSO, K3, K2 tog, YO; repeat from ★ across to last 3 sts, K3.

Row 27: K4, P5, ★ K8, P5; repeat from ★ across to last 4 sts, K4.

Row 28: K4, YO, slip 1, K1, PSSO, K1, K2 tog, YO, ★ K8, YO, slip 1, K1, PSSO, K1, K2 tog, YO; repeat from ★ across to last 4 sts, K4.

Row 29: Purl across.

Row 30: K5, YO, [slip 1, K2 tog, PSSO *(Figs. 26a & b, page 584)*], YO, ★ K 10, YO, slip 1, K2 tog, PSSO, YO; repeat from ★ across to last 5 sts, K5.

Rows 31 and 32: Knit across.

Row 33: Purl across.

Row 34: K2 tog twice, YO, (K1, YO) 5 times, ★ K2 tog 4 times, YO, (K1, YO) 5 times; repeat from ★ across to last 4ce: 180 sts.

Rows 35 and 36: Knit across.

Row 37: Purl across.

Row 38: K2 tog twice, YO, (K1, YO) 7 times, ★ K2 tog 4 times, YO, (K1, YO) 7 times; repeat from ★ across to last 4 sts, K2 tog twice: 228 sts.

Rows 39 and 40: Knit across.

Row 41: Purl across.

Row 42: K2 tog 3 times, YO, (K1, YO) 7 times, ★ K2 tog 6 times, YO, (K1, YO) 7 times; repeat from ★ across to last 6 sts, K2 tog 3 times: 252 sts.

Rows 43 and 44: Knit across.

Row 45: Purl across.

Row 46: K2 tog 3 times, YO, (K1, YO) 9 times, ★ K2 tog 6 times, YO, (K1, YO) 9 times; repeat from ★ across to last 6 sts, K2 tog 3 times: 300 sts.

Rows 47 and 48: Knit across.

Row 49: Purl across.

Row 50: K2 tog 4 times, YO, (K1, YO) 9 times, ★ K2 tog 8 times, YO, (K1, YO) 9 times; repeat from ★ across to last 8 sts, K2 tog 4 times: 324 sts.

Rows 51 and 52: Knit across.

Row 53: Purl across.

Row 54: K2 tog 4 times, YO, (K1, YO) 11 times, ★ K2 tog 8 times, YO, (K1, YO) 11 times; repeat from ★ across to last 8 sts, K2 tog 4 times: 372 sts.

SKIRT
Rows 1 and 2: Knit across.

Dress Only - Row 3: P 62, bind off 62 sts **loosely**, P 123, bind off 62 sts **loosely**, purl across: 248 sts.

Gown Only - Row 3: P 124, slip 62 sts just worked onto st holder (Sleeve), P 186, slip 62 sts just worked onto second st holder (Sleeve), P 62: 248 sts.

Dress or Gown - Row 4: K2 tog 5 times, YO, (K1, YO) 11 times, ★ K2 tog 10 times, YO, (K1, YO) 11 times; repeat from ★ across to last 10 sts, K2 tog 5 times: 264 sts.

Rows 5 and 6: Knit across.

Row 7: Purl across.

Row 8: K2 tog 5 times, K1, (YO, K1) 12 times, ★ K2 tog 10 times, K1, (YO, K1) 12 times; repeat from ★ across to last 10 sts, K2 tog 5 times: 280 sts.

Rows 9 and 10: Knit across.

Row 11: Purl across.

Row 12: K2 tog 6 times, YO, (K1, YO) 11 times, ★ K2 tog 12 times, YO, (K1, YO) 11 times; repeat from ★ across to last 12 sts, K2 tog 6 times.

Rows 13 and 14: Knit across.

Repeat Rows 11-14 until Dress measures approximately 9{10-11}"/23{25.5-28} cm **or** Gown measures approximately 18{19-20}"/45.5{48-51} cm from cast on edge **or to desired length**, ending by working Row 14.

Bind off all sts **loosely**.

SLEEVES - Gown Only

With **right** side facing, slip 62 sts from st holder onto needle.

Row 1: K2 tog 5 times, YO, (K1, YO) 11 times, K2 tog 10 times, YO, (K1, YO) 11 times, K2 tog 5 times: 66 sts.

Rows 2 and 3: Knit across.

Row 4: Purl across.

Row 5: K2 tog 5 times, K1, (YO, K1) 12 times, K2 tog 10 times, K1, (YO, K1) 12 times, K2 tog 5 times: 70 sts.

Rows 6 and 7: Knit across.

Row 8: Purl across.

Row 9: K2 tog 6 times, YO, (K1, YO) 11 times, K2 tog 12 times, YO, (K1, YO) 11 times, K2 tog 6 times.

Rows 10 and 11: Knit across.

Rows 12-23: Repeat Rows 8-11, 3 times.

Bind off all sts **loosely**.

Sew Sleeve seam.

Repeat for second Sleeve.

FINISHING

Sew back seam, leaving a 3" (7.5 cm) neck opening.

EDGING

With **wrong** side facing, join yarn with slip st to top left back neck opening **(see Crochet Stitches, pages 588 & 589)**.

Row 1: Sc evenly spaced down left side and up right side.

Row 2: Ch 3, turn; skip first 2 sc, sc in next sc (button loop made), sc in each sc across; finish off.

Add button.

SACQUE ▰▰▰▰ EXPERIENCED

Size: Newborn, 3 months and 6 months

Note: Yarn amounts, Gauge and length are given for Newborn, with 3 months and 6 months in braces { }. Proper measurement is obtained by using different needle sizes as recommended under Materials.

MATERIALS

Baby Yarn, approximately:
2{2¼-2½} ounces, 350{395-440} yards,
[60{65-70} grams, 320{361-402} meters]
For Newborn size ONLY:
    24" (61 cm) Circular needle, size 3 (3.25 mm)
        or size needed for gauge
For 3 months size ONLY:
    24" (61 cm) Circular needle, size 4 (3.5 mm)
        or size needed for gauge
For 6 months size ONLY:
    24" (61 cm) Circular needle, size 5 (3.75 mm)
        or size needed for gauge
2 Stitch holders
Button

GAUGE: One pattern (35 sts) = 3{3¼-3½}"/
7.5{8.25-9} cm;
26 rows = 2¼{2½-2¾}"/
5.75{6.25-7} cm

Work Gauge Swatch as follows:
Cast on 35 sts **loosely**.
Rows 1 and 2: Knit across.
Row 3: Purl across.
Row 4: K2 tog 6 times *(Fig. 17, page 583)*, YO *(Fig. 16a, page 582)*, (K1, YO) 11 times, K2 tog 6 times.
Rows 5-24: Repeat Rows 1-4, 5 times.
Rows 25 and 26: Knit across.
Bind off all sts **loosely**.

YOKE

Cast on 55 sts **loosely**.

Rows 1 and 2: Knit across.

Row 3 (Buttonhole row)**:** K1, K2 tog *(Fig. 17, page 583)*, YO *(Fig. 16a, page 582)*, knit across.

Rows 4-6: Knit across.

Instructions continued on page 364.

Row 7: K4, P3, ★ K1, P3; repeat from ★ across to last 4 sts, K4.

Row 8 (Right side)**:** K3, P1, ★ K1, (YO, K1) twice, P1; repeat from ★ across to last 3 sts, K3: 79 sts.

Note: Loop a short piece of yarn around any stitch to mark Row 8 as **right** side.

Row 9: K4, P5, ★ K1, P5; repeat from ★ across to last 4 sts, K4.

Row 10: K3, P1, ★ K5, P1; repeat from ★ across to last 3 sts, K3,

Row 11: K4, P5, ★ K1, P5; repeat from ★ across to last 4 sts, K4.

Row 12: K3, P1, ★ K2, YO, K1, YO, K2, P1; repeat from ★ across to last 3 sts, K3: 103 sts.

Row 13: K4, P7, ★ K1, P7; repeat from ★ across to last 4 sts, K4.

Row 14: K3, P1, ★ K7, P1; repeat from ★ across to last 3 sts, K3.

Row 15 (Buttonhole row)**:** K1, K2 tog, YO, ★ K1, P7; repeat from ★ across to last 4 sts, K4.

Row 16: K3, P1, ★ K3, YO, K1, YO, K3, P1; repeat from ★ across to last 3 sts, K3: 127 sts.

Row 17: K4, P9, ★ K1, P9; repeat from ★ across to last 4 sts, K4.

Row 18: K3, P1, ★ K9, P1; repeat from ★ across to last 3 sts, K3.

Row 19: K4, P9, ★ K1, P9; repeat from ★ across to last 4 sts, K4.

Row 20: K3, P1, ★ K4, YO, K1, YO, K4, P1; repeat from ★ across to last 3 sts, K3: 151 sts.

Row 21: K4, P 11, ★ K1, P 11; repeat from ★ across to last 4 sts, K4.

Row 22: K3, P1, ★ K 11, P1; repeat from ★ across to last 3 sts, K3.

Row 23: K4, P 11, ★ knit into the front **and** into the back of the next st, P 11; repeat from ★ across to last 4 sts, K4: 162 sts.

Row 24: K4, YO, [slip 1, K1, PSSO *(Figs. 19a & b, page 583)*], K7, K2 tog, YO, ★ K2, YO, slip 1, K1, PSSO, K7, K2 tog, YO; repeat from ★ across to last 4 sts, K4.

Row 25: K5, P9, ★ K4, P9; repeat from ★ across to last 5 sts, K5.

Row 26: K5, YO, slip 1, K1, PSSO, K5, K2 tog, YO, ★ K4, YO, slip 1, K1, PSSO, K5, K2 tog, YO; repeat from ★ across to last 5 sts, K5.

Row 27: K3, purl across to last 3 sts, K3.

Row 28: K6, YO, slip 1, K1, PSSO, K3, K2 tog, YO, ★ K6, YO, slip 1, K1, PSSO, K3, K2 tog, YO; repeat from ★ across to last 6 sts, K6.

Row 29 (Buttonhole row)**:** K1, K2 tog, YO, K4, P5, ★ K8, P5; repeat from ★ across to last 7 sts, K7.

Row 30: K7, YO, slip 1, K1, PSSO, K1, K2 tog, YO, ★ K8, YO, slip 1, K1, PSSO, K1, K2 tog, YO; repeat from ★ across to last 7 sts, K7.

Row 31: K3, purl across to last 3 sts, K3.

Row 32: K8, YO, [slip 1, K2 tog, PSSO *(Figs. 26a & b, page 584)*], YO, ★ K 10, YO, slip 1, K2 tog, PSSO, YO; repeat from ★ across to last 8 sts, K8.

Rows 33 and 34: Knit across.

Row 35: K3, purl across to last 3 sts, K3.

Row 36: K3, K2 tog twice, YO, (K1, YO) 5 times, ★ K2 tog 4 times, YO, (K1, YO) 5 times; repeat from ★ across to last 7 sts, K2 tog twice, K3: 186 sts.

Rows 37 and 38: Knit across.

Row 39: K3, purl across to last 3 sts, K3.

Row 40: K3, K2 tog twice, YO, (K1, YO) 7 times, ★ K2 tog 4 times, YO, (K1, YO) 7 times; repeat from ★ across to last 7g twice, K3: 234 sts.

Rows 41-43: Repeat Rows 37-39.

Row 44: K3, K2 tog 3 times, YO, (K1, YO) 7 times, ★ K2 tog 6 times, YO, (K1, YO) 7 times; repeat from ★ across to last 9 sts, K2 tog 3 times, K3: 258 sts.

Rows 45-47: Repeat Rows 37-39.

Row 48: K3, K2 tog 3 times, YO, (K1, YO) 9 times, ★ K2 tog 6 times, YO, (K1, YO) 9 times; repeat from ★ across to last 9 sts, K2 tog 3 times, K3: 306 sts.

Rows 49-51: Repeat Rows 37-39.

Row 52: K3, K2 tog 4 times, YO, (K1, YO) 9 times, ★ K2 tog 8 times, YO, (K1, YO) 9 times; repeat from ★ across to last 11 sts, K2 tog 4 times, K3: 330 sts.

Rows 53-55: Repeat Rows 37-39.

Row 56: K3, K2 tog 4 times, YO, (K1, YO) 11 times, ★ K2 tog 8 times, YO, (K1, YO) 11 times; repeat from ★ across to last 11 sts, K2 tog 4 times, K3: 378 sts.

BODY

Rows 1 and 2: Knit across.

Row 3: K3, P 124, slip 62 sts just worked onto st holder (Sleeve), P 186, slip 62 sts just worked onto second st holder (Sleeve), P 62, K3: 254 sts.

Row 4: K3, K2 tog 5 times, YO, (K1, YO) 11 times, ★ K2 tog 10 times, YO, (K1, YO) 11 times; repeat from ★ across to last 13270 sts.

Rows 5 and 6: Knit across.

Row 7: K3, purl across to last 3 sts, K3.

Row 8: K3, K2 tog 5 times, K1, (YO, K1) 12 times, ★ K2 tog 10 times, K1, (YO, K1) 12 times; repeat from ★ across to last 13 sts, K2 tog 5 times, K3: 286 sts.

Rows 9 and 10: Knit across.

Row 11: K3, purl across to last 3 sts, K3.

Row 12: K3, K2 tog 6 times, YO, (K1, YO) 11 times, ★ K2 tog 12 times, YO, (K1, YO) 11 times; repeat from ★ across to last 15 sts, K2 tog 6 times, K3.

Rows 13 and 14: Knit across.

Rows 15-18: Repeat Rows 11-14.

Bind off all sts **loosely**.

Add buttons.

SLEEVES

Work same as Gown, page 363.

BONNET ◼◼◼◼▶ EXPERIENCED

Size: Newborn, 3 months and 6 months

Note: Yarn amounts, Gauge and length are given for Newborn, with 3 months and 6 months in braces { }. Proper measurement is obtained by using different needle sizes as recommended under Materials.

MATERIALS

Baby Yarn, approximately: **⟨SUPER FINE 1⟩**
    $^3/_4${1-1$^1/_4$} ounces, 130{175-220} yards,
    [20{30-40} grams, 119{160-201} meters]
For Newborn size ONLY:
    Straight knitting needles, size 3 (3.25 mm)
        or size needed for gauge
For 3 months size ONLY:
    Straight knitting needles, size 4 (3.5 mm)
        or size needed for gauge
For 6 months size ONLY:
    Straight knitting needles, size 5 (3.75 mm)
        or size needed for gauge
1/4" (7 mm) wide Ribbon - 1 yard (.9 meters)

GAUGE: One pattern (35 sts) = 3{3$^1/_4$-3$^1/_2$}"/ 7.5{8.25-9} cm; 26 rows = 2$^1/_4${2$^1/_2$-2$^3/_4$}"/ 5.75{6.25-7} cm

Work Gauge Swatch as follows:
Cast on 35 sts **loosely**.
Rows 1 and 2: Knit across.
Row 3: Purl across.
Row 4: K2 tog 6 times *(Fig. 17, page 583)*, YO *(Fig. 16a, page 582)*, (K1, YO) 11 times, K2 tog 6 times.
Rows 5-24: Repeat Rows 1-4, 5 times.
Rows 25 and 26: Knit across.
Bind off all sts **loosely**.

Cast on 17 sts **loosely**.

Row 1: Purl across.

Row 2 (Right side)**:** P1, ★ K1, [YO *(Fig. 16a, page 582)*, K1] twice, P1; repeat from ★ across: 25 sts.

Note: Loop a short piece of yarn around any stitch to mark Row 2 as **right** side.

Instructions continued on page 366.

Row 3: K1, ★ P5, K1; repeat from ★ across.

Row 4: P1, ★ K2, YO, K1, YO, K2, P1; repeat from ★ across: 33 sts.

Row 5: K1, ★ P7, K1; repeat from ★ across.

Row 6: P1, ★ K3, YO, K1, YO, K3, P1; repeat from ★ across: 41 sts.

Row 7: K1, ★ P9, K1; repeat from ★ across.

Row 8: P1, ★ K4, YO, K1, YO, K4, P1; repeat from ★ across: 49 sts.

Row 9: K1, ★ P 11, K1; repeat from ★ across.

Row 10: P1, ★ K5, YO, K1, YO, K5, P1; repeat from ★ across: 57 sts.

Row 11: K1, ★ P 13, K1; repeat from ★ across.

Row 12: P1, ★ K6, YO, K1, YO, K6, P1; repeat from ★ across: 65 sts.

Row 13: K1, ★ P 15, K1; repeat from ★ across.

Row 14: P1, ★ K7, YO, K1, YO, K7, P1; repeat from ★ across: 73 sts.

Row 15: K1, P 17, ★ knit into the front and into the back of the next st, P 17; repeat from ★ across to last st, K1: 76 sts.

Place marker at each end of Row 15.

Row 16: K1, YO, [slip 1, K1, PSSO *(Figs. 19a & b, page 583)*], K 13, K2 tog *(Fig. 17, page 583)*, YO, ★ K2, YO, slip 1, K1, PSSO, K 13, K2 tog, YO; repeat from ★ across to last st, K1.

Row 17: Purl across.

Row 18: K2, YO, slip 1, K1, PSSO, K 11, K2 tog, YO, ★ K4, YO, slip 1, K1, PSSO, K 11, K2 tog, YO; repeat from ★ across to last 2 sts, K2.

Row 19: K3, P 13, ★ K6, P 13; repeat from ★ across to last 3 sts, K3.

Row 20: K3, YO, slip 1, K1, PSSO, K9, K2 tog, YO, ★ K6, YO, slip 1, K1, PSSO, K9, K2 tog, YO; repeat from ★ across to last 3 sts, K3.

Row 21: Purl across.

Row 22: K4, YO, slip 1, K1, PSSO, K7, K2 tog, YO, ★ K8, YO, slip 1, K1, PSSO, K7, K2 tog, YO; repeat from ★ across to last 4 sts, K4.

Row 23: K5, P9, ★ K 10, P9; repeat from ★ across to last 5 sts, K5.

Row 24: K5, YO, slip 1, K1, PSSO, K5, K2 tog, YO, ★ K 10, YO, slip 1, K1, PSSO, K5, K2 tog, YO; repeat from ★ across to last 5 sts, K5.

Row 25: Purl across.

Row 26: K6, YO, slip 1, K1, PSSO, K3, K2 tog, YO, ★ K 12, YO, slip 1, K1, PSSO, K3, K2 tog, YO; repeat from ★ across to last 6 sts, K6.

Row 27: K7, P5, ★ K 14, P5; repeat from ★ across to last 7 sts, K7.

Row 28: K7, YO, slip 1, K1, PSSO, K1, K2 tog, YO, ★ K 14, YO, slip 1, K1, PSSO, K1, K2 tog, YO; repeat from ★ across to last 7 sts, K7.

Row 29: Purl across.

Row 30: K8, YO, [slip 1, K2 tog, PSSO *(Figs. 26a & b, page 584)*], YO, ★ K 16, YO, slip 1, K2 tog, PSSO, YO; repeat from ★ across to last 8 sts, K8.

Rows 31 and 32: Knit across.

Row 33: Purl across.

Row 34: K2 tog 3 times, YO, (K1, YO) 7 times, ★ K2 tog 6 times, YO, (K1, YO) 7 times; repeat from ★ across to last 6 sts, K2 tog 3 times: 84 sts.

Rows 35 and 36: Knit across.

Row 37: Purl across.

Row 38: K2 tog 3 times, YO, (K1, YO) 9 times, ★ K2 tog 6 times, YO, (K1, YO) 9 times; repeat from ★ across to last 6 sts, K2 tog 3 times: 100 sts.

Rows 39 and 40: Knit across.

Row 41: Purl across.

Row 42: K2 tog 4 times, YO, (K1, YO) 9 times, ★ K2 tog 8 times, YO, (K1, YO) 9 times; repeat from ★ across to last 8 sts, K2 tog 4 times: 108 sts.

Instructions continued on page 368.

Rows 43 and 44: Knit across.

Rows 45: Purl across.

Row 46: K2 tog 4 times, YO, (K1, YO) 11 times, ★ K2 tog 8 times, YO, (K1, YO) 11 times; repeat from ★ across to last 8 sts, K2 tog 4 times: 124 sts.

Rows 47-49: Repeat Rows 43-45.

Row 50: K2 tog 5 times, YO, (K1, YO) 11 times, ★ K2 tog 10 times, YO, (K1, YO) 11 times; repeat from ★ across to last 10 sts, K2 tog 5 times: 132 sts.

Rows 51 and 52: Knit across.

Row 53: Purl across.

Row 54: K2 tog 5 times, K1, (YO, K1) 12 times, ★ K2 tog 10 times, K1, (YO, K1) 12 times; repeat from ★ across to last 10 sts, K2 tog 5 times: 140 sts.

Rows 55 and 56: Knit across.

Row 57: Purl across.

Row 58: K2 tog 6 times, YO, (K1, YO) 11 times, ★ K2 tog 12 times, YO, (K1, YO) 11 times; repeat from ★ across to last 12 sts, K2 tog 6 times.

Row 59: Knit across.

Row 60: ★ K2, K2 tog; repeat from ★ across: 105 sts.

Bind off all sts **loosely**.

FINISHING

Weave yarn through cast on stitches; draw up tightly.

Sew back seam to markers.

NECK BAND

With **right** side facing, pick up 50 sts evenly spaced across neck edge *(Fig. 34a, page 586)*.

Rows 1-5: Knit across.

Bind off all sts **loosely**.

Sew on ribbon for ties using photo as a guide for placement.

BOOTIES ◀▬▬▶ EXPERIENCED

Size: Newborn, 3 months and 6 months

Note: Yarn amounts, Gauge and length are given for Newborn, with 3 months and 6 months in braces { }. Proper measurement is obtained by using different needle sizes as recommended under Materials.

MATERIALS

SUPER FINE
1

Baby Yarn, approximately:
$1/2${$3/4$-1} ounce, 90{130-175} yards,
[15{20-30} grams, 82{119-160} meters]
For Newborn size ONLY:
Straight knitting needles, size 3 (3.25 mm)
or size needed for gauge
For 3 months size ONLY:
Straight knitting needles, size 4 (3.5 mm)
or size needed for gauge
For 6 months size ONLY:
Straight knitting needles, size 5 (3.75 mm)
or size needed for gauge
2 Stitch holders
$1/4$" (7 mm) wide Ribbon - 1 yard (.9 meters)

GAUGE: One pattern (35 sts) = 3{$3^1/4$-$3^1/2$}"/
7.5{8.25-9} cm;
26 rows = $2^1/4${$2^1/2$-$2^3/4$}"/
5.75{6.25-7} cm

Work Gauge Swatch as follows:
Cast on 35 sts **loosely**.
Rows 1 and 2: Knit across.
Row 3: Purl across.
Row 4: K2 tog 6 times *(Fig. 17, page 583)*, YO *(Fig. 16a, page 582)*, (K1, YO) 11 times, K2 tog 6 times.
Rows 5-24: Repeat Rows 1-4, 5 times.
Rows 25 and 26: Knit across.
Bind off all sts **loosely**.

CUFF

Cast on 30 sts **loosely**.

Row 1 (Right side)**:** Knit across.

Note: Loop a short piece of yarn around any stitch to mark Row 1 as **right** side.

Row 2 (Eyelet row)**:** K2, ★ YO *(Fig. 16a, page 582)*, K2 tog *(Fig. 17, page 583)*; repeat from ★ across.

Rows 3-5: Knit across.

Row 6: Purl across.

Row 7: K2 tog twice, YO, (K1, YO) 7 times, K2 tog 4 times, YO, (K1, YO) 7 times, K2 tog twice: 38 sts.

Rows 8 and 9: Knit across.

Row 10: Purl across.

Row 11: K2 tog 3 times, YO, (K1, YO) 7 times, K2 tog 6 times, YO, (K1, YO) 7 times, K2 tog 3 times: 42 sts.

Rows 12-14: Repeat Rows 8-10.

Row 15: K2 tog 4 times, YO, (K1, YO) 5 times, K2 tog 8 times, YO, (K1, YO) 5 times, K2 tog 4 times: 38 sts.

Rows 16 and 17: Knit across.

Bind off all sts **loosely**.

INSTEP

With **right** side facing, pick up 30 sts along cast on edge **(Fig. 34b, page 586)**.

Row 1 (Wrong side)**:** Knit across.

Row 2: K 20, slip remaining 10 sts onto st holder: 20 sts.

Row 3: K 10, slip remaining 10 sts onto second st holder: 10 sts.

Rows 4-23: Knit across; at end of Row 23, cut yarn.

SIDES

Row 1: With **right** side facing, slip sts from st holder onto empty needle, pick up 10 sts along right side of Instep **(Fig. 34a, page 586)**, K 10, pick up 10 sts along left side of Instep, slip sts from st holder onto empty needle, knit across: 50 sts.

Rows 2-12: Knit across.

Row 13: K3, K2 tog, K 15, K2 tog, K6, K2 tog, K 15, K2 tog, K3: 46 sts.

Row 14: Knit across.

Bind off all sts.

FINISHING

Sew seam.

Weave Ribbon through Eyelet row.

BLANKET ◀■■▶ EXPERIENCED

Size: Approximately 31" (78.5 cm) square

MATERIALS

Baby Yarn, approximately:
11 ounces, 1,925 yards
(310 grams, 1,760 meters)
24" (61 cm) Circular needle, size 7 (4.5 mm)
or size needed for gauge

Note: Entire Blanket is worked holding two strands of yarn together.

GAUGE: Working double strand,
2 patterns (34 sts) = 6" (15.25 cm);
27 rows = 3^1/$_2$" (9 cm)

Work Gauge Swatch as follows:
Cast on 34 sts **loosely**.
Rows 1-3: Knit across.
Row 4: Purl across.
Row 5: K2 tog 3 times **(Fig. 17, page 583)**, YO **(Fig. 16a, page 582)**, (K1, YO) 5 times, K2 tog 3 times.
Rows 6 and 7: Knit across.
Rows 8-27: Repeat Rows 4-7, 5 times.
Rows 25 and 26: Knit across.
Bind off all sts **loosely**.

Cast on 176 sts **loosely**.

Rows 1-3: Knit across.

Row 4: K3, purl across to last 3 sts, K3.

Row 5: K3, K2 tog 3 times **(Fig. 17, page 583)**, YO **(Fig. 16a, page 582)**, (K1, YO) 5 times, ★ K2 tog 6 times, YO, (K1, YO) 5 times; repeat from ★ across to last 9 sts, K2 tog 3 times, K3.

Rows 6 and 7: Knit across.

Repeat Rows 4-7 until Blanket measures approximately 31" (78.5 cm) or to desired length, ending by working Row 7.

Bind off all sts **loosely**.

Designs by Jeannine.

HEARTS PULLOVER ◖■■▭ INTERMEDIATE

Size: 6 months, 12 months, and 18 months

Size Note: Instructions are written for size 6 months with sizes 12 and 18 months in braces { }. Instructions will be easier to read, if you circle all the numbers pertaining to your size. If only one number is given, it applies to all sizes.

MATERIALS

SUPER FINE
1

Fingering Weight Yarn, approximately:
  2³/₄{3¹/₄-4} ounces, 395{465-570} yards
  [80{90-110} grams, 361{425-521} meters]
Straight knitting needles, sizes 2 (2.75 mm) **and**
  3 (3.25 mm) **or** sizes needed for gauge
2 Stitch holders
Yarn needle
Crochet hook, size E (2.5 mm)

GAUGE: With larger size needles,
  in Stockinette Stitch,
  28 sts and 36 rows = 4" (10 cm)

FRONT
RIBBING

With smaller size needles, cast on 70{74-78} sts **loosely**.

Work in K1, P1 ribbing for ³/₄" (2 cm) increasing 9 sts evenly spaced across last row *(see Increases, page 581)*: 79{83-87} sts.

BODY

Change to larger size needles.

Row 1 (Wrong side)**:** P9{11-13}, † K2, P2, K2, P 10, K2, P2, K2 †, P 17, repeat from † to † once, P9{11-13}.

To work Right Twist 2 (abbreviated RT2), skip next st on left needle, knit next st, knit skipped st, slip both sts off left needle.

Row 2: K9{11-13}, † P2, RT2, P2, K 10, P2, RT2, P2 †, K 17, repeat from † to † once, K9{11-13}.

Repeat Rows 1 and 2, 2{5-3} times; then repeat Row 1 once **more**.

HEART PATTERN

Row 1 (Right side)**:** K9{11-13}, † P2, RT2, P2, K 10, P2, RT2, P2 †, K6, K2 tog *(Fig. 17, page 583)*, YO *(Fig. 16a, page 582)*, K1, YO, SSK *(Figs. 21a-c, page 584)*, K6, repeat from † to † once, K9{11-13}.

Row 2 AND ALL WRONG SIDE ROWS:
P9{11-13}, † K2, P2, K2, P 10, K2, P2, K2 †, P 17, repeat from † to † once, P9{11-13}.

Row 3: K9{11-13}, † P2, RT2, P2, K 10, P2, RT2, P2 †, K5, K2 tog, YO, K3, YO, SSK, K5, repeat from † to † once, K9{11-13}.

Row 5: K9{11-13}, † P2, RT2, P2, K 10, P2, RT2, P2 †, K4, K2 tog, YO, K5, YO, SSK, K4, repeat from † to † once, K9{11-13}.

Row 7: K9{11-13}, † P2, RT2, P2, K 10, P2, RT2, P2 †, K3, K2 tog, YO, K7, YO, SSK, K3, repeat from † to † once, K9{11-13}.

Row 9: K9{11-13}, † P2, RT2, P2, K 10, P2, RT2, P2 †, K2, K2 tog, YO, K9, YO, SSK, K2, repeat from † to † once, K9{11-13}.

Row 11: K9{11-13}, † P2, RT2, P2, K 10, P2, RT2, P2 †, K3, YO, SSK, K3, YO, K1, YO, K3, K2 tog, YO, K3, repeat from † to † once, K9{11-13}: 81{85-89} sts.

Row 13: K9{11-13}, † P2, RT2, P2, K 10, P2, RT2, P2 †, K4, YO, slip 2 sts as if to **knit**, K2 tog, P2SSO, YO, K3, YO, slip 2 sts as if to **knit**, K2 tog, P2SSO, YO, K4, repeat from † to † once, K9{11-13}: 79{83-87} sts.

Row 15: K9{11-13}, † P2, RT2, P2, K 10, P2, RT2, P2 †, K 17, repeat from † to † once, K9{11-13}.

Row 16: P9{11-13}, † K2, P2, K2, P 10, K2, P2, K2 †, P 17, repeat from † to † once, P9{11-13}.

Rows 17-20: Repeat Rows 15 and 16 twice.

Repeat Rows 1-20 for pattern until Front measures approximately 8{8³/₄-10¹/₂}"/ 20.5{22-26.5} cm from cast on edge, ending by working Pattern Row 19.

Instructions continued on page 372.

Neck Shaping

Note: Both sides of Neck are worked at the same time, using separate yarn for **each** side. Maintain established pattern throughout.

Row 1: Work across 30{32-32} sts, slip next 19{19-23} sts onto st holder; with second yarn, work across: 30{32-32} sts **each** side.

Row 2 (Decrease row): Work across to within 2 sts of Neck edge, decrease **(see Decreases, pages 583 & 584)**; with second yarn, decrease, work across: 29{31-31} sts **each** side.

Row 3: Work across; with second yarn, work across.

Rows 4-12: Repeat Rows 2 and 3, 4 times; then repeat Row 2 once **more**: 24{26-26} sts **each** side.

Work even until Front measures approximately 10^1/$_2${11^1/$_4$-13}"/26.5{28.5-33} cm from cast on edge, ending by working a **right** side row.

Decrease Row: P9{11-13}, K2 tog, P2 tog **(Fig. 18, page 583)**, K2 tog, P9{9-7}; with second yarn, P9{9-7}, K2 tog, P2 tog, K2 tog, P9{11-13}: 21{23-23} sts **each** side.

Bind off all sts.

BACK
RIBBING
Work same as Front, page 370: 79{83-87} sts.

BODY
Row 1 (Wrong side)**:** P9{11-13}, † K2, P2, K2, P 10, K2, P2, K2 †, P 17, repeat from † to † once, P9{11-13}.

Row 2: K9{11-13}, † P2, RT2, P2, K 10, P2, RT2, P2 †, K 17, repeat from † to † once, K9{11-13}.

Repeat Rows 1 and 2 until Back measures same as Front, ending by working Row 2.

Decrease Row: P9{11-13}, † K2 tog, P2 tog, K2 tog, P 10, K2 tog, P2 tog, K2 tog †, P 17, repeat from † to † once, P9{11-13}: 67{71-75} sts.

Next Row: Bind off 21{23-23} sts, work across 24{24-28} sts, slip 25{25-29} sts just worked onto st holder, bind off remaining sts.

SLEEVE (Make 2)
RIBBING
With smaller size needles, cast on 40{42-44} sts **loosely**.

Work in K1, P1 ribbing for 1^1/$_2$" (4 cm) increasing 10 sts evenly spaced across last row: 50{52-54} sts.

BODY
Change to larger size needles.

Row 1 (Wrong side)**:** P 14{15-16}, K2, P2, K2, P 10, K2, P2, K2, P 14{15-16}.

Row 2: K 14{15-16}, P2, RT2, P2, K 10, P2, RT2, P2, K 14{15-16}.

Row 3: P 14{15-16}, K2, P2, K2, P 10, K2, P2, K2, P 14{15-16}.

Row 4 (Increase row)**:** Increase, K 13{14-15}, P2, RT2, P2, K 10, P2, RT2, P2, K 13{14-15}, increase: 52{54-56} sts.

Maintaining pattern, continue to increase one stitch at **each** edge, every fourth row, 2{0-3} times **more (see Zeros, page 577)**; then increase every sixth row, 3{6-7} times: 62{66-76} sts.

Work even until Sleeve measures approximately 6{7-9}"/15{18-23} cm from cast on edge, ending by working a **right** side row.

Decrease Row: P 20{22-27}, K2 tog, P2 tog, K2 tog, P 10, K2 tog, P2 tog, K2 tog, purl across: 56{60-70} sts.

Bind off all sts **loosely**.

FINISHING
Sew left shoulder seam.

NECK RIBBING
With **right** side facing and smaller size needles, knit 25{25-29} sts from Back st holder, pick up 20{20-19} sts along left Neck edge **(Fig. 34a, page 586)**, knit 19{19-23} sts from Front st holder, pick up 20{20-19} sts along right Neck edge: 84{84-90} sts.

Work in K1, P1 ribbing for ^{3}/$_4$" (4 cm).

Bind off all sts **loosely** in ribbing.

Sew right shoulder seam.
Sew Sleeves to Sweater matching center to shoulder seam and beginning 4{4$\frac{1}{4}$-5}"/10{11-12.5} cm down from seam.
Sew underarm and side in one continuous seam.

PICOT NECK EDGING

With **right** side facing, using crochet hook and working around stitches in first row of Neck Ribbing, join yarn with slip st at left shoulder seam *(see Crochet Stitches, pages 588 & 589)*; ★ sc in next st, ch 3, slip st in base of sc just worked, slip st in each of next 2 sts; repeat from ★ around; join with slip st to first st, finish off.

SHORT PANTS ◼◼◻◻ EASY

Note: For Long Pants, see page 380.

Size: 6 months, 12 months, and 18 months

Size Note: Instructions are written for size 6 months with sizes 12 and 18 months in braces { }. Instructions will be easier to read, if you circle all the numbers pertaining to your size. If only one number is given, it applies to all sizes.

MATERIALS

SUPER FINE **1**

Fingering Weight Yarn, approximately:
    1$\frac{1}{2}${1$\frac{3}{4}$-2} ounces, 215{250-285} yards
    [40{50-60} grams, 197{229-261} meters]
Straight knitting needles, sizes 2 (2.75 mm) **and**
    3 (3.25 mm) **or** sizes needed for gauge
Yarn needle
$\frac{3}{8}$" (10 mm) Elastic - 19{20-21}"/
    48.5{51-53.5} meters

GAUGE: With larger size needles,
        in Stockinette Stitch,
        28 sts and 36 rows = 4" (10 cm)

BACK

With larger size needles, cast on 22 sts **loosely**.

Beginning with a **purl** row, work in Stockinette Stitch (knit one row, purl one row) until Back measures approximately $\frac{1}{2}$" (1.25 cm) from cast on edge, ending by working a **purl** row.

SHAPING

Add on 2 sts **loosely** at the beginning of the next 16{18-18} rows *(Figs. 5a & b, page 580)*, work across: 54{58-58} sts.

Add on 3 sts **loosely** at the beginning of the next 6{6-8} rows, work across: 72{76-82} sts.

Work even until Back measures approximately 6$\frac{1}{4}${7$\frac{1}{4}$-8$\frac{1}{4}$}"/16{18.5-21} cm from cast on edge, ending by working a **purl** row.

WAISTBAND

Change to smaller size needles.

Work in K1, P1 ribbing for 1$\frac{1}{2}$" (4 cm).

Bind off all sts **very loosely** in ribbing.

FRONT

With larger size needles, cast on 22 sts **loosely**.

Beginning with a **purl** row, work in Stockinette Stitch until Front measures approximately 1" (2.5 cm) from cast on edge, ending by working a **purl** row.

SHAPING

Add on 2 sts **loosely** at the beginning of the next 12{14-14} rows, work across: 46{50-50} sts.

Add on 3 sts **loosely** at the beginning of the next 4{4-6} rows, work across: 58{62-68} sts.

Add on 7 sts **loosely** at the beginning of the next 2 rows, work across: 72{76-82} sts.

Work even until Front measures same as Back to Waistband, ending by working a **purl** row.

WAISTBAND

Work same as Back.

FINISHING

Sew Front and Back cast on edges together.

LEG RIBBING

With **right** side facing and smaller size needles, pick up 72{78-84} sts evenly spaced along leg opening *(Figs. 34a & b, page 586)*.

Work in K1, P1 ribbing for 1$\frac{1}{2}$" (4 cm).

Bind off all sts **very loosely** in ribbing.

Repeat for second leg opening.

Sew side seams.
Fold Leg Ribbing in half to inside and sew **loosely** to base of first row.

Instructions continued on page 374.

Cut elastic 1" (2.5 cm) more than desired waist measurement; overlapping ends ¹/₂" (1.25 cm), sew firmly in a circle. Place elastic along wrong side of Waistband, fold Waistband to inside and sew in place, being careful not to catch elastic.

HEARTS BOOTIES ◼️◼️◻️◻️ EASY

Size: 6 months ONLY

MATERIALS
Fingering Weight yarn, approximately:
¹/₂ ounce, 70 yards (20 grams, 64 meters)
Straight knitting needles, sizes 2 (2.75 mm) **and**
3 (3.25 mm) **or** sizes needed for gauge
3 Stitch holders
Yarn needle
Crochet hook, size E (2.5 mm)

GAUGE: With larger size needles,
in Stockinette Stitch,
28 sts and 36 rows = 4" (10 cm)

RIBBING
With smaller size needles, cast on 40 sts **loosely**.

Work in K1, P1 ribbing 2" (5 cm).

INSTEP
Change to larger size needles.

Row 1 (Right side): Work across 15 sts, slip 15 sts just worked onto st holder, P1, increase *(see Increases, page 581)*, P1, increase in each of next 4 sts, P1, increase, P1, slip last 15 sts onto st holder: 16 sts.

Row 2: K1, P2, K1, P8, K1, P2, K1.

To work Right Twist 2 (abbreviated RT2), skip next st on left needle, knit next st, knit skipped st, slip both sts off left needle.

Row 3: P1, RT2, P1, K8, P1, RT2, P1.

Repeat Rows 2 and 3 until Instep measures approximately 1¹/₂", ending by working Row 3.

Cut yarn; slip sts onto st holder.

SIDES
With **right** side facing and larger size needles, knit 15 sts from first st holder, pick up 8 sts evenly spaced along right side of Instep *(Fig. 34a, page 586)*, knit 16 sts from Instep st holder, pick up 8 sts evenly spaced along left side of Instep, slip 15 sts from last st holder onto empty needle and knit across: 62 sts.

Work in Garter Stitch (knit every row) for ³/₄" (2 cm), ending by working a **right** side row.

Next Row: K 23, ★ K2 tog *(Fig. 17, page 583)*, K1; repeat from ★ 3 times **more**, K2 tog twice, knit across: 56 sts.

SOLE
Row 1: K 32, K2 tog; turn, leave remaining 22 sts unworked.

Rows 2-35: K9, K2 tog; turn, leave remaining sts unworked.

Row 36: K9, K2 tog, K5: 20 sts.

Bind off remaining sts.

FINISHING
Sew back seam. Sew back of Sole to Sides.

PICOT EDGING
With **right** side facing, using crochet hook and working in last row of Cuff, join yarn with slip st in first st at back seam *(see Crochet Stitches, pages 588 & 589)*; sc in next st, ch 3, slip st in base of sc just worked, ★ slip st in each of next 2 sts, sc in next st, ch 3, slip st in base of sc just worked; repeat from ★ around; join with slip st to first st, finish off.

HEARTS BONNET ◼️◼️◻️◻️ EASY

Size: 6 months ONLY

MATERIALS
Fingering Weight Yarn, approximately:
³/₄ ounce, 110 yards (20 grams, 101 meters)
Straight knitting needles, sizes 2 (2.75 mm) **and**
3 (3.25 mm) **or** sizes needed for gauge
Yarn needle
Crochet hook, size E (2.5 mm)
³/₈" (10 mm) Ribbon - 36" (91.5 cm)

GAUGE: With larger size needles, in Stockinette Stitch, 28 sts and 36 rows = 4" (10 cm)

FRONT BAND
With smaller size needles, cast on 85 sts **loosely**.

Row 1 (Wrong side)**:** P1, (K1, P1) across.

Row 2: K1, (P1, K1) across.

Repeat Rows 1 and 2 until Front Band measures approximately 1" (2.5 cm), ending by working Row 2.

CROWN
Change to larger size needles.

Row 1: P 28, K2, P2, K2, P 17, K2, P2, K2, P 28.

To work Right Twist 2 (abbreviated RT2), skip next st on left needle, knit next st, knit skipped st, slip both sts off left needle.

Row 2: K 28, P2, RT2, P2, K 17, P2, RT2, P2, K 28.

Rows 3-9: Repeat Rows 1 and 2, 3 times; then repeat Row 1 once **more**.

Row 10: K 28, P2, RT2, P2, K6, K2 tog *(Fig. 17, page 583)*, YO *(Fig. 16a, page 582)*, K1, YO, SSK *(Figs. 21a-c, page 584)*, K6, P2, RT2, P2, K 28.

Row 11 AND ALL WRONG SIDE ROWS: P 28, K2 P2, K2, P 17, K2, P2, K2, P 28.

Row 12: K 28, P2, RT2, P2, K5, K2 tog, YO, K3, YO, SSK, K5, P2, RT2, P2, K 28.

Row 14: K 28, P2, RT2, P2, K4, K2 tog, YO, K5, YO, SSK, K4, P2, RT2, P2, K 28.

Row 16: K 28, P2, RT2, P2, K3, K2 tog, YO, K7, YO, SSK, K3, P2, RT2, P2, K 28.

Row 18: K 28, P2, RT2, P2, K2, K2 tog, YO, K9, YO, SSK, K2, P2, RT2, P2, K 28.

Row 20: K 28, P2, RT2, P2, K3, YO, SSK, K3, YO, K1, YO, K3, K2 tog, YO, K3, P2, RT2, P2, K 28: 87 sts.

Row 22: K 28, P2, RT2, P2, K4, YO, slip 2 sts as if to **knit**, K2 tog, P2SSO, YO, K3, YO, slip 2 sts as if to **knit**, K2 tog, P2SSO, YO, K4, P2, RT2, P2, K 28: 85 sts.

Row 24: K 28, P2, RT2, P2, K 17, P2, RT2, P2, K 28.

Row 25: P 28, K2, P2, K2, P 17, K2, P2, K2, P 28.

Repeat Rows 24 and 25 until Crown measures approximately 5" (12.5 cm) from cast on edge, ending by working Row 25.

BACK
Note: Maintain established pattern throughout.

Rows 1 and 2: Bind off 28 sts at the beginning of the next 2 rows, work across: 29 sts.

Work even until Back measures approximately 4" (10 cm) from bound off sts, ending by working a **wrong** side row.

Bind off all sts.

FINISHING
Sew sides of Back to bound off edges of Crown.

NECK RIBBING
With **right** side facing and smaller size needles, pick up 87 sts evenly spaced along lower edge of Bonnet *(Figs. 34a & b, page 586)*.

Row 1 (Wrong side)**:** P1, (K1, P1) across.

Row 2: K1, (P1, K1) across.

Repeat Rows 1 and 2 until Neck Ribbing measures approximately 1" (2.5 cm), ending by working Row 1.

Bind off all sts **loosely** in ribbing.

PICOT EDGING
With **right** side facing, using crochet hook and working in last row of Front Band, join yarn with slip st in first st at left side of Front Band *(see Crochet Stitches, pages 588 & 589)*; sc in next st, ch 3, slip st in base of sc just worked, ★ slip st in each of next 2 sts, sc in next st, ch 3, slip st in base of sc just worked; repeat from ★ across; finish off.

Attach an 18" (45.5 cm) length of Ribbon for each tie, using Photo as a guide for placement.

Instructions continued on page 376.

HEARTS BLANKET ◀▬▬▭ INTERMEDIATE

Finished Size: 32" x 41" (81.5 cm x 104 cm)

MATERIALS

Sport Weight Yarn, approximately:
9³/₄ ounces, 1,225 yards
(280 grams, 1,120 meters)
24" (61 cm) Circular needle, size 8 (5 mm) **or**
size needed for gauge

GAUGE: In Stockinette Stitch,
20 sts and 26 rows = 4" (10 cm)

Cast on 163 sts **loosely**.

Rows 1-7: K1, (P1, K1) across (Seed Stitch).

Row 8 (Right side)**:** (K1, P1) 3 times, K 21, ★ P1, (K1, P1) twice, K 21; repeat from ★ across to last 6 sts, (P1, K1) 3 times.

Row 9: K1, (P1, K1) twice, P 23, ★ K1, P1, K1, P 23; repeat from ★ across to last 5 sts, K1, (P1, K1) twice.

Rows 10-13: Repeat Rows 8 and 9 twice.

Row 14: (K1, P1) 3 times, K8, K2 tog **(Fig. 17, page 583)**, YO **(Fig. 16a, page 582)**, K1, YO, SSK **(Figs. 21a-c, page 584)**, K8, ★ P1, (K1, P1) twice, K8, K2 tog, YO, K1, YO, SSK, K8; repeat from ★ across to last 6 sts, (P1, K1) 3 times.

Row 15: K1, (P1, K1) twice, P 23, ★ K1, P1, K1, P 23; repeat from ★ across to last 5 sts, K1, (P1, K1) twice.

Row 16: (K1, P1) 3 times, K7, K2 tog, YO, K3, YO, SSK, K7, ★ P1, (K1, P1) twice, K7, K2 tog, YO, K3, YO, SSK, K7; repeat from ★ across to last 6 sts, (P1, K1) 3 times.

Row 17: K1, (P1, K1) twice, P 23, ★ K1, P1, K1, P 23; repeat from ★ across to last 5 sts, K1, (P1, K1) twice.

Row 18: (K1, P1) 3 times, K6, K2 tog, YO, K5, YO, SSK, K6, ★ P1, (K1, P1) twice, K6, K2 tog, YO, K5, YO, SSK, K6; repeat from ★ across to last 6 sts, (P1, K1) 3 times.

Row 19: K1, (P1, K1) twice, P 23, ★ K1, P1, K1, P 23; repeat from ★ across to last 5 sts, K1, (P1, K1) twice.

Row 20: (K1, P1) 3 times, K5, K2 tog, YO, K7, YO, SSK, K5, ★ P1, (K1, P1) twice, K5, K2 tog, YO, K7, YO, SSK, K5; repeat from ★ across to last 6 sts, (P1, K1) 3 times.

Row 21: K1, (P1, K1) twice, P 23, ★ K1, P1, K1, P 23; repeat from ★ across to last 5 sts, K1, (P1, K1) twice.

Row 22: (K1, P1) 3 times, K4, K2 tog, YO, K9, YO, SSK, K4, ★ P1, (K1, P1) twice, K4, K2 tog, YO, K9, YO, SSK, K4; repeat from ★ across to last 6 sts, (P1, K1) 3 times.

Row 23: K1, (P1, K1) twice, P 23, ★ K1, P1, K1, P 23; repeat from ★ across to last 5 sts, K1, (P1, K1) twice.

Row 24: (K1, P1) 3 times, K5, YO, SSK, K3, YO, K1, YO, K3, K2 tog, YO, K5, ★ P1, (K1, P1) twice, K5, YO, SSK, K3, YO, K1, YO, K3, K2 tog, YO, K5; repeat from ★ across to last 6 sts, (P1, K1) 3 times: 175 sts.

Rows 25: K1, (P1, K1) twice, P 25, ★ K1, P1, K1, P 25; repeat from ★ across to last 5 sts, K1, (P1, K1) twice.

Row 26: (K1, P1) 3 times, K6, YO, slip 2 sts as if to knit, K2 tog, P2SSO, YO, K3, YO, slip 2 sts as if to knit, K2 tog, P2SSO, YO, K6, ★ P1, (K1, P1) twice, K6, YO, slip 2 sts as if to knit, K2 tog, P2SSO, YO, K3, YO, slip 2 sts as if to knit, K2 tog, P2SSO, YO, K6; repeat from ★ across to last 6 sts, (P1, K1) 3 times: 163 sts.

Row 27: K1, (P1, K1) twice, P 23, ★ K1, P1, K1, P 23; repeat from ★ across to last 5 sts, K1, (P1, K1) twice.

Rows 28-33: Repeat Rows 8 and 9, 3 times.

Rows 34-39: K1, (P1, K1) across (Seed Stitch).

Repeat Rows 8-39 for pattern until Blanket measures approximately 40" (102 cm) from cast on edge, ending by working Pattern Row 39.

Bind off all sts **loosely** in pattern.

Holding two strands of yarn together, each 7" (18cm) in length, add fringe in every other stitch along cast on and bound off edges **(Figs. 37a & b, page 588)**.

Designs by Carole Prior.

ARAN LAYETTE

ARAN PULLOVER ■■■□ INTERMEDIATE

Size: 6 months, 12 months, and 18 months

Size Note: Instructions are written for size 6 months with sizes 12 and 18 months in braces { }. Instructions will be easier to read, if you circle all the numbers pertaining to your size. If only one number is given, it applies to all sizes.

MATERIALS

SUPER FINE (1)

Fingering Weight Yarn, approximately:
  2³/₄{3¹/₄-4} ounces, 395{465-570} yards
  [80{90-110} grams, 361{425-521} meters]
Straight knitting needles, sizes 2 (2.75 mm) **and**
  3 (3.25 mm) **or** sizes needed for gauge
16" (40.5 cm) Circular needle, size 2 (2.75 mm)
3 Stitch holders
Markers
Yarn needle
Buttons - 2

GAUGE: With larger size needles,
  in Stockinette Stitch,
  28 sts and 36 rows = 4" (10 cm)

Cable 4 Front, *abbreviated C4F* (4 sts): Slip 2 sts onto cable needle and hold in **front** of work, K2 from left needle, K2 from cable needle.
Cable 4 Back, *abbreviated C4B* (4 sts): Slip 2 sts onto cable needle and hold in **back** of work, K2 from left needle, K2 from cable needle.
Cable 5 Front, *abbreviated C5F* (5 sts): Slip 3 sts onto cable needle and hold in **front** of work, K2 from left needle, slip **purl** st from cable needle back onto left needle and purl this st, K2 from cable needle.
Cable 5 Back, *abbreviated C5B* (5 sts): Slip 3 sts onto cable needle and hold in **back** of work, K2 from left needle, slip **purl** st from cable needle back onto left needle and purl this st, K2 from cable needle.

FRONT
RIBBING
With smaller size needles, cast on 72{76-80} sts **loosely**.

Work in K1, P1 ribbing for ³/₄" (2 cm).

Increase Row: (K1, P1) 1{2-3} time(s), [increase **(Figs. 10a & b, page 581)**, P1] 4 times, (K1, P1) 5 times, increase, P1, (K1, P1) 3 times, (increase, P1) 9 times, (K1, P1) 4 times, increase, P1, (K1, P1) 3 times, (increase, P1) 5 times, (K1, P1) 0{1-2} time(s) **(see Zeros, page 577)**: 92{96-100} sts.

BODY
Change to larger size needles.

Note: when instructed to slip a stitch, always slip as if to **purl** unless otherwise specified.

Row 1 AND ALL WRONG SIDE ROWS:
P 15{17-19}, K3, P1, K3, P4, K3, P1, K3, P2, (K1, P2) 8 times, K3, P1, K3, P4, K3, P1, K3, P 15{17-19}.

Row 2: K 15{17-19}, P3, WYB slip 1, P3, C4F, P3, WYB slip 1, P3, K2, (P1, C5F) 4 times, P3, WYB slip 1, P3, C4B, P3, WYB slip 1, P3, K 15{17-19}.

Row 4: K 15{17-19}, P3, WYB slip 1, P3, K4, P3, WYB slip 1, P3, K2, (P1, K2) 8 times, P3, WYB slip 1, P3, K4, P3, WYB slip 1, P3, K 15{17-19}.

Row 6: K 15{17-19}, P3, WYB slip 1, P3, C4F, P3, WYB slip 1, P3, (C5B, P1) 4 times, K2, P3, WYB slip 1, P3, C4B, P3, WYB slip 1, P3, K 15{17-19}.

Row 8: Repeat Row 4.

Repeat Rows 1-8 for pattern until Front measures approximately 6¹/₂{7-8}"/16.5{18-20.5} cm from cast on edge, ending by working a **wrong** side row.

Instructions continued on page 378.

Armhole Shaping

Rows 1 and 2: Bind off 3 sts at the beginning of the next 2 rows, work across: 86{90-94} sts.

Row 3: (Decrease row)**:** [Slip 1 as if to **knit**, K1, PSSO *(Figs. 19a & b, page 583)*], work across to last 2 sts, K2 tog *(Fig. 17, page 583)*: 84{88-92} sts.

Row 4: Work across.

Repeat Rows 3 and 4 twice.

Work even until Armholes measure approximately 2{2^1/$_4$-3}"/5{5.5-7.5} cm, ending by working a **wrong** side row.

Neck Shaping

Row 1: (Decrease row)**:** Work across 27{29-31} sts, K2 tog, (P1, K2 tog) 8 times, work across: 71{75-79} sts.

Note: Both sides of Neck are worked at the same time, using separate yarn for **each** side.

Row 2: Work across 21{23-24} sts, slip 29{29-31} sts onto st holder; with second yarn, work across: 21{23-24} sts **each** side.

Row 3: (Decrease row)**:** Work across to within 2 sts of Neck edge, decrease; with second yarn, decrease, work across: 20{22-23} sts **each** side.

Row 4: Work across; with second yarn, work across.

Repeat Rows 3 and 4, 3{3-4} times: 17{19-19} sts **each** side.

Work even until Armholes measure approximately 4{4^1/$_4$-5}"/10{11-12.5} cm, ending by working a **wrong** side row.

Bind off all sts.

BACK
RIBBING

With smaller size needles, cast on 72{76-80} sts **loosely.**

Work in K1, P1 ribbing for ^{3}/$_4$" (2 cm).

BODY

Change to larger size needles.

Work in Stockinette Stitch (knit one row, purl one row) until Back measures same as Front to Armhole Shaping, ending by working a **purl** row.

Armhole Shaping

Rows 1 and 2: Bind off 3 sts at the beginning of the next 2 rows, work across: 66{70-74} sts.

Row 3 (Decrease row)**:** Slip 1 as if to **knit**, K1, PSSO, knit across to last 2 sts, K2 tog: 64{68-72} sts.

Row 4: Purl across.

Repeat Rows 3 and 4 twice: 60{64-68} sts.

Work even until Armholes measure same as Front to Neck Shaping, ending by working a **purl** row.

Placket Opening

Row 1: K 32{34-36}; with second yarn, add on 4 sts **loosely** *(Figs. 5a & b, page 580)*, knit across: 32{34-36} sts **each** side.

Row 2: Purl across to last 4 sts, K4; with second yarn, K4, purl across.

Row 3: Knit across; with second yarn, knit across.

Rows 4-10: Repeat Rows 2 and 3, 3 times; then repeat Row 2 once **more.**

Row 11 (Buttonhole row)**:** Knit across to last 4 sts, K2 tog, YO *(Fig. 16a, page 582)*, K2; with second yarn, knit across.

Work even until Back measures same as Front, ending by working a **wrong** side row.

Next Row: Bind off 17{19-19} sts, knit across, slip 15{15-17} sts just worked onto st holder; with second yarn, K 15{15-17} sts, slip 15{15-17} sts just worked onto st holder, bind off remaining sts.

SLEEVE (Make 2)
RIBBING

With smaller size needles, cast on 40{42-44} sts **loosely**.

Work in K1, P1 ribbing for 1¹/₂" increasing 6 sts evenly spaced across last row: 46{48-50} sts.

BODY

Change to larger size needles.

Row 1 (Wrong side)**:** P 14{15-16}, place marker **(Fig. 1, page 578)**, K3, P1, K3, P4, K3, P1, K3, place marker, purl across.

Row 2: Knit to marker, P3, WYB slip 1, P3, K4, P3, WYB slip 1, P3, knit across.

Row 3: Purl to marker, K3, P1, K3, P4, K3, P1, K3, purl across.

Row 4 (Increase row)**:** Increase, knit to marker, P3, WYB slip 1, P3, C4F, P3, WYB slip 1, P3, knit across to last st, increase: 48{50-52} sts.

Maintaining pattern, continue to increase one stitch at **each** edge, every fourth row, 1{0-0} time(s) **more (see Zeros, page 577)**; then increase every sixth row, 4{6-8} times: 58{62-68} sts.

Work even until Sleeve measures approximately 6{7-9}"/15{18-23} cm from cast on edge, ending by working a **wrong** side row.

SLEEVE CAP

Note: Maintain established pattern throughout.

Rows 1 and 2: Bind off 3 sts at the beginning of the next 2 rows, work across: 52{56-62} sts.

Row 3 (Decrease row)**:** Slip 1 as if to **knit**, K1, PSSO, work across to last 2 sts, K2 tog: 50{54-60} sts.

Row 4: Work across.

Continue to decrease one stitch at **each** edge, ever other row, 2{4-6} times **more**; then decrease every row, 13{13-14} times: 20 sts.

Bind off 2 sts at the beginning of the next 4 rows, work across: 12 sts.

Bind off remaining sts.

Instructions continued on page 380.

FINISHING

Sew shoulder seams.
Set in Sleeves matching center to shoulder seam.
Sew underarm and side in one continuous seam.
Sew bottom edge of Placket to Sweater, lapping right Placket over left Placket.

NECK RIBBING

With **right** side facing and circular needle, knit 15{15-17} sts from left Back st holder, pick up 16 sts along left Neck edge **(Fig. 34a, page 586)**, knit 29{29-31} sts from Front st holder, pick up 16 sts along right Neck edge, knit 15{15-17} sts from right Back st holder: 91{91-97} sts.

Row 1 (Wrong side)**:** K4, P1, (K1, P1) across to last 4 sts, K4.

Row 2: K5, P1, (K1, P1) across to last 5 sts, K5.

Row 3: K4, P1, (K1, P1) across to last 4 sts, K4.

Row 4 (Buttonhole row)**:** K5, (P1, K1) across to last 4 sts, K2 tog, YO, K2.

Rows 5-7: Repeat Rows 1-3.

Bind off all sts **loosely** in pattern.

Add Buttons.

LONG PANTS ◂■▭▭ EASY

Note: For Short Pants, see page 373.

Size: 6 months, 12, months, and 18 months

Size Note: Instructions are written for size 6 months with sizes 12 and 18 months in braces { }. Instructions will be easier to read, if you circle all the numbers pertaining to your size. If only one number is given, it applies to all sizes.

MATERIALS

Fingering Weight Yarn, approximately:
  $2^1/4${$2^3/4$-$3^1/2$} ounces, 320{395-500} yards
  [70{80-100} grams, 293{361-457} meters]
Straight knitting needles, sizes 2 (2.75 mm) **and**
  3 (3.25 mm) **or** sizes needed for gauge
Yarn needle
$^3/_8$" Elastic - 19{20-21}" 48.5{51-53.5} meters

GAUGE: With larger size needles,
in Stockinette Stitch,
28 sts and 36 rows = 4" (10 cm)

LEG (Make 2)
RIBBING

With smaller size needles, cast on 46{50-56} sts **loosely**.

Work in K1, P1 ribbing for $1^1/2$" (4 cm) increasing 20 sts evenly spaced across last row **(see Increases, page 581)**: 66{70-76} sts.

BODY

Change to larger size needles.

Work in Stockinette Stitch (knit one row, purl one row) until Leg measures approximately 7{8-10}"/ 18{20.5-25.5} cm from cast on edge, ending by working a **purl** row.

Shaping
Row 1 (Increase row)**:** Increase **(Figs. 10a & b, page 581)**, knit across to last st, increase: 68{72-78} sts.

Row 2: Purl across.

Rows 3-6: Repeat Rows 1 and 2 twice: 72{76-82} sts.

Note: Tie a short piece of yarn around the first and last stitch of last row worked to mark end of Shaping.

Work even in Stockinette Stitch until piece measures approximately $6^1/4${$7^1/4$-$8^1/4$}"/ 16{18.5-21} cm from markers.

WAISTBAND

Change to smaller size needles.

Work in K1, P1 ribbing for $1^1/2$" (4 cm).

Bind off all sts **very loosely** in ribbing.

FINISHING

Sew center front and back seams from top of Waistband to marker. Sew inseam.
Cut elastic 1" (2.5 cm) more than desired waist measurement; overlapping ends $^1/2$" (1.25 cm), sew firmly in a circle. Place elastic along wrong side of Waistband, fold Waistband to inside and sew in place, being careful not to catch elastic.

ARAN BOOTIES ▬▬◻◻ EASY

Size: 6 months ONLY

MATERIALS

SUPER FINE
1

Fingering Weight Yarn, approximately:
  1/2 ounce, 70 yards (20 grams, 64 meters)
Straight knitting needles, sizes 2 (2.75 mm) **and**
  3 (3.25 mm) **or** sizes needed for gauge
3 Stitch holders
Cable needle
Yarn needle

GAUGE: With larger size needles,
        in Stockinette Stitch,
        28 sts and 36 rows = 4" (10 cm)

With smaller size needles, cast on 40 sts **loosely**.

Work in K1, P1 ribbing for 2" (5 cm).

INSTEP
Change to larger size needles.

Note: When instructed to slip a stitch, always slip as if
to **purl**.

Row 1 (Right side)**:** Work across 15 sts, slip 15 sts just
worked onto st holder, increase **(Figs. 10a & b,
page 581)**, WYB slip 1, increase, slip last 15 sts onto
st holder: 16 sts.

Row 2: K2, P1, K3, P4, K3, P1, K2.

Row 3: P2, WYB slip 1, P3, [slip 2 sts onto cable
needle and hold in front of work, K2 from left needle,
K2 from cable needle **(Cable 4 Front made,
abbreviated C4F)**], P3, WYB slip 1, P2.

Row 4: K2, P1, K3, P4, K3, P1, K2.

Row 5: P2, WYB slip 1, P3, K4, P3, WYB slip 1, P2.

Repeat Rows 2-5 for pattern until Instep measures
approximately 1 1/2" (4 cm), ending by working a **wrong**
side row.

Cut yarn; slip sts onto st holder.

SIDES
With **right** side facing and larger size needles, knit
15 sts from first st holder, pick up 8 sts evenly spaced
along right side of Instep **(Fig. 34a, page 586)**,
slip 16 sts from Instep st holder onto empty needle,
maintaining pattern work 16 sts from needle, pick up
8 sts evenly spaced along left side of Instep, slip 16 sts
from last st holder onto empty needle and knit across:
62 sts.

Row 1 (Wrong side)**:** P 23, work across 16 sts in
pattern, P 23.

Row 2: K 23, work across 16 sts in pattern, K 23.

Repeat Rows 1 and 2 until Sides measure
approximately 3/4" (2 cm), ending by working Row 2.

Next Row: P 23, K2 tog, P1, K2 tog **(Fig. 17,
page 583)**, K1, P2 tog twice **(Fig. 18, page 583)**,
K1, K2 tog, P1, K2 tog, P 23: 56 sts.

SOLE
Row 1: K 32, K2 tog; turn, leave remaining 22 sts
unworked.

Row 2: P9, P2 tog; turn, leave remaining sts
unworked.

Row 3: K9, K2 tog; turn, leave remaining sts
unworked.

Rows 4-35: Repeat Rows 2 and 3, 16 times.

Row 36: P9, P2 tog, P5: 20 sts.

Bind off remaining sts.

FINISHING
Sew back seam. Sew back of Sole to Sides.

Instructions continued on page 382.

ARAN BONNET ◖■□□ EASY

Size: 6 months ONLY

MATERIALS
Fingering Weight Yarn, approximately: **SUPER FINE ❶**
$^3/_4$ ounce, 110 yards (20 grams, 101 meters)
Straight knitting needles, sizes 2 (2.75 mm) **and**
3 (3.25 mm) **or** sizes needed for gauge
Cable needle
Yarn needle
Button - 1

GAUGE: With larger size needles,
in Stockinette Stitch,
28 sts and 36 rows - 4" (10 cm)

With larger size needles, cast on 10 sts **loosely**.

Row 1 (Right side)**:** K1, increase in each of the next
8 sts **(Figs. 10a & b, page 581)**, K1: 18 sts.

Row 2 AND ALL WRONG SIDE ROWS: Purl
across.

Row 3: ★ K2, YO **(Fig. 16a, page 582)**; repeat from
★ across to last 2 sts, K2: 26 sts.

Row 5: (K3, YO) across to last 2 sts, K2: 34 sts.

Row 7: (K4, YO) across to last 2 sts, K2: 42 sts.

Row 9: (K5, YO) across to last 2 sts, K2: 50 sts.

Row 11: (K6, YO) across to last 2 sts, K2: 58 sts.

Row 13: (K7, YO) across to last 2 sts, K2: 66 sts.

Row 15: (K8, YO) across to last 2 sts, K2: 74 sts.

Row 17: (K9, YO) across to last 2 sts, K2: 82 sts.

Row 19: (K 10, YO) across to last 2 sts, K2: 90 sts.

Row 21: (K 11, YO) across to last 2 sts, K2: 98 sts.

Row 22: Purl across.

CROWN
Row 1: Bind off 3 sts, knit across: 95 sts.

Row 2: Bind off 3 sts, P 39, increase **(Fig. 11, page 581)**, (P1, increase) 5 times, purl across: 98 sts.
Note: When instructed to slip a stitch, always slip as if
to **purl**.

Row 3: K 40, P3, WYB slip 1, P3, [slip 2 sts onto
cable needle and hold in **front** of work, K2 from left
needle, K2 from cable needle **(Cable 4 Front made, abbreviated C4F)**], P3, WYB slip 1, P3, K 40.

Row 4: P 40, K3, P1, K3, P4, K3, P1, K3, P 40.

Row 5: K 40, P3, WYB slip 1, P3, K4, P3,
WYB slip 1, P3, K 40.

Row 6: P 40, K3, P1, K3, P4, K3, P1, K3, P 40.

Repeat Rows 3-6 for pattern until Crown measures
approximately $3^1/_4$" (8.5 cm) from bound off sts,
ending by working a **wrong** side row.

FRONT BAND
Row 1 (Right side)**:** K2 tog **(Fig. 17, page 583)**,
(P1, K1) across: 97 sts.

Row 2: P1, (K1, P1) across.

Row 3: K1, (P1, K1) across.

Rows 4-9: Repeat Rows 2 and 3, 3 times.

Bind off all sts **loosely** in ribbing.

FINISHING
Sew back seam.

NECK BAND
With **right** side facing and smaller size needles, pick up
65 sts evenly spaced along lower edge **(Figs. 34a & b, page 586)**, add on 22 sts **loosely** **(Figs. 5a & b, page 580)**: 87 sts.

Row 1 (Wrong side)**:** P1, (K1, P1) across.

Row 2: K1, (P1, K1) across.

Row 3 (Buttonhole row)**:** P1, K2 tog, YO, (K1, P1)
across.

Row 4: K1, (P1, K1) across.

Row 5: P1, (K1, P1) across.

Rows 6-9: Repeat Rows 4 and 5 twice.

Bind off all sts **loosely** in ribbing.

Add Button.

ARAN BLANKET ▰▰▰▱ INTERMEDIATE

Finished Size: 36" x 42" (91.5 cm x 106.5 cm)

MATERIALS

Sport Weight Yarn, approximately:
13 ounces, 1,635 yards
(370 grams, 1,495 meters)
Straight knitting needles, size 8 (5 mm) **or** size
needed for gauge
Cable needle
Yarn needle

GAUGE: In Stockinette Stitch,
20 sts and 26 rows = 4" (10 cm)

Cable 4 Front, *abbreviated C4F* (4 sts): Slip 2 sts onto cable needle and hold in **front** of work, K2 from left needle, K2 from cable needle.
Cable 4 Back, *abbreviated C4B* (4 sts): Slip 2 sts onto cable needle and hold in **back** of work, K2 from left needle, K2 from cable needle.
Cable 5 Front, *abbreviated C5F* (5 sts): Slip 3 sts onto cable needle and hold in **front** of work, K2 from left needle, slip **purl** st from cable needle back onto left needle and purl this st, K2 from cable needle.
Cable 5 Back, *abbreviated C5B* (5 sts): Slip 3 sts onto cable needle and hold in **back** of work, K2 from left needle, slip **purl** st from cable needle back onto left needle and purl this st, K2 from cable needle.

STRIP (Make 3)

Cast on 62 sts **loosely**.

Work in Garter Stitch (knit every row) for 8 rows.

Row 1 (Wrong side)**:** K 14, increase *(Figs. 10a & b, page 581)*, K 11, increase in each of next 10 sts, K 11, increase, K 14: 74 sts.

Note: When instructed to slip a stitch, always slip as if to **purl**.

Row 2: K6, P3, WYB slip 1, P3, K4, P3, WYB slip 1, P3, K2, (P1, K2) 8 times, P3, WYB slip 1, P3, K4, P3, WYB slip 1, P3, K6.

Row 3 AND ALL WRONG SIDE ROWS: K9, P1, K3, P4, K3, P1, K3, P2, (K1, P2) 8 times, K3, P1, K3, P4, K3, P1.

Row 4: K6, P3, WYB slip 1, P3, C4F, P3, WYB slip 1, P3, K2, (P1, C5F) 4 times, P3, WYB slip 1, P3, C4B, P3, WYB slip 1, P3, K6.

Row 6: Repeat Row 2.

Row 8: K6, P3, WYB slip 1, P3, C4F, P3, WYB slip 1, P3, (C5B, P1) 4 times, K2, P3, WYB slip 1, P3, C4B, P3, WYB slip 1, P3, K6.

Repeat Rows 2-9 for pattern until Strip measures approximately 41" (104 cm) from cast on edge, ending by working Pattern Row 2.

Decrease Row: K 14, K2 tog *(Fig. 17, page 583)*, K 11, K2 tog 10 times, K 11, K2 tog, K 14: 62 sts.

Work in Garter Stitch for 8 rows.

Bind off all sts.

FINISHING

Sew Strips together making sure the bottom of each Strip (cast on edge) is at the same end.

Designs by Carole Prior.

BOOTIE BOUTIQUE

BASIC SOLE

GAUGE: In Garter St, 10 sts and 20 rows = 2"

Gauge Swatch: 2" square
Cast on 10 sts.
Work in Garter Stitch for 19 rows.
Bind off all sts in **knit**.

Cast on 38{44} sts.

Row 1 (Right side)**:** Knit across.

Row 2: K 18{20}, place marker *(Fig. 1, page 578)*, increase *(Figs. 10a & b, page 581)*, K 0{2} *(see Zeros, page 577)*, increase, place marker, knit across: 40{46} sts.

Rows 3-6: Knit across to first marker, increase, knit across to within one st of next marker, increase, knit across: 48{54} sts.

Row 7: Knit across to first marker, remove marker, increase, knit across to within one st of next marker, increase, remove marker, knit across: 50{56} sts.

1. TRIPLE-BUTTON BOOTIES
◼◼◻◻ EASY

Sizes: 0-3 months - approximately 3³/₄" heel to toe
3-6 months - approximately 4" heel to toe

Size Note: Instructions are written for size 0-3 months with size 3-6 months in braces { }. Instructions will be easier to read if you circle all the numbers pertaining to your size. If only one number is given, it applies to both sizes.

MATERIALS
Sport Weight Yarn - 40{50} yards
Straight knitting needles, size 7 (4.5 mm) **or** size needed for gauge
Stitch holder
¹/₄" Pearl buttons - 6
Sewing needle and thread
Yarn needle

RIGHT BOOTIE
SOLE
Work Basic Sole, this page: 50{56} sts.

INSTEP
Row 1: K 14{16}, place marker, [slip 1 as if to **knit**, K1, PSSO *(Figs. 19a & b, page 583)*], K 18{20}, K2 tog *(Fig. 17, page 583)*, place marker, knit across: 48{54} sts.

Rows 2-5: Knit across to first marker, slip 1 as if to **knit**, K1, PSSO, knit across to within 2 sts of next marker, K2 tog, knit across: 40{46} sts.

Row 6: Knit across to first marker, remove marker, slip 1 as if to **knit**, K1, PSSO, knit across to within 2 sts of next marker, K2 tog, remove marker, knit across: 38{44} sts.

Row 7: K 14{16}, slip 1 as if to **knit**, K1, PSSO, K1, slip 16{18} sts just worked onto st holder, bind off next 4{6} sts, K2 tog, knit across: 16{18} sts.

FIRST SIDE
Row 1: Knit across to last 4 sts, K2 tog twice: 14{16} sts.

Row 2: (Slip 1 as if to **knit**, K1, PSSO) twice, knit across: 12{14} sts.

Row 3: Knit across.

Row 4: Add on 12{14} sts *(Figs. 5a & b, page 580)*, knit across: 24{28} sts.

Row 5 (Buttonhole row)**:** Knit across to last 2 sts, YO *(Fig. 16a, page 582)*, K2 tog.

Row 6: Bind off 12{14} sts **loosely** in **knit**, knit across: 12{14} sts.

Rows 7-13: Repeat Rows 3-6 once, then repeat Rows 3-5 once **more**.

Bind off all sts **loosely** in **knit**.

Instructions continued on page 386.

1

2

3

4

5

6

SECOND SIDE

Row 1: Slip 16{18} sts from st holder onto empty needle, (slip 1 as if to **knit**, K1, PSSO) twice, knit across: 14{16} sts.

Row 2: Knit across to last 4 sts, K2 tog twice: 12{14} sts.

Rows 3-13: Knit across.

Bind off all sts **loosely** in **knit**.

Sew Sole and back in one continuous seam.

Sew buttons to side opposite straps.

LEFT BOOTIE
SOLE
Cast on 38{44} sts.

Row 1: Knit across.

Row 2 (Right side)**:** K 18{20}, place marker, increase, K 0{2}, increase, place marker, knit across: 40{46} sts.

Rows 3-7: Work same as Rows 3-7 of Basic Sole: 50{56} sts.

Complete same as Right Bootie.

2. FRENCH BOWS

Sizes: 0-3 months - approximately 3³/₄" heel to toe
3-6 months - approximately 4" heel to toe

Size Note: Instructions are written for size 0-3 months with size 3-6 months in braces { }. Instructions will be easier to read if you circle all the numbers pertaining to your size. If only one number is given, it applies to both sizes.

MATERIALS
Sport Weight Yarn - 40{50} yards ![FINE 2]
Straight knitting needles, size 7 (4.5 mm) **or** size needed for gauge
Stitch holder
¹/₈"w Ribbon - two 18" lengths for laces
Yarn needle

SOLE
Work Basic Sole, page 384: 50{56} sts.

INSTEP AND SIDES

Row 1: K 14{16}, place marker, [slip 1 as if to **knit**, K1, PSSO *(Figs. 19a & b, page 583)*], K 18{20}, K2 tog *(Fig. 17, page 583)*, place marker, knit across: 48{54} sts.

Rows 2-6: Knit across to first marker, slip 1 as if to **knit**, K1, PSSO, knit across to within 2 sts of next marker, K2 tog, knit across: 38{44} sts.

Row 7: Knit across to first marker, remove marker, slip 1 as if to **knit**, K1, PSSO, knit across to within 2 sts of next marker, K2 tog, remove marker, knit across: 36{42} sts.

Row 8: K 15{17}, slip 15{17} sts just worked onto st holder, bind off next 6{8} sts, knit across: 15{17} sts.

FIRST SIDE

Row 1: Knit across to last 2 sts, K2 tog: 14{16} sts.

Row 2: Knit across.

Row 3: Knit across to last 2 sts, K2 tog: 13{15} sts.

Rows 4 thru 5{7}: Knit across.

Next Row (Eyelet row)**:** ★ K2 tog, YO *(Fig. 16a, page 582)*; repeat from ★ across to last st, K1.

Last Row: Knit across.

Bind off all sts **loosely** in **knit**.

SECOND SIDE

Row 1: Slip 15{17} sts from st holder onto empty needle, K2 tog, knit across: 14{16} sts.

Row 2: Knit across.

Row 3: K2 tog, knit across: 13{15} sts.

Rows 4 thru 5{7}: Knit across.

Next Row (Eyelet row)**:** (K2 tog, YO) across to last st, K1.

Last Row: Knit across.

Bind off all sts **loosely** in **knit**.

Sew Sole and back in one continuous seam.

Weave an 18" length of ribbon through Eyelet row.

3. JOGGERS

Sizes: 0-3 months - approximately 3³/₄" heel to toe
3-6 months - approximately 4" heel to toe

Size Note: Instructions are written for size 0-3 months with size 3-6 months in braces { }. Instructions will be easier to read if you circle all the numbers pertaining to your size. If only one number is given, it applies to both sizes.

MATERIALS

Sport Weight Yarn: **FINE 2**
  White - 40{45} yards
  Blue - 20{24} yards
Straight knitting needles, size 7 (4.5 mm) **or** size needed for gauge
Bobbins - 2
Stitch holders - 2
¹/₁₆"w Ribbon - two 16" lengths for laces
Yarn needle

Note: Before beginning Booties, wind 10{12} yards of Blue onto each of 2 bobbins **(see Using Colors, page 585)**.

SOLE

With White, work Basic Sole, page 384, through Row 4: 44{50} sts.

Rows 5 and 6: With Blue on bobbin knit across to first marker, increase, knit across to within one st of next marker, increase, knit across: 48{54} sts.

Row 7: With White K2{4}, with Blue K2, with White K2, with Blue K2, with White K 10, remove marker, increase, K 10{12}, increase, remove marker, K 10, with Blue on next bobbin K2, with White K2, with Blue K2, with White K2{4}: 50{56} sts.

INSTEP AND SIDES

Note #1: When instructed to slip a stitch, slip as if to **purl** unless otherwise instructed.

Note #2: When working wrong side rows, Blue yarn will need to be stranded so that it will be in correct position to work right side rows.

Row 1: K2{4}, with yarn in front, slip 2, pick up White from beneath Blue, K2, with yarn in front, slip 2, pick up White from beneath Blue, K6, [slip 1 as if to **knit**, K1, PSSO **(Figs. 19a & b, page 583)**], K 18{20}, K2 tog **(Fig. 17, page 583)**, K6, with yarn in front, slip 2, pick up White from beneath Blue, K2, with yarn in front, slip 2, K2{4}: 48{54} sts.

Note: Continue stranding Blue in same manner on wrong side rows throughout.

Row 2: K3{5}, with Blue K2, with White K2, with Blue K2, with White K5, slip 1 as if to **knit**, K1, PSSO, K 16{18}, K2 tog, K5, with Blue K2, with White K2, with Blue K2, with White K3{5}: 46{52} sts.

Row 3: K3{5}, with yarn in front, slip 2, K2, with yarn in front, slip 2, K5, slip 1 as if to **knit**, K1, PSSO, K 14{16}, K2 tog, K5, with yarn in front, slip 2, K2, with yarn in front, slip 2, K3{5}: 44{50} sts.

Row 4: K4{6}, with Blue K2, with White K2, with Blue K2, with White K4, slip 1 as if to **knit**, K1, PSSO, K 12{14}, K2 tog, K4, with Blue K2, with White K2, with Blue K2, with White K4{6}: 42{48} sts.

Row 5: K4{6}, with yarn in front, slip 2, K2, with yarn in front, slip 2, K4, slip 1 as if to **knit**, K1, PSSO, K 10{12}, K2 tog, K4, with yarn in front, slip 2, K2, with yarn in front, slip 2, K4{6}: 40{46} sts.

Row 6: K5{7}, with Blue K2, with White K2, with Blue K2, with White K3, slip 1 as if to **knit**, K1, PSSO, K8{10}, K2 tog, K3, with Blue K2, with White K2, with Blue K2, with White K5{7}: 38{44} sts.

Row 7: K5{7}, with yarn in front, slip 2, K2, with yarn in front, slip 2, K3, slip 1 as if to **knit**, K1, PSSO, K6{8}, K2 tog, K3, with yarn in front, slip 2, K2, with yarn in front, slip 2, K5{7}: 36{42} sts.

FIRST SIDE

Row 1: K6{8}, with Blue K2, with White K2, with Blue K2, **turn**; with White add on 4 sts **(Figs. 5a & b, page 580)**, **turn**; slip next 12{14} sts onto st holder, slip remaining 12{14} sts onto second st holder: 16{18} sts.

Row 2: K4, with yarn in front, slip 2, K2, with yarn in front, slip 2, K6{8}.

Row 3: K7{9}, with Blue K2, with White K2, with Blue K2, with White K1, YO **(Fig. 16a, page 582)** (eyelet), K2 tog.

Row 4: K3, with yarn in front, slip 2, K2, with yarn in front, slip 2, K7{9}.

Instructions continued on page 388.

Row 5: K8{10}, (with Blue K2, with White K2) twice.

Row 6: Slip 1 as if to **knit**, K1, PSSO, YO (eyelet), with yarn in front, slip 2, K2, with yarn in front, slip 2, K8{10}.

Row 7: K9{11}, with Blue K2, with White K2, with Blue K2, with White K1.

Row 8: K1, with yarn in front, slip 2, K2, with yarn in front, slip 2, K9{11}.

Row 9: K 10{12}, with Blue K2, with White K2, with Blue YO (eyelet), K2 tog.

Row 10: K2, with White K2, with yarn in front, slip 2, K 10{12}.

With White bind off 9{11} sts **loosely** in **knit**, with Blue bind off next 2 sts **loosely** in **knit**, with White bind off next 2 sts **loosely** in **knit**, with Blue bind off last 2 sts **loosely** in **knit**.

SECOND SIDE

Row 1: Slip 12{14} sts from second st holder onto empty needle, with White add on 4 sts, K4, with Blue K2, with White K2, with Blue K2, with White K6{8}: 16{18} sts.

Row 2: K6{8}, with yarn in front, slip 2, K2, with yarn in front, slip 2, K4.

Row 3: Slip 1 as if **to knit**, K1, PSSO, YO (eyelet), K1, with Blue K2, with White K2, with Blue K2, with White K7{9}.

Row 4: K7{9}, with yarn in front, slip 2, K2, with yarn in front, slip 2, K3.

Row 5: K2, with Blue K2, with White K2, with Blue K2, with White K8{10}.

Row 6: K8{10}, with yarn in front, slip 2, K2, with yarn in front, slip 2, YO (eyelet), K2 tog.

Row 7: K1, with Blue K2, with White K2, with Blue K2, with White K9{11}.

Row 8: K9{11}, with yarn in front, slip 2, K2, with yarn in front, slip 2, K1.

Row 9: Slip 1 as if to **knit**, with Blue K1, PSSO, YO (eyelet), with White K2, with Blue K2, with White K 10{12}.

Row 10: K 10{12}, with yarn in front, slip 2, with White K2, with Blue K2.

With Blue bind off one st **loosely** in **knit**, with White bind off next 2 sts **loosely** in **knit**, with Blue bind off next 2 sts **loosely** in **knit**, with White bind off last 10{12} sts **loosely** in **knit**.

TONGUE

Row 1: Slip 12{14} sts from remaining st holder onto empty needle, with White pick up one st between First Side and first st on needle (**Fig. 34b, page 586**), K2, slip 1 as if to **knit**, K1, PSSO, K4{6}, K2 tog, K2, pick up one st between last st on needle and Second Side: 12{14} sts.

Row 2: K3, slip 1 as if to **knit**, K1, PSSO, K2{4}, K2 tog, K3: 10{12} sts.

Row 3: K3, slip 1 as if to **knit**, K1, PSSO, K 0{2}, K2 tog, K3: 8{10} sts.

Rows 4-11: Knit across.

Row 12: Slip 1 as if to **knit**, K1, PSSO, knit across to last 2 sts, K2 tog: 6{8} sts.

Bind off all sts **loosely** in **knit**.

Sew Sole and back in one continuous seam.

Lace 16" length of ribbon through eyelets.

4. T-STRAP BOOTIES

Sizes: 0-3 months - approximately 3³/₄" heel to toe
3-6 months - approximately 4" heel to toe

Size Note: Instructions are written for size 0-3 months with size 3-6 months in braces { }. Instructions will be easier to read if you circle all the numbers pertaining to your size. If only one number is given, it applies to both sizes.

MATERIALS
Sport Weight Yarn - 40{45} yards
Straight knitting needles, size 7 (4.5 mm) **or** size needed for gauge
Stitch holders - 2
³/₈" Buttons - 4
Sewing needle and thread
Yarn needle

SOLE
Work Basic Sole, page 384: 50{56} sts.

INSTEP AND SIDES

Row 1: K 14{16}, place marker, [slip 1 as if to **knit**, K1, PSSO *(Figs. 19a & b, page 583)*], K 18{20}, K2 tog *(Fig. 17, page 583)*, place marker, knit across: 48{54} sts.

Rows 2-6: Knit across to first marker, slip 1 as if to **knit**, K1, PSSO, knit across to within 2 sts of next marker, K2 tog, knit across: 38{44} sts.

Row 7: Knit across to first marker, remove marker, slip 1 as if to **knit**, K1, PSSO, knit across to within 2 sts of next marker, K2 tog, remove marker, knit across: 36{42} sts.

Row 8: K 10{12}, slip 10{12} sts just worked onto st holder, bind off next 6 sts, K3{5}, slip 4{6} sts just worked onto second st holder, bind off next 6 sts, knit across: 10{12} sts.

FIRST SIDE

Rows 1-5: Knit across.

Bind off all sts **loosely** in **knit**.

SECOND SIDE

Row 1: Slip 10{12} sts from first st holder onto empty needle, knit across: 10{12} sts.

Rows 2-5: Knit across.

Bind off all sts **loosely** in **knit**.

T-STRAP

Row 1: Slip 4{6} sts from remaining st holder onto empty needle, knit across: 4{6} sts.

Rows 2 thru 3{5}: Knit across.

Row 4{6} and 5{7}: Add on 5 sts *(Figs. 5a & b, page 580)*, knit across: 14{16} sts.

Row 6{8} (Buttonhole row): K2 tog, YO *(Fig. 16a, page 582)*, K 10{12}, YO, K2 tog.

Row 7{9}: K5{6}, K2 tog twice, K5{6}: 12{14} sts.

Row 8{10}: K2 tog, K1, slip first st on right needle over second st and off needle, bind off 7{9} sts **loosely** in **knit**, K2 tog, slip first st on right needle over last st and off needle.

Sew Sole and back in one continuous seam.

Sew buttons to sides.

5. TUBE SOCKS

Sizes: 0-3 months - approximately 3³/₄" heel to toe
3-6 months - approximately 4" heel to toe

Size Note: Instructions are written for size 0-3 months with size 3-6 months in braces { }. Instructions will be easier to read if you circle all the numbers pertaining to your size. If only one number is given, it applies to both sizes.

MATERIALS

Sport Weight Yarn: 🏷️ **2** FINE
White - 55{65} yards
Green - 10 yards
Straight knitting needles, sizes 6 (4 mm) and 7 (4.5 mm) **or** sizes needed for gauge
Yarn needle

SOLE

With White and larger size needles, work Basic Sole, page 384: 50{56} sts.

INSTEP AND SIDES

Row 1: K 13{15}, place marker, [slip 1 as if to **knit**, K1, PSSO *(Figs. 19a & b, page 583)*], K 20{22}, K2 tog *(Fig. 17, page 583)*, place marker, knit across: 48{54} sts.

Rows 2-10: Knit across to first marker, slip 1 as if to **knit**, K1, PSSO, knit across to within 2 sts of next marker, K2 tog, knit across: 30{36} sts.

Row 11: Knit across to first marker, remove marker, slip 1 as if to **knit**, K1, PSSO, K 0{2} *(see Zeros, page 577)*, K2 tog, remove marker, knit across: 28{34} sts.

CUFF

Rows 1 thru 19{21}: Knit across working in the following Stripe Sequence: 10{12} rows White, 2 rows Green, 2 rows White, 2 rows Green, 3 rows White; at end of Row 19{21}, cut Green.

Change to smaller size needles.

Last 3 Rows: (K1, P1) across.

Bind off all sts **loosely** in pattern.

Sew Sole and back in one continuous seam.

6. WALKERS

Sizes: 0-3 months - approximately 3³/₄" heel to toe
3-6 months - approximately 4" heel to toe

Size Note: Instructions are written for size 0-3 months with size 3-6 months in braces { }. Instructions will be easier to read if you circle all the numbers pertaining to your size. If only one number is given, it applies to both sizes.

MATERIALS
Sport Weight Yarn - 50{55} yards
Straight knitting needles, size 7 (4.5 mm) **or** size needed for gauge
Stitch holders - 2
¹/₁₆"w Ribbon - two 18" lengths for laces
Yarn needle

SOLE
Work Basic Sole, page 384: 50{56} sts.

INSTEP AND SIDES
Row 1: K 14{16}, place marker, **[**slip 1 as if to **knit**, K1, PSSO *(Figs. 19a & b, page 583)]*, K 18{20}, K2 tog *(Fig. 17, page 583)*, place marker, knit across: 48{54} sts.

Rows 2-6: Knit across to first marker, slip 1 as if to **knit**, K1, PSSO, knit across to within 2 sts of next marker, K2 tog, knit across: 38{44} sts.

Row 7: Knit across to first marker, remove marker, slip 1 as if to **knit**, K1, PSSO, knit across to within 2 sts of next marker, K2 tog, remove marker, knit across: 36{42} sts.

3-6 MONTHS ONLY
Rows 8 and 9: Knit across.

FIRST SIDE
Row 1: K 12{14}, **turn**; add on 4 sts *(Figs. 5a & b, page 580)*, **turn**; slip next 12{14} sts onto st holder, slip remaining 12{14} sts onto second st holder: 16{18} sts.

Row 2: Knit across.

Row 3: Knit across to last 2 sts, YO *(Fig. 16a, page 582)* (eyelet), K2 tog.

Rows 4 and 5: Knit across.

Row 6: K2 tog, YO (eyelet), knit across.

Rows 7 and 8: Knit across.

Rows 9-14: Repeat Rows 3-8.

Bind off all sts **loosely** in **knit**.

SECOND SIDE
Row 1: Slip 12{14} sts from second st holder onto empty needle, add on 4 sts, knit across: 16{18} sts.

Row 2: Knit across.

Row 3: K2 tog, YO (eyelet), knit across.

Rows 4 and 5: Knit across.

Row 6: Knit across to last 2 sts, YO (eyelet), K2 tog.

Rows 7 and 8: Knit across.

Rows 9-14: Repeat Rows 3-8.

Bind off all sts **loosely** in **knit**.

TONGUE
Row 1: Slip 12{14} sts from remaining st holder onto empty needle, pick up one st between First Side and first st on needle *(Fig. 34b, page 586)*, K2, slip 1 as if to **knit**, K1, PSSO, K4{6}, K2 tog, K2, pick up one st between last st on needle and Second Side: 12{14} sts.

Row 2: K3, slip 1 as if to **knit**, K1, PSSO, K2{4}, K2 tog, K3: 10{12} sts.

Row 3: K3, slip 1 as if to **knit**, K1, PSSO, K 0{2}, K2 tog, K3: 8{10} sts.

Rows 4 thru 14{16}: Knit across.

Rows 15{17} and 16{18}: Slip 1 as if to **knit**, K1, PSSO, knit across to last 2 sts, K2 tog: 4{6} sts.

Bind off all sts **loosely** in **knit**.

Sew sole and back in one continuous seam.

Lace 18" length of ribbon through eyelets.

All Bootie designs by Sandra J. Patterson.

SMOCKED BUBBLE

◼◼◼◻ INTERMEDIATE

Shown on page 393.

Size: 3{6-12} months
Finished Measurement: 20{22-24}"/51{56-61} cm

Size Note: Instructions are written for size 3 months, with sizes 6 and 12 months in braces { }. Instructions will be easier to read, if you circle all the numbers pertaining to your size. If only one number is given, it applies to all sizes.

MATERIALS

Sport Weight Yarn, approximately:
MC (White)
3(3³/₄-4¹/₂) ounces, 375(470-565) yards
[90(105-130) grams, 343{430-517} meters]
CC (Pink) - small amount
Straight knitting needles, sizes 3 (3.25 mm) **and**
5 (3.75 mm) **or** sizes needed for gauge
Stitch holders - 5
Snap tape - 5" (12.5 cm)
Buttons - 3
Yarn needle
Sewing needle and thread

GAUGE: With larger size needles,
in Stockinette Stitch,
24 sts and 32 rows = 4" (10 cm)

YOKE

With MC and using smaller size needles, cast on 60{70-80} sts **loosely**.

Rows 1-5: Work across in K1, P1 ribbing.

Row 6 (Right side)**:** With CC, knit across.

Row 7 (Increase row)**:** Knit across increasing 27{29-31} sts evenly spaced *(Figs. 10a & b, page 581)*: 87{99-111} sts.

Change to larger size needles.

Row 8: With MC, knit across.

Row 9: K1, P1, (K3, P1) across to last st, K1.

Row 10: P1, K1, (P3, K1) across to last st, P1.

Row 11: K1, P1, tie a scrap piece of yarn around last st worked for Smocking placement, (K3, P1) across to last st, K1.

Row 12 (Increase row)**:** P1, (increase, P3) across to last 2 sts, K1, P1: 108{123-138} sts.

Row 13: K1, P1, (K4, P1) across to last st, K1.

Row 14: P1, K1, (P4, K1) across to last st, P1.

Row 15: K1, P1, (K4, P1) across to last st, K1.

Row 16 (Increase row)**:** P1, (increase, P4) across to last 2 sts, K1, P1: 129{147-165} sts.

Row 17: K1, P1, (K5, P1) across to last st, K1.

Row 18: P1, K1, (P5, K1) across to last st, P1.

Row 19: K1, P1, (K5, P1) across to last st, K1.

Row 20: With CC, knit across.

Row 21 (Increase row)**:** Knit across increasing 57{59-61} sts evenly spaced: 186{206-226} sts.

With MC and beginning with a **knit** row, work in Stockinette Stitch until Yoke measures approximately 4¹/₂{4³/₄-5}"/11.5{12-12.5} cm from cast on edge, ending by working a **purl** row; at end of last row, cut yarn.

FRONT

Row 1: With **right** side facing, slip first 26{29-33} sts onto st holder (right Back), slip next 38{42-44} sts onto second st holder (first Sleeve), with MC, increase 2{2-1} time(s), K 54{60-70}, increase 2{2-1} time(s), slip next 38{42-44} sts onto third st holder (second Sleeve), slip last 26{29-33} sts onto fourth st holder (left Back): 62{68-74} sts.

Work in Stockinette Stitch until piece measures approximately 11(13-15)"/28{33-38} cm from cast on edge, ending by working a **purl** row.

LEG SHAPING

Rows 1 and 2: Bind off 7{9-10} sts at the beginning of the next 2 rows, work across: 48{50-54} sts.

Bind off 2 sts at the beginning of the next 0{10-8} rows **(see Zeros, page 577)**, work across: 48{30-38} sts.

Instructions continued on page 392.

Next Row (Decrease row)**:** [Slip 1, K1, PSSO *(Figs. 19a & b, page 583)*], work across to last 2 sts, K2 tog *(Fig. 17, page 583)*: 46{28-36} sts.

Continue to decrease one stitch at each edge in same manner, every other row, 13{3-6} times **more**: 20{22-24} sts.

Work even until piece measures approximately 15(17½-20)"/38{44.5-51} cm from cast on edge, ending by working a **purl** row.

Slip remaining sts onto st holder; cut yarn.

BACK
With larger size needles, slip sts from right Back st holder onto empty needle, then slip sts from left Back st holder onto same needle: 52{58-66} sts.

Row 1 (Right side)**:** With MC and working across left Back first, increase 2{2-1} time(s), K 24{27-32}, **turn**; add on 6 sts *(Figs. 5a & b, page 580)*, **turn**; K 24{27-32}, increase 2{2-1} time(s): 62{68-74} sts.

Work in Stockinette Stitch until piece measures approximately 11(13-15)"/28{33-38} cm from cast on edge, ending by working a **purl** row.

LEG SHAPING
Row 1 (Decrease row)**:** Slip 1, K1, PSSO, knit across to last 2 sts, K2 tog: 60{66-72} sts.

Continue to decrease one stitch at each edge in same manner, every fourth row, 1{3-5} time(s); then decrease every other row, 13{11-9} times: 32{38-44} sts.

Next 2 Rows: Bind off 6{8-10} sts, work across: 20{22-24} sts.

Slip remaining sts onto st holder; cut yarn.

SLEEVE
With larger size needles, slip sts from first Sleeve st holder onto empty needle: 38{42-44} sts.

Row 1 (Right side)**:** With MC, increase, knit across to last st, increase: 40{44-46} sts.

Work in Stockinette Stitch until Sleeve measures approximately 1½(1¾-2)"/4{4.5-5} cm from underarm, ending by working a **purl** row.

RIBBING
Change to smaller size needles.

Rows 1-6: Work across in K1, P1 ribbing. Bind off all sts **loosely** in ribbing.

Repeat for second Sleeve.

FINISHING
Weave underarm and side in one continuous seam *(Fig. 36, page 587)*, ending at beginning of Leg Shaping.

LEG RIBBING
With **right** side facing, using smaller size needles and MC, pick up 30{36-42} sts evenly spaced across Front and 18{24-30} sts evenly spaced across Back of Leg opening *(Figs. 34a & b, page 586)*: 48{60-72} sts.

Rows 1-5: Work across in K1, P1 ribbing.

Bind off all sts **loosely** in ribbing.

Repeat for second Leg opening.

BOTTOM RIBBING
With **right** side of Front facing, using smaller size needles and MC, pick up 4 sts evenly spaced across end of Leg Ribbing, slip sts from Front st holder onto empty needle and knit across, pick up 4 sts evenly spaced across end of Leg Ribbing: 28{30-32} sts.

Rows 1-5: Work across in K1, P1 ribbing.

Bind off all sts in ribbing.

Repeat for Back.

Sew snap tape to Bottom Ribbings.

LEFT PLACKET RIBBING
With **right** side facing, using smaller size needles and MC, pick up 37{39-41} sts evenly spaced across Left Placket opening: 37{39-41} sts.

Row 1: P1, (K1, P1) across.

Row 2: K1, (P1, K1) across.

Rows 3-9: Repeat Rows 1 and 2, 3 times; then repeat Row 1 once **more**.

Bind off all sts in ribbing.

RIGHT PLACKET RIBBING

With **right** side facing, using smaller size needles and MC, pick up 37{39-41} sts evenly spaced across Right Placket opening: 37{39-41} sts.

Row 1: P1, (K1, P1) across.

Row 2: K1, (P1, K1) across.

Rows 3 and 4: Repeat Rows 1 and 2.

Row 5 (Buttonhole row)**:** (P1, K1) 2(3-2) times, YO **(Fig. 16a, page 582)**, K2 tog, ★ (P1, K1) 6{6-7} times, YO, K2 tog; repeat from ★ once **more**, P1, K1, P1.

Row 6: K1, (P1, K1) across.

Rows 7-9: Repeat Rows 1 and 2 once, then repeat Row 1 once **more**.

Bind off all sts in ribbing.

Sew Placket loosely in place, lapping right over left.

Add buttons.

Instructions continued on page 394.

SMOCKING

With **right** side of Back facing, neck down and using CC, bring yarn up at left of marked stitch (third stitch) on first vertical line *(Point A, Fig. A)*. Insert needle from right to left through corresponding stitch on next vertical line *(Point B, Fig. A)*, then through first stitch, pulling yarn until lines meet (not too tightly). Stitch again over same stitch, pulling the yarn to the wrong side at Point B.

Bring yarn up at left of seventh stitch on second vertical line *(Point C, Fig. B)*. Insert needle from right to left through corresponding stitch on next vertical line *(Point D, Fig. B)*, then through first stitch, pulling yarn until lines meet. Stitch again over same stitch, pulling yarn to the wrong side at Point D. Bring yarn up at left of third stitch on third vertical line *(Point E, Fig. B)*.

Repeat this process across, working through third and seventh stitch on vertical lines.

With **right** side of Back facing, neck down and using CC, bring yarn up at left of eleventh stitch on first vertical line. Insert needle from right to left through corresponding stitch on next vertical line, then through first stitch, pulling yarn until lines meet. Stitch again over same stitch, pulling the yarn to the wrong side.

Bring yarn up at left of eleventh stitch on third vertical line. Insert needle from right to left through corresponding stitch on next vertical line, then through first stitch, pulling yarn until lines meet. Stitch again over same stitch, pulling yarn to the wrong side. Repeat this process across, working through eleventh stitch on vertical lines.

Design by Joan Beebe.

Fig. A

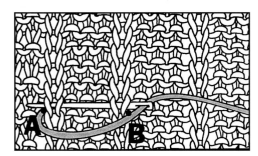

Fig. B

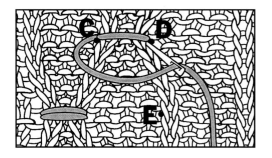

CABLED BUBBLE

◼︎◼︎◼︎◻︎ INTERMEDIATE

Shown on page 397.

Size: 3{6-12} months
Finished Measurement:
20{22-24}"/51{56-61} cm

Size Note: Instructions are written for size 3 months, with sizes 6 and 12 months in braces { }. Instructions will be easier to read, if you circle all the numbers pertaining to your size. If only one number is given, it applies to all sizes.

MATERIALS

Sport Weight Yarn, approximately:
  3{3$\frac{1}{2}$-4$\frac{1}{4}$} ounces, 375{440-535} yards
  [90{100-120} grams, 343{402-489} meters]
Straight knitting needles, sizes 3 (3.25 mm) **and**
  5 (3.75 mm) **or** sizes needed for gauge
Cable needle
Stitch holders - 5
Snap tape - 5" (12.5 cm)
Buttons - 3
Yarn needle
Sewing needle and thread

GAUGE: With larger size needles,
  in Stockinette Stitch,
  24 sts and 32 rows = 4" (10 cm)

Note: Row gauge is very important in this design.

YOKE

With smaller size needles, cast on 60{70-80} sts **loosely**.

Rows 1-6: Work across in K1, P1 ribbing.

Row 7 (Increase row)**:** Work across in K1, P1 ribbing increasing 6{8-10} sts evenly spaced *(see Increases, page 581)*: 66{78-90} sts.

Change to larger size needles.

Row 8 (Right side)**:** K 10{12-13}, † YO *(Fig. 16a, page 582)*, K1, YO, K8{10-14}, YO, K1, YO †, K 26{30-32}, repeat from † to † once, K 10{12-13}: 74{86-98} sts.

Row 9: P2, K1, P4, K1, † P6{9-12}, K1, P4, K1 †, repeat from † to † once **more**, (P2, K1, P4, K1) twice, repeat from † to † twice, P2.

To work Cable, slip next 2 sts onto cable needle and hold in **front** of work, K2 from left needle, K2 from cable needle.

Row 10: K3, work Cable, † K4{6-7}, YO, K1, YO, K3{4-6}, work Cable, K3{4-6}, YO, K1, YO, K4{6-7}, work Cable †, (K4, work Cable) twice, repeat from † to † once, K3: 82{94-106} sts.

Row 11: P2, K1, P4, K1, † P8{11-14}, K1, P4, K1 †, repeat from † to † once **more**, (P2, K1, P4, K1) twice, repeat from † to † twice, P2.

Row 12: K 12{14-15}, † YO, K1, YO, K 12{14-18}, YO, K1, YO †, K 30{34-36}, repeat from † to † once, K 12{14-15}: 90{102-114} sts.

Row 13: P2, K1, P4, K1, † P 10{13-16}, K1, P4, K1 †, repeat from † to † once **more**, (P2, K1, P4, K1) twice, repeat from † to † twice, P2.

Row 14: K3, work Cable, † K6{8-9}, YO, K1, YO, K5{6-8}, work Cable, K5{6-8}, YO, K1, YO, K6{8-9}, work Cable †, (K4, work Cable) twice, repeat from † to † once, K3: 98{110-122} sts.

Row 15: P2, K1, P4, K1, † P 12{15-18}, K1, P4, K1 †, repeat from † to † once **more**, (P2, K1, P4, K1) twice, repeat from † to † twice, P2.

Row 16: K 14{16-17}, † YO, K1, YO, K 16{18-22}, YO, K1, YO †, K 34{38-40}, repeat from † to † once, K 14{16-17}: 106{118-130} sts.

Row 17: P2, K1, P4, K1, † P 14{17-20}, K1, P4, K1 †, repeat from † to † once **more**, (P2, K1, P4, K1) twice, repeat from † to † twice, P2.

Row 18: K3, work Cable, † K8{10-11}, YO, K1, YO, K7{8-10}, work Cable, K7{8-10}, YO, K1, YO, K8{10-11}, work Cable †, (K4, work Cable) twice, repeat from † to † once, K3: 114{126-138} sts.

Row 19: P2, K1, P4, K1, † P 16{19-22}, K1, P4, K1 †, repeat from † to † once **more**, (P2, K1, P4, K1) twice, repeat from † to † twice, P2.

Row 20: K 16{18-19}, † YO, K1, YO, K 20{22-26}, YO, K1, YO †, K 38{42-44}, repeat from † to † once, K 16{18-19}: 122{134-146} sts.

Row 21: P2, K1, P4, K1, † P 18{21-24}, K1, P4, K1 †, repeat from † to † once **more**, (P2, K1, P4, K1) twice, repeat from † to † twice, P2.

Row 22: K3, work Cable, † K 10{12-13}, YO, K1, YO, K9{10-12}, work Cable, K9{10-12}, YO, K1, YO, K 10{12-13}, work Cable †, (K4, work Cable) twice, repeat from † to † once, K3: 130{142-154} sts.

Row 23: P2, K1, P4, K1, † P 20{23-26}, K1, P4, K1 †, repeat from † to † once **more**, (P2, K1, P4, K1) twice, repeat from † to † twice, P2.

Row 24: K 18{20-21}, † YO, K1, YO, K 24{26-30}, YO, K1, YO †, K 42{46-48}, repeat from † to † once, K 18{20-21}: 138{150-162} sts.

Row 25: P2, K1, P4, K1, † P 22{25-28}, K1, P4, K1 †, repeat from † to † once **more**, (P2, K1, P4, K1) twice, repeat from † to † twice, P2.

Row 26: K3, work Cable, † K 12{14-15}, YO, K1, YO, K 11{12-14}, work Cable, K 11{12-14}, YO, K1, YO, K 12{14-15}, work Cable †, (K4, work Cable) twice, repeat from † to † once, K3: 146{158-170} sts.

Row 27: P2, K1, P4, K1, † P 24{27-30}, K1, P4, K1 †, repeat from † to † once **more**, (P2, K1, P4, K1) twice, repeat from † to † twice, P2.

Row 28: K 20{22-23}, † YO, K1, YO, K 28{30-34}, YO, K1, YO †, K 46{50-52}, repeat from † to † once, K 20{22-23}: 154{166-178} sts.

Instructions continued on page 396.

Row 29: P2, K1, P4, K1, † P 26{29-32}, K1, P4, K1 †, repeat from † to † once **more**, (P2, K1, P4, K1) twice, repeat from † to † twice, P2.

Row 30: K3, work Cable, † K 14{16-17}, YO, K1, YO, K 13{14-16}, work Cable, K 13{14-16}, YO, K1, YO, K 14{16-17}, work Cable †, (K4, work Cable) twice, repeat from † to † once, K3: 162{174-186} sts.

Row 31: P2, K1, P4, K1, † P 28{31-34}, K1, P4, K1 †, repeat from † to † once **more**, (P2, K1, P4, K1) twice, repeat from † to † twice, P2.

Row 32: K 22{24-25}, † YO, K1, YO, K 32{34-38}, YO, K1, YO †, K 50{54-56}, repeat from † to † once, K 22{24-25}: 170{182-194} sts.

Row 33: P2, K1, P4, K1, † P 30{33-36}, K1, P4, K1 †, repeat from † to † once **more**, (P2, K1, P4, K1) twice, repeat from † to † twice, P2.

Row 34: K3, work Cable, † K 16{18-19}, YO, K1, YO, K 15{16-18}, work Cable, K 15{16-18}, YO, K1, YO, K 16{18-19}, work Cable †, (K4, work Cable) twice, repeat from † to † once, K3: 178{190-202} sts.

Row 35: P2, K1, P4, K1, † P 32{35-38}, K1, P4, K1 †, repeat from † to † once **more**, (P2, K1, P4, K1) twice, repeat from † to † twice, P2.

Row 36: K 24{26-27}, † YO, K1, YO, K 36{38-42}, YO, K1, YO †, K 54{58-60}, repeat from † to † once, K 24{26-27}: 186{198-210} sts.

Row 37: P2, K1, P4, K1, † P 34{37-40}, K1, P4, K1 †, repeat from † to † once **more**, (P2, K1, P4, K1) twice, repeat from † to † twice, P2.

Size 3 months ONLY
Cut yarn.

Size 6 months ONLY
Row 38: K3, work Cable, † K 20, YO, K1, YO, K 18, work Cable, K 18, YO, K1, YO, K 20, work Cable †, (K4, work Cable) twice, repeat from † to † once, K3: 206 sts.

Row 39: P2, K1, P4, K1, (P 39, K1, P4, K1) twice, (P2, K1, P4, K1) twice, (P 39, K1, P4, K1) twice, P2; cut yarn.

Size 12 months ONLY
Row 38: K3, work Cable, † K 21, YO, K1, YO, K 20, work Cable, K 20, YO, K1, YO, K 21, work Cable †, (K4, work Cable) twice, repeat from † to † once, K3: 218 sts.

Row 39: P2, K1, P4, K1, (P 42, K1, P4, K1) twice, (P2, K1, P4, K1) twice, (P 42, K1, P4, K1) twice, P2.

Row 40: K 29, † YO, K1, YO, K 46, YO, K1, YO †, K 64, repeat from † to † once, K 29: 226 sts.

Row 41: P2, K1, P4, K1, (P 44, K1, P4, K1) twice, (P2, K1, P4, K1) twice, (P 44, K1, P4, K1) twice, P2; cut yarn.

FRONT
Size 3 months ONLY
Row 1: With **right** side facing, slip first 26 sts onto st holder (right Back), slip next 38 sts onto second st holder (first Sleeve), increase twice, K 17, work Cable, (K4, work Cable) twice, K 17, increase twice, slip next 38 sts onto third st holder (second Sleeve), slip last 26 sts onto fourth st holder (left Back): 62 sts.

Size 6 months ONLY
Row 1: With **right** side facing, slip first 29 sts onto st holder (right Back), slip next 42 sts onto second st holder (first Sleeve), increase twice, K 60, increase twice, slip next 42 sts onto third st holder (second Sleeve), slip last 29 sts onto fourth st holder (left Back): 68 sts.

Size 12 months ONLY
Row 1: With **right** side facing, slip first 33 sts onto st holder (right Back), slip next 44 sts onto second st holder (first Sleeve), increase, K 25, work Cable, (K4, work Cable) twice, K 25, increase, slip next 44 sts onto third st holder (second Sleeve), slip last 33 sts onto fourth st holder (left Back): 74 sts.

All Sizes
Rows 2 and 3: Knit across.

Row 4: Purl across.

Row 5: K4, P1, (K5, P1) across to last 3 sts, K3.

Row 6: Purl across.

Row 7: Knit across.

Row 8: Purl across.

Row 9: K1, P1, (K5, P1) across to last 6 sts, K6.

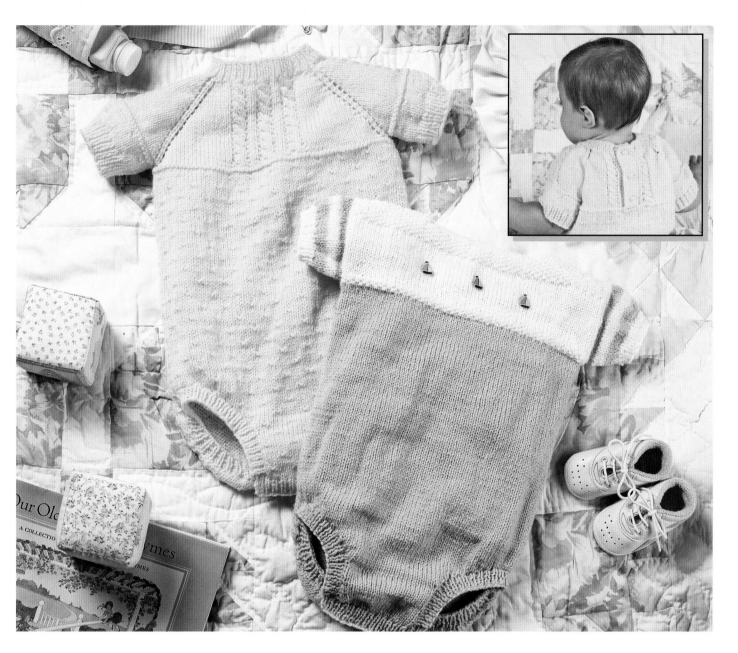

Row 10: Purl across.

Row 11: Knit across.

Repeat Rows 4-11 for pattern until piece measures approximately 11{13-15}"/28{33-38} cm from cast on edge, ending by working a **purl** row.

LEG SHAPING
Note: Maintain established pattern throughout.

Rows 1 and 2: Bind off 7{9-10} sts at the beginning of the next 2 rows, work across: 48{50-54} sts. Bind off 2 sts at the beginning of the next 0{10-8} rows (*see Zeros, page 577*), work across: 48{30-38} sts.

Next Row (Decrease row)**:** [Slip 1, K1, PSSO (*Figs. 19a & b, page 583*)], work across to last 2 sts, K2 tog (*Fig. 17, page 583*): 46{28-36} sts.

Continue to decrease one stitch at each edge in same manner, every other row, 13{3-6} times **more**: 20{22-24} sts.

Work even until piece measures approximately 15{17^1/$_2$-20}"/38{44.5-51} cm from cast on edge, ending by working a **purl** row.

Slip remaining sts onto st holder; cut yarn.

BACK
With larger size needles, slip sts from right Back st holder onto empty needle, then slip sts from left Back st holder onto same needle: 52{58-66} sts.

Instructions continued on page 398.

Size 3 months ONLY
Row 1 (Right side)**:** Working across left Back first, increase twice, K 17, work Cable, K3, **turn**; add on 6 sts *(Figs. 5a & b, page 580)*, **turn**; K3, work Cable, K 17, increase twice: 62 sts.

Size 6 months ONLY
Row 1 (Right side)**:** Working across left Back first, increase twice, K 27, **turn**; add on 6 sts *(Figs. 5a & b, page 580)*, **turn**; K 27, increase twice: 68 sts.

Size 12 months ONLY
Row 1 (Right side)**:** Working across left Back first, increase, K 25, work Cable, K3, **turn**; add on 6 sts *(Figs. 5a & b, page 580)*, **turn**; K3, work Cable, K 25, increase: 74 sts.

All Sizes
Rows 2 and 3: Knit across.

Row 4: Purl across.

Row 5: K4, P1, (K5, P1) across to last 3 sts, K3.

Row 6: Purl across.

Row 7: Knit across.

Row 8: Purl across.

Row 9: K1, P1, (K5, P1) across to last 6 sts, K6.

Row 10: Purl across.

Row 11: Knit across.

Repeat Rows 4-11 for pattern until piece measures approximately 11{13-15}"/28{33-38} cm from cast on edge, ending by working a **purl** row.

LEG SHAPING

Note: Maintain established pattern throughout.

Row 1 (Decrease row)**:** Slip 1, K1, PSSO, work across to last 2 sts, K2 tog: 60{66-72} sts.

Continue to decrease one stitch at each edge in same manner, every fourth row, 1{3-5} times; then decrease every other row, 13{11-9} times: 32{38-44} sts.

Next 2 Rows: Bind off 6{8-10} sts, work across: 20{22-24} sts.

Slip remaining sts onto st holder; cut yarn.

SLEEVE
With larger size needles, slip sts from first Sleeve st holder onto empty needle: 38{42-44} sts.

Size 3 months ONLY
Row 1 (Right side)**:** Increase, K 16, work Cable, K 16, increase: 40 sts.

Size 6 months ONLY
Row 1 (Right side)**:** Increase, knit across to last st, increase: 44 sts.

Size 12 months ONLY
Row 1 (Right side)**:** Increase, K 19, work Cable, K 19, increase: 46 sts.

All Sizes
Rows 2 and 3: Knit across.

Row 4: Purl across.

Row 5: K3{4-1}, P1, (K5, P1) across to last 6{3-2} sts, K6{3-2}.

Row 6: Purl across.

Row 7: Knit across.

Row 8: Purl across.

Row 9: K6{1-4}, P1, (K5, P1) across to last 3{6-5} sts, K3{6-5}.

Row 10: Purl across.

Row 11: Knit across.

Row 12: Purl across.

RIBBING
Change to smaller size needles.

Rows 1-6: Work across in K1, P1 ribbing.

Bind off all sts **loosely** in ribbing.

Repeat for second Sleeve.

FINISHING
Weave underarm and side in one continuous seam *(Fig. 3b, page 587)*, ending at beginning of Leg Shaping.

LEG RIBBING

With **right** side facing and using smaller size needles, pick up 30{36-42} sts evenly spaced across Front and 18{24-30} sts evenly spaced across Back of Leg opening *(Figs. 34a & b, page 586)*: 48{60-72} sts.

Rows 1-5: Work across in K1, P1 ribbing.

Bind off all sts **loosely** in ribbing.

Repeat for second Leg opening.

BOTTOM RIBBING

With **right** side of Front facing and using smaller size needles, pick up 4 sts evenly spaced across end of Leg Ribbing, slip sts from Front st holder onto empty needle and knit across, pick up 4 sts evenly spaced across end of Leg Ribbing: 28{30-32} sts.

Rows 1-5: Work across in K1, P1 ribbing.

Bind off all sts in ribbing.

Repeat for Back.

LEFT PLACKET RIBBING

With **right** side facing and using smaller size needles, pick up 37{39-41} sts evenly spaced across Left Placket opening: 37{39-41} sts.

Row 1: P1, (K1, P1) across.

Row 2: K1, (P1, K1) across.

Rows 3-9: Repeat Rows 1 and 2, 3 times; then repeat Row 1 once **more**.

Bind off all sts in ribbing.

RIGHT PLACKET RIBBING

With **right** side facing and using smaller size needles, pick up 37{39-41} sts evenly spaced across Right Placket opening: 37{39-41} sts.

Row 1: P1, (K1, P1) across.

Row 2: K1, (P1, K1) across.

Rows 3 and 4: Repeat Rows 1 and 2.

Row 5 (Buttonhole row)**:** (P1, K1) 2{3-2} times, YO, K2 tog, ★ (P1, K1) 6{6-7} times, YO, K2 tog; repeat from ★ once **more**, P1, K1, P1.

Row 6: K1, (P1, K1) across.

Rows 7-9: Repeat Rows 1 and 2 once, then repeat Row 1 once **more**.

Bind off all sts in ribbing.

Sew Placket loosely in place, lapping right over left.
Sew snap tape to Bottom Ribbings.
Add buttons.

Design by Joan Beebe.

SAILOR BUBBLE

◖■■◻ INTERMEDIATE

Shown on page 397.

Size: 3(6-12) months
Finished Measurement:
20(22-24)"/51{56-61} cm

Size Note: Instructions are written for size 3 months, with sizes 6 and 12 months in braces { }. Instructions will be easier to read, if you circle all the numbers pertaining to your size.

MATERIALS

Sport Weight Yarn, approximately:
    MC (Blue)
    2¼(2¾-3½) ounces, 285(345-440) yards
    [65(80-100) grams, 261{315-402} meters]
    CC (White)
    1(1¼-1¼) ounces, 125(155-155) yards
    [30(35-35) grams, 114{142-142} meters]
Straight knitting needles, sizes 3 (3.25 mm) **and**
    5 (3.75 mm) **or** sizes needed for gauge
Stitch holders - 2
Snap tape - 5" (12.5 cm)
Buttons - 3 (for placket)
Yarn needle
Sewing needle and thread
Optional - 3 Decorative buttons for trim

Instructions continued on page 400.

GAUGE: With larger size needles, in Stockinette Stitch, 24 sts and 32 rows = 4"

Note: Row gauge is very important in this design.

YOKE
FRONT

With CC and using larger size needles, cast on 62{68-74} sts **loosely**.

Row 1 (Right side)**:** (K1, P1) across.

Row 2: (P1, K1) across.

Rows 3 and 4: Repeat Rows 1 and 2 (Seed Stitch).

Rows 5 thru 22(24-26): Beginning with a **knit** row, work in Stockinette Stitch.

Next 8 Rows: Repeat Rows 1 and 2, 4 times.

NECK OPENING

Note: Maintain established Seed Stitch pattern throughout, unless otherwise instructed.

Row 1: Work across 18{20-22} sts, bind off next 26{28-30} sts in knit (neck opening), work across remaining sts: 18{20-22} sts **each** side.

*Note: Both sides of Neck are worked at the same time, using separate yarn for **each** side.*

Rows 2-8: Work across; with second yarn, work across.

Rows 9 and 10: Work across; with second yarn, add on 16{17-18} sts *(Figs. 5a & b, page 580)*, work across: 34{37-40} sts **each** side.

BACK

Rows 1 and 2: Work across; with second yarn, work across.

Row 3 (Buttonhole row)**:** Work across; with second yarn, work across 2 sts, decrease *(see Decreases, page 583)*, YO *(Figs. 16a or b, page 582)*, work across.

Rows 4-6: Work across; with second yarn, work across.

Rows 7-10: Beginning with a **knit** row, work in Stockinette Stitch across to last 6 sts, work last 6 sts in Seed Stitch (left placket); with second yarn, work next 6 sts in Seed Stitch (right placket), work in Stockinette Stitch across.

Row 11 (Buttonhole row)**:** Knit across to last 6 sts, work last 6 sts in Seed Stitch; with second yarn, work 2 sts in Seed Stitch, decrease, YO, work 2 sts in Seed Stitch, knit across.

Rows 12-18: Work in Stockinette Stitch across to last 6 sts, work last 6 sts in Seed Stitch; with second yarn, work next 6 sts in Seed Stitch, work in Stockinette Stitch across.

Row 19 (Buttonhole row)**:** Repeat Row 11.

Rows 20 thru 24(26-28): Work in Stockinette Stitch across to last 6 sts, work last 6 sts in Seed Stitch; with second yarn, work next 6 sts in Seed Stitch, work in Stockinette Stitch across.

Next 4 Rows: Work in Seed Stitch across; with second yarn, work in Seed Stitch across.

Bind off all sts **loosely** in knit.

Note: Yoke should measure 7^1/$_2$(8-8^1/$_2$)"/ 19{20.5-21.5} cm from cast on edge.

FRONT

With **right** side of Yoke Front facing, using larger size needles and MC, pick up 62{68-74} sts evenly spaced across cast on edge *(Fig. 34b, page 586)*: 62{68-74} sts.

Beginning with a **purl** row, work in Stockinette Stitch until Front measures approximately 7^1/$_4${9-10^3/$_4$}"/18.5{23-27.5} cm from Yoke, ending by working a **purl** row.

LEG SHAPING

Rows 1 and 2: Bind off 7{9-10} sts at the beginning of the next 2 rows, work across: 48{50-54} sts.

Bind off 2 sts at the beginning of the next 0{10-8} rows *(see Zeros, page 577)*, work across: 48{30-38} sts.

Next Row (Decrease row)**:** [Slip 1, K1, PSSO *(Figs. 19a & b, page 583)*], work across to last 2 sts, K2 tog *(Fig. 17, page 583)*: 46{28-36} sts.

Continue to decrease one stitch at each edge in same manner, every other row, 13{3-6} times **more**: 20{22-24} sts.

Work even until piece measures approximately 11$\frac{1}{4}${13$\frac{1}{2}$-15$\frac{3}{4}$}"/28.5{34.5-40} cm from Yoke, ending by working a **purl** row.

Slip remaining sts onto st holder; cut yarn.

BACK
Sew placket loosely in place, lapping right over left.

With **right** side of Yoke Back facing, using larger size needles and MC, pick up 62{68-74} sts evenly spaced across bound off edge working through both thicknesses of placket: 62{68-74} sts.

Beginning with a **purl** row, work in Stockinette Stitch until Back measures approximately 7$\frac{1}{4}${9-10$\frac{3}{4}$}"/18.5{23-27.5} cm from Yoke, ending by working a **purl** row.

LEG SHAPING
Row 1 (Decrease row)**:** Slip 1, K1, PSSO, knit across to last 2 sts, K2 tog: 60{66-72} sts.

Continue to decrease one stitch at each edge in same manner, every fourth row, 1{3-5} time(s); then decrease every other row, 13{11-9} times: 32{38-44} sts.

Next 2 Rows: Bind off 6{8-10} sts, work across: 20{22-24} sts.

Slip remaining sts onto st holder; cut yarn.

SLEEVE
With **right** side facing, using larger size needles and MC, pick up 46{50-54} sts evenly spaced along side of Yoke *(Fig. 34a, page 586)*: 46{50-54} sts.

Row 1: Purl across.

Row 2: Knit across.

Row 3: Purl across.

Rows 4-7: With CC, repeat Rows 2 and 3 twice.

Rows 8-11: With MC, repeat Rows 2 and 3 twice.

Row 12: With CC, K4{1-3}, K2 tog, (K3, K2 tog) 7{9-9} times, K5{2-4}: 38{40-44} sts.

RIBBING
Change to smaller size needles.

Rows 1-5: Work across in K1, P1 ribbing.

Bind off all sts **loosely** in ribbing.

Repeat for second Sleeve.

FINISHING
Weave underarm and side in one continuous seam *(Fig. 36, page 587)*, ending at beginning of Leg Shaping.

LEG RIBBING
With **right** side facing, using smaller size needles and MC, pick up 30{36-42} sts evenly spaced across Front and 18{24-30} sts evenly spaced across Back of Leg opening: 48{60-72} sts.

Rows 1-5: Work across in K1, P1 ribbing.

Bind off all sts **loosely** in ribbing.

Repeat for second Leg opening.

BOTTOM RIBBING
With **right** side of Front facing, using smaller size needles and MC, pick up 4 sts evenly spaced across end of Leg Ribbing, slip sts from Front st holder onto empty needle and knit across, pick up 4 sts evenly spaced across end of Leg Ribbing: 28{30-32} sts.

Rows 1-5: Work across in K1, P1 ribbing.

Bind off all sts in ribbing.

Repeat for Back.

Sew snap tape to Bottom Ribbings.

Add buttons.

Design by Joan Beebe.

SIMPLE SUNDRESS

◼◼◼◻ INTERMEDIATE

Size	Finished Chest Measurement	
6 months	18"	(45.5 cm)
12 months	19"	(48.5 cm)
18 months	20"	(51 cm)
24 months	21"	(53.5 cm)

Size Note: Instructions are written for size 6 months with sizes 12, 18 and 24 months in braces { }. Instructions will be easier to read if you circle all the numbers pertaining to your size. If only one number is given, it applies to all sizes.

MATERIALS

Fingering Weight Yarn
SUPER FINE 1
[1³/₄ ounces, 226 yards
(50 grams, 206 meters) per skein]:
2{3-3-4} skeins
Note: If length of Dress is adjusted, yarn amounts should be adjusted accordingly.
Knitting needles, size 3 (3.25 mm) **or** size needed for gauge
Stitch holder
Sewing needle and thread
¹/₂" (12 mm) Buttons - 4

GAUGE: In pattern (slightly stretched),
24 sts and 32 rows = 3" (7.5 cm)

Gauge Swatch: 3" (7.5 cm) square
Cast on 24 sts.
Row 1: ★ K2 tog *(Fig. 17, page 583)*, YO *(Fig. 16a, page 582)*, [slip 1, K1, PSSO *(Figs. 19a & b, page 583)*]; repeat from ★ across: 18 sts.
Row 2 (Right side)**:** K1, (K, P) **all** in next st, ★ K2, (K, P) **all** in next st; repeat from ★ across to last st, K1: 24 sts.
Rows 3-32: Repeat Rows 1 and 2, 15 times.
Bind off all sts in **knit**.

FRONT
SKIRT
Cast on 150{158-166-174} sts.

When instructed to slip a stitch, always slip as if to **knit**.

Row 1: K1, ★ K2 tog *(Fig. 17, page 583)*, YO *(Fig. 16a, page 582)*, [slip 1, K1, PSSO *(Figs. 19a & b, page 583)*]; repeat from ★ across to last st, K1: 113{119-125-131} sts.

Row 2 (Right side)**:** K2, ★ (K, P) **all** in next st, K2; repeat from ★ across: 150{158-166-174} sts.

Row 3: K1, (K2 tog, YO, slip 1, K1, PSSO) across to last st, K1: 113{119-125-131} sts.

Repeat Rows 2 and 3 for pattern until Skirt measures approximately 8{9-10-11}"/ 20.5{23-25.5-28} cm from cast on edge, ending by working Row 2.

Instructions continued on page 404.

BODICE

Row 1 (Wrong side)**:** K1, K2 tog across to last st, K1: 76{80-84-88} sts.

Row 2: K2 tog, knit across to last 2 sts, K2 tog: 74{78-82-86} sts.

Row 3: K1, (K2 tog, YO, slip 1, K1, PSSO) across to last st, K1: 56{59-62-65} sts.

Row 4: K2, ★ (K, P) **all** in next st, K2; repeat from ★ across: 74{78-82-86} sts.

Rows 5 thru 22{22-26-26}: Repeat Rows 3 and 4, 9{9-11-11} times: 74{78-82-86} sts.

Row 23{23-27-27}: Bind off 8 sts in **knit**, (K2 tog, YO, slip 1, K1, PSSO) across to last st, K1: 50{53-56-59} sts.

Row 24{24-28-28}: Bind off 6 sts, K1, ★ (K, P) **all** in next st, K2; repeat from ★ across: 58{62-66-70} sts.

Row 25{25-29-29}: K1, (K2 tog, YO, slip 1, K1, PSSO) across to last st, K1: 44{47-50-53} sts.

Row 26{26-30-30}: K1, K4 tog, (K, P) **all** in next st, ★ K2, (K, P) **all** in next st; repeat from ★ across to last 5 sts, K4 tog, K1: 50{54-58-62} sts.

Rows 27{27-31-31} and 28{28-32-32}: Repeat last 2 rows: 42{46-50-54} sts.

Row 29{29-33-33}: K1, (K2 tog, YO, slip 1, K1, PSSO) across to last st, K1: 32{35-38-41} sts.

Next Row: K2, ★ (K, P) **all** in next st, K2; repeat from ★ across: 42{46-50-54} sts.

Next Row: K1, (K2 tog, YO, slip 1, K1, PSSO) across to last st, K1: 32{35-38-41} sts.

Repeat last 2 rows, 6{6-7-9} times: 32{35-38-41} sts.

FIRST STRAP

Row 1: K2, [(K, P) **all** in next st, K2] twice, slip 10 sts just worked onto st holder, bind off next 16{19-22-25} sts in **knit**, K1, [(K, P) **all** in next st, K2] twice: 10 sts.

Row 2: K1, (K2 tog, YO, slip 1, K1, PSSO) twice, K1: 8 sts.

Row 3: K2, ★ (K, P) **all** in next st, K2; repeat from ★ once **more**: 10 sts.

Repeat Rows 2 and 3 until Strap measures 9{10-11-12}"/23{25.5-28-30.5} cm **or** to desired length, ending by working Row 3.

Bind off all sts in **knit**.

SECOND STRAP
Slip sts from st holder onto empty needle.

With **wrong** side facing and beginning with Row 2, complete same as First Strap.

BACK
Work same as Front through Row 20{20-24-24} of Bodice: 74{78-82-86} sts.

Buttonhole Row: K1, (K2 tog, YO, slip 1, K1, PSSO) 5 times, K2 tog, YO twice (for buttonhole), slip 1, K1, PSSO, (K2 tog, YO, slip 1, K1, PSSO) 6{7-8-9} times, K2 tog, YO twice (for buttonhole), slip 1, K1, PSSO, (K2 tog, YO, slip 1, K1, PSSO) 5 times, K1: 58{61-64-67} sts.

Last Row: K2, [(K, P) **all** in next st, K2] 5 times, (K, P) **all** in next YO letting second YO drop off of left needle, K2, [(K, P) **all** in next st, K2] 6{7-8-9} times, (K, P) **all** in next YO letting second YO drop off of left needle, K2, [(K, P) **all** in next st, K2] across: 74{78-82-86} sts.

Bind off all sts in **knit**.

FINISHING
Weave side seams *(Fig. 36, page 587)*.

Sew 2 buttons to end of each Strap, spacing 1$^{1}/_{2}$" (4 cm) apart. Cross Straps in back to button.

Design by Larisa Scott.

BREEZY PINAFORE
INTERMEDIATE

Size	Finished Chest Measurement	
6 months	21"	(53.5 cm)
12 months	22"	(56 cm)
18 months	23"	(58.5 cm)
24 months	24"	(61 cm)

Size Note: Instructions are written for size 6 months with sizes 12, 18 and 24 months in braces { }. Instructions will be easier to read if you circle all the numbers pertaining to your size. If only one number is given, it applies to all sizes.

MATERIALS
SUPER FINE 1
Fingering Weight Yarn
  [1³/₄ ounces, 226 yards
  (50 grams, 206 meters) per skein]:
    3{3-4-4} skeins
  Note: If length of Dress is adjusted, yarn
    amounts should be adjusted accordingly.
Knitting needles, size 3 (3.25 mm) **or** size
  needed for gauge
Tapestry needle
Sewing needle and thread
⁵/₈" (16 mm) Buttons - 9{10-10-10}

GAUGE: In pattern,
        21 sts and 32 rows = 3" (7.5 cm)
        In Stockinette Stitch,
        21 sts and 32 rows = 3¹/₄" (8.25 cm)

Gauge Swatch: 3" (7.5 cm) square
Cast on 21 sts.
Row 1: Purl across.

Row 2: K1, K2 tog *(Fig. 17, page 583)*, YO *(Fig. 16a, page 582)*, K1, YO, [slip 1, K1, PSSO *(Figs. 19a & b, page 583)*], ★ K2, K2 tog, YO, K1, YO, slip 1, K1, PSSO; repeat from ★ once **more**, K1.
Row 3: Purl across.
Row 4: ★ K2 tog, YO, K3, YO, slip 1, K1, PSSO; repeat from ★ across.
Rows 5-32: Repeat Rows 1-4, 7 times.
Bind off all sts in **knit**.

FRONT
SKIRT
Cast on 135{142-149-156} sts.

Row 1: K1, purl across to last st, K1.

When instructed to slip a stitch, always slip as if to **knit**.

Row 2 (Right side)**:** K2, ★ K2 tog *(Fig. 17, page 583)*, YO *(Fig. 16a, page 582)*, K1, YO, [slip 1, K1, PSSO *(Figs. 19a & b, page 583)*], K2; repeat from ★ across.

Row 3: K1, purl across to last st, K1.

Row 4: K1, ★ K2 tog, YO, K3, YO, slip 1, K1, PSSO; repeat from ★ across to last st, K1.

Row 5: K1, purl across to last st, K1.

Row 6: K2, ★ K2 tog, YO, K1, YO, slip 1, K1, PSSO, K2; repeat from ★ across.

Rows 7 thru 85{93-105-117}: Repeat Rows 3-6, 19{21-24-27} times; then repeat Rows 3-5 once **more**.

Instructions continued on page 408.

BODICE

Row 1 (Right side): K1{1-2-2}, K2 tog across to last 0{1-1-2} st(s) *(see Zeros, page 577)*, K 0{1-1-2}: 68{72-76-80} sts.

Row 2: [K1, (P1, K1) twice (band)], purl across to last 5 sts, [K1, (P1, K1) twice (band)].

Row 3: (K1, P1) twice, knit across to last 4 sts, (P1, K1) twice.

Rows 4 thru 10{10-12-14}: Repeat Rows 2 and 3, 3{3-4-5} times; then repeat Row 2 once **more**.

Row 11{11-13-15} (Decrease row): (K1, P1) twice, K2 tog, knit across to last 6 sts, slip 1, K1, PSSO, (P1, K1) twice: 66{70-74-78} sts.

Row 12{12-14-16}: K1, (P1, K1) twice, purl across to last 5 sts, K1, (P1, K1) twice.

Rows 13{13-15-17} thru 36{36-40-42}: Repeat last 2 rows, 12{12-13-13} times: 42{46-48-52} sts.

Row 37{37-41-43}: (K1, P1) twice, knit across to last 6 sts, slip 1, K1, PSSO, (P1, K1) twice: 41{45-47-51} sts.

Rows 38{38-42-44} thru 40{40-46-48}: K1, (P1, K1) across.

Row 41{41-47-49} (Buttonhole row): (K1, P1) twice, bind off next 2 sts (buttonhole begun), (P1, K1) across to last 6 sts, bind off next 2 sts (buttonhole begun), K1, P1, K1: 37{41-43-47} sts.

Row 42{42-48-50}: (K1, P1) twice, **turn**; [add on 2 sts *(Figs. 5a & b, page 580)* (buttonhole completed)], **turn**; K1, (P1, K1) across to last 4 sts, **turn**; [add on 2 sts (buttonhole completed)], **turn**; (P1, K1) twice: 41{45-47-51} sts.

Last 2 Rows: K1, (P1, K1) across.

Bind off all sts in pattern.

RIGHT BACK
SKIRT

Cast on 71{78-78-85} sts.

Row 1: [K1, (P1, K1) 3 times (band)], purl across to last st, K1.

Row 2 (Right side): K2, ★ K2 tog, YO, K1, YO, slip 1, K1, PSSO, K2; repeat from ★ across to last 6 sts, (P1, K1) 3 times.

Row 3: K1, (P1, K1) 3 times, purl across to last st, K1.

Row 4: K1, ★ K2 tog, YO, K3, YO, slip 1, K1, PSSO; repeat from ★ across to last 7 sts, K1, (P1, K1) 3 times.

Rows 5 thru 85{93-105-117}: Repeat Rows 1-4, 20{22-25-28} times; then repeat Row 1 once **more**.

BODICE

Row 1 (Right side): K2{1-1-2}, K2 tog across to last 7 sts, K1, (P1, K1) 3 times: 40{43-43-47} sts.

Row 2: K1, (P1, K1) 3 times, purl across to last 5 sts, K1, (P1, K1) twice.

Row 3: (K1, P1) twice, knit across to last 6 sts, (P1, K1) 3 times.

Rows 4 thru 8{8-8-12}: Repeat Rows 2 and 3, 2{2-2-4} times; then repeat Row 2 once **more**.

Row 9{9-9-13}: (K1, P1) twice, knit across to last 10 sts, [slip 1, K2 tog, PSSO *(Figs. 26a & b, page 584)*], K1, (P1, K1) 3 times: 38{41-41-45} sts.

Place a marker on Row 9{9-9-13} of band for top button placement.

Row 10{10-10-14}: K1, (P1, K1) 3 times, purl across to last 5 sts, K1, (P1, K1) twice.

SIZE 6 MONTHS ONLY
Row 11 (Decrease row): K1, (P1, K1) twice, K2 tog, knit across to last 10 sts, slip 1, K2 tog, PSSO, K1, (P1, K1) 3 times: 35 sts.

Instructions continued on page 410.

Row 12: K1, (P1, K1) 3 times, purl across to last 5 sts, K1, (P1, K1) twice.

Rows 13 and 14: Repeat Rows 11 and 12: 32 sts.

Row 15 (Decrease row)**:** K1, (P1, K1) twice, K2 tog, knit across to last 9 sts, slip 1, K1, PSSO, K1, (P1, K1) 3 times: 30 sts.

Row 16: K1, (P1, K1) 3 times, purl across to last 5 sts, K1, (P1, K1) twice.

Rows 17-28: Repeat Rows 15 and 16, 6 times: 18 sts.

Row 29: K1, (P1, K1) twice, K2 tog, K2, slip 1, K1, PSSO, K1, (P1, K1) 3 times: 16 sts.

Row 30: K1, (P1, K1) 3 times, P4, K1, (P1, K1) twice.

Row 31: K1, (P1, K1) twice, K2 tog, slip 1, K1, PSSO, K1, (P1, K1) 3 times: 14 sts.

Row 32: K1, (P1, K1) 3 times, P2, K1, (P1, K1) twice.

Row 33: K1, (P1, K1) twice, slip 1, K1, PSSO, K1, (P1, K1) 3 times: 13 sts.

Row 34: K1, (P1, K1) across.

Row 35: K1, P1, K2, slip 1, K1, PSSO, K1, (P1, K1) 3 times: 12 sts.

Row 36: K1, (P1, K1) 3 times, P2, K1, P1, K1.

Row 37: K1, P1, K1, slip 1, K1, PSSO, K1, (P1, K1) 3 times: 11 sts.

Row 38: K1, (P1, K1) across.

Row 39: K1, P1, slip 1, K1, PSSO, K1, (P1, K1) 3 times: 10 sts.

Row 40: K1, (P1, K1) 3 times, P2, K1.

Row 41: K1, slip 1, K1, PSSO, K1, (P1, K1) 3 times: 9 sts.

Continue with ALL SIZES - STRAP, page 411.

SIZE 12 MONTHS ONLY

Row 11 (Decrease row)**:** K1, (P1, K1) twice, K2 tog, knit across to last 10 sts, slip 1, K2 tog, PSSO, K1, (P1, K1) 3 times: 38 sts.

Row 12: K1, (P1, K1) 3 times, purl across to last 5 sts, K1, (P1, K1) twice.

Rows 13-20: Repeat Rows 11 and 12, 4 times: 26 sts.

Row 21 (Decrease row)**:** K1, (P1, K1) twice, K2 tog, knit across to last 9 sts, slip 1, K1, PSSO, K1, (P1, K1) 3 times: 24 sts.

Row 22: K1, (P1, K1) 3 times, purl across to last 5 sts, K1, (P1, K1) twice.

Rows 23-30: Repeat Rows 21 and 22, 4 times: 16 sts.

Row 31: K1, (P1, K1) twice, K2 tog, slip 1, K1, PSSO, K1, (P1, K1) 3 times: 14 sts.

Row 32: K1, (P1, K1) 3 times, P2, K1, (P1, K1) twice.

Row 33: K1, (P1, K1) twice, slip 1, K1, PSSO, K1, (P1, K1) 3 times: 13 sts.

Row 34: K1, (P1, K1) across.

Row 35: (K1, P1) twice, slip 1, K1, PSSO, K1, (P1, K1) 3 times: 12 sts.

Row 36: K1, (P1, K1) 3 times, P2, K1, P1, K1.

Row 37: K1, P1, K1, slip 1, K1, PSSO, K1, (P1, K1) 3 times: 11 sts.

Row 38: K1, (P1, K1) across.

Row 39: K1, P1, slip 1, K1, PSSO, K1, (P1, K1) 3 times: 10 sts.

Row 40: K1, (P1, K1) 3 times, P2, K1.

Row 41: K1, slip 1, K1, PSSO, K1, (P1, K1) 3 times: 9 sts.

Continue with ALL SIZES - STRAP.

SIZE 18 MONTHS ONLY
Row 11: (K1, P1) twice, knit across to last 10 sts, slip 1, K2 tog, PSSO, K1, (P1, K1) 3 times: 39 sts.

Row 12: K1, (P1, K1) 3 times, purl across to last 5 sts, K1, (P1, K1) twice.

Row 13: K1, (P1, K1) twice, K2 tog, knit across to last 10 sts, slip 1, K2 tog, PSSO, K1, (P1, K1) 3 times: 36 sts.

Row 14: K1, (P1, K1) 3 times, purl across to last 5 sts, K1, (P1, K1) twice.

Row 15 (Decrease row)**:** K1, (P1, K1) twice, K2 tog, knit across to last 9 sts, slip 1, K1, PSSO, K1, (P1, K1) 3 times: 34 sts.

Row 16: K1, (P1, K1) 3 times, purl across to last 5 sts, K1, (P1, K1) twice.

Rows 17-34: Repeat Rows 15 and 16, 9 times: 16 sts.

Row 35: K1, (P1, K1) twice, K2 tog, slip 1, K1, PSSO, K1, (P1, K1) 3 times: 14 sts.

Row 36: K1, (P1, K1) 3 times, P2, K1, (P1, K1) twice.

Row 37: K1, (P1, K1) twice, slip 1, K1, PSSO, K1, (P1, K1) 3 times: 13 sts.

Row 38: K1, (P1, K1) across.

Row 39: (K1, P1) twice, slip 1, K1, PSSO, K1, (P1, K1) 3 times: 12 sts.

Row 40: K1, (P1, K1) 3 times, P2, K1, P1, K1.

Row 41: K1, P1, K1, slip 1, K1, PSSO, K1, (P1, K1) 3 times: 11 sts.

Row 42: K1, (P1, K1) across.

Row 43: K1, P1, slip 1, K1, PSSO, K1, (P1, K1) 3 times: 10 sts.

Row 44: K1, (P1, K1) 3 times, P2, K1.

Row 45: K1, slip 1, K1, PSSO, K1, (P1, K1) 3 times: 9 sts.

Continue with ALL SIZES - STRAP.

SIZE 24 MONTHS ONLY
Row 15: K1, (P1, K1) twice, K2 tog, knit across to last 10 sts, slip 1, K2 tog, PSSO, K1, (P1, K1) 3 times: 42 sts.

Row 16: K1, (P1, K1) 3 times, purl across to last 5 sts, K1, (P1, K1) twice.

Row 17 (Decrease row)**:** K1, (P1, K1) twice, K2 tog, knit across to last 9 sts, slip 1, K1, PSSO, K1, (P1, K1) 3 times: 40 sts.

Row 18: K1, (P1, K1) 3 times, purl across to last 5 sts, K1, (P1, K1) twice.

Rows 19-42: Repeat Rows 17 and 18, 12 times: 16 sts.

Row 43: K1, (P1, K1) twice, K2 tog, slip 1, K1, PSSO, K1, (P1, K1) 3 times: 14 sts.

Row 44: K1, (P1, K1) 3 times, P2, K1, (P1, K1) twice.

Row 45: K1, (P1, K1) twice, slip 1, K1, PSSO, K1, (P1, K1) 3 times: 13 sts.

Row 46: K1, (P1, K1) across.

Row 47: (K1, P1) twice, slip 1, K1, PSSO, K1, (P1, K1) 3 times: 12 sts.

Row 48: K1, (P1, K1) 3 times, P2, K1, P1, K1.

Row 49: K1, P1, K1, slip 1, K1, PSSO, K1, (P1, K1) 3 times: 11 sts.

ALL SIZES - STRAP
Row 1: K1, (P1, K1) across: 9{9-9-11} sts.

Repeat Row 1 until Strap measures 8" (20.5 cm) **or** to desired length.

Bind off all sts in pattern.

Instructions continued on page 412.

Place a marker on band for bottom button placement, 1$\frac{1}{2}${1$\frac{1}{2}$-2-2$\frac{1}{2}$}"/4 {4-5-6.5} cm from cast on edge. Evenly space remaining 3 {4-4-4} buttons between top and bottom marker.

LEFT BACK
SKIRT
Cast on 71{78-78-85} sts.

Row 1: K1, purl across to last 7 sts, [K1, (P1, K1) 3 times (band)].

Row 2 (Right side)**:** (K1, P1) 3 times, ★ K2, K2 tog, YO, K1, YO, slip 1, K1, PSSO; repeat from ★ across to last 2 sts, K2.

Row 3: K1, purl across to last 7 sts, K1, (P1, K1) 3 times.

Row 4: (K1, P1) 3 times, K1, ★ K2 tog, YO, K3, YO, slip 1, K1, PSSO; repeat from ★ across to last st, K1.

Repeat Rows 1-4 for pattern until Skirt measures same as Right Back to first button marker, ending by working a **wrong** side row.

Buttonhole Row: K1, P1, K1, bind off next 2 sts (buttonhole begun), work across in pattern.

Next Row: K1, purl across to last 5 sts, K1, P1, **turn**; add on 2 sts (buttonhole completed), **turn**; K1, P1, K1.

Continue in pattern, working buttonholes as you reach each marker, until Skirt measures same as Right Back, ending by working Row 1.

BODICE
Row 1 (Right side)**:** K1, (P1, K1) 3 times, K2 tog across to last 2{1-1-2} st(s), K2{1-1-2}: 40{43-43-47} sts.

Row 2: K1, (P1, K1) twice, purl across to last 7 sts, K1, (P1, K1) 3 times.

Row 3: (K1, P1) 3 times, knit across to last 4 sts, (P1, K1) twice.

Rows 4 thru 8{8-8-12}: Repeat Rows 2 and 3, 2{2-2-4} times; then repeat Row 2 once **more**.

Row 9{9-9-13} (Buttonhole row)**:** K1, P1, K1, bind off next 2 sts (buttonhole begun), K1, slip 1, K2 tog, PSSO, knit across to last 4 sts, (P1, K1) twice: 36{39-39-43} sts.

Row 10{10-10-14}: K1, (P1, K1) twice, purl across to last 5 sts, K1, P1, **turn**; add on 2 sts (buttonhole completed), **turn**; K1, P1, K1: 38{41-41-45} sts.

SIZE 6 MONTHS ONLY
Row 11 (Decrease row)**:** K1, (P1, K1) 3 times, slip 1, K2 tog, PSSO, knit across to last 7 sts, slip 1, K1, PSSO, K1, (P1, K1) twice: 35 sts.

Row 12: K1, (P1, K1) twice, purl across to last 7 sts, K1, (P1, K1) 3 times.

Rows 13 and 14: Repeat Rows 11 and 12: 32 sts.

Row 15 (Decrease row)**:** K1, (P1, K1) 3 times, K2 tog, knit across to last 7 sts, slip 1, K1, PSSO, K1, (P1, K1) twice: 30 sts.

Row 16: K1, (P1, K1) twice, purl across to last 7 sts, K1, (P1, K1) 3 times.

Rows 17-28: Repeat Rows 15 and 16, 6 times: 18 sts.

Row 29: K1, (P1, K1) 3 times, K2 tog, K2, slip 1, K1, PSSO, K1, (P1, K1) twice: 16 sts.

Row 30: K1, (P1, K1) twice, P4, K1, (P1, K1) 3 times.

Row 31: K1, (P1, K1) 3 times, K2 tog, slip 1, K1, PSSO, K1, (P1, K1) twice: 14 sts.

Row 32: K1, (P1, K1) twice, P2, K1, (P1, K1) 3 times.

Row 33: K1, (P1, K1) 3 times, K2 tog, K1, (P1, K1) twice: 13 sts.

Row 34: K1, (P1, K1) across.

Row 35: K1, (P1, K1) 3 times, K2 tog, (P1, K1) twice: 12 sts.

Row 36: K1, P1, K1, P2, K1, (P1, K1) 3 times.

Row 37: K1, (P1, K1) 3 times, K2 tog, K1, P1, K1: 11 sts.

Row 38: K1, (P1, K1) across.

Row 39: K1, (P1, K1) 3 times, K2 tog, P1, K1: 10 sts.

Row 40: K1, P2, K1, (P1, K1) 3 times.

Row 41: K1, (P1, K1) 3 times, K2 tog, K1: 9 sts.

Continue with ALL SIZES - STRAP, page 414.

SIZE 12 MONTHS ONLY
Row 11 (Decrease row)**:** K1, (P1, K1) 3 times, slip 1, K2 tog, PSSO, knit across to last 7 sts, slip 1, K1, PSSO, K1, (P1, K1) twice: 38 sts.

Row 12: K1, (P1, K1) twice, purl across to last 7 sts, K1, (P1, K1) 3 times.

Rows 13-20: Repeat Rows 11 and 12, 4 times: 26 sts.

Row 21 (Decrease row)**:** K1, (P1, K1) 3 times, K2 tog, knit across to last 7 sts, slip 1, K1, PSSO, K1, (P1, K1) twice: 24 sts.

Row 22: K1, (P1, K1) twice, purl across to last 7 sts, K1, (P1, K1) 3 times.

Rows 23-28: Repeat Rows 21 and 22, 3 times: 18 sts.

Row 29: K1, (P1, K1) 3 times, K2 tog, K2, slip 1, K1, PSSO, K1, (P1, K1) twice: 16 sts.

Row 30: K1, (P1, K1) twice, P4, K1, (P1, K1) 3 times.

Row 31: K1, (P1, K1) 3 times, K2 tog, slip 1, K1, PSSO, K1, (P1, K1) twice: 14 sts.

Row 32: K1, (P1, K1) twice, P2, K1, (P1, K1) 3 times.

Row 33: K1, (P1, K1) 3 times, K2 tog, K1, (P1, K1) twice: 13 sts.

Row 34: K1, (P1, K1) across.

Row 35: K1, (P1, K1) 3 times, K2 tog, (P1, K1) twice: 12 sts.

Row 36: K1, P1, K1, P2, K1, (P1, K1) 3 times.

Row 37: K1, (P1, K1) 3 times, K2 tog, K1, P1, K1: 11 sts.

Row 38: K1, (P1, K1) across.

Row 39: K1, (P1, K1) 3 times, K2 tog, P1, K1: 10 sts.

Row 40: K1, P2, K1, (P1, K1) 3 times.

Row 41: K1, (P1, K1) 3 times, K2 tog, K1: 9 sts.

Continue with ALL SIZES - STRAP, page 414.

SIZE 18 MONTHS ONLY
Row 11: K1, (P1, K1) 3 times, slip 1, K2 tog, PSSO, knit across to last 4 sts, (P1, K1) twice: 39 sts.

Row 12: K1, (P1, K1) twice, purl across to last 7 sts, K1, (P1, K1) 3 times.

Row 13: K1, (P1, K1) 3 times, slip 1, K2 tog, PSSO, knit across to last 7 sts, slip 1, K1, PSSO, K1, (P1, K1) twice: 36 sts.

Row 14: K1, (P1, K1) twice, purl across to last 7 sts, K1, (P1, K1) 3 times.

Row 15 (Decrease row)**:** K1, (P1, K1) 3 times, K2 tog, knit across to last 7 sts, slip 1, K1, PSSO, K1, (P1, K1) twice: 34 sts.

Row 16: K1, (P1, K1) twice, purl across to last 7 sts, K1, (P1, K1) 3 times.

Rows 17-32: Repeat Rows 15 and 16, 8 times: 18 sts.

Instructions continued on page 414.

Row 33: K1, (P1, K1) 3 times, K2 tog, K2, slip 1, K1, PSSO, K1, (P1, K1) twice: 16 sts.

Row 34: K1, (P1, K1) twice, P4, K1, (P1, K1) 3 times.

Row 35: K1, (P1, K1) 3 times, K2 tog, slip 1, K1, PSSO, K1, (P1, K1) twice: 14 sts.

Row 36: K1, (P1, K1) twice, P2, K1, (P1, K1) 3 times.

Row 37: K1, (P1, K1) 3 times, K2 tog, K1, (P1, K1) twice: 13 sts.

Row 38: K1, (P1, K1) across.

Row 39: K1, (P1, K1) 3 times, K2 tog, (P1, K1) twice: 12 sts.

Row 40: K1, P1, K1, P2, K1, (P1, K1) 3 times.

Row 41: K1, (P1, K1) 3 times, K2 tog, K1, P1, K1: 11 sts.

Row 42: K1, (P1, K1) across.

Row 43: K1, (P1, K1) 3 times, K2 tog, P1, K1: 10 sts.

Row 44: K1, P2, K1, (P1, K1) 3 times.

Row 45: K1, (P1, K1) 3 times, K2 tog, K1: 9 sts.

Continue with ALL SIZES - STRAP.

SIZE 24 MONTHS ONLY
Row 15: K1, (P1, K1) 3 times, slip 1, K2 tog, PSSO, knit across to last 7 sts, slip 1, K1, PSSO, K1, (P1, K1) twice: 42 sts.

Row 16: K1, (P1, K1) twice, purl across to last 7 sts, K1, (P1, K1) 3 times.

Row 17 (Decrease row)**:** K1, (P1, K1) 3 times, K2 tog, knit across to last 7 sts, slip 1, K1, PSSO, K1, (P1, K1) twice: 40 sts.

Row 18: K1, (P1, K1) twice, purl across to last 7 sts, K1, (P1, K1) 3 times.

Rows 19-40: Repeat Rows 17 and 18, 11 times: 18 sts.

Row 41: K1, (P1, K1) 3 times, K2 tog, K2, slip 1, K1, PSSO, K1, (P1, K1) twice: 16 sts.

Row 42: K1, (P1, K1) twice, P4, K1, (P1, K1) 3 times.

Row 43: K1, (P1, K1) 3 times, K2 tog, slip 1, K1, PSSO, K1, (P1, K1) twice: 14 sts.

Row 44: K1, (P1, K1) twice, P2, K1, (P1, K1) 3 times.

Row 45: K1, (P1, K1) 3 times, K2 tog, K1, (P1, K1) twice: 13 sts.

Row 46: K1, (P1, K1) across.

Row 47: K1, (P1, K1) 3 times, K2 tog, (P1, K1) twice: 12 sts.

Row 48: K1, P1, K1, P2, K1, (P1, K1) 3 times.

Row 49: K1, (P1, K1) 3 times, K2 tog, K1, P1, K1: 11 sts.

ALL SIZES - STRAP
Row 1: K1, (P1, K1) across: 9{9-9-11} sts.

Repeat Row 1 until Strap measures 8" (20.5 cm) **or** to desired length.

Bind off all sts in pattern.

FINISHING
Weave side seams *(Fig. 36, page 587)*, ending at Row 10{10-10-14} of Bodice.

Sew buttons to Right Back at markers and sew 2 buttons to end of each Strap, spacing 1¹/₂" (4 cm) apart. Cross Straps in back to button.

Design by Larisa Scott.

SWEETHEART CARDIGAN

Shown on page 417.

BACK

LEFT FRONT

SLEEVE

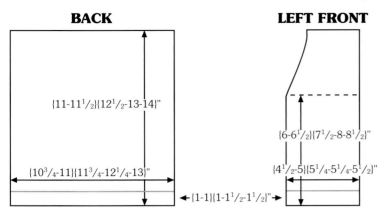

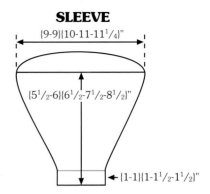

■■■□ INTERMEDIATE

Size: {3 months-6 months}
{12 months-18 months-24 months}

Finished Chest Measurement:
{21-21¹/₂}{23-24-25}"

Size Note: Instructions are written for sizes 3 months and 6 months in the first set of braces { }, with sizes 12 months, 18 months, and 24 months in the second set of braces. Instructions will be easier to read if you circle all the numbers pertaining to your child's size. If only one number is given, it applies to all sizes.

MATERIALS

Baby Sport Weight Yarn: **[FINE 2]**
  White - {3-3¹/₂}{4-4¹/₂-5} ounces,
    [{90-100}{110-130-140} ounces
    {320-370}{425-480-530} yards]
  Pink - 20 yards
  Green - 20 yards
Straight knitting needles, sizes 5 (3.75 mm) **and**
  6 (4 mm) **or** sizes needed for gauge
24" Circular needle, size 5 (3.75 mm)
Bobbins - 2
Stitch holder
Markers
⁷/₁₆" Buttons - 4
Yarn needle

GAUGE: With larger size needles,
    in Stockinette Stitch,
    22 sts and 30 rows = 4"

STITCH GUIDE

TWIST (uses next 2 sts)
K2 tog *(Fig. 17, page 583)* making sure **not** to drop off, then knit the first stitch letting both stitches drop off left needle together.

BACK
RIBBING

With White and smaller size straight needles, cast on {59-61}{65-67-71} sts **loosely** *(Figs. 2a-e, page 9)*.

Row 1: P1, (K1, P1) across.

Row 2 (Right side)**:** Knit across.

Row 3: P1, (K1, P1) across.

Rows 4 thru {9-9}{9-13-13}: Repeat Rows 2 and 3, {3-3}{3-5-5} times.

BODY

Change to larger size needles.

Row 1: Knit across.

Row 2: Purl across.

When instructed to slip a stitch, always slip as if to **knit**.

Row 3: K{4-5}{7-8-2}, YO *(Fig. 16a, page 582)*, [slip 1, K2 tog, PSSO *(Figs. 26a & b, page 584)*], (YO, K5, YO, slip 1, K2 tog, PSSO) {6-6}{6-6-8} times, YO, K{4-5}{7-8-2}.

Instructions continued on page 416.

Row 4: Purl across.

Row 5: K{5-6}{8-9-3}, YO, [slip 1, K1, PSSO **(Figs. 19a & b, page 583)]**, (K6, YO, slip 1, K1, PSSO) {6-6}{6-6-8} times, K{4-5}{7-8-2}.

Row 6: Purl across.

Row 7: Knit across.

Row 8: Purl across.

Row 9: K{8-1}{3-4-6}, YO, slip 1, K2 tog, PSSO, (YO, K5, YO, slip 1, K2 tog, PSSO) {5-7}{7-7-7} times, YO, K{8-1}{3-4-6}.

Row 10: Purl across.

Row 11: K{9-2}{4-5-7}, YO, slip 1, K1, PSSO, (K6, YO, slip 1, K1, PSSO) {5-7}{7-7-7} times, K{8-1}{3-4-6}.

Row 12: Purl across.

Row 13: Knit across.

Row 14: Purl across.

Row 15: K{4-5}{7-8-2}, YO, slip 1, K2 tog, PSSO, (YO, K5, YO, slip 1, K2 tog, PSSO) {6-6}{6-6-8} times, YO, K{4-5}{7-8-2}.

Row 16: Purl across.

Row 17: K{5-6}{8-9-3}, YO, slip 1, K1, PSSO, (K6, YO, slip 1, K1, PSSO) {6-6}{6-6-8} times, K{4-5}{7-8-2}.

Row 18: Purl across.

Repeat Rows 7-18 until Back measures approximately {11-11¹/₂}{12¹/₂-13-14}" from cast on edge, ending by working a **wrong** side row.

Last Row: Bind off {20-21}{22-23-25} sts, knit next {18-18}{20-20-20} sts, slip {19-19}{21-21-21} sts just worked onto st holder; bind off remaining sts.

LEFT FRONT
RIBBING
With White and smaller size straight needles, cast on {25-27}{29-29-31} sts **loosely**.

Row 1: P1, (K1, P1) across.

Row 2 (Right side)**:** Knit across.

Row 3: P1, (K1, P1) across.

Rows 4 thru {9-9}{9-13-13}: Repeat Rows 2 and 3, {3-3}{3-5-5} times.

BODY
Change to larger size needles.

Wind a small amount of Green onto one bobbin and a small amount of Pink onto another bobbin **(see Bobbin Knitting, page 585)**.

CHART

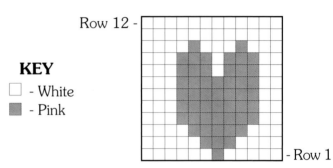

Row 12 -

KEY
☐ - White
⬛ - Pink

- Row 1

FOR SIZES 3 AND 6 MONTHS ONLY
Row 1: K{11-13}, place marker **(Fig. 1, page 578)**, with Green work Twist **(Fig. 30, page 585)**, knit across.

Row 2: P 12, with Green P2, with White purl across.

Row 3: K{6-8}, YO, slip 1, K2 tog, PSSO, YO, K2, with Green work Twist, work Row 1 of Chart **(see Following A Chart, page 586)**.

Row 4: Work next row of Chart, with Green P2, with White purl across.

Row 5: K{7-9}, YO, slip 1, K1, PSSO, K2, with Green work Twist, work next row of Chart.

Instructions continued on page 418.

Row 6: Work next row of Chart, with Green P2, with White purl across.

Row 7: Knit across to marker, with Green work Twist, work next row of Chart.

Row 8: Work next row of Chart, with Green P2, with White purl across.

Row 9: K{2-4}, YO, slip 1, K2 tog, PSSO, YO, K6, with Green work Twist, work next row of Chart.

Row 10: Work next row of Chart, with Green P2, with White purl across.

Row 11: K{3-5}, YO, slip 1, K1, PSSO, K6, with Green work Twist, work next row of Chart.

Row 12: Work next row of Chart, with Green P2, with White purl across.

Row 13: Knit across to marker, with Green work Twist, work next row of Chart.

Row 14: Work next row of Chart, with Green P2, with White purl across.

FOR SIZES 12, 18, AND 24 MONTHS ONLY

Row 1: K{15-15-17}, place marker *(Fig. 1, page 578)*, with Green work Twist *(Fig. 30, page 585)*, knit across.

Row 2: P 12, with Green P2, with White purl across.

Row 3: K{2-2-4}, YO, slip 1, K2 tog, PSSO, YO, K5, YO, slip 1, K2 tog, PSSO, YO, K2, with Green work Twist, work Row 1 of Chart *(see Following A Chart, page 586)*.

Row 4: Work next row of Chart, with Green P2, with White purl across.

Row 5: K{3-3-5}, YO, slip 1, K1, PSSO, K6, YO, slip 1, K1, PSSO, K2, with Green work Twist, work next row of Chart.

Row 6: Work next row of Chart, with Green P2, with White purl across.

Row 7: Knit across to marker, with Green work Twist, work next row of Chart.

Row 8: Work next row of Chart, with Green P2, with White purl across.

Row 9: K{6-6-8}, YO, slip 1, K2 tog, PSSO, YO, K6, with Green work Twist, work next row of Chart.

Row 10: Work next row of Chart, with Green P2, with White purl across.

Row 11: K{7-7-9}, YO, slip 1, K1, PSSO, K6, with Green work Twist, work next row of Chart.

Row 12: Work next row of Chart, with Green P2, with White purl across.

Row 13: Knit across to marker, with Green work Twist, work next row of Chart.

Row 14: Work next row of Chart, with Green P2, with White purl across.

FOR ALL SIZES
Repeat Rows 3-14 until Left Front measures approximately {6-6$^1/_2$}{7$^1/_2$-8-8$^1/_2$}" from cast on edge, ending by working a **wrong** side row.

NECK SHAPING
Note: Maintain established patterns throughout and continue to follow Chart.

Row 1 (Decrease row)**:** Work across to within 3 sts of marker, K2 tog, K1, work across, place marker around last st to mark beginning of Neck Shaping: {24-26}{28-28-30} sts.

Row 2: Work across.

Continue to decrease every fourth row, {0-3}{6-3-0} times *(see Zeros, page 577)*; then decrease every sixth row, {4-2}{0-2-5} times: {20-21}{22-23-25} sts.

Work even until Left Front measures same as Back, ending by working a **purl** row.

Bind off remaining sts in **knit**.

RIGHT FRONT
RIBBING

With White and smaller size straight needles, cast on {25-27}{29-29-31} sts **loosely**.

Row 1: P1, (K1, P1) across.

Row 2 (Right side)**:** Knit across.

Row 3: P1, (K1, P1) across.

Rows 4 thru {9-9}{9-13-13}: Repeat Rows 2 and 3, {3-3}{3-5-5} times.

BODY

Change to larger size needles.

Wind a small amount of Green onto one bobbin and a small amount of Pink onto another bobbin.

FOR SIZES 3, 6, AND 12 MONTHS ONLY

Row 1: K 12, with Green work Twist, place marker, with White knit across.

Row 2: Purl across to marker, with Green P2, with White purl across.

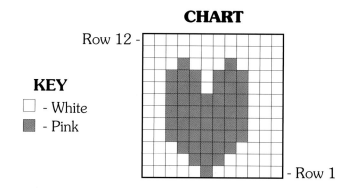

CHART

Row 12 -

KEY
☐ - White
■ - Pink

- Row 1

Row 3: Work Row 1 of Chart, with Green work Twist, with White K2, YO, slip 1, K2 tog, PSSO, YO, knit across.

Row 4: Purl across to marker, with Green P2, work next row of Chart.

Row 5: Work next row of Chart, with Green work Twist, with White K3, YO, slip 1, K1, PSSO, knit across.

Row 6: Purl across to marker, with Green P2, work next row of Chart.

Row 7: Work next row of Chart, with Green work Twist, with White knit across.

Row 8: Purl across, with Green P2, work next row of Chart.

Row 9: Work next row of Chart, with Green work Twist, with White K6, YO, slip 1, K2 tog, PSSO, YO, knit across.

Row 10: Purl across to marker, with Green P2, work next row of Chart.

Row 11: Work next row of Chart, with Green work Twist, with White K7, YO, slip 1, K1, PSSO, knit across.

Row 12: Purl across to marker, with Green P2, work next row of Chart.

Row 13: Work next row of Chart, with Green work Twist, with White knit across.

Row 14: Purl across to marker, with Green P2, work next row of Chart.

FOR SIZES 18 AND 24 MONTHS ONLY

Row 1: K 12, with Green work Twist, place marker, with White knit across.

Row 2: Purl across to marker, with Green P2, with White purl across.

Row 3: Work Row 1 of Chart, work Twist, with White K2, YO, slip 1, K2 tog, PSSO, YO, K5, YO, slip 1, K2 tog, PSSO, YO, knit across.

Row 4: Purl across to marker, with Green P2, work next row of Chart.

Row 5: Work next row of Chart, with Green work Twist, with White K3, YO, slip 1, K1, PSSO, K6, YO, slip 1, K1, PSSO, knit across.

Instructions continued on page 420.

Row 6: Purl across to marker, with Green P2, work next row of Chart.

Row 7: Work next row of Chart, with Green work Twist, with White knit across.

Row 8: Purl across, with Green P2, work next row of Chart.

Row 9: Work next row of Chart, with Green work Twist, with White K6, YO, slip 1, K2 tog, PSSO, YO, knit across.

Row 10: Purl across to marker, with Green P2, work next row of Chart.

Row 11: Work next row of Chart, with Green work Twist, with White K7, YO, slip 1, K1, PSSO, knit across.

Row 12: Purl across to marker, with Green P2, work next row of Chart.

Row 13: Work next row of Chart, with Green work Twist, with White knit across.

Row 14: Purl across to marker, with Green P2, work next row of Chart.

FOR ALL SIZES
Repeat Rows 3-14 until Left Front measures approximately {6-6^1/$_2$}{7^1/$_2$-8-8^1/$_2$}" from cast on edge, ending by working a **wrong** side row.

NECK SHAPING
Note: Maintain established patterns throughout and continue to follow Chart.

Row 1 (Decrease row)**:** Work across to marker, K1, SSK *(Figs. 21a-c, page 584)*, work across, place marker around first st to mark beginning of Neck Shaping: {24-26}{28-28-30} sts.

Rows 2 and 3: Work across.

Beginning with **next** row, decrease every fourth row, {0-3}{6-3-0} times; then decrease every sixth row, {4-2}{0-2-5} times: {20-21}{22-23-25} sts.

Work even until Right Front measures same as Back, ending by working a **wrong** side row.

Bind off remaining sts in **knit**.

SLEEVE (Make 2)
RIBBING
With White and smaller size straight needles, cast on {35-35}{37-39-39} sts **loosely**.

Row 1: P1, (K1, P1) across.

Row 2 (Right side)**:** Knit across.

Row 3: P1, (K1, P1) across.

Rows 4 thru {8-8}{8-12-12}: Repeat Rows 2 and 3, {2-2}{2-4-4} times; then repeat Row 2 once **more**.

Row {9-9}{9-13-13}: P1, (K1, P1) across increasing one st: {36-36}{38-40-40} sts.

BODY
Change to larger size needles.

Row 1: Knit across.

Row 2: Purl across.

Row 3: K1, Right Invisible Increase *(Fig. 12a, page 581)*, K{4-4}{5-6-6}, YO, slip 1, K2 tog, PSSO, (YO, K5, YO, slip 1, K2 tog, PSSO) 3 times, YO, K{3-3}{4-5-5}, Left Invisible Increase *(Figs. 13a & b, page 581)*, K1: {38-38}{40-42-42} sts.

Row 4: Purl across.

Row 5: K1, Right Invisible Increase, K{6-6}{7-8-8}, YO, slip 1, K1, PSSO, (K6, YO, slip 1, K1, PSSO) 3 times, K{4-4}{5-6-6}, Left Invisible Increase, K1: {40-40}{42-44-44} sts.

Row 6: Purl across.

Row 7: Knit across.

Row 8: Purl across.

Row 9: K1, Right Invisible Increase, K{2-2}{3-4-4}, YO, slip 1, K2 tog, PSSO, (YO, K5, YO, slip 1, K2 tog, PSSO) 4 times, YO, K{1-1}{2-3-3}, Left Invisible Increase, K1: {42-42}{44-46-46} sts.

Row 10: Purl across.

Row 11: K{5-5}{6-7-7}, YO, slip 1, K1, PSSO, (K6, YO, slip 1, K1, PSSO) 4 times, K{3-3}{4-5-5}.

Row 12: Purl across.

Beginning with next row and working new stitches in pattern, increase one stitch at **each** edge, every fourth row, {4-4}{6-7-8} times: {50-50}{56-60-62} sts.

Work even until Sleeve measures approximately {5^1/$_2$-6}{6^1/$_2$-7^1/$_2$-8^1/$_2$}" from cast on edge, ending by working a **wrong** side row.

SLEEVE SHAPING
Rows 1-8: Bind off {5-5}{6-7-7} sts at the beginning of the row, work across: {10-10}{8-4-6} sts.

Bind off remaining sts **loosely** in **knit**.

FINISHING
Sew shoulder seams.

BAND
With **right** side facing, using White and circular needle, pick up {36-38}{44-48-52} sts evenly spaced across Right Front to marker **(Figs. 34a & b, page 586)**, do **not** remove marker, pick up {26-32}{32-32-36} sts along Right Front Neck edge, knit {19-19}{21-21-21} sts from Back st holder, pick up {26-32}{32-32-36} sts across Left Front Neck edge to marker, do **not** remove marker, pick up {36-38}{44-48-52} sts evenly spaced across Left Front: {143-159}{173-181-197} sts.

Mark placement of buttons on Left Front, placing first marker ^{1}/$_2$" from cast on edge and second marker ^{1}/$_2$" down from Neck Shaping marker; evenly space markers for remaining 2 buttons.

Row 1: P1, (K1, P1) across.

Row 2: Knit across.

Row 3: P1, (K1, P1) across.

Row 4 (Buttonhole row)**:** Knit across to first marker, **[K2 tog, YO, (buttonhole made)]**, (knit across to next marker, K2 tog, YO) 3 times, knit across.

Row 5: P1, (K1, P1) across.

Row 6: Knit across.

Row 7: P1, (K1, P1) across.

Bind off all sts **loosely** in **knit**.

Sew Sleeves to Sweater, matching center of last row on Sleeve Shaping to shoulder seam and beginning {4^1/$_2$-4^1/$_2$}{5-5^1/$_2$-5^1/$_2$}" down from seam.

Weave underarm and side in one continuous seam **(Fig. 36, page 587)**.

Sew buttons opposite buttonholes.

Design by Lois J. Long.

HANDSOME CARDIGAN

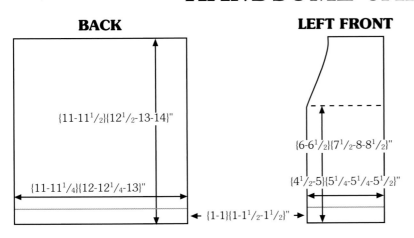

BACK

LEFT FRONT

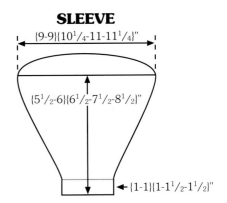

SLEEVE

Size: {3 months-6 months}
{12 months-18 months-24 months}

Finished Chest Measurement:
{21-22}{23-24-25$^1/_2$}"

Size Note: Instructions are written for sizes
3 months and 6 months in the first set of braces { },
with sizes 12 months, 18 months, and 24 months
in the second set of braces. Instructions will be
easier to read if you circle all the numbers
pertaining to your child's size. If only one number is
given, it applies to all sizes.

MATERIALS

Baby Sport Weight Yarn:
Blue - {3$^1/_2$-4}{4$^1/_2$-5-5$^1/_2$} ounces,
[{100-110}{130-140-160} grams,
{370-425}{480-530-585} yards]
White - 20 yards
Straight knitting needles, sizes 5 (3.75 mm) **and**
6 (4.00 mm) **or** sizes needed for gauge
24" Circular needle, size 5 (3.75 mm)
Cable needle
Markers
Stitch holder
$^1/_2$" Buttons - 4
Yarn needle

GAUGE: With larger size needles, in pattern,
22 sts and 30 rows = 4"

STITCH GUIDE

BACK CABLE (uses next 3 sts)
Slip next 2 stitches onto cable needle and hold in
back of work, knit next stitch from left needle,
K2 from cable needle.

FRONT CABLE (uses next 3 sts)
Slip next stitch onto cable needle and hold in
front of work, knit next 2 stitches from left
needle, K1 from cable needle.

BACK
RIBBING
FOR SIZES 3, 6, & 12 MONTHS ONLY
With Blue and smaller size straight needles, cast on
{59-61}{65} sts **loosely** *(Figs. 2a-e, page 9)*.

Row 1: P1, (K1, P1) across.

Row 2 (Right side)**:** Knit across.

Row 3: P1, (K1, P1) across.

Row 4: With White, knit across.

Row 5: P1, (K1, P1) across; cut White.

Row 6: With Blue, knit across.

Row 7: P1, (K1, P1) across.

Row 8: Knit across.

Instructions continued on page 424.

FOR SIZES 18 AND 24 MONTHS ONLY

With Blue and smaller size straight needles, cast on {67-71} sts **loosely (Figs. 2a-e, page 9)**.

Row 1: P1, (K1, P1) across.

Row 2 (Right side)**:** Knit across.

Row 3: P1, (K1, P1) across.

Row 4: Knit across.

Row 5: P1, (K1, P1) across.

Row 6: With White, knit across.

Row 7: P1, (K1, P1) across; cut White.

Row 8: With Blue, knit across.

Row 9: P1, (K1, P1) across.

Row 10: Knit across.

Row 11: P1, (K1, P1) across.

Row 12: Knit across.

FOR ALL SIZES

Row {9-9}{9-13-13}: P1, (K1, P1) across increasing one st **(see Increases, page 581)**: {60-62}{66-68-72} sts.

BODY

Change to larger size needles.

Row 1: K{2-3}{5-6-2}, P2, (K4, P2) {9-9}{9-9-11} times, K{2-3}{5-6-2}.

Row 2: Purl across.

Row 3: K{5-6}{2-3-5}, P2, (K4, P2) {8-8}{10-10-10} times, K{5-6}{2-3-5}.

Row 4: Purl across.

Repeat Rows 1-4 until Back measures approximately {11-11¹/₂}{12¹/₂-13-14}" from cast on edge, ending by working a **wrong** side row.

Last Row: Bind off {20-21}{22-23-25} sts, knit next {19-19}{21-21-21} sts, slip {20-20}{22-22-22} sts just worked onto st holder; bind off remaining sts.

LEFT FRONT
RIBBING
FOR SIZES 3, 6, & 12 MONTHS ONLY

With Blue and smaller size straight needles, cast on {25-27}{29} sts **loosely**.

Row 1: P1, (K1, P1) across.

Row 2 (Right side)**:** Knit across.

Row 3: P1, (K1, P1) across.

Row 4: With White, knit across.

Row 5: P1, (K1, P1) across; cut White.

Row 6: With Blue, knit across.

Row 7: P1, (K1, P1) across.

Row 8: Knit across.

FOR SIZES 18 AND 24 MONTHS ONLY

With Blue and smaller size straight needles, cast on {29-31} sts **loosely**.

Row 1: P1, (K1, P1) across.

Row 2 (Right side)**:** Knit across.

Row 3: P1, (K1, P1) across.

Row 4: Knit across.

Row 5: P1, (K1, P1) across.

Row 6: With White, knit across.

Row 7: P1, (K1, P1) across; cut White.

Row 8: With Blue, knit across.

Row 9: P1, (K1, P1) across.

Row 10: Knit across.

Row 11: P1, (K1, P1) across.

Row 12: Knit across.

FOR ALL SIZES
Row {9-9}{9-13-13}: P1, (K1, P1) across increasing one st: {26-28}{30-30-32} sts.

BODY
Change to larger size needles.

Row 1: K{1-3}{5-5-1}, P2, (K4, P2) {2-2}{2-2-3} times, place marker *(Fig. 1, page 578)*, K9, P1, K1.

Row 2: P2, K1, purl across.

Row 3: K{4-6}{2-2-4}, P2, (K4, P2) {1-1}{2-2-2} time(s), K 12, P1, K1.

Row 4: P2, K1, purl across.

Row 5: K{1-3}{5-5-1}, P2, (K4, P2) {2-2}{2-2-3} times, K1, work Front Cable, work Back Cable, K2, P1, K1.

Row 6: P2, K1, purl across.

Row 7: K{4-6}{2-2-4}, (P2, K4) {2-2}{3-3-3} times, work Front Cable, work Back Cable, K2, P1, K1.

Row 8: P2, K1, purl across.

Row 9: K{1-3}{5-5-1}, P2, (K4, P2) {2-2}{2-2-3} times, K1, work Front Cable, work Back Cable, K2, P1, K1.

Row 10: P2, K1, purl across.

Row 11: K{4-6}{2-2-4}, P2, (K4, P2) {1-1}{2-2-2} time(s), K 12, P1, K1.

Row 12: P2, K1, purl across.

Row 13: K{1-3}{5-5-1}, P2, (K4, P2) {2-2}{2-2-3} times, K9, P1, K1.

Row 14: P2, K1, purl across.

Row 15: K{4-6}{2-2-4}, (P2, K4) {2-2}{3-3-3} times, work Front Cable, work Back Cable, K2, P1, K1.

Row 16: P2, K1, purl across.

Row 17: K{1-3}{5-5-1}, P2, (K4, P2) {2-2}{2-2-3} times, K1, work Front Cable, work Back Cable, K2, P1, K1.

Row 18: P2, K1, purl across.

Row 19: K{4-6}{2-2-4}, (P2, K4) {2-2}{3-3-3} times, work Front Cable, work Back Cable, K2, P1, K1.

Row 20: P2, K1, purl across.

Row 21: K{1-3}{5-5-1}, P2, (K4, P2) {2-2}{2-2-3} times, K9, P1, K1.

Row 22: P2, K1, purl across.

Repeat Rows 3-22 until Left Front measures approximately {6-6$\frac{1}{2}$}{7$\frac{1}{2}$-8-8$\frac{1}{2}$}" from cast on edge, ending by working a **wrong** side row.

NECK SHAPING
Note: Maintain established pattern throughout.

Row 1 (Decrease row)**:** Work across to within 3 sts of marker, K2 tog *(Fig. 17, page 583)*, K1, work across, place marker around last st to mark beginning of Neck Shaping: {25-27}{29-29-31} sts.

Rows 2 and 3: Work across.

Continue to decrease every fourth row, {1-4}{7-4-1} time(s); then decrease every sixth row, {4-2}{0-2-5} times *(see Zeros, page 577)*: {20-21}{22-23-25} sts.

Work even until Left Front measures same as Back, ending by working a **purl** row.

Bind off remaining sts **loosely** in **knit**.

Instructions continued on page 426.

RIGHT FRONT
RIBBING
FOR SIZES 3, 6, & 12 MONTHS ONLY

With Blue and smaller size straight needles, cast on {25-27}{29} sts **loosely**.

Row 1: P1, (K1, P1) across.

Row 2 (Right side)**:** Knit across.

Row 3: P1, (K1, P1) across.

Row 4: With White, knit across.

Row 5: P1, (K1, P1) across; cut White.

Row 6: With Blue, knit across.

Row 7: P1, (K1, P1) across.

Rows 8: Knit across.

FOR SIZES 18 AND 24 MONTHS ONLY

With Blue and smaller size straight needles, cast on {29-31} sts **loosely**.

Row 1: P1, (K1, P1) across.

Row 2 (Right side)**:** Knit across.

Row 3: P1, (K1, P1) across.

Row 4: Knit across.

Row 5: P1, (K1, P1) across.

Row 6: With White, knit across.

Row 7: P1, (K1, P1) across; cut White.

Row 8: With Blue, knit across.

Row 9: P1, (K1, P1) across.

Row 10: Knit across.

Row 11: P1, (K1, P1) across.

Row 12: Knit across.

FOR ALL SIZES

Row {9-9}{9-13-13}: P1, (K1, P1) across increasing one st: {26-28}{30-30-32} sts.

BODY

Change to larger size needles.

Row 1: K1, P1, K9, place marker, P2, (K4, P2) {2-2}{2-2-3} times, K{1-3}{5-5-1}.

Row 2: Purl across to last 3 sts, K1, P2.

Row 3: K1, P1, K 12, P2, (K4, P2) {1-1}{2-2-2} time(s), K{4-6}{2-2-4}.

Row 4: Purl across to last 3 sts, K1, P2.

Row 5: K1, P1, K2, work Front Cable, work Back Cable, K1, P2, (K4, P2) {2-2}{2-2-3} times, K{1-3}{5-5-1}.

Row 6: Purl across to last 3 sts, K1, P2.

Row 7: K1, P1, K2, work Front Cable, work Back Cable, (K4, P2) {2-2}{3-3-3} times, K{4-6}{2-2-4}.

Row 8: Purl across to last 3 sts, K1, P2.

Row 9: K1, P1, K2, work Front Cable, work Back Cable, K1, P2, (K4, P2) {2-2}{2-2-3} times, K{1-3}{5-5-1}.

Row 10: Purl across to last 3 sts, K1, P2.

Row 11: K1, P1, K 12, P2, (K4, P2) {1-1}{2-2-2} time(s), K{4-6}{2-2-4}.

Row 12: Purl across to last 3 sts, K1, P2.

Row 13: K1, P1, K9, P2, (K4, P2) {2-2}{2-2-3} times, K{1-3}{5-5-1}.

Row 14: Purl across to last 3 sts, K1, P2.

Row 15: K1, P1, K2, work Front Cable, work Back Cable, (K4, P2) {2-2}{3-3-3} times, K{4-6}{2-2-4}.

Row 16: Purl across to last 3 sts, K1, P2.

Row 17: K1, P1, K2, work Front Cable, work Back Cable, K1, P2, (K4, P2) {2-2}{2-2-3} times, K{1-3}{5-5-1}.

Row 18: Purl across to last 3 sts, K1, P2.

Row 19: K1, P1, K2, work Front Cable, work Back Cable, (K4, P2) {2-2}{3-3-3} times, K{4-6}{2-2-4}.

Row 20: Purl across to last 3 sts, K1, P2.

Row 21: K1, P1, K9, P2, (K4, P2) {2-2}{2-2-3} times, K{1-3}{5-5-1}.

Row 22: Purl across to last 3 sts, K1, P2.

Repeat Rows 3-22 until Right Front measures same as Left Front to Neck Shaping, ending by working a **wrong** side row.

NECK SHAPING
Note: Maintain established pattern throughout.

Row 1 (Decrease row)**:** Work across to marker, K1, SSK *(Figs. 21a-c, page 584)*, work across, place marker around first st to mark beginning of Neck Shaping: {25-27}{29-29-31} sts.

Row 2: Purl across to marker, K2, P6, K2, P2.

Continue to decrease every fourth row, {1-4}{7-4-1} time(s); then decrease every sixth row, {4-2}{0-2-5} times: {20-21}{22-23-25} sts.

Work even until Right Front measures same as Back, ending by working a **wrong** side row.

Bind off remaining sts **loosely** in **knit**.

SLEEVE (Make 2)
RIBBING
FOR SIZES 3, 6, & 12 MONTHS ONLY
With Blue and smaller size straight needles, cast on {35-35}{37} sts **loosely**.

Row 1: P1, (K1, P1) across.

Row 2 (Right side)**:** Knit across.

Row 3: P1, (K1, P1) across.

Row 4: With White, knit across.

Row 5: P1, (K1, P1) across; cut White.

Row 6: With Blue, knit across.

Row 7: P1, (K1, P1) across.

Rows 8: Knit across.

FOR SIZES 18 AND 24 MONTHS ONLY
With Blue and smaller size straight needles, cast on {39-39} sts **loosely**.

Row 1: P1, (K1, P1) across.

Row 2 (Right side)**:** Knit across.

Row 3: P1, (K1, P1) across.

Row 4: Knit across.

Row 5: P1, (K1, P1) across.

Row 6: With White, knit across.

Row 7: P1, (K1, P1) across; cut White.

Row 8: With Blue, knit across.

Row 9: P1, (K1, P1) across.

Row 10: Knit across.

Row 11: P1, (K1, P1) across.

Row 12: Knit across.

FOR ALL SIZES
Row {9-9}{9-13-13}: P1, (K1, P1) across increasing one st *(see Increases, page 581)*: {36-36}{38-40-40} sts.

Instructions continued on page 428.

BODY

Change to larger size needles.

Row 1: K{2-2}{3-4-4}, P2, (K4, P2) 5 times, K{2-2}{3-4-4}.

Row 2: Purl across.

Row 3: K1, Right Invisible Increase *(Fig. 12a, page 581)*, K{4-4}{5-0-0}, P2, (K4, P2) {4-4}{4-6-6} times, K{4-4}{5-0-0}, Left Invisible Increase *(Figs. 13a & b, page 581)*, K1: {38-38}{40-42-42} sts.

Row 4: Purl across.

Row 5: K1, Right Invisible Increase, K{2-2}{3-4-4}, P2, (K4, P2) 5 times, K{2-2}{3-4-4}, Left Invisible Increase, K1: {40-40}{42-44-44} sts.

Row 6: Purl across.

Row 7: K{1-1}{2-3-3}, P2, (K4, P2) 6 times, K{1-1}{2-3-3}.

Row 8: Purl across.

Beginning with next row and working new stitches in pattern, increase one stitch at **each** edge, every fourth row, {5-5}{7-8-9} times: {50-50}{56-60-62} sts.

Work even until Sleeve measures approximately {5¹/₂-6}{6¹/₂-7¹/₂-8¹/₂}" from cast on edge, ending by working a **wrong** side row.

SLEEVE SHAPING
Rows 1-8: Bind off {5-5}{6-7-7} sts at the beginning of the row, work across: {10-10}{8-4-6} sts.

Bind off remaining sts **loosely** in **knit**.

FINISHING
Sew shoulder seams.

BAND

With **right** side facing, using Blue and circular needle, pick up {36-38}{44-48-52} sts evenly spaced across Right Front to marker *(Figs. 34a & b, page 586)*, do **not** remove marker, pick up {26-32}{32-32-36} sts along Right Front Neck edge, knit {20-20}{22-22-22} sts from Back st holder, pick up {25-31}{31-31-35} sts across Left Front Neck edge to marker, do **not** remove marker, pick up {36-38}{44-48-52} sts evenly spaced across Left Front: {143-159}{173-181-197} sts.

Mark placement of buttons on Left Front, placing first marker ¹/₂" from cast on edge and second marker ¹/₂" down from Neck Shaping marker; evenly space markers for remaining 3 buttons.

Row 1: P1, (K1, P1) across.

Row 2: Knit across.

Row 3: P1, (K1, P1) across.

Row 4 (Buttonhole row)**:** With White, knit across to first marker, [K2 tog, YO *(Fig. 16a, page 582)*, **(buttonhole made)]**, (knit across to next marker, K2 tog, YO) 3 times, knit across.

Row 5: P1, (K1, P1) across; cut White.

Row 6: With Blue, knit across.

Row 7: P1, (K1, P1) across.

Bind off all sts **loosely** in **knit**.

Sew Sleeves to Cardigan, matching center of last row on Sleeve Shaping to shoulder seam and beginning {4¹/₂-4¹/₂}{5-5¹/₂-5¹/₂}" down from seam.

Weave underarm and side in one continuous seam *(Fig. 36, page 587)*.

Sew buttons opposite buttonholes on Band.

Design by Lois J. Long.

PRECIOUS PULLOVER
■■■□ INTERMEDIATE
Shown on page 431.

Size:	1	2	4
Finished			
Measurement:	21"	22"	23"
	53.5 cm	56 cm	58.5 cm

Size Note: Instructions are written for size 1 with sizes 2 and 4 in braces { }. Instructions will be easier to read, if you circle all the numbers pertaining to your size. If only one number is given, it applies to all sizes.

MATERIALS
Sport Weight Yarn, approximately: FINE **2**
  MC (White)
    $3^1/_2${$4^1/_2$-$5^1/_2$} ounces, 350{450-550} yards
    [100{130-160} grams, 320{411-503} meters]
  Color A (Pink) - 5 yards (4.5 meters)
  Color B (Green) - 10 yards (9 meters)
  Straight knitting needles, sizes 3 (3.25 mm) **and**
    5 (3.75 mm) **or** sizes needed for gauge
  16" (40.5 cm) Circular needle, size 3 (3.25 mm)
  Markers
  3 Stitch holders
  Bobbins
  $^5/_8$" (16 mm) Buttons - 3
  Yarn needle

GAUGE: With larger size needles,
    in Stockinette Stitch,
    24 sts and 32 rows = 4" (10 cm)

BACK
RIBBING
With smaller size needles and MC, cast on 64{68-70} sts **loosely**.

Work in K1, P1 ribbing for $1^1/_2$" (4 cm) increasing one stitch at end of last row: 65{69-71} sts.

BODY
Change to larger size needles.

Work in Stockinette Stitch until Back measures approximately $9^1/_2${11-$12^1/_2$}"/24{28-32} cm from cast on edge, ending by working a **purl** row.

PLACKET
Note: Both sides of Placket are worked at the same time, using separate yarn for **each** side.

Row 1: K 30{32-33}, place marker *(see Markers, page 578)*, K5; with second yarn, add on 5 sts *(Figs. 5a & b, page 580)*, K5, place marker, knit across: 35{37-38} sts **each** side.

Row 2: Purl to marker, K5; with second yarn, K5, purl across.

Row 3: Knit across; with second yarn, knit across.

Rows 4-6: Repeat Rows 2 and 3 once, then repeat Row 2 once **more**.

Row 7 (Buttonhole row)**:** Knit to marker, K1, K2 tog *(Fig. 17, page 583)*, YO *(Fig. 16a, page 582)*, K2; with second yarn, knit across.

Rows 8-12: Repeat Rows 2 and 3 twice, then repeat Row 2 once **more**.

Row 13: Repeat Row 7.

Rows 14-16: Repeat Rows 2 and 3 once, then repeat Row 2 once **more**.

Row 17: Bind off 20{21-22} sts, knit across, slip 15{16-16} sts just worked onto st holder; with second yarn, K 15{16-16}, slip sts just worked onto st holder, bind off remaining 20{21-22} sts.

FRONT
RIBBING
With smaller size needles and MC, cast on 64{68-70} sts **loosely**.

Work in K1, P1 ribbing for $1^1/_2$" (4 cm).

Instructions continued on page 430.

BODY

Change to larger size needles.

Beginning with a **knit** row, work in Stockinette Stitch for 2{6-10} rows.

Note: Work in Stockinette Stitch throughout, following Charts as indicated *(see Using Colors, page 585)*.

Next 9 Rows: Work across following Chart A, page 433.

Work in Stockinette Stitch for 7{9-11} rows.

Next 9 Rows: Work across following Chart B.

Work in Stockinette Stitch for 7{9-11} rows.

Next 9 Rows: Work across following Chart A.

Work in Stockinette Stitch for 7{9-11} rows.

Next 10 Rows: Work across following Chart C.

Work in Stockinette Stitch for 7{9-11} rows.

Next 3 Rows: Work across following Chart D.

NECK SHAPING

Note: Continue to follow Chart D throughout.

Row 1: K 40{43-44}, slip 16{18-18} sts just worked onto st holder, knit across: 24{25-26} sts **each** side.

Note: Both sides of Neck are worked at the same time, using separate yarn for each side.

Row 2: Purl across; with second yarn, purl across.

Row 3 (Decrease row): Knit across to within 3 sts of Neck edge, K2 tog, K1; with second yarn, K1, [slip 1, K1, PSSO *(Figs. 19a & b, page 583)*], knit across: 23{24-25} sts **each** side.

Rows 4-9: Repeat Rows 2 and 3, 3 times: 20{21-22} sts **each** side.

Work even until Front measures same as Back, ending by working a **purl** row.

Bind off remaining sts.

Sew shoulder seams.

Place a marker on each side of Front and Back, $4^1/_2${5-5$^1/_2$}"/11.5{12.5-14} cm down from shoulder.

SLEEVE (Make 2)

With **right** side facing, using larger size needles and MC, pick up 54{60-66} sts evenly spaced between markers *(Fig. 34a, page 586)*.

Rows 1-5: Beginning with a **purl** row, work in Stockinette Stitch.

Row 6: K8{11-14}, place marker, K 38, place marker, knit across.

Rows 7-9: Work across following Chart E between markers.

Row 10 (Decrease row): Slip 1, K1, PSSO, knit across to last 2 sts following Chart E between markers, K2 tog: 52{58-64} sts.

Rows 11-15: Work across following Chart E between markers.

Row 16: Knit across.

Row 17: Purl across.

Row 18: Slip 1, K1, PSSO, knit across to last 2 sts, K2 tog: 50{56-62} sts.

Work in Stockinette Stitch for 4{6-7} rows.

SIZE 4 ONLY: Repeat Row 18: 60 sts.

ALL SIZES - Next 9 Rows: Work across following Chart F between markers and decreasing one stitch at **each** edge on Row 4{2-8}: 48{54-58} sts.

Instructions continued on page 432.

SIZE 4 ONLY: Work in Stockinette Stitch for 6 rows.

ALL SIZES - Next Row: Repeat Row 18: 46{52-56} sts.

Continue to decrease one stitch at **each** edge, every 8 rows, 0{1-0} time(s) **(see Zeros, page 577)**; then decrease every 6 rows, 1{2-4} times: 44{46-48} sts.

Work even until Sleeve measures approximately 5^1/$_2${7^1/$_2$-9}"/14{19-23} cm, ending by working a **knit** row.

RIBBING

Change to smaller size needles.

Row 1 (Ridge)**:** Knit across decreasing 6 sts evenly spaced: 38{40-42} sts.

Work in K1, P1 ribbing for 1^1/$_2$" (4 cm).

Bind off all sts **loosely** in ribbing.

FINISHING
NECK RIBBING

With **right** side facing, using circular needle and MC, knit 15{16-16} sts from left Back st holder, pick up 11 sts along left Front neck edge, knit 16{18-18} sts from Front st holder, pick up 12 sts along right Front neck edge, knit 15{16-16} sts from right Back st holder: 69{73-73} sts.

Row 1 (Ridge)**:** Knit across.

Row 2: K1, (P1, K1) across.

Row 3 (Buttonhole row)**:** K2, P1, YO **(Fig. 16a, page 582)**, P2 tog **(Fig. 17, page 583)**, (K1, P1) across to last 2 sts, K2.

Row 4: K1, (P1, K1) across.

Row 5: K2, P1, (K1, P1) across to last 2 sts, K2.

Rows 6 and 7: Repeat Rows 4 and 5.

Bind off all sts **loosely** in ribbing.

NECK RUFFLE

With **right** side facing and Neck Ribbing toward you, using circular needle and MC, pick up one st in each st of Ridge, leaving first 5 and last 5 sts unworked: 59{63-63} sts.

Row 1: Increase in next st **(see Increases, page 581)**, (P1, increase in next st) across: 89{95-95} sts.

Row 2: K2, YO, (K1, YO) across to last 2 sts, K2: 175{187-187} sts.

Row 3: K2, purl across to last 2 sts, K2.

Row 4: Knit across.

Bind off all sts **loosely** in knit.

CUFF RUFFLE

With **right** side facing and Sleeve Ribbing toward you, using circular needle and MC, pick up one st in each st of Ridge, leaving first and last st unworked: 36{38-40} sts.

Row 1: Increase in next st, (P2, increase in next st) across to last 2{1-0} sts, P2{1-0}: 48{51-54} sts.

Row 2: K2, YO, (K1, YO) across to last 2 sts, K2: 93{99-105} sts.

Row 3: K2, purl across to last 2 sts, K2.

Row 4: Knit across.

Bind off all sts **loosely** in knit.

Lapping right over left, sew bottom of Placket to Sweater.

Weave underarm and side in one continuous seam **(Fig. 36, page 587)**.

Weave Cuff Ruffle seam.

Add Buttons to Placket.

Design by Carole Prior.

CHART A

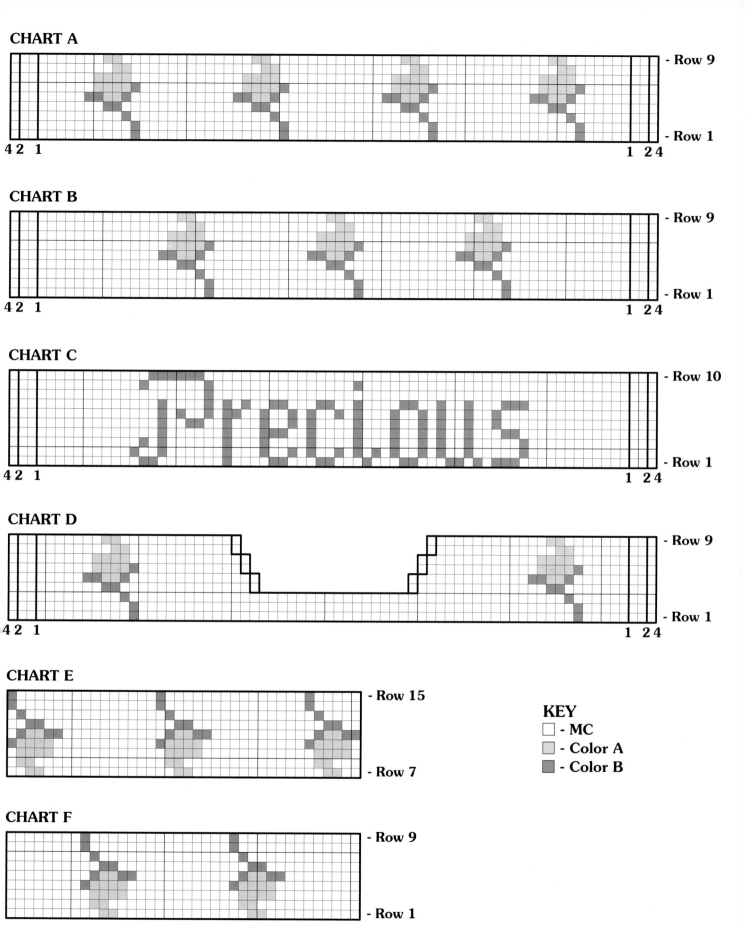

- Row 9

- Row 1

4 2 1   1 2 4

CHART B

- Row 9

- Row 1

4 2 1   1 2 4

CHART C

- Row 10

- Row 1

4 2 1   1 2 4

CHART D

- Row 9

- Row 1

4 2 1   1 2 4

CHART E

- Row 15

- Row 7

CHART F

- Row 9

- Row 1

KEY
☐ - MC
▨ - Color A
▩ - Color B

**On right side rows, follow Charts from right to left;
on wrong side rows, follow Charts from left to right.**

ALL-BOY PULLOVER

INTERMEDIATE

Size:	1	2	4
Finished			
Measurement:	21"	22"	23"
	53.5 cm	56 cm	58.5 cm

Size Note: Instructions are written for size 1 with sizes 2 and 4 in braces { }. Instructions will be easier to read, if you circle all the numbers pertaining to your size. If only one number is given, it applies to all sizes.

MATERIALS

Sport Weight Yarn, approximately:
  MC (White)
    3¹/₂{4¹/₂-5¹/₂} ounces, 350{450-550} yards
    [100{130-160} grams, 320{411-503} meters]
  CC (Blue) - 1 ounce, 100 yards (30 grams, 91.5 meters)
Straight knitting needles, sizes 3 (3.25 mm) **and**
  5 (3.75 mm) **or** sizes needed for gauge
16" (40.5 cm) Circular needle, size 3 (3.25 mm)
Markers
3 Stitch holders
Bobbins
⁵/₈" (16 mm) Buttons - 3
Yarn needle

GAUGE: With larger size needles,
in Stockinette Stitch,
24 sts and 32 rows = 4" (10 cm)

BACK
RIBBING

With smaller size needles and MC, cast on 64{68-70} sts **loosely**.

Work in K1, P1 ribbing for 1¹/₂" (4 cm) increasing one stitch at end of last row: 65{69-71} sts.

BODY

Change to larger size needles.

Work in Stockinette Stitch until Back measures approximately 9¹/₂{11-12¹/₂}"/24{28-32} cm from cast on edge, ending by working a **purl** row.

PLACKET

Note: Both sides of Placket are worked at the same time, using separate yarn for **each** side.

Row 1: K 30{32-33}, place marker *(see Markers, page 578)*, K5; with second yarn, add on 5 sts *(Figs. 5a & b, page 580)*, K5, place marker, knit across: 35{37-38} sts **each** side.

Row 2: Purl to marker, K5; with second yarn, K5, purl across.

Row 3: Knit across; with second yarn, knit across.

Rows 4-6: Repeat Rows 2 and 3 once, then repeat Row 2 once **more**.

Row 7 (Buttonhole row)**:** Knit to marker, K1, K2 tog *(Fig. 17, page 583)*, YO *(Fig. 16a, page 582)*, K2; with second yarn, knit across.

Rows 8-16: Repeat Rows 2-7 once, then repeat Rows 2-4 once **more**.

Row 17: Bind off 20{21-22} sts, knit across, slip 15{16-16} sts just worked onto st holder; with second yarn, K 15{16-16}, slip sts just worked onto st holder, bind off remaining 20{21-22} sts.

FRONT
RIBBING

With smaller size needles and MC, cast on 64{68-70} sts **loosely**.

Work in K1, P1 ribbing for 1¹/₂" (4 cm) increasing one stitch at end of last row: 65{69-71} sts.

BODY

Change to larger size needles.

Beginning with a **purl** row, work in Stockinette Stitch for 7{9-13} rows.

Next Row: K7{9-10}, place marker, K 52, place marker, K6{8-9}.

SAILBOATS

Rows 1-15: Work across, following Chart A, page 436, between markers *(see Using Colors, page 585)*; remove markers at end of last row.

Instructions continued on page 436.

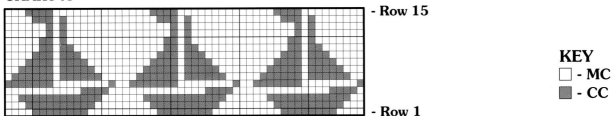

- Row 15

- Row 1

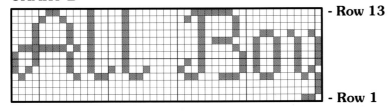

- Row 13

- Row 1

KEY

☐ - MC

■ - CC

On right side rows, follow Charts from right to left; on wrong side rows, follow Charts from left to right.

With MC, work in Stockinette Stitch for 8{10-14} rows.

DIAMONDS

Row 1: K4{6-7}, P1, (K7, P1) across to last 4{6-7} sts, K4{6-7}.

Row 2: P3{5-6}, K1, P1, K1, (P5, K1, P1, K1) across to last 3{5-6} sts, P3{5-6}.

Row 3: K2{4-5}, P1, (K3, P1) across to last 2{4-5} sts, K2{4-5}.

Row 4: P1{3-4}, K1, P5, K1, (P1, K1, P5, K1) across to last 1{34} sts, P1{34}.

Row 5: K 0{2-3} *(see Zeros, page 577)*, P1, (K7, P1) across to last 0{23} sts, K 0{2-3}.

Row 6: Repeat Row 4.

Row 7: Repeat Row 3.

Row 8: Repeat Row 2.

Row 9: Repeat Row 1.

Work in Stockinette Stitch for 7{9-13} rows.

Next Row: K 10{12-13}, place marker, K 45, place marker, K 10{1213}.

ALL BOY

Note: Rows 1-13 can be knit in MC and later worked in Duplicate Stitch *(Figs. 32a & b, page 586)*.

Rows 1-13: Work across, following Chart B between markers; remove markers at end of last row.

With MC, continue in Stockinette Stitch until Front measures approximately 10{11^1/$_2$-13}"/25.5{29-33} cm from cast on edge, ending by working a **purl** row.

NECK SHAPING

Row 1: K 41{44-45}, slip 17{19-19} sts just worked onto st holder, knit across: 24{25-26} sts **each** side.

Note: Both sides of Neck are worked at the same time, using separate yarn for each side.

Row 2: Purl across; with second yarn, purl across.

Row 3 (Decrease row)**:** Knit across to within 3 sts of Neck edge, K2 tog, K1; with second yarn, K1, [slip 1, K1, PSSO *(Figs. 19a & b, page 583)*], knit across: 23{24-25} sts **each** side.

Rows 4-9: Repeat Rows 2 and 3, 3 times: 20{21-22} sts **each** side.

Work even until Front measures same as Back, ending by working a **purl** row.

Bind off remaining sts.

Sew shoulder seams.
Place a marker on each side of Front and Back, 4^1/$_2${5-5^1/$_2$}"/11.5{12.5-14} cm down from shoulder.

SLEEVE (Make 2)

With **right** side facing, using larger size needles and MC, pick up 53{61-69} sts evenly spaced between markers *(Fig. 34a, page 586)*.

Row 1: Purl across.

Row 2: K2, P1, (K7, P1) across to last 2 sts, K2.

Row 3: (P1, K1) twice, (P5, K1, P1, K1) across to last st, P1.

Row 4: K4, P1, (K3, P1) across to last 4 sts, K4.

Row 5: P5, (K1, P1, K1, P5) across.

Row 6: K6, P1, (K7, P1) across to last 6 sts, K6.

Row 7: Repeat Row 5.

Row 8: Repeat Row 4.

Row 9: Repeat Row 3.

Row 10: Slip 1, K1, PSSO, P1, (K7, P1) across to last 2 sts, K2 tog: 51{59-67} sts.

Rows 11-15: Work in Stockinette Stitch for 5 rows.

Row 16: K1, P1, (K7, P1) across to last st, K1.

Row 17: P2, K1, P5, K1, (P1, K1, P5, K1) across to last 2 sts, P2.

Row 18: Slip 1, K1, PSSO, K1, P1, (K3, P1) across to last 3 sts, K1, K2 tog: 49{57-65} sts.

Row 19: P3, K1, P1, K1, (P5, K1, P1, K1) across to last 3 sts, P3.

Row 20: K4, P1, (K7, P1) across to last 4 sts, K4.

Row 21: Repeat Row 19.

Row 22: K2, P1, (K3, P1) across to last 2 sts, K2.

Row 23: P1, (K1, P5, K1, P1) across.

Row 24: K8, P1, (K7, P1) across to last 8 sts, K8.

Row 25: Purl across.

Row 26: Slip 1, K1, PSSO, knit across to last 2 sts, K2 tog: 47{55-63} sts.

Rows 27-29: Work in Stockinette Stitch for 3 rows.

Row 30: K7, (P1, K7) across.

Row 31: P6, K1, P1, K1, (P5, K1, P1, K1) across to last 6 sts, P6.

SIZE 1 ONLY
Row 32: Slip 1, K1, PSSO, K3, (P1, K3) across to last 2 sts, K2 tog: 45 sts.

Row 33: (P1, K1) twice, (P5, K1, P1, K1) across to last st, P1.

Row 34: K2, P1, (K7, P1) across to last 2 sts, K2.

Row 35: (P1, K1) twice, (P5, K1, P1, K1) across to last st, P1.

Row 36: K4, P1, (K3, P1) across to last 4 sts, K4.

Row 37: P5, (K1, P1, K1, P5) across.

Row 38: Slip 1, K1, PSSO, K4, P1, (K7, P1) across to last 6 sts, K4, K2 tog: 43 sts.

SIZES 2 and 4 ONLY
Row 32: K1, P1, (K3, P1) across to last st, K1.

Row 33: P2, K1, P1, K1, (P5, K1, P1, K1) across to last 2 sts, P2.

Row 34: Slip 1, K1, PSSO, K1, P1, (K7, P1) across to last 3 sts, K1, K2 tog: {53-61} sts.

Row 35: (P1, K1) twice, (P5, K1, P1, K1) across to last st, P1.

Row 36: K4, P1, (K3, P1) across to last 4 sts, K4.

Row 37: P5, (K1, P1, K1, P5) across.

Row 38: K6, P1, (K7, P1) across to last 6 sts, K6.

Rows 39-41: Work in Stockinette Stitch for 3 rows.

Row 42: Slip 1, K1, PSSO, knit across to last 2 sts, K2 tog: {51-59} sts.

Row 43: Purl across.

Row 44: K5, P1, (K7, P1) across to last 5 sts, K5.

Instructions continued on page 438.

Row 45: P4, K1, P1, K1, (P5, K1, P1, K1) across to last 4 sts, P4.

Row 46: K3, (P1, K3) across.

Row 47: P2, K1, P5, K1, (P1, K1, P5, K1) across to last 2 sts, P2.

Row 48: Slip 1, K1, PSSO, K7, (P1, K7) across to last 2 sts, K2 tog: {49-57} sts.

Row 49: P1, (K1, P5, K1, P1) across.

Row 50: K2, P1, (K3, P1) across to last 2 sts, K2.

Row 51: P3, K1, P1, K1, (P5, K1, P1, K1) across to last 3 sts, P3.

Row 52: K4, P1, (K7, P1) across to last 4 sts, K4.

Row 53: Purl across.

Row 54: Slip 1, K1, PSSO, knit across to last 2 sts, K2 tog: {47-55} sts.

SIZE 4 ONLY
Rows 55-57: Work in Stockinette Stitch for 3 rows.

Row 58: K3, P1, (K7, P1) across to last 3 sts, K3.

Row 59: P2, K1, P1, K1, (P5, K1, P1, K1) across to last 2 sts, P2.

Row 60: Slip 1, K1, PSSO, K3, (P1, K3) across to last 2 sts, K2 tog: 53 sts.

Row 61: P5, (K1, P1, K1, P5) across.

Row 62: K6, P1, (K7, P1) across to last 6 sts, K6.

Row 63: Repeat Row 61.

Row 64: K4, P1, (K3, P1) across to last 4 sts, K4.

Row 65: (P1, K1) twice, (P5, K1, P1, K1) across to last st, P1.

Row 66: Slip 1, K1, PSSO, P1, (K7, P1) across to last 2 sts, K2 tog: 51 sts.

ALL SIZES
Work in Stockinette Stitch until Sleeve measures approximately 5^1/$_2${7^1/$_2$-9}"/14{19-23} cm, ending by working a **purl** row.

RIBBING
Change to smaller size needles.

Row 1: With CC, knit across decreasing 5{7-9} sts evenly spaced: 38{40-42} sts.

Work in K1, P1 ribbing for 1^1/$_2$" (4 cm).

Bind off all sts **loosely** in ribbing.

FINISHING
NECK RIBBING
With **right** side facing, using circular needle and CC, knit 15{16-16} sts from left Back st holder, pick up 12 sts along left Front neck edge, knit 17{19-19} sts from Front st holder, pick up 12 sts along right Front neck edge, knit 15{16-16} sts from right Back st holder: 71{75-75} sts.

Row 1: K2, P1, (K1, P1) across to last 2 sts, K2.

Row 2: K1, (P1, K1) across.

Row 3 (Buttonhole row)**:** K2, P1, YO *(Fig. 16b, page 582)*, P2 tog *(Fig. 18, page 583)*, (K1, P1) across to last 2 sts, K2.

Row 4: K1, (P1, K1) across.

Row 5: K2, P1, (K1, P1) across to last 2 sts, K2.

Rows 6 and 7: Repeat Rows 4 and 5.

Bind off all sts **loosely** in ribbing.

Lapping right over left, sew bottom of Placket to Sweater.

Weave underarm and side in one continuous seam *(Fig. 36, page 587)*.

Add Buttons to Placket.

With 2 strands of CC, add French Knots to center of each Diamond on Front *(Fig. 34, page 37)*.

WINTER WONDERLAND SET

■■□□ **EASY**

Shown on page 441.

Size:	1	2	4
Finished			
Measurement:	21"	22"	23"
	53.5 cm	56 cm	58.5 cm

Size Note: Pullover instructions are written for size 1 with sizes 2 and 4 in braces { }. Cap instructions are written for sizes 1 and 2. Instructions will be easier to read, if you circle all the numbers pertaining to your size. If only one number is given, it applies to all sizes.

MATERIALS

Sport Weight Yarn, approximately:
  6{7-8} ounces, 565{660-755} yards
  [170{200-230} grams, 517{604-690 meters]
Straight knitting needles, sizes 4 (3.5 mm) **and**
  6 (4 mm) **or** sizes needed for gauge
16" (40.5 cm) Circular knitting needle, size 4 (3.5 mm)
Stitch holders - 2
Markers
Yarn needle

GAUGE: With larger size needles,
  in Stockinette Stitch,
  22 sts and 30 rows = 4" (10 cm)

PULLOVER
BACK
RIBBING

With smaller size needles, cast on 59{63-67} sts **loosely**.

Row 1: P1, (K1, P1) across.

Row 2: K1 tbl, (P1, K1 tbl) across.

Repeat Rows 1 and 2 until Ribbing measures approximately 1¹/₂" (4 cm), ending by working Row 1.

BODY

Change to larger size needles.

Row 1 (Right side): K9{11-13}, P1, K2, P1, (K 16, P1) twice, K2, P1, K9{11-13}.

Row 2: P5{7-9}, K2, P3, K1, P2, K1, P6, K2, P6, K3, P6, K2, P6, K1, P2, K1, P3, K2, P5{7-9}.

Row 3: K 11{13-15}, P1, K2, P1, K 12, P2, K1, P2, K 12, P1, K2, P1, K 11{13-15}.

Row 4: P5{7-9}, K2, P5, K1, P2, K1, (P4, K2) twice, P3, (K2, P4) twice, K1, P2, K1, P5, K2, P5{7-9}.

Row 5: K 13{15-17}, P1, K2, P1, K8, P2, K5, P2, K8, P1, K2, P1, K 13{15-17}.

Row 6: P5{7-9}, K2, P7, (K1, P2) twice, K2, P2, K2, P7, K2, P2, K2, (P2, K1) twice, P7, K2, P5{7-9}.

Row 7: K 13{15-17}, P1, K2, P1, K7, P2, K3, P1, K3, P2, K7, P1, K2, P1, K 13{15-17}.

Row 8: P5{7-9}, K2, P5, K1, P2, K1, P4, K2, P3, K4, P1, K4, P3, K2, P4, K1, P2, K1, P5, K2, P5{7-9}.

Row 9: K 11{13-15}, P1, K2, P1, K 11, P2, K3, P2, K 11, P1, K2, P1, K 11{13-15}.

Row 10: P5{7-9}, K2, P3, K1, P2, K1, P6, K2, P 15, K2, P6, K1, P2, K1, P3, K2, P5{7-9}.

Repeat Rows 1-10 until Back measures approximately 10³/₄{12¹/₂-13³/₄}"/ 27.5{32-35} cm from cast on edge, ending by working a **wrong** side row.

NECK SHAPING

Note: Both sides of Neck are worked at the same time, using separate yarn for **each** side. Maintain established pattern throughout.

Row 1: Work across 17{18-19} sts, slip next 25{27-29} sts onto st holder; with second yarn, work across: 17{18-19} sts **each** side.

Row 2: Work across; with second yarn, work across.

Row 3: Work across to within 3 sts of Neck edge, K2 tog *(Fig. 17, page 583)*, K1; with second yarn, K1, [slip 1, K1, PSSO *(Figs. 19a & b, page 583)]*, work across: 16{17-18} sts **each** side.

Instructions continued on page 440.

Row 4: Work across; with second yarn, work across.

Bind off all sts.

FRONT

Work same as Back until Front measures approximately 9³/4{11¹/2-12³/4}"/25{29-32.5} cm from cast on edge, ending by working a **wrong** side row: 59{63-67} sts.

NECK SHAPING

Note: Both sides of Neck are worked at the same time, using separate yarn for **each** side. Maintain established pattern throughout.

Row 1: Work across 20{21-22} sts, slip next 19{21-23} sts onto st holder; with second yarn, work across: 20{21-22} sts **each** side.

Row 2: Work across; with second yarn, work across.

Row 3 (Decrease row): Work across to within 3 sts of Neck edge, K2 tog, K1; with second yarn, K1, slip 1, K1, PSSO, work across: 19{20-21} sts **each** side.

Rows 4-9: Repeat Rows 2 and 3, 3 times: 16{17-18} sts **each** side.

Work even until Front measures same as Back, ending by working a **wrong** side row.

Bind off all sts.

Sew shoulder seams.

Place a marker on each side of Front and Back, 4¹/2{5-5¹/2}"/11.5{12.5-14} cm down from shoulder seam.

SLEEVE (Size 1 ONLY)
BODY

With **right** side facing and using larger size needles, pick up 49 sts evenly spaced between markers **(Fig. 34a, page 586)**.

Row 1: P 13, K2, P 19, K2, purl across.

Row 2 (Right side): K 21, P2, K3, P2, knit across.

Row 3: P 13, K2, P5, K4, P1, K4, P5, K2, purl across.

Row 4: K 19, P2, K3, P1, K3, P2, knit across.

Row 5: P 13, K2, P4, K2, P7, K2, P4, K2, purl across.

Row 6: K 20, P2, K5, P2, knit across.

Row 7: P 13, K2, P6, K2, P3, K2, P6, K2, purl across.

Row 8 (Decrease row): K1, slip 1, K1, PSSO, K 19, P2, K1, P2, knit across to last 3 sts, K2 tog, K1: 47 sts.

Row 9: P 12, K2, P8, K3, P8, K2, purl across.

Row 10: K 23, P1, knit across.

Row 11: P 12, K2, P 19, K2, purl across.

Row 12: K 20, P2, K3, P2, knit across.

Row 13: P 12, K2, P5, K4, P1, K4, P5, K2, purl across.

Row 14: K 18, P2, K3, P1, K3, P2, knit across.

Row 15: P 12, K2, P4, K2, P7, K2, P4, K2, purl across.

Row 16 (Decrease row): K1, slip 1, K1, PSSO, K 16, P2, K5, P2, knit across to last 3 sts, K2 tog, K1: 45 sts.

Rows 17-36: Maintaining pattern, continue to decrease one stitch at each **edge**, every eighth row once **more**; then decrease every sixth row, 2 times: 39 sts.

Row 37: P8, K2, P6, K2, P3, K2, P6, K2, purl across.

Row 38: K 17, P2, K1, P2, knit across.

Row 39: P8, K2, P8, K3, P8, K2, purl across.

Row 40: K 19, P1, knit across.

Row 41: Work across in pattern decreasing 4 sts evenly spaced: 35 sts.

RIBBING

Change to smaller size needles.

Row 1: K1 tbl, (P1, K1 tbl) across.

Row 2: P1, (K1, P1) across.

Repeat Rows 1 and 2 until Ribbing measures approximately 1¹/2" (4 cm), ending by working Row 2.

Instructions continued on page 442.

Bind off all sts **loosely** in pattern.

Repeat for second Sleeve.-

SLEEVE (Size 2 ONLY)
BODY
With **right** side facing and using larger size needles, pick up 55 sts evenly spaced between markers *(Fig. 34a, page 586)*.

Row 1: P 16, K2, P 19, K2, purl across.

Row 2 (Right side)**:** Knit across.

Row 3: P 16, K2, P 19, K2, purl across.

Row 4: K 24, P2, K3, P2, knit across.

Row 5: P 16, K2, P5, K4, P1, K4, P5, K2, purl across.

Row 6: K 22, P2, K3, P1, K3, P2, knit across.

Row 7: P 16, K2, P4, K2, P7, K2, P4, K2, purl across.

Row 8 (Decrease row)**:** K1, slip 1, K1, PSSO, K 20, P2, K5, P2, knit across to last 3 sts, K2 tog, K1: 53 sts.

Row 9: P 15, K2, P6, K2, P3, K2, P6, K2, purl across.

Row 10: K 24, P2, K1, P2, knit across.

Row 11: P 15, K2, P8, K3, P8, K2, purl across.

Row 12: K 26, P1, knit across.

Row 13: P 15, K2, P 19, K2, purl across.

Row 14: K 23, P2, K3, P2, knit across.

Row 15: P 15, K2, P5, K4, P1, K4, P5, K2, purl across.

Row 16 (Decrease row)**:** K1, slip 1, K1, PSSO, K 18, P2, K3, P1, K3, P2, knit across to last 3 sts, K2 tog, K1: 51 sts.

Rows 17-50: Maintaining pattern, continue to decrease one stitch at each edge, every eighth row, 2 times **more**; then decrease every sixth row, 3 times: 41 sts.

Row 51: P9, K2, P8, K3, P8, K2, purl across.

Row 52: K 20, P1, knit across.

Row 53: P9, K2, P 19, K2, purl across.

Row 54: Knit across.

Rows 55 and 56: Repeat Rows 53 and 54.

Row 57: Work across in pattern decreasing 4 sts evenly spaced: 37 sts.

RIBBING
Work same as Sleeve (Size 1), page 440.

Repeat for second Sleeve.

SLEEVE (Size 4 ONLY)
BODY
With **right** side facing and using larger size needles, pick up 61 sts evenly spaced between markers *(Fig. 34a, page 586)*.

Row 1: P 19, (K2, P 19) twice.

Row 2 (Right side)**:** Knit across.

Row 3: P 19, (K2, P 19) twice.

Row 4: K 27, P2, K3, P2, knit across.

Row 5: P 19, K2, P5, K4, P1, K4, P5, K2, purl across.

Row 6: K 25, P2, K3, P1, K3, P2, knit across.

Row 7: P 19, K2, P4, K2, P7, K2, P4, K2, purl across.

Row 8 (Decrease row)**:** K1, slip 1, K1, PSSO, K 23, P2, K5, P2, knit across to last 3 sts, K2 tog, K1: 59 sts.

Row 9: P 18, K2, P6, K2, P3, K2, P6, K2, purl across.

Row 10: K 27, P2, K1, P2, knit across.

Row 11: P 18, K2, P8, K3, P8, K2, purl across.

Row 12: K 29, P1, knit across.

Row 13: P 18, K2, P 19, K2, purl across.

Row 14: K 26, P2, K3, P2, knit across.

Row 15: P 18, K2, P5, K4, P1, K4, P5, K2, purl across.

Row 16 (Decrease row)**:** K1, slip 1, K1, PSSO, K 21, P2, K3, P1, K3, P2, knit across to last 3 sts, K2 tog, K1: 57 sts.

Rows 17-62: Maintaining pattern, continue to decrease one stitch at **each** edge, every eighth row, 2 times **more**; then decrease every sixth row, 5 times: 43 sts.

Row 63: P 10, K2, P 19, K2, purl across.

Row 64: Knit across.

Rows 65 and 66: Repeat Rows 63 and 64.

Row 67: Work across in pattern decreasing 4 sts evenly spaced: 39 sts.

RIBBING
Work same as Sleeve (Size 1), page 440.

Repeat for second Sleeve.

FINISHING
NECK RIBBING
With **right** side facing, using circular needle and beginning at left shoulder seam, pick up 11 sts along left Front neck edge, slip 19{21-23} sts from Front st holder onto empty needle and knit across, pick up 15 sts along right neck edge, slip 25{27-29} sts from Back st holder onto empty needle and knit across, pick up 4 sts along left Back neck edge, place marker *(see Markers, page 578)*: 74{78-82} sts.

Rnd 1: (K1 tbl, P1) around.

Rnd 2: (K1, P1) around.

Rnds 3-7: Repeat Rnds 1 and 2 twice, then repeat Rnd 1 once **more**.

Bind off all sts **loosely** in ribbing.

Weave underarm and side in one continuous seam *(Fig. 36, page 587)*.

CAP
RIBBING
With smaller size needles, cast on 99 sts **loosely**.

Row 1: P1, (K1, P1) across.

Row 2: K1 tbl, (P1, K1 tbl) across.

Rows 3-6: Repeat Rows 1 and 2 twice.

Row 7: Increase *(see Increases, page 581)*, work across in established ribbing: 100 sts.

BODY
Change to larger size needles.

Row 1 (Right side): Knit across.

Row 2: P6, K2, (P 15, K2) 5 times, P7.

Rows 3-6: Repeat Rows 1 and 2 twice.

Row 7: (K 16, P1) 5 times, K 15.

Row 8: P6, K2, (P6, K3, P6, K2) 5 times, P7.

Row 9: K 14, P2, K1, P2, (K 12, P2, K1, P2) 4 times, K 13.

Row 10: P6, K2, P4, K2, P3, K2, ★ (P4, K2) twice, P3, K2; repeat from ★ 3 times **more**, P4, K2, P7.

Row 11: K 12, P2, K5, P2, (K8, P2, K5, P2) 4 times, K 11.

Row 12: P6, K2, P2, K2, P7, K2, ★ (P2, K2) twice, P7, K2; repeat from ★ 3 times **more**, P2, K2, P7.

Row 13: K 11, P2, K3, P1, K3, P2, (K6, P2, K3, P1, K3, P2) 4 times, K 10.

Row 14: P6, K2, (P3, K4, P1, K4, P3, K2) 5 times, P7.

Row 15: K 13, P2, K3, P2, (K 10, P2, K3, P2) 4 times, K 12.

Row 16: P6, K2, (P 15, K2) 5 times, P7.

Rows 17-20: Repeat Rows 1 and 2 twice.

CROWN
Row 1: K3, K2 tog, (K5, K2 tog) across to last 4 sts, K4: 86 sts.

Instructions continued on page 444.

Rows 2-5: Knit across.

Row 6: Purl across.

Row 7: Knit across.

Row 8: P2, (P2 tog, P4) across: 72 sts.

Rows 9-13: Work in Stockinette Stitch for 5 rows.

Row 14: P2, (P2 tog, P3) across: 58 sts.

Rows 15-17: Work in Stockinette Stitch for 3 rows.

Row 18: P2, (P2 tog, P2) across: 44 sts.

Rows 19-21: Work in Stockinette Stitch for 3 rows.

Row 22: P2, (P2 tog, P1) across: 30 sts.

Row 23: Knit across.

Row 24: P1, P2 tog across to last st, P1: 16 sts.

Row 25: K2 tog across; cut yarn leaving an 18" (45.5 cm) end for sewing: 8 sts.

Thread yarn needle with end and weave through remaining sts; gather **tightly**. Weave back seam.

Designs by Carole Prior.

SNOWBALLS SWEATER

◼◼◼◻ INTERMEDIATE

Size:	1	2	4
Finished			
Measurement:	21"	22"	23"
	53.5 cm	56 cm	58.5 cm

Size Note: Instructions are written for size 1 with sizes 2 and 4 in braces { }. Instructions will be easier to read, if you circle all the numbers pertaining to your size. If only one number is given, it applies to all sizes.

MATERIALS

Sport Weight Yarn, approximately: FINE 2

5{6-7^1/$_4$} ounces, 470{565-685} yards
[140{170-210} grams, 430{517-626} meters]
Straight knitting needles, sizes 4 (3.5 mm) **and**
6 (4 mm) **or** sizes needed for gauge
16" (40.5 cm) Circular knitting needle, size 4 (3.5 mm)
Stitch holders - 2
Markers
Yarn needle

GAUGE: With larger size needles, in pattern,
23 sts and 28 rows = 4" (10 cm)

BACK
RIBBING

With smaller size needles,
cast on 59{61-65} sts **loosely**.

Row 1: P1, (K1, P1) across.

Row 2: K1, (P1, K1) across.

Repeat Rows 1 and 2 until Ribbing measures approximately 1^1/$_2$" (4 cm), ending by working Row 2.

Increase Row: Work across in established ribbing increasing 3{5-5} sts evenly spaced *(see Increases, page 581)*: 62{66-70} sts.

BODY
Change to larger size needles.

Row 1 (Right side): Knit across.

Note: See Yarn Overs *(Figs. 16a, b, & d, page 582)*.

Row 2: P2, (YO, P2, pass YO over both purl sts, P2) across.

Rows 3-5: Work in Stockinette Stitch for 3 rows.

Row 6: P4, YO, P2, pass YO over both purl sts, (P2, YO, P2, pass YO over both purl sts) across to last 4 sts, P4.

Rows 7-9: Work in Stockinette Stitch for 3 rows.

Instructions continued on page 446.

Repeat Rows 2-9 until Back measures approximately 10³/₄{12¹/₂-13³/₄}"/ 27.5{32-35} cm from cast on edge, ending by working a **wrong** side row.

NECK SHAPING

Note: Both sides of Neck are worked at the same time, using separate yarn for **each** side. Maintain established pattern throughout.

Row 1: Work across 20{21-22} sts, slip next 22{24-26} sts onto st holder; with second yarn, work across: 20{21-22} sts **each** side.

Row 2: Work across; with second yarn, work across.

Note: When instructed to slip a stitch, always slip as if to **knit**.

Row 3: Work across to within 3 sts of Neck edge, K2 tog *(Fig. 17, page 583)*, K1; with second yarn, K1, [slip 1, K1, PSSO *(Figs. 19a & b, page 583)*], work across: 19{20-21} sts **each** side.

Row 4: Work across; with second yarn, work across.

Bind off all sts.

FRONT
RIBBING

With smaller size needles, cast on 59{61-65} sts **loosely**.

Row 1: P1, (K1, P1) across.

Row 2: K1, (P1, K1) across.

Repeat Rows 1 and 2 until Ribbing measures approximately 1¹/₂" (4 cm), ending by working Row 2.

Increase Row: Work across in established ribbing increasing 6{8-8} sts evenly spaced: 65{69-73} sts.

BODY

Change to larger size needles.

Row 1 (Right side): K 22{24-26}, place marker *(see Markers, page 578)*, P1, K1 tbl, YO, slip 1, K1, PSSO, K1 tbl, (P5, K1 tbl) twice, YO, slip 1, K1, PSSO, K1 tbl, P1, place marker, K 22{24-26}.

Row 2: P2{4-2}, (YO, P2, pass YO over both purl sts, P2) across to marker, K1, P1 tbl, YO, slip 1, K1, PSSO, P1 tbl, (K5, P1 tbl) twice, YO, slip 1, K1, PSSO, P1 tbl, K1, (P2, YO, P2, pass YO over both purl sts) 5{5-6} times, P2{4-2}.

Row 3: Knit to marker, P1, K1 tbl, YO, slip 1, K1, PSSO, K1 tbl, (P5, K1 tbl) twice, YO, slip 1, K1, PSSO, K1 tbl, P1, knit across.

Row 4: Purl to marker, K1, P1 tbl, YO, slip 1, K1, PSSO, P1 tbl, (K5, P1 tbl) twice, YO, slip 1, K1, PSSO, P1 tbl, K1, purl across.

Row 5: Repeat Row 3.

Row 6: P4{2-4}, YO, P2, pass YO over both purl sts, (P2, YO, P2, pass YO over both purl sts) 3{4-4} times, P4, K1, P1 tbl, YO, slip 1, K1, PSSO, P1 tbl, (K5, P1 tbl) twice, YO, slip 1, K1, PSSO, P1 tbl, K1, P4, YO, P2, pass YO over both purl sts, (P2, YO, P2, pass YO over both purl sts) 3{4-4} times, P4{2-4}.

Rows 7 and 8: Repeat Rows 3 and 4.

To work Bobble, (K, P, K, P, K) **all** in the next st, **turn**, P5, **turn**, K5, pass second, third, fourth, and fifth sts on **right** needle over first st.

Row 9: Knit to marker, P1, K1 tbl, YO, slip 1, K1, PSSO, K1 tbl, P3, work Bobble, P1, K1 tbl, P1, work Bobble, P3, K1 tbl, YO, slip 1, K1, PSSO, K1 tbl, P1, knit across.

Row 10: Repeat Row 2.

Row 11: Repeat Row 9.

Row 12: Repeat Row 4.

Row 13: Knit to marker, P1, K1 tbl, YO, slip 1, K1, PSSO, K1 tbl, P5, work Bobble, P5, K1 tbl, YO, slip 1, K1, PSSO, K1 tbl, P1, knit across.

Row 14: P4{2-4}, YO, P2, pass YO over both purl sts, (P2, YO, P2, pass YO over both purl sts) 3{4-4} times, P4, K1, P1 tbl, YO, slip 1, K1, PSSO, P1 tbl, K 11, P1 tbl, YO, slip 1, K1, PSSO, P1 tbl, K1, P4, YO, P2, pass YO over both purl sts, (P2, YO, P2, pass YO over both purl sts) 3{4-4} times, P4{2-4}.

Row 15: Knit to marker, P1, K1 tbl, YO, slip 1, K1, PSSO, K1 tbl, P 11, K1 tbl, YO, slip 1, K1, PSSO, K1 tbl, P1, knit across.

Row 16: Purl to marker, K1, P1 tbl, YO, slip 1, K1, PSSO, P1 tbl, K 11, P1 tbl, YO, slip 1, K1, PSSO, P1 tbl, K1, purl across.

Row 17: Knit to marker, P1, K1 tbl, YO, slip 1, K1, PSSO, K1 tbl, (P5, K1 tbl) twice, YO, slip 1, K1, PSSO, K1 tbl, P1, knit across.

Repeat Rows 2-17 until Front measures approximately 9³/₄{11¹/₂-12³/₄}"/25{29-32.5} cm from cast on edge, ending by working a **wrong** side row.

NECK SHAPING

Note: Both sides of Neck are worked at the same time, using separate yarn for **each** side. Maintain established pattern throughout.

Row 1: Work across 22{23-24} sts, slip next 21{23-25} sts onto st holder; with second yarn, work across: 22{23-24} sts **each** side.

Row 2: Work across; with second yarn, work across.

Row 3 (Decrease row)**:** Work across to within 3 sts of Neck edge, K2 tog, K1; with second yarn, K1, slip 1, K1, PSSO, work across: 21{22-23} sts **each** side.

Rows 4-7: Repeat Rows 2 and 3 twice: 19{20-21} sts **each** side.

Work even until Front measures same as Back, ending by working a **wrong** side row.

Bind off all sts.

Sew shoulder seams.

Place a marker on **each** side of Front and Back, 4¹/₂{5-5¹/₂}"/11.5{12.5-14} cm down from shoulder seam.

SLEEVE
BODY

With **right** side facing and using larger size needles, pick up 52{58-64} sts evenly spaced between markers *(Fig. 34a, page 586)*.

Row 1: Purl across.

Row 2 (Right side)**:** Knit across.

Row 3: P3{2-1}, YO, P2, pass YO over both purl sts, (P2, YO, P2, pass YO over both purl sts) across to last 3{2-1} sts, P3{2-1}.

Rows 4-6: Work in Stockinette Stitch for 3 rows.

Row 7: P1{4-3}, YO, P2, pass YO over both purl sts, (P2, YO, P2, pass YO over both purl sts) across to last 1{4-3} sts, P1{4-3}.

Rows 8 and 9: Work in Stockinette Stitch for 2 rows.

Row 10 (Decrease row)**:** K1, slip 1, K1, PSSO, knit across to last 3 sts, K2 tog, K1: 50{56-62} sts.

Maintaining pattern, continue to decrease one stitch at **each** edge, every eighth row, 3{4-3} times **more**; then decrease every sixth row, 0{1-4} times: 44{46-48} sts.

Work even until Sleeve measures approximately 5¹/₂{7¹/₂-9}"/14{19-23} cm, ending by working a **knit** row.

Decrease Row: Purl across decreasing 9 sts evenly spaced: 35{37-39} sts.

RIBBING

Change to smaller size needles.

Row 1: K1, (P1, K1) across.

Row 2: P1, (K1, P1) across.

Repeat Rows 1 and 2 until Ribbing measures approximately 1¹/₂" (4 cm), ending by working Row 2.

Bind off all sts **loosely** in ribbing.

Repeat for second Sleeve.

Instructions continued on page 448.

FINISHING
NECK RIBBING
With **right** side facing, using circular needle and beginning at left shoulder seam, pick up 11 sts along left Front Neck edge, slip 21{23-25} sts from Front st holder onto empty needle and knit across, pick up 14 sts along right Neck edge, slip 22{24-26} sts from Back st holder onto empty needle and knit across, pick up 4 sts along left Back Neck edge, place marker: 72{76-80} sts.

Work in K1, P1 ribbing around for 1" (2.5 cm).

Bind off all sts **loosely** in ribbing.

Weave underarm and side in one continuous seam **(Fig. 36, page 587)**.

Design by Carole Prior.

FROSTY DIAMONDS PULLOVER
◖■□□ EASY

Size:	1	2	4
Finished			
Measurement:	21"	22"	23"
	53.5 cm	56 cm	58.5 cm

Size Note: Instructions are written for size 1 with sizes 2 and 4 in braces. Instructions will be easier to read, if you circle all the numbers pertaining to your size. If only one number is given, it applies to all sizes.

MATERIALS
FINE
(2)

Sport Weight Yarn, approximately:
 5{6-7¼} ounces, 470{565-685} yards
 [140{170-210} grams, 430{517-626} meters]
Straight knitting needles, sizes 4 (3.5 mm) **and**
 6 (4 mm) **or** sizes needed for gauge
16" (40.5 cm) Circular knitting needle,
 size 4 (3.5 mm)
Stitch holders - 2
Markers
Yarn needle

GAUGE: With larger size needles, in pattern,
 24 sts and 29 rows = 4" (10 cm)

BACK
RIBBING
With smaller size needles, cast on 59{63-65} sts **loosely**.

Row 1: P1, (K1, P1) across.

Row 2: K1, (P1, K1) across.

Repeat Rows 1 and 2 until Ribbing measures approximately 1¹/₂" (4 cm), ending by working Row 2.

Increase Row: Work across in established ribbing increasing 6 sts evenly spaced **(see Increases, page 581)**: 65{69-71} sts.

BODY
Change to larger size needles.

Row 1 (Right side)**:** K8{2-3}, P1, (K7, P1) across to last 8{2-3} sts, K8{2-3}.

Row 2: P8{2-3}, K1, (P7, K1) across to last 8{2-3} sts, P8{2-3}.

Row 3: K 0{1-2} **(see Zeros, page 577)**, P 0{1-1}, K1, (P1, K5, P1, K1) across to last 0{2-3} sts, P 0{1-1}, K 0{1-2}.

Row 4: P 0{1-2}, K 0{1-1}, P1, (K1, P5, K1, P1) across to last 0{2-3} sts, K 0{1-1}, P 0{1-2}.

Row 5: K2{4-1}, P1, (K3, P1) across to last 2{4-1} sts, K2{4-1}.

Row 6: P2{4-1}, K1, (P3, K1) across to last 2{4-1} sts, P2{4-1}.

Row 7: K3{5-6}, P1, K1, P1, (K5, P1, K1, P1) across to last 3{5-6} sts, K3{5-6}.

Row 8: P3{5-6}, K1, P1, K1, (P5, K1, P1, K1) across to last 3{5-6} sts, P3{5-6}.

Row 9: K4{6-7}, P1, (K7, P1) across to last 4{6-7} sts, K4{6-7}.

Instructions continued on page 450.

Row 10: P4{6-7}, K1, (P7, K1) across to last 4{6-7} sts, P4{6-7}.

Rows 11 and 12: Repeat Rows 7 and 8.

Rows 13 and 14: Repeat Rows 5 and 6.

Rows 15 and 16: Repeat Rows 3 and 4.

Repeat Rows 1-16 until Back measures approximately 10³/₄{12¹/₂-13³/₄}"/27.5{32-35} cm from cast on edge, ending by working a **wrong** side row.

NECK SHAPING

Note: Both sides of Neck are worked at the same time, using separate yarn for **each** side. Maintain established pattern throughout.

Row 1: Work across 21{22-22} sts, slip next 23{25-27} sts onto st holder; with second yarn, work across: 21{22-22} sts **each** side.

Row 2: Work across; with second yarn, work across.

Row 3: Work across to within 3 sts of Neck edge, K2 tog *(Fig. 17, page 583)*, K1; with second yarn, K1, [slip 1, K1, PSSO *(Figs. 19a & b, page 583)*], work across: 20{21-21} sts **each** side.

Row 4: Work across; with second yarn, work across.

Bind off all sts.

FRONT

Work same as Back until Front measures approximately 9³/₄{11¹/₂-12³/₄}"/25{29-32.5} cm from cast on edge, ending by working a **wrong** side row: 65{69-71} sts.

NECK SHAPING

Note: Both sides of Neck are worked at the same time, using separate yarn for **each** side. Maintain established pattern throughout.

Row 1: Work across 23{24-24} sts, slip next 19{21-23} sts onto st holder; with second yarn, work across: 23{24-24} sts **each** side.

Row 2: Work across; with second yarn, work across.

Row 3 (Decrease row)**:** Work across to within 3 sts of Neck edge, K2 tog, K1; with second yarn, K1, slip 1, K1, PSSO, work across: 22{23-23} sts **each** side.

Rows 4-7: Repeat Rows 2 and 3 twice: 20{21-21} sts **each** side.

Work even until Front measures same as Back, ending by working a **wrong** side row.

Bind off all sts.

Sew shoulder seams.

Place a marker on **each** side of Front and Back, 4¹/₂(5-5¹/₂}"/11.5{12.5-14} cm down from shoulder seam.

SLEEVE
BODY

With **right** side facing and using larger size needles, pick up 55{61-67} sts evenly spaced between markers *(Fig. 34a, page 586)*.

Row 1: Purl across.

Row 2 (Right side)**:** K 15{18-21}, P1, (K7, P1) 3 times, knit across.

Row 3: P 15{18-21}, K1, (P7, K1) 3 times, purl across.

Row 4: K 14{17-20}, P1, K1, P1, (K5, P1, K1, P1) 3 times, knit across.

Row 5: P 14{17-20}, K1, P1, K1, (P5, K1, P1, K1) 3 times, purl across.

Row 6: K 13{16-19}, P1, (K3, P1) 7 times, knit across.

Row 7: P 13{16-19}, K1, (P3, K1) 7 times, purl across.

Row 8: K 12{15-18}, P1, K5, P1, (K1, P1, K5, P1) 3 times, knit across.

Row 9: P 12{15-18}, K1, P5, K1, (P1, K1, P5, K1) 3 times, purl across.

Row 10 (Decrease row)**:** K1, slip 1, K1, PSSO, K8{11-14}, P1, (K7, P1) 4 times, K8{11-14}, K2 tog, K1: 53{59-65} sts.

Row 11: P 10{13-16}, K1, (P7, K1) 4 times, purl across.

Row 12: K 11{14-17}, P1, K5, P1, (K1, P1, K5, P1) 3 times, knit across.

Row 13: P 11{14-17}, K1, P5, K1, (P1, K1, P5, K1) 3 times, purl across.

Row 14: K 12{15-18}, P1, (K3, P1) 7 times, knit across.

Row 15: P 12{15-18}, K1, (P3, K1) 7 times, purl across.

Row 16: K 13{16-19}, P1, K1, P1, (K5, P1, K1, P1) 3 times, knit across.

Row 17: P 13{16-19}, K1, P1, K1, (P5, K1, P1, K1) 3 times, purl across.

Row 18 (Decrease row)**:** K1, slip 1, K1, PSSO, K 11{14-17}, P1, (K7, P1) 3 times, K 11{14-17}, K2 tog, K1: 51{57-63} sts.

Row 19: P 13{16-19}, K1, (P7, K1) 3 times, purl across.

Maintaining pattern, continue to decrease one stitch at **each** edge, every eighth row, 0{1-1} time(s) **more**; then decrease every sixth row, 3{4-6} times: 45{47-49} sts.

Work even until Sleeve measures approximately 5¹/₂{7¹/₂-9}"/14{19-23} cm, ending by working a **right** side row.

Decrease Row: Purl across decreasing 10 sts evenly spaced **(Fig. 18, page 583)**: 35{37-39} sts.

RIBBING

Change to smaller size needles.

Row 1: K1, (P1, K1) across.

Row 2: P1, (K1, P1) across.

Repeat Rows 1 and 2 until Ribbing measures approximately 1¹/₂" (4 cm), ending by working Row 2.

Bind off all sts **loosely** in ribbing.

Repeat for second Sleeve.

FINISHING
NECK RIBBING

With **right** side facing, using circular needle and beginning at left shoulder seam, pick up 11 sts along left Front neck edge, slip 19{21-23} sts from Front st holder onto empty needle and knit across, pick up 15 sts along right neck edge, slip 23{25-27} sts from Back st holder onto empty needle and knit across, pick up 4 sts along left Back neck edge, place marker **(see Markers, page 578)**: 72{76-80} sts.

Work in K1, P1 ribbing for 1" (2.5 cm).

Bind off all sts **loosely** in ribbing.

Weave underarm and side in one continuous seam **(Fig. 36, page 587)**.

Design by Carole Prior.

SIMPLY SWEET ◼◼◼◻ INTERMEDIATE

Finished Size: 36¹/₂" x 44" (92.5 cm x 112 cm)

MATERIALS
Worsted Weight Yarn: **[MEDIUM 4]**
17 ounces, 1,135 yards
(480 grams, 1,038 meters)
29" (73.5 cm) Circular needles, sizes 9 (5.5 mm)
and 10 (6 mm) **or** sizes needed for gauge
Yarn needle

GAUGE: With larger size needle,
in pattern, 21 sts = 5" (12.75 cm);
24 rows = 4¹/₂" (11.5 cm)

Gauge Swatch: 4" (10 cm) square
With larger size needle, cast on 16 sts.
Beginning with a **purl** row, work in Stockinette
Stitch for 20 rows.
Bind off all sts in **purl**.

AFGHAN BODY
With larger size needle, cast on 141 sts.

Row 1: Purl across.

Row 2 (Right side): K1, **[**K2 tog **(Fig. 17, page 583)**, YO **(Fig. 16a, page 582)]** twice, K1, **[**YO, SSK **(Figs. 21a-c, page 584)]** twice, ★ P1, (K2 tog, YO) twice, K1, (YO, SSK) twice; repeat from ★ across to last st, K1.

Row 3: P 10, K1, (P9, K1) across to last 10 sts, P 10.

Row 4: K2, K2 tog, YO, K3, YO, SSK, ★ K1, P1, K1, K2 tog, YO, K3, YO, SSK; repeat from ★ across to last 2 sts, K2.

Row 5: P 10, K1, (P9, K1) across to last 10 sts, P 10.

Row 6: K1, (K2 tog, YO) twice, K1, (YO, SSK) twice, ★ P1, (K2 tog, YO) twice, K1, (YO, SSK) twice; repeat from ★ across to last st, K1.

Row 7: P 10, K1, (P9, K1) across to last 10 sts, P 10.

Repeat Rows 4-7 for pattern until Afghan Body measures approximately 41" (104 cm) from cast on edge, ending by working Row 7.

Bind off all sts in **knit**.

MITERED EDGING
FIRST SIDE
With **right** side facing, using smaller size needle, and leaving a long end for sewing, pick up an odd number of stitches evenly spaced across bound off edge **(Fig. 34b, page 586)**.

Row 1 (Wrong side): P2, K1, (P1, K1) across to last 2 sts, P2.

Row 2: K2, M1 **(Figs. 14a & b, page 582)**, P1, (K1, P1) across to last 2 sts, M1, K2.

Row 3: P3, K1, (P1, K1) across to last 3 sts, P3.

Row 4: K2, M1P **(Figs. 15a & b, page 582)**, K1, (P1, K1) across to last 2 sts, M1P, K2.

Rows 5-9: Repeat Rows 1-4 once, then repeat Row 1 once **more**.

Bind off all sts in pattern.

SECOND SIDE
With **right** side facing, using smaller size needle, and leaving a long end for sewing, pick up an odd number of stitches evenly spaced across cast on edge.

Rows 1-9: Work same as First Side.

Bind off all sts in pattern.

THIRD AND FOURTH SIDES
With **right** side facing, using smaller size needle, and leaving a long end for sewing, pick up an odd number of stitches evenly spaced across long edge of Afghan Body **(Fig. 34a, page 586)**.

Rows 1-9: Work same as First Side.

Bind off all sts in pattern.

Design by Melissa Leapman.

TENDER TOUCHES ◀■■■◻ INTERMEDIATE

Finished Size: 35" x 44$^1/_2$" (89 cm x 113 cm)

MATERIALS

Worsted Weight Yarn: **MEDIUM 4**
  17 ounces, 1,135 yards
  (480 grams, 1,038 meters)
29" (73.5 cm) Circular needles, sizes 9 (5.5 mm)
  and 10 (6 mm) **or** sizes needed for gauge
Yarn needle

GAUGE: With larger size needle,
  in pattern, 2 repeats (16 sts)
  and 20 rows = 4" (10 cm)

Gauge Swatch: 4" (10 cm) square
With larger size needle, cast on 16 sts.
Beginning with a **purl** row, work in Stockinette
Stitch for 20 rows.
Bind off all sts in **purl**.

STITCH GUIDE

LEFT TWIST (uses next 2 sts)
Skip next st on left needle, knit the next st
through back loop *(Fig. 4a, page 580)*, then
knit the skipped st, slipping both sts off left
needle together.

RIGHT TWIST (uses next 2 sts)
K2 tog *(Fig. 17, page 583)* making sure **not**
to drop sts off left needle, then knit the first st
letting both sts drop off left needle together.

AFGHAN BODY

With larger size needle, cast on 129 sts.

Row 1: Purl across.

Row 2 (Right side)**:** K3, K2 tog *(Fig. 17, page 583)*, YO *(Fig. 16a, page 582)*, work Left Twist, ★ K4, K2 tog, YO, work Left Twist; repeat from ★ across to last 2 sts, K2.

Row 3: Purl across.

Row 4: K2, work Right Twist, YO, SSK *(Figs. 21a-c, page 584)*, ★ K4, work Right Twist, YO, SSK; repeat from ★ across to last 3 sts, K3.

Row 5: Purl across.

Row 6: K3, K2 tog, YO, work Left Twist, ★ K4, K2 tog, YO, work Left Twist; repeat from ★ across to last 2 sts, K2.

Row 7: Purl across.

Row 8: K2, work Right Twist, YO, SSK, ★ K4, work Right Twist, YO, SSK; repeat from ★ across to last 3 sts, K3.

Row 9: Purl across.

Repeat Rows 6-9 for pattern until Afghan Body measures approximately 41$^1/_2$" (105.5 cm) from cast on edge, ending by working Row 9.

Bind off all sts in **knit**.

EDGING

Work Mitered Edging, page 452.

Design by Melissa Leapman.

BABY BLOCKS

◼◼◻◻ EASY

Finished Size: 37" x 47$\frac{1}{2}$"

MATERIALS
Baby Sport Weight Yarn: **LIGHT 3**
  White - 26 ounces, (740 grams, 2,390 yards)
  Blue - 8$\frac{1}{4}$ ounces, (235 grams, 760 yards)
  24" Circular knitting needles, sizes 10 (6.00 mm)
    and 10$\frac{1}{2}$ (6.50 mm) **or** sizes needed
      for gauge

Entire Afghan is worked holding two strands of yarn together.

GAUGE: With larger size needle, in pattern,
        10 sts and 18 rows = 2$\frac{1}{2}$"

Gauge Swatch: 7"w x 3$\frac{3}{4}$"h
With smaller size needle and White, cast on 27 sts.
Work same as Afghan for 25 rows.
Bind off all sts in **knit**.

AFGHAN
With smaller size needle and White, cast on 147 sts.

Rows 1-7: Knit across.

Change to larger size needle.

Row 8 (Right side)**:** Knit across.

Row 9: K4, purl across to last 4 sts, K4.

Row 10: Knit across.

Row 11: K4, purl across to last 4 sts, K4.

Both side borders of Afghan are worked at the same time, using separate yarn for each side. When instructed to slip a stitch, always slip as if to **purl**.

Row 12: K4 (side border), drop White *(Fig. 30, page 585)*; with Blue K1, slip 1, K1, slip 3, K1, ★ (slip 1, K1) 3 times, slip 3, K1; repeat from ★ across to last 6 sts, slip 1, K1, drop Blue; with next White K4 (side border).

Row 13: K4, WYF drop White; with Blue K1, WYF slip 1, WYB K1, WYF slip 3, WYB K1, ★ (WYF slip 1, WYB K1) 3 times, WYF slip 3, WYB K1; repeat from ★ across to last 6 sts, WYF slip 1, WYB K1, WYF drop Blue; with next White K4.

Carry yarn not being used **loosely** along inside edge.

Row 14: Knit across to last 4 sts, drop White; with next White K4.

Row 15: K4, WYF drop White; with next White purl across to last 4 sts, K4.

Rows 16-27: Repeat Rows 12-15, 3 times.

Row 28: Knit across to last 4 sts, drop White; with next White K4.

Row 29: K4, WYF drop White; with next White purl across to last 4 sts, K4.

Repeat Rows 12-29 for pattern until Afghan measures approximately 45$\frac{1}{4}$" from cast on edge, ending by working Row 24.

Next Row: K4, WYF cut White; with Blue K1, WYF slip 1, WYB K1, WYF slip 3, WYB K1, ★ (WYF slip 1, WYB K1) 3 times, WYF slip 3, WYB K1; repeat from ★ across to last 6 sts, WYF slip 1, WYB K1, WYF cut Blue; with next White K4.

Next 4 Rows: Repeat Rows 8-11.

Change to smaller size needle.

Last 7 Rows: Knit across.

Bind off all sts in **knit**.

Design by Kay Meadors.

ROSEBUD PRINCESS

◼◼◻◻ **EASY**

Finished Size: 37" x 49"

MATERIALS
Worsted Weight Yarn: **(4)** MEDIUM
  24 ounces, (680 grams, 1,160 yards)
  29" Circular knitting needles, size 10 (6.00 mm)
  or size needed for gauge

GAUGE: In Stockinette Stitch, 16 sts and 22 rows = 4"

STITCH GUIDE

BOBBLE
(K1, YO, K1) in next st, **turn**; P1, **[P1, YO (Fig. 16b, page 582),** P1] in next st, P1, **turn**; K5, **turn**; P2 tog **(Fig. 18, page 583),** P1, P2 tog, **turn**; [slip 1, K2 tog, PSSO **(Figs. 26a & b, page 584)]**.

AFGHAN
Cast on 147 sts.

Rows 1-6: Knit across.

Row 7 (Right side)**:** K8, K2 tog **(Fig. 17, page 583),** YO **(Fig. 16a, page 582),** K1, YO, SSK **(Figs. 21a-c, page 584),** (K 13, K2 tog, YO, K1, YO, SSK) across to last 8 sts, K8.

Row 8: K4, purl across to last 4 sts, K4.

Row 9: K7, K2 tog, K1, (YO, K1) twice, SSK, ★ K 11, K2 tog, K1, (YO, K1) twice, SSK; repeat from ★ across to last 7 sts, K7.

Row 10: K4, purl across to last 4 sts, K4.

Row 11: K6, K2 tog, K2, YO, K1, YO, K2, SSK, (K9, K2 tog, K2, YO, K1, YO, K2, SSK) across to last 6 sts, K6.

Row 12: K4, purl across to last 4 sts, K4.

Row 13: K5, K2 tog, K3, YO, K1, YO, K3, SSK, (K7, K2 tog, K3, YO, K1, YO, K3, SSK) across to last 5 sts, K5.

Row 14: K4, purl across to last 4 sts, K4.

Row 15: K 10, work Bobble, (K 17, work Bobble) across to last 10 sts, K 10.

Row 16: K4, purl across to last 4 sts, K4.

Row 17: K 17, K2 tog, YO, K1, YO, SSK, (K 13, K2 tog, YO, K1, YO, SSK) across to last 17 sts, K 17.

Row 18: K4, purl across to last 4 sts, K4.

Row 19: K 16, K2 tog, K1, (YO, K1) twice, SSK, ★ K 11, K2 tog, K1, (YO, K1) twice, SSK; repeat from ★ across to last 16 sts, K 16.

Row 20: K4, purl across to last 4 sts, K4.

Row 21: K 15, K2 tog, K2, YO, K1, YO, K2, SSK, (K9, K2 tog, K2, YO, K1, YO, K2, SSK) across to last 15 sts, K 15.

Row 22: K4, purl across to last 4 sts, K4.

Row 23: K 14, K2 tog, K3, YO, K1, YO, K3, SSK, (K7, K2 tog, K3, YO, K1, YO, K3, SSK) across to last 14 sts, K 14.

Row 24: K4, purl across to last 4 sts, K4.

Row 25: K 19, work Bobble, (K 17, work Bobble) across to last 19 sts, K 19.

Row 26: K4, purl across to last 4 sts, K4.

Row 27: K8, K2 tog, YO, K1, YO, SSK, (K 13, K2 tog, YO, K1, YO, SSK) across to last 8 sts, K8.

Repeat Rows 8-27 for pattern until Afghan measures approximately 48" from cast on *edge*, ending by working Row 16.

Last 7 Rows: Knit across.

Bind off all sts in **knit**.

Design by Melissa Leapman.

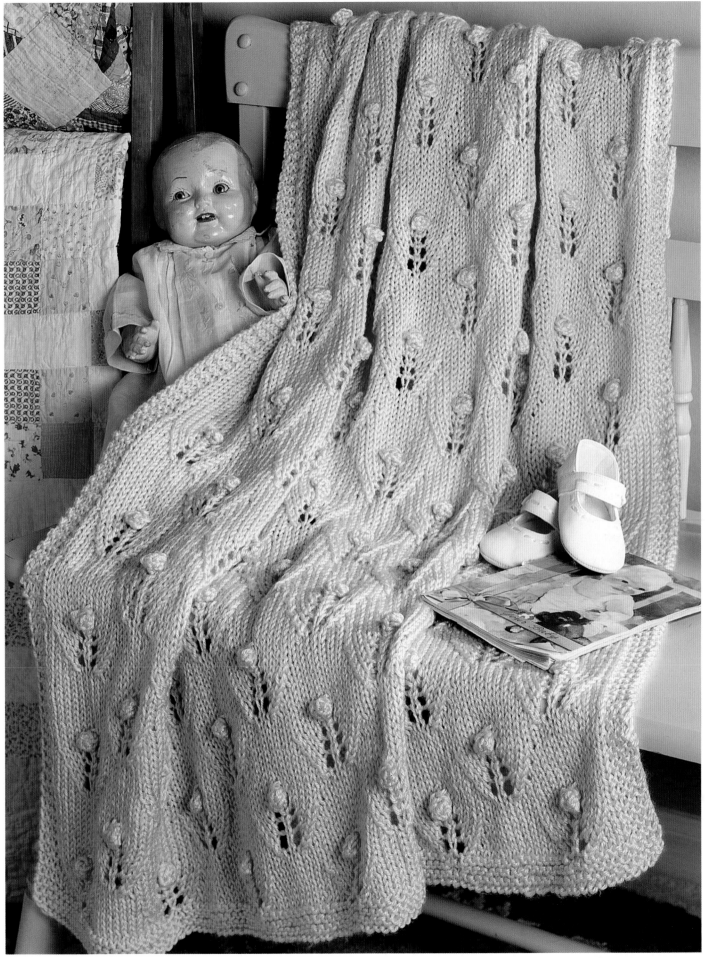

LITTLE PRINCE

Finished Size: 37" x 49"

MATERIALS
Worsted Weight Yarn: **4 MEDIUM**
   21 ounces, (600 grams, 1,015 yards)
   29" Circular knitting needles, size 10 (6.00 mm)
   or size needed for gauge

GAUGE: In Stockinette Stitch, 16 sts and
          22 rows = 4"

AFGHAN
Cast on 148 sts.

Rows 1-6: Knit across.

Row 7 (Right side)**:** K4, K2 tog *(Fig. 17, page 583)*, ★ YO *(Fig. 16a, page 582)*, K5, K2 tog; repeat from ★ across to last 9 sts, YO, K9.

Row 8: K4, purl across to last 4 sts, K4.

Row 9: K6, YO, SSK *(Figs. 21a-c, page 584)*, (K5, YO, SSK) across to last 7 sts, K7.

Row 10: K4, purl across to last 4 sts, K4.

Row 11: K7, YO, SSK, (K5, YO, SSK) across to last 6 sts, K6.

Row 12: K4, purl across to last 4 sts, K4.

Row 13: K8, (YO, SSK, K5) across.

Row 14: K4, purl across to last 4 sts, K4.

Row 15: K9, YO, SSK, (K5, YO, SSK) across to last 4 sts, K4.

Row 16: K4, purl across to last 4 sts, K4.

Row 17: K7, K2 tog, (YO, K5, K2 tog) across to last 6 sts, YO, K6.

Row 18: K4, purl across to last 4 sts, K4.

Row 19: K6, K2 tog, (YO, K5, K2 tog) across to last 7 sts, YO, K7.

Row 20: K4, purl across to last 4 sts, K4.

Row 21: K5, K2 tog, (YO, K5, K2 tog) across to last 8 sts, YO, K8.

Row 22: K4, purl across to last 4 sts, K4.

Row 23: K4, K2 tog, (YO, K5, K2 tog) across to last 9 sts, YO, K9.

Repeat Rows 8-23 for pattern until Afghan measures approximately 48" from cast on edge, ending by working Row 15.

Last 6 Rows: Knit across.

Bind off all sts in **knit.**

Design by Melissa Leapman.

SOFT & DREAMY

▰▰▱▱ EASY

Finished Size: 33" x 44"

MATERIALS

Double Knitting Weight Yarn: **3** LIGHT

Yellow - 7½ ounces, (210 grams, 705 yards)
White - 7½ ounces, (210 grams, 705 yards)
31" Circular knitting needles, sizes 13 (9 mm)
and 15 (10 mm) **or** sizes needed for gauge

Note: Afghan is made holding one strand of Yellow and one strand of White together.

GAUGE: With larger size needle, in Stockinette Stitch, 11 sts and 14 rows = 4"

Gauge Swatch: 4" square
With larger size needle, cast on 11 sts.
Work in Stockinette Stitch for 13 rows.
Bind off all sts.

With smaller size needle, cast on 89 sts.

Rows 1-13: K1, (P1, K1) across.

Change to larger size needle.

Rows 14-17: (K1, P1) 4 times, knit across to last 8 sts, (P1, K1) 4 times.

Row 18 (Right side)**:** K1, (P1, K1) 4 times, ★ K2 tog **(Fig. 17, page 583)**, YO **(Fig. 16a, page 582)**; repeat from ★ across to last 10 sts, K2, (P1, K1) 4 times.

Row 19: K1, (P1, K1) 4 times, purl across to last 9 sts, K1, (P1, K1) 4 times.

Rows 20-24: (K1, P1) 4 times, knit across to last 8 sts, (P1, K1) 4 times.

Row 25: K1, (P1, K1) 4 times, purl across to last 9 sts, K1, (P1, K1) 4 times.

Row 26: (K1, P1) 4 times, knit across to last 8 sts, (P1, K1) 4 times.

Rows 27-45: Repeat Rows 25 and 26, 9 times; then repeat Row 25 once **more**.

Rows 46-49: (K1, P1) 4 times, knit across to last 8 sts, (P1, K1) 4 times.

Row 50: K1, (P1, K1) 4 times, (K2 tog, YO) across to last 10 sts, K2, (P1, K1) 4 times.

Rows 51-151: Repeat Rows 19-50, 3 times; then repeat Rows 19-23 once **more**.

Change to smaller size needle.

Rows 152-164: K1, (P1, K1) across.

Bind off all sts in pattern.

Design by Evelyn A. Clark.

ROCK-A-BYE

◼◼◻◻ EASY

Finished Size: 33" x 42"

MATERIALS
Double Knitting Weight Yarn:
Variegated - 10½ ounces, (300 grams, 990 yards)
White - 10½ ounces, (300 grams, 990 yards)
31" Circular knitting needle, size 15 (10 mm) **or** size needed for gauge
Markers

Note: Afghan is made holding one strand of Variegated and one strand of White together.

GAUGE: In Garter Stitch, 11 sts and 18 rows = 4"

Gauge Swatch: 4" square
Cast on 11 sts.
Work in Garter Stitch for 17 rows.
Bind off all sts.

FIRST CORNER
Cast on 3 sts.

Rows 1 and 2: Knit across.

Row 3: Increase *(Figs 10a & b, page 581)*, K1, increase: 5 sts.

Row 4: Knit across.

Row 5: K1, (increase, K1) twice: 7 sts.

Row 6: Knit across.

Row 7: K2, increase, K1, increase, K2: 9 sts.

Row 8: Knit across.

Row 9: K3, increase, K1, increase, K3: 11 sts.

Row 10: Knit across.

Row 11: K4, increase, K1, increase, K4: 13 sts.

Row 12: Knit across.

Row 13: K5, increase, K1, increase, K5: 15 sts.

Row 14: Knit across.

Row 15: K6, increase, K1, increase, K6: 17 sts.

Row 16: Knit across.

Row 17: K8, place marker *(see Markers, page 578)*, YO *(Fig. 16a, page 582)*, K1, YO, place marker, K8: 19 sts.

Note: There should be 8 sts before the first marker and after the second marker at **all** times.

Row 18: Knit across.

Row 19: K8, slip marker, YO, knit across to next marker, YO, slip marker, K8: 21 sts.

Row 20: Knit across.

Rows 21-120: Repeat Rows 19 and 20, 50 times: 121 sts.

Instructions continued on page 466.

SECOND CORNER

Note: Begin working in short rows *(see Wrapping Stitches, page 467)*.

Row 1: K7, wrap next st, **turn**.

Row 2: K7.

Row 3: K6, wrap next st, turn.

Row 4: K6.

Row 5: K5, wrap next st, turn.

Row 6: K5.

Row 7: K4, wrap next st, turn.

Row 8: K4.

Row 9: K3, wrap next st, turn.

Row 10: K3.

Row 11: K2, wrap next st, turn.

Row 12: K2.

Row 13: K1, wrap next st, turn.

Row 14: K1.

Row 15: K2 *(Fig. A, page 467)*, turn.

Row 16: WYB slip one st as if to **purl**, K1.

Row 17: K3, turn.

Row 18: WYB slip one st as if to **purl**, K2.

Row 19: K4, turn.

Row 20: WYB slip one st as if to **purl**, K3.

Row 21: K5, turn.

Row 22: WYB slip one st as if to **purl**, K4.

Row 23: K6, turn.

Row 24: WYB slip one st as if to **purl**, K5.

Row 25: K7, turn.

Row 26: WYF slip one st as if to **purl**, K6.

Row 27: K8, slip marker, YO, K3 tog *(Fig. 23, page 584)*, knit across to next marker, YO, slip marker, K8: 121 sts.

Row 28: Knit across.

Row 29: K8, slip marker, YO, K3 tog, knit across to next marker, YO, slip marker, K8.

Rows 30-69: Repeat Rows 28 and 29, 20 times.

THIRD CORNER
Rows 1-26: Work same as Second Corner.

Row 27: Knit across: 121 sts.

Row 28: K8, slip marker, YO, K3 tog, knit across to within 3 sts of next marker, K3 tog, YO, slip marker, K8: 119 sts.

Row 29: Knit across.

Rows 30-127: Repeat Rows 28 and 29, 49 times: 21 sts.

FOURTH CORNER
Row 1: K8, remove marker, YO, slip next 2 sts as if to **purl**, K3 tog, with the left needle bring the 2 slipped sts over the st just made and off the needle, YO, remove marker, K8: 19 sts.

Row 2: Knit across.

Row 3: K7, K2 tog *(Fig. 17, page 583)*, K1, K2 tog, K7: 17 sts.

Row 4: Knit across.

Row 5: K6, K2 tog, K1, K2 tog, K6: 15 sts.

Row 6: Knit across.

Row 7: K5, K2 tog, K1, K2 tog, K5: 13 sts.

Row 8: Knit across.

Row 9: K4, K2 tog, K1, K2 tog, K4: 11 sts.

Row 10: Knit across.

Row 11: K3, K2 tog, K1, K2 tog, K3: 9 sts.

Row 12: Knit across.

Row 13: K2, K2 tog, K1, K2 tog, K2: 7 sts.

Row 14: Knit across.

Row 15: K1, (K2 tog, K1) twice: 5 sts.

Row 16: Knit across.

Row 17: K2 tog, K1, K2 tog: 3 sts.

Bind off all sts in **knit**.

Design by Evelyn A. Clark.

WRAPPING STITCHES
When working short rows (not working all of the stitches on the left needle before turning), it is necessary to wrap the yarn around an unworked stitch before turning in order to prevent holes.

Wrap the stitch indicated as follows:
With yarn to the back, slip next stitch as if to **purl**, bring yarn to the **front** and slip the same stitch back onto the left needle. Leave remaining stitches unworked.

When meeting the wrapped stitch, knit the wrap and the stitch it wraps together *(Fig. A)*.

Fig. A

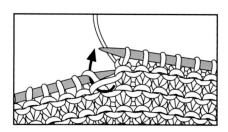

RIBBED RIPPLE

■■□□ EASY

Finished Size: 35" x 45"

MATERIALS

Worsted Weight Yarn: (MEDIUM 4)
18 ounces, (510 grams, 1,180 yards)
29" Circular knitting needles, sizes 8 (5 mm)
and 10 (6 mm) **or** sizes needed for gauge

GAUGE: With larger size needle,
In pattern, 22 sts and 22 rows = $4^1/_2$"
In Stockinette Stitch, 18 sts = 4"

AFGHAN

With smaller size needle, cast on 171 sts.

Rows 1-6: Knit across.

Change to larger size needle.

To increase, knit into the front **and** into the back of the next stitch.

Row 7 (Right side)**:** K3, increase, K3, [slip 2 tog as if to **knit**, K1, P2SSO *(Figs. 29a & b, page 585)*], K3, ★ increase twice, K3, slip 2 tog as if to **knit**, K1, P2SSO, K3; repeat from ★ across to last 4 sts, increase, K3.

Row 8: K3, purl across to last 3 sts, K3.

Row 9: K3, increase, K3, slip 2 tog as if to **knit**, K1, P2SSO, K3, ★ increase twice, K3, slip 2 tog as if to **knit**, K1, P2SSO, K3; repeat from ★ across to last 4 sts, increase, K3.

Repeat Rows 8 and 9 for pattern until Afghan measures approximately $44^1/_4$" from cast on edge, ending by working Row 9.

Change to smaller size needle.

Last 6 Rows: Knit across.

Bind off all sts in **knit**.

Design by Melissa Leapman.

EMBOSSED RIPPLE

■■□□ EASY

Finished Size: 37" x 48"

MATERIALS

Worsted Weight Yarn: **MEDIUM 4**
22 ounces, (620 grams, 1,445 yards)
29" Circular knitting needles, sizes 8 (5 mm)
and 10 (6 mm) **or** sizes needed for gauge

GAUGE: With larger size needle,
In pattern, 15 sts and 22 rows = $3^1/4$"
In Stockinette Stitch, 18 sts = 4"

AFGHAN

With smaller size needle, cast on 172 sts.

Rows 1-6: Knit across.

Change to larger size needle.

Row 7 (Right side)**:** K3, K2 tog *(Fig. 17, page 583)*, K5, YO *(Fig. 16a, page 582)*, K2, YO, K5, ★ [slip 2 tog as if to **knit**, K1, P2SSO *(Figs. 29a & b, page 585)*], K5, YO, K2, YO, K5; repeat from ★ across to last 5 sts, SSK *(Figs. 21a-c, page 584)*, K3.

Row 8: K3, purl across to last 3 sts, K3.

Row 9: K3, K2 tog, K5, YO, K2, YO, K5, ★ slip 2 tog as if to **knit**, K1, P2SSO, K5, YO, K2, YO, K5; repeat from ★ across to last 5 sts, SSK, K3.

Rows 10 and 11: Repeat Rows 8 and 9.

Rows 12 and 13: K3, purl across to last 3 sts, K3.

Row 14: Knit across.

Rows 15 and 16: K3, purl across to last 3 sts, K3.

Row 17: K3, K2 tog, K5, YO, K2, YO, K5, ★ slip 2 tog as if to **knit**, K1, P2SSO, K5, YO, K2, YO, K5; repeat from ★ across to last 5 sts, SSK, K3.

Repeat Rows 8-17 for pattern until Afghan measures approximately $47^1/4$" from cast on edge, ending by working Row 11.

Change to smaller size needle.

Last 6 Rows: Knit across.

Bind off all sts in **knit**.

Design by Melissa Leapman.

DREAMLAND WRAP

Finished Size: 35¹/₂" x 48" (90 cm x 122 cm)

MATERIALS

Medium/Worsted Weight Yarn: **MEDIUM 4**
   25 ounces, 1,250 yards
   (710 grams, 1,143 meters)
   29" (73.5 cm) Circular needles, sizes
   8 (5 mm) **and** 10 (6 mm) **or** sizes needed
   for gauge

GAUGE: In pattern, with larger size needle,
   20 sts and 28 rows = 4¹/₂" (11.5 cm)
   In Stockinette Stitch, 18 sts = 4" (10 cm)

THROW

With smaller size needle, cast on 157 sts.

Rows 1-6: Knit across.

Change to larger size needle.

Row 7 (Right side)**:** Knit across.

Row 8: K3, purl across to last 3 sts, K3.

Row 9: K3, **[**slip 1 as if to **knit**, K2 tog, PSSO *(Figs. 26a & b, page 584)]*, K1, ★ **[**YO *(Fig. 16a, page 582)*, K1**]** 4 times, **[**slip 2 tog as if to **knit**, K3 tog, P2SSO *(Figs. A-C)]*, K1; repeat from ★ across to last 10 sts, (YO, K1) 3 times, YO, K3 tog, K4.

Rows 10 and 11: Knit across.

Row 12: K3, purl across to last 3 sts, K3.

Row 13: K3, slip 1 as if to **knit**, K2 tog, PSSO, K1, ★ (YO, K1) 4 times, slip 2 tog as if to **knit**, K3 tog, P2SSO, K1; repeat from ★ across to last 10 sts, (YO, K1) 3 times, YO, K3 tog, K4.

Repeat Rows 10-13 for pattern until Throw measures approximately 47¹/₂" (120.5 cm) from cast on edge, ending by working Row 11.

Change to smaller size needle.

Last 6 Rows: Knit across.

Bind off all sts in **knit**.

Design by Melissa Leapman.

Fig. A

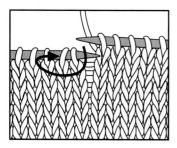

Fig. B

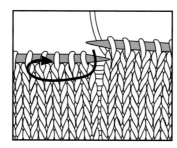

Fig. C

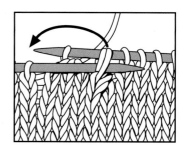

TEA TIME

EASY

Finished Size: 47" x 61"

MATERIALS

MEDIUM 4

Worsted Weight Yarn:
  33 ounces, (940 grams, 2,170 yards)
  29" Circular knitting needles, size 17
    (12.75 mm) **or** size needed for gauge

Note: Afghan is worked holding two strands of yarn together.

GAUGE: In Stockinette Stitch, 9 sts and
  12 rows = 4"

AFGHAN

Cast on 106 sts.

Rows 1-10: Knit across.

Row 11 (Right side): K 14, P2, K2, P2, (K 12, P2, K2, P2) across to last 14 sts, K 14.

Row 12: K3, P1, K8, ★ P2, (K2, P2) twice, K8; repeat from ★ across to last 4 sts, P1, K3.

Row 13: K4, P8, ★ K2, (P2, K2) twice, P8; repeat from ★ across to last 4 sts, K4.

Row 14: K3, P 11, K2, P2, K2, (P 12, K2, P2, K2) across to last 14 sts, P 11, K3.

Rows 15-18: Repeat Rows 11-14.

Row 19: Knit across.

Row 20: K3, (P2, K2) twice, (P 12, K2, P2, K2) across to last 5 sts, P2, K3.

Row 21: K5, P2, K2, P2, ★ K2, P8, (K2, P2) twice; repeat from ★ across to last 5 sts, K5.

Row 22: K3, P2, (K2, P2) twice, ★ K8, P2, (K2, P2) twice; repeat from ★ across to last 3 sts, K3.

Row 23: K5, P2, K2, P2, (K 12, P2, K2, P2) across to last 5 sts, K5.

Rows 24-27: Repeat Rows 20-23.

Row 28: K3, purl across to last 3 sts, K3.

Repeat Rows 11-28 for pattern until Afghan measures approximately 58" from cast on edge, ending by working Row 28.

Last 10 Rows: Knit across.

Bind off all sts.

Design by Carole Prior.

TWILIGHT

Finished Size: 45" x 58"

MATERIALS

Worsted Weight Yarn: **④** MEDIUM
44¹/₂ ounces, (1,260 grams, 2,900 yards)
29" Circular knitting needles, size 17
(12.75 mm) **or** size needed for gauge

Note: Afghan is worked holding two strands of yarn together.

GAUGE: In Stockinette Stitch, 9 sts and
12 rows = 4"

AFGHAN

Cast on 102 sts.

Rows 1-12: Knit across.

Row 13 (Right side)**:** K8, P3, (K5, P3) across to last 11 sts, K 11.

Row 14: K8, P4, (K3, P5) across to last 10 sts, K 10.

Row 15: K8, P1, (K5, P3) across to last 13 sts, K 13.

Row 16: K9, P5, (K3, P5) across to last 8 sts, K8.

Row 17: K 12, (P3, K5) across to last 10 sts, P2, K8.

Row 18: K 11, (P5, K3) across to last 11 sts, P3, K8.

Row 19: K 10, P3, (K5, P3) across to last 9 sts, K9.

Row 20: K8, P2, K3, (P5, K3) across to last 9 sts, P1, K8.

Repeat Rows 13-20 for pattern until Afghan measures approximately 55" from cast on edge, ending by working Row 20.

Last 12 Rows: Knit across.

Bind off all sts.

Design by Linda Luder.

ASSURANCE

Finished Size: 47" x 62"

MATERIALS

Worsted Weight Yarn: [MEDIUM 4]
    47 ounces, (1,330 grams, 3,225 yards)
    29" Circular knitting needles, size 17
        (12.75 mm) **or** size needed for gauge

Note: Afghan is worked holding two strands of yarn together.

GAUGE: In Stockinette Stitch, 9 sts and
        12 rows = 4"

STITCH GUIDE

SLIP 1, PURL 2 TOGETHER, PASS SLIPPED STITCH OVER
(abbreviated slip 1, P2 tog, PSSO)
Slip one stitch as if to **purl** *(Fig. A)*, then purl the next two stitches together *(Fig. B)*. With the left needle, bring the slipped stitch over the stitch just made *(Fig. C)*, and off the needle.

Fig. A   **Fig. B**

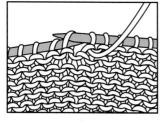   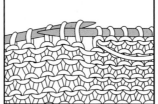

Fig. C

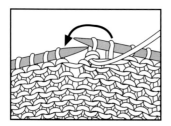

AFGHAN
Cast on 143 sts.

Rows 1-4: Knit across.

Note: When instructed to slip a stitch, always slip as if to **purl**, with yarn held in front.

Row 5 (Right side)**:** K3, P2, ★ M1 *(Figs. 14a & b, page 582)*, K3, P2, [slip 1, P2 tog, PSSO *(Figs. A-C)*], P2, K3, M1, P2; repeat from ★ across to last 3 sts, K3.

Row 6: (K5, P4) twice, (K2, P4, K5, P4) across to last 5 sts, K5.

Row 7: K3, P2, ★ M1, K4, P1, slip 1, P2 tog, PSSO, P1, K4, M1, P2; repeat from ★ across to last 3 sts, K3.

Row 8: K5, P5, K3, P5, (K2, P5, K3, P5) across to last 5 sts, K5.

Row 9: K3, P2, ★ M1, K5, slip 1, P2 tog, PSSO, K5, M1, P2; repeat from ★ across to last 3 sts, K3.

Row 10: K5, P6, K1, P6, (K2, P6, K1, P6) across to last 5 sts, K5.

Repeat Rows 5-10 for pattern until Afghan measures approximately 61" from cast on edge, ending by working Row 10.

Last 3 Rows: Knit across.

Bind off all sts.

Design by Carole Prior.

COMFORT

Finished Size: 47" x 58"

MATERIALS

Worsted Weight Yarn: 🧶 **4** 🧶 (MEDIUM)
44 ounces, (1,250 grams, 3,015 yards)
29" Circular knitting needles, size 17
(12.75 mm) **or** size needed for gauge

Note: Afghan is worked holding two strands of yarn together.

GAUGE: In Stockinette Stitch, 9 sts and
12 rows = 4"

AFGHAN

Cast on 107 sts.

Rows 1-12: Knit across.

Row 13 (Right side)**:** Knit across.

Row 14: K 12, P3, (K5, P3) across to last
12 sts, K 12.

Row 15: K8, P4, K3, (P5, K3) across to last
12 sts, P4, K8.

Row 16: K 12, P3, (K5, P3) across to last
12 sts, K 12.

Row 17: Knit across.

Row 18: K8, P3, (K5, P3) across to last 8 sts,
K8.

Row 19: K 11, P5, (K3, P5) across to last
11 sts, K 11.

Row 20: K8, P3, (K5, P3) across to last 8 sts,
K8.

Repeat Rows 13-20 for pattern until Afghan
measures approximately 55" from cast on edge,
ending by working Row 16 or Row 20.

Last 12 Rows: Knit across.

Bind off all sts.

Design by Linda Luder.

VISION

■■□□ **EASY**

Finished Size: 48" x 68"

MATERIALS
Worsted Weight Yarn: **MEDIUM 4**
  57 ounces, (1,620 grams, 3,325 yards)
29" Circular knitting needles, size 15
  (10.00 mm) **or** size needed for gauge
Cable needle

Note: Afghan is worked holding two strands of yarn together.

GAUGE: In Stockinette Stitch,
      11 sts and 14 rows = 4"

STITCH GUIDE

POPCORN (uses one st)
(K, P, K, P, K) **all** in next stitch, pass second, third, fourth, and fifth stitch on right needle **over** first stitch.

CABLE (uses 6 sts)
Slip 3 stitches onto cable needle and hold in **back** of work, K3 from left needle, K3 from cable needle.

AFGHAN
Cast on 132 sts.

Row 1: (K1, P1) across.

Row 2: (P1, K1) across.

Rows 3-9: Repeat Rows 1 and 2, 3 times; then repeat Row 1 once **more**.

Note: See Yarn Overs *(Figs. 16a, c, & d, page 582)*.

Row 10 (Right side)**:** P1, (K1, P1) 3 times, K7, YO, K2 tog twice *(Fig. 17, page 583)*, YO, (K6, YO, K2 tog twice, YO) twice, P1, (K4, P1) twice, YO, K2 tog twice, YO, (K6, YO, K2 tog twice, YO) 3 times, P1, (K4, P1) twice, (YO, K2 tog twice, YO, K6) 3 times, (P1, K1) 4 times.

Row 11: K1, (P1, K1) 3 times, P 31, K1, P3, K3, P3, K1, P 34, K1, P3, K3, P3, K1, P 30, (K1, P1) 4 times.

Row 12: P1, (K1, P1) 3 times, K7, YO, K2 tog twice, YO, (K6, YO, K2 tog twice, YO) twice, P1, K2, P5, K2, P1, YO, K2 tog twice, YO, (K6, YO, K2 tog twice, YO) 3 times, P1, K2, P5, K2, P1, (YO, K2 tog twice, YO, K6) 3 times, (P1, K1) 4 times.

Row 13: K1, (P1, K1) 3 times, P 31, K1, P1, K3, work Popcorn, K3, P1, K1, P 34, K1, P1, K3, work Popcorn, K3, P1, K1, P 30, (K1, P1) 4 times.

Row 14: Repeat Row 12.

Row 15: Repeat Row 11.

Row 16: (P1, K1) 4 times, (work Cable, YO, K2 tog twice, YO) 3 times, P1, (K4, P1) twice, YO, K2 tog twice, YO, (work Cable, YO, K2 tog twice, YO) 3 times, P1, (K4, P1) twice, (YO, K2 tog twice, YO, work Cable) 3 times, (P1, K1) 4 times.

Row 17: K1, (P1, K1) 3 times, P 31, K1, P9, K1, P 34, K1, P9, K1, P 30, (K1, P1) 4 times.

Rows 18-225: Repeat Rows 10-17, 26 times.

Row 226: (P1, K1) across.

Row 227: (K1, P1) across.

Row 228: (P1, K1) across.

Rows 229-234: Repeat Rows 227 and 228, 3 times.

Bind off all sts in pattern.

Design by Lee Tribett.

BLISS

Finished Size: 45" x 60"

MATERIALS

Worsted Weight Yarn: 🧶**4**🧶 MEDIUM
   33 ounces, (940 grams, 2,075 yards)
   29" Circular knitting needles, size 17
     (12.75 mm) **or** size needed for gauge

Note: Afghan is worked holding two strands of yarn together.

GAUGE: In Stockinette Stitch,
       9 sts and 12 rows = 4"

STITCH GUIDE

RIGHT TWIST *(abbreviated RT)* (uses 2 sts)
Knit second stitch on left needle making sure **not** to drop off, then purl the first stitch letting both stitches drop off left needle together *(Figs. 7a & b, page 580)*.

LEFT TWIST *(abbreviated LT)* (uses 2 sts)
Working behind first stitch on left needle, purl into the back of second stitch making sure **not** to drop off, then knit the first stitch letting both stitches drop off left needle together *(Figs. 6a & b, page 580)*.

AFGHAN

Cast on 98 sts.

Rows 1-5: Knit across.

Row 6: K5, P1, K2, (P2, K2) across to last 6 sts, P1, K5.

Row 7 (Right side)**:** K6, P1, RT, LT, P1, (K2, P1, RT, LT, P1) across to last 6 sts, K6.

Row 8: K5, P1, K1, P1, K2, P1, K1, (P2, K1, P1, K2, P1, K1) across to last 6 sts, P1, K5.

Row 9: K6, RT, P2, LT, (K2, RT, P2, LT) across to last 6 sts, K6.

Row 10: K5, P2, K4, (P4, K4) across to last 7 sts, P2, K5.

Row 11: Knit across.

Row 12: K5, P1, K2, (P2, K2) across to last 6 sts, P1, K5.

Row 13: K5, (LT, P1, K2, P1, RT) across to last 5 sts, K5.

Row 14: K6, P1, K1, P2, K1, P1, (K2, P1, K1, P2, K1, P1) across to last 6 sts, K6.

Row 15: K5, P1, LT, K2, RT, (P2, LT, K2, RT) across to last 6 sts, P1, K5.

Row 16: K7, P4, (K4, P4) across to last 7 sts, K7.

Row 17: Knit across.

Repeat Rows 6-17 for pattern until Afghan measures approximately 58" from cast on edge, ending by working Row 16.

Last 6 Rows: Knit across.

Bind off all sts.

Design by Anita Lewis.

1. BOXED BOBBLES PILLOW

MATERIALS

MEDIUM 4

Worsted Weight Yarn:
   7 ounces, (200 grams, 455 yards)
Knitting needles, size 8 (5.00 mm) **or** size
   needed for gauge
Yarn needle
Pillow form - 16" square

GAUGE: In pattern, 12 sts and 18 rows = 3"

STITCH GUIDE

BOBBLE (uses one st)
(K, P, K) **all** in next st, **turn**; P3, **turn**;
[slip 1, K2 tog, PSSO *(Figs. 26a & b,
page 584)*].

PILLOW COVER (Make 2)

Cast on 63 sts **loosely**.

Row 1 (Right side)**:** Knit across.

Row 2: Purl across.

Row 3: K4, P1, (K1, P1) 3 times, ★ K5, P1,
(K1, P1) 3 times; repeat from ★ across to last
4 sts, K4.

Row 4: P3, ★ K1, (P1, K1) 4 times, P3; repeat
from ★ across.

Row 5: K4, P1, (K5, P1) across to last 4 sts,
K4.

Row 6: P3, (K1, P7, K1, P3) across.

Rows 7 and 8: Repeat Rows 5 and 6.

Row 9: K4, P1, K2, work Bobble, K2, P1, (K5,
P1, K2, work Bobble, K2, P1) across to last
4 sts, K4.

Row 10: P3, (K1, P7, K1, P3) across.

Row 11: K4, P1, (K5, P1) across to last 4 sts,
K4.

Row 12: Repeat Row 4.

Row 13: Repeat Row 3.

Row 14: Purl across.

Rows 15-84: Repeat Rows 1-14, 5 times.

Bind off all sts **loosely** in **knit**.

With **wrong** sides together, matching stitches and
rows, sew around three sides, insert pillow form
and sew last side.

Design by Susan Ackerman Carter.

2. FANCY FRINGE PILLOW
Shown on page 487.

● □ □ □ BEGINNER

MATERIALS

Bulky Weight Yarn: 🅑 **5**
11 ounces, (310 grams, 340 yards)
Knitting needles, size 8 (5.00 mm) **or** size
needed for gauge
Yarn needle
Crochet hook for fringe
Pillow form - 14" square

GAUGE: In pattern, 10 sts = 3"

PILLOW COVER (Make 2)
Cast on 43 sts.

Purl each row until piece measures approximately
13" from cast on edge.

Bind off all sts in **purl**.

With **wrong** sides together, matching stitches and
rows, sew around three sides, insert pillow form
and sew last side.

Design by Valesha Marshell Kirksey.

FRINGE

Cut a piece of cardboard 3" x 8". Wind the yarn
loosely and **evenly** around the length of the
cardboard until the card is filled, then cut across
one end; repeat as needed.
Hold together 2 strands of yarn; fold in half.
With **front** facing and using a crochet hook,
draw the folded end up through a stitch or a row
around the seam and pull the loose ends through
the folded end *(Fig. A)*; draw the knot up **tightly**
(Fig. B). Repeat, spacing as desired.
Lay flat on a hard surface and trim the ends.
Knot ends of each strand.

Fig. A   **Fig. B**

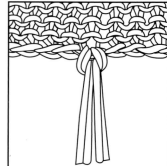

3. DISTINCTIVE DIAMONDS PILLOW

Shown on page 487.

◼◼◻◻ EASY

MATERIALS
Worsted Weight Yarn: 🧶 **4**
 5 ounces, (140 grams, 290 yards)
Knitting needles, size 9 (5.5 mm) **or** size
 needed for gauge
Yarn needle
Pillow form - 16" square
Fabric - ¹/₂ yard for lining (optional)

GAUGE: In Stockinette Stitch, 12 sts and
 18 rows = 3"

PILLOW COVER (Make 2)
Cast on 63 sts.

Rows 1-8: P1, (K1, P1) across.

Row 9: (P1, K1) 3 times, purl across to last
6 sts, (K1, P1) 3 times.

Row 10 (Right side)**:** P1, (K1, P1) twice, knit
across to last 5 sts, P1, (K1, P1) twice.

Rows 11 and 12: Repeat Rows 9 and 10.

Row 13: (P1, K1) 3 times, P 14, K1, P 21, K1,
P 14, (K1, P1) 3 times.

Row 14: P1, (K1, P1) twice, K 13, K2 tog
(Fig. 17, page 583), YO *(Fig. 16a,
page 582)*, K1, YO, **[**slip 1, K1, PSSO
*(Figs. 19a & b, page 583)***]**, K 17, K2 tog, YO,
K1, YO, slip 1, K1, PSSO, K 13, P1, (K1, P1)
twice.

Row 15: (P1, K1) 3 times, P 13, K1, P1, K1,
P 19, K1, P1, K1, P 13, (K1, P1) 3 times.

Row 16: P1, (K1, P1) twice, K 12, K2 tog, YO,
K1, P1, K1, YO, slip 1, K1, PSSO, K 15,
K2 tog, YO, K1, P1, K1, YO, slip 1, K1, PSSO,
K 12, P1, (K1, P1) twice.

Row 17: (P1, K1) 3 times, P 12, K1, (P1, K1)
twice, P 17, K1, (P1, K1) twice, P 12, (K1, P1) 3
times.

Row 18: P1, (K1, P1) twice, K 11, K2 tog, YO,
K1, (P1, K1) twice, YO, slip 1, K1, PSSO, K 13,
K2 tog, YO, K1, (P1, K1) twice, YO, slip 1, K1,
PSSO, K 11, P1, (K1, P1) twice.

Row 19: (P1, K1) 3 times, P 11, K1, (P1, K1)
3 times, P 15, K1, (P1, K1) 3 times, P 11, (K1,
P1) 3 times.

Row 20: P1, (K1, P1) twice, K 10, K2 tog, YO,
K1, (P1, K1) 3 times, YO, slip 1, K1, PSSO,
K 11, K2 tog, YO, K1, (P1, K1) 3 times, YO,
slip 1, K1, PSSO, K 10, P1, (K1, P1) twice.

Row 21: (P1, K1) 3 times, P 10, K1, (P1, K1)
4 times, P 13, K1, (P1, K1) 4 times, P 10, (K1,
P1) 3 times.

Row 22: P1, (K1, P1) twice, K9, ★ K2 tog,
YO, K1, (P1, K1) 4 times, YO, slip 1, K1,
PSSO, K9; repeat from ★ once **more**, P1, (K1,
P1) twice.

Row 23: (P1, K1) 3 times, P9, K1, (P1, K1) 5
times, P 11, K1, (P1, K1) 5 times, P9, (K1, P1)
3 times.

Row 24: P1, (K1, P1) twice, K8, K2 tog, YO,
K1, (P1, K1) 5 times, YO, slip 1, K1, PSSO, K7,
K2 tog, YO, K1, (P1, K1) 5 times, YO, slip 1,
K1, PSSO, K8, P1, (K1, P1) twice.

Row 25: (P1, K1) 3 times, P8, K1, (P1, K1) 6
times, P9, K1, (P1, K1) 6 times, P8, (K1, P1) 3
times.

Row 26: P1, (K1, P1) twice, K7, K2 tog, YO,
K1, (P1, K1) 6 times, YO, slip 1, K1, PSSO, K5,
K2 tog, YO, K1, (P1, K1) 6 times, YO, slip 1,
K1, PSSO, K7, P1, (K1, P1) twice.

Row 27: (P1, K1) 3 times, P7, ★ K1, (P1, K1)
7 times, P7; repeat from ★ once **more**, (K1, P1)
3 times.

Instructions continued on page 490.

Row 28: P1, (K1, P1) twice, K6, K2 tog, YO, K1, (P1, K1) 7 times, YO, slip 1, K1, PSSO, K3, K2 tog, YO, K1, (P1, K1) 7 times, YO, slip 1, K1, PSSO, K6, P1, (K1, P1) twice.

Row 29: (P1, K1) 3 times, P6, K1, (P1, K1) 8 times, P5, K1, (P1, K1) 8 times, P6, (K1, P1) 3 times.

Row 30: P1, (K1, P1) twice, K6, YO, slip 1, K1, PSSO, P1, (K1, P1) 7 times, K2 tog, YO, K3, YO, slip 1, K1, PSSO, P1, (K1, P1) 7 times, K2 tog, YO, K6, P1, (K1, P1) twice.

Row 31: (P1, K1) 3 times, P7, ★ K1, (P1, K1) 7 times, P7; repeat from ★ once **more**, (K1, P1) 3 times.

Row 32: P1, (K1, P1) twice, K7, YO, slip 1, K1, PSSO, P1, (K1, P1) 6 times, K2 tog, YO, K5, YO, slip 1, K1, PSSO, P1, (K1, P1) 6 times, K2 tog, YO, K7, P1, (K1, P1) twice.

Row 33: (P1, K1) 3 times, P8, K1, (P1, K1) 6 times, P9, K1, (P1, K1) 6 times, P8, (K1, P1) 3 times.

Row 34: P1, (K1, P1) twice, K8, YO, slip 1, K1, PSSO, P1, (K1, P1) 5 times, K2 tog, YO, K7, YO, slip 1, K1, PSSO, P1, (K1, P1) 5 times, K2 tog, YO, K8, P1, (K1, P1) twice.

Row 35: (P1, K1) 3 times, P9, K1, (P1, K1) 5 times, (P5, K1) twice, (P1, K1) 5 times, P9, (K1, P1) 3 times.

Row 36: P1, (K1, P1) twice, K9, YO, slip 1, K1, PSSO, P1, (K1, P1) 4 times, K2 tog, YO, K3, P3, K3, YO, slip 1, K1, PSSO, P1, (K1, P1) 4 times, K2 tog, YO, K9, P1, (K1, P1) twice.

Row 37: (P1, K1) 3 times, P 10, K1, (P1, K1) 4 times, P5, K3, P5, K1, (P1, K1) 4 times, P 10, (K1, P1) 3 times.

Row 38: P1, (K1, P1) twice, K 10, YO, slip 1, K1, PSSO, P1, (K1, P1) 3 times, K2 tog, YO, K3, P2, K1, P2, K3, YO, slip 1, K1, PSSO, P1, (K1, P1) 3 times, K2 tog, YO, K 10, P1, (K1, P1) twice.

Row 39: (P1, K1) 3 times, P 11, K1, (P1, K1) 3 times, P5, K2, P1, K2, P5, K1, (P1, K1) 3 times, P 11, (K1, P1) 3 times.

Row 40: P1, (K1, P1) twice, K 11, YO, slip 1, K1, PSSO, P1, (K1, P1) twice, K2 tog, YO, K3, (P2, K3) twice, YO, slip 1, K1, PSSO, P1, (K1, P1) twice, K2 tog, YO, K 11, P1, (K1, P1) twice.

Row 41: (P1, K1) 3 times, P 12, K1, (P1, K1) twice, P5, K2, P3, K2, P5, K1, (P1, K1) twice, P 12, (K1, P1) 3 times.

Row 42: P1, (K1, P1) twice, K 12, YO, slip 1, K1, PSSO, P1, K1, P1, K2 tog, YO, K3, P2, K2 tog, YO, K1, YO, slip 1, K1, PSSO, P2, K3, YO, slip 1, K1, PSSO, P1, K1, P1, K2 tog, YO, K 12, P1, (K1, P1) twice.

Row 43: (P1, K1) 3 times, P 13, K1, P1, K1, P5, (K2, P5) twice, K1, P1, K1, P 13, (K1, P1) 3 times.

Row 44: P1, (K1, P1) twice, K 13, YO, slip 1, K1, PSSO, P1, K2 tog, YO, K3, P2, K2 tog, K1, (YO, K1) twice, slip 1, K1, PSSO, P2, K3, YO, slip 1, K1, PSSO, P1, K2 tog, YO, K 13, P1, (K1, P1) twice.

Row 45: (P1, K1) 3 times, P 14, K1, P5, K2, P7, K2, P5, K1, P 14, (K1, P1) 3 times.

Row 46: P1, (K1, P1) twice, K 13, K2 tog, YO, K1, YO, slip 1, K1, PSSO, K2, P2, K2 tog, K2, YO, K1, YO, K2, slip 1, K1, PSSO, P2, K2, K2 tog, YO, K1, YO, slip 1, K1, PSSO, K 13, P1, (K1, P1) twice.

Row 47: (P1, K1) 3 times, P 13, K1, P1, K1, P3, K2, P9, K2, P3, K1, P1, K1, P 13, (K1, P1) 3 times.

Row 48: P1, (K1, P1) twice, K 12, K2 tog, YO, K1, P1, K1, YO, slip 1, K1, PSSO, K2, P1, YO, slip 1, K1, PSSO, K5, K2 tog, YO, P1, K2, K2 tog, YO, K1, P1, K1, YO, slip 1, K1, PSSO, K 12, P1, (K1, P1) twice.

Row 49: (P1, K1) 3 times, P 12, K1, (P1, K1) twice, P3, K2, P7, K2, P3, K1, (P1, K1) twice, P 12, (K1, P1) 3 times.

Row 50: P1, (K1, P1) twice, K 11, K2 tog, YO, K1, (P1, K1) twice, YO, slip 1, K1, PSSO, K2, P1, YO, slip 1, K1, PSSO, K3, K2 tog, YO, P1, K2, K2 tog, YO, K1, (P1, K1) twice, YO, slip 1, K1, PSSO, K 11, P1, (K1, P1) twice.

Row 51: (P1, K1) 3 times, P 11, K1, (P1, K1) 3 times, P3, K2, P5, K2, P3, K1, (P1, K1) 3 times, P 11, (K1, P1) 3 times.

Row 52: P1, (K1, P1) twice, K 10, K2 tog, YO, K1, (P1, K1) 3 times, YO, slip 1, K1, PSSO, K2, P1, YO, slip 1, K1, PSSO, K1, K2 tog, YO, P1, K2, K2 tog, YO, K1, (P1, K1) 3 times, YO, slip 1, K1, PSSO, K 10, P1, (K1, P1) twice.

Row 53: (P1, K1) 3 times, P 10, K1, (P1, K1) 4 times, P3, (K2, P3) twice, K1, (P1, K1) 4 times, P 10, (K1, P1) 3 times.

Row 54: P1, (K1, P1) twice, K9, K2 tog, YO, K1, (P1, K1) 4 times, YO, slip 1, K1, PSSO, K2, P1, YO, [slip 1, K2 tog, PSSO *(Figs. 26a & b, page 584)*], YO, P1, K2, K2 tog, YO, K1, (P1, K1) 4 times, YO, slip 1, K1, PSSO, K9, P1 (K1, P1) twice.

Row 55: (P1, K1) 3 times, P9, K1, (P1, K1) 5 times, P3, K2, P1, K2, P3, K1, (P1, K1) 5 times, P9, (K1, P1) 3 times.

Row 56: P1, (K1, P1) twice, K8, K2 tog, YO, K1, (P1, K1) 5 times, YO, slip 1, K1, PSSO, K2, P3, K2, K2 tog, YO, K1, (P1, K1) 5 times, YO, slip 1, K1, PSSO, K8, P1, (K1, P1) twice.

Row 57: (P1, K1) 3 times, P8, K1, (P1, K1) 6 times, P3, K3, P3, K1, (P1, K1) 6 times, P8, (K1, P1) 3 times.

Row 58: P1, (K1, P1) twice, K7, K2 tog, YO, K1, (P1, K1) 6 times, YO, slip 1, K1, PSSO, K2, P1, K2, K2 tog, YO, K1, (P1, K1) 6 times, YO, slip 1, K1, PSSO, K7, P1, (K1, P1) twice.

Rows 59-66: Repeat Rows 27-34.

Row 67: (P1, K1) 3 times, P9, K1, (P1, K1) 5 times, P 11, K1, (P1, K1) 5 times, P9, (K1, P1) 3 times.

Row 68: P1, (K1, P1) twice, K9, ★ YO, slip 1, K1, PSSO, P1, (K1, P1) 4 times, K2 tog, YO, K9; repeat from ★ once **more**, P1, (K1, P1) twice.

Row 69: (P1, K1) 3 times, P 10, K1, (P1, K1) 4 times, P 13, K1, (P1, K1) 4 times, P 10, (K1, P1) 3 times.

Row 70: P1, (K1, P1) twice, K 10, YO, slip 1, K1, PSSO, P1, (K1, P1) 3 times, K2 tog, YO, K 11, YO, slip 1, K1, PSSO, P1, (K1, P1) 3 times, K2 tog, YO, K 10, P1, (K1, P1) twice.

Row 71: (P1, K1) 3 times, P 11, K1, (P1, K1) 3 times, P 15, K1, (P1, K1) 3 times, P 11, (K1, P1) 3 times.

Row 72: P1, (K1, P1) twice, K 11, YO, slip 1, K1, PSSO, P1, (K1, P1) twice, K2 tog, YO, K 13, YO, slip 1, K1, PSSO, P1, (K1, P1) twice, K2 tog, YO, K 11, P1, (K1, P1) twice.

Row 73: (P1, K1) 3 times, P 12, K1, (P1, K1) twice, P 17, K1, (P1, K1) twice, P 12, (K1, P1) 3 times.

Row 74: P1, (K1, P1) twice, K 12, YO, slip 1, K1, PSSO, P1, K1, P1, K2 tog, YO, K 15, YO, slip 1, K1, PSSO, P1, K1, P1, K2 tog, YO, K 12, P1, (K1, P1) twice.

Row 75: (P1, K1) 3 times, P 13, K1, P1, K1, P 19, K1, P1, K1, P 13, (K1, P1) 3 times.

Row 76: P1, (K1, P1) twice, K 13, YO, slip 1, K1, PSSO, P1, K2 tog, YO, K 17, YO, slip 1, K1, PSSO, P1, K2 tog, YO, K 13, P1, (K1, P1) twice.

Row 77: (P1, K1) 3 times, P 14, K1, P 21, K1, P 14, (K1, P1) 3 times.

Row 78: P1, (K1, P1) twice, knit across to last 5 sts, P1, (K1, P1) twice.

Row 79: (P1, K1) 3 times, purl across to last 6 sts, (K1, P1) 3 times.

Instructions continued on page 492.

Rows 80-82: Repeat Rows 78 and 79 once, then repeat Row 78 once **more**.

Rows 83-90: P1, (K1, P1) across.

Bind off all sts in pattern.

Cover pillow form with fabric, if desired.

With **wrong** sides together, matching stitches and rows, sew around three sides, insert pillow form and sew last side.

Design by Patty Kowaleski.

4. DIAGONAL RIDGES PILLOW
Shown on page 487.

◼◼◻◻ EASY

MATERIALS
Worsted Weight Chenille Yarn: MEDIUM 4
    5 ounces, (140 grams, 310 yards)
Knitting needles, size 7 (4.50 mm) **or** size
    needed for gauge
Yarn needle
Pillow form - 14" square

GAUGE: In pattern, 12 sts = 3"

STITCH GUIDE

RIGHT TWIST *(abbreviated RT)*
    (uses next 2 sts)
K2 tog *(Fig. 17, page 583)* making sure
not to drop off, then knit the first st letting
both sts drop off left needle together.

PILLOW COVER (Make 2)
Cast on 54 sts **loosely**.

Row 1 AND ALL WRONG SIDE ROWS:
Purl across.

Row 2 (Right side)**:** K3, RT, (K4, RT) across to last st, K1.

Row 4: K2, RT, (K4, RT) across to last 2 sts, K2.

Row 6: K1, RT, (K4, RT) across to last 3 sts, K3.

Row 8: K6, (RT, K4) across.

Row 10: K5, RT, (K4, RT) across to last 5 sts, K5.

Row 12: (K4, RT) across to last 6 sts, K6.

Repeat Rows 1-12 for pattern until piece measures approximately $13^1/_2$" from cast on edge, ending by working a **purl** row.

Bind off all sts **loosely** in **knit**.

With **wrong** sides together, matching stitches and rows, sew around three sides, insert pillow form and sew last side.

Design by Patty Kowaleski.

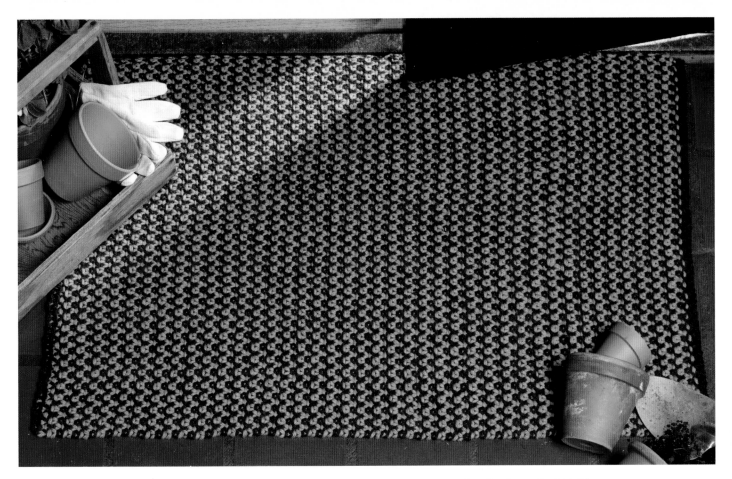

GARDEN CHECKERBOARD RUG

■□□□ BEGINNER

Finished Sizes: Approximately 2' x 3'{3' x 4'-2' x 8'}

Size Note: Instructions are written for size 2' x 3' with sizes 3' x 4' and 2' x 8' in braces { }. Instructions will be easier to read if you circle all the numbers pertaining to your size. If only one number is given, it applies to all sizes.

MATERIALS

Worsted Weight Yarn, approximately:

MC (Dark Green) - 7¹/₂{15-20} ounces, [210{430-570} grams, 470{945-1,255} yards]

CC (Green) - 7¹/₂{15-20} ounces, [210{430-570} grams, 470{945-1,255} yards]

31" Circular knitting needle, size 15 (10 mm) **or** size needed for gauge

MEDIUM 4

Note: Entire Rug is worked holding two strands of yarn together.

GAUGE: In pattern, 12 sts and 20 rows = 4"

With MC, cast on 72{108-72} sts.

Row 1 (Right side): ★ With yarn in back, K1, with yarn in front, slip 1 as if to **purl**; repeat from ★ across.

Row 2: ★ With yarn in front, P1, with yarn in back, slip 1 as if to **purl**; repeat from ★ across.

Note: Carry unused yarn **loosely** along edge.

Rows 3 and 4: With CC, repeat Rows 1 and 2.

Rows 5 and 6: With MC, repeat Rows 1 and 2.

Rows 7-182{242-482}: Repeat Rows 3-6, 44{59-119} times.

Bind off all sts in **knit**.

Design by Candi Jensen.

RUSTIC STRIPES RUG

Finished Sizes: Approximately 2' x 3'{3' x 4'-2' x 8'}

Size Note: Instructions are written for size 2' x 3' with sizes 3' x 4' and 2' x 8' in braces { }. Instructions will be easier to read if you circle all the numbers pertaining to your size. If only one number is given, it applies to all sizes.

MATERIALS

Worsted Weight Yarn, approximately:

MC (Light Green) - $5^1/_2${$10^1/_2$-$14^1/_2$} ounces,
  [160{300-410} grams, 345{660-910} yards]
Color A (Green) - 5{10-13} ounces,
  [140{280-370} grams, 315{630-815} yards]
Color B (Dark Green) - $4^1/_2${9-12} ounces,
  [130{260-340} grams, 285{565-755} yards]
31" Circular knitting needle, size 15 (10 mm)
  or size needed for gauge

Note: Entire Rug is worked holding two strands of yarn together.

GAUGE: In pattern, 12 sts and 20 rows = 4"

Note: Carry unused yarn **loosely** along edge, unless otherwise instructed.

With MC, cast on 72{108-72} sts.

Row 1 (Right side): ★ With yarn in back, K1, with yarn in front, slip 1 as if to **purl**; repeat from ★ across.

Row 2: ★ With yarn in front, P1, with yarn in back, slip 1 as if to **purl**; repeat from ★ across.

Rows 3-5: Repeat Rows 1 and 2 once, then repeat Row 1 once **more**.

Row 6: Using Color A, ★ with yarn in front, P1, with yarn in back, slip 1 as if to **purl**; repeat from ★ across.

Row 7: ★ With yarn in back, K1, with yarn in front, slip 1 as if to **purl**; repeat from ★ across.

Rows 8 and 9: With MC, repeat Rows 6 and 7. Cut MC.

Rows 10-18: With Color A, repeat Rows 6 and 7, 4 times; then repeat Row 6 once **more**.

Rows 19 and 20: With Color B, repeat Rows 1 and 2.

Rows 21 and 22: With Color A, repeat Rows 1 and 2. Cut Color A.

Rows 23-31: With Color B, repeat Rows 1 and 2, 4 times; then repeat Row 1 once **more**.

Rows 32 and 33: With MC, repeat Rows 6 and 7.

Rows 34 and 35: With Color B, repeat Rows 6 and 7. Cut Color B.

Rows 36-44: With MC, repeat Rows 6 and 7, 4 times; then repeat Row 6 once **more**.

Rows 45 and 46: With Color A, repeat Rows 1 and 2.

Rows 47 and 48: With MC, repeat Rows 1 and 2. Cut MC.

Rows 49-57: With Color A, repeat Rows 1 and 2, 4 times; then repeat Row 1 once **more**.

Rows 58 and 59: With Color B, repeat Rows 6 and 7.

Rows 60 and 61: With Color A, repeat Rows 6 and 7. Cut Color A.

Rows 62-70: With Color B, repeat Rows 6 and 7, 4 time(s); then repeat Row 6 once **more**.

Rows 71 and 72: With MC, repeat Rows 1 and 2.

Rows 73 and 74: With Color B, repeat Rows 1 and 2. Cut Color B.

Rows 75-83: With MC, repeat Rows 1 and 2, 4 times; then repeat Row 1 once **more**.

Rows 84-198{238-472}: Repeat Rows 6-83, 1{1-4} times; then repeat Rows 6-42{82-82} once **more**.

Bind off all sts in **knit**.

Add fringe *(Figs. 37a & b, page 588)*.

Design by Candi Jensen.

SHADES OF TWEED RUG

◼☐☐☐ BEGINNER

Finished Sizes: Approximately 2' x 3'{3' x 4'-2' x 8'}

Size Note: Instructions are written for size 2' x 3' with sizes 3' x 4' and 2' x 8' in braces { }. Instructions will be easier to read if you circle all the numbers pertaining to your size. If only one number is given, it applies to all sizes.

MATERIALS

MEDIUM 4

Worsted Weight Yarn, approximately:
Color A (Dark Green) - 3{6-8} ounces, [90{170-230} grams, 190{375-505} yards]
Color B (Green) - $2^1/_2${$4^1/_2$-6} ounces, [70{130-170} grams, 155{285-375} yards]
Color C (Dark Blue) - $2^1/_2${$4^1/_2$-6} ounces, [70{130-170} grams, 155{285-375} yards]
Color D (Blue) - 3{$5^1/_2$-7} ounces, [90{160-200} grams, 190{345-440} yards]
Color E (Dark Purple) - $2^1/_2${$4^1/_2$-6} ounces, [70{130-170} grams, 155{285-375} yards]
Color F (Purple) - $2^1/_2${5-$6^1/_2$} ounces, [70{140-190} grams, 155{315-410} yards]
31" Circular knitting needle, size 15 (10 mm) **or** size needed for gauge

Note: Entire Rug is worked holding two strands of yarn together.

GAUGE: In pattern, 12 sts and 20 rows = 4"

With Color A, cast on 72{108-72} sts.

Row 1 (Right side)**:** ★ With yarn in back, K1, with yarn in front, slip 1 as if to **purl**; repeat from ★ across.

Row 2: ★ With yarn in front, P1, with yarn in back, slip 1 as if to **purl**; repeat from ★ across.

Rows 3 and 4: Repeat Rows 1 and 2.

Cut Color A.

Rows 5-8: With Color B, repeat Rows 1 and 2 twice.

Cut Color B.

Rows 9-12: With Color C, repeat Rows 1 and 2 twice.

Cut Color C.

Rows 13-16: With Color D, repeat Rows 1 and 2 twice.

Cut Color D.

Rows 17-20: With Color E, repeat Rows 1 and 2 twice.

Cut Color E.

Rows 21-24: With Color F, repeat Rows 1 and 2 twice.

Cut Color F.

Rows 25-28: With Color A, repeat Rows 1 and 2 twice.

Cut Color A.

Rows 29-172{244-484}: Repeat Rows 5-28, 6{9-19} times.

Bind off all sts in **knit**.

Design by Candi Jensen.

EASY-DOES-IT DISHCLOTHS

Finished Size:
9" square unless otherwise noted

MATERIALS
100% Cotton Worsted Weight Yarn: MEDIUM **4**
  One ball
Straight knitting needles, size 7 (4.5 mm) **or**
  size needed for gauge

GAUGE: In Stockinette Stitch, 5 sts = 1"

1. SQUARE TEXTURES
◧◼◻◻ EASY

STITCH GUIDE

RIGHT TWIST *(abbreviated RT)*
(uses 2 sts) K2 tog *(Fig. 17, page 583)*
making sure **not** to drop off, then knit the
first st letting both sts drop off needle.

DISHCLOTH
Cast on 46 sts.

Row 1: (K1, P1) across.

Row 2 (Right side)**:** (P1, K1) across.

Row 3: K1, (P1, K1) 5 times, P9, K1, (P1, K1)
3 times, P9, (K1, P1) across.

Row 4: P1, (K1, P1) 5 times, RT 4 times, (K1,
P1) 4 times, RT 4 times, K1, (P1, K1) across.

Row 5: K1, (P1, K1) 5 times, P9, K1, (P1, K1)
3 times, P9, (K1, P1) across.

Row 6: (P1, K1) 6 times, RT 3 times, K2, (P1,
K1) 4 times, RT 3 times, K2, (P1, K1) across.

Rows 7-12: Repeat Rows 3-6 once, then
repeat Rows 3 and 4 once **more**.

Row 13: K1, P1, K1, P9, ★ K1, (P1, K1) 3
times, P9; repeat from ★ once **more**, K1, P1.

Row 14: P1, K1, P1, RT 4 times, ★ (K1, P1) 4
times, RT 4 times; repeat from ★ once **more**,
K1, P1, K1.

Row 15: K1, P1, K1, P9, ★ K1, (P1, K1) 3
times, P9; repeat from ★ once **more**, K1, P1.

Row 16: (P1, K1) twice, RT 3 times, K2,
★ (P1, K1) 4 times, RT 3 times, K2; repeat from
★ once **more**, P1, K1.

Rows 17-22: Repeat Rows 13-16 once, then
repeat Rows 13 and 14 once **more**.

Rows 23-62: Repeat Rows 3-22 twice.

Row 63: (K1, P1) across.

Row 64: (P1, K1) across.

Bind off all sts in pattern.

Design by Linda Luder.

1

2

3

4

5

6

7

8

Easy-Does-It Dishcloths   **499**

2. TEXTURED RIDGES

Shown on page 499.

◼◼◻◻ EASY

STITCH GUIDE

KNIT 1 BELOW *(abbreviated K1 below)*
When instructed to K1 below, insert needle into st **below** next st and knit *(Fig. A)*, allowing st on needle to fall to the back.

Fig. A

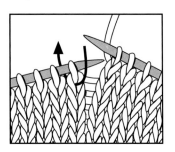

DISHCLOTH
Cast on 43 sts.

Rows 1-4: Purl across.

Row 5 (Right side)**:** P3, K1, ★ P2 tog *(Fig. 18, page 583)*, YO *(Fig. 16b, page 582)*, P1, K1; repeat from ★ across to last 3 sts, P3.

Row 6: Purl across.

Row 7: P3, K1 below, (P1, YO, P2 tog, K1 below) across to last 3 sts, P3.

Row 8: Purl across.

Row 9: P3, K1 below, (P2 tog, YO, P1, K1 below) across to last 3 sts, P3.

Repeat Rows 6-9 for pattern until Dishcloth measures approximately 8½" from cast on edge, ending by working a **wrong** side row.

Last 4 Rows: Purl across.

Bind off all sts in **purl**.

Design by Sue Galucki.

3. FIGURE EIGHTS

Shown on page 499.

◼◼◻◻ EASY

STITCH GUIDE

LEFT TWIST *(abbreviated LT)* (uses 2 sts)
Working **behind** first st on left needle, knit into the back of second st *(Fig. A)* making sure **not** to drop off, then knit the first st *(Fig. B)* letting both sts drop off needle.

Fig. A   ### Fig. B

 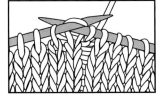

RIGHT TWIST *(abbreviated RT)*
(uses 2 sts)
K2 tog *(Fig. 17, page 583)* making sure **not** to drop off, then knit the first st letting both sts drop off needle.

DISHCLOTH
Cast on 45 sts.

Rows 1-4: Purl across.

Row 5 (Right side)**:** P6, K6, (P3, K6) 3 times, P6.

Row 6 AND ALL WRONG SIDE ROWS: Purl across.

Rows 7-10: Repeat Rows 5 and 6 twice.

Row 11: P3, K3, (LT, K2, RT, K3) 4 times, P3.

Row 13: P3, K4, LT, RT, (K5, LT, RT) 3 times, K4, P3.

Row 15: P3, K5, RT, (K7, RT) 3 times, K5, P3.

Row 17: P3, K4, RT, LT, (K5, RT, LT) 3 times, K4, P3.

Row 19: P3, K3, (RT, K2, LT, K3) 4 times, P3.

Row 20: Purl across.

Rows 21-52: Repeat Rows 5-20 twice.

Rows 53-57: Repeat Rows 5 and 6 twice, then repeat Row 5 once **more**.

Rows 58-61: Purl across.

Bind off all sts in **purl**.

Design by Linda Luder.

4. SIMPLE WEAVE
Shown on page 499.

◀■□□ EASY

DISHCLOTH
Cast on 47 sts.

Rows 1-6: Knit across.

Row 7: K7, P1, (K3, P1) across to last 7 sts, K7.

Row 8 (Right side)**:** Knit across.

Row 9 and 10: Repeat Rows 7 and 8.

Row 11: K5, P1, (K3, P1) across to last 5 sts, K5.

Row 12: Knit across.

Row 13 and 14: Repeat Rows 11 and 12.

Repeat Rows 7-14 for pattern until Dishcloth measures approximately 8" from cast on edge, ending by working Row 9 or Row 13.

Last 6 Rows: Knit across.

Bind off all sts in **knit**.

Design by Susan Ackerman.

5. LACY EYELETS

Shown on page 499.

◀■■□□ EASY

DISHCLOTH

Cast on 45 sts.

Rows 1-5: K1, (P1, K1) across.

Row 6 (Right side)**:** K1, (P1, K1) twice, ★ YO *(Fig. 16a, page 582)*, slip 1 as if to **purl**, K2 tog, PSSO, YO, K1; repeat from ★ across to last 4 sts, (P1, K1) twice.

Row 7: K1, (P1, K1) twice, (P3, K1) across to last 4 sts, (P1, K1) twice.

Row 8: K1, (P1, K1) twice, (YO, slip 1 as if to **purl**, K2 tog, PSSO, YO, K1) across to last 4 sts, (P1, K1) twice.

Repeat Rows 7 and 8 for pattern until Dishcloth measures approximately 8½" from cast on edge, ending by working Row 7.

Last 5 Rows: K1, (P1, K1) across.

Bind off all sts in pattern.

Design by Patty Kowaleski.

6. VERTICAL STRIPES

Shown on page 499.

◀■■□□ EASY

DISHCLOTH

Cast on 43 sts.

Rows 1-4: Knit across.

See Yarn Overs, page 582.

Row 5 (Right side)**:** K3, ★ K2 tog *(Fig. 17, page 583)*, YO, K3; repeat from ★ across.

Row 6: K3, P2 tog *(Fig. 18, page 583)*, (YO, P3, P2 tog) across to last 3 sts, YO, K3.

Row 7: K3, (K2 tog, YO, K3) across.

Row 8: K3, P2 tog, (YO, P3, P2 tog) across to last 3 sts, YO, K3.

Repeat Rows 7 and 8 for pattern until Dishcloth measures approximately 8½" from cast on edge, ending by working Row 7.

Last 4 Rows: Knit across.

Bind off all sts in **knit**.

Design by Sue Galucki.

7. RIDGED FURROWS

Shown on page 499.

■■□□ EASY

DISHCLOTH

Cast on 44 sts.

Row 1: (K1, P1) across.

Row 2 (Right side)**:** (P1, K1) across.

Rows 3-5: Repeat Rows 1 and 2 once, then repeat Row 1 once **more**.

See Yarn Overs, page 582.

Row 6: (P1, K1) 3 times, YO, P2 tog *(Fig. 18, page 583)*, (K1, P1, K2, YO, P2 tog) across to last 6 sts, K2, (P1, K1) twice.

Row 7: (K1, P1) 3 times, K2, (P4, K2) 5 times, P2, (K1, P1) twice.

Row 8: (P1, K1) 3 times, P2 tog, YO, K2, (P1, K1, P2 tog, YO, K2) across to last 4 sts, (P1, K1) twice.

Row 9: (K1, P1) 3 times, K2, (P4, K2) 5 times, P2, (K1, P1) twice.

Repeat Rows 6-9 for pattern until Dishcloth measures approximately 8¹/₂" from cast on edge, ending by working a **wrong** side row.

Next Row: (P1, K1) across.

Next 4 Rows: Repeat Rows 2-5.

Bind off all sts in pattern.

Design by Patty Kowaleski.

8. MINI CABLES

Shown on page 499.

■■□□ EASY

STITCH GUIDE

RIGHT TWIST *(abbreviated RT)* (uses 2 sts) K2 tog *(Fig. 17, page 583)* making sure **not** to drop off, then knit the first st letting both sts drop off needle.

DISHCLOTH

Cast on 44 sts.

Rows 1-5: Knit across.

Row 6 (Right side)**:** K5, P1, RT, P1, (K2, P1, RT, P1) across to last 5 sts, K5.

Row 7: K5, purl across to last 5 sts, K5.

Row 8: K5, P1, K2, P1, (RT, P1, K2, P1) across to last 5 sts, K5.

Row 9: K5, purl across to last 5 sts, K5.

Repeat Rows 6-9 for pattern until Dishcloth measures approximately 8¹/₂" from cast on edge, ending by working Row 6.

Last 5 Rows: Knit across.

Bind off all sts in **knit**.

Design by Susan Ackerman.

1. VALENTINE HEARTS

◼️◼️◻️◻️ EASY

Finished Size: 9¹/₂" (24 cm) square

MATERIALS

100% Cotton Medium/Worsted **MEDIUM 4** Weight Yarn
   [122 yards (111.5 meters) per ball**]**: 1 ball
Straight knitting needles, size 7 (4.5 mm) **or** size needed for gauge

GAUGE: In Stockinette Stitch, 5 sts = 1" (2.5 cm)

DISHCLOTH

Cast on 47 sts.

Rows 1-5: K1, (P1, K1) across.

Row 6 (Right side)**:** K1, (P1, K1) twice, P6, K1, (P 11, K1) twice, P6, K1, (P1, K1) twice.

Row 7: (K1, P1) twice, K6, P3, (K9, P3) twice, K6, (P1, K1) twice.

Row 8: K1, (P1, K1) twice, P5, K3, (P9, K3) twice, P5, K1, (P1, K1) twice.

Row 9: (K1, P1) twice, K5, P5, (K7, P5) twice, K5, (P1, K1) twice.

Row 10: K1, (P1, K1) twice, P3, K7, (P5, K7) twice, P3, K1, (P1, K1) twice.

Row 11: (K1, P1) twice, K3, (P9, K3) 3 times, (P1, K1) twice.

Row 12: K1, (P1, K1) twice, P2, K9, (P3, K9) twice, P2, K1, (P1, K1) twice.

Row 13: (K1, P1) twice, K3, (P9, K3) 3 times, (P1, K1) twice.

Row 14: K1, (P1, K1) twice, P2, K4, P1, K4, (P3, K4, P1, K4) twice, P2, K1, (P1, K1) twice.

Row 15: (K1, P1) 3 times, (K2, P2, K3, P2, K2, P1) 3 times, K1, (P1, K1) twice.

Row 16: (K1, P1) twice, K2, P 11, (K1, P 11) twice, K2, (P1, K1) twice.

Row 17: K1, (P1, K1) twice, P2, K9, (P3, K9) twice, P2, K1, (P1, K1) twice.

Row 18: (K1, P1) twice, K3, (P9, K3) 3 times, (P1, K1) twice.

Row 19: K1, (P1, K1) twice, P3, K7, (P5, K7) twice, P3, K1, (P1, K1) twice.

Row 20: (K1, P1) twice, K5, P5, (K7, P5) twice, K5, (P1, K1) twice.

Row 21: K1, (P1, K1) twice, P5, K3, (P9, K3) twice, P5, K1, (P1, K1) twice.

Row 22: (K1, P1) twice, K6, P3, (K9, P3) twice, K6, (P1, K1) twice.

Row 23: K1, (P1, K1) twice, P5, K3, (P9, K3) twice, P5, K1, (P1, K1) twice.

Row 24: (K1, P1) 3 times, (K4, P3, K4, P1) 3 times, K1, (P1, K1) twice.

Row 25: (K1, P1) twice, K3, (P2, K2, P1, K2, P2, K3) 3 times, (P1, K1) twice.

Repeat Rows 6-25 for pattern until Dishcloth measures approximately 9" (23 cm) from cast on edge, ending by working a **wrong** side row.

Last 5 Rows: K1, (P1, K1) across.

Bind off all sts in pattern.

1

2

3

4

5

2. BASIC DIAMONDS

Shown on page 505.

■■□□ EASY

Finished Size: 9" (23 cm) square

MATERIALS

100% Cotton Medium/Worsted Weight Yarn
    MEDIUM 4
    [120 yards (109 meters) per ball**]**: 1 ball
Straight knitting needles, size 7 (4.5 mm) **or** size needed for gauge

GAUGE: In Stockinette Stitch, 5 sts = 1" (2.5 cm)

DISHCLOTH

Cast on 45 sts.

Rows 1-4: Knit across.

Row 5 (Right side)**:** K7, P1, (K5, P1) 5 times, K7.

Row 6: K4, P2, K1, P1, K1, (P3, K1, P1, K1) 5 times, P2, K4.

Row 7: K5, P1, K3, P1, (K1, P1, K3, P1) 5 times, K5.

Row 8: K5, P5, (K1, P5) 5 times, K5.

Row 9: K5, P1, K3, P1, (K1, P1, K3, P1) 5 times, K5.

Row 10: K4, P2, K1, P1, K1, (P3, K1, P1, K1) 5 times, P2, K4.

Repeat Rows 5-10 for pattern until Dishcloth measures approximately 8½" (21.5 cm) from cast on edge, ending by working Row 5.

Last 4 Rows: Knit across.

Bind off all sts in **knit**.

Design by Susan Carter.

3. CROCUS BUDS

Shown on page 505.

■■■□ INTERMEDIATE

Finished Size: 9¹/₂" (24 cm) square

MATERIALS

100% Cotton Medium/Worsted
Weight Yarn
[120 yards (109 meters) per ball]: 1 ball
Straight knitting needles, size 7 (4.5 mm) **or** size
needed for gauge

GAUGE: In Stockinette Stitch, 5 sts = 1" (2.5 cm)

DISHCLOTH

Cast on 45 sts.

Rows 1-5: K1, (P1, K1) across.

Row 6 (Right side): (K1, P1) 3 times, YO
(Fig. 16c, page 582), ★ K2, YO *(Fig. 16a, page 582)*; repeat from ★ across to last 7 sts, K3, (P1, K1) twice: 62 sts.

Row 7: K1, (P1, K1) twice, P4, with left needle bring the third st on right needle over the first 2 sts and off the needle, ★ P3, with left needle bring the third st on right needle over the first 2 sts and off the needle; repeat from ★ across to last 5 sts, K1, (P1, K1) twice: 45 sts.

Row 8: (K1, P1) twice, K3, (YO, K2) across to last 4 sts, (P1, K1) twice: 62 sts.

Row 9: K1, (P1, K1) twice, ★ P3, with left needle bring the third st on right needle over the first 2 sts and off the needle; repeat from ★ across to last 6 sts, (P1, K1) 3 times: 45 sts.

Row 10: (K1, P1) 3 times, YO, (K2, YO) across to last 7 sts, K3, (P1, K1) twice: 62 sts.

Repeat Rows 7-10 for pattern until Dishcloth measures approximately 9" (23 cm) from cast on edge, ending by working a **wrong** side row.

Last 5 Rows: K1, (P1, K1) across.

Bind off all sts in pattern.

4. CLIMBING LATTICE

Shown on page 505.

■■■□ INTERMEDIATE

Finished Size: 9" (23 cm) square

MATERIALS

100% Cotton Medium/Worsted
Weight Yarn
    [95 yards (86 meters) per ball]: 1 ball
Straight knitting needles, size 7 (4.5 mm) **or** size
needed for gauge

GAUGE: In Stockinette Stitch, 5 sts = 1" (2.5 cm)

STITCH GUIDE

LEFT TWIST *(abbreviated LT)* (uses 2 sts)
Working **behind** first st on left needle, knit into
the back of second st *(Fig. A)* making sure **not** to
drop off, then knit the first st *(Fig. B)* letting both
sts drop off needle.

Fig. A   **Fig. B**

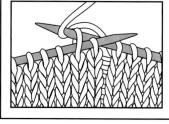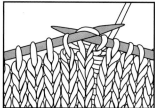

DISHCLOTH

Cast on 44 sts.

Row 1: (K1, P1) across.

Row 2 (Right side)**:** (P1, K1) across.

Rows 3-5: Repeat Rows 1 and 2 once, then
repeat Row 1 once **more**.

Row 6: P1, (K1, P1) twice, LT twice, ★ [YO
(Fig. 16a, page 582), K2 tog *(Fig. 17,
page 583)*] 3 times, LT twice; repeat from ★
2 times **more**, K1, (P1, K1) twice.

Row 7: K1, (P1, K1) twice, purl across to last
4 sts, (K1, P1) twice.

Row 8: P1, (K1, P1) twice, LT twice, ★ (K2 tog,
YO) 3 times, LT twice; repeat from ★ 2 times
more, K1, (P1, K1) twice.

Row 9: K1, (P1, K1) twice, purl across to last
4 sts, (K1, P1) twice.

Row 10: P1, (K1, P1) twice, LT twice, ★ (YO,
K2 tog) 3 times, LT twice; repeat from ★ 2 times
more, K1, (P1, K1) twice.

Repeat Rows 7-10 for pattern until Dishcloth
measures approximately 8$^1/_2$" (21.5 cm) from cast
on edge, ending by working a **wrong** side row.

Next Row: (P1, K1) across.

Last 4 Rows: Repeat Rows 1 and 2 twice.

Bind off all sts in pattern.

Design by Patty Kowaleski.

5. ELFIN LACE

Shown on page 505.

Finished Size: 9" (23 cm) square

MATERIALS

100% Cotton Medium/Worsted Weight Yarn
[122 yards (112 meters) per ball]: 1 ball
Straight knitting needles, size 7 (4.5 mm) **or** size needed for gauge

GAUGE: In Stockinette Stitch, 5 sts = 1" (2.5 cm)

DISHCLOTH

Cast on 47 sts.

Rows 1-5: K1, (P1, K1) across.

Note: When instructed to slip sts, always slip as if to **knit**.

Row 6 AND ALL WRONG SIDE ROWS: K1, (P1, K1) twice, purl across to last 5 sts, K1, (P1, K1) twice.

Row 7 (Right side)**:** (K1, P1) twice, K7, YO *(Fig. 16a, page 582)*, SSK *(Figs. 21a-c, page 584)*, (K6, YO, SSK) 3 times, K6, (P1, K1) twice.

Row 9: (K1, P1) twice, K5, K2 tog *(Fig. 17, page 583)*, YO, K1, YO, SSK, (K3, K2 tog, YO, K1, YO, SSK) 3 times, K5, (P1, K1) twice.

Row 11: (K1, P1) twice, K4, K2 tog, YO, K3, YO, SSK, (K1, K2 tog, YO, K3, YO, SSK) 3 times, K4, (P1, K1) twice.

Row 13: (K1, P1) twice, K6, YO, [slip 2, K1, P2SSO *(Figs. 27a & b, page 585)*], YO, (K5, YO, slip 2, K1, P2SSO, YO) 3 times, K6, (P1, K1) twice.

Row 15: (K1, P1) twice, K3, YO, SSK, (K6, YO, SSK) 4 times, K2, (P1, K1) twice.

Row 17: K1, (P1, K1) twice, K2 tog, YO, K1, YO, SSK, (K3, K2 tog, YO, K1, YO, SSK) 4 times, K1, (P1, K1) twice.

Row 19: (K1, P1) twice, K2 tog, YO, K3, YO, SSK, (K1, K2 tog, YO, K3, YO, SSK) 4 times, (P1, K1) twice.

Row 21: (K1, P1) twice, K2, YO, slip 2, K1, P2SSO, YO, (K5, YO, slip 2, K1, P2SSO, YO) 4 times, K2, (P1, K1) twice.

Repeat Rows 6-21 for pattern until Dishcloth measures approximately 8¹/₂" (21.5 cm) from cast on edge, ending by working a **wrong** side row.

Last 5 Rows: K1, (P1, K1) across.

Bind off all sts in pattern.

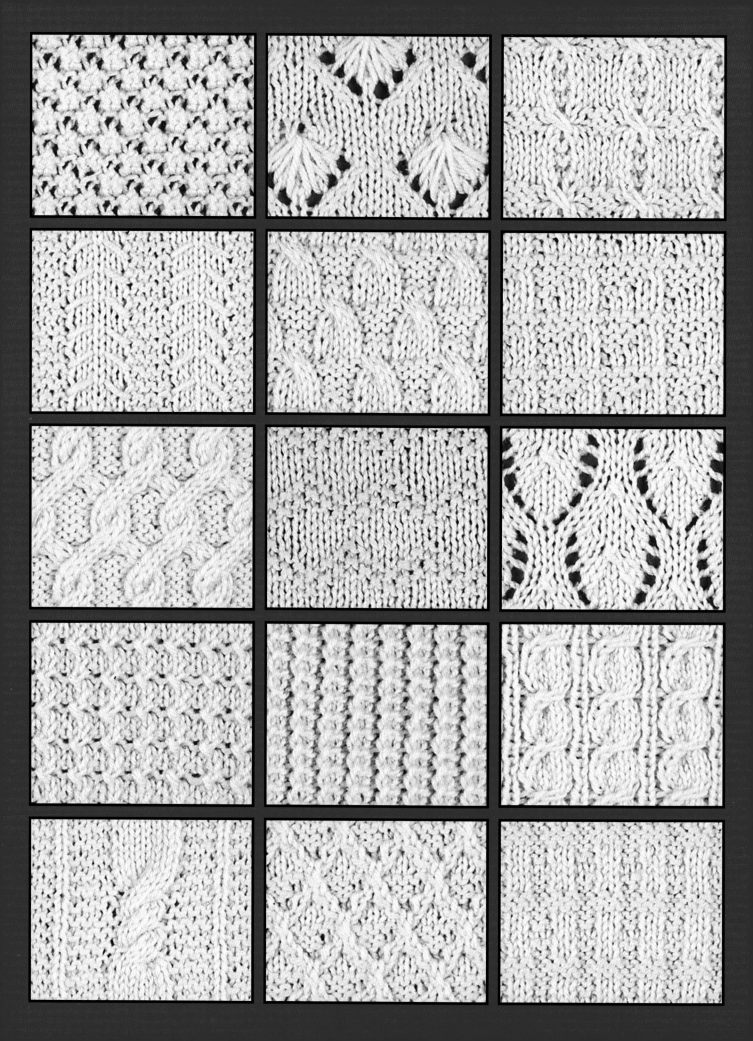

99 knit stitches

A s easy to use as a dictionary, this giant knitting section includes step-by-step instructions and close-up photos for 99 beautiful pattern stitches. You'll consult this handy reference time and time again to experiment with new stitches and spice up your knitting. The alphabetical arrangement makes it simple to find your favorites. Seven eye-catching projects — two mufflers, two pillows, two sweaters, and an afghan — are presented to show how the pattern stitches can be used. With all these irresistible pattern stitches at your fingertips, you're set for a lifetime of exciting knitting!

PATTERN STITCHES

1. Bee Stitch

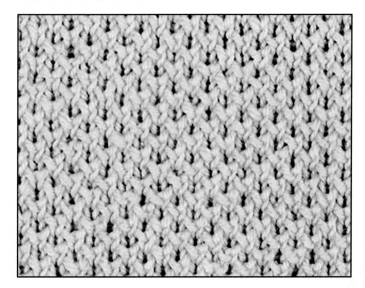

Multiple of 2 sts + 1.

Row 1: Knit across.

Row 2 (Right side)**:** K1, ★ K1 below *(Fig. A, page 500)*, K1; repeat from ★ across.

Row 3: Knit across.

Row 4: K2, K1 below, (K1, K1 below) across to last 2 sts, K2.

Repeat Rows 1-4 for pattern.

2. Berry Stitch

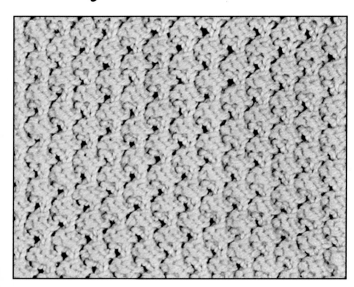

Multiple of 4 sts + 3.

Row 1 (Right side)**:** K1, [K, K tbl *(Fig. 4a, page 580)*, K] **all** in next st, ★ P3, (K, K tbl, K) **all** in next st; repeat from ★ across to last st, K1.

Row 2: K4, P3 tog *(Fig. 24, page 584)*, (K3, P3 tog) across to last 4 sts, K4.

Row 3: K1, P3, ★ (K, K tbl, K) **all** in next st, P3; repeat from ★ across to last st, K1.

Row 4: K1, P3 tog, (K3, P3 tog) across to last st, K1.

Repeat Rows 1-4 for pattern.

3. Bordered Diamonds

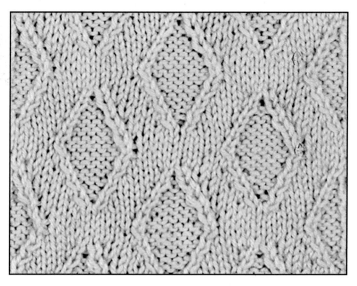

Multiple of 18 sts + 2.

Row 1: P6, K8, (P 10, K8) across to last 6 sts, P6.

Row 2 (Right side)**:** K5, work Back Cross *(Figs. 8a & b, page 580)*, P6, work Front Cross *(Figs. 9a & b, page 580)*, ★ K8, work Back Cross, P6, work Front Cross; repeat from ★ across to last 5 sts, K5.

Row 3: P7, K6, (P 12, K6) across to last 7 sts, P7.

Row 4: K1, ★ LT *(Figs. 6a & b, page 580)*, K3, work Back Cross, P4, work Front Cross, K3, RT *(Figs. 7a & b, page 580)*; repeat from ★ across to last st, K1.

Row 5: K2, (P6, K4, P6, K2) across.

Row 6: P2, ★ LT, K3, work Back Cross, P2, work Front Cross, K3, RT, P2; repeat from ★ across.

Row 7: K3, P6, K2, P6, (K4, P6, K2, P6) across to last 3 sts, K3.

Row 8: P3, LT, K3, work Back Cross, work Front Cross, K3, RT, ★ P4, LT, K3, work Back Cross, work Front Cross, K3, RT; repeat from ★ across to last 3 sts, P3.

Row 9: K4, P 12, (K6, P 12) across to last 4 sts, K4.

Row 10: P4, LT, K8, RT, (P6, LT, K8, RT) across to last 4 sts, P4.

Row 11: K5, P 10, (K8, P 10) across to last 5 sts, K5.

Row 12: P4, work Front Cross, K8, work Back Cross, (P6, work Front Cross, K8, work Back Cross) across to last 4 sts, P4.

Row 13: K4, P 12, (K6, P 12) across to last 4 sts, K4.

Row 14: P3, work Front Cross, K3, RT, LT, K3, work Back Cross, ★ P4, work Front Cross, K3, RT, LT, K3, work Back Cross; repeat from ★ across to last 3 sts, P3.

Row 15: K3, P6, K2, P6, (K4, P6, K2, P6) across to last 3 sts, K3.

Row 16: P2, ★ work Front Cross, K3, RT, P2, LT, K3, work Back Cross, P2; repeat from ★ across.

Row 17: K2, (P6, K4, P6, K2) across.

Row 18: K1, ★ work Front Cross, K3, RT, P4, LT, K3, work Back Cross; repeat from ★ across to last st, K1.

Row 19: P7, K6, (P 12, K6) across to last 7 sts, P7.

Row 20: K5, RT, P6, LT, (K8, RT, P6, LT) across to last 5 sts, K5.

Repeat Rows 1-20 for pattern.

4. Cable - Boxes & Bells

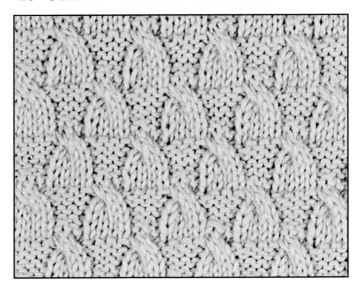

Multiple of 8 sts + 6.

Additional materials: Cable needle

Cable 4 Front (abbreviated **C4F**) (uses next 4 sts) Slip next 2 sts onto cable needle and hold in **front** of work, K2 from left needle, K2 from cable needle.

Row 1 (Right side)**:** K5, P4, (K4, P4) across to last 5 sts, K5.

Row 2: P5, K4, (P4, K4) across to last 5 sts, P5.

Rows 3 and 4: Repeat Rows 1 and 2.

Row 5: K1, C4F, (K4, C4F) across to last st, K1.

Row 6: K5, P4, (K4, P4) across to last 5 sts, K5.

Row 7: P5, K4, (P4, K4) across to last 5 sts, P5.

Row 8: K5, P4, (K4, P4) across to last 5 sts, K5.

Rows 9 and 10: Repeat Rows 7 and 8.

Row 11: K5, C4F, (K4, C4F) across to last 5 sts, K5.

Row 12: P5, K4, (P4, K4) across to last 5 sts, P5.

Repeat Rows 1-12 for pattern.

5. Cable - Cable & Eyelets

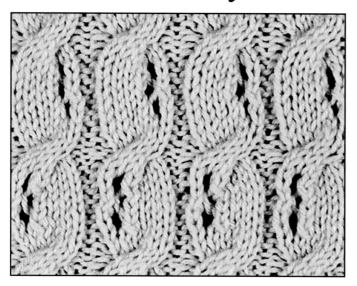

Multiple of 8 sts + 2.

Additional materials: Cable needle

Cable 6 Back *(abbreviated C6B)* (uses next 6 sts)
Slip next 3 sts onto cable needle and hold in **back** of work, K3 from left needle, K3 from cable needle.

Row 1 AND ALL WRONG SIDE ROWS: K2, (P6, K2) across.

Row 2 (Right side)**:** P2, (K6, P2) across.

Row 4: P2, (C6B, P2) across.

Row 6: P2, (K6, P2) across.

Row 8: P2, ★ K1, YO *(Fig. 16a, page 582)*, K2 tog *(Fig. 17, page 583)*, K3, P2; repeat from ★ across.

Row 10: P2, ★ [slip 1 as if to **knit**, K1, PSSO *(Figs. 19a & b, page 583)*], YO, K4, P2; repeat from ★ across.

Row 12: P2, (K1, YO, K2 tog, K3, P2) across.

Row 14: P2, (K6, P2) across.

Row 16: P2, (C6B, P2) across.

Row 18: P2, (K6, P2) across.

Row 20: P2, ★ K3, slip 1 as if to **knit**, K1, PSSO, YO, K1, P2; repeat from ★ across.

Row 22: P2, (K4, YO, K2 tog, P2) across.

Row 24: P2, ★ K3, slip 1 as if to **knit**, K1, PSSO, YO, K1, P2; repeat from ★ across.

Repeat Rows 1-24 for pattern.

6. Cable - Cable & Garter Fabric

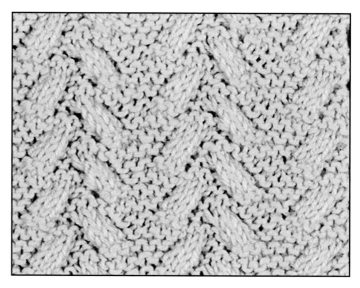

Multiple of 13 sts + 2.

Additional materials: Cable needle

Cable 4 Right *(abbreviated C4R)* (uses next 4 sts)
Slip next st onto cable needle and hold in **back** of work, K3 from left needle, K1 from cable needle.

Cable 4 Left *(abbreviated C4L)* (uses next 4 sts)
Slip next 3 sts onto cable needle and hold in **front** of work, K1 from left needle, K3 from cable needle.

Row 1: K2, (P3, K 10) across.

Row 2 (Right side)**:** K3, C4R, K3, C4L, (K2, C4R, K3, C4L) across to last st, K1.

Row 3: K9, P3, (K 10, P3) across to last 3 sts, K3.

Row 4: K2, (C4R, K9) across.

Row 5: (K 10, P3) across to last 2 sts, K2.

Row 6: K1, C4R, K3, C4L, (K2, C4R, K3, C4L) across to last 3 sts, K3.

Row 7: K3, P3, (K 10, P3) across to last 9 sts, K9.

Row 8: (K9, C4L) across to last 2 sts, K2.

Repeat Rows 1-8 for pattern.

7. Cable - Cable & Lace

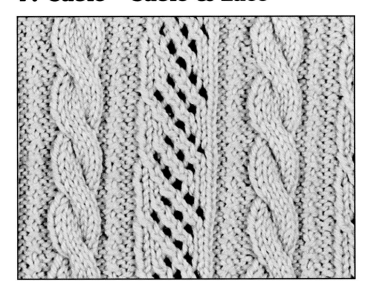

Multiple of 23 sts + 7.

Additional materials: Cable needle

Cable 6 Front *(abbreviated C6F)* (uses next 6 sts)
Slip next 3 sts onto cable needle and hold in **front** of work, K3 from left needle, K3 from cable needle.

Row 1 AND ALL WRONG SIDE ROWS: P7, (K5, P6, K5, P7) across.

Row 2 (Right side)**:** K3, YO *(Fig. 16a, page 582)*, **[**slip 1 as if to **knit**, K1, PSSO *(Figs. 19a & b, page 583)***]**, K2, ★ P2, K1, P2, C6F, P2, K1, P2, K3, YO, slip 1 as if to **knit**, K1, PSSO, K2; repeat from ★ across.

Row 4: K2, (YO, slip 1 as if to **knit**, K1, PSSO) twice, ★ (K1, P2) twice, K6, P2, K1, P2, K2, (YO, slip 1 as if to **knit**, K1, PSSO) twice; repeat from ★ across to last st, K1.

Row 6: K1, (YO, slip 1 as if to **knit**, K1, PSSO) 3 times, ★ P2, K1, P2, K6, (P2, K1) twice, (YO, slip 1 as if to **knit**, K1, PSSO) 3 times; repeat from ★ across.

Row 8: K2, (YO, slip 1 as if to **knit**, K1, PSSO) twice, ★ (K1, P2) twice, K6, P2, K1, P2, K2, (YO, slip 1 as if to **knit**, K1, PSSO) twice; repeat from ★ across to last st, K1.

Repeat Rows 1-8 for pattern.

8. Cable - Cable Panels

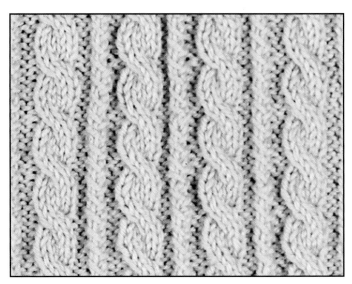

Multiple of 10 sts + 4.

Additional materials: Cable needle

Cable 4 Front *(abbreviated C4F)* (uses next 4 sts) Slip next 2 sts onto cable needle and hold in **front** of work, K2 from left needle, K2 from cable needle.

Twist (uses next 2 sts)
With yarn in back, insert right needle through next st as if to **purl**, knit second st on needle and draw loop through first st *(Fig. A)* being careful **not** to drop off, then knit into the **back** of first st *(Fig. B)* letting both sts drop off needle together.

Fig. A   **Fig. B**

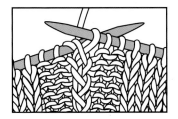   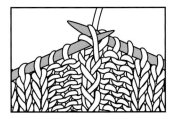

Row 1 AND ALL WRONG SIDE ROWS: K1, P2, (K2, P4, K2, P2) across to last st, K1.

Row 2 (Right side)**:** P1, work Twist, (P2, C4F, P2, work Twist) across to last st, P1.

Row 4: P1, work Twist, (P2, K4, P2, work Twist) across to last st, P1.

Row 6: P1, work Twist, (P2, K4, P2, work Twist) across to last st, P1.

Repeat Rows 1-6 for pattern.

9. Cable - Cables & Twists

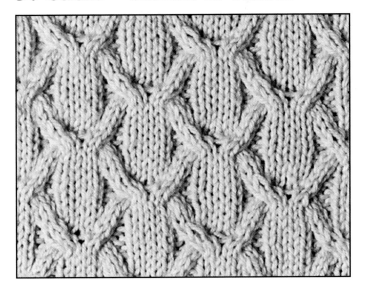

Multiple of 16 sts + 2.

Additional materials: Cable needle

Cable 4 Back *(abbreviated C4B)* (uses next 4 sts)
Slip next 2 sts onto cable needle and hold in **back** of work, K2 from left needle, K2 from cable needle.

Cable 4 Front *(abbreviated C4F)* (uses next 4 sts)
Slip next 2 sts onto cable needle and hold in **front** of work, K2 from left needle, K2 from cable needle.

Twist 3 Back *(abbreviated T3B)* (uses next 3 sts)
Slip next st onto cable needle and hold in **back** of work, K2 from left needle, P1 from cable needle.

Twist 3 Front *(abbreviated T3F)* (uses next 3 sts)
Slip next 2 sts onto cable needle and hold in **front** of work, P1 from left needle, K2 from cable needle.

Row 1: P3, K2, P8, K2, (P4, K2, P8, K2) across to last 3 sts, P3.

Row 2 (Right side)**:** K3, P2, C4B, C4F, P2, (K4, P2, C4B, C4F, P2) across to last 3 sts, K3.

Row 3: Repeat Row 1.

Row 4: K3, P1, T3B, K4, T3F, P1, (K4, P1, T3B, K4, T3F, P1) across to last 3 sts, K3.

Row 5: P3, K1, P2, K1, (P4, K1, P2, K1) across to last 3 sts, P3.

Row 6: K3, T3B, P1, K4, P1, T3F, (K4, T3B, P1, K4, P1, T3F) across to last 3 sts, K3.

Row 7: P5, K2, P4, K2, (P8, K2, P4, K2) across to last 5 sts, P5.

Row 8: K1, (C4F, P2, K4, P2, C4B) across to last st, K1.

Row 9: P5, K2, P4, K2, (P8, K2, P4, K2) across to last 5 sts, P5.

Row 10: K3, T3F, P1, K4, P1, T3B, (K4, T3F, P1, K4, P1, T3B) across to last 3 sts, K3.

Row 11: P3, K1, P2, K1, (P4, K1, P2, K1) across to last 3 sts, P3.

Row 12: K3, P1, T3F, K4, T3B, P1, (K4, P1, T3F, K4, T3B, P1) across to last 3 sts, K3.

Repeat Rows 1-12 for pattern.

10. Cable - Corkscrew Panels

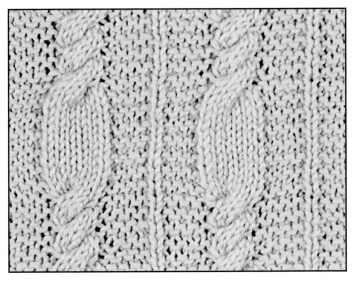

Multiple of 15 sts + 5.

Additional materials: Cable needle

Cable 6 Back *(abbreviated C6B)* (uses next 6 sts)
Slip next 3 sts onto cable needle and hold in **back** of work, K3 from left needle, K3 from cable needle.

Row 1 (Right side)**:** Knit across.

Row 2 AND ALL WRONG SIDE ROWS: K2, P1, (K4, P6, K4, P1) across to last 2 sts, K2.

Row 3: Knit across.

Row 5: K7, C6B, (K9, C6B) across to last 7 sts, K7.

Row 7: Knit across.

Row 9: K7, C6B, (K9, C6B) across to last 7 sts, K7.

Row 11: Knit across.

Row 13: K7, C6B, (K9, C6B) across to last 7 sts, K7.

Row 15: Knit across.

Row 17: Knit across.

Row 19: Knit across.

Row 21: Knit across.

Row 23: Knit across.

Row 25: Knit across.

Repeat Rows 2-25 for pattern.

11. Cable - Diagonal Lozenge

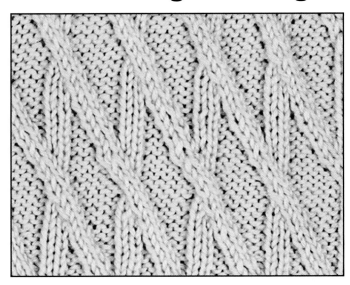

Multiple of 8 sts + 4.

Additional materials: Cable needle

Cable 3 Front *(abbreviated C3F)* (uses next 3 sts)
Slip next 2 sts onto cable needle and hold in **front** of work, K1 from left needle, K2 from cable needle.

Twist 3 Front *(abbreviated T3F)* (uses next 3 sts)
Slip next 2 sts onto cable needle and hold in **front** of work, P1 from left needle, K2 from cable needle.

Row 1: K1, P2, (K6, P2) across to last st, K1.

Row 2 (Right side)**:** P1, (C3F, P5) across to last 3 sts, K2, P1.

Row 3: K1, P2, (K5, P3) across to last st, K1.

Row 4: P1, (K1, C3F, P4) across to last 3 sts, K2, P1.

Row 5: K1, P2, (K4, P4) across to last st, K1.

Row 6: P1, K2, (T3F, P3, K2) across to last st, P1.

Row 7: K1, P2, (K3, P2, K1, P2) across to last st, K1.

Row 8: P1, K2, P1, (T3F, P2, K2, P1) across.

Row 9: K1, P2, (K2, P2) across to last st, K1.

Row 10: P1, K2, (P2, T3F, P1, K2) across to last st, P1.

Row 11: (K1, P2) twice, K3, P2, (K1, P2, K3, P2) across to last st, K1.

Row 12: P1, K2, (P3, T3F, K2) across to last st, P1.

Row 13: K1, (P4, K4) across to last 3 sts, P2, K1.

Row 14: P1, K2, (P4, T3F, K1) across to last st, P1.

Row 15: K1, (P3, K5) across to last 3 sts, P2, K1.

Row 16: P1, K2, (P5, T3F) across to last st, P1.

Repeat Rows 1-16 for pattern.

12. Cable - Dotted Fabric

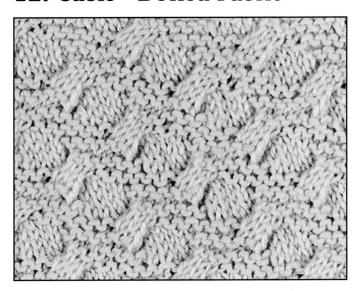

Multiple of 12 sts + 2.

Additional materials: Cable needle

Cable 6 Back *(abbreviated C6B)* (uses next 6 sts)
Slip next 3 sts onto cable needle and hold in **back** of work, K3 from left needle, K3 from cable needle.

Row 1 (Right side)**:** Knit across.

Row 2: P3, K6, (P6, K6) across to last 5 sts, P5.

Row 3: Knit across.

Row 4: P1, (K6, P6) across to last st, K1.

Row 5: K1, C6B, (K6, C6B) across to last 7 sts, K7.

Row 6: K5, P6, (K6, P6) across to last 3 sts, K3.

Row 7: Knit across.

Row 8: K3, P6, (K6, P6) across to last 5 sts, K5.

Row 9: Knit across.

Row 10: K1, (P6, K6) across to last st, P1.

Row 11: K7, C6B, (K6, C6B) across to last st, K1.

Row 12: P5, K6, (P6, K6) across to last 3 sts, P3.

Repeat Rows 1-12 for pattern.

13. Cable - Grillwork Lattice

Multiple of 8 sts + 2.

Additional materials: Cable needle

Cable 4 Back *(abbreviated C4B)* (uses next 4 sts)
Slip next 2 sts onto cable needle and hold in **back** of work, K2 from left needle, K2 from cable needle.

Twist 4 Back *(abbreviated T4B)* (uses next 4 sts)
Slip next 2 sts onto cable needle and hold in **back** of work, K2 from left needle, P2 from cable needle.

Twist 4 Front *(abbreviated T4F)* (uses next 4 sts)
Slip next 2 sts onto cable needle and hold in **front** of work, P2 from left needle, K2 from cable needle.

Row 1 (Right side): P1, K2, P4, (K4, P4) across to last 3 sts, K2, P1.

Row 2: K1, P2, K4, (P4, K4) across to last 3 sts, P2, K1.

Row 3: P1, K2, P4, (C4B, P4) across to last 3 sts, K2, P1.

Row 4: K1, P2, K4, (P4, K4) across to last 3 sts, P2, K1.

Row 5: P1, (T4F, T4B) across to last st, P1.

Row 6: K3, P4, (K4, P4) across to last 3 sts, K3.

Row 7: P3, C4B, (P4, C4B) across to last 3 sts, P3.

Row 8: K3, P4, (K4, P4) across to last 3 sts, K3.

Row 9: P3, K4, (P4, K4) across to last 3 sts, P3.

Rows 10-20: Repeat Rows 6-9 twice, then repeat Rows 6-8 once **more**.

Row 21: P1, (T4B, T4F) across to last st, P1.

Row 22: K1, P2, K4, (P4, K4) across to last 3 sts, P2, K1.

Row 23: P1, K2, P4, (C4B, P4) across to last 3 sts, K2, P1.

Row 24: K1, P2, K4, (P4, K4) across to last 3 sts, P2, K1.

Repeat Rows 1-24 for pattern.

14. Cable - Honeycomb Trellis

Multiple of 6 sts + 2.

Additional materials: Cable needle

Row 1 (Right side): K2, (P4, K2) across.

Row 2: P2, (K4, P2) across.

Row 3: K1, ★ slip next st onto cable needle and hold in **front** of work, P2 from left needle, K1 from cable needle, slip next 2 sts onto cable needle and hold in **back** of work, K1 from left needle, P2 from cable needle; repeat from ★ across to last st, K1.

Row 4: K3, P2, (K4, P2) across to last 3 sts, K3.

Row 5: P3, K2, (P4, K2) across to last 3 sts, P3.

Row 6: K3, P2, (K4, P2) across to last 3 sts, K3.

Row 7: K1, ★ slip next 2 sts onto cable needle and hold in **back** of work, K1 from left needle, P2 from cable needle, slip next st onto cable needle and hold in **front** of work, P2 from left needle, K1 from cable needle; repeat from ★ across to last st, K1.

Row 8: P2, (K4, P2) across.

Repeat Rows 1-8 for pattern.

15. Cable - Hourglass Stripes

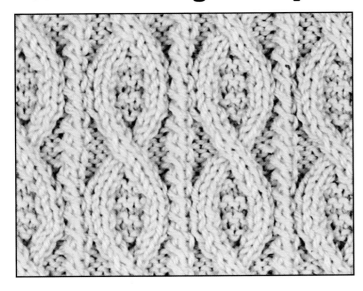

Multiple of 12 sts + 4.

Additional materials: Cable needle

Twist 3 Back *(abbreviated T3B)* (uses next 3 sts)
Slip next st onto cable needle and hold in **back** of work, K2 from left needle, P1 from cable needle.

Twist 3 Front *(abbreviated T3F)* (uses next 3 sts)
Slip next 2 sts onto cable needle and hold in **front** of work, P1 from left needle, K2 from cable needle.

Cable 3 Back *(abbreviated C3B)* (uses next 3 sts)
Slip next st onto cable needle and hold in **back** of work, K2 from left needle, K1 from cable needle.

Cable 3 Front *(abbreviated C3F)* (uses next 3 sts)
Slip next 2 sts onto cable needle and hold in **front** of work, K1 from left needle, K2 from cable needle.

Cable 4 Front *(abbreviated C4F)* (uses next 4 sts)
Slip next 2 sts onto cable needle and hold in **front** of work, K2 from left needle, K2 from cable needle.

Row 1: K1, P2, K1, ★ P2, K4, (P2, K1) twice; repeat from ★ across.

Row 2 (Right side)**:** P1, work Back Cross *(Figs. 8a & b, page 580)*, P1, (K8, P1, work Back Cross, P1) across.

Row 3: K1, P2, K1, ★ P2, K4, (P2, K1) twice; repeat from ★ across.

Row 4: P1, work Back Cross, P1, ★ T3F, K2, T3B, P1, work Back Cross, P1; repeat from ★ across.

Row 5: K1, P2, (K2, P2) across to last st, K1.

Row 6: P1, work Back Cross, ★ P2, T3F, T3B, P2, work Back Cross; repeat from ★ across to last st, P1.

Row 7: K1, P2, (K3, P4, K3, P2) across to last st, K1.

Row 8: P1, work Back Cross, ★ P3, C4F, P3, work Back Cross; repeat from ★ across to last st, P1.

Row 9: K1, P2, (K3, P4, K3, P2) across to last st, K1.

Row 10: P1, work Back Cross, ★ P2, C3B, C3F, P2, work Back Cross; repeat from ★ across to last st, P1.

Row 11: K1, P2, (K2, P2) across to last st, K1.

Row 12: P1, work Back Cross, P1, ★ C3B, K2, C3F, P1, work Back Cross, P1; repeat from ★ across.

Row 13: K1, P2, K1, ★ P2, K4, (P2, K1) twice; repeat from ★ across.

Row 14: P1, work Back Cross, P1, (K8, P1, work Back Cross, P1) across.

Repeat Rows 1-14 for pattern.

16. Cable - Ribbed Cables

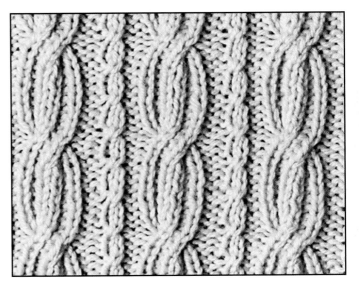

Multiple of 14 sts + 2.

Additional materials: Cable needle

Row 1: P2, (K2, P1, K2, P2) across.

Row 2 (Right side)**:** K2, (P2, K1, P2, K2) across.

Row 3: P2, (K2, P1, K2, P2) across.

Row 4: Work Front Cross *(Figs. 9a & b, page 580)*, ★ P2, K1, P2, K2, P2, K1, P2, work Front Cross; repeat from ★ across.

Rows 5-11: Repeat Rows 1-4 once, then repeat Rows 1-3 once **more**.

Row 12: Work Front Cross, ★ P2, slip next 4 sts onto cable needle and hold in **back** of work, (K1, P2, K1) from left needle, (K1, P2, K1) from cable needle, P2, work Front Cross; repeat from ★ across.

Repeat Rows 1-12 for pattern.

17. Cable - Shadow Cable

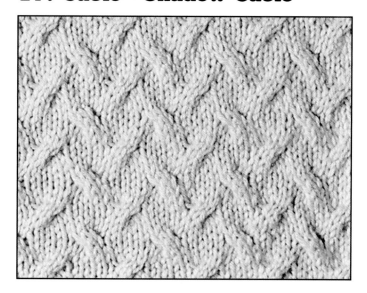

Multiple of 8 sts + 2.

Additional materials: Cable needle

Cable 4 Back *(abbreviated C4B)* (uses next 4 sts)
Slip next 2 sts onto cable needle and hold in **back** of work, K2 from left needle, K2 from cable needle.

Cable 4 Front *(abbreviated C4F)* (uses next 4 sts)
Slip next 2 sts onto cable needle and hold in **front** of work, K2 from left needle, K2 from cable needle.

Row 1 AND ALL WRONG SIDE ROWS: Purl across.

Row 2 (Right side)**:** Knit across.

Row 4: K1, C4B, (K4, C4B) across to last 5 sts, K5.

Row 6: Knit across.

Row 8: K5, C4F, (K4, C4F) across to last st, K1.

Repeat Rows 1-8 for pattern.

18. Cable - Six Stitch Cable

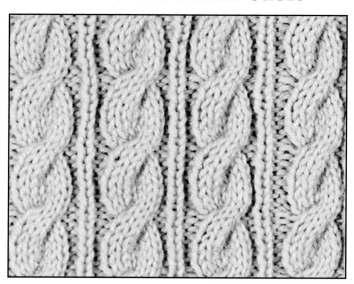

Multiple of 11 sts + 1.

Additional materials: Cable needle

Cable 6 Back *(abbreviated C6B)* (uses next 6 sts)
Slip next 3 sts onto cable needle and hold in **back** of work, K3 from left needle, K3 from cable needle.

Row 1 AND ALL WRONG SIDE ROWS: P1, (K2, P6, K2, P1) across.

Row 2 (Right side)**:** K1, (P2, K6, P2, K1) across.

Row 4: K1, (P2, K6, P2, K1) across.

Row 6: K1, (P2, C6B, P2, K1) across.

Row 8: K1, (P2, K6, P2, K1) across.

Repeat Rows 1-8 for pattern.

19. Cable - Small Wheatear

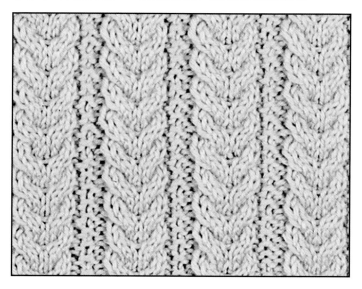

Multiple of 11 sts + 3.

Additional materials: Cable needle

> **Cable 4 Back** *(abbreviated C4B)* (uses next 4 sts)
> Slip next 2 sts onto cable needle and hold in **back** of work, K2 from left needle, K2 from cable needle.
>
> **Cable 4 Front** *(abbreviated C4F)* (uses next 4 sts)
> Slip next 2 sts onto cable needle and hold in **front** of work, K2 from left needle, K2 from cable needle.

Row 1: K3, (P8, K3) across.

Row 2 (Right side)**:** P1, K1, P1, (C4B, C4F, P1, K1, P1) across.

Row 3: K3, (P8, K3) across.

Row 4: P1, K1, P1, (K8, P1, K1, P1) across.

Repeat Rows 1-4 for pattern.

20. Cable - Twisted Cable

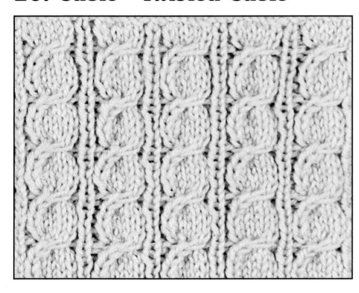

Multiple of 8 sts + 1.

Additional materials: Cable needle

Row 1 AND ALL WRONG SIDE ROWS: P1, (K1, P5, K1, P1) across.

Row 2 (Right side)**:** K1, ★ P1, slip next 4 sts onto cable needle and hold in **back** of work, K1 from left needle, slip last 3 sts from cable needle back onto left needle and knit them, K1 from cable needle, P1, K1; repeat from ★ across.

Row 4: K1, (P1, K5, P1, K1) across.

Row 6: K1, (P1, K5, P1, K1) across.

Repeat Rows 1-6 for pattern.

21. Cable - Woven Lattice

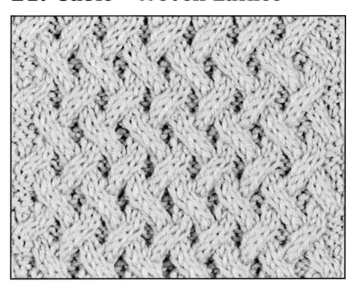

Multiple of 6 sts + 2.

Additional materials: Cable needle

> **Cable 4 Back** *(abbreviated C4B)* (uses next 4 sts)
> Slip next 2 sts onto cable needle and hold in **back** of work, K2 from left needle, K2 from cable needle.
>
> **Cable 4 Front** *(abbreviated C4F)* (uses next 4 sts)
> Slip next 2 sts onto cable needle and hold in **front** of work, K2 from left needle, K2 from cable needle.
>
> **Twist 4 Back** *(abbreviated T4B)* (uses next 4 sts)
> Slip next 2 sts onto cable needle and hold in **back** of work, K2 from left needle, P2 from cable needle.
>
> **Twist 4 Front** *(abbreviated T4F)* (uses next 4 sts)
> Slip next 2 sts onto cable needle and hold in **front** of work, P2 from left needle, K2 from cable needle.

Row 1: K3, P4, (K2, P4) across to last st, K1.

Row 2 (Right side)**:** P1, C4F, (P2, C4F) across to last 3 sts, P3.

Row 3: K3, P4, (K2, P4) across to last st, K1.

Row 4: P3, (K2, T4B) across to last 5 sts, K4, P1.

Row 5: K1, P4, (K2, P4) across to last 3 sts, K3.

Row 6: P3, C4B, (P2, C4B) across to last st, P1.

Row 7: K1, P4, (K2, P4) across to last 3 sts, K3.

Row 8: P1, K4, (T4F, K2) across to last 3 sts, P3.

Repeat Rows 1-8 for pattern.

22. Chalice

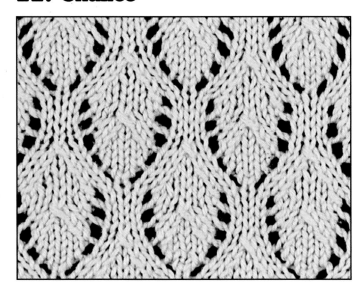

Multiple of 10 sts + 3.

Note: When instructed to slip a st, always slip as if to **knit**.

Row 1 (Right side)**:** K2, YO *(Fig. 16a, page 582)*, K1, **[**slip 1, K1, PSSO *(Figs. 19a & b, page 583)***]**, K3, K2 tog *(Fig. 17, page 583)*, K1, ★ (YO, K1) twice, slip 1, K1, PSSO, K3, K2 tog, K1; repeat from ★ across to last 2 sts, YO, K2.

Row 2 AND ALL WRONG SIDE ROWS: Purl across.

Row 3: K3, ★ YO, K1, slip 1, K1, PSSO, K1, K2 tog, K1, YO, K3; repeat from ★ across.

Row 5: K4, YO, K1, **[**slip 1, K2 tog, PSSO *(Figs. 26a & b, page 584)***]**, K1, ★ YO, K5, YO, K1, slip 1, K2 tog, PSSO, K1; repeat from ★ across to last 4 sts, YO, K4.

Row 7: K2, K2 tog, K1, YO, K3, YO, K1, slip 1, K1, PSSO, ★ K1, K2 tog, K1, YO, K3, YO, K1, slip 1, K1, PSSO; repeat from ★ across to last 2 sts, K2.

Row 9: K1, slip 1, K1, PSSO, K2, YO, K3, YO, K2, ★ slip 1, K2 tog, PSSO, K2, YO, K3, YO, K2; repeat from ★ across to last 3 sts, K2 tog, K1.

Row 11: K3, ★ K2 tog, K1, (YO, K1) twice, slip 1, K1, PSSO, K3; repeat from ★ across.

Row 13: K2, K2 tog, K1, YO, K3, YO, K1, slip 1, K1, PSSO, ★ K1, K2 tog, K1, YO, K3, YO, K1, slip 1, K1, PSSO; repeat from ★ across to last 2 sts, K2.

Row 15: K1, slip 1, K1, PSSO, K1, YO, K5, YO, K1, ★ slip 1, K2 tog, PSSO, K1, YO, K5, YO, K1; repeat from ★ across to last 3 sts, K2 tog, K1.

Row 17: K3, ★ YO, K1, slip 1, K1, PSSO, K1, K2 tog, K1, YO, K3; repeat from ★ across.

Row 19: K3, ★ YO, K2, slip 1, K2 tog, PSSO, K2, YO, K3; repeat from ★ across.

Row 20: Purl across.

Repeat Rows 1-20 for pattern.

23. Checkered Fleurette

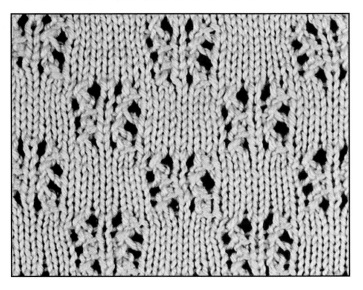

Multiple of 12 sts + 7.

Row 1 AND ALL WRONG SIDE ROWS: Purl across.

Row 2 (Right side)**:** K1, P2 tog *(Fig. 18, page 583)*, YO *(Fig. 16d, page 582)*, K1, YO *(Fig. 16c, page 582)*, P2 tog, (K7, P2 tog, YO, K1, YO, P2 tog) across to last st, K1.

Row 4: K1, YO, P2 tog, K1, P2 tog, (YO, K7, YO, P2 tog, K1, P2 tog) across to last st, YO, K1.

Row 6: Repeat Row 4.

Row 8: K1, P2 tog, YO, K1, YO, P2 tog, (K7, P2 tog, YO, K1, YO, P2 tog) across to last st, K1.

Row 10: K7, (P2 tog, YO, K1, YO, P2 tog, K7) across.

Row 12: K7, (YO, P2 tog, K1, P2 tog, YO, K7) across.

Row 14: Repeat Row 12.

Row 16: Repeat Row 10.

Repeat Rows 1-16 for pattern.

24. Cloverleaf Eyelet

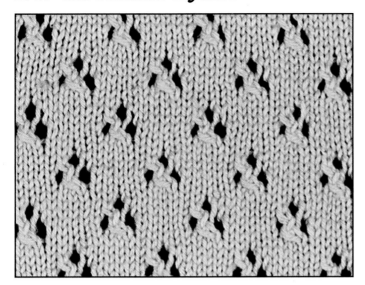

Multiple of 8 sts + 7.

Note: When instructed to slip a st, always slip as if to **knit**.

Row 1 AND ALL WRONG SIDE ROWS: Purl across.

Row 2 (Right side)**:** Knit across.

Row 4: K2, YO *(Fig. 16a, page 582)*, **[**slip 1, K2 tog, PSSO *(Figs. 26a & b, page 584)***]**, (YO, K5, YO, slip 1, K2 tog, PSSO) across to last 2 sts, YO, K2.

Row 6: K3, YO, SSK *(Figs. 21a-c, page 584)*, (K6, YO, SSK) across to last 2 sts, K2.

Row 8: Knit across.

Row 10: K6, YO, slip 1, K2 tog, PSSO, (YO, K5, YO, slip 1, K2 tog, PSSO) across to last 6 sts, YO, K6.

Row 12: K7, (YO, SSK, K6) across.

Repeat Rows 1-12 for pattern.

25. Cluster Rib

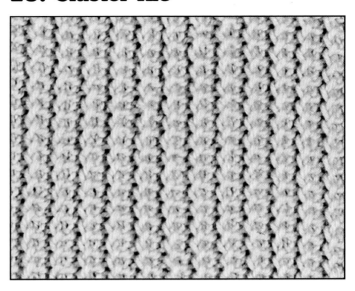

Multiple of 3 sts + 1.

Row 1 (Right side)**:** P1, (K2, P1) across.

Row 2: K1, ★ YO *(Fig. 16a, page 582)*, K2, with left needle bring the YO over the 2 knit sts and off the right needle, K1; repeat from ★ across.

Row 3: P1, (K2, P1) across.

Row 4: K1, ★ YO, K2, with left needle bring the YO over the 2 knit sts and off the right needle, K1; repeat from ★ across.

Repeat Rows 3 and 4 for pattern.

26. Cogwheel Eyelets

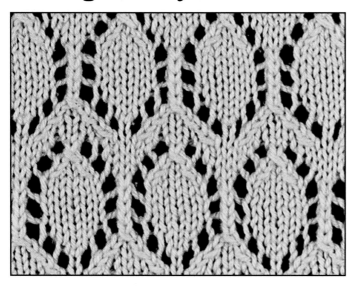

Multiple of 8 sts + 1.

Note: When instructed to slip sts, always slip as if to **knit**.

Row 1 (Right side)**:** K2, K2 tog *(Fig. 17, page 583)*, YO *(Fig. 16a, page 582)*, K1, YO, [slip 1, K1, PSSO *(Figs. 19a & b, page 583)*], ★ K3, K2 tog, YO, K1, YO, slip 1, K1, PSSO; repeat from ★ across to last 2 sts, K2.

Row 2 AND ALL WRONG SIDE ROWS: Purl across.

Row 3: K1, ★ K2 tog, YO, K3, YO, slip 1, K1, PSSO, K1; repeat from ★ across.

Row 5: K2 tog, YO, K5, ★ YO, [slip 1, K2 tog, PSSO *(Figs. 26a & b, page 584)*], YO, K5; repeat from ★ across to last 2 sts, YO, slip 1, K1, PSSO.

Row 7: Slip 1, K1, PSSO, YO, K5, ★ YO, [slip 2 tog, K1, P2SSO *(Figs. 29a & b, page 585)*], YO, K5; repeat from ★ across to last 2 sts, YO, K2 tog.

Row 9: Repeat Row 7.

Row 11: K2, YO, slip 1, K1, PSSO, K1, K2 tog, ★ YO, K3, YO, slip 1, K1, PSSO, K1, K2 tog; repeat from ★ across to last 2 sts, YO, K2.

Row 13: K3, YO, slip 1, K2 tog, PSSO, ★ YO, K5, YO, slip 1, K2 tog, PSSO; repeat from ★ across to last 3 sts, YO, K3.

Row 15: K1, ★ YO, slip 1, K1, PSSO, K3, K2 tog, YO, K1; repeat from ★ across.

Row 17: K2, YO, slip 1, K1, PSSO, K1, K2 tog, ★ YO, K3, YO, slip 1, K1, PSSO, K1, K2 tog; repeat from ★ across to last 2 sts, YO, K2.

Row 19: K3, YO, slip 1, K2 tog, PSSO, ★ YO, K5, YO, slip 1, K2 tog, PSSO; repeat from ★ across to last 3 sts, YO, K3.

Row 21: K3, YO, slip 2 tog, K1, P2SSO, ★ YO, K5, YO, slip 2 tog, K1, P2SSO; repeat from ★ across to last 3 sts, YO, K3.

Row 23: Repeat Row 21.

Row 25: K1, ★ K2 tog, YO, K3, YO, slip 1, K1, PSSO, K1; repeat from ★ across.

Row 27: K2 tog, YO, K5, ★ YO, slip 1, K2 tog, PSSO, YO, K5; repeat from ★ across to last 2 sts, YO, slip 1, K1, PSSO.

Row 28: Purl across.

Repeat Rows 1-28 for pattern.

27. Corona

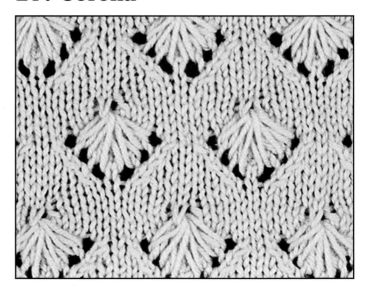

Multiple of 10 sts + 1.

Note: When instructed to slip a st, always slip as if to **knit**.

Row 1 (Right side)**:** K3, K2 tog *(Fig. 17, page 583)*, YO *(Fig. 16a, page 582)*, K1, YO, [slip 1, K1, PSSO *(Figs. 19a & b, page 583)*], ★ K5, K2 tog, YO, K1, YO, slip 1, K1, PSSO; repeat from ★ across to last 3 sts, K3.

Row 2: Purl across.

Row 3: K2, K2 tog, YO, K3, YO, slip 1, K1, PSSO, ★ K3, K2 tog, YO, K3, YO, slip 1, K1, PSSO; repeat from ★ across to last 2 sts, K2.

Row 4: Purl across.

Row 5: K1, ★ K2 tog, YO, K5, YO, slip 1, K1, PSSO, K1; repeat from ★ across.

Row 6: Purl across.

Row 7: Knit across.

Row 8: Purl across.

Note: A crochet hook may be helpful to pull yarn through spaces.

Row 9: K6, working from **right** to **left**, insert right needle or crochet hook in first space 4 rows below and pull up a loop even with loop on needle, pull up a loop in next 5 spaces *(Fig. A)*, ★ K 10, working from **right** to **left**, insert right needle or crochet hook in next space 4 rows below and pull up a loop even with loop on needle, pull up a loop in next 5 spaces; repeat from ★ across to last 5 sts, K5.

Fig. A

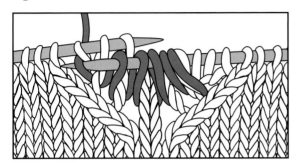

Row 10: P5, P7 tog, (P9, P7 tog) across to last 5 sts, P5.

Row 11: Knit across.

Row 12: Purl across.

Row 13: K1, ★ YO, slip 1, K1, PSSO, K5, K2 tog, YO, K1; repeat from ★ across.

Row 14: Purl across.

Row 15: K2, YO, slip 1, K1, PSSO, K3, K2 tog, ★ YO, K3, YO, slip 1, K1, PSSO, K3, K2 tog; repeat from ★ across to last 2 sts, YO, K2.

Row 16: Purl across.

Row 17: K3, YO, slip 1, K1, PSSO, K1, K2 tog, ★ YO, K5, YO, slip 1, K1, PSSO, K1, K2 tog; repeat from ★ across to last 3 sts, YO, K3.

Row 18: Purl across.

Row 19: Knit across.

Row 20: Purl across.

Row 21: K1, working from **right** to **left**, insert right needle or crochet hook in first space 8 rows below and pull up a loop even with loop on needle, pull up a loop in next 2 spaces, K 10, ★ working from **right** to **left**, insert right needle or crochet hook in next space 4 rows below and pull up a loop even with loop on needle, pull up a loop in next 5 spaces, K 10; repeat from ★ across, working from **right** to **left**, insert right needle or crochet hook in first space 4 rows below and pull up a loop even with loop on needle, pull up a loop in last 2 spaces.

Row 22: P4 tog, P9, (P7 tog, P9) across to last 4 sts, P4 tog.

Row 23: Knit across.

Row 24: Purl across.

Repeat Rows 1-24 for pattern.

28. Crocus Buds

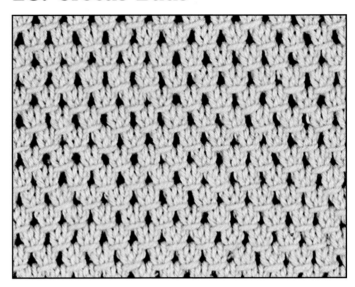

Multiple of 2 sts + 1.

Row 1 (Right side)**:** K1, ★ YO *(Fig. 16a, page 582)*, K2; repeat from ★ across.

Row 2: P4, with left needle bring the third st on right needle over the first 2 sts and off the needle, ★ P3, with left needle bring the third st on right needle over the first 2 sts and off the needle; repeat from ★ across.

Row 3: (K2, YO) across to last st, K1.

Row 4: ★ P3, with left needle bring the third st on right needle over the first 2 sts and off the needle; repeat from ★ across to last st, P1.

Repeat Rows 1-4 for pattern.

29. Cross Stitch Ladders

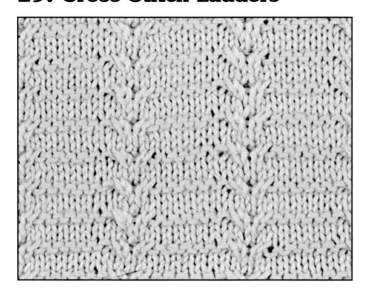

Multiple of 10 sts.

Row 1 (Right side): Knit across.

Row 2: K4, P2, (K8, P2) across to last 4 sts, K4.

Row 3: K3, work Front Cross *(Figs. 9a & b, page 580)*, work Back Cross *(Figs. 8a & b, page 580)*, (K6, work Front Cross, work Back Cross) across to last 3 sts, K3.

Row 4: Purl across.

Repeat Rows 1-4 for pattern.

30. Cross Stitch Lattice

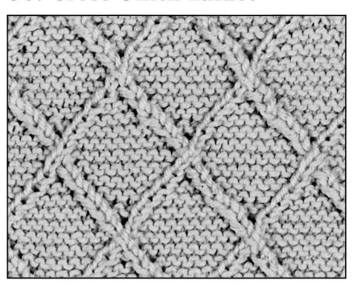

Multiple of 12 sts + 4.

Row 1: K7, P2, (K 10, P2) across to last 7 sts, K7.

Row 2 (Right side): K7, work Front Cross *(Figs. 9a & b, page 580)*, (K 10, work Front Cross) across to last 7 sts, K7.

Row 3: K7, P2, (K 10, P2) across to last 7 sts, K7.

Row 4: K6, work Front Cross, work Back Cross *(Figs. 8a & b, page 580)*, (K8, work Front Cross, work Back Cross) across to last 6 sts, K6.

Row 5: K6, P1, K2, P1, (K8, P1, K2, P1) across to last 6 sts, K6.

Row 6: K5, work Front Cross, K2, work Back Cross, (K6, work Front Cross, K2, work Back Cross) across to last 5 sts, K5.

Row 7: K5, P1, K4, P1, (K6, P1, K4, P1) across to last 5 sts, K5.

Row 8: K4, (work Front Cross, K4, work Back Cross, K4) across.

Row 9: K4, (P1, K6, P1, K4) across.

Row 10: K3, work Front Cross, K6, work Back Cross, (K2, work Front Cross, K6, work Back Cross) across to last 3 sts, K3.

Row 11: K3, P1, K8, P1, (K2, P1, K8, P1) across to last 3 sts, K3.

Row 12: K2, (work Front Cross, K8, work Back Cross) across to last 2 sts, K2.

Row 13: K1, P2, (K 10, P2) across to last st, K1.

Row 14: K1, work Back Cross, (K 10, work Back Cross) across to last st, K1.

Row 15: K1, P2, (K 10, P2) across to last st, K1.

Row 16: K2, (work Back Cross, K8, work Front Cross) across to last 2 sts, K2.

Row 17: K3, P1, K8, P1, (K2, P1, K8, P1) across to last 3 sts, K3.

Row 18: K3, work Back Cross, K6, work Front Cross, (K2, work Back Cross, K6, work Front Cross) across to last 3 sts, K3.

Row 19: K4, (P1, K6, P1, K4) across.

Row 20: K4, (work Back Cross, K4, work Front Cross, K4) across.

Row 21: K5, P1, K4, P1, (K6, P1, K4, P1) across to last 5 sts, K5.

Row 22: K5, work Back Cross, K2, work Front Cross, (K6, work Back Cross, K2, work Front Cross) across to last 5 sts, K5.

Row 23: K6, P1, K2, P1, (K8, P1, K2, P1) across to last 6 sts, K6.

Row 24: K6, work Back Cross, work Front Cross, (K8, work Back Cross, work Front Cross) across to last 6 sts, K6.

Repeat Rows 1-24 for pattern.

31. Cross Stitch Lozenge

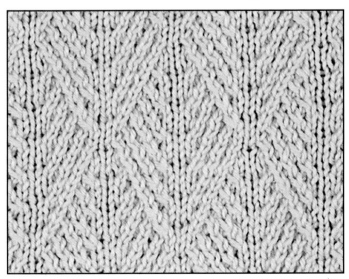

Multiple of 16 sts + 1.

Row 1 AND ALL WRONG SIDE ROWS: Purl across.

Row 2 (Right side)**:** K1, ★ work Back Cross *(Figs. 8a & b, page 580)*, work Front Cross twice *(Figs. 9a & b, page 580)*, K3, work Back Cross twice, work Front Cross, K1; repeat from ★ across.

Row 4: K2, work Back Cross, work Front Cross twice, K1, work Back Cross twice, work Front Cross, ★ K3, work Back Cross, work Front Cross twice, K1, work Back Cross twice, work Front Cross; repeat from ★ across to last 2 sts, K2.

Row 6: K1, ★ work Back Cross twice, work Front Cross, K3, work Back Cross, work Front Cross twice, K1; repeat from ★ across.

Row 8: K2, work Back Cross twice, work Front Cross, K1, work Back Cross, work Front Cross twice, ★ K3, work Back Cross twice, work Front Cross, K1, work Back Cross, work Front Cross twice; repeat from ★ across to last 2 sts, K2.

Row 10: K1, ★ work Back Cross 3 times, K3, work Front Cross 3 times, K1; repeat from ★ across.

Row 12: K2, work Back Cross 3 times, K1, work Front Cross 3 times, ★ K3, work Back Cross 3 times, K1, work Front Cross 3 times; repeat from ★ across to last 2 sts, K2.

Row 14: Repeat Row 10.

Row 16: Repeat Row 8.

Row 18: Repeat Row 6.

Row 20: Repeat Row 4.

Row 22: Repeat Row 2.

Row 24: K2, work Front Cross 3 times, K1, work Back Cross 3 times, ★ K3, work Front Cross 3 times, K1, work Back Cross 3 times; repeat from ★ across to last 2 sts, K2.

Row 26: K1, ★ work Front Cross 3 times, K3, work Back Cross 3 times, K1; repeat from ★ across.

Row 28: Repeat Row 24.

Repeat Rows 1-28 for pattern.

32. Cross Stitch Zigzag

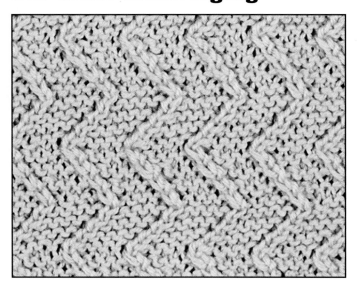

Multiple of 6 sts + 1.

Row 1 (Right side)**:** K1, ★ work Back Cross *(Figs. 8a & b, page 580)*, K4; repeat from ★ across.

Row 2: K4, P1, (K5, P1) across to last 2 sts, K2.

Row 3: K2, work Back Cross, (K4, work Back Cross) across to last 3 sts, K3.

Row 4: K3, P1, (K5, P1) across to last 3 sts, K3.

Row 5: K3, work Back Cross, (K4, work Back Cross) across to last 2 sts, K2.

Row 6: K2, P1, (K5, P1) across to last 4 sts, K4.

Row 7: (K4, work Back Cross) across to last st, K1.

Row 8: K1, (P1, K5) across.

Row 9: ★ K4, work Front Cross *(Figs. 9a & b, page 580)*; repeat from ★ across to last st, K1.

Row 10: K2, P1, (K5, P1) across to last 4 sts, K4.

Row 11: K3, work Front Cross, (K4, work Front Cross) across to last 2 sts, K2.

Row 12: K3, P1, (K5, P1) across to last 3 sts, K3.

Row 13: K2, work Front Cross, (K4, work Front Cross) across to last 3 sts, K3.

Row 14: K4, P1, (K5, P1) across to last 2 sts, K2.

Row 15: K1, (work Front Cross, K4) across.

Row 16: (K5, P1) across to last st, K1.

Repeat Rows 1-16 for pattern.

33. Diagonal Texture

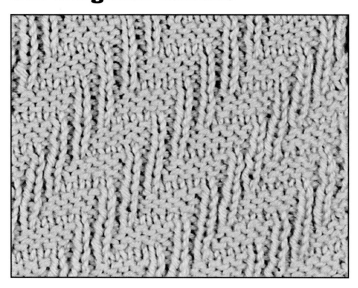

Multiple of 8 sts.

Row 1 (Right side)**:** (K1, P1, K1, P5) across.

Row 2: (K5, P1, K1, P1) across.

Row 3: (K1, P1, K5, P1) across.

Rows 4 and 5: (K1, P5, K1, P1) across.

Row 6: (K1, P1, K5, P1) across.

Row 7: (K5, P1, K1, P1) across.

Row 8: (K1, P1, K1, P5) across.

Row 9: P4, (K1, P1, K1, P5) across to last 4 sts, (K1, P1) twice.

Row 10: (K1, P1) twice, (K5, P1, K1, P1) across to last 4 sts, K4.

Row 11: K3, P1, K1, P1, (K5, P1, K1, P1) across to last 2 sts, K2.

Rows 12 and 13: P2, K1, P1, K1, (P5, K1, P1, K1) across to last 3 sts, P3.

Row 14: K3, P1, K1, P1, (K5, P1, K1, P1) across to last 2 sts, K2.

Row 15: (K1, P1) twice, (K5, P1, K1, P1) across to last 4 sts, K4.

Row 16: P4, (K1, P1, K1, P5) across to last 4 sts, (K1, P1) twice.

Repeat Rows 1-16 for pattern.

34. Diamond & Block

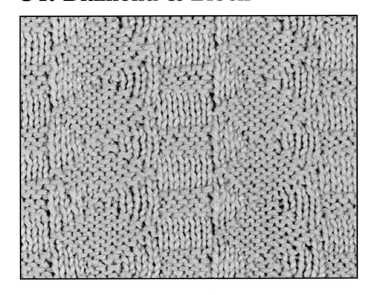

Multiple of 14 sts + 5.

Row 1 (Right side): P5, (K4, P1, K4, P5) across.

Row 2: K5, (P3, K3, P3, K5) across.

Row 3: K7, P5, (K9, P5) across to last 7 sts, K7.

Row 4: P6, K7, (P7, K7) across to last 6 sts, P6.

Row 5: K5, (P9, K5) across.

Row 6: P6, K7, (P7, K7) across to last 6 sts, P6.

Row 7: K7, P5, (K9, P5) across to last 7 sts, K7.

Row 8: K5, (P3, K3, P3, K5) across.

Repeat Rows 1-8 for pattern.

35. Divided Boxes

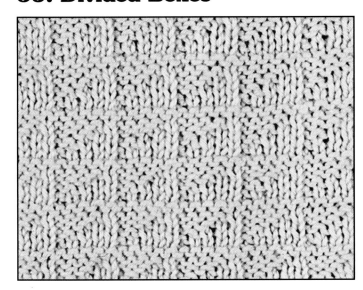

Multiple of 5 sts.

Row 1 (Right side): Knit across.

Row 2: (K1, P4) across.

Rows 3 and 4: (K3, P2) across.

Row 5: (K1, P4) across.

Rows 6 and 7: Knit across.

Repeat Rows 2-7 for pattern.

36. Double Parallelogram

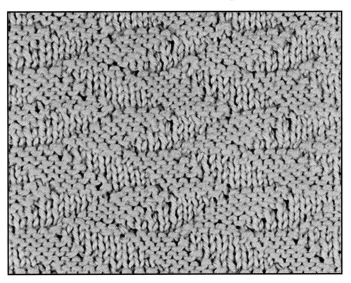

Multiple of 10 sts + 4.

Row 1 (Right side): K2, (P5, K5) across to last 2 sts, P2.

Row 2: K3, (P5, K5) across to last st, P1.

Row 3: (P5, K5) across to last 4 sts, P4.

Row 4: (K5, P5) across to last 4 sts, K4.

Row 5: P3, (K5, P5) across to last st, K1.

Row 6: K1, (P5, K5) across to last 3 sts, P3.

Row 7: K4, (P5, K5) across.

Row 8: P4, (K5, P5) across.

Row 9: P1, (K5, P5) across to last 3 sts, K3.

Row 10: P2, (K5, P5) across to last 2 sts, K2.

Repeat Rows 1-10 for pattern.

37. Elfin Lace

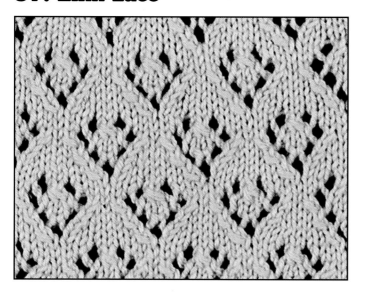

Multiple of 8 sts + 1.

Note: When instructed to slip sts, always slip as if to **knit**.

Row 1 AND ALL WRONG SIDE ROWS: Purl across.

Row 2 (Right side)**:** K2, YO *(Fig. 16a, page 582)*, SSK *(Figs. 21a-c, page 584)*, (K6, YO, SSK) across to last 5 sts, K5.

Row 4: K3, YO, SSK, ★ K3, K2 tog *(Fig. 17, page 583)*, YO, K1, YO, SSK; repeat from ★ across to last 4 sts, K4.

Row 6: K4, YO, SSK, (K1, K2 tog, YO, K3, YO, SSK) across to last 3 sts, K3.

Row 8: K2, K2 tog, YO, K5, ★ YO, [slip 2, K1, P2SSO *(Figs. 27a & b, page 585)*], YO, K5; repeat from ★ across.

Row 10: (K6, YO, SSK) across to last st, K1.

Row 12: K4, K2 tog, (YO, K1, YO, SSK, K3, K2 tog) across to last 3 sts, YO, K3.

Row 14: K3, K2 tog, (YO, K3, YO, SSK, K1, K2 tog) across to last 4 sts, YO, K4.

Row 16: K5, (YO, slip 2, K1, P2SSO, YO, K5) across to last 4 sts, YO, K2 tog, K2.

Repeat Rows 1-16 for pattern.

38. Elm Seeds

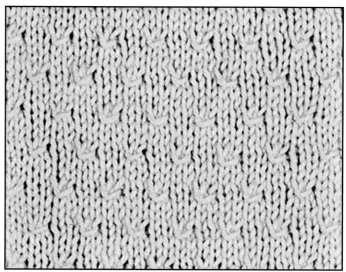

Multiple of 4 sts + 2.

Row 1 (Right side)**:** Knit across.

Row 2: P1, YO *(Fig. 16b, page 582)*, P2, with left needle bring YO over the 2 purl sts just made and off the right needle, ★ P2, YO, P2, with left needle bring YO over the 2 purl sts just made and off the right needle; repeat from ★ across to last 3 sts, P3.

Row 3: Knit across.

Row 4: Purl across.

Row 5: Knit across.

Row 6: P3, YO, P2, with left needle bring YO over the 2 purl sts just made and off the right needle, ★ P2, YO, P2, with left needle bring YO over the 2 purl sts just made and off the right needle; repeat from ★ across to last st, P1.

Row 7: Knit across.

Row 8: Purl across.

Repeat Rows 1-8 for pattern.

39. Fancy Lozenge

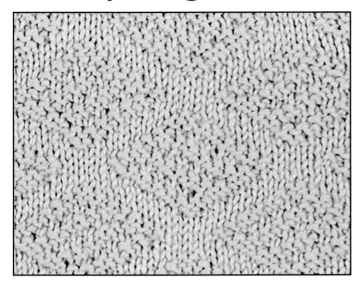

Multiple of 18 sts + 2.

Row 1: K2, (P4, K2, P2, K4, P4, K2) across.

Row 2 (Right side)**:** P3, K4, P2, K2, P2, K4, (P4, K4, P2, K2, P2, K4) across to last 3 sts, P1, K1, P1.

Row 3: P2, K2, P4, K4, P4, (K2, P2, K2, P4, K4, P4) across to last 4 sts, K4.

Row 4: P1, (K2, P2, K4, P2, K4, P4) across to last st, K1.

Row 5: K2, P2, K2, P8, K2, ★ (P2, K2) twice, P8, K2; repeat from ★ across to last 4 sts, P2, K2.

Row 6: K1, P2, K2, P2, K6, P4, ★ (K2, P2) twice, K6, P4; repeat from ★ across to last 3 sts, K2, P1.

Row 7: (P2, K2) twice, P4, ★ K2, (P2, K2) 3 times, P4; repeat from ★ across to last 8 sts, (K2, P2) twice.

Row 8: P1, K2, P4, K6, ★ (P2, K2) twice, P4, K6; repeat from ★ across to last 7 sts, P2, K2, P2, K1.

Row 9: K2, P2, K2, P8, K2, ★ (P2, K2) twice, P8, K2; repeat from ★ across to last 4 sts, P3, K1.

Row 10: K1, (P4, K4, P2, K4, P2, K2) across to last st, P1.

Row 11: P2, K2, P4, K4, P4, (K2, P2, K2, P4, K4, P4) across to last 4 sts, K4.

Row 12: P3, K4, P2, K2, P2, K4, (P4, K4, P2, K2, P2, K4) across to last 3 sts, P3.

Row 13: K2, (P4, K4, P2, K2, P4, K2) across.

Row 14: K5, P2, (K2, P2) twice, ★ K8, P2, (K2, P2) twice; repeat from ★ across to last 5 sts, K5.

Row 15: P4, K4, (P2, K2) twice, ★ P6, K4, (P2, K2) twice; repeat from ★ across to last 4 sts, P4.

Row 16: K3, P2, (K2, P2) 3 times, ★ K4, P2, (K2, P2) 3 times; repeat from ★ across to last 3 sts, K3.

Row 17: P4, (K2, P2) twice, K4, ★ P6, (K2, P2) twice, K4; repeat from ★ across to last 4 sts, P4.

Row 18: K5, P2, (K2, P2) twice, ★ K8, P2, (K2, P2) twice; repeat from ★ across to last 5 sts, K5.

Repeat Rows 1-18 for pattern.

40. Flame Chevron

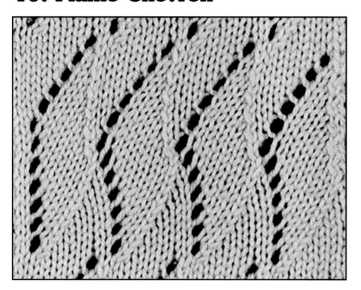

Multiple of 7 sts + 3.

Row 1 AND ALL WRONG SIDE ROWS: Purl across.

Row 2 (Right side)**:** K1, SSK *(Figs. 21a-c, page 584)*, K5, ★ YO *(Fig. 16a, page 582)*, SSK, K5; repeat from ★ across to last 2 sts, YO, K2.

Row 4: K1, SSK, K4, (YO, K1, SSK, K4) across to last 3 sts, YO, K3.

Row 6: K1, SSK, K3, (YO, K2, SSK, K3) across to last 4 sts, YO, K4.

Row 8: K1, SSK, K2, (YO, K3, SSK, K2) across to last 5 sts, YO, K5.

Row 10: K1, SSK, K1, (YO, K4, SSK, K1) across to last 6 sts, YO, K6.

Row 12: K1, SSK, (YO, K5, SSK) across to last 7 sts, YO, K7.

Row 14: K6, K2 tog *(Fig. 17, page 583)*, (YO, K5, K2 tog) across to last 2 sts, YO, K2.

Row 16: K5, K2 tog, K1, (YO, K4, K2 tog, K1) across to last 2 sts, YO, K2.

Row 18: K4, K2 tog, K2, (YO, K3, K2 tog, K2) across to last 2 sts, YO, K2.

Row 20: K3, K2 tog, K3, (YO, K2, K2 tog, K3) across to last 2 sts, YO, K2.

Row 22: K2, K2 tog, K4, (YO, K1, K2 tog, K4) across to last 2 sts, YO, K2.

Row 24: K1, K2 tog, K5, (YO, K2 tog, K5) across to last 2 sts, YO, K2.

Repeat Rows 1-24 for pattern.

41. Garter Stitch

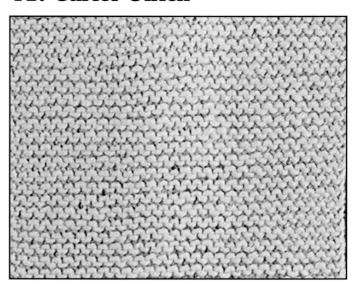

Can be worked on any number of sts.

Row 1: Knit across.

Repeat Row 1 for pattern.

42. Garter Stitch Chevron

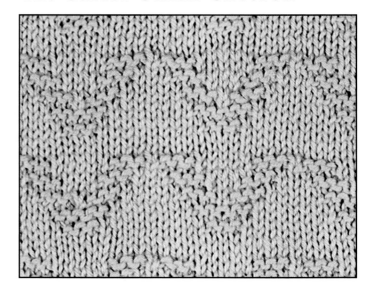

Multiple of 12 sts + 1.

Row 1 (Right side)**:** Knit across.

Row 2: P5, K3, (P9, K3) across to last 5 sts, P5.

Row 3 AND ALL RIGHT SIDE ROWS: Knit across.

Row 4: P4, K5, (P7, K5) across to last 4 sts, P4.

Row 6: P3, K3, P1, K3, (P5, K3, P1, K3) across to last 3 sts, P3.

Row 8: P2, K3, (P3, K3) across to last 2 sts, P2.

Row 10: P1, (K3, P5, K3, P1) across.

Row 12: Purl across.

Repeat Rows 1-12 for pattern.

43. Goblets

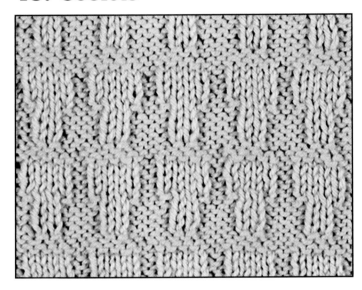

Multiple of 6 sts + 2.

Row 1 (Right side): P3, K2, (P4, K2) across to last 3 sts, P3.

Row 2: K3, P2, (K4, P2) across to last 3 sts, K3.

Rows 3 and 4: Repeat Rows 1 and 2.

Row 5: P2, (K4, P2) across.

Row 6: K2, (P4, K2) across.

Rows 7 and 8: Repeat Rows 5 and 6.

Row 9: Purl across.

Row 10: Knit across.

Repeat Rows 1-10 for pattern.

44. Harris Tweed Ribbing

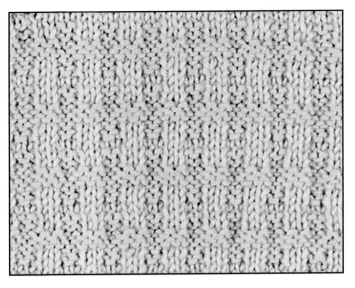

Multiple of 4 sts + 2.

Row 1 (Right side): K2, (P2, K2) across.

Row 2: P2, (K2, P2) across.

Row 3: Knit across.

Row 4: Purl across.

Row 5: K2, (P2, K2) across.

Row 6: P2, (K2, P2) across.

Row 7: Purl across.

Row 8: Knit across.

Repeat Rows 1-8 for pattern.

45. Hodgepodge Diamonds

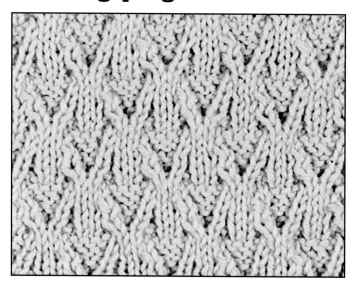

Multiple of 8 sts + 2.

Row 1: K1, P1, K2, (P2, K2) across to last 2 sts, P1, K1.

Row 2 (Right side)**:** P1, K1, P1, RT *(Figs. 7a & b, page 580)*, LT *(Figs. 6a & b, page 580)*, P1, (K2, P1, RT, LT, P1) across to last 2 sts, K1, P1.

Row 3: (K1, P1) twice, K2, (P1, K1, P2, K1, P1, K2) across to last 4 sts, (P1, K1) twice.

Row 4: P1, K1, RT, P2, LT, (K2, RT, P2, LT) across to last 2 sts, K1, P1.

Row 5: K1, P2, K4, (P4, K4) across to last 3 sts, P2, K1.

Row 6: Knit across.

Row 7: K1, P1, K2, (P2, K2) across to last 2 sts, P1, K1.

Row 8: P1, (LT, P1, K2, P1, RT) across to last st, P1.

Row 9: K2, (P1, K1, P2, K1, P1, K2) across.

Row 10: P2, (LT, K2, RT, P2) across.

Row 11: K3, P4, (K4, P4) across to last 3 sts, K3.

Row 12: Knit across.

Repeat Rows 1-12 for pattern.

46. Honeycomb Variation

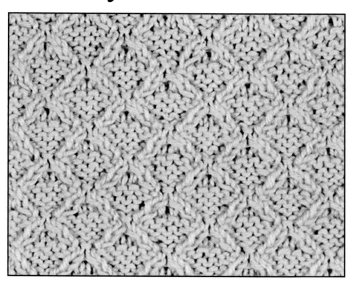

Multiple of 8 sts + 2.

Row 1: P4, K2, (P6, K2) across to last 4 sts, P4.

Row 2 (Right side)**:** K2, ★ RT *(Figs. 7a & b, page 580)*, P2, LT *(Figs. 6a & b, page 580)*, K2; repeat from ★ across.

Row 3: P3, K4, (P4, K4) across to last 3 sts, P3.

Row 4: K1, (RT, P4, LT) across to last st, K1.

Row 5: K2, (P6, K2) across.

Row 6: P2, (LT, K2, RT, P2) across.

Row 7: K3, P4, (K4, P4) across to last 3 sts, K3.

Row 8: P3, LT, RT, (P4, LT, RT) across to last 3 sts, P3.

Repeat Rows 1-8 for pattern.

47. Horseshoe Print

Multiple of 10 sts + 1.

Note: When instructed to slip a st always slip as if to **knit**.

Row 1: Purl across.

Row 2 (Right side)**:** K1, ★ YO *(Fig. 16a, page 582)*, K3, [slip 1, K2 tog, PSSO *(Figs. 26a & b, page 584)*], K3, YO, K1; repeat from ★ across.

Row 3: Purl across.

Row 4: P1, ★ K1, YO, K2, slip 1, K2 tog, PSSO, K2, YO, K1, P1; repeat from ★ across.

Row 5: K1, (P9, K1) across.

Row 6: P1, ★ K2, YO, K1, slip 1, K2 tog, PSSO, K1, YO, K2, P1; repeat from ★ across.

Row 7: K1, (P9, K1) across.

Row 8: P1, ★ K3, YO, slip 1, K2 tog, PSSO, YO, K3, P1; repeat from ★ across.

Repeat Rows 1-8 for pattern.

48. Imitation Lattice

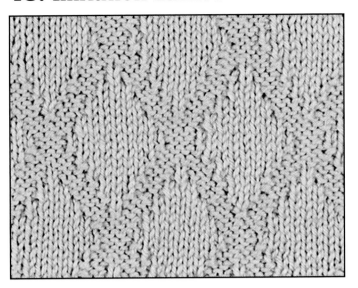

Multiple of 12 sts + 1.

Row 1 (Right side)**:** K4, P5, (K7, P5) across to last 4 sts, K4.

Row 2: P4, K5, (P7, K5) across to last 4 sts, P4.

Row 3: K3, P3, K1, P3, (K5, P3, K1, P3) across to last 3 sts, K3.

Row 4: P3, K3, P1, K3, (P5, K3, P1, K3) across to last 3 sts, P3.

Row 5: K2, P3, (K3, P3) across to last 2 sts, K2.

Row 6: P2, K3, (P3, K3) across to last 2 sts, P2.

Row 7: K1, (P3, K5, P3, K1) across.

Row 8: P1, (K3, P5, K3, P1) across.

Row 9: P3, K7, (P5, K7) across to last 3 sts, P3.

Row 10: K3, P7, (K5, P7) across to last 3 sts, K3.

Row 11: P2, K9, (P3, K9) across to last 2 sts, P2.

Row 12: K2, P9, (K3, P9) across to last 2 sts, K2.

Rows 13 and 14: Repeat Rows 9 and 10.

Rows 15 and 16: Repeat Rows 7 and 8.

Rows 17 and 18: Repeat Rows 5 and 6.

Rows 19 and 20: Repeat Rows 3 and 4.

Rows 21 and 22: Repeat Rows 1 and 2.

Row 23: K5, P3, (K9, P3) across to last 5 sts, K5.

Row 24: P5, K3, (P9, K3) across to last 5 sts, P5.

Repeat Rows 1-24 for pattern.

49. Inverness Diamond

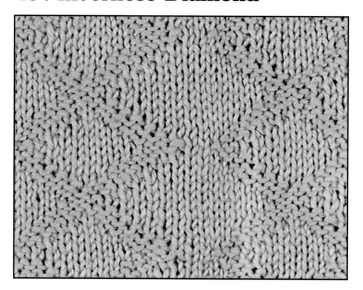

Multiple of 17 sts.

Row 1: P1, K3, P9, K3, (P2, K3, P9, K3) across to last st, P1.

Row 2 (Right side)**:** K2, P3, K7, P3, (K4, P3, K7, P3) across to last 2 sts, K2.

Row 3: P3, K3, P5, K3, (P6, K3, P5, K3) across to last 3 sts, P3.

Row 4: K4, P3, K3, P3, (K8, P3, K3, P3) across to last 4 sts, K4.

Row 5: P5, K3, P1, K3, (P 10, K3, P1, K3) across to last 5 sts, P5.

Row 6: K6, P5, (K 12, P5) across to last 6 sts, K6.

Row 7: P7, K3, (P 14, K3) across to last 7 sts, P7.

Row 8: K6, P5, (K 12, P5) across to last 6 sts, K6.

Row 9: P5, K3, P1, K3, (P 10, K3, P1, K3) across to last 5 sts, P5.

Row 10: K4, P3, K3, P3, (K8, P3, K3, P3) across to last 4 sts, K4.

Row 11: P3, K3, P5, K3, (P6, K3, P5, K3) across to last 3 sts, P3.

Row 12: K2, P3, K7, P3, (K4, P3, K7, P3) across to last 2 sts, K2.

Repeat Rows 1-12 for pattern.

50. Lacy Lattice

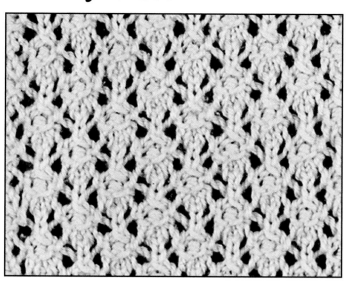

Multiple of 6 sts + 1.

Note: When instructed to slip a st, always slip as if to **knit**.

Row 1 (Right side)**:** K1, ★ YO *(Fig. 16c, page 582)*, P1, P3 tog *(Fig. 24, page 584)*, P1, YO *(Fig. 16d, page 582)*, K1; repeat from ★ across.

Row 2 AND ALL WRONG SIDE ROWS: Purl across.

Row 3: K2, YO *(Fig. 16a, page 582)*, [slip 1, K2 tog, PSSO *(Figs. 26a & b, page 584)*], (YO, K3, YO, slip 1, K2 tog, PSSO) across to last 2 sts, YO, K2.

Row 5: P2 tog *(Fig. 18, page 583)*, P1, YO, K1, YO, P1, (P3 tog, P1, YO, K1, YO, P1) across to last 2 sts, P2 tog.

Row 7: K2 tog, YO, K3, (YO, slip 1, K2 tog, PSSO, YO, K3) across to last 2 sts, YO, [slip 1, K1, PSSO *(Figs. 19a & b, page 583)*].

Row 8: Purl across.

Repeat Rows 1-8 for pattern.

51. Little Fountain

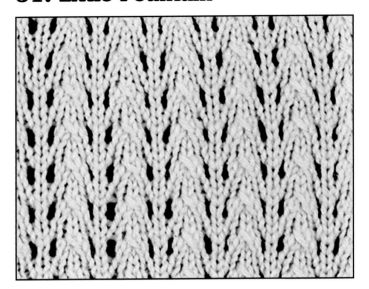

Multiple of 4 sts + 1.

Row 1 (Right side)**:** K1, ★ YO *(Fig. 16a, page 582)*, K3, YO, K1; repeat from ★ across.

Row 2: Purl across.

Row 3: K2, [slip 1 as if to **knit**, K2 tog, PSSO *(Figs. 26a & b, page 584)*], (K3, slip 1 as if to **knit**, K2 tog, PSSO) across to last 2 sts, K2.

Row 4: Purl across.

Repeat Rows 1-4 for pattern.

52. Little Shells

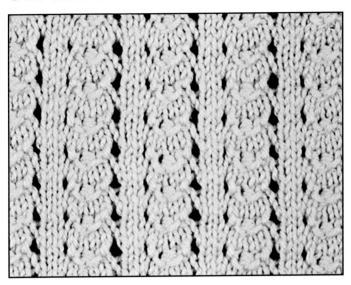

Multiple of 7 sts + 2.

Row 1 (Right side)**:** Knit across.

Row 2: Purl across.

Row 3: K2, ★ YO *(Fig. 16c, page 582)*, P1, P3 tog *(Fig. 24, page 584)*, P1, YO *(Fig. 16d, page 582)*, K2; repeat from ★ across.

Row 4: Purl across.

Repeat Rows 1-4 for pattern.

53. Little Tent

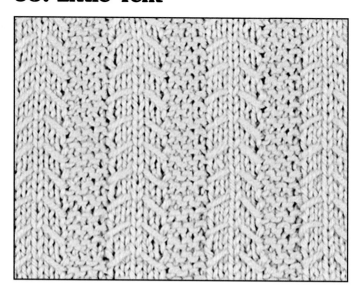

Multiple of 8 sts + 1.

Note: When instructed to slip 5 stitches, always slip as if to **purl**, with yarn held loosely in **front**.

Row 1: K2, P5, (K3, P5) across to last 2 sts, K2.

Row 2 (Right side)**:** K2, slip 5, (K3, slip 5) across to last 2 sts, K2.

Row 3: K2, P5, (K3, P5) across to last 2 sts, K2.

Row 4: K4, insert right needle under loose strand and knit next st on left needle, pulling st under strand *(Fig. A)*, ★ K7, insert right needle under loose strand and knit next st on left needle, pulling st under strand; repeat from ★ across to last 4 sts, K4.

Repeat Rows 1-4 for pattern.

Fig. A

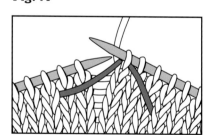

54. Moss & Rib Block

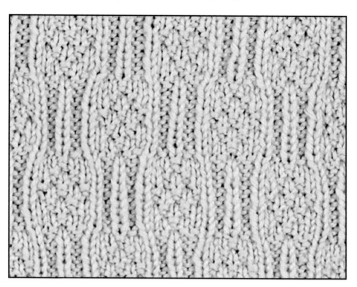

Multiple of 12 sts + 7.

Row 1 (Right side)**:** K3, P1, K3, ★ P2, K1, P2, K3, P1, K3; repeat from ★ across.

Row 2: P3, K1, P3, ★ K2, P1, K2, P3, K1, P3; repeat from ★ across.

Row 3: K2, P1, K1, P1, K2, ★ P2, K1, P2, K2, P1, K1, P1, K2; repeat from ★ across.

Row 4: P2, K1, P1, K1, P2, ★ K2, P1, K2, P2, K1, P1, K1, P2; repeat from ★ across.

Row 5: K1, (P1, K1) 3 times, ★ (P2, K1) twice, (P1, K1) 3 times; repeat from ★ across.

Row 6: P1, (K1, P1) 3 times, ★ (K2, P1) twice, (K1, P1) 3 times; repeat from ★ across.

Rows 7 and 8: Repeat Rows 3 and 4.

Rows 9 and 10: Repeat Rows 1 and 2.

Row 11: (K1, P2) twice, ★ K3, P1, K3, P2, K1, P2; repeat from ★ across to last st, K1.

Row 12: (P1, K2) twice, ★ P3, K1, P3, K2, P1, K2; repeat from ★ across to last st, P1.

Row 13: (K1, P2) twice, ★ K2, P1, K1, P1, K2, P2, K1, P2; repeat from ★ across to last st, K1.

Row 14: (P1, K2) twice, ★ P2, K1, P1, K1, P2, K2, P1, K2; repeat from ★ across to last st, P1.

Row 15: K1, (P2, K1) twice, ★ (P1, K1) 3 times, (P2, K1) twice; repeat from ★ across.

Row 16: P1, (K2, P1) twice, ★ (K1, P1) 3 times, (K2, P1) twice; repeat from ★ across.

Rows 17 and 18: Repeat Rows 13 and 14.

Rows 19 and 20: Repeat Rows 11 and 12.

Repeat Rows 1-20 for pattern.

55. Moss Stitch

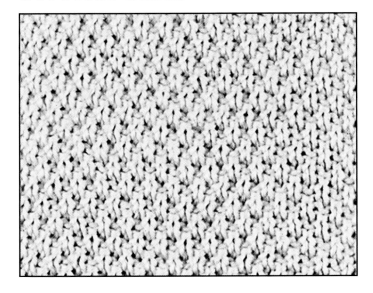

Multiple of 2 sts.

Row 1 (Right side): (K1, P1) across.

Row 2: (K1, P1) across.

Row 3: (P1, K1) across.

Row 4: (P1, K1) across.

Repeat Rows 1-4 for pattern.

56. Moss Stitch Panels

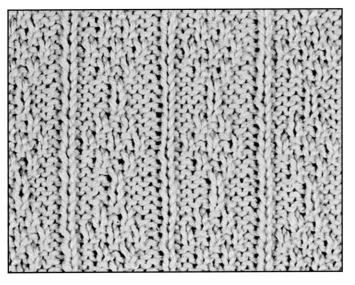

Multiple of 8 sts + 1.

Row 1: P1, (K3, P1) across.

Row 2 (Right side): K1, (P3, K1) across.

Row 3: P1, (K2, P1, K1, P1, K2, P1) across.

Row 4: K1, (P2, K1, P1, K1, P2, K1) across.

Row 5: P1, (K1, P1) across.

Row 6: K1, (P1, K1) across.

Row 7: P1, (K2, P1, K1, P1, K2, P1) across.

Row 8: K1, (P2, K1, P1, K1, P2, K1) across.

Row 9: P1, (K3, P1) across.

Row 10: K1, (P3, K1) across.

Repeat Rows 1-10 for pattern.

57. Moss Stitch Zigzag

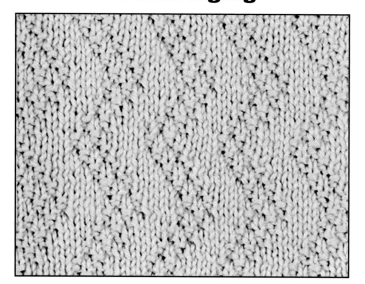

Multiple of 7 sts.

Row 1 (Right side): (P1, K1, P1, K4) across.

Row 2: (P4, K1, P1, K1) across.

Row 3: (K1, P1) twice, (K4, P1, K1, P1) across to last 3 sts, K3.

Row 4: P3, K1, P1, K1, (P4, K1, P1, K1) across to last st, P1.

Row 5: K2, P1, K1, P1, (K4, P1, K1, P1) across to last 2 sts, K2.

Row 6: P2, K1, P1, K1, (P4, K1, P1, K1) across to last 2 sts, P2.

Row 7: K3, P1, K1, P1, (K4, P1, K1, P1) across to last st, K1.

Row 8: (P1, K1) twice, (P4, K1, P1, K1) across to last 3 sts, P3.

Row 9: (K4, P1, K1, P1) across.

Row 10: (K1, P1, K1, P4) across.

Rows 11 and 12: Repeat Rows 7 and 8.

Rows 13 and 14: Repeat Rows 5 and 6.

Rows 15 and 16: Repeat Rows 3 and 4.

Repeat Rows 1-16 for pattern.

58. Panel - Anchor

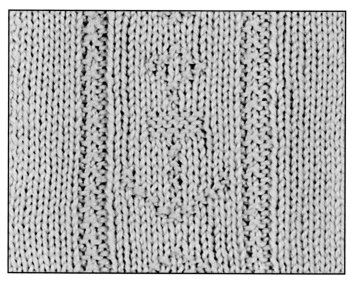

Panel of 17 sts on a background of Stockinette Stitch.

Row 1 (Right side): P3, K 11, P3.

Row 2: K1, P1, K1, (P5, K1) twice, P1, K1.

Row 3: P3, K4, P1, K1, P1, K4, P3.

Row 4: K1, P1, K1, P3, K1, (P1, K1) twice, P3, K1, P1, K1.

Row 5: P3, K2, P1, K5, P1, K2, P3.

Row 6: K1, (P1, K1) twice, (P3, K1) twice, (P1, K1) twice.

Row 7: P3, K1, P1, K7, P1, K1, P3.

Row 8: K1, P1, K1, (P5, K1) twice, P1, K1.

Row 9: P3, K 11, P3.

Rows 10 and 11: Repeat Rows 8 and 9.

Row 12: K1, P1, K1, P3, K5, P3, K1, P1, K1.

Row 13: P3, K3, P5, K3, P3.

Row 14: K1, P1, K1, P3, K5, P3, K1, P1, K1.

Row 15: P3, K 11, P3.

Row 16: K1, P1, K1, (P5, K1) twice, P1, K1.

Rows 17 and 18: Repeat Rows 15 and 16.

Row 19: P3, K4, P1, K1, P1, K4, P3.

Row 20: K1, P1, K1, (P3, K1) 3 times, P1, K1.

Row 21: P3, K4, P1, K1, P1, K4, P3.

Row 22: K1, P1, K1, (P5, K1) twice, P1, K1.

Row 23: P3, K 11, P3.

Row 24: K1, P1, K1, P 11, K1, P1, K1.

Repeat Rows 1-24 for pattern.

59. Panel - Cable Gate

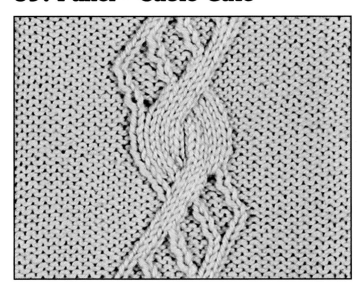

Panel of 16 sts on a background of Reverse Stockinette Stitch.

Additional materials: Cable needle

Twist 3 Back *(abbreviated T3B)* (uses next 3 sts)
Slip next st onto cable needle and hold in **back** of work, K2 from left needle, P1 from cable needle.

Row 1 (Right side)**:** P2, (K5, P2) twice.

Row 2: K2, (P5, K2) twice.

Work **increases** by purling into front **and** back of next st.

Row 3: P1, increase, K4, [slip 1 as if to **knit**, K1, PSSO *(Figs. 19a & b, page 583)*], K2 tog *(Fig. 17, page 583)*, K4, increase, P1.

Row 4: K3, P 10, K3.

Row 5: P2, increase, K2, slip 1 as if to **knit**, K1, PSSO, slip next st onto cable needle and hold in **back** of work, K4 from left needle, P1 from cable needle, LT *(Figs. 6a & b, page 580)*, P2.

Row 6: K2, P1, K2, P7, K4.

Row 7: P3, increase, slip 1 as if to **knit**, K1, PSSO, slip next st onto cable needle and hold in **back** of work, K4 from left needle, P1 from cable needle, P2, LT, P1.

Row 8: K1, P1, K4, P5, K5.

Row 9: P5, slip next st onto cable needle and hold in **back** of work, K3 from left needle, P1 from cable needle, LT, P3, LT.

Row 10: P1, K4, P1, K2, P3, K5.

Row 11: P4, slip next st onto cable needle and hold in **back** of work, K3 from left needle, P1 from cable needle, P2, LT, P2, RT *(Figs. 7a & b, page 580)*.

Row 12: K1, P1, K2, P1, K4, P3, K4.

Row 13: P3, T3B, LT, P3, LT, RT, P1.

Row 14: K2, P2, K4, P1, K2, P2, K3.

Row 15: P2, T3B, P2, LT, P2, T3B, P2.

Row 16: K3, P2, K2, P1, K4, P2, K2.

Row 17: P1, RT, LT, P3, LT, T3B, P3.

Row 18: K4, P3, K4, P1, K2, P1, K1.

Row 19: RT, P2, LT, P2, slip next st onto cable needle and hold in **back** of work, K3 from left needle, P1 from cable needle, P4.

Row 20: K5, P3, K2, P1, K4, P1.

Row 21: LT, P3, LT, slip next st onto cable needle and hold in **back** of work, K3 from left needle, K1 from cable needle, P5.

Row 22: K5, P5, K4, P1, K1.

Row 23: P1, LT, P2, slip next st onto cable needle and hold in **back** of work, K4 from left needle, knit into front **and** back of st on cable needle, K1, P2 tog *(Fig. 18, page 583)*, P3.

Row 24: K4, P7, K2, P1, K2.

Row 25: P2, LT, slip next st onto cable needle and hold in **back** of work, K4 from left needle, knit into front **and** back of st on cable needle, K3, P2 tog, P2.

Row 26: K3, P 10, K3.

Row 27: P1, P2 tog, K5, insert left needle from front under horizontal strand between sts *(Fig. A)*, purl into back **and** front of strand, K5, P2 tog, P1.

Row 28: K2, (P5, K2) twice.

Repeat Rows 1-28 for pattern.

Fig. A

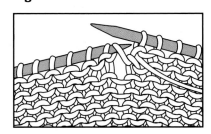

60. Panel - Cable & Seed Stitch

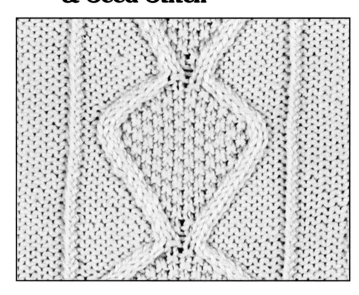

Panel of 24 sts on a background of Reverse Stockinette Stitch.

Additional materials: Cable needle

Cable 3 Back *(abbreviated C3B)* (uses next 3 sts)
Slip next st onto cable needle and hold in **back** of work, K2 from left needle, K1 from cable needle.

Cable 3 Front *(abbreviated C3F)* (uses next 3 sts)
Slip next 2 sts onto cable needle and hold in **front** of work, K1 from left needle, K2 from cable needle.

Twist 3 Back *(abbreviated T3B)* (uses next 3 sts)
Slip next st onto cable needle and hold in **back** of work, K2 from left needle, P1 from cable needle.

Twist 3 Front *(abbreviated T3F)* (uses next 3 sts)
Slip next 2 sts onto cable needle and hold in **front** of work, P1 from left needle, K2 from cable needle.

Twist 4 Back *(abbreviated T4B)* (uses next 4 sts)
Slip next 2 sts onto cable needle and hold in **back** of work, K2 from left needle, P2 from cable needle.

Twist 4 Front *(abbreviated T4F)* (uses next 4 sts)
Slip next 2 sts onto cable needle and hold in **front** of work, P2 from left needle, K2 from cable needle.

Row 1: P1 tbl *(Fig. 4a, page 580)*, K9, P4, K9, P1 tbl.

Row 2 (Right side)**:** K1 tbl, P8, C3B, T3F, P8, K1 tbl.

Row 3: P1 tbl, K8, P3, K1, P2, K8, P1 tbl.

Row 4: K1 tbl, P7, T3B, K1, P1, C3F, P7, K1 tbl.

Row 5: P1 tbl, K7, P2, K1, P1, K1, P3, K7, P1 tbl.

Row 6: K1 tbl, P6, C3B, (P1, K1) twice, T3F, P6, K1 tbl.

Row 7: P1 tbl, K6, P3, K1, (P1, K1) twice, P2, K6, P1 tbl.

Row 8: K1 tbl, P5, T3B, (K1, P1) 3 times, C3F, P5, K1 tbl.

Row 9: P1 tbl, K5, P2, K1, (P1, K1) 3 times, P3, K5, P1 tbl.

Row 10: K1 tbl, P4, C3B, (P1, K1) 4 times, T3F, P4, K1 tbl.

Row 11: P1 tbl, K4, P3, K1, (P1, K1) 4 times, P2, K4, P1 tbl.

Row 12: K1 tbl, P3, T3B, (K1, P1) 5 times, C3F, P3, K1 tbl.

Row 13: P1 tbl, K3, P2, K1, (P1, K1) 5 times, P3, K3, P1 tbl.

Row 14: K1 tbl, P2, C3B, (P1, K1) 6 times, T3F, P2, K1 tbl.

Row 15: P1 tbl, K2, P3, K1, (P1, K1) 6 times, P2, K2, P1 tbl.

Row 16: K1 tbl, P2, K3, P1, (K1, P1) 6 times, K2, P2, K1 tbl.

Row 17: P1 tbl, K2, P3, K1, (P1, K1) 6 times, P2, K2, P1 tbl.

Row 18: K1 tbl, P2, T4F, (K1, P1) 5 times, T4B, P2, K1 tbl.

Row 19: P1 tbl, K4, P3, K1, (P1, K1) 4 times, P2, K4, P1 tbl.

Row 20: K1 tbl, P4, T4F, (K1, P1) 3 times, T4B, P4, K1 tbl.

Row 21: P1 tbl, K6, P3, K1, (P1, K1) twice, P2, K6, P1 tbl.

Row 22: K1 tbl, P6, T4F, K1, P1, T4B, P6, K1 tbl.

Repeat Rows 1-22 for pattern.

61. Panel - Cross Stitch

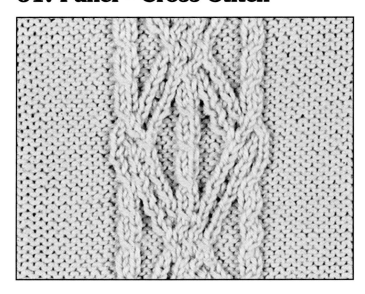

Panel of 20 sts on a background of Reverse Stockinette Stitch.

Row 1: K1, P2, K4, P6, K4, P2, K1.

Row 2 (Right side)**:** P1, work Front Cross *(Figs. 9a & b, page 580)*, P4, work Back Cross 3 times *(Figs. 8a & b, page 580)*, P4, work Back Cross, P1.

Row 3: K1, P2, K4, P6, K4, P2, K1.

Row 4: P1, K2, P3, work Front Cross 3 times, work Back Cross, P3, K2, P1.

Row 5: K1, P2, K3, P8, K3, P2, K1.

Row 6: P1, work Front Cross, P2, work Front Cross, RT *(Figs. 7a & b, page 580)*, work Back Cross, LT *(Figs. 6a & b, page 580)*, work Back Cross, P2, work Back Cross, P1.

Row 7: K1, P2, K2, P3, K1, P2, K1, P3, K2, P2, K1.

Row 8: P1, K2, P1, work Front Cross, RT, P1, K2, P1, LT, work Back Cross, P1, K2, P1.

Row 9: K1, P2, K1, P3, K2, P2, K2, P3, K1, P2, K1.

Row 10: P1, work Front Cross twice, RT, P2, work Back Cross, P2, LT, work Back Cross twice, P1.

Row 11: K1, P5, K3, P2, K3, P5, K1.

Row 12: Work Front Cross twice, RT, P3, K2, P3, LT, work Back Cross twice.

Row 13: P5, K4, P2, K4, P5.

Row 14: K1, work Front Cross twice, P4, work Back Cross, P4, work Back Cross twice, K1.

Row 15: P5, K4, P2, K4, P5.

Row 16: LT, work Front Cross, work Back Cross, P3, K2, P3, work Front Cross, work Back Cross, RT.

Row 17: K1, P5, K3, P2, K3, P5, K1.

Row 18: P1, work Front Cross, LT, (work Back Cross, P2) twice, work Front Cross, RT, work Back Cross, P1.

Row 19: K1, P2, K1, P3, K2, P2, K2, P3, K1, P2, K1.

Row 20: P1, K2, P1, LT, work Back Cross, P1, K2, P1, work Front Cross, RT, P1, K2, P1.

Row 21: K1, P2, K2, P3, K1, P2, K1, P3, K2, P2, K1.

Row 22: P1, work Front Cross, P2, LT, work Back Cross twice, work Front Cross, RT, P2, work Back Cross, P1.

Row 23: K1, P2, K3, P8, K3, P2, K1.

Row 24: P1, K2, P3, LT, work Front Cross twice, RT, P3, K2, P1.

Repeat Rows 1-24 for pattern.

62. Panel - Diamond Net Mask

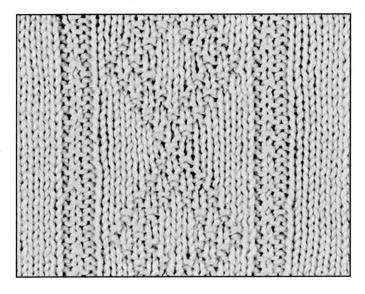

Panel of 19 sts on a background of Stockinette Stitch.

Row 1 (Right side)**:** P3, K6, P1, K6, P3.

Row 2: K1, P1, K1, (P6, K1) twice, P1, K1.

Row 3: P3, K5, P1, K1, P1, K5, P3.

Row 4: K1, P1, K1, (P5, K1, P1, K1) twice.

Row 5: P3, K4, P1, (K1, P1) twice, K4, P3.

Instructions continued on page 544.

Row 6: K1, P1, K1, P4, K1, (P1, K1) twice, P4, K1, P1, K1.

Row 7: P3, K3, P1, (K1, P1) 3 times, K3, P3.

Row 8: K1, P1, K1, P3, K1, (P1, K1) 3 times, P3, K1, P1, K1.

Row 9: P3, K2, P1, K1, P1, K3, P1, K1, P1, K2, P3.

Row 10: K1, P1, K1, P2, K1, P1, K1, P3, K1, P1, K1, P2, K1, P1, K1.

Row 11: P3, (K1, P1) twice, K5, (P1, K1) twice, P3.

Row 12: K1, (P1, K1) 3 times, P5, K1, (P1, K1) 3 times.

Rows 13 and 14: Repeat Rows 9 and 10.

Rows 15 and 16: Repeat Rows 7 and 8.

Rows 17 and 18: Repeat Rows 5 and 6.

Rows 19 and 20: Repeat Rows 3 and 4.

Repeat Rows 1-20 for pattern.

63. Panel - Eyelet Butterflies

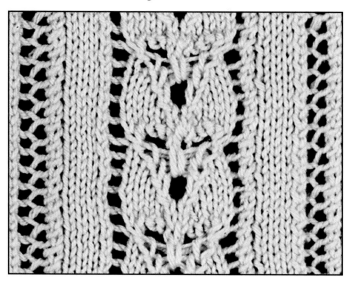

Panel of 30 sts on a background of Stockinette Stitch.

Note: When instructed to slip a st, always slip as if to **knit**.

Row 1: Purl across.

Row 2 (Right side)**:** K2 tog *(Fig. 17, page 583)*, YO *(Fig. 16a, page 582)*, K5, K2 tog, YO, K4, K2 tog, [slip 1, K1, PSSO *(Figs. 19a & b, page 583)*], K4, YO, K2 tog, K5, YO, K2 tog.

Row 3: P2, YO *(Fig. 16b, page 582)*, P2 tog *(Fig. 18, page 583)*, P 20, P2 tog, YO, P2.

Row 4: K2 tog, YO, K5, K2 tog, YO, K3, K2 tog, YO 3 times, slip 1, K1, PSSO, K3, YO, K2 tog, K5, YO, K2 tog.

Row 5: P2, YO, P2 tog, P9, drop 3 YOs off left needle, P9, P2 tog, YO, P2.

Row 6: K2 tog, YO, K5, K2 tog, YO, K2, K2 tog, YO 3 times, slip 1, K1, PSSO, K2, YO, K2 tog, K5, YO, K2 tog.

Row 7: P2, YO, P2 tog, P8, drop 3 YOs off left needle, P8, P2 tog, YO, P2.

Row 8: K2 tog, YO, K5, K2 tog, YO, K1, K2 tog, YO 4 times, slip 1, K1, PSSO, K1, YO, K2 tog, K5, YO, K2 tog.

Row 9: P2, YO, P2 tog, P7, drop 4 YOs off left needle, P7, P2 tog, YO, P2.

Row 10: K2 tog, YO, K5, K2 tog, YO, K2 tog, **turn**, add on 5 sts *(Figs. 5a & b, page 580)*, **turn**, insert right needle under 6 horizontal strands, YO and draw up a st *(Fig. A)*, place st on left needle and knit this st, **turn**, add on 4 sts, **turn**, slip 1, K1, PSSO, YO, K2 tog, K5, YO, K2 tog.

Fig. A

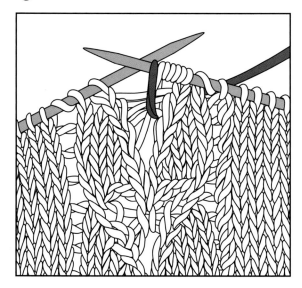

Row 11: P2, YO, P2 tog, P 22, P2 tog, YO, P2.

Repeat Rows 2-11 for pattern.

64. Panel - Five Stitch Cable with Bobbles

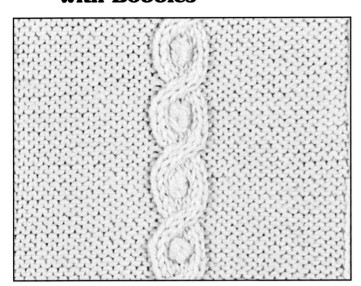

Panel of 5 sts on a background of Reverse Stockinette Stitch.

Additional materials: Cable needle

Row 1 (Right side)**:** Slip next 3 sts onto cable needle and hold in **back** of work, K2 from left needle, K3 from cable needle.

Row 2 AND ALL WRONG SIDE ROWS: P5.

Row 3: K5.

Row 5: K2, (K, P, K, P, K) **all** in next st, pass second, third, fourth, and fifth sts on right needle over first st, K2.

Row 7: K5.

Row 8: P5.

Repeat Rows 1-8 for pattern.

65. Panel - Lace Diamond Chain

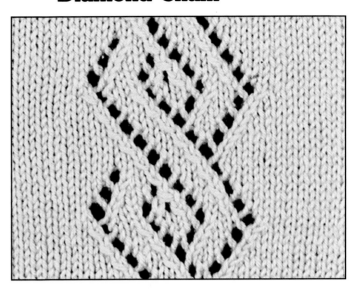

Panel of 16 sts on a background of Stockinette Stitch.

Row 1 AND ALL WRONG SIDE ROWS: Purl across.

Row 2 (Right side)**:** K5, YO *(Fig. 16a, page 582)*, SSK *(Figs. 21a-c, page 584)*, K2, YO, SSK, K5.

Row 4: K3, K2 tog *(Fig. 17, page 583)*, YO, K1, YO, SSK, K2, YO, SSK, K4.

Row 6: K2, K2 tog, YO, K3, YO, SSK, K2, YO, SSK, K3.

Row 8: K1, K2 tog, YO, K2, K2 tog, YO, K1, (YO, SSK, K2) twice.

Row 10: K2 tog, YO, K2, K2 tog, YO, K3, YO, SSK, K2, YO, SSK, K1.

Row 12: (K2, YO, SSK) twice, YO, K2 tog, YO, K2, K2 tog, YO, K2 tog.

Row 14: K3, YO, SSK, K2, YO, [slip 1 as if to **knit**, K2 tog, PSSO *(Figs. 26a & b, page 584)*], YO, K2, K2 tog, YO, K2.

Row 16: K4, YO, SSK, K2, YO, SSK, K1, K2 tog, YO, K3.

Repeat Rows 1-16 for pattern.

66. Panel - Saxon Braid

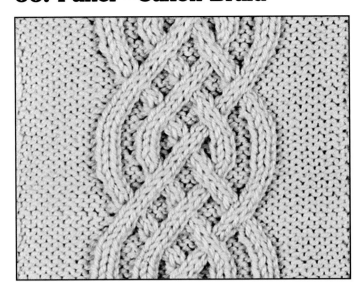

Panel of 24 sts on a background of Reverse Stockinette Stitch.

Additional materials: Cable needle

Cable 4 Back *(abbreviated C4B)* (uses next 4 sts)
Slip next 2 sts onto cable needle and hold in **back** of work, K2 from left needle, K2 from cable needle.

Cable 4 Front *(abbreviated C4F)* (uses next 4 sts)
Slip next 2 sts onto cable needle and hold in **front** of work, K2 from left needle, K2 from cable needle.

Twist 3 Back *(abbreviated T3B)* (uses next 3 sts)
Slip next st onto cable needle and hold in **back** of work, K2 from left needle, P1 from cable needle.

Twist 3 Front *(abbreviated T3F)* (uses next 3 sts)
Slip next 2 sts onto cable needle and hold in **front** of work, P1 from left needle, K2 from cable needle.

Twist 4 Back *(abbreviated T4B)* (uses next 4 sts)
Slip next 2 sts onto cable needle and hold in **back** of work, K2 from left needle, P2 from cable needle.

Twist 4 Front *(abbreviated T4F)* (uses next 4 sts)
Slip next 2 sts onto cable needle and hold in **front** of work, P2 from left needle, K2 from cable needle.

Row 1: K2, P4, (K4, P4) twice, K2.

Row 2 (Right side)**:** P2, C4B, (P4, C4B) twice, P2.

Row 3: K2, P4, (K4, P4) twice, K2.

Row 4: P1, T3B, (T4F, T4B) twice, T3F, P1.

Row 5: K1, P2, K3, P4, K4, P4, K3, P2, K1.

Row 6: T3B, P3, C4F, P4, C4B, P3, T3F.

Row 7: P2, K4, (P4, K4) twice, P2.

Row 8: K2, P3, T3B, T4F, T4B, T3F, P3, K2.

Row 9: (P2, K3) twice, P4, (K3, P2) twice.

Row 10: (K2, P3) twice, C4B, (P3, K2) twice.

Row 11: (P2, K3) twice, P4, (K3, P2) twice.

Row 12: K2, P3, T3F, T4B, T4F, T3B, P3, K2.

Row 13: P2, K4, (P4, K4) twice, P2.

Row 14: T3F, P3, C4F, P4, C4B, P3, T3B.

Row 15: K1, P2, K3, P4, K4, P4, K3, P2, K1.

Row 16: P1, T3F, (T4B, T4F) twice, T3B, P1.

Repeat Rows 1-16 for pattern.

67. Panel - Tight Braid Cable

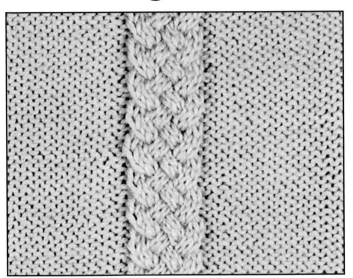

Panel of 10 sts on a background of Reverse Stockinette Stitch.

Additional materials: Cable needle

Cable 4 Back *(abbreviated C4B)* (uses next 4 sts)
Slip next 2 sts onto cable needle and hold in **back** of work, K2 from left needle, K2 from cable needle.

Cable 4 Front *(abbreviated C4F)* (uses next 4 sts)
Slip next 2 sts onto cable needle and hold in **front** of work, K2 from left needle, K2 from cable needle.

Row 1: P 10.

Row 2 (Right side)**:** K2, C4F twice.

Row 3: P 10.

Row 4: C4B twice, K2.

Repeat Rows 1-4 for pattern.

68. Panel - Traveling Rope

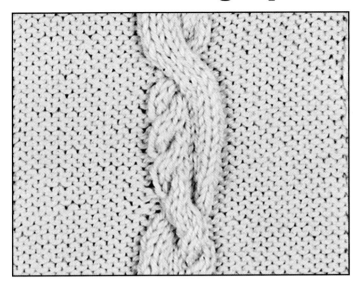

Panel of 8 sts on a background of Reverse Stockinette Stitch.

Additional materials: Cable needle

Cable 4 Back *(abbreviated C4B)* (uses next 4 sts)
Slip next 2 sts onto cable needle and hold in **back** of work, K2 from left needle, K2 from cable needle.

Cable 8 Front *(abbreviated C8F)* (uses next 8 sts)
Slip next 4 sts onto cable needle and hold in **front** of work, K4 from left needle, K4 from cable needle.

Row 1: P8.

Row 2 (Right side)**:** C8F.

Row 3: P8.

Row 4: C4B, K4.

Row 5: P8.

Row 6: K8.

Rows 7-17: Repeat Rows 3-6 twice, then repeat Rows 3-5 once **more**.

Row 18: C8F.

Row 19: P8.

Row 20: K4, C4B.

Row 21: P8.

Row 22: K8.

Rows 23-32: Repeat Rows 19-22 twice, then repeat Rows 19 and 20 once **more**.

Repeat Rows 1-32 for pattern.

69. Panel - Twisted Eyelet

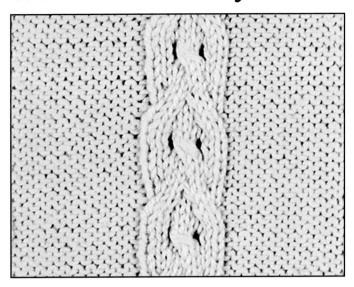

Panel of 8 sts on a background of Reverse Stockinette Stitch.

Additional materials: Cable needle

Cable 3 Back *(abbreviated C3B)* (uses next 3 sts)
Slip next st onto cable needle and hold in **back** of work, K2 from left needle, K1 from cable needle.

Cable 3 Front *(abbreviated C3F)* (uses next 3 sts)
Slip next 2 sts onto cable needle and hold in **front** of work, K1 from left needle, K2 from cable needle.

Row 1 (Right side)**:** K8.

Row 2 AND ALL WRONG SIDE ROWS: P8.

Row 3: K2, slip next 2 sts onto cable needle and hold in **front** of work, YO *(Fig. 16a, page 582)*, K2 tog from left needle *(Fig. 17, page 583)*, [slip 1 as if to **knit**, K1, PSSO from cable needle *(Figs. 19a & b, page 583)*], YO, K2.

Row 5: K8.

Row 7: C3F, K2, C3B.

Row 9: K1, C3F, C3B, K1.

Row 10: P8.

Repeat Rows 1-10 for pattern.

70. Panel - Willow Bud Tree

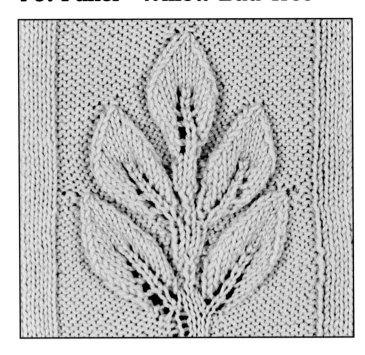

Panel of 29 sts on a background of Stockinette Stitch.

Note: When instructed to slip a st, always slip as if to **knit**.

Row 1: K 11, P7, K 11.

Row 2 (Right side)**:** P 12, K5, P 12.

Row 3: K 12, P5, K 12.

Row 4: P 13, K3, P 13.

Row 5: K 13, P3, K 13.

Rows 6-11: Repeat Rows 4 and 5, 3 times.

Row 12: P 11, P2 tog *(Fig. 18, page 583)*, knit into front **and** into back of next st **(knit increase made)**, K1, knit increase, P2 tog, P 11.

Row 13: K 12, P5, K 12.

Row 14: P 10, P2 tog, YO *(Fig. 16d, page 582)*, K1, YO *(Fig. 16a, page 582)*, K3, YO, K1, YO *(Fig. 16c, page 582)*, P2 tog, P 10.

Row 15: K 11, P3, purl into front **and** into back of next st **(purl increase made)**, P1, purl increase, P3, K 11.

Row 16: P9, P2 tog, K1, (YO, K1) twice, (P2, K1) twice, (YO, K1) twice, P2 tog, P9.

Row 17: K 10, P5, K1, knit increase, P1, knit increase, K1, P5, K 10.

Row 18: P8, P2 tog, K2, YO, K1, YO, K2, P3, K1, P3, K2, YO, K1, YO, K2, P2 tog, P8.

Row 19: K9, P7, K1, knit increase, K1, P1, K1, knit increase, K1, P7, K9.

Row 20: P7, P2 tog, K3, YO, K1, YO, K3, (P3, K3) twice, YO, K1, YO, K3, P2 tog, P7.

Row 21: K8, P9, K1, knit increase, K1, P3, K1, knit increase, K1, P9, K8.

Row 22: P6, P2 tog, K4, YO, K1, YO, K4, P4, K3, P4, K4, YO, K1, YO, K4, P2 tog, P6.

Row 23: K7, P 11, K1, knit increase, K2, P3, K2, knit increase, K1, P 11, K7.

Row 24: P5, P2 tog, [slip 1, K1, PSSO *(Figs. 19a & b, page 583)*], K7, K2 tog *(Fig. 17, page 583)*, P5, K3, P5, slip 1, K1, PSSO, K7, K2 tog, P2 tog, P5.

Row 25: K6, P9, K5, purl increase, P1, purl increase, K5, P9, K6.

Row 26: P4, P2 tog, slip 1, K1, PSSO, K5, K2 tog, P5, YO, K1, YO, P1, K1, P1, YO, K1, YO, P5, slip 1, K1, PSSO, K5, K2 tog, P2 tog, P4.

Row 27: K5, P7, K5, P3, knit increase, P1, knit increase, P3, K5, P7, K5.

Row 28: P3, P2 tog, slip 1, K1, PSSO, K3, K2 tog, P5, K1, (YO, K1) twice, (P2, K1) twice, (YO, K1) twice, P5, slip 1, K1, PSSO, K3, K2 tog, P2 tog, P3.

Row 29: K4, P5, K5, P5, K1, knit increase, P1, knit increase, K1, P5, K5, P5, K4.

Row 30: P2, P2 tog, slip 1, K1, PSSO, K1, K2 tog, P5, K2, YO, K1, YO, K2, P3, K1, P3, K2, YO, K1, YO, K2, P5, slip 1, K1, PSSO, K1, K2 tog, P2 tog, P2.

Row 31: K3, P3, K5, P7, K1, knit increase, P3, knit increase, K1, P7, K5, P3, K3.

Row 32: P1, P2 tog, K3 tog *(Fig. 23, page 584)*, P5, K3, YO, K1, YO, K3, (P3, K3) twice, YO, K1, YO, K3, P5, K3 tog, P2 tog, P1.

Rows 33-35: Repeat Rows 21-23.

Row 36: P5, P2 tog, slip 1, K1, PSSO, K7, K2 tog, P6, YO, K1, YO, P6, slip 1, K1, PSSO, K7, K2 tog, P2 tog, P5.

Row 37: K6, P9, K6, P3, K6, P9, K6.

Row 38: P6, slip 1, K1, PSSO, K5, K2 tog, P6, K1, (YO, K1) twice, P6, slip 1, K1, PSSO, K5, K2 tog, P6.

Row 39: K6, P7, K6, P5, K6, P7, K6.

Row 40: P6, slip 1, K1, PSSO, K3, K2 tog, P6, K2, YO, K1, YO, K2, P6, slip 1, K1, PSSO, K3, K2 tog, P6.

Row 41: K6, P5, K6, P7, K6, P5, K6.

Row 42: P6, slip 1, K1, PSSO, K1, K2 tog, P6, K3, YO, K1, YO, K3, P6, slip 1, K1, PSSO, K1, K2 tog, P6.

Row 43: K6, P3, K6, P9, K6, P3, K6.

Row 44: P6, K3 tog, P6, K4, YO, K1, YO, K4, P6, K3 tog, P6.

Row 45: K 13, P 11, K 13.

Row 46: P 13, slip 1, K1, PSSO, K7, K2 tog, P 13.

Row 47: K 13, P9, K 13.

Row 48: P 13, slip 1, K1, PSSO, K5, K2 tog, P 13.

Row 49: K 13, P7, K 13.

Row 50: P 13, slip 1, K1, PSSO, K3, K2 tog, P 13.

Row 51: K 13, P5, K 13.

Row 52: P 13, slip 1, K1, PSSO, K1, K2 tog, P 13.

Row 53: K 13, P3, K 13.

Row 54: P 13, K3 tog, P 13.

Row 55: K 12, knit increase, K1, knit increase, K 12.

Row 56: Purl across.

Row 57: Knit across.

Rows 58-60: Repeat Rows 56 and 57 once, then repeat Row 56 once **more**.

Repeat Rows 1-60 for pattern.

71. Panel - Zigzag with Diamonds

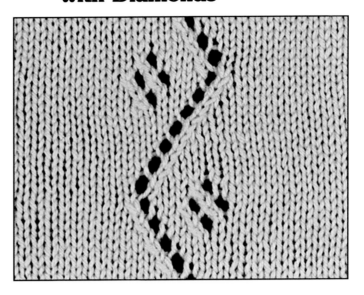

Panel of 9 sts on a background of Stockinette Stitch.

Note: When instructed to slip a st, always slip as if to **knit**.

Row 1 (Right side)**:** K2, YO *(Fig. 16a, page 582)*, [slip 1, K1, PSSO *(Figs. 19a & b, page 583)*], K5.

Row 2 AND ALL WRONG SIDE ROWS: Purl across.

Row 3: K3, YO, slip 1, K1, PSSO, K4.

Row 5: K4, YO, slip 1, K1, PSSO, K3.

Row 7: K5, YO, slip 1, K1, PSSO, K2.

Row 9: (K2, YO, slip 1, K1, PSSO) twice, K1.

Row 11: K1, (YO, slip 1, K1, PSSO) twice, K2, YO, slip 1, K1, PSSO.

Row 13: K2, YO, slip 1, K1, PSSO, K2, K2 tog *(Fig. 17, page 583)*, YO, K1.

Row 15: K5, K2 tog, YO, K2.

Row 17: K4, K2 tog, YO, K3.

Row 19: K3, K2 tog, YO, K4.

Row 21: K2, K2 tog, YO, K5.

Row 23: K1, K2 tog, YO, K3, YO, slip 1, K1, PSSO, K1.

Row 25: K2 tog, YO, K3, (YO, slip 1, K1, PSSO) twice.

Row 27: K1, YO, slip 1, K1, PSSO, K3, YO, slip 1, K1, PSSO, K1.

Row 28: Purl across.

Repeat Rows 1-28 for pattern.

72. Pinecones

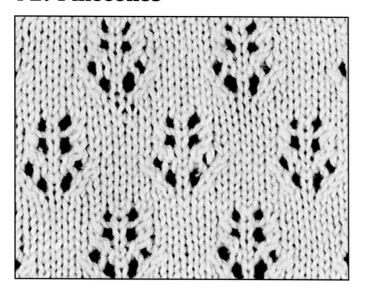

Multiple of 10 sts + 1.

Note: When instructed to slip a st, always slip as if to **knit**.

Row 1 (Right side): Knit across.

Row 2 AND ALL WRONG SIDE ROWS: Purl across.

Row 3: K3, K2 tog *(Fig. 17, page 583)*, YO *(Fig. 16a, page 582)*, K1, YO, [slip 1, K1, PSSO *(Figs. 19a & b, page 583)*], ★ K5, K2 tog, YO, K1, YO, slip 1, K1, PSSO; repeat from ★ across to last 3 sts, K3.

Row 5: K2, K2 tog, YO, K3, YO, slip 1, K1, PSSO, ★ K3, K2 tog, YO, K3, YO, slip 1, K1, PSSO; repeat from ★ across to last 2 sts, K2.

Row 7: K3, K2 tog, YO, K1, YO, slip 1, K1, PSSO, ★ K5, K2 tog, YO, K1, YO, slip 1, K1, PSSO; repeat from ★ across to last 3 sts, K3.

Row 9: Repeat Row 7.

Row 11: Knit across.

Row 13: K1, ★ YO, slip 1, K1, PSSO, K5, K2 tog, YO, K1; repeat from ★ across.

Row 15: K2, YO, slip 1, K1, PSSO, K3, K2 tog, ★ YO, K3, YO, slip 1, K1, PSSO, K3, K2 tog; repeat from ★ across to last 2 sts, YO, K2.

Row 17: K1, ★ YO, slip 1, K1, PSSO, K5, K2 tog, YO, K1; repeat from ★ across.

Row 19: Repeat Row 17.

Row 21: Knit across.

Repeat Rows 2-21 for pattern.

73. Polperro Northcott

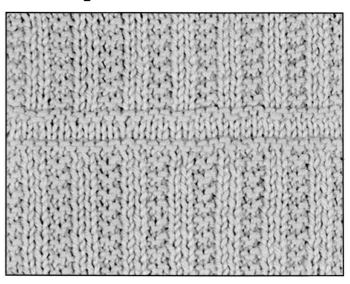

Multiple of 4 sts + 2.

Rows 1-3: Knit across.

Row 4: K2, (P2, K2) across.

Row 5 (Right side): Knit across.

Row 6: K2, (P2, K2) across.

Rows 7-24: Repeat Rows 5 and 6, 9 times.

Rows 25-27: Knit across.

Row 28: Purl across.

Repeat Rows 1-28 for pattern.

74. Reverse Stockinette Stitch

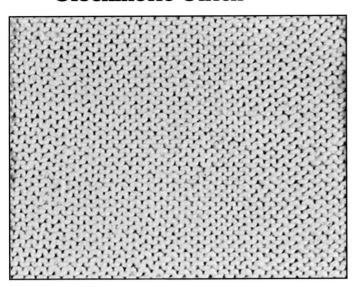

Can be worked on any number of sts.

Row 1 (Right side): Purl across.

Row 2: Knit across.

Repeat Rows 1 and 2 for pattern.

75. Rib & Arrow

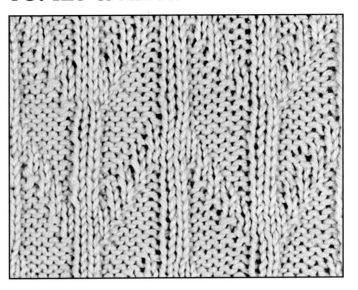

Multiple of 14 sts + 2.

Row 1 (Right side): K2, (P4, K4, P4, K2) across.

Row 2: P2, (K4, P4, K4, P2) across.

Row 3: K2, (P3, K6, P3, K2) across.

Row 4: P2, (K3, P6, K3, P2) across.

Row 5: K2, P2, K2, (P1, K2) twice, ★ (P2, K2) twice, (P1, K2) twice; repeat from ★ across to last 4 sts, P2, K2.

Row 6: P2, K2, P2, (K1, P2) twice, ★ (K2, P2) twice, (K1, P2) twice; repeat from ★ across to last 4 sts, K2, P2.

Row 7: K2, ★ P1, K2, (P2, K2) twice, P1, K2; repeat from ★ across.

Row 8: P2, ★ K1, P2, (K2, P2) twice, K1, P2; repeat from ★ across.

Row 9: K4, P3, K2, P3, (K6, P3, K2, P3) across to last 4 sts, K4.

Row 10: P4, K3, P2, K3, (P6, K3, P2, K3) across to last 4 sts, P4.

Row 11: K3, P4, K2, P4, (K4, P4, K2, P4) across to last 3 sts, K3.

Row 12: P3, K4, P2, K4, (P4, K4, P2, K4) across to last 3 sts, P3.

Row 13: K2, (P5, K2) across.

Row 14: P2, (K5, P2) across.

Repeat Rows 1-14 for pattern.

76. Rib Stitch - 1 x 1

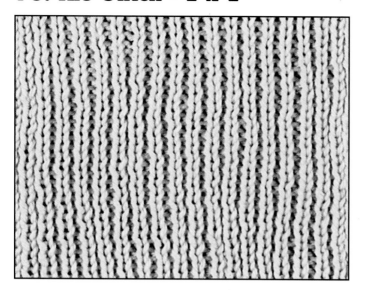

Multiple of 2 sts.

Row 1: (K1, P1) across.

Repeat Row 1 for pattern.

77. Rib Stitch - 2 x 2

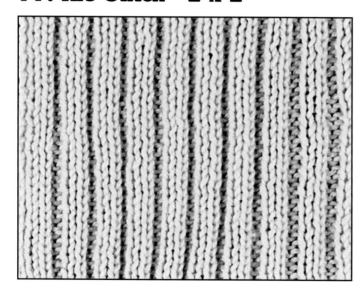

Multiple of 4 sts.

Row 1: (K2, P2) across.

Repeat Row 1 for pattern.

78. Rib & Twist Panels

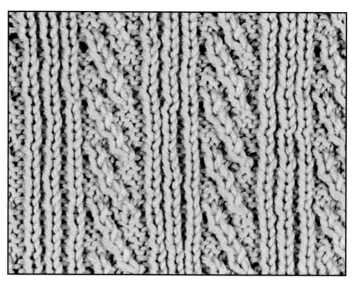

Multiple of 12 sts + 7.

Row 1: (K2, P1) twice, ★ (K1, P1) 3 times, (K2, P1) twice; repeat from ★ to last st, K1.

Row 2 (Right side)**:** P1, **[**LT *(Figs. 6a & b, page 580)*, P1**]** twice, ★ (K1, P1) 3 times, (LT, P1) twice; repeat from ★ across.

Row 3: K4, P1, K2, ★ P1, (K1, P1) twice, K4, P1, K2; repeat from ★ across.

Row 4: P2, LT, P3, ★ K1, (P1, K1) twice, P2, LT, P3; repeat from ★ across.

Row 5: ★ (K3, P1) twice, (K1, P1) twice; repeat from ★ across to last 7 sts, K3, P1, K3.

Row 6: P3, LT, P2, ★ K1, (P1, K1) twice, P3, LT, P2; repeat from ★ across.

Repeat Rows 1-6 for pattern.

79. Ridge & Diamond Stripes

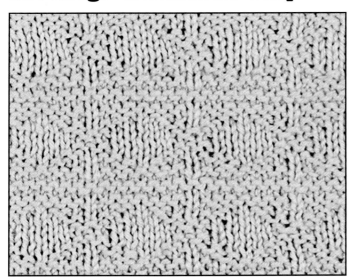

Multiple of 8 sts + 7.

Row 1 (Right side): P7, (K1, P7) across.

Row 2: K3, P1, (K2, P3, K2, P1) across to last 3 sts, K3.

Row 3: P2, K3, P2, (K1, P2, K3, P2) across.

Row 4: K1, P5, (K3, P5) across to last st, K1.

Row 5: K7, (P1, K7) across.

Row 6: K1, P5, (K3, P5) across to last st, K1.

Row 7: P2, K3, P2, (K1, P2, K3, P2) across.

Row 8: K3, P1, (K2, P3, K2, P1) across to last 3 sts, K3.

Row 9: P7, (K1, P7) across.

Rows 10-12: Purl across.

Repeat Rows 1-12 for pattern.

80. Ripples

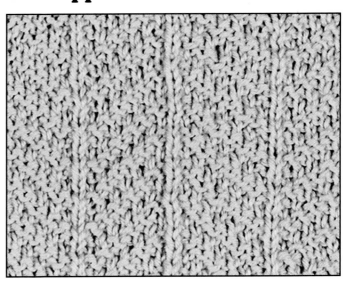

Multiple of 16 sts + 1.

Row 1 (Right side): (K2, P2) twice, K1, P2, K2, P2, (K3, P2, K2, P2, K1, P2, K2, P2) across to last 2 sts, K2.

Row 2: P1, (K2, P2, K2, P3, K2, P2, K2, P1) across.

Row 3: K1, (P1, K2, P2, K5, P2, K2, P1, K1) across.

Row 4: P3, K2, P2, K1, P1, K1, P2, K2, (P5, K2, P2, K1, P1, K1, P2, K2) across to last 3 sts, P3.

Repeat Rows 1-4 for pattern.

81. Rosebuds

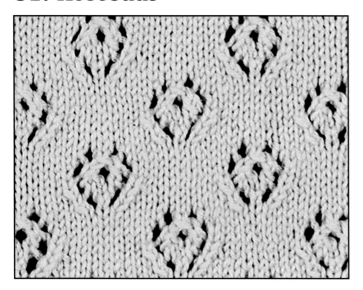

Multiple of 14 sts + 11.

Note: When instructed to slip a st, always slip as if to **knit**.

Row 1 AND ALL WRONG SIDE ROWS: Purl across.

Row 2 (Right side)**:** K 10, K2 tog *(Fig. 17, page 583)*, YO *(Fig. 16a, page 582)*, K1, YO, SSK *(Figs. 21a-c, page 584)*, (K9, K2 tog, YO, K1, YO, SSK) across to last 10 sts, K 10.

Row 4: K9, K2 tog, YO, K3, YO, SSK, (K7, K2 tog, YO, K3, YO, SSK) across to last 9 sts, K9.

Row 6: K 10, YO, SSK, YO, K3 tog *(Fig. 23, page 584)*, ★ YO, K9, YO, SSK, YO, K3 tog; repeat from ★ across to last 10 sts, YO, K 10.

Row 8: K 11, ★ YO, [slip 1, K2 tog, PSSO *(Figs. 26a & b, page 584)*], YO, K 11; repeat from ★ across.

Row 10: K3, K2 tog, YO, K1, YO, SSK, (K9, K2 tog, YO, K1, YO, SSK) across to last 3 sts, K3.

Row 12: K2, K2 tog, YO, K3, YO, SSK, (K7, K2 tog, YO, K3, YO, SSK) across to last 2 sts, K2.

Row 14: K3, YO, SSK, YO, K3 tog, (YO, K9, YO, SSK, YO, K3 tog) across to last 3 sts, YO, K3.

Row 16: K4, YO, slip 1, K2 tog, PSSO, (YO, K 11, YO, slip 1, K2 tog, PSSO) across to last 4 sts, YO, K4.

Repeat Rows 1-16 for pattern.

82. Sculptured Terrace

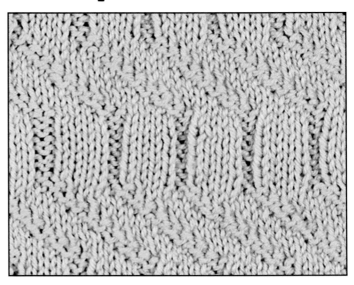

Multiple of 6 sts + 2.

Row 1 (Right side)**:** P2, (K4, P2) across.

Row 2: K2, (P4, K2) across.

Rows 3-8: Repeat Rows 1 and 2, 3 times.

Row 9: K1, (P2, K4) across to last st, P1.

Row 10: (P4, K2) across to last 2 sts, P2.

Row 11: K3, P2, (K4, P2) across to last 3 sts, K3.

Row 12: P2, (K2, P4) across.

Row 13: P1, (K4, P2) across to last st, K1.

Row 14: K2, (P4, K2) across.

Rows 15 and 16: Repeat Rows 9 and 10.

Row 17: K3, P2, (K4, P2) across to last 3 sts, K3.

Row 18: P3, K2, (P4, K2) across to last 3 sts, P3.

Rows 19-24: Repeat Rows 17 and 18, 3 times.

Row 25: (K4, P2) across to last 2 sts, K2.

Row 26: P1, (K2, P4) across to last st, K1.

Row 27: P2, (K4, P2) across.

Row 28: K1, (P4, K2) across to last st, P1.

Row 29: K2, (P2, K4) across.

Row 30: P3, K2, (P4, K2) across to last 3 sts, P3.

Row 31-32: Repeat Rows 25 & 26.

Repeat Rows 1-32 for pattern.

83. Seed Stitch

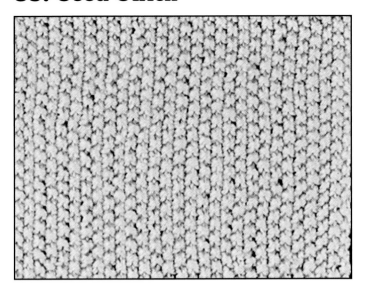

Multiple of 2 sts.

Row 1 (Right side)**:** (K1, P1) across.

Row 2: (P1, K1) across.

Repeat Rows 1 and 2 for pattern.

84. Seed Stitch Zigzag

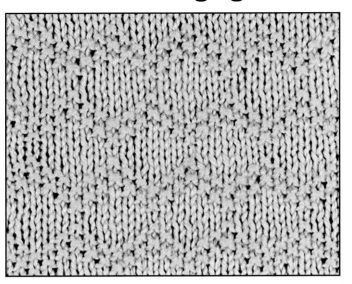

Multiple of 6 sts + 1.

Row 1 (Right side)**:** Knit across.

Row 2: Purl across.

Row 3: P1, (K5, P1) across.

Row 4: P1, (K1, P3, K1, P1) across.

Rows 5 and 6: P1, (K1, P1) across.

Row 7: K2, P1, K1, P1, (K3, P1, K1, P1) across to last 2 sts, K2.

Row 8: P3, K1, (P5, K1) across to last 3 sts, P3.

Row 9: Knit across.

Row 10: Purl across.

Row 11: K3, P1, (K5, P1) across to last 3 sts, K3.

Row 12: P2, K1, P1, K1, (P3, K1, P1, K1) across to last 2 sts, P2.

Rows 13 and 14: K1, (P1, K1) across.

Row 15: K1, (P1, K3, P1, K1) across.

Row 16: K1, (P5, K1) across.

Repeat Rows 1-16 for pattern.

85. Semi-Woven Lattice

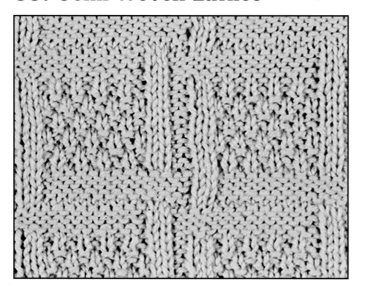

Multiple of 15 sts + 6.

Row 1 (Right side): K2, (P 13, K2) across to last 4 sts, P4.

Row 2: K4, P2, (K 13, P2) across.

Row 3: K2, (P 13, K2) across to last 4 sts, P4.

Row 4: Purl across.

Row 5: K2, P2, K2, ★ P1, (K1, P1) 4 times, K2, P2, K2; repeat from ★ across.

Row 6: P2, K2, P2, ★ K1, (P1, K1) 4 times, P2, K2, P2; repeat from ★ across.

Row 7: K2, P2, ★ K3, P1, (K1, P1) 3 times, K3, P2; repeat from ★ across to last 2 sts, K2.

Row 8: P2, K2, ★ P3, K1, (P1, K1) 3 times, P3, K2; repeat from ★ across to last 2 sts, P2.

Rows 9-14: Repeat Rows 5-8 once, then repeat Rows 5 and 6 once **more**.

Row 15: P4, K2, (P 13, K2) across.

Row 16: P2, (K 13, P2) across to last 4 sts, K4.

Row 17: P4, K2, (P 13, K2) across.

Row 18: Purl across.

Repeat Rows 1-18 for pattern.

86. Slip Stitch Boxes

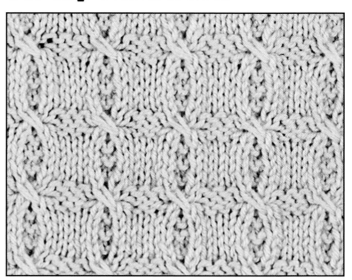

Multiple of 7 sts + 1.

Additional materials: Cable needle

Note: When instructed to slip a st, always slip as if to **purl**.

Row 1 (Right side): Knit across.

Row 2: P3, K2, (P5, K2) across to last 3 sts, P3.

Row 3: Knit across.

Rows 4 and 5: Repeat Rows 2 and 3.

Row 6: (K2, WYF slip 1) twice, (K3, WYF slip 1, K2, WYF slip 1) across to last 2 sts, K2.

Row 7: P2, WYB slip 1, K2, WYB slip 1, (P3, WYB slip 1, K2, WYB slip 1) across to last 2 sts, P2.

Row 8: (K2, WYF slip 1) twice, (K3, WYF slip 1, K2, WYF slip 1) across to last 2 sts, K2.

Row 9: K2, slip next st onto cable needle and hold in **front** of work, knit third st on left needle making sure **not** to drop off, knit first and second sts letting all 3 sts drop off needle, K1 from cable needle, ★ K3, slip next st onto cable needle and hold in **front** of work, knit third st on left needle making sure **not** to drop off, knit first and second sts letting all 3 sts drop off needle, K1 from cable needle; repeat from ★ across to last 2 sts, K2.

Row 10: P3, K2, (P5, K2) across to last 3 sts, P3.

Repeat Rows 1-10 for pattern.

87. Snowflakes

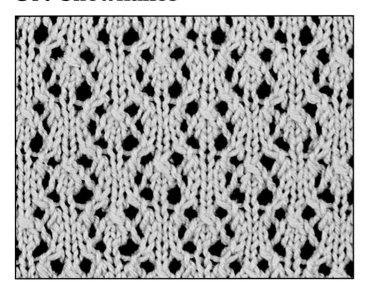

Multiple of 6 sts + 1.

Note: When instructed to slip a st, always slip as if to **knit**.

Row 1 (Right side): K1, ★ YO *(Fig. 16a, page 582)*, [slip 1, K1, PSSO *(Figs. 19a & b, page 583)*], K1, K2 tog *(Fig. 17, page 583)*, YO, K1; repeat from ★ across.

Row 2 AND ALL WRONG SIDE ROWS: Purl across.

Row 3: K2, (YO, K3) across to last 2 sts, YO, K2.

Row 5: K2 tog, YO, slip 1, K1, PSSO, K1, K2 tog, ★ YO, [slip 1, K2 tog, PSSO *(Figs. 26a & b, page 584)*], YO, slip 1, K1, PSSO, K1, K2 tog; repeat from ★ across to last 2 sts, YO, slip 1, K1, PSSO.

Row 7: K1, ★ K2 tog, YO, K1, YO, slip 1, K1, PSSO, K1; repeat from ★ across.

Row 9: K2, (YO, K3) across to last 2 sts, YO, K2.

Row 11: K1, ★ K2 tog, YO, slip 1, K2 tog, PSSO, YO, slip 1, K1, PSSO, K1; repeat from ★ across.

Row 12: Purl across.

Repeat Rows 1-12 for pattern.

88. Spiral Columns

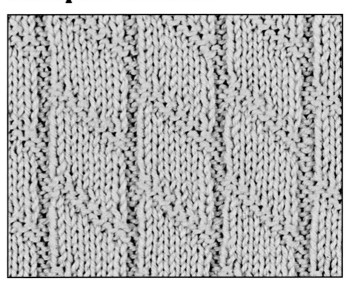

Multiple of 8 sts.

Row 1 (Right side): P1, K6, (P2, K6) across to last st, P1.

Row 2: K1, P5, (K3, P5) across to last 2 sts, K2.

Row 3: P3, K4, (P4, K4) across to last st, P1.

Row 4: K1, P3, K2, P1, (K2, P3, K2, P1) across to last st, K1.

Row 5: P1, K2, (P2, K2) across to last st, P1.

Row 6: K1, P1, K2, P3, (K2, P1, K2, P3) across to last st, K1.

Row 7: P1, K4, (P4, K4) across to last 3 sts, P3.

Row 8: K2, P5, (K3, P5) across to last st, K1.

Row 9: P1, K6, (P2, K6) across to last st, P1.

Row 10: K1, P6, (K2, P6) across to last st, K1.

Repeat Rows 1-10 for pattern.

89. Stockinette Stitch

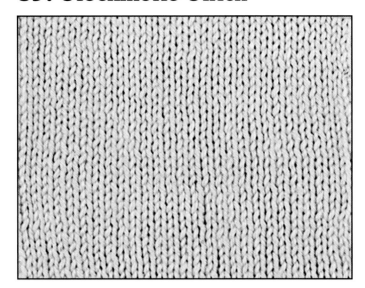

Can be worked on any number of sts.

Row 1 (Right side): Knit across.

Row 2: Purl across.

Repeat Rows 1 and 2 for pattern.

90. Textured Lozenge

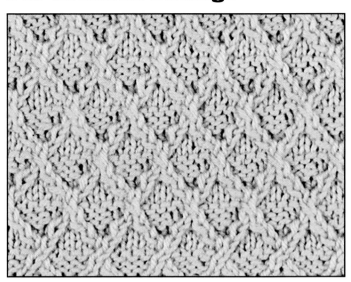

Multiple of 6 sts + 2.

Row 1: Purl across.

Row 2 (Right side): P1, ★ LT *(Figs. 6a & b, page 580)*, K2, RT *(Figs. 7a & b, page 580)*; repeat from ★ across to last st, P1.

Row 3: K2, (P4, K2) across.

Row 4: P2, (LT, RT, P2) across.

Row 5: K3, P2, (K4, P2) across to last 3 sts, K3.

Row 6: K3, work Back Cross *(Figs. 8a & b, page 580)*, (K4, work Back Cross) across to last 3 sts, K3.

Row 7: Purl across.

Row 8: K2, (RT, LT, K2) across.

Row 9: P3, K2, (P4, K2) across to last 3 sts, P3.

Row 10: K1, (RT, P2, LT) across to last st, K1.

Row 11: P2, (K4, P2) across.

Row 12: Work Back Cross, (K4, work Back Cross) across.

Repeat Rows 1-12 for pattern.

91. Textured Stripes

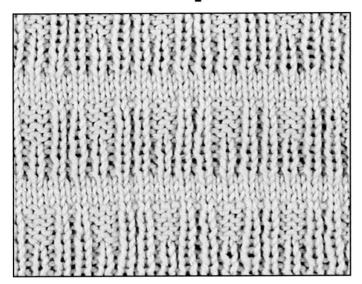

Multiple of 6 sts + 3.

Row 1 (Right side): Knit across.

Row 2: Purl across.

Rows 3 and 4: Repeat Rows 1 and 2.

Row 5: K1, (P1, K1) across.

Row 6: P1, (K1, P1) across.

Rows 7 and 8: Repeat Rows 5 and 6.

Row 9: K1, P1, K1, (P3, K1, P1, K1) across.

Row 10: P1, K1, P1, (K3, P1, K1, P1) across.

Rows 11 and 12: Repeat Rows 9 and 10.

Repeat Rows 1-12 for pattern.

92. Trinity Stitch

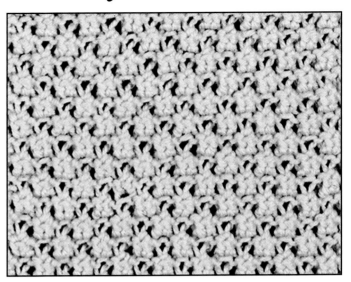

Multiple of 4 sts.

Row 1: ★ (K, P, K) **all** in next st, P3 tog **(Fig. 24, page 584)**; repeat from ★ across.

Row 2 (Right side): Purl across.

Row 3: ★ P3 tog, (K, P, K) **all** in next st; repeat from ★ across.

Row 4: Purl across.

Repeat Rows 1-4 for pattern.

93. Twisted Chains

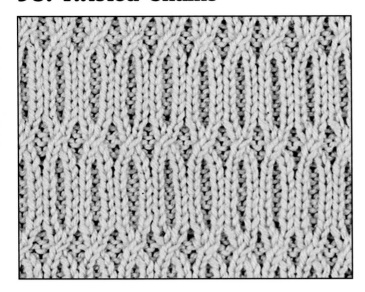

Multiple of 4 sts + 2.

Row 1 (Right side)**:** P1, K1, P2, (K2, P2) across to last 2 sts, K1, P1.

Row 2: K1, P1, K2, (P2, K2) across to last 2 sts, P1, K1.

Rows 3 and 4: Repeat Rows 1 and 2.

Row 5: P1, ★ LT *(Figs. 6a & b, page 580)*, RT *(Figs. 7a & b, page 580)*; repeat from ★ across to last st, P1.

Row 6: K2, (P2, K2) across.

Row 7: P2, ★ work Front Cross *(Figs. 9a & b, page 580)*, P2; repeat from ★ across.

Row 8: K2, (P2, K2) across.

Row 9: P1, (RT, LT) across to last st, P1.

Row 10: K1, P1, K2, (P2, K2) across to last 2 sts, P1, K1.

Row 11: P1, K1, P2, (K2, P2) across to last 2 sts, K1, P1.

Row 12: K1, P1, K2, (P2, K2) across to last 2 sts, P1, K1.

Rows 13-16: Repeat Rows 11 and 12 twice.

Repeat Rows 5-16 for pattern.

94. Twisted Texture

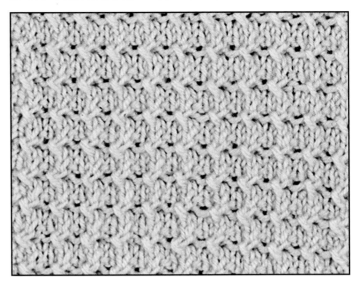

Multiple of 3 sts + 1.

Row 1: Purl across.

Row 2 (Right side)**:** P1, ★ work Back Cross *(Figs. 8a & b, page 580)*, P1; repeat from ★ across.

Row 3: K1, ★ working in front of first st on left needle, purl second st *(Fig. A)* making sure **not** to drop off, then purl first st *(Fig. B)* letting both sts drop off needle, K1; repeat from ★ across.

Row 4: Knit across.

Repeat Rows 1-4 for pattern.

Fig. A

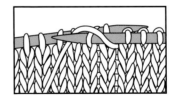

Fig. B

95. Valentine Hearts

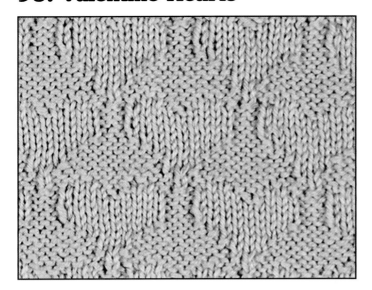

96. Waffle Stitch

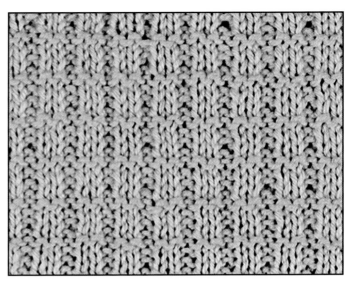

Multiple of 12 sts + 1.

Row 1 (Right side): P6, K1, (P 11, K1) across to last 6 sts, P6.

Row 2: K5, P3, (K9, P3) across to last 5 sts, K5.

Row 3: P5, K3, (P9, K3) across to last 5 sts, P5.

Row 4: K4, P5, (K7, P5) across to last 4 sts, K4.

Row 5: P3, K7, (P5, K7) across to last 3 sts, P3.

Row 6: K2, P9, (K3, P9) across to last 2 sts, K2.

Row 7: P2, K9, (P3, K9) across to last 2 sts, P2.

Row 8: K2, P9, (K3, P9) across to last 2 sts, K2.

Row 9: P2, K4, P1, K4, (P3, K4, P1, K4) across to last 2 sts, P2.

Row 10: P1, (K2, P2, K3, P2, K2, P1) across.

Row 11: K1, (P 11, K1) across.

Row 12: P2, K9, (P3, K9) across to last 2 sts, P2.

Row 13: K2, P9, (K3, P9) across to last 2 sts, K2.

Row 14: P3, K7, (P5, K7) across to last 3 sts, P3.

Row 15: K4, P5, (K7, P5) across to last 4 sts, K4.

Row 16: P5, K3, (P9, K3) across to last 5 sts, P5.

Row 17: K5, P3, (K9, P3) across to last 5 sts, K5.

Row 18: P5, K3, (P9, K3) across to last 5 sts, P5.

Row 19: P1, (K4, P3, K4, P1) across.

Row 20: K2, P2, K2, P1, K2, P2, (K3, P2, K2, P1, K2, P2) across to last 2 sts, K2.

Repeat Rows 1-20 for pattern.

Multiple of 3 sts + 1.

Row 1 (Right side): P1, (K2, P1) across.

Row 2: K1, (P2, K1) across.

Row 3: P1, (K2, P1) across.

Row 4: Knit across.

Repeat Rows 1-4 for pattern.

97. Wheatear Stitch

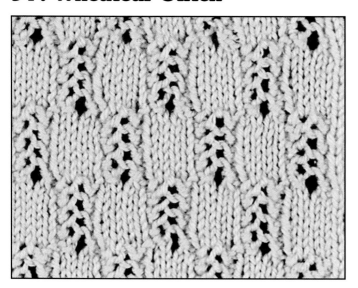

Multiple of 8 sts.

Note: When instructed to slip a st, always slip as if to **knit**.

Row 1: P6, K2, YO *(Fig. 16a, page 582)*, [slip 1, K1, PSSO *(Figs. 19a & b, page 583)*], (P4, K2, YO, slip 1, K1, PSSO) across to last 6 sts, P6.

Row 2 (Right side)**:** K6, P2, YO *(Fig. 16b, page 582)*, P2 tog *(Fig. 18, page 583)*, (K4, P2, YO, P2 tog) across to last 6 sts, K6.

Rows 3-8: Repeat Rows 1 and 2, 3 times.

Row 9: P2, K2, YO, slip 1, K1, PSSO, (P4, K2, YO, slip 1, K1, PSSO) across to last 2 sts, P2.

Row 10: K2, P2, YO, P2 tog, (K4, P2, YO, P2 tog) across to last 2 sts, K2.

Rows 11-16: Repeat Rows 9 and 10, 3 times.

Repeat Rows 1-16 for pattern.

98. Yarn Over Cable

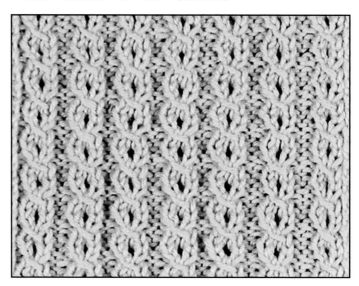

Multiple of 5 sts + 2.

Row 1 (Right side)**:** P2, ★ [slip 1 as if to **knit**, K2, PSSO *(Figs. 25a & b, page 584)*], P2; repeat from ★ across.

Row 2: K2, ★ P1, YO *(Fig. 16b, page 582)*, P1, K2; repeat from ★ across.

Row 3: P2, (K3, P2) across.

Row 4: K2, (P3, K2) across.

Repeat Rows 1-4 for pattern.

99. Zigzag Eyelet

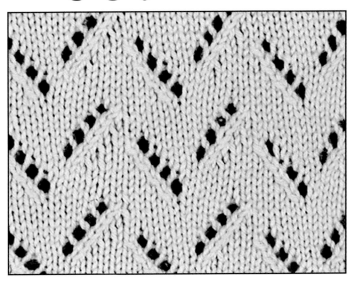

Multiple of 11 sts + 2.

Row 1 AND ALL WRONG SIDE ROWS: Purl across.

Row 2 (Right side)**:** K6, YO *(Fig. 16a, page 582)*, SSK *(Figs. 21a-c, page 584)*, (K9, YO, SSK) across to last 5 sts, K5.

Row 4: K7, YO, SSK, (K9, YO, SSK) across to last 4 sts, K4.

Row 6: K3, K2 tog *(Fig. 17, page 583)*, YO, K3, YO, SSK, (K4, K2 tog, YO, K3, YO, SSK) across to last 3 sts, K3.

Row 8: K2, (K2 tog, YO, K5, YO, SSK, K2) across.

Row 10: K1, K2 tog, (YO, K9, K2 tog) across to last 10 sts, YO, K 10.

Row 12: K2 tog, (YO, K9, K2 tog) across to last 11 sts, YO, K 11.

Repeat Rows 1-12 for pattern.

*Now Turn The Page
to See How to Use
These Pattern Stitches
in Your Projects!*

PROJECTS

The seven pretty sweaters and accessories shown on the following pages were designed especially to help you understand how to incorporate one of our 99 pattern stitches into a specific project. As you become more familiar with multiples and gauge, you'll want to experiment with substituting other pattern stitches in these projects or in using the patterns in your own projects.

MEN'S MUFFLER

◀▬▭▭ **EASY**

We used Cross Stitch Ladders, page 526, for our Muffler.

Finished Size: 7½ " x 45"

MATERIALS
Worsted Weight Yarn:
   5¾ ounces, (160 grams, 395 yards)
Straight knitting needles, sizes 8 (5 mm) **or** size needed for gauge
Crochet hook

GAUGE: In Stockinette Stitch, 18 sts and 24 rows = 4"

Gauge Swatch: 4" square
Cast on 18 sts **loosely**.
Work in Stockinette Stitch for 23 rows.
Bind off all sts in pattern.

Cast on 33 sts **loosely**.

Rows 1-4: Knit across.

Row 5 (Right side)**:** K7, increase **(see Figs. 10a & b, page 581)**, (K8, increase) twice, K7: 36 sts.

Row 6: K3, purl across to last 3 sts, K3.

Row 7: Knit across.

Row 8: K7, P2, (K8, P2) twice, K7.

Row 9: K6, ★ work Front Cross **(Figs. 9a & b, page 580)**, work Back Cross **(Figs. 8a & b, page 580)**, K6; repeat from ★ 2 times **more**.

Repeat Rows 6-9 for pattern until piece measures approximately 44" from cast on edge, ending by working a **wrong** side row.

Next Row: K7, K2 tog **(Fig. 17, page 583)**, (K8, K2 tog) twice, K7: 33 sts.

Last 4 Rows: Knit across.

Bind off all sts in **knit**.

Holding 6 strands of yarn together, each 18" long, add fringe across short edges of Muffler **(Figs. 37a & b, page 588)**.

WOMEN'S MUFFLER

◖◼◻◻ EASY

We used Slip Stitch Boxes, page 556, for our Muffler.

Finished Size: 8" x 45"

MATERIALS
Worsted Weight Yarn: **MEDIUM 4**
    6 ounces, (170 grams, 410 yards)
Straight knitting needles, size 8 (5 mm) **or** size
    needed for gauge
Cable needle
Crochet hook

GAUGE: In Stockinette Stitch, 18 sts and 24 rows = 4"

Gauge Swatch: 4" square
Cast on 18 sts **loosely**.
Work in Stockinette Stitch for 23 rows.
Bind off all sts in pattern.
Cast on 37 sts **loosely**.

Rows 1-4: Knit across.

Row 5 (Right side)**:** K6, increase *(see Figs. 10a & b, page 581)*, (K5, increase) across to last 6 sts, K6: 42 sts.

Row 6: K3, P3, K2, (P5, K2) across to last 6 sts, P3, K3.

Row 7: Knit across.

Rows 8 and 9: Repeat Rows 6 and 7.

Note: When instructed to slip a st, always slip as if to **purl**.

Row 10: K5, WYF slip 1, K2, WYF slip 1, (K3, WYF slip 1, K2, WYF slip 1) across to last 5 sts, K5.

Row 11: K3, P2, WYB slip 1, K2, WYB slip 1, (P3, WYB slip 1, K2, WYB slip 1) across to last 5 sts, P2, K3.

Row 12: Repeat Row 10.

Row 13: K5, slip next st onto cable needle and hold in **front** of work, knit third st on left needle making sure **not** to drop off, knit first and second sts letting all 3 sts drop off needle, K1 from cable needle, ★ K3, slip next st onto cable needle and hold in **front** of work, knit third st on left needle making sure **not** to drop off, knit first and second sts letting all 3 sts drop off needle, K1 from cable needle; repeat from ★ across to last 5 sts, K5.

Rows 14-19: Repeat Rows 6 and 7, 3 times.
Repeat Rows 10-19 for pattern until piece measures approximately 44" from cast on edge, ending by working a **wrong** side row.

Next Row: K6, K2 tog *(Fig. 17, page 583)*, (K5, K2 tog) across to last 6 sts, K6: 37 sts.

Last 4 Rows: Knit across.

Bind off all sts in **knit**.

Holding 6 strands of yarn together, each 18" long, add fringe across short edges of Muffler *(Figs. 37a & b, page 588)*.

SAXON BRAID PILLOW

◼◼◻◻ EASY

We used Panel - Saxon Braid, page 546, for our Pillow.

Finished Size: 14" square

MATERIALS
Worsted Weight Yarn: MEDIUM **4**
  6½ ounces, (180 grams, 445 yards)
  Straight knitting needles, size 8 (5 mm) **or** size
    needed for gauge
14" Pillow form
Cable needle
Yarn needle

GAUGE: In pattern, 29 sts = 4⅜"; 16 rows = 2¼"
      In Stockinette Stitch, 18 sts and 24 rows = 4"

Gauge Swatch: 4" square
Cast on 18 sts **loosely**.
Work in Stockinette Stitch for 23 rows.
Bind off all sts in pattern.

STITCH GUIDE

CABLE 4 BACK *(abbreviated C4B)*
  (uses next 4 sts)
  Slip next 2 sts onto cable needle and hold in **back** of
  work, K2 from left needle, K2 from cable needle.

CABLE 4 FRONT *(abbreviated C4F)*
  (uses next 4 sts)
  Slip next 2 sts onto cable needle and hold in **front** of
  work, K2 from left needle, K2 from cable needle.

TWIST 3 BACK *(abbreviated T3B)*
  (uses next 3 sts)
  Slip next st onto cable needle and hold in **back** of
  work, K2 from left needle, P1 from cable needle.

TWIST 3 FRONT *(abbreviated T3F)*
  (uses next 3 sts)
  Slip next 2 sts onto cable needle and hold in **front** of
  work, P1 from left needle, K2 from cable needle.

TWIST 4 BACK *(abbreviated T4B)*
  (uses next 4 sts)
  Slip next 2 sts onto cable needle and hold in **back** of
  work, K2 from left needle, P2 from cable needle.

TWIST 4 FRONT *(abbreviated T4F)*
  (uses next 4 sts)
  Slip next 2 sts onto cable needle and hold in **front** of
  work, P2 from left needle, K2 from cable needle.

FRONT
Cast on 90 sts **loosely**.

Row 1 (Right side): K1, P6, K4, (P4, K4) twice, ★ P8, K4, (P4, K4) twice; repeat from ★ once **more**, P6, K1.

Row 2: P1, K6, P4, (K4, P4) twice, ★ K8, P4, (K4, P4) twice; repeat from ★ once **more**, K6, P1.

Row 3: K1, P6, C4B, (P4, C4B) twice, ★ P8, C4B, (P4, C4B) twice; repeat from ★ once **more**, P6, K1.

Row 4: P1, K6, P4, (K4, P4) twice, ★ K8, P4, (K4, P4) twice; repeat from ★ once **more**, K6, P1.

Row 5: K1, P5, T3B, (T4F, T4B) twice, T3F, ★ P6, T3B, (T4F, T4B) twice, T3F; repeat from ★ once **more**, P5, K1.

Row 6: P1, K5, P2, K3, P4, K4, P4, K3, P2, ★ K6, P2, K3, P4, K4, P4, K3, P2; repeat from ★ once **more**, K5, P1.

Row 7: K1, P4, ★ T3B, P3, C4F, P4, C4B, P3, T3F, P4; repeat from ★ 2 times **more**, K1.

Row 8: P1, K4, ★ P2, K4, (P4, K4) twice, P2, K4; repeat from ★ 2 times **more**, P1.

Row 9: K1, P4, ★ K2, P3, T3B, T4F, T4B, T3F, P3, K2, P4; repeat from ★ 2 times **more**, K1.

Row 10: P1, K4, ★ (P2, K3) twice, P4, (K3, P2) twice, K4; repeat from ★ 2 times **more**, P1.

Row 11: K1, P4, ★ (K2, P3) twice, C4B, (P3, K2) twice, P4; repeat from ★ 2 times **more**, K1.

Row 12: P1, K4, ★ (P2, K3) twice, P4, (K3, P2) twice, K4; repeat from ★ 2 times **more**, P1.

Row 13: K1, P4, ★ K2, P3, T3F, T4B, T4F, T3B, P3, K2, P4; repeat from ★ 2 times **more**, K1.

Row 14: P1, K4, ★ P2, K4, (P4, K4) twice, P2, K4; repeat from ★ 2 times **more**, P1.

Row 15: K1, P4, ★ T3F, P3, C4F, P4, C4B, P3, T3B, P4; repeat from ★ 2 times **more**, K1.

Row 16: P1, K5, P2, K3, P4, K4, P4, K3, P2, ★ K6, P2, K3, P4, K4, P4, K3, P2; repeat from ★ once **more**, K5, P1.

Row 17: K1, P5, T3F, (T4B, T4F) twice, T3B, ★ P6, T3F, (T4B, T4F) twice, T3B; repeat from ★ once **more**, P5, K1.

Repeat Rows 2-17 for pattern until piece measures approximately 13" from cast on edge, ending by working a **wrong** side row.

Bind off all sts in **purl**.

BACK
Work same as Front.

ASSEMBLY
With **wrong** sides of Front and Back together, sew pieces together inserting pillow form before closing.

TRINITY PILLOW

■■□□ EASY

We used Trinity Stitch, page 559, for our Pillow.

Finished Size: 14" square

MATERIALS
Worsted Weight Yarn: **MEDIUM 4**
6 ounces, (170 grams, 410 yards)
Straight knitting needles, size 8 (5 mm) **or** size needed for gauge
14" Pillow form
Yarn needle

GAUGE: In pattern, 16 sts and 17 rows = 2½ "

Gauge Swatch: 2¾"w x 2½"h
Cast on 18 sts **loosely**.
Work same as Front for 16 rows
Bind off all sts in **purl**.

FRONT
Cast on 82 sts **loosely**.

Row 1 (Right side)**:** Purl across.

Row 2: K1, ★ (K, P, K) **all** in next st, P3 tog *(Fig. 24, page 584)*; repeat from ★ across to last st, K1.

Row 3: Purl across.

Row 4: K1, ★ P3 tog, (K, P, K) **all** in next st; repeat from ★ across to last st, K1.

Row 5: Purl across.

Repeat Rows 2-5 for pattern until piece measures approximately 13" from cast on edge, ending by working a **wrong** side row.

Bind off all sts in **purl**.

BACK
Work same as Front.

ASSEMBLY
With **wrong** sides of Front and Back together, sew pieces together inserting pillow form before closing.

GIRLS' SWEATER

◖◖▢▢ EASY

We used Seed Stitch Zigzag, page 555, for our Sweater.

Size:	Finished Chest Measurement
Small	26"
Medium	29"
Large	32"

Size Note: Instructions are written for size Small with sizes Medium and Large in braces { }. Instructions will be easier to read if you circle all the numbers pertaining to your size. If only one number is given, it applies to all sizes.

MATERIALS

MEDIUM 4

Worsted Weight Yarn:
6½{8½-11} ounces,
  [180{240-310} grams, 425{560-725} yards]
Straight knitting needles, sizes 5 (3.75 mm) **and**
  7 (4.5 mm) **or** sizes needed for gauge
Yarn needle

GAUGE: With larger size needles, in Stockinette Stitch,
  20 sts and 26 rows = 4"

Gauge Swatch: 4" square
With larger size needles, cast on 20 sts **loosely**.
Work in Stockinette Stitch for 25 rows.
Bind off all sts in pattern.

FRONT
BORDER

With smaller size needles, cast on
66{74-82} sts **loosely**.

Row 1: (K1, P1) across.

Row 2: (P1, K1) across.

Rows 3-11: Repeat Rows 1 and 2, 4 times; then repeat Row 1 once **more**.

BODY

Change to larger size needles.

Row 1 (Right side)**:** Knit across to last st, increase *(Figs. 10a & b, page 581)*: 67{75-83} sts.

Beginning with a **purl** row, work in Stockinette Stitch until piece measures approximately 8½{10½-12½}" from cast on edge, ending by working a **purl** row.

SLEEVES

Row 1: Add on 27{32-37} sts **loosely** for Sleeve *(Figs. 5a & b, page 580)*, K1, P1, knit across: 94{107-120} sts.

Row 2: Add on 27{32-37} sts **loosely** for Sleeve, K1, P1, K1, purl across to last 3 sts, K1, P1, K1: 121{139-157} sts.

Row 3: K1, P1, knit across to last 2 sts, P1, K1.

Row 4: K1, P1, K1, purl across to last 3 sts, K1, P1, K1.

Row 5: (K1, P1) twice, (K5, P1) across to last 3 sts, K1, P1, K1.

Row 6: K1, (P1, K1) twice, P3, K1, (P1, K1, P3, K1) across to last 4 sts, (P1, K1) twice.

Rows 7 and 8: K1, (P1, K1) across.

Row 9: K1, (P1, K3, P1, K1) across.

Row 10: K1, P1, K1, P3, K1, (P5, K1) across to last 6 sts, P3, K1, P1, K1.

Row 11: K1, P1, knit across to last 2 sts, P1, K1.

Row 12: K1, P1, K1, purl across to last 3 sts, K1, P1, K1.

Row 13: K1, P1, K4, P1, (K5, P1) across to last 6 sts, K4, P1, K1.

Row 14: K1, P1, K1, P2, K1, P1, K1, (P3, K1, P1, K1) across to last 5 sts, P2, K1, P1, K1.

Rows 15 and 16: K1, P1, K2, P1, (K1, P1) across to last 4 sts, K2, P1, K1.

Row 17: K1, P1, K2, P1, K3, P1, (K1, P1, K3, P1) across to last 4 sts, K2, P1, K1.

Row 18: K1, P1, K2, P5, (K1, P5) across to last 4 sts, K2, P1, K1.

Repeat Rows 3-18 for pattern until Sleeves measure approximately 5½{6½-7½}", ending by working a **wrong** side row.

Bind off all sts **loosely** in knit.

BACK

Work same as Front.

FINISHING

Sew shoulder seams leaving a 7{7½-8}" neck opening. With **right** sides together, sew Sleeve and side in one continuous seam.

FRONT & BACK

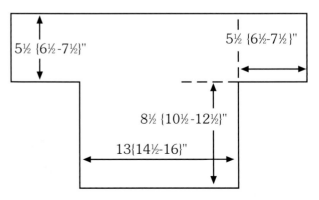

5½ {6½-7½}"

5½ {6½-7½}"

8½ {10½-12½}"

13{14½-16}"

WOMEN'S SWEATER

 EASY

We used Ridge & Diamond Stripes, page 553, for our Sweater.

Size:	Finished Chest Measurement
Small	36"
Medium	40"
Large	44"

Size Note: Instructions are written for size Small with sizes Medium and Large in braces { }. Instructions will be easier to read if you circle all the numbers pertaining to your size. If only one number is given, it applies to all sizes.

MATERIALS

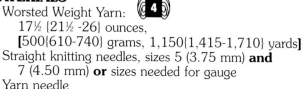

Worsted Weight Yarn:
17½ {21½ -26} ounces,
[500{610-740} grams, 1,150{1,415-1,710} yards]
Straight knitting needles, sizes 5 (3.75 mm) **and**
7 (4.50 mm) **or** sizes needed for gauge
Yarn needle

GAUGE: With larger size needles, in Stockinette Stitch,
20 sts and 26 rows = 4"

Gauge Swatch: 4" square
With larger size needles, cast on 20 sts **loosely**.
Work in Stockinette Stitch for 25 rows.
Bind off all sts in pattern.

FRONT
BORDER
With smaller size needles, cast on 92{102-112} sts **loosely**.

Row 1: (K1, P1) across.

Row 2: (P1, K1) across.

Rows 3-11: Repeat Rows 1 and 2, 4 times; then repeat Row 1 once **more**.

BODY
Change to larger size needles.

Row 1 (Right side)**:** Knit across to last st, increase *(Figs. 10a & b, page 581)*: 93{103-113} sts.

Beginning with a **purl** row, work in Stockinette Stitch until piece measures approximately 14½ {15½ -16½}" from cast on edge, ending by working a **purl** row.

SLEEVES
Row 1: Add on 44{51-58} sts **loosely** for Sleeve *(Figs. 5a & b, page 580)*, K1, P1, knit across: 137{154-171} sts.

Row 2: Add on 44{51-58} sts **loosely** for Sleeve, K1, P1, K1, purl across to last 3 sts, K1, P1, K1: 181{205-229} sts.

Rows 3 and 4: K1, P1, K1, purl across to last 3 sts, K1, P1, K1.

Row 5: K1, P1, K1, (P7, K1) across to last 2 sts, P1, K1.

Row 6: K1, P1, K4, P1, (K2, P3, K2, P1) across to last 6 sts, K4, P1, K1.

Row 7: K1, P1, K1, (P2, K3, P2, K1) across to last 2 sts, P1, K1.

Row 8: K1, P1, K2, P5, (K3, P5) across to last 4 sts, K2, P1, K1.

Row 9: K1, P1, K8, P1, (K7, P1) across to last 10 sts, K8, P1, K1.

Row 10: K1, P1, K2, P5, (K3, P5) across to last 4 sts, K2, P1, K1.

Row 11: K1, P1, K1, (P2, K3, P2, K1) across to last 2 sts, P1, K1.

Row 12: K1, P1, K4, P1, (K2, P3, K2, P1) across to last 6 sts, K4, P1, K1.

Row 13: K1, P1, K1, (P7, K1) across to last 2 sts, P1, K1.

Rows 14-16: K1, P1, K1, purl across to last 3 sts, K1, P1, K1.

Repeat Rows 5-16 for pattern until Sleeves measure approximately 9{10-11}", ending by working a **wrong** side row.

Bind off all sts **loosely** in knit.

BACK
Work same as Front.

FINISHING
Sew shoulder seams leaving a 8½{9-9½}" neck opening.

With **right** sides together, sew Sleeve and side in one continuous seam.

FRONT & BACK

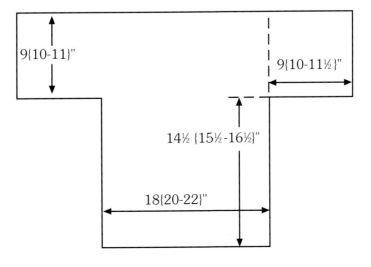

9{10-11}"

9{10-11½}"

14½ {15½-16½}"

18{20-22}"

SAMPLER AFGHAN

▰▰▰▱ INTERMEDIATE

We made our Afghan using the following patterns:
Strip A - Moss Stitch Panels, page 539.
Strip B - Panel - Diamond Net Mask, page 543.
Strip C - Cable - Twisted Cable, page 521.
Strip D - Cogwheel Eyelets, page 524.
Strip E - Panel - Cable Gate, page 541.
Strip F - Little Shells, page 537.

Finished Size: 48" x 61"

MATERIALS

MEDIUM 4

Worsted Weight Yarn:
48 ounces, (1,360 grams, 3,290 yards)
Straight knitting needles, size 8 (5 mm) **or** size needed for gauge
Cable needle
Yarn needle
Crochet hook

GAUGE: In Stockinette Stitch, 18 sts and 24 rows = 4"
Strip A = 8¼"w
Strip B = 8"w
Strip C = 7¾"w
Strip D = 8½"w
Strip E = 7¾"w
Strip F = 8"w

Gauge Swatch: 4" square
Cast on 18 sts **loosely**.
Work in Stockinette Stitch for 23 rows.
Bind off all sts in pattern.

STITCH GUIDE

TWIST 3 BACK *(abbreviated T3B)*
(uses next 3 sts)
Slip next st onto cable needle and hold in **back** of work, K2 from left needle, P1 from cable needle.

INCREASE
Purl into front **and** back of next st *(Fig. 11, page 581)*.

MAKE ONE PURL *(abbreviated M1P)*
Insert left needle from the back under horizontal strand between sts *(Fig. A)*; then purl into the **front** of the strand *(Fig. B)*.

Fig. A   **Fig. B**

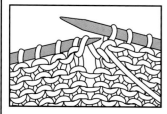   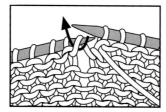

STRIP A

Cast on 39 sts **loosely**.

Rows 1-3: K1, (P1, K1) across.

Row 4 (Right side)**:** K1, P1, K1, purl across to last 3 sts, K1, P1, K1.

Row 5: (K1, P1) twice, K3, (P1, K3) across to last 4 sts, (P1, K1) twice.

Row 6: K1, P1, K2, P3, (K1, P3) across to last 4 sts, K2, P1, K1.

Row 7: (K1, P1) twice, (K2, P1, K1, P1, K2, P1) across to last 3 sts, K1, P1, K1.

Row 8: K1, P1, K2, P2, K1, P1, K1, P2, (K1, P2, K1, P1, K1, P2) across to last 4 sts, K2, P1, K1.

Row 9: K1, (P1, K1) across.

Row 10: K1, P1, K2, P1, (K1, P1) across to last 4 sts, K2, P1, K1.

Rows 11 and 12: Repeat Rows 7 and 8.

Rows 13 and 14: Repeat Rows 5 and 6.

Repeat Rows 5-14 for pattern until piece measures approximately 60" from cast on edge, ending by working a **wrong** side row.

Last 3 Rows: K1, (P1, K1) across.
Bind off all sts in pattern.

STRIP B

Cast on 39 sts **loosely**.

Rows 1-3: K1, (P1, K1) across.

Row 4 (Right side)**:** K1, P1, K8, P3, K6, P1, K6, P3, K8, P1, K1.

Row 5: K1, P1, K1, P7, K1, P1, K1, (P6, K1) twice, P1, K1, P7, K1, P1, K1.

Row 6: K1, P1, K8, P3, K5, P1, K1, P1, K5, P3, K8, P1, K1.

Row 7: K1, P1, K1, P7, K1, P1, K1, (P5, K1, P1, K1) twice, P7, K1, P1, K1.

Row 8: K1, P1, K8, P3, K4, P1, (K1, P1) twice, K4, P3, K8, P1, K1.

Row 9: K1, P1, K1, P7, K1, P1, K1, P4, K1, (P1, K1) twice, P4, K1, P1, K1, P7, K1, P1, K1.

Row 10: K1, P1, K8, P3, K3, P1, (K1, P1) 3 times, K3, P3, K8, P1, K1.

Row 11: K1, P1, K1, P7, K1, P1, K1, P3, K1, (P1, K1) 3 times, P3, K1, P1, K1, P7, K1, P1, K1.

Row 12: K1, P1, K8, P3, K2, P1, K1, P1, K3, P1, K1, P1, K2, P3, K8, P1, K1.

Row 13: K1, P1, K1, P7, K1, P1, K1, P2, K1, P1, K1, P3, K1, P1, K1, P2, K1, P1, K1, P7, K1, P1, K1.

Row 14: K1, P1, K8, P3, (K1, P1) twice, K5, (P1, K1) twice, P3, K8, P1, K1.

Row 15: K1, P1, K1, P7, K1, (P1, K1) 3 times, P5, K1, (P1, K1) 3 times, P7, K1, P1, K1.

Rows 16 and 17: Repeat Rows 12 and 13.

Rows 18 and 19: Repeat Rows 10 and 11.

Rows 20 and 21: Repeat Rows 8 and 9.

Rows 22 and 23: Repeat Rows 6 and 7.

Repeat Rows 4-23 for pattern until piece measures approximately 60" from cast on edge, ending by working a **wrong** side row.

Last 3 Rows: K1, (P1, K1) across.

Bind off all sts in pattern.

STRIP C

Cast on 37 sts **loosely**.

Rows 1-3: K1, (P1, K1) across.

Row 4: (K1, P1) 3 times, **[**M1P **(Figs. A & B, page 572)**, P1**]** twice, ★ (K1, P1) twice, (M1P, P1) twice; repeat from ★ across to last 5 sts, K1, (P1, K1) twice: 47 sts.

Row 5 (Right side)**:** K1, P1, K2, P1, slip next 4 sts onto cable needle and hold in **back** of work, K1 from left needle, slip last 3 sts from cable needle back onto left needle and knit them, K1 from cable needle, P1, ★ K1, P1, slip next 4 sts onto cable needle and hold in **back** of work, K1 from left needle, slip last 3 sts from cable needle back onto left needle and knit them, K1 from cable needle, P1; repeat from ★ across to last 4 sts, K2, P1, K1.

Row 6: K1, (P1, K1) twice, P5, K1, (P1, K1, P5, K1) across to last 4 sts, (P1, K1) twice.

Row 7: K1, P1, K2, P1, K5, P1, (K1, P1, K5, P1) across to last 4 sts, K2, P1, K1.

Row 8: K1, (P1, K1) twice, P5, K1, (P1, K1, P5, K1) across to last 4 sts, (P1, K1) twice.

Row 9: K1, P1, K2, P1, K5, P1, (K1, P1, K5, P1) across to last 4 sts, K2, P1, K1.

Instructions continued on page 574.

Row 10: K1, (P1, K1) twice, P5, K1, (P1, K1, P5, K1) across to last 4 sts, (P1, K1) twice.

Repeat Rows 5-10 for pattern until piece measures approximately 60" from cast on edge, ending by working a **right** side row.

Next Row: K1, (P1, K1) twice, P2 tog *(Fig. 18, page 583)*, P1, P2 tog, ★ K1, P1, K1, P2 tog, P1, P2 tog; repeat from ★ across to last 5 sts, K1, (P1, K1) twice: 37 sts.

Last 3 Rows: K1, (P1, K1) across.

Bind off all sts in pattern.

STRIP D
Cast on 39 sts **loosely**.

Rows 1-3: K1, (P1, K1) across.

Note: When instructed to slip sts, always slip as if to **knit**.

Row 4 (Right side)**:** K1, P1, K3, K2 tog *(Fig. 17, page 583)*, YO *(Fig. 16a, page 582)*, K1, YO, [slip 1, K1, PSSO *(Figs. 19a & b, page 583)*], ★ K3, K2 tog, YO, K1, YO, slip 1, K1, PSSO; repeat from ★ 2 times **more**, K3, P1, K1.

Row 5 AND ALL WRONG SIDE ROWS: K1, P1, K1, purl across to last 3 sts, K1, P1, K1.

Row 6: K1, P1, K2, K2 tog, YO, K3, YO, slip 1, K1, PSSO, ★ K1, K2 tog, YO, K3, YO, slip 1, K1, PSSO; repeat from ★ 2 times **more**, K2, P1, K1.

Row 8: K1, P1, K1, K2 tog, YO, K5, ★ YO, [slip 1, K2 tog, PSSO *(Figs. 26a & b, page 584)*], YO, K5; repeat from ★ 2 times **more**, YO, slip 1, K1, PSSO, K1, P1, K1.

Row 10: K1, P1, K1, slip 1, K1, PSSO, YO, K5, ★ YO, [slip 2 tog, K1, P2SSO *(Figs. 29a & b, page 585)*], YO, K5; repeat from ★ 2 times **more**, YO, K2 tog, K1, P1, K1.

Row 12: K1, P1, K1, slip 1, K1, PSSO, YO, K5, ★ YO, slip 2 tog, K1, P2SSO, YO, K5; repeat from ★ 2 times **more**, YO, K2 tog, K1, P1, K1.

Row 14: K1, P1, K3, YO, slip 1, K1, PSSO, K1, K2 tog, ★ YO, K3, YO, slip 1, K1, PSSO, K1, K2 tog; repeat from ★ 2 times **more**, YO, K3, P1, K1.

Row 16: K1, P1, K4, YO, slip 1, K2 tog, PSSO, ★ YO, K5, YO, slip 1, K2 tog, PSSO; repeat from ★ 2 times **more**, YO, K4, P1, K1.

Row 18: K1, P1, K2, YO, slip 1, K1, PSSO, K3, K2 tog, ★ YO, K1, YO, slip 1, K1, PSSO, K3, K2 tog; repeat from ★ 2 times **more**, YO, K2, P1, K1.

Row 20: Repeat Row 14.

Row 22: Repeat Row 16.

Row 24: K1, P1, K4, YO, slip 2 tog, K1, P2SSO, ★ YO, K5, YO, slip 2 tog, K1, P2SSO; repeat from ★ 2 times **more**, YO, K4, P1, K1.

Row 26: Repeat Row 24.

Row 28: Repeat Row 6.

Row 30: Repeat Row 8.

Row 31: K1, P1, K1, purl across to last 3 sts, K1, P1, K1.

Repeat Rows 4-31 for pattern until piece measures approximately 60" from cast on edge, ending by working a **wrong** side row.

Last 3 Rows: K1, (P1, K1) across.

Bind off all sts in pattern.

STRIP E
Cast on 36 sts **loosely**.

Row 1: (K1, P1) across.

Row 2 (Right side)**:** (P1, K1) across.

Row 3: (K1, P1) across.

Row 4: P1, K1, P 10, K5, P2, K5, P9, K1, P1, K1.

Row 5: K1, P1, K 10, P5, K2, P5, K9, P1, K1, P1.

Row 6: P1, K1, P9, increase *(Fig. 11, page 581)*, K4, [slip 1 as if to **knit**, K1, PSSO *(Figs. 19a & b, page 583)*], K2 tog *(Fig. 17, page 583)*, K4, increase, P8, K1, P1, K1.

Row 7: K1, P1, K 11, P 10, K 10, P1, K1, P1.

Row 8: P1, K1, P 10, increase, K2, slip 1 as if to **knit**, K1, PSSO, slip next st onto cable needle and hold in **back** of work, K4 from left needle, P1 from cable needle, LT *(Figs. 6a & b, page 580)*, P9, K1, P1, K1.

Row 9: K1, P1, K 10, P1, K2, P7, K 11, P1, K1, P1.

Row 10: P1, K1, P 11, increase, slip 1 as if to **knit**, K1, PSSO, slip next st onto cable needle and hold in **back** of work, K4 from left needle, P1 from cable needle, P2, LT, P8, K1, P1, K1.

Row 11: K1, P1, K9, P1, K4, P5, K 12, P1, K1, P1.

Row 12: P1, K1, P 13, slip next st onto cable needle and hold in **back** of work, K3 from left needle, P1 from cable needle, LT, P3, LT, P7, K1, P1, K1.

Row 13: K1, P1, K8, P1, K4, P1, K2, P3, K 12, P1, K1, P1.

Row 14: P1, K1, P 12, slip next st onto cable needle and hold in **back** of work, K3 from left needle, P1 from cable needle, P2, LT, P2, RT *(Figs. 7a & b, page 580)*, P7, K1, P1, K1.

Row 15: K1, P1, K9, P1, K2, P1, K4, P3, K 11, P1, K1, P1.

Row 16: P1, K1, P 11, T3B, LT, P3, LT, RT, P8, K1, P1, K1.

Row 17: K1, P1, K 10, P2, K4, P1, K2, P2, K 10, P1, K1, P1.

Row 18: P1, K1, P 10, T3B, P2, LT, P2, T3B, P9, K1, P1, K1.

Row 19: K1, P1, K 11, P2, K2, P1, K4, P2, K9, P1, K1, P1.

Row 20: P1, K1, P9, RT, LT, P3, LT, T3B, P 10, K1, P1, K1.

Row 21: K1, P1, K 12, P3, K4, P1, K2, P1, K8, P1, K1, P1.

Row 22: P1, K1, P8, RT, P2, LT, P2, slip next st onto cable needle and hold in **back** of work, K3 from left needle, P1 from cable needle, P 11, K1, P1, K1.

Row 23: K1, P1, K 13, P3, K2, P1, K4, P1, K7, P1, K1, P1.

Row 24: P1, K1, P8, LT, P3, LT, slip next st onto cable needle and hold in **back** of work, K3 from left needle, K1 from cable needle, P 12, K1, P1, K1.

Row 25: K1, P1, K 13, P5, K4, P1, K8, P1, K1, P1.

Row 26: P1, K1, P9, LT, P2, slip next st onto cable needle and hold in **back** of work, K4 from left needle, knit into front **and** back of st on cable needle, K1, P2 tog *(Fig. 18, page 583)*, P 10, K1, P1, K1.

Row 27: K1, P1, K 12, P7, K2, P1, K9, P1, K1, P1.

Row 28: P1, K1, P 10, LT, slip next st onto cable needle and hold in **back** of work, K4 from left needle, knit into front **and** back of st on cable needle, K3, P2 tog, P9, K1, P1, K1.

Row 29: K1, P1, K 11, P 10, K 10, P1, K1, P1.

Row 30: P1, K1, P9, P2 tog, K5, insert left needle from front under horizontal strand between sts *(Fig. A, page 541)*, purl into back **and** front of strand, K5, P2 tog, P8, K1, P1, K1.

Row 31: K1, P1, K 10, P5, K2, P5, K9, P1, K1, P1.

Repeat Rows 4-31 for pattern until piece measures approximately 60" from cast on edge, ending by working a **wrong** side row.

Next Row: (P1, K1) across.

Next Row: (K1, P1) across.

Last Row: (P1, K1) across.

Bind off all sts in pattern.

STRIP F
Cast on 36 sts **loosely.**

Row 1: (K1, P1) across.

Row 2 (Right side)**:** (P1, K1) across.

Row 3: (K1, P1) across.

Row 4: P1, K1, P1, knit across to last 2 sts, P1, K1.

Row 5: K1, P1, K1, purl across to last 2 sts, K1, P1.

Row 6: P1, K1, P1, ★ K2, YO *(Fig. 16c, page 582)*, P1, P3 tog *(Fig. 24, page 584)*, P1, YO *(Fig. 16d, page 582)*; repeat from ★ across to last 5 sts, K3, P1, K1.

Row 7: K1, P1, K1, purl across to last 2 sts, K1, P1. Repeat Rows 4-7 for pattern until piece measures approximately 60" from cast on edge, ending by working a **wrong** side row.

Next Row: (P1, K1) across.

Next Row: (K1, P1) across.

Last Row: (P1, K1) across.
Bind off all sts in pattern.

ASSEMBLY
Sew strips together in the following order:
Strip A, Strip B, Strip C, Strip D, Strip E, Strip F.

Holding 4 strands of yarn together, each 18" long, add fringe across short edges of Afghan *(Figs. 37a & b, page 588)*.

GENERAL INSTRUCTIONS

Note: For additional knitting information, see Learn to Knit, pages 6-57.

ABBREVIATIONS

BC	Back Cable
BT	Back Twist
C3B	Cable 3 Back
C3F	Cable 3 Front
C4B	Cable 4 Back
C4F	Cable 4 Front
C4L	Cable 4 Left
C4R	Cable 4 Right
C5B	Cable 5 Back
C5F	Cable 5 Front
C6B	Cable 6 Back
C6F	Cable 6 Front
C8F	Cable 8 Front
CC	Contrasting Color
ch(s)	chain(s)
cm	centimeters
FC	Front Cable
FT	Front Twist
K	knit
LT	Left Twist
M1	Make One
M1P	Make One Purlwise
MC	Main Color
mm	millimeters
P	purl
PSSO	pass slipped stitch over
P2SSO	pass 2 slipped stitches over
Rnd(s)	Round(s)
RT	Right Twist
RT2	Right Twist 2
sc	single crochet(s)
SSK	slip, slip, knit
SSP	slip, slip, purl
st(s)	stitch(es)
T3B	Twist 3 Back
T3F	Twist 3 Front
T4B	Twist 4 Back
T4F	Twist 4 Front
tbl	through back loop
tog	together
WYB	with yarn in back
WYF	with yarn in front
YO(s)	yarn over(s)

★ — work instructions following ★ as many **more** times as indicated in addition to the first time.

† to † — work all instructions from first † to second † as many times as specified.

( ) or **[ ]** — work enclosed instructions **as many** times as specified by the number immediately following **or** work all enclosed instructions in the stitch indicated **or** contains explanatory remarks.

colon (:) — the number(s) given after a colon at the end of a row or round denote(s) the number of stitches or spaces you should have on that row or round.

work even — work without increasing or decreasing in the established pattern.

KNIT TERMINOLOGY	
UNITED STATES	**INTERNATIONAL**
gauge =	tension
bind off =	cast off
yarn over (YO) =	yarn forward (yfwd) **or**
	yarn around needle (yrn)

GAUGE

Exact gauge is **essential** for proper fit. Needle size given in instructions is merely a guide and should never be used without first making a sample swatch approximately 4" (10 cm) square in the stitch, yarn, and needle specified. Then measure it, counting your stitches and rows carefully. If your swatch is larger or smaller than specified, **make another, changing needle size to get the correct gauge**. If you have more rows per inch than specified, use a larger needle for the purl rows. If you have fewer rows per inch, use a smaller needle on the purl rows. Keep trying until you find the size needles that will give you the specified gauge. Once proper gauge is obtained, measure width of piece approximately every 3" (7.5 cm) to be sure gauge remains consistent.

MULTIPLES

The multiple for each pattern stitch in the 99 Knit Stitches, pages 512-563, is listed after the ID Photo. The multiple indicates the number of stitches required to form one complete pattern of the design.

Different pattern stitches produce a different number of stitches and/or rows per inch with the same yarn and the same size needles. Therefore, patterns which share the same multiple will not necessarily be interchangeable, because each may produce a different gauge.

Panels are patterns worked over a certain number of stitches without necessarily being repeated. Panels list only the number of stitches required to form one complete pattern. To work any of the panels you must cast on enough stitches to work the panel plus the desired number of background stitches on each side.

SIZING

When choosing what size to make, you may want to measure a favorite sweater with similar styling and knit the size that has the nearest finished measurement. Once you have chosen a size, you may adjust the body length and the sleeve length to accommodate the actual measurements while adjusting the amount of yarn purchased accordingly.

ZEROS

To consolidate the length of an involved pattern, Zeros are sometimes used so that all sizes can be combined. For example, decrease one stitch at **each** edge, every row, 0{6-4} times means the first size would do nothing, the second size would decrease 6 times, and the largest size would decrease 4 times.

Yarn Weight Symbol & Names	SUPER FINE 1	FINE 2	LIGHT 3	MEDIUM 4	BULKY 5	SUPER BULKY 6
Type of Yarns in Category	Sock, Fingering Baby	Sport, Baby	DK, Light Worsted	Worsted, Afghan, Aran	Chunky, Craft, Rug	Bulky, Roving
Knit Gauge Ranges in Stockinette St to 4" (10 cm)	27-32 sts	23-26 sts	21-24 sts	16-20 sts	12-15 sts	6-11 sts
Advised U.S. Needle Size Range	1-3	3-5	5-7	7-9	9-11	11 and larger

METRIC CONVERSIONS	
UNITED STATES	**INTERNATIONAL**
1 inch	= 2.54 centimeters
1 yard	= .9144 meter
1 ounce	= 28.4 grams

KNITTING NEEDLES															
U.S.	0	1	2	3	4	5	6	7	8	9	10	10½	11	13	15	17
U.K.	13	12	11	10	9	8	7	6	5	4	3	2	1	00	000	---
Metric - mm	2	2.25	2.75	3.25	3.5	3.75	4	4.5	5	5.5	6	6.5	8	9	10	12.75

■□□□ BEGINNER	Projects for first-time knitters using basic knit and purl stitches. Minimal shaping.
■■□□ EASY	Projects using basic stitches, repetitive stitch patterns, simple color changes, and simple shaping and finishing.
■■■□ INTERMEDIATE	Projects with a variety of stitches, such as basic cables and lace, simple intarsia, double-pointed needles and knitting in the round needle techniques, mid-level shaping and finishing.
■■■■ EXPERIENCED	Projects using advanced techniques and stitches, such as short rows, fair isle, more intricate intarsia, cables, lace patterns, and numerous color changes.

BASIC FABRICS
GARTER STITCH
When working in **rows**, knit every row.
When working in **rounds**, knit one round, purl one round.
Two rows/rounds of knitting make one horizontal ridge in your fabric *(Photo A)*.

Photo A

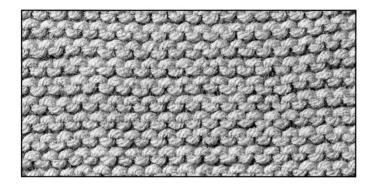

STOCKINETTE STITCH
When working in **rows**, knit one row, purl one row.
When working in **rounds**, knit every round.
The right side is smooth *(Photo B)* and the wrong side is bumpy *(Photo C)*.

Photo B

Photo C

DOUBLE MOSS STITCH
Moss Stitch, also known as Seed Stitch, is a reversible fabric that does not curl at the edges *(Photo D)*. Alternate the knit and purl stitches on the first row. On the following rows, knit the purl stitches and purl the knit stitches as they face you. For Double Moss Stitch, alternate 2 knit stitches with 2 purl stitches every 2 rows *(Photo D)*.

Photo D

Photo E

MARKERS
As a convenience to you, we have used markers to help distinguish the beginning of a pattern, placement of buttonholes, or the beginning of a round. Place markers as instructed. You may use purchased markers or tie a length of contrasting color yarn around the needle. When you reach a marker on each row or round, slip it from the left needle to the right needle *(Fig. 1)*; remove it when no longer needed.

Fig. 1

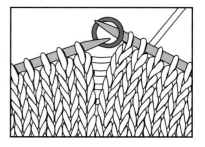

HOW TO MEASURE

When measuring a garment, it is important to lay the piece flat on a hard, smooth surface. **Figs. 2a & b** illustrate how to measure from the cast on edge of a piece.

Fig. 2a   **Fig. 2b**

KNITTING IN THE ROUND

Using a circular needle, cast on all stitches as instructed. Untwist and straighten the stitches on the needle before beginning Rnd 1.

Place a marker after the last stitch to mark the beginning of a round. Hold the needle so that the ball of yarn is attached to the stitch closest to the **right** hand point.

To begin working in the round, knit the stitches on the left hand point *(Fig. 3a)*.

Fig. 3a

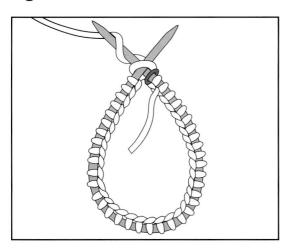

Continue working each round as instructed **without turning the work**; but for the first three rounds or so, check to be sure that the cast on edge has not twisted around the needle. If it has, it is impossible to untwist it. The only way to fix this is to rip it out and return to the cast on row.

When working a project that is too small to use a circular needle, or the size circular needle is unavailable in the length needed, double pointed needles are required. Divide the stitches into thirds or fourths and slip $1/3$ or $1/4$ of the stitches onto each of the double pointed needles forming a triangle or square. With the last needle, knit across the first needle *(Fig. 3b)*. You will now have an empty needle with which to knit the stitches from the next needle. Work the first stitch of each needle firmly to prevent gaps.

Fig. 3b

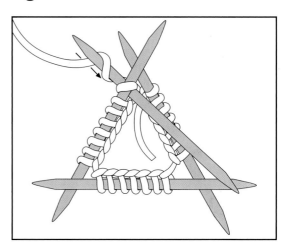

THROUGH BACK LOOP
(abbreviated tbl)

When instructed to work through back loop of a stitch, insert right needle as indicated *(Fig. 4a)*. The result will be twisted stitches *(Fig. 4b)*.

Fig. 4a

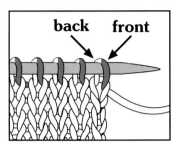
back   front

Fig. 4b

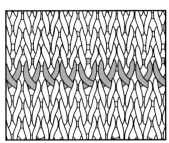

ADDING NEW STITCHES

Insert the right needle into stitch as if to **knit**, yarn over and pull loop through *(Fig. 5a)*, insert the left needle into the loop just worked from **front** to **back** and slip the loop onto the left needle *(Fig. 5b)*. Repeat for required number of stitches.

Fig. 5a

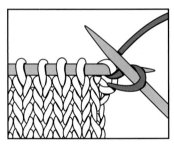

Fig. 5b

LEFT TWIST
(abbreviated LT) (uses 2 sts)

Working **behind** first stitch on left needle, purl into the back of second stitch *(Fig. 6a)* making sure **not** to drop off, then knit the first stitch *(Fig. 6b)* letting both stitches drop off needle.

Fig. 6a

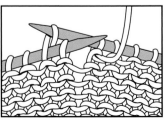

Fig. 6b

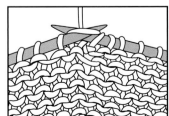

RIGHT TWIST
(abbreviated RT) (uses 2 sts)

Knit second stitch on left needle *(Fig. 7a)* making sure **not** to drop off, then purl the first stitch *(Fig. 7b)* letting both stitches drop off needle.

Fig. 7a

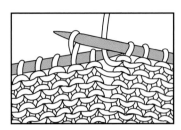

Fig. 7b

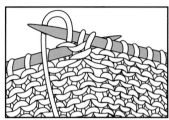

BACK CROSS (uses 2 sts)

Working **behind** first stitch on left needle, knit into the back of second stitch *(Fig. 8a)* making sure **not** to drop off, then knit the first stitch *(Fig. 8b)* letting both stitches drop off needle.

Fig. 8a

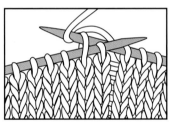

Fig. 8b

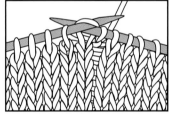

FRONT CROSS (uses 2 sts)

Knit second stitch on left needle *(Fig. 9a)* making sure not to drop off, then knit the first stitch *(Fig. 9b)* letting both stitches drop off needle.

Fig. 9a

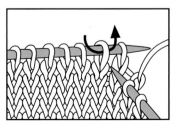

Fig. 9b

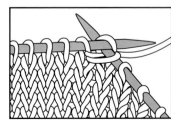

INCREASES
INCREASING EVENLY ACROSS A ROW/ROUND

Add one to the number of increases required and divide that number into the number of stitches on the needle. Subtract one from the result and the new number is the approximate number of stitches to be worked between each increase. Adjust the number as needed.

KNIT INCREASE

Knit the next stitch but do **not** slip the old stitch off the left needle *(Fig. 10a)*. Insert the right needle into the back loop of the **same** stitch and knit it *(Fig. 10b)*, then slip the old stitch off the left needle.

Fig. 10a

Fig. 10b

 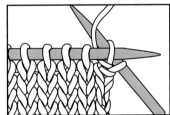

PURL INCREASE

Purl the next stitch but do **not** slip the old stitch off the left needle. Insert the right needle into the **back** loop of the **same** stitch from **back** to **front** *(Fig. 11)* and purl it. Slip the old stitch off the left needle.

Fig. 11

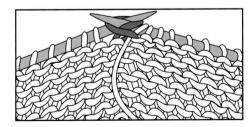

RIGHT INVISIBLE INCREASE
KNIT

Insert the right needle from the **front** into the side of the stitch **below** the next stitch on the left needle *(Fig. 12a)* and knit it.

PURL

Insert the right needle from the **back** into the top of the stitch **below** the next stitch on the left needle *(Fig. 12b)*, slip it onto the left needle and purl it.

Fig. 12a   **Fig. 12b**

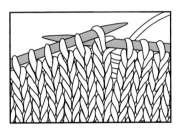 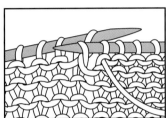

LEFT INVISIBLE INCREASE
KNIT

Insert the left needle from the **back** into the side of the stitch 2 rows **below** the stitch on the right needle *(Fig. 13a)*, pull it up and knit into the back loop *(Fig. 13b)*.

PURL

Insert the left needle from the **front** into the top of the stitch 2 rows **below** the stitch on the right needle *(Fig. 13c)*, pull it up and purl it.

Fig. 13a   **Fig. 13b**

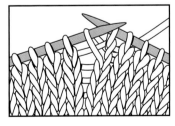 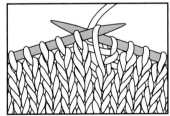

Fig. 13c

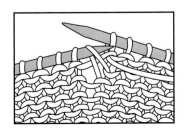

MAKE ONE (abbreviated M1)

Insert the **left** needle under the horizontal strand between the stitches from the **front** *(Fig. 14a)*. Then knit into the **back** of the strand *(Fig. 14b)*.

Fig. 14a   **Fig. 14b**

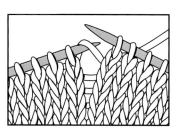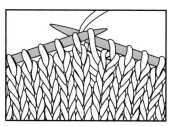

MAKE ONE PURLWISE
(abbreviated M1P)

Insert the **left** needle under the horizontal strand between the stitches from the **back** *(Fig. 15a)*. Then purl the strand *(Fig. 15b)*.

Fig. 15a   **Fig. 15b**

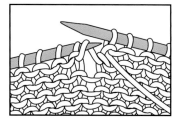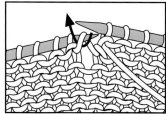

YARN OVER (abbreviated YO)
After a knit stitch, before a knit stitch

Bring the yarn forward **between** the needles, then back **over** the top of the right hand needle, so that it is now in position to knit the next stitch *(Fig. 16a)*.

Fig. 16a

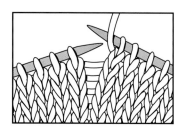

After a purl stitch, before a purl stitch

Take yarn **over** the right hand needle to the back, then forward **under** it, so that it is now in position to purl the next stitch *(Fig. 16b)*.

Fig. 16b

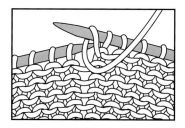

After a knit stitch, before a purl stitch

Bring yarn forward **between** the needles, then back over the top of the right hand needle and forward **between** the needles again, so that it is now in position to purl the next stitch *(Fig. 16c)*.

Fig. 16c

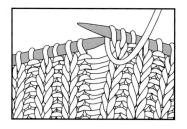

After a purl stitch, before a knit stitch

Take yarn over right hand needle to the back, so that it is now in position to knit the next stitch *(Fig. 16d)*.

Fig. 16d

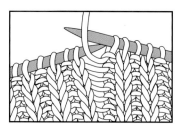

DECREASES
DECREASING EVENLY IN A ROUND

Add one to the number of decreases required and divide that number into the number of stitches on the needle(s). Subtract one from the result and the new number is the approximate number of stitches to be worked between each decrease. Adjust the number as needed.

KNIT 2 TOGETHER
(abbreviated K2 tog)

Insert the right needle into the **front** of the first two stitches on the left needle as if to **knit** *(Fig. 17)*, then **knit** them together as if they were one stitch.

Fig. 17

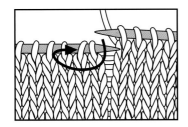

PURL 2 TOGETHER
(abbreviated P2 tog)

Insert the right needle into the **front** of the first two stitches on the left needle as if to **purl** *(Fig. 18)*, then **purl** them together as if they were one stitch.

Fig. 18

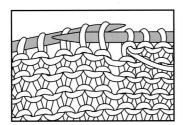

SLIP 1, KNIT 1, PASS SLIPPED STITCH OVER
(abbreviated slip 1, K1, PSSO)

Slip one stitch as if to **knit** *(Fig. 19a)*. Knit the next stitch. With the left needle, bring the slipped stitch over the knit stitch *(Fig. 19b)* and off the needle.

Fig. 19a   **Fig. 19b**

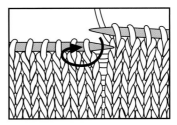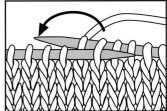

PURL 2 TOGETHER THROUGH THE BACK LOOP
(abbreviated P2 tog tbl)

Insert the right needle into the **back** of both stitches from **back** to **front** *(Fig. 20)*, then **purl** them together as if they were one stitch.

Fig. 20

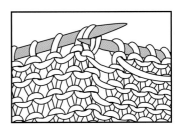

SLIP, SLIP, KNIT (abbreviated SSK)

With yarn in back of work, separately slip two stitches as if to **knit (Fig. 21a)**. Insert the **left** needle into the **front** of both slipped stitches **(Fig. 21b)** and knit them together **(Fig. 21c)**.

Fig. 21a

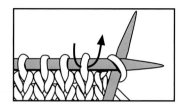

Fig. 21b

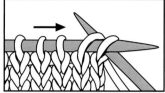

Fig. 21c

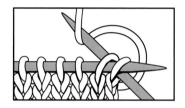

SLIP, SLIP, PURL (abbreviated SSP)

With yarn held in front of work, separately slip two stitches as if to **knit**. Place these two stitches back onto the left needle. Insert the right needle into the **back** of both stitches from **back** to **front (Fig. 22)** and purl them together as if they were one stitch.

Fig. 22

KNIT 3 TOGETHER
(abbreviated K3 tog)

Insert the right needle into the **front** of the first three stitches on the left needle as if to **knit (Fig. 23)**, then **knit** them together as if they were one stitch.

Fig. 23

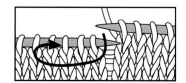

PURL 3 TOGETHER
(abbreviated P3 tog)

Insert the right needle into the **front** of the first three stitches on the left needle as if to **purl (Fig. 24)**, then **purl** them together as if they were one stitch.

Fig. 24

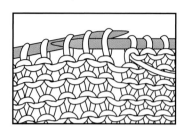

SLIP 1, KNIT 2, PASS SLIPPED STITCH OVER
(abbreviated slip 1, K2, PSSO)

Slip one stitch as if to **knit (Fig. 25a)**, then knit the next two stitches. With the left needle, bring the slipped stitch over the two knit stitches **(Fig. 25b)** and off the needle.

Fig. 25a

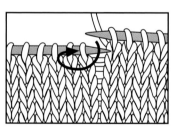

Fig. 25b

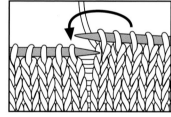

SLIP 1, KNIT 2 TOGETHER, PASS SLIPPED STITCH OVER
(abbreviated slip 1, K2 tog, PSSO)

Slip one stitch as if to **knit (Fig. 26a)**, then knit the next two stitches together. With the left needle, bring the slipped stitch over the stitch just made **(Fig. 26b)** and off the needle.

Fig. 26a

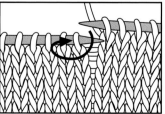

Fig. 26b

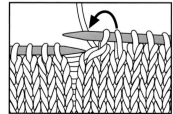

SLIP 2, KNIT 1, PASS 2 SLIPPED STITCHES OVER

(abbreviated slip 2, K1, P2SSO)

Separately slip two stitches as if to **knit** *(Fig. 27a)*, then knit the next stitch. With the left needle, bring the two slipped stitches over the stitch just made *(Fig. 27b)* and off the needle.

Fig. 27a   **Fig. 27b**

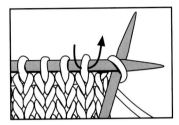

PURL 3 TOGETHER THROUGH THE BACK LOOP

(abbreviated P3 tog tbl)

With yarn held in front of work, insert the right needle into the **back** of the first three stitches on the left needle from **back** to **front** *(Fig. 28)*, then **purl** them together as if they were one stitch.

Fig. 28

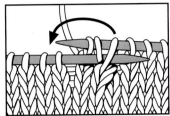

SLIP 2 TOGETHER, KNIT 1, PASS 2 SLIPPED STITCHES OVER

(abbreviated slip 2 tog, K1, P2SSO)

Slip two stitches together as if to **knit** *(Fig. 29a)*, then knit the next stitch. With the left needle, bring the two slipped stitches over the stitch just made *(Fig. 29b)* and off the needle.

Fig. 29a   **Fig. 29b**

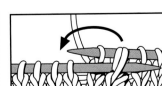

USING COLORS
CHANGING COLORS

When changing colors, always pick up the new color yarn from **beneath** the dropped yarn and keep the color which has just been worked to the left *(Fig. 30)*. This will prevent holes in the finished piece. Take extra care to keep your tension even. For proper fit, it is essential to maintain gauge when following Charts.

Fig. 30

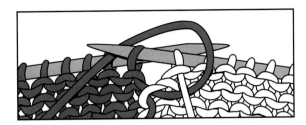

BOBBIN KNITTING

In Intarsia knitting, better known as Bobbin knitting, there are usually large areas of color. Bobbins are used to hold the small amount of yarn needed to work each color change and also to help keep the different color yarns from tangling. You'll need to wind a bobbin for each color change, using as many bobbins as necessary to avoid carrying the yarn across the back, except when there are so few stitches of the new color that it would be easier to carry the unused color loosely across the back *(Fig. 31)*.

Fig. 31

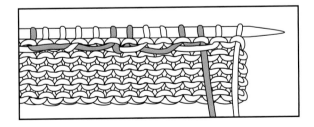

Start each bobbin as you would a new ball of yarn, leaving a 6" (15 cm) end to weave in later. Always keep the bobbins on the **wrong** side of your work and only unfasten enough yarn to work the area comfortably, otherwise the yarn will tangle.

FOLLOWING A CHART

It is easier to follow a Chart than written instructions and you can also see what the pattern looks like. The chart shows each stitch as a square indicating what color each stitch should be. Visualize the chart as your fabric, beginning at the bottom edge.

If the chart is symmetrical, it doesn't matter which direction the chart is followed.
If the chart is **not** symmetrical, work as follows: On **right** side rows, follow the chart from **right** to **left**; on **wrong** side rows, follow the chart from **left** to **right**.

For ease in following the chart, place a ruler on the chart above the row being worked to help keep your place.

FAIR ISLE KNITTING

See pages 352-354.

DUPLICATE STITCH

Thread yarn needle with an 18" (45.5 cm) strand of yarn. With **right** side facing, bring needle up from wrong side and draw yarn through bottom of stitch, leaving a short end at back to be woven in later. Needle should always go **between** strands of yarn. Insert needle from **right** to **left** around knit stitch above **(Fig. 32a)**, keeping yarn on top of stitch, and draw through. Insert needle back through bottom of same stitch where first stitch began **(Fig. 32b, Duplicate Stitch completed)**. Continuing to follow Chart, bring needle up through next stitch and repeat for all charted stitches. Keep tension even with tension of knit fabric to avoid puckering.

Fig. 32a   **Fig. 32b**

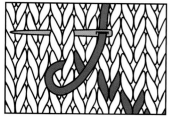   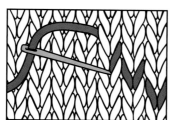

3-NEEDLE BIND OFF

Holding pieces with **right** sides together and needles parallel to each other, insert a third needle as if to **knit** into the first stitch on the front needle **and** into the first stitch on the back needle **(Fig. 33)**. Knit these two stitches together and slip them off the needle. ★ Knit the next stitch on each needle together and slip them off the needle. To bind off, insert the left needle into the first stitch on the right needle and pull the first stitch over the second stitch and off the right needle; repeat from ★ across until all of the stitches on the right needle have been bound off.

Fig. 33

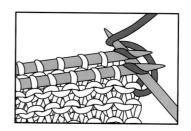

PICKING UP STITCHES

When instructed to pick up stitches, insert the needle from the **front** to the **back** under two strands at the edge of the worked piece **(Figs. 34a & b)**. Put the yarn around the needle as if to **knit**, then bring the needle with the yarn back through the stitch to the right side, resulting in a stitch on the needle.
Repeat this along the edge, picking up the required number of stitches.
A crochet hook may be helpful to pull yarn through.

Fig. 34a   **Fig. 34b**

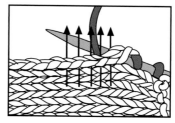   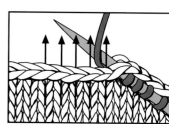

FINISHING
SEWING IN SLEEVES

With **right** sides together and referring to Diagram below, sew bound off edge of Sleeve to Body, matching center of last row on Sleeve to shoulder seam and corners indicated at the X's and sewing the bound off sts at Armhole Shaping to side edges of Sleeve.

DIAGRAM

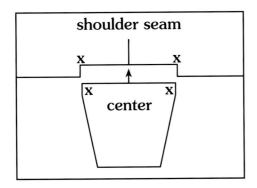

WEAVING SHOULDER AND SIDE SEAMS

Shoulder and side seams that are joined by this method appear seamless. With **right** side of both pieces facing you and the edges even, bring the needle from behind the work and through the center of the first stitch, leaving a long end to be woven in later.

★ Bring the needle over the edge and pick up both loops of the corresponding stitch on the second side **(Fig. 35a)**. Bring the needle back over the seam and pick up the inverted "V" of the next stitch **(Fig. 35b)**. Repeat from ★ across. Pull the yarn gently ever 2 or 3 stitches, being careful to maintain even tension.

Fig. 35a   **Fig.35b**

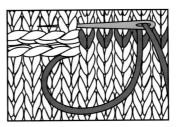 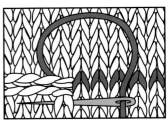

WEAVING SEAMS ONE STITCH IN

With the **right** side of both pieces facing you and edges even, sew through both sides once to secure the seam. Insert the needle under the bar **between** the first and second stitches on the row and pull the yarn through **(Fig. 36)**. Insert the needle under the next bar on the second side. Repeat from side to side, being careful to match rows. If the edges are different lengths, it may be necessary to insert the needle under two bars at one edge.

Fig. 36

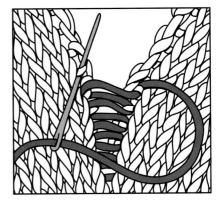

FRINGE

Cut a piece of cardboard 3" (7.5 cm) wide and
$1/2$" (12 mm) longer than you want your finished
fringe to be. Wind the yarn **loosely** and **evenly**
lengthwise around the cardboard until the card is
filled, then cut across one end; repeat as needed.
Hold together as many strands as specified in
individual instructions; fold in half.

With **wrong** side facing and using a crochet
hook, draw the folded end up through a stitch or
space and pull the loose ends through the folded
end *(Fig. 37a)*; draw the knot up **tightly**
(Fig. 37b). Repeat, spacing as specified in
individual instructions.

Lay flat on a hard surface and trim the ends.

Fig. 37a

Fig. 37b

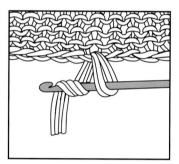

POM-POM

Cut a piece of cardboard 3" (7.5 cm) wide and as
long as you want the diameter of your finished
pom-pom to be. Wind the yarn around the
cardboard until it is approximately $1/2$" (12 mm)
thick in the middle *(Fig. 38a)*. Carefully slip the
yarn off the cardboard and firmly tie an 18"
(45.5 cm) length of yarn around the middle
(Fig. 38b). Leave yarn ends long enough to attach
the pom-pom. Cut the loops on both ends and
trim the pom-pom into a smooth ball *(Fig. 38c)*.

Fig. 38a **Fig. 38b**

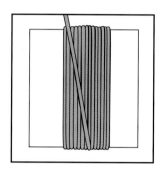
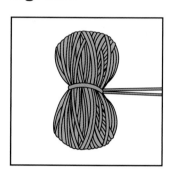

Fig. 38c

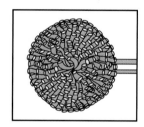

CROCHET STITCHES

YARN OVER *(abbreviated YO)*

Bring the yarn over the top of the hook from
back to **front**, catching the yarn with the hook
and turning the hook slightly toward you to keep
the yarn from slipping off *(Fig. 39)*.

Fig. 39

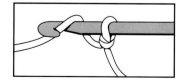

CHAIN *(abbreviated ch)*

YO, draw the yarn through the stitch on the
hook *(Fig. 40)*.

Fig. 40

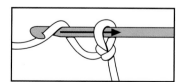

SLIP STITCH (abbreviated slip st)

Insert hook in stitch indicated, YO and draw through stitch and through loop on hook (*Fig. 41*).

Fig. 41

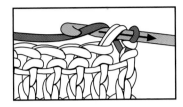

SINGLE CROCHET (abbreviated sc)

Insert hook in stitch indicated, YO and pull up a loop, YO and draw through both loops on hook (*Fig. 42*).

Fig. 42

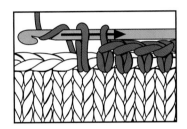

JOINING WITH SLIP ST

When instructed to join with slip st, begin with a slip knot on hook. Insert hook in stitch indicated, YO and draw through stitch **and** through loop on hook.

JOINING WITH SC

When instructed to join with sc, begin with a slip knot on hook. Insert hook in stitch indicated, YO and pull up a loop, YO and draw through both loops on hook.

BACK OR FRONT LOOP ONLY

Work only in loop(s) indicated by arrow (*Fig. 43*).

Fig. 43

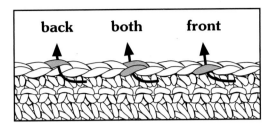

REVERSE SINGLE CROCHET
(*abbreviated reverse sc*)

Working from **left** to **right**, insert hook in stitch to right of hook (*Fig. 44a*), YO and draw through, under and to left of loop on hook (2 loops on hook) (*Fig. 44b*), YO and draw through both loops on hook (*Fig. 44c*) (**reverse sc made,** *Fig. 44d*); repeat from ★ around.

Fig. 44a

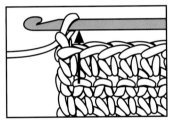

Fig. 44b

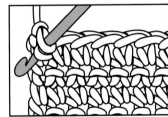

Fig. 44c

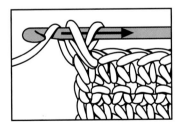

Fig. 44d

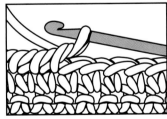

FINISH OFF

Cut yarn about 8" (20.5 cm) from hook. YO and pull loose end all the way through the loop on hook; pull end to tighten.

Keeping a Knitting Journal

Do you ever wish you could remember a certain detail about an item you knitted in the past? That you could recall the type of yarn used for a favorite sweater? Or find the same pattern again? Or just know how many afghans you've made and given away?

Then what you could do is start keeping a knitting journal! It can be as brief or as detailed as you like. Just have fun with it!

To help you get started, we recommend that you obtain a sturdy 3-ring binder and use the fill-in-the-blanks journal page given opposite. You can punch holes in the pages or insert them in clear protective plastic sleeves like those that scrapbookers use.

Filling in the Blanks

Keep a supply of photocopies of the blank journal page. Then all you have to do is fill in the blanks whenever you complete a project. Keep in mind that you are keeping a history, and you'll want to be able to understand your musings even many years from now.

■ Be thorough when filling in your information.

■ Make note of any instructions you'd enjoy using again. Conversely, if you didn't like working a particular pattern, note that too.

■ Washing care information is extremely important, not only for yourself but if the item is a gift. The recipient of your beautiful knitting will appreciate knowing that he or she can call on you in the future if unsure of how to take care of the new treasure.

■ Don't forget to make it personal. Record why you made a particular piece for a particular person, what was going on in your life when you were making a project, or whether or not you were pleased with the outcome of the project. Whatever is important for you to remember is worth writing down.

■ If you'd like, use archival-safe glue to attach a photo of your completed item (or a photocopy of the pattern book image) to the journal page. A picture tells a thousand words!

■ Use the plastic page protector sleeve as a catch-all for other things you'd like to keep in reference to the project: yarn labels, swatches of yarn, a thank-you note from the recipient, even the project instructions themselves, if they will fit.

My Knitting Journal

Project name or description: _____

Made for: _____

In honor of: _____

Date begun: _____Date completed: _____

Yarn or other fiber used: _____

Knitting needle sizes used: _____

Instructions used: _____

Special care instructions: _____

_____

Other important notes: _____

_____

_____

Project Index